THE HAMLYN ENCYCLOPEDIA OF

CHILD HEALTH

PRISCA MIDDLEMISS

CONSULTANT PAEDIATRICIAN: ALEX HABEL MB, ChB, FRCP

hamlyn

First published in Great Britain in 1998 by Hamlyn
an imprint of Octopus Publishing Group Limited
2–4 Heron Quays, London, E14 4JP

This paperback edition first published 2001

ISBN 0 600 60403 9

A CIP catalogue record for this book is available from the British Library.

Produced by Toppan
Printed in China

Publishing Director: Laura Bamford
Executive Editor: Jane McIntosh
Creative Director: Keith Martin
Project Manager: Casey Horton
Design Manager: Bryan Dunn
Designer: Martin Topping
Editors: Casey Horton, Arlene Sobel, Jill Cropper
Assistant Editor: Meredith White
Proofreader: Anne Crane
Picture Research: Liz Fowler
Special Photography: Gary Holder
Jacket Photography: Peter Myers
Jacket Design: Geoff Borin

Illustrations:
Ailments: Virginia Gray
Body systems: Liz Gray
First aid: Jackie Harland

Additional text: Casey Horton

Senior Production Controller: Katherine Hockley

Note
This book is not intended as a substitute for personal medical advice. The reader should consult a physician in all matters relating to health and particularly in respect of any symptoms which may require diagnosis or medical attention. While the advice and information are believed to be accurate and true at the time of going to press, neither the authors nor the publisher can accept any legal responsibility or liability for any errors or omissions that may be made.

CONTENTS

Common Ailments

INTRODUCTION

PARENTS TODAY FACE MANY MORE RESPONSIBILITIES and choices than their grandparents did in bringing up their children – responsibilities and choices that can make child-rearing seem a daunting prospect. While every effort may be made to ensure that the home is a happy, healthy and secure environment, influences from outside can not only cause illness and disease, but can also exert enormous pressures on children to behave in a way that is in direct opposition to the family's principles and beliefs.

In such situations parents are often ill-equipped to deal with every crisis and emergency, and understandably so. They may also be unsure of where they can turn for help, or what the nature of that help should be. In the field of medicine alone the choices are often multiple. Should they have their child vaccinated or forego vaccination altogether and strive for prevention? Should they treat a child with abdominal pain at home, take them to hospital or call the doctor? Is it necessary to call the doctor every time their child is feverish or can they deal with it themselves? Will a hyperactive child gain most benefit from music therapy, nutritional therapy, drug treatment or psychological counselling?

Before parents can make intelligent decisions about how they will raise and care for their child they need information and guidance from professionals who, with their extensive knowledge and experience, can discuss the various practices and methods of child care objectively.

This publication brings together the knowledge and wisdom of a number of such professionals, who come from what used to be seen as two radically opposed sides of the medical divide: orthodox and complementary medicine. Today this division is becoming increasingly blurred: more and more medical doctors are acknowledging the valuable contributions that acupuncture, homeopathy and osteopathy, among others, can make to the well being of their patients, while responsible, qualified complementary practitioners will always recommend patients to take orthodox medical advice when necessary. And in many hospitals staff are making use of therapies such as relaxation and aromatherapy to deal with the emotional and mental effects of hospitalization and surgery.

The modern approach to child care is epitomized within these pages: an emphasis on positive health at all stages of development; a broad approach to the treatment of childhood ailments and emotional problems; and the help and support of specialized agencies and organizations in times of difficulty. Parents at all levels of experience will find encouragement here, as well as valuable advice and information on which to base their personal philosophy of child care. In the end good parenting and child care are processes that benefit from the intuitiveness and originality of the individuals involved, not hard and fast rules to be followed blindly.

HOW TO USE THIS BOOK

The *Encyclopedia of Child Health* is a practical, authoritative reference that for ease of access has been organized in four major sections: the first deals with the important subject of positive health during the three main stages of childhood; the second covers common children's ailments, and is introduced by a guide to symptoms; the third is concerned with the developmental stages of childhood; and the fourth with first aid and safety. Section one concludes with an essay on complementary medicine that outlines those practices and therapies that are most suitable for children. The book concludes with information on how to care for a sick child at home and in hospital, a directory of useful organizations and agencies, a glossary and a cross-referenced index.

POSITIVE HEALTH

The positive aspects of infant, child and adolescent health are discussed in separate chapters in section one. Infant health includes an assessment of the bonding process, the question of post-natal depression and its possible effects on the infant, breast- and bottle-feeding, weaning, nutrition and safety equipment for babies. Promoting physical and mental health, how the child's position in the family can affect behaviour and learning, road safety and nutrition are some of the subjects dealt with in the chapter on child health. Positive health in adolescence is concerned with problems that often face parents and teenagers – such as smoking, drinking, sexual activity and drugs – and offers guidance on dealing with these serious matters.

COMPLEMENTARY MEDICINE

Sixteen complementary treatments are described on pages 48-63: homeopathy, the Bach flower remedies, aromatherapy, nutritional therapy, Western herbalism, chiropractic, osteopathy, play therapy, arts therapies, reflexology, Chinese herbalism, tai chi and chi kung, acupuncture, kinesiology, relaxation, and massage. There is information on who may most benefit from treatment, any possible contraindications, the consultation and method of treatment, and whether parents can treat the child themselves. Information on how to find qualified practitioners is given in the Directory.

GUIDE TO SYMPTOMS

A guide to symptoms immediately precedes the section on childhood ailments. This provides a quick reference to symptoms often seen in children, pinpoints their possible causes and tells you where in the book you can find information on the relevant ailments, developmental problems or first aid treatment.

THE AILMENTS

Common childhood ailments make up a large proportion of the book. With one exception they are grouped according to the body system or systems that they mainly affect, under 12 headings: Growth; Infections; Brain, nerves and muscles; Bones and joints, Hormones and glands; Skin, hair and nails; Eyes; Ears, nose throat and respiration, Mouth and teeth; Feeding and digestion; Heart, blood and circulation; and Genitals, urinary tract and kidneys.

Each of the 12 sections has been given a coloured symbol to help you find the information you need quickly and efficiently. For example, Growth has a rust symbol, and you would look here for the article on Growing pains. Other features in this section include lists of common symptoms, set off by bullet points •, under the heading 'You may notice'; clear instructions about what to do and, where applicable, details on medical diagnoses, tests and treatment. There is also a diagnosis page at the beginning of each ailment section; this gives a detailed picture of the common symptoms that are relevant to the illnesses in that particular section.

It is a unique feature of this book that suitable complementary treatments are given for each ailment, providing parents with comprehensive information on available methods of

managing their child's illness. Each treatment has its own colour symbol (see below) for easy identification. In this way, by glancing under the heading Complementary treatment for, say, mumps, you would see that Western herbalism, osteopathy and homeopathy were suitable treatments.

Where applicable, additional guidelines or practical advice on the ailment is highlighted in coloured boxes adjacent to the main text. Cross-references are given in those cases where further information about an ailment or associated condition can be found elsewhere in the book.

- **Homeopathy**
- **Chinese herbalism**
- **Western herbalism**
- **Massage**
- **Aromatherapy**
- **Chiropractic**
- **Osteopathy**
- **Acupuncture**
- **Tai chi and chi kung**
- **Kinesiology**
- **Arts therapy**
- **Play therapy**
- **Reflexology**
- **Relaxation**
- **Bach flower remedies**
- **Nutritional therapy**

CHILD DEVELOPMENT

The child from 0 to 15 and the various stages of physical, emotional and mental development are the concerns of the third section. As in the chapters on positive health the subject is covered in three parts: the infant, the growing child and the adolescent. It begins with a guide to how infants develop, from the first months of life until the age of five, under headings such as hearing and talking, moving, handling objects, seeing and moving. This allows parents to plan games and other activities that are appropriate to their child's level of development. The physical and emotional development of school age children, from five to fifteen, is also covered in detail. Sources of advice and information for the problems discussed in this section are given in the Directory.

FIRST AID AND SAFETY

The latest first aid instructions for the most common accidents and emergencies are given here, together with advice and tips on making your child's environment as safe and secure as possible. This section contains detailed illustrations that add considerably to the written instructions.

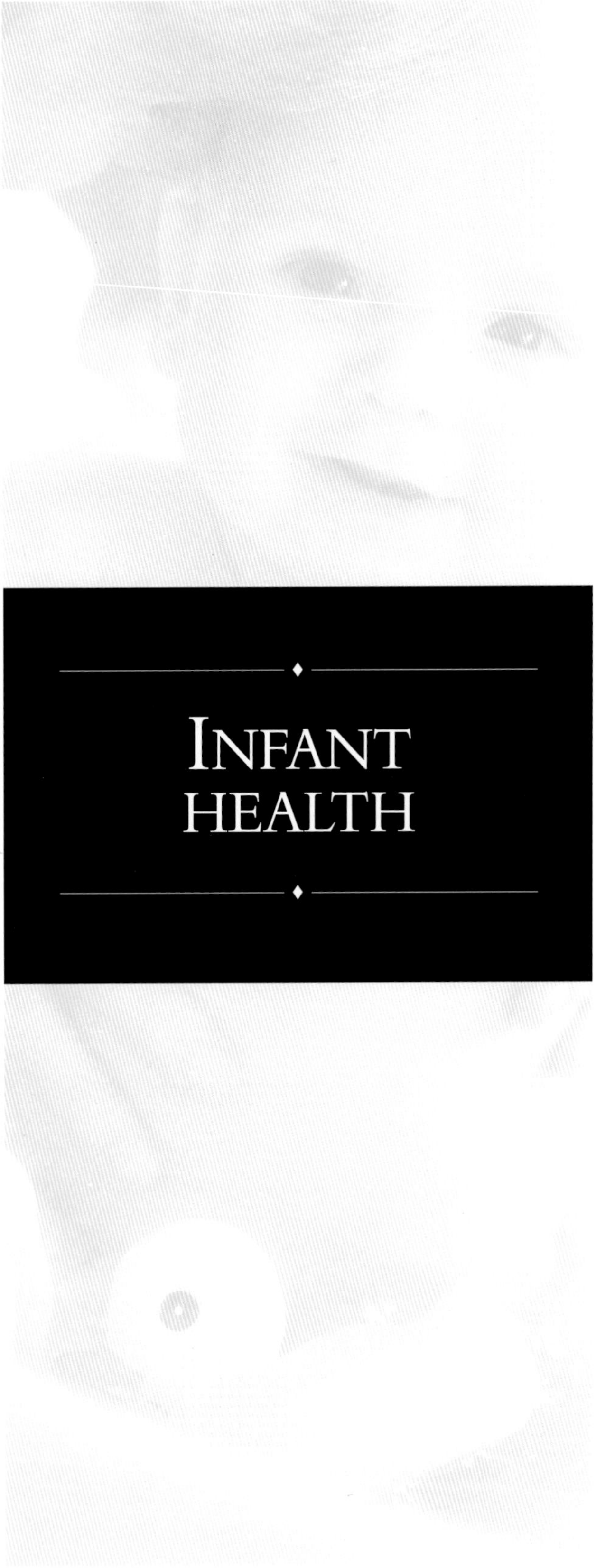

INFANT HEALTH

Fragile and dependent as new infants look, they are actually born survivors. Modern lifestyles and improvements in medicine mean that the newly born now begin life in better health than they have ever done before – and the vast majority of them remain that way. Survival statistics show that, in the United Kingdom, 994 infants out of every 1000 celebrate their first birthdays in good health. Only a generation ago three times as many infants died before they were one year of age, so in the developed countries of northern Europe and North America the prospects for new infants have never before been so promising.

Infants in the developed world have never been healthier than they are today. Good nutrition and healthcare as well as widespread immunization mean that for many the childhood years are free from serious disease. However parents still worry over their children's health, which is only natural.

Bonding

For an infant to survive emotionally, bonding is a necessity. Babies do not thrive if only their physical needs are attended to, but as long as their emotional needs are met, most of them develop into caring and empathetic children. What is more, there is evidence that babies who have securely bonded with their mothers develop their innate capacities more fully than babies who do not develop such strong attachments.

What is bonding?

Babies need one special person whom they love and who loves them, and initially this is the person the baby spends most time with when awake – usually the mother, but it can be a father, grandparent or a paid carer. (A baby who has more than one special person to care for them – a father and a mother, and perhaps a grandparent as well – is additionally fortunate.) During the first year of life an infant becomes increasingly attached to these special people.

From the mother's point of view, bonding is the process whereby she becomes irrevocably committed to her baby.

Some mothers fall in love instantly with their babies. For others the strong feelings of a caring concern and commitment take weeks or even months to flower. The emotional commitment can begin before birth; in fact, in one study almost four mothers in ten reported positive feelings towards their unborn babies. The infant's foetal movements were important to these mothers, perhaps because they encouraged the realization that the bump was a baby. Almost exactly the same number of mothers fell in love with their babies during birth or on the first day, with most of the remaining mothers starting to feel positive about the infant a day or two following the birth. For these mothers, important issues were being able to be alone with their new baby and having the opportunity to hold them.

Close body contact calms infant and parent, and makes them feel more attuned to each other. The power of touch in the process of bonding has been under-rated, but is now widely acknowledged: one study showed that blindfolded new mothers could identify their babies by touching their hands.

Unfortunately there are a number of mothers who simply do not bond with their babies, at least in the first few weeks or months. There can be many reasons. Postnatal depression (see right) is one, and so is the infant's temperament. Some babies are not responsive. Others have spent weeks or even months in a neonatal intensive care unit where the opportunities for the simple activities known to promote bonding – holding the infant, communicating with them – are not possible or are limited. One mother of a very premature baby, born at 26 weeks, found that she didn't dare love her baby daughter in case the baby died. She hoped that once she got her baby home and she no longer had to ask permission to hold her, her love would flower. However, this failed to occur. Then, when she was two years old, the toddler slipped as she was coming downstairs. 'I suddenly felt an overwhelming surge of love for her. I couldn't stop loving her. I'd always loved her, but you know when you have really bonded. Now I just love her to bits.' This is an excellent illustration of the fact that it is never too late.

Postnatal depression

At a stage when a baby's emotional well being is closely intertwined with the mother's, it would seem obvious that depression can have far-reaching consequences. Not surprisingly, there is now evidence that babies do suffer harm when their mothers are depressed in the months following birth, especially where the depression is severe and long lasting.

Depression following childbirth is extremely common. Over half of all new mothers feel tearful and upset in the first few days after childbirth; they have postnatal blues, probably caused by the swift fall in progesterone and oestrogen that all women experience immediately after delivery. Yet this experience of 'baby blues' is quite distinct from postnatal depression. With postnatal depression, one woman in eight will feel so low within three to six months of the birth that she will need professional help to get her through the experience. Mothers who have had depression prior to the birth are at greater risk, as are women with a family history of depression.

Diagnosis

There is no test for postnatal depression, so doctors have to rely on a cluster of symptoms to reach their diagnosis. If you are not sure whether your feelings are caused by exhaustion – exacerbated by concern about family circumstances, lack of money and support at home – or real depression, try asking yourself the following questions (derived from the Edinburgh Postnatal Depression Scale).

In the past week, have you:

- Been unable to laugh and see the funny side of things?
- Stopped looking forward with enjoyment?
- Blamed yourself when things went wrong?
- Felt unreasonably anxious or worried?
- Felt unreasonably frightened or panicky?
- Felt things were getting on top of you?
- Been so unhappy that you had difficulty sleeping?
- Felt sad or miserable?
- Been so unhappy that you have been crying?
- Thought about harming yourself?

If you find that most of your answers are yes, talk to your health visitor or doctor. It is definitely worth seeking treatment not only because treatment for postnatal depression works for the vast majority of women, but because it gives you some protection against further attacks of depression.

Treatment

Women with postnatal depression certainly need to know that they will get better. They need support, reassurance and explanation. Beyond this, meeting other mothers of young babies helps to banish isolation. A more balanced life style is important. It should allow time initially for rest (depression can bring overwhelming feelings of tiredness) and, as recovery begins, time for exercise, personal interests and a healthy diet. Priorities need to be set, at first by someone else. Talking to someone else who has been through the same experience is frequently helpful, but more formal counselling may be needed, perhaps provided by a counsellor working in a doctor's surgery, a volunteer working through a local support group or even a psychologist or psychiatrist. Some women have been helped by cognitive therapy, which challenges negative thoughts and substitutes more reasonable alternatives. Other women respond better to a physical treatment, particularly when it is backed by supportive counselling.

Treatment with hormones – progesterone or oestrogen patches – can work, although like all drug treatment, hormone treatment has side effects, and, to date, has only been tried on seriously depressed women. Antidepressants work by lifting the mood sufficiently for people to begin tackling their problems themselves. However many mothers do not want to take antidepressants for fear they will affect a breastfed infant. Many doctors will agree with this attitude of caution, although conclusive research is lacking. As there is more evidence for the safety of the older tricyclic antidepressants, such as imipramine and amitriptyline, these are likely to be considered safer for breastfeeding women, although most manufacturers advise against this.

Safety equipment

Over half the accidents that happen to children under five years of age occur at home, and while the peak age for accident-prone behaviour is around two, babies enter the danger zone at about nine months, when they become mobile. In the early days your baby will need complete protection. A watchful, caring eye is essential, but safety equipment both helps to protect infants in high-risk areas, such as a sitting room or kitchen, and gives parents peace of mind.

Research suggests that, in the United Kingdom, every year around 15,000 under-fives are injured in accidents involving nursery equipment. Safety equipment that is bought second-hand, or is not repaired or replaced when worn or faulty, can itself cause accidents. Second-hand equipment does not usually come with fitting or assembly instructions and may only conform to out-of-date safety standards. It may also have worn or missing components. To keep young babies safe, it is best to buy new equipment that conforms with national or international safety standards, or to use equipment handed down by a relative or friend, the origin and history of which is well known.

Car safety seats in particular must always be replaced after a crash because of the risk of unseen structural damage to the shell or the harness. If replacement is not possible, parents should check that the seat conforms with safety standards, using information from the Child Accident Prevention Trust (see Directory for details).

The first few months

Equipment needed initially includes the following: a non-slip bath mat for a baby bath; a safe cot (see Safety in the bedroom, page 362); a safe pushchair with a five-point safety harness; a car safety seat; and a highchair with a five-point safety harness.

Pushchairs suitable from birth must be fully reclining to allow babies to lie flat until they can sit unsupported. They must have good brakes and a safety locking device to ensure they don't fold up unexpectedly. They must also have a safety harness, and should have a guard or shopping tray behind the footrest to stop trailing feet reaching the ground. They should have a deep hood to protect a baby from direct sunlight as well as a place where you can attach a parasol. A lightweight buggy is suitable after a baby can sit up straight: a lie-back buggy is suitable after three months.

There are two suitable types of child safety seat for babies under one year of age: a rear-facing seat with an integral harness for babies up to 10–13 kg/22–29 lb, and a forward-facing seat with integral harness, secured by a fitting kit or a lap belt with or without a diagonal belt. The latter are suitable for babies weighing between 9 and 18 kg/20 and 40 lb. All seats should now comply with a new European safety standard and be marked ECE R44.03.

The highchair should have a wide, stable base. Make sure it does not have any sharp edges or places where the baby can trap their fingers. Don't leave a baby in a highchair near a table, as they can reach out for dangerous objects or food.

Additional equipment

Once a baby is mobile, much more equipment becomes necessary. However, before you spend any money, lie down on the floor to put yourself at the baby's level, so you can see unexpected hazards and observe your baby's environment. (Never allow a baby under 12 months into the kitchen, as this is the highest-risk environment in the house; see Safety in the kitchen, page 361)

A safety gate is a priority purchase for parents keen to protect their mobile and inquisitive toddler from danger. From the stage when children are just walking until the point where they are able to clamber over it, the safety gate enables parents to keep their child out of the most hazardous danger zones in the home.

At the age of 11–12 months you will probably need: safety gates to block access to stairs and high-risk rooms such as the kitchen (screw-in designs are sturdier than pressure-mounted styles); corner protectors to stop your child from banging themself on furniture; electricity socket protectors; a fireguard to protect a mobile baby from coming close to a fire; cupboard, door, fridge and video locks to discourage unwanted inquisitiveness; safety film on low level glass tables, doors and windows.

Some families find playpens useful. If you use one, look for a design with deep sides – more than 60 cm/2 ft high – and safe spacing between any bars. Don't tie strings across the playpen, as anything over 20 cm/8 inches can strangle a baby, and only keep small toys inside – resourceful babies can easily climb out. Baby walkers are popular because they allow a baby who is not quite walking to move around in apparent safety. However, they can be the cause of accidents if the baby is able to reach higher than they otherwise could and, for example, pull down a tablecloth. They can also tip a baby down the stairs. If a baby spends too long in a walker and their feet only just touch the ground, this encourages tiptoe walking. Ideally, babies should never use a walker and they certainly shouldn't once they are walking. To be used safely, a baby in a walker has to be constantly supervised.

Warmth

Every human's body temperature is controlled by a thermostat housed in the brain. Infants also control their temperature in this way, but they differ from adults in that they lose heat through their skin quickly because they are thin, they have little insulating fat and their skin area is relatively large compared with their body mass. Young infants therefore need to be kept warm, and are usually comfortable at around 16–20°C/61–68°F, a temperature that is also comfortable for an adult in light clothing. However, once undressed, babies cool down quickly, particularly if their skin is wet; so before you massage or bath your baby the room needs heating.

In winter you should wrap your baby warmly when you go outside, and pay particular attention to the head, which has a large surface area and therefore loses heat rapidly. Even on a summer's day, winds can chill. Once babies come inside, however, their outdoor clothing should be loosened or taken off immediately. In this case, inside includes getting into a heated car, going into a shop or into a shopping centre.

In many homes, an infant is, however, more likely to overheat than to become cold. The sign of an overheated infant is that they look flushed and sweaty. Cool by first removing a layer or two of clothing and offering a drink – a breastfeed or cooled, boiled water.

Outside, babies' skin is extremely vulnerable to the sun's ultraviolet rays, so use a shade on a pushchair to protect the infant from direct sunlight. An infant under six months should never be left in the sun, and an older baby should be dressed in a wide-brimmed hat with a dense weave, and light clothes to cover most of the body. Protect the baby's skin with a suncream that has an SPF (sun protection factor) of at least 15. Inside a car, glass filters some of the ultraviolet rays, but a baby should have a blind for shade.

Smoking

In spite of all the evidence against smoking in pregnancy and around small children, one of the few groups of people who

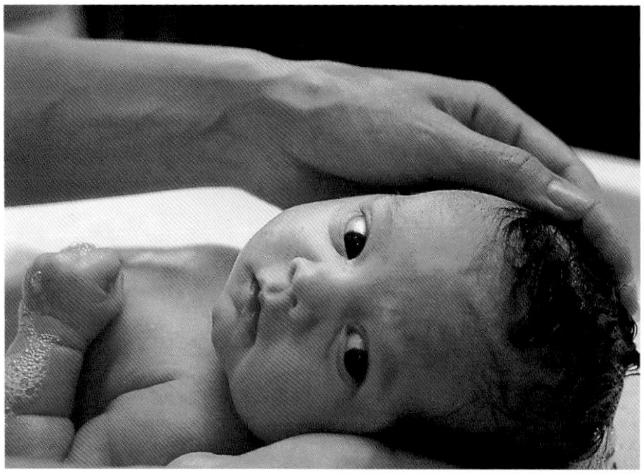

A baby's skin has a superfine protective layer of natural oils, which is why it feels so silky to the touch. To keep it that way, avoid bathing with soaps, detergents or any product that foams. Use lotions instead, massaging in oils or moisturizers to add to the skin's natural oils.

are actually smoking more today is young women. Of those women who are persuaded to stop smoking while pregnant, the majority start again as soon as their baby is born. Yet one of the most protective steps anyone can take on behalf of children is to keep them well away from cigarette smoke at all times. The toll of diseases suffered by the children of smokers rises almost annually.

Not only do women who smoke while pregnant run a greater risk of complications and also of miscarriage, but one study has shown that their daughters do too, while their sons have an increased chance of minor abnormalities such as undescended testicles.

Infants exposed to cigarette smoke during pregnancy are more likely to be born underweight or premature than infants born to non-smoking mothers, and they are more likely to grow slowly. It is possible that they are also more likely to be born with a limb abnormality. They run a greater risk of sudden infant death syndrome (formerly known as cot death) and, in the first six months, they are more likely to develop respiratory problems such as breathlessness and wheezing. In the longer term, these children are more prone to asthma. All of these respiratory effects stem from the fact that their airways are smaller. The children of fathers who smoke may also run an increased cancer risk, possibly because smoking can cause genetic damage to the sperm.

Smoking in the presence of infants and young children only makes matters worse. Children who grow up in smoking households are more likely to get coughs, asthma, and ear and chest infections.

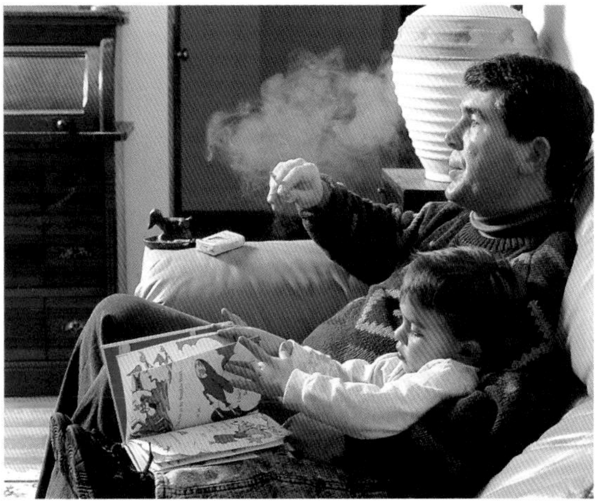

The effects of smoking on the pregnant woman and foetus are perhaps better known and accepted than the effects of passive smoking on children, but they are just as serious. It is now thought that fathers who smoke may also harm their child's health through genetic damage to their sperm.

The most effective ways to stop smoking

- You must really want to stop
- You must be clear about your reasons for stopping (your children's health; your health; money)
- Throw away all your cigarettes, ashtrays and lighters and avoid any places where you feel tempted to smoke
- Ask for other people's support. Tell them you are giving up
- Give up with a friend
- Do something else when you feel like smoking – run up and down stairs, do some exercises, go for a walk, ring a friend
- Stop completely, but take it one cigarette at a time, then one day at a time

Breastfeeding

There is no argument about the best way to feed a baby. Apart from being practical, cheap, safe, hygienic and immediately available at the correct temperature, breastmilk provides all the food and drink a baby needs for at least the first four to six months of life. Even during weaning, breastmilk continues to provide the baby with important nutrients.

Breastmilk contains exactly the right nutrients in the right proportions, even for premature babies, and as the baby grows the composition of milk changes to meet the baby's needs. The creamy yellow colostrum produced in the first few days contains more protein and minerals (as well as antibodies against infections to which the baby is especially vulnerable) and less carbohydrate and fat than mature breastmilk, because that is what babies need at that time.

The contents of breastmilk

Mature breastmilk is still very different from cows' milk. It contains only about 1.2 per cent protein, much less than the milk of other mammals, because a human infant grows more slowly than other mammal infants. Some of the protein nourishes the baby and some plays a role in the immune system. Mature milk contains enough fats to supply over 50 per cent of the baby's energy needs. Lipase, one of some 70 enzymes in breastmilk, is responsible for the almost total digestion and absorption of the fats. Unlike cows' milk, breastmilk contributes to the healthy development of the brain and retina by supplying the long-chain polyunsaturated fatty acids docosahexaenoic acid (DHA) and arachidonic acid (AA). This is especially important for preterm babies and some full-term babies who cannot synthesize these fatty acids efficiently from the essential fatty acids linoleic and alpha-linolenic acid.

There are lower levels of most minerals in human than in cows' milk, but infants absorb more of the important minerals such as calcium and iron. However, breastmilk contains high concentrations of vitamins A, C and E.

Benefits to the baby

In general, breastfed babies are healthier and less liable to catch infections than babies who are bottle-fed. This is because breastmilk contains immunoglobulins – antibodies against infection, antiviral substances and lymphocytes to help infants resist infections until they can protect themselves. As the mother creates antibodies to infective agents in her own environment she passes them on to the baby, who is at risk from the same infections. Breastmilk also contains at least 10 to 20 times more lactoferrin than cows' milk. Lactoferrin is a protein that binds iron and acts in a variety of ways as an anti-infective factor. Breastfed babies are less likely to suffer from gastroenteritis and even colds, coughs, respiratory, middle ear and urinary tract infections. When they are immunized, breastfed babies make more antibodies, suggesting that their immune systems are already more mature. And it is possible that breastfeeding may protect babies against sudden infant death syndrome.

Breastfeeding has other effects on health as well. Breastfed babies tend to be slimmer at age one than bottle-fed infants, and breastfeeding delays the onset of symptoms of allergic ailments such as asthma and eczema, and may help to prevent them developing. This may be in part because a breastfed infant is exposed to much less foreign food protein, and because breastmilk encourages the intestines to mature early. Even tiny premature infants born so young that they have to be fed intravenously are given a small quantity of breastmilk – less than a 5 ml/1 teaspoon – to help their bowels to mature. Even this amount helps to protect against infections.

Many of the benefits of breastmilk are not yet fully understood. Scientists think, for example, that there may be long-term health benefits from the changing proportions of fats and fatty acids during the feed – thirst-quenching thinner milk (foremilk) followed by more satisfying fat-rich hindmilk – but what these benefits are has not yet been proven.

Benefits to the mother

Breastfeeding also benefits the mother. In terms of energy, it possibly uses up as much as 600–800 calories a day, a proportion of these taken from the mother's daily diet and a proportion from fat stores. This helps women to regain their shape and weight prior to pregnancy. Early breastfeeding also stimulates the uterus to contract, so bleeding after childbirth is completed more quickly. More importantly, breastfeeding is a force for empowerment, helping mothers in the early, uncertain days of parenting to feel confident and fulfilled.

Breastfeeding is, however, a major commitment at a time of major life change. It is a skill that has to be learned and it is not always easy. No mother should feel bullied into breastfeeding. Unfortunately this can happen today, when hospitals are keen to increase their breastfeeding rates. There can be worries with breastfeeding. Even if getting started is easy, some babies take time and need practice to get used to the idea. At this point a bottle may seem a simple solution.

Common concerns of breastfeeding mothers

A common concern is whether the baby is getting enough milk. In fact, breastfeeding babies do not need as much milk as bottle-fed babies because they use it so efficiently. As long as a baby is happy, growing and producing wet nappies regularly, then it is unlikely that there is anything to worry about. If you don't think you are producing enough milk, offer the infant the breast frequently, take enough rest and make sure you are eating and drinking in sufficient amounts.

Sore nipples put a lot of mothers off breastfeeding, but often simple measures such as checking that the baby is in the right position for feeding, keeping the nipples dry and avoiding soap can help. Sometimes a thrush infection (see page 100) in the baby's mouth can make nipples sore. Engorged breasts can make feeding difficult for the baby, and the answer to this is frequent feeds or expressing milk between feeds. Blocked ducts or mastitis can make the breasts feel tender and make the mother feel feverish. Keep on breastfeed-

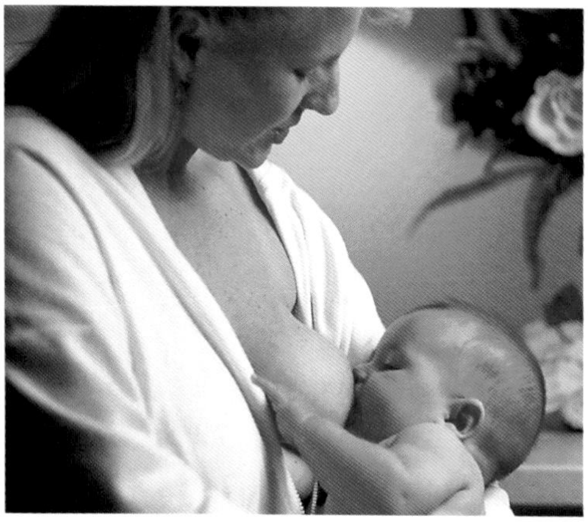

Breastfeeding gives every baby the best possible start in life. Health benefits to the baby include protection against a wide range of infections and allergies, while for the mother it can be a means to effortless weight loss and a return to her former figure.

ing, offering the breast with a blocked duct first, massage the lump towards the nipple and express milk after a feed to make sure the breast is empty. To help relieve the tenderness, apply warm face cloths to the breast or soak in a warm bath. Contact a doctor if the symptoms persist after 24 hours. In all of these situations, the support of a friend, counsellor or health visitor who is currently breastfeeding or who has recently breastfed is invaluable.

When to stop

Once breastfeeding is going well it can be difficult to know when to stop. Some organizations suggest stopping after a year, others – such as UNICEF and the World Health Organisation (WHO) suggest two years. As long as both mother and baby are enjoying it and as long as solid foods are introduced any time between four and six months, there is no reason to stop. In fact, continuing breastfeeding helps to protect a baby against infection into the second half of the first year. Some babies decide to call a halt themselves, while others cut down until they are only taking one feed a day, or just turn for comfort to the breast. As long as the infant continues to feed, the breast will continue to supply milk.

Stopping can be immediate or gradual, depending on what you can cope with. If you cut down gradually it helps to have a supportive partner to feed the baby at the time you would have done, and if possible to leave at least three days between dropping each feed. It is better not to cut down quickly, but if you have to, a change of routine can help to mask the signals your baby might otherwise pick up.

Bottle-feeding

Breastmilk is always the first option for babies, but occasionally a mother cannot breastfeed. Some women have to take drugs, such as antidepressants, which pass into their breastmilk and could affect the infant. Occasionally, too, a baby cannot breastfeed without great difficulty; although some succeed, babies with a cleft palate, for example, may find breastfeeding difficult. One-third of mothers in the United Kingdom bottle-feed their babies from the early days, and by six weeks, six out of ten infants are being fed with a bottle.

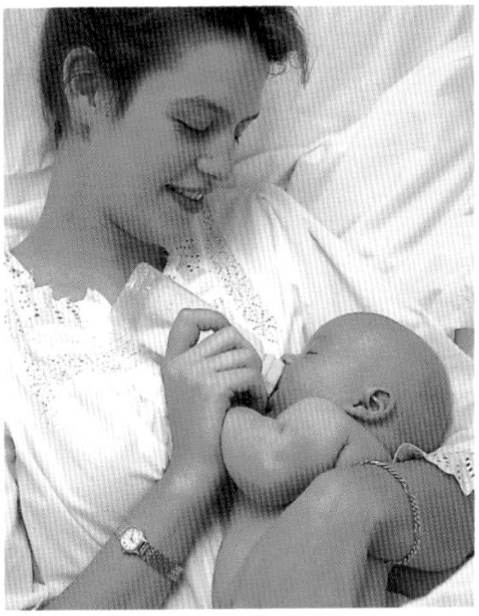

Although 'breast is best', there are several reasons why some mothers bottle-feed their babies; for example, some babies requires a special formula for a medical condition, or the mother may be unable to breastfeed. Whatever the reason, the mother can become as emotionally involved with her baby as a mother who breastfeeds.

Advantages and disadvantages

Formula milk may not be the perfect substitute for breastmilk, but in a caring and careful family in a developed country it is a satisfactory one. It is of course based on cows' milk, which is modified so that it resembles human milk as closely as possible. Constituents such as sodium and protein are reduced to amounts that a young baby's kidneys can cope with; the natural fat is replaced with blends of dairy and vegetable fats and there are added essential vitamins, trace elements and minerals, as well as the milk sugar lactose.Yet it still lacks many of the substances to be found in breastmilk. It does not contain antibodies to protect against infection, nor enzymes such as lipase to help in the digestion of fats. It usually does not contain long-chain polyunsaturated fatty acids, important for healthy brain and eye development.

Moreover, formula milks have been involved in a succession of health scares, some more worrying than others. For example, a number of brands were revealed to contain phthalates, chemicals used to make plastics flexible and found in animal tests to affect fertility. However, the amounts in formula milk are not considered to present a problem.

It was then revealed that soya milks, prescribed for babies who are intolerant of cows' milk protein and lactose, and chosen by some vegan families, not only contain tooth-damaging sugars, but also phytoestrogens, hormones that are structurally similar to oestrogen. It is not yet clear whether this helps or harms infants and the long-term effects are not known. Most recently, one brand of formula was withdrawn because of presumed contamination with a rare type of salmonella, *Salmonella anatum*.

In spite of this there are a few advantages to bottle-feeding. Bottle milks are fortified with iron, and studies have shown that infants given the follow-on milks that are especially formulated for infants over six months (containing more protein, iron and vitamin C) are protected against iron-deficiency anaemia in the second half of the first year. They can be used while mothers are decreasing breastfeeds, and are much more suitable than ordinary cows' milk, which is not recommended for infants under a year old.

It is possible to become as close emotionally to a bottle-fed infant as to a breastfed one, and to enjoy the experience just as much. When the IQ-boosting effects of breastfeeding are discussed, it is probable that it is these ways of behaving – being very close physically to the baby and communicating

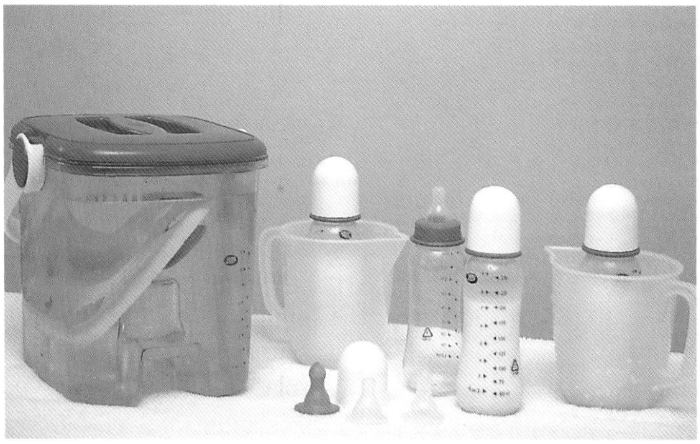

Bottle-feeds should be prepared very carefully, always following the manufacturer's directions, and bottles and teats should be washed thoroughly before sterilizing. There are several methods for doing this, including the chemical method, the equipment for which is shown here.

with them intimately during a feed – that play the most important determining role.

Hygiene

If you do decide to give your baby bottles, remember the following points. First, make the feeds up as hygienically as possible. Only use bottles and teats sterilized chemically, by boiling, steaming or microwaving. Wash your own hands well before preparing feeds. Follow the instructions on the packet precisely and never top up the feed with an extra spoonful or add anything to it, such as crumbled rusk or baby rice. Even more damaging is the practice prevalent among certain ethnic groups of sweetening formula with honey or sugar. Sucking a sweetened liquid does no more than bathe the teeth in a sugared glaze and induce dental decay.

In the early months the only way a baby can feed is by sucking, but by weaning age babies develop a range of other feeding techniques. Bottle-fed babies should be encouraged off the bottle and on to a cup by the age of six months, in order to promote other ways of handling food. They should certainly have stopped sucking for nutrition by the age of one year. One of the factors influencing obesity is continuing to bottle-feed large quantities of milk at the same time as establishing a full weaning diet.

Weaning

Breastmilk provides all that young babies need in the way of food and drink, but as babies grow they need more energy and a broader range of nutrients. By the time the baby is six months old, milk alone no longer provides enough protein, vitamins A and D, iron or zinc. It is time to start the gradual process of moving from one method of feeding to another.

Weaning involves much more than providing nutritious food for a growing baby. It is concerned with beginning to enjoy food and getting into the habit of pleasant family mealtimes. Therefore from the early days of introducing new textures and tastes, babies should enjoy the experience. At each stage, being sensitive to the infant's food preferences and never cajoling or forcing food means that monumental battles can be avoided, and the lesson can be taught that eating is a relaxed and enjoyable activity.

To eat solid or semi-solid food, a baby needs new skills. By five months, many infants have discovered how to move food from the tip of the tongue to the back of the throat and then swallow it. Around the same age, a baby learns to put objects in their mouth and suck them, a skill that will prove vital when they come to hold food and feed themselves. Given the opportunity, from six months they can learn to chew. It is a good idea to have introduced babies to a range of tastes and textures – before another important skill develops around seven months – pressing the lips together and refusing food.

Beginning

In the early weeks, starting any time between four and six months, the idea is to get the baby used to sipping food from a spoon instead of sucking it from a nipple. The amounts of extra food the baby takes in are negligible, so breastmilk or formula are still the most important part of their diet. Offer smooth, bland foods such as puréed rice, mashed potato, plain yoghurt or puréed vegetables.

Although an infant's kidneys and intestines have matured enough to cope with some solid food by now, there are still foods they cannot manage, especially foods that have been commonly associated with allergic reactions. In the early weeks the walls of the intestines are highly permeable, allowing large molecules through into the bloodstream, which can provoke an immunological response. The gut walls gradually 'close', so that an infant can eat a wider range of foods without fear that they will cause an inappropriate reaction. However, at this stage babies still cannot manage wheat-based foods, nuts, spicy foods, fatty foods, eggs or citrus fruits.

Once a baby is taking different foods from a spoon two or three times a day they should be taking in enough nutrients to make a difference to their diet. The key nutrients the diet should provide are: proteins (from fish and meat as well as milk); fat, mostly from milk, and as cows' milk shouldn't be given in the first year as a drink (although it can be used in cooking from four months), that means breastmilk, formula or a follow-on milk; and starchy carbohydrates. However, large amounts of unrefined cereals are not recommended as they are too bulky for babies and contain high levels of phytates, which impair the absorption of zinc and iron.

Minerals are also important. Inherited iron stores are low by now and iron is not supplied in large quantities by milk. Many of the foods commonly used in weaning diets are also low in iron. By 6–8 months, infants therefore need either meat, which is a good source of haem iron (iron from meat sources), or a plentiful supply of iron-rich vegetables and vitamin C to aid absorption. Eating enough meat also ensures that an infant's zinc stores are topped up.

The wide range of other minerals needed for healthy growth are best guaranteed by moving an infant gradually on to a diet that contains a rich variety of meat, fish, cereals, fresh fruits, vegetables and dairy produce. These minerals include: calcium, phosphorus, magnesium, sodium, potassium, selenium, iodine and copper. Taking supplements is not sensible – except prescribed iron supplements for premature infants – because of a real risk of producing an imbalance.

Vitamins are a vital constituent of the weaning diet, and one of the first extra foods is juice or fruit containing vitamin C. Again, the best way to ensure that a baby being weaned is getting enough vitamins is to give them varied foods. Give recommended vitamin drops if the baby is breastfed.

Six to twelve months

At six to nine months, an infant can experiment with stronger tastes and varied textures and start to eat soft finger foods like banana, cooked green beans and carrot, toast, pitta bread, rice cakes and soft fruit. Family foods can be mashed or blended to leave a few lumps, without adding salt or sugar. Drinks of water or fresh fruit juice diluted five parts water to one part juice should be given in a cup rather than a bottle.

By nine to twelve months, babies can follow the family's eating pattern, with three main meals, adapted from family foods (chopped or mashed and with no salt or added sugar). As these foods may not be high enough in fats and protein, snacks need to be added – small pieces of fruit, cooked and salad vegetables, potatoes and cheese – but no high-sugar biscuits or cakes. Babies can now cope with a higher level of fibre, so they can start to eat more wholemeal foods.

By 12 months, an infant can eat food that is broadly similar to an adult's. But essential differences remain: toddlers and young children need a higher fat intake than adults, so their drinking milk should be full-fat until at least the age of two and they should not drink skimmed milk until they are five.

Foods to avoid

During weaning, some foods shouldn't be given at all and some should be delayed until later. Foods you shouldn't give:

- Cows' milk as a drink. You can use it in cooking
- Added salt – an infant's kidneys cannot excrete it. There is enough natural salt in foods already
- Added sugar – it provides no nutrients, only energy, and is a major cause of tooth decay. Instead, encourage your baby to eat savoury or naturally sweet foods as far as possible
- Tea – tannin binds with iron and stops it being absorbed
- Soft drinks, colas – they may contain sugar and/or artificial sweeteners. Their acidity also contributes to tooth erosion
- Unpasteurized milk
- Goats' or sheeps' milk – they are no healthier than cows' milk and are low in folic acid
- Spoonable honey – in rare cases it can cause botulism
- Whole nuts
- Soya milk (unless recommended by a paediatrician)

Foods you shouldn't give until an infant is six months old are wheat products, eggs (cooked until both white and yolk are solid), citrus fruits, nut butters or peanut butter. If you come from a family with allergies, wait even longer.

The family bed

Parenting is a 24-hour-a-day job and as if to reinforce the message, toddlers and young children often creep out of their cots and into their parents' beds night after night. Some parents start the trend themselves, bringing a colicky young infant into bed with them for a breastfeed or for the rest of the night. Estimates put the rate of family bedsharing on even an occasional basis at 75 per cent, but it is still a controversial practice. So what are the arguments for and against it?

Advocates of co-sleeping argue that young babies who have not differentiated themselves from their mothers in their minds are too young to be left alone. They say that an adult lying close to an infant at an age when respiration is unstable will sense, even when asleep, if the baby's breathing movements falter. Further, the baby will be stimulated to breathe by the movement of the adult's chest. They point to research that suggests that mothers who are close to their babies are more responsive and are quicker to notice and take action on potential danger signs like unusual breathing or bringing back part of a feed. Advocates also point to the breastfeeding benefits. Co-sleeping makes night feeds part of the natural night-time continuum. What is more, levels of the milk-producing hormone prolactin are highest at night.

There are, however, strong arguments against bedsharing. Aside from the psychological arguments – that all children want to come between their parents and bedsharing allows them to do so, interfering with their sexual relationship in a very real way; that very young children can be exposed to the realities of sex; and that co-sleeping spoils the child and leaves parents with the eventual problem of moving them out – there are physical arguments.

These are clear: a child who sleeps on the edge of the bed can fall out; an infant can suffocate in adult pillows or bed-

Bedsharing is the natural sleeping arrangement for many families and can solve children's sleep problems. Advocates insist that a child needs no prompting to leave the parental bed – when they are ready to go.

clothes; adults can roll over on to babies, although normally only when drunk or drugged; warm parents' bodies and bedclothes can combine to overheat a baby, which can present a real risk if the baby is already feverish; long hair can wind round a baby's neck, so parents need to tie it back. Most serious is the concern that co-sleeping is a factor in sudden infant death syndrome. However, this only holds true if the mother or her partner are smokers.

Current official advice in Britain is not to bedshare as usual practice with infants under six months old. This does not of course mean that parents don't do it. There are, however, times when parents should certainly not co-sleep. These include: when either parent smokes or is extremely overweight; when the parent is ill, drunk or drugged; when the bed is deep and soft. They should also not co-sleep if the infant is feverish or unable to move freely – if they are in a splint or plaster, for example.

Immunization

It is arguable that the single most important single step you can take to protect your children against serious illness is to have them immunized. The vast majority of people, including health professionals, would say that it is not arguable, it is certain. Since vaccination against smallpox began on a large scale at the start of the nineteenth century, the numbers of children dying from common infectious diseases have plummeted. The UK Department of Health points out that before vaccination against measles began in 1968, around 400,000 children a year suffered from this common childhood illness. In 1995, only 22 children caught measles.

Vaccines work by priming the body to anticipate illness. The vaccine contains a version of the virus or bacterium that normally causes the infection, or enough of it to trick the immune system into reacting as though it had met the real thing. White blood cells – B-lymphocytes – then make antibodies to the germs and these linger in the body, ready to annihilate the real thing should it ever arrive. The reason the child does not develop the infection when they are immunized is that the virus or bacterium has been pre-treated to make it harmless. Sometimes it is heated or treated with chemicals, or only a small part of it is used. Diphtheria and tetanus vaccines, for example, only contain pretreated toxins.

In the UK, some infants start their immunization programme within a few days of birth with a BCG immunization against tuberculosis. This depends where you live and whether there is any special reason why your baby should be vulnerable. Other infants start at two months old, when they receive a combination vaccine against whooping cough, diphtheria, tetanus and Hib – *Haemophilus influenzae* type B, a cause of bacterial meningitis. At the same time they have a dose of polio vaccine by mouth. This is repeated after one month and again one month later. The next vaccine comes between a child's first birthday and 15 months, when another combination vaccine is given against measles, mumps and rubella. The whole programme is reinforced before the child starts school with two booster doses, one against measles, mumps and rubella, and the other against diptheria and tetanus, as well as a polio booster. Schoolchildren aged 10–13 are tested for tuberculin sensitivity and if necessary vaccinated, and school leavers get a final injection of diphtheria and tetanus and a final anti-polio dose by mouth.

Vaccines commonly have minor adverse effects. For example, some babies are fretful within 48 hours of the DTPHib injection. More worrying for parents, vaccines can also have acute adverse effects. Out of 14 million doses of vaccine given to UK children in 1995, there were 152 officially reported serious reactions. Some of these were probably a coincidence – illnesses that happened to develop just after immunization. Others were linked to the vaccine. Anaphylactic reactions are known to occur extremely rarely after a vaccine is given, which is why every nurse or doctor administering a vaccine is trained in resuscitation. In three years from 1992, there were only 87 reports of anaphylaxis out of 55 million doses of vaccine. The possibility of a severe reaction to immunization is why infants are usually kept under supervision until they are seen to be well.

Opponents of vaccination worry, however, whether there are other effects. A research group at the Royal Free Hospital in London has raised the question of whether measles vaccination may – rarely – make the development of inflammatory

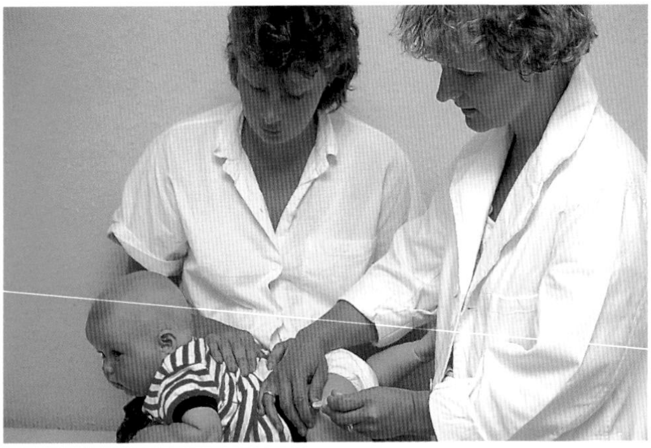

Immunization has changed the face of childhood illnesses beyond recognition. Of the common infectious diseases of childhood that every family used to expect to suffer, only chickenpox remains. A vaccine against chickenpox has already been licensed in the United States.

bowel disease in later life more likely. In the absence of proof one way or the other, current advice is to remember the millions of lives saved by immunization and be vaccinated.

By not vaccinating a child, a parent not only leaves their own child prey to the illness but also lowers the overall level of immunity in the community. Once the overall level drops, the infection can gain a foothold again. This poses very real risks for infants too young for vaccination and for children with weakened immune systems, for example, children being treated for leukaemia.

Baby teeth

By the time an infant is six months old, their first teeth may be just coming through. By 12 months, they may well have ten teeth – eight you can see at the front of the mouth and two molars in the bottom jaw. As soon as the first teeth come through, it is time to start regular daily toothcare.

In the early days of toothbrushing, an infant is unlikely to have a build-up of food remains, so a brush isn't vital. If the infant accepts a soft cloth, finger or wisp of cotton wool more easily at first, use that, and graduate to a brush as more teeth erupt and the baby eats more solid food. When brushing starts, the inside of the front teeth is an area that is frequently missed. The important part of brushing at this stage is the toothpaste and that is because of the fluoride it contains. Fluoride helps damaged tooth enamel to reform, but it needs to be present in the right quantities. Too much and the teeth can become mottled and stained; too little and it doesn't work. Low fluoride toothpastes contain 400–600 parts per million (ppm) of fluoride, which is probably enough to protect baby teeth so long as it is used daily and the water supply is fluoridated to around 1 ppm. A dentist or the local water company will know the fluoride level of the local supply.

Infants can, and should, be registered with a dentist at any time from birth, although they don't normally need a check-up until they are two. If you take an infant with you when you visit the dentist, they will get used to the surroundings.

The other way to keep baby teeth perfect is to avoid added sugar. Sugars occur naturally in foods such as fruit and vegetables and are contained within the cellular structure of the food. These sugars do not damage teeth and nor does lactose, which is found in milk. Cariogenic sugars, which cause tooth decay, occur either outside the cell walls – as in concentrated fruit juices – or are added during manufacture. Cariogenic sugars include sucrose, glucose, dextrose, fructose and maltose. To avoid these, no sugar should be added to baby food and babies should never be given sweetened drinks, above all at bedtime. To put a sweetened drink in a bottle simply bathes vulnerable teeth in a sugar glaze and is just about the worst thing that can be done. However 'natural' they may be, concentrated fruit syrups also contain large amounts of sugar. The only drink an infant needs is water (milk is a food).

Vitamin K

Everyone needs vitamin K to help their blood clot. In fact, the K stands for 'koagulation', spelt with a 'k' instead of a 'c' by the Danish discoverer of the vitamin. All babies are born with low levels of vitamin K and in a tiny number this can cause a serious illness – haemorrhagic disease of the newborn – where the baby may develop life-threatening bleeding, sometimes into the brain. Fortunately, the disease can be prevented by giving newborn infants vitamin K.

Toothcare becomes an important part of a baby's daily routine from the time when his first teeth appear around the age of six months. Early signs of impending teething include gnawing at the fingers and fist, and dribbling. A visit to the dentist at this age will familiarize the baby with the clinical surroundings.

All babies are given vitamin K just after birth. Some infants have their dose by mouth, others by injection, and parents should be allowed to discuss the options with the midwife or doctor. General medical opinion is that injected vitamin K offers better protection against the disease developing either in the baby's first week of life or later on in the first three months. However, important studies a few years ago suggested a possible link between injected vitamin K and childhood cancers, although this was later disputed.

As oral vitamin K has never been associated with cancer, for some time it was recommended that infants should have vitamin K by mouth. A first dose at birth was followed by a second within a week. Subsequent research unfortunately revealed a small number of infants who developed haemorrhagic disease later, despite having been given vitamin K by mouth. Infants who are given oral vitamin K and are fed only on breastmilk now receive a third dose a month later.

Most recently, studies in Germany and England have again failed to find any link between injected vitamin K and childhood cancers. It is now believed that the cumulative evidence almost certainly excludes any association, so most hospitals are reverting to giving vitamin K by injection, which is also the method for preterm infants and those born by Caesarean.

Sudden infant death syndrome (SIDS)

In recent years the number of babies dying of sudden infant death syndrome has fallen by 70 per cent. The chief reason for the fall is believed to be that parents are following advice to lay their babies on their backs or their sides to sleep. Even though sudden infant death syndrome remains the most common cause of death in babies over a month old but under the age of one, it is very unlikely to happen. It is natural for parents to worry about it, but this shouldn't interfere with their enjoyment of their babies.

Not all the causes of sudden infant death syndrome are known yet, but there are a number steps that can be taken to reduce the risk:

- When you put your baby down to sleep in their cot, lay them on their back without a pillow and with their feet near the end of the cot. The bedclothes should cover no further than their shoulders. This is so that they cannot wriggle down until the bedding covers their face. For the same reason, tuck bedding in securely. Babies shouldn't sleep with a duvet or in a baby nest or have a pillow or cot bumper until the age of 12 months. Sometimes there may be a medical reason for a baby to lie on their stomach. In this case the doctor will explain why. Even if your baby is lying on their stomach, make sure that they cannot slip down beneath the bedclothes. Once a baby is old enough to roll over, at around six months, the risk of sudden infant death syndrome is reduced. Eight out of ten cases of sudden infant death syndrome happen before a baby is six months old
- Smoke in the air damages infants' lungs before and after birth, so parents should not smoke or allow anyone to smoke in a room where there is an infant. Infants should not be taken into smoky rooms and if possible no one should smoke indoors where there are children. To protect an infant against sudden infant death syndrome, and for other health benefits, neither parent, and certainly not the mother, should smoke during pregnancy
- Infants shouldn't be allowed to get too hot or too cold. Indoors, rooms should be at a temperature at which adults feel comfortable in light clothes – around 18°C /64°F – but even in winter this doesn't necessarily mean that all-night heating needs to be left on. A room thermometer can be a useful way of checking
- In their cot, infants need a mattress that is firm, clean, dry and well-fitting and complies with safety standards, currently BS1877 and BS7177. One sheet and three layers of light blankest are normally just right for a baby dressed in a vest, nappy and babygrow. However, the best guide is the baby themself. If they look flushed or sweaty, they are too hot, so remove a blanket or two until they are cooler
- Outdoors in cold weather, infants need wrapping up warmly, especially in the first month. But outdoor clothes and wrappings should come off as soon as the baby is brought indoors Infants are often ill. It can sometimes be hard to distinguish between a minor infection and a more serious illness, so if your baby is unwell and you are unsure how ill they are, don't hesitate to phone your doctor

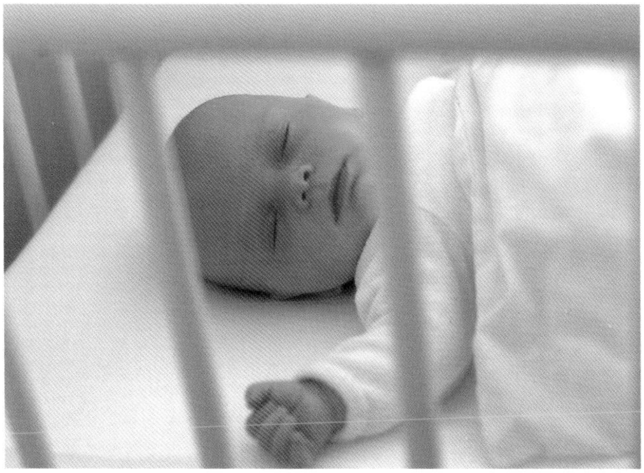

This sleeping position, recommended to reduce the risk of cot death, has recently been shown to bring other health benefits. Infants who slept on their backs are less likely to have coughs, fevers or stomach cramps. Only the risk of cradle cap and nappy rash were raised.

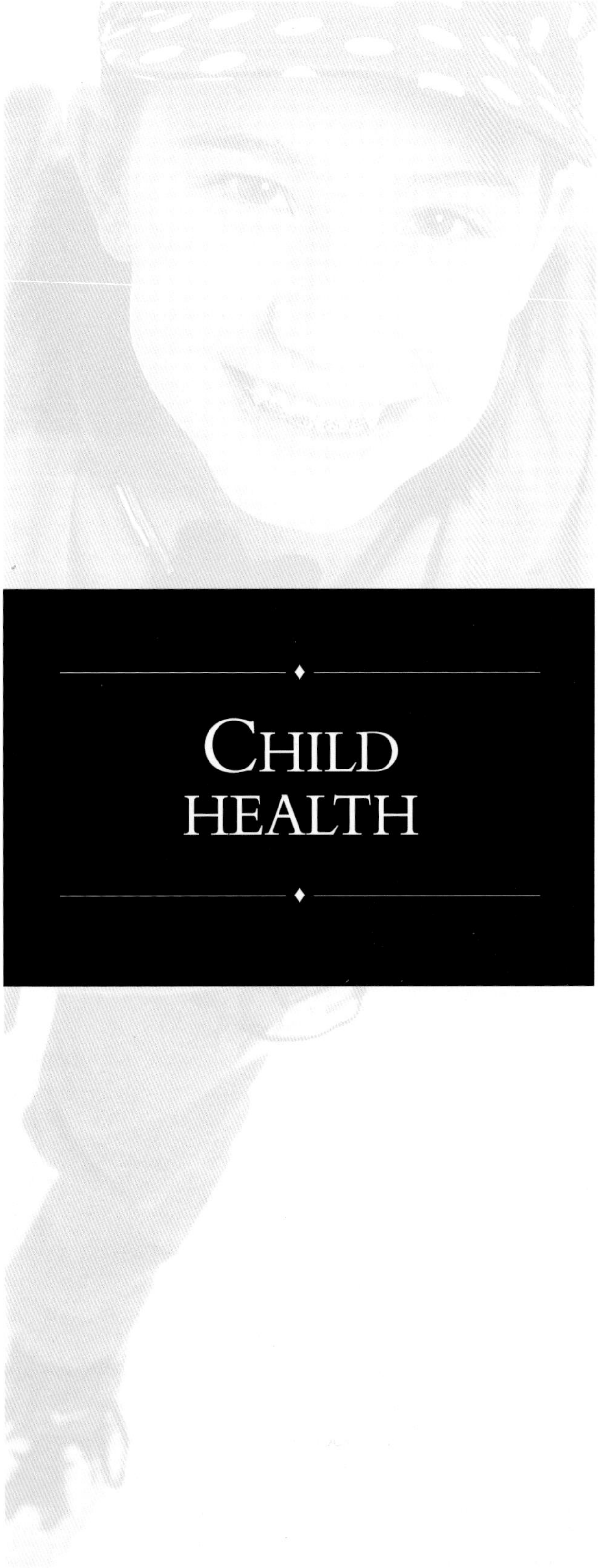

CHILD HEALTH

What does being healthy mean to you? Being fit enough to bound up two flights of stairs without feeling breathless? Having a clear skin and a sheen to your hair? Waking up in the morning and springing out of bed, ready to take whatever the day brings? Feeling good about yourself? Since becoming a parent, the chances are that these feelings are a distant memory, but they will come back. In the meantime, nearly everyone agrees that being healthy means much more than not being ill.

It is just the same for children. A healthy child is not just a 'not-sick' child. A healthy child has energy to spare, is eager and maddeningly inquisitive and enjoys life. Healthy children sleep well and eat as much as they need – even if their appetite seems bird-like to you. Their lives show a balance between spells of intense, quiet concentration and equally intense activity.

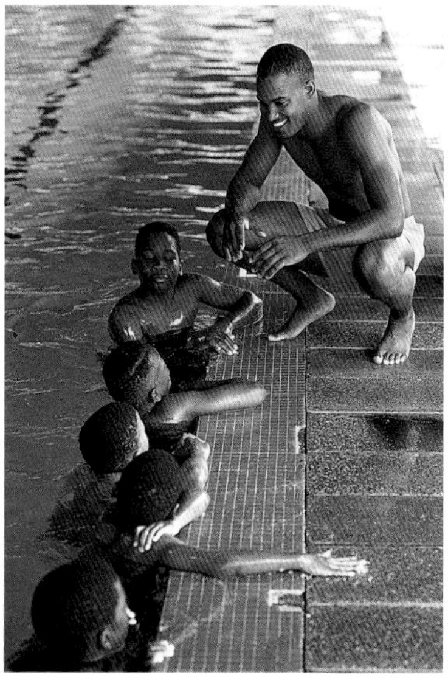

Swimming is an important skill for young children to acquire. As well as increasing their self confidence it provides a moderate to vigorous form of exercise that many will continue. Surveys show that a quarter of young men and women under 25 choose to swim as a leisure activity.

Promoting mental and physical health

Children need to be physically healthy because they are already laying down the foundations for a healthy adulthood and old age. We know that many adult health problems originate in childhood (or even earlier, in pregnancy) but by endowing children with the best possible health, many of them can be prevented. Children who are physically robust also stand the best chance of throwing off the inevitable infections of childhood without developing serious or unpleasant complications. Diseases that have only mild effects in a healthy population play havoc in undernourished children living in poor conditions.

As infections have become less of a threat in childhood, so diseases that relate to our way of life have increased. All the diseases of atopy (allergic conditions such as asthma, eczema and hay fever) are on the increase, as are nutritional diseases. These are not diseases of want, but of plenty. An increasing number of children are now overweight, and while being a podgy pre-schooler does not predict an overweight adult, being overweight as an adolescent does. Overweight predisposes to a wide range of diseases: respiratory infections are more common in childhood, and asthma and diabetes are harder to control; in adulthood high blood pressure, coronary thrombosis and heart failure are more common, as are diabetes, menstrual problems, certain sex hormone-sensitive cancers and osteoarthritis of the weight-bearing joints.

Emotional health is also important in childhood. What good is it to be bounding with unbridled energy if you are consumed with self-doubt? Many factors play a role in determining emotional health. Not all of them are amenable to change, but some of them are.

Friendships are especially important to schoolchildren, whose days are spent in a socially demanding group environment. While boys will often make group friendships, girls more typically pair off and feel jealous if they are abandoned for a new friend.

Mental health is now a key issue in child health. Children are as subject to stress as adults, and many children no longer enjoy the supportive family structure that in the past acted as a buffer. Children increasingly need to be taught to relax and to adopt behaviour that keep them and others around them as stress-free as possible.

The seeds of much addictive behaviour – smoking, drinking too much, abusing solvents – that is more common in the teenage years are sown in childhood. However as these assume greater prominence in adolescence, they are considered in the section on Teenage health (see page 38).

Parents have a unique power to influence positively their children's health. Pregnancy is a time when women are more open to messages about good health than at any other time, yet it is easy to let good habits slip. Many families eat well and exercise well until their children reach school age, when peer pressure combines with the power of the commercialized media to corrupt the messages. Yet it is those early habits that are most important. Good – and bad – health habits are taught, not caught. The best way we can teach our children to lead healthy lives is to do so ourselves.

The importance of family position

What difference does it make to a child to be one of a large family, one of a pair or an only child? We know that there are immediate effects on health for children with older siblings. They tend to catch common cough-and-cold-type infections earlier than first-born children because their older brothers or sisters pick up these infections at school or nursery. This is not necessarily a bad thing. While it is sensible to keep very young infants away from toddlers with streaming noses, there is no reason to protect an otherwise healthy infant over six months of age from the inevitable upper respiratory tract infections. In fact there is a suggestion that early exposure to infection may protect against allergy. One plausible explanation for the recent increase in asthma and eczema is that catching viral infections when young may exert a protective influence. The argument is that as children are increasingly protected against infections so the incidence of allergies rises.

Most concerns about family position centre on the child's social relationships. Will an only child suffer? Or, conversely, what are the effects on the child of belonging to a large family? Here there is some evidence. Most recent research shows that the major differences between families are between those with one or two children and those with several children.

Only children

Only children do not, as prejudice suggests, grow into spoilt and lonely misfits. Research shows that, on a range of personality and behaviour tests (evaluating factors such as maturity, anxiety, happiness and self-control), only children are much the same as children with siblings. They are different in that their parents tend to expect a lot of them, but this can work in their favour as, on average, only children talk early and have advanced reading skills throughout their school career.

However, while children with brothers and sisters cut their social teeth in the privacy of their own homes – learning the painful lessons about sharing, taking turns and seeing the other person's point of view – only children have to do this in public, at mother-and-toddler groups, playgroups and at school. There is also a certain amount of evidence that because only children have missed out on the rough and ready lessons that sibling rivalry teaches, an unease and an anxiety may later on underlie relationships that appear superficially straightforward.

First children

First children start life as only children. They receive more social interaction, stimulation and play with their parents than any later children, although at the same time their parents tend to be more anxious about them and more controlling, and to apply more pressure. This means that they tend to achieve more both academically and professionally, that they are at the same time more intelligent and less confident in their own abilities and that they are more traditional and conformist in their outlook than subsequent children in the family. In terms of their anxieties and insecurities, the way the second child is introduced to the family plays an important role (see Jealousy and sibling rivalry, page 324). There is a tendency for first children to be more bossy and dominant in their relationships with younger brothers and sisters, and to use their superior power or understanding, and this tendency may remain throughout life.

Middle or second children

Middle or second children tend not to achieve as highly as their older brother or sister or, if they do, to choose a different field. They are more radical – even rebellious – and more free-thinking in their attitudes. When they grow up they tend to be less anxious and more easy-going.

Youngest children

Youngest children tend to be the most confident family members of all, and they tend to be tough. However a large age gap can make them less independent. Boys in particular tend to be resourceful in terms of finding ways around difficult situations, and girls tend to be tomboyish and less concerned with appearances than are their older sisters.

Whether or not a child has brothers and/or sisters can have important consequences for their future social development. It appears that those children who grew up with one or more siblings may be more realistic and relaxed in their dealings with other children. Conversely, children without siblings may find it more difficult to socialize.

Children of multiple births

Families with twins and other children of multiple births (triplets, and so on) are becoming increasingly common. Since the early 1980s, when infertility treatment became more widespread, there has been a steady rise year-on-year in multiple births.

The first sign of a multiple pregnancy may be a high level of alpha-fetoprotein (AFP) when a woman is tested for a neural tube defect, or an ultrasound scan shows two amniotic sacs. An ultrasound performed by a skilled operator can detect more than one heartbeat in the seventh week of a pregnancy.

It is very likely that twins will be born early; on average, a twin pregnancy lasts 37 weeks and a triplet pregnancy 34 weeks. Starting maternity leave early and avoiding excessive tiredness may help to prevent an extremely early birth, but apart from that there is little you or anyone else can do to prevent prematurity in a multiple birth.

Breastfeeding is the best way to feed all babies, and breast milk is especially important for premature infants. It is perfectly possible to breastfeed twins and triplets, but it is hard work, especially if the babies do not suck strongly at first. Contact with a mother who has succeeded in breastfeeding twins or triplets is the most useful form of support (see breastfeeding, page 16).

Behaviour

Behaviour problems are common in twins and particularly in identical male twins. A twin whose behaviour improves when they are alone with one parent may be sending a signal that they need more one-to-one adult attention, and the routine needs to be reorganized to allow each twin to spend some time alone with a parent every day.

Twins – especially identical twins – need to know that they are different. They need to look different from each other; if they have to wear the same school uniform, individual hairstyles can set them apart. Other people should be encouraged strongly to call each child by their name, and not to refer to them as 'the twins' or 'the boys'. As they mature it becomes increasingly important that they have some private space, even if it is only the corner of a room.

Development

Proper speech and language development requires regular adult input, which is not easy to organize with children of multiple birth. Forty per cent of twins develop a private language; this does not matter, provided they also develop speech that others can understand. Research shows that mothers of twins use particularly short, simple phrases and answer questions fully when the first twin asks them, but only briefly the second time around. To help twins' speech develop well, parents need to spend time every day playing and talking with each child separately, and need to make an effort to answer questions from each child in detail.

When twins start school, parents need to decide whether to keep them together or to separate them. It is important to consider whether, on the one hand, the twins very obviously have different ability levels or if, on the other hand, they make very similar progress; whether they egg each other on to behave badly; and whether one twin is very dependent on the other. Children who are very dependent on each other can find it helpful to start school together. If they have to separate it can be even more traumatic than for a single child who has to leave their mother for the first time.

Once the children start school, it can be tempting to make comparisons. However comparisons between children who achieve at very different levels are destructive to both children. Should such comparisons arise, the children may do better if they attend different secondary schools.

Emotional health

It is impossible to underestimate the importance of looking after children's emotional health. To be fully healthy, children need more than a balanced diet, a safe and unpolluted environment and immunizations to protect them from physical illness. Yet it is a sad truth that behavioural and emotional disorders and mental health problems in children are increasing. What can parents do to protect their children?

First, children need parents who not only love them unconditionally, but are in a position to show it. Parents should be available when they are needed – in the very early months and years, at times of transition, at bedtimes and when children are ill. This can be inconvenient for full-time working parents and needs negotiation with a sympathetic employer, but in the end it is in the child's best interests.

Temperament

Temperament differences make some children more vulnerable than others. From the start, some infants are easy to handle, cheerful and adaptable. Others dislike change, are slow to adapt and seem to need constant reassurance and comfort. The type of child you have is very much in the lap of the gods, although once you have worked out your child's temperament you can usually see which traits are inherited – and from whom. If you do have a difficult infant you should pay particular attention to their emotional health as the child gets older. Children need their parents' undivided attention. 'Quality time' is all very well, but it is lost on a child who is hungry, tired or plain grumpy. Any relationship needs accommodation on both sides and that may mean giving your attention when the child needs it rather than when you want to give it. As children grow older, shared interests and activities can bring them closer to their parents.

Consistent boundaries

Children also need a positive atmosphere at home, with plenty of praise when they do things right. However parents need to set clear boundaries for their behaviour and be prepared to restrain them when they go too far. Parents need to agree these boundaries between themselves so that they give consistent messages. It is best to avoid criticism: children who are criticized themselves tend to have critical relationships with others. As long as they feel good about themselves they will be able to make friends outside the home. In the early years they need to try a wide variety of different activities, partly because this builds up their base of skills and self-confidence, and partly because in this way they can discover what they are good at. And every child is good at something.

Children thrive on consistency. When they know what is expected of them they find it much easier to conform. Young lives are full enough of change without having to cope with unnecessary inconsistencies. A change of school or home, or a change in carer are major events in a child's life and need to be sensitively prepared for. A sameness that adults may find boring can often provide a healthily supportive atmosphere in which growing children thrive.

Hygiene and food hygiene

Many bacteria and other germs are spread directly from person to person, but by teaching your children some simple steps you can help to keep them healthy. Teach them to use a tissue rather than a cloth handkerchief when they sneeze or blow their noses; to turn their head away from other people to blow their nose, sneeze or cough; and, whenever possible, to wash their hands afterwards.

Children should be taught to wash their hands thoroughly, washing both sides in soap and warm water, rubbing between the fingers and round the nails before rinsing in clean water. Everyone should do this after going to the lavatory, and each family member should have their own towel. If anyone has a stomach upset or diarrhoea, handwashing is especially important and contact surfaces – the lavatory seat, the flush handle, the taps and the door handle – should be wiped down daily with antiseptic.

Once children are active, especially outdoors, they should wash daily. It is easier to give young children a bath, but once they are steady on their feet and do not mind being splashed with water, showers are better. If you do not have one, fit a shower attachment to your bath taps. Frequent washing with soap or using bubble bath may dry out sensitive skin; use a mild cleansing lotion instead or smooth moisturizing lotion into a child's skin after a bath. There is no need to wash hair more than once a week.

Food hygiene

Food hygiene is extremely important. Always buy food as fresh as possible and if you are buying chilled or frozen foods in warm weather, buy them last and transport them in a cool-box or frozen food bag. Your freezer should be kept at –18°C or less and your fridge should be between 0 and 5°C. Use a fridge thermometer to check that the temperature is not too high. Store the most perishable foods, such as cooked meats, in the coldest part of the fridge, and wrap each food item separately or put it in a plastic container. Store uncooked meat and defrosting foods in a drip-proof, covered container at the bottom of the fridge. Keep eggs in the fridge and throw away any that are cracked or broken. If you are putting cooked food into the fridge, let it cool for about an hour first.

Before cooking, and after handling rubbish or emptying the bins, wash your hands and dry them on a hand towel or kitchen paper. If you have an open wound on your hand, cover it with a waterproof plaster before cooking. Wash work surfaces frequently and clear up spills immediately, and use separate chopping boards for bread, cheese, vegetables and meat. The most hygienic way to wash dishes and cutlery is to use a dishwasher, but if you do not have one, wash them in hot water and washing up liquid, rinse and leave to dry.

If you are cooking food taken from the freezer, let it thaw fully first, then make sure it is cooked right through. If you use a microwave or reheat food, make sure the food is piping hot right through. For infants, or a child who is ill, eggs should be cooked until the white and yolk are solid, and children should never be given dishes made with uncooked eggs. Wash all salads, fruit and vegetables before use, especially if they are to be eaten raw. Throw away any milk drinks left outside the fridge for more than an hour, and don't eat food after the 'use by' date.

Some foods contain natural poisons. For example, raw kidney beans contain substances called lectins, which can cause stomach ache and vomiting, but are destroyed when the beans are soaked overnight in cold water for 12 hours and then boiled in fresh water at a vigorous roll for ten minutes or more. The green and sprouting parts of potatoes contain high levels of substances called glycoalkaloids. These parts should be cut out and the whole potato thrown away if it still tastes bitter. Damaged or mouldy apples can contain a toxin called patulin, especially near the damaged sections of the fruit, and should not be eaten. It is also unwise to eat food that shows any sign of mould.

If you use canned food, wipe the top of the can before opening it. Don't leave any food in the can once it is opened, and always wash the can opener after use.

Road safety

From the age of about eight, many children are allowed out alone on the roads. What are the principal hazards that await them and what can parents do to make sure their children behave as safely as possible on the roads?

Here are some facts:

- Children cannot safely cross any road alone, even under the supervision of an adult standing on the sidelines, until they are about 8–9 years old
- Over 95 per cent of child pedestrian accidents happen in urban areas
- Most accidents to child pedestrians happen while they are crossing a road. A large number occur when a child crosses a road where there are parked cars
- Boys have more accidents than girls. Although boys and girls behave in a similar way when approaching roads, boys may react more slowly to unexpected events
- Most accidents happen when children are coming to and from school, particularly in the summer
- Three out of five accidents involving pre-school children occur when the child is playing in the street

The objectives of cycling proficiency schemes is to teach young riders about the rules of the road, basic road skills and the control of the bicycle, as well as simple bicycle maintenance. Cycling awareness programmes develop the young rider's skills in recognizing, assessing and responding to road dangers. Children attending these programmes are therefore more likely to be safe riders.

Knowing this, what should you teach your child about road safety? First, discourage a child from using or crossing main roads. Where possible, a child should use a bridge or underpass. Once children have been taught how, they can use pedestrian crossings. When you are out walking, even with a young child, tell them what you are doing: stopping at the edge of the pavement; looking and listening for traffic; waiting for a gap in the traffic before you cross; looking for safe places to cross, such as a pedestrian crossing or an underpass.

When children reach five or six years of age, teach them to use the right procedure for crossing a road. Teach the key points of the Green Cross Code: Stop! Look! Listen! Practise first on quiet roads near your home. Show your child what to do, then let them lead you across. Finally, let them cross while you watch. At this age, never let a child cross a road without an adult watching. When children are seven to nine years of age, you can teach the full Green Cross Code.

The Green Cross Code

1. Find a safe place to cross, then stop
2. Stand on the pavement near the kerb
3. Look all around for traffic and listen
4. If traffic is coming, let it pass. Look all around again
5. When there is no traffic near, walk straight across the road
6. Keep looking and listening for traffic while you cross

Practise this with your child on quiet roads near your home

By the time children are ten years old, they may be ready to walk to school alone. Walk the route with them until you are certain they are safe. Make sure they wear light or bright clothing, or carry a bright or fluorescent bag. If they have to walk after dark, they will need reflective clothing.

Cycling

It is estimated that, in the United Kingdom, 150,000 children every year attend hospital following a cycling accident. Boys are more likely than girls to be seriously injured. One reason children have cycling accidents is that their bicycles are not properly maintained. Brakes or tyres in poor condition or riding a bike of the wrong size increases the likelihood of accidents. Some children simply lack the necessary skill to ride their bicycle safely or are unable to judge hazards, either because they are inexperienced or because they are too confident. Motorists often do not see cyclists in the road ahead of them, partly because the cyclists are not wearing bright or reflective clothing. It is unwise to allow children to cycle at night or in the rain, but if they have to, they should use front and rear lights.

The most effective step that parents can take to prevent serious injury is to ensure that their children wear a properly fitting helmet; eight out of ten child cycling deaths are caused by head injuries. Children under the age of nine should never be allowed to cycle on the road, and they should take a cycling proficiency course or follow a cycling awareness programme before they do. Parents should always accompany their child on the road until their child is fully competent. They should also plan cycle routes so that children do not need to make risky right hand turns: some three-quarters of all cycling accidents in traffic involve a turn at a junction.

Healthy eating

Healthy eating for children means a lot more than balancing a list of essential and desirable nutrients. Eating is both a social activity and a focal point of family life. Providing food is a way of expressing care and love, and meals are times that should be enjoyable.

The United Kingdom Department of Health recently published *Eight Guidelines for a Healthy Diet**. The first piece of advice is, enjoy your food. The other guidelines are as relevant to young people as they are to adults.

The healthy diet

- Eat a variety of different foods
- Eat the right quantity to be a healthy weight
- Eat foods containing lots of starch and fibre
- Don't eat too much fat
- Don't eat sugary foods too often
- Pay attention to the vitamins and minerals in your food.

The eighth guideline concerns sensible drinking (see page 46).

Once infants have been weaned there is no reason why they should not eat the same food as the rest of the family. By the time children have reached school age, their diet should follow the same pattern as that of adults, with carbohydrates

*Reprinted with kind permission of the Health Education Authority

providing 50 per cent of their energy, fats providing 35 per cent and proteins 15 per cent. But what does that mean in practice?

Food groups

Imagine an empty plate. Put on a good helping of starchy food (pasta, cereals, rice, bread, potatoes); add an equally good helping of vegetables and fruit, with as much variety as you like; next add a smaller helping of a food that is high in protein (fish, eggs, meat, poultry, nuts, pulses); and finish the plate off with a helping of a dairy food (cheese, milk, yoghurt, fromage frais). The plate now contains a healthy, balanced meal. The only foods that are missing are foods that should be eaten sparingly: fatty, oily and sugary foods.

Good proportions

Many children do not eat large platefuls of food. Instead, they skip meals and snack, or 'graze'. In terms of nutrition, this probably does not matter, provided the daily proportions of foods on the imagined plate add up as follows: starchy, carbohydrate-rich foods, five to eleven helpings; vegetables or fruit, five to nine helpings; protein, three helpings; and dairy produce, two to three helpings.

Snacks may actually be beneficial for young children because they need higher energy and nutrient levels than adults to fuel their rapid growth. For pre-school children the snacks can be relatively high in fat: fingers of cheese, whole-milk yoghurts or a glass of full-fat milk or, for children over the age of two, semi-skimmed milk. Children over the age of five do not need such high-energy foods and can drink skimmed milk and eat low-fat dairy produce.

Within the four broad food groups no single food is healthy or unhealthy. It is the combination of foods that is important. Children who eat a wide variety of foods are likely to get all the minerals and vitamins they need. Foods that do not appear in the four groups, such as sugary and fried foods, are not essential and should be kept to a minimum.

Children's food choices

The question is, will children eat this sort of food? The evidence shows that they will, as long as they are not presented with high-fat, high-sugar alternatives and they don't fill up on drinks. Young children may drink too much if they are not weaned from a bottle by the age of 12 months. Once a child is eating a range of solid foods, 600 ml/1 pint of milk (including the milk used in cooking) is enough to meet daily needs. Drinking large quantities of squash or fruit juice fills a child up while providing few nutrients, apart from sugar.

Young children tend to eat the same foods as their parents, but as they grow more independent their choices are influenced by their friends, by school meals and by commercial pressures such as television. Advertisements shown in children's prime viewing time frequently feature food that is far from healthy – most often confectionery, highly sweetened breakfast cereals and fast food – and only rarely promote healthy food such as fruit and vegetables.

Partly as a result of these commercial pressures, in the United Kingdom children's diets are not as healthy as they ought to be. They tend to be high in fat and sugar, and low in certain nutrients. There are gender differences too, with girls eating more fruit and drinking more fruit juice, while boys eat bulkier foods, such as breakfast cereals, baked beans and chips, as well as drinking more milk.

Food and health

From a physical point of view, healthy eating has obvious immediate benefits. Children who eat a good diet have better teeth, a better build, suffer less anaemia and may possibly be more intelligent. The links between poor thinking ability and poor nourishment are disputed, and while for most children there is no evidence that the ability to learn is limited by the quality of their diet, there is concern about a minority of children with subclinical vitamin and mineral deficiencies.

Preparing for a healthy adulthood

Attitudes and behaviour towards food are established in childhood, and diet in childhood plays a vital role in determining health in adulthood. The process that leads to coronary heart disease starts no later than childhood, with evidence that weight, blood cholesterol levels and blood pressure carry through into adult life. Both high cholesterol levels and high blood pressure are important risk factors for coronary heart disease, and as eating fat-containing food has a strong influence on cholesterol levels, children can protect their future by eating a diet that is low in fat.

High blood pressure tends to persist from childhood into adult life, and as blood pressure is affected by sodium intake, establishing a taste for foods without added salt helps to keep blood pressure in the normal range in adulthood. Children who are overweight in middle childhood are likely to stay overweight as adults. Obesity in adults contributes to a range of modern diseases, including high blood pressure, hyperlipidaemia and insulin resistance (see Overweight, page 78).

The disease processes that lead to osteoporosis and cancer may also start in childhood. Osteoporosis is affected by calcium intake and levels of exercise, so to protect against bone-weakening and fractures in old age, children – particularly girls – should eat a calcium-rich diet. Diet may be involved in around one-third of all cancers, and diets that are rich in fruit, vegetables and salads seem to be linked with a lower chance of developing cancers of the lung, bowel, stomach and oesophagus. It is the antioxidant vitamins C and E in these foods that are accepted as exerting the protective effect.

School dinners

Once children are at school their main source of nutrition each day may be their school dinner, which contributes one-third of their average daily energy intake. But how nutritious is this meal? What is provided depends on the education authority, the caterer and the school, and although school meal providers follow general guidelines, they may not have to conform to set nutritional guidelines. Schools that have a cafeteria system may actually supply unhealthy meals. One British survey has shown that among teenagers, school meals were the source of over half their weekday consumption of chips.

School meals are not compulsory, and around half of all parents send their child to school with a packed lunch instead. Unfortunately the traditional British packed lunch (sandwiches made with white bread, crisps, chocolate bar, sugary drink) is high in fat, sugar and salt, and low in vitamins and micronutrients. However it is much easier for parents to improve the quality of packed lunches than to improve the quality of school meals.

What about beef?

Many parents in parts of the Western world are increasingly worried about letting their children eat beef. New variant Creutzfeldt–Jakob disease – an extremely rare but incurable neuropsychiatric disorder that is eventually fatal – has probably been transmitted from cows infected with bovine spongiform encephalopathy (BSE). The disease develops inside the brain for an estimated 10–15 years, or even longer, so it does not appear in children. although it is possible to come into contact with the infectious agent in childhood.

The government of the United Kingdom is clear in its statements that current practices in slaughterhouses should have made new variant Creutzfeldt–Jakob infection acquired in this way a thing of the past, and that beef, cows' milk and gelatin derived from beef are safe to consume. However as the agent behind the disease has not yet been identified, some parents are cautious about allowing their children to eat beef, gelatin or even to drink milk. Schools provide a choice of dishes so no child should have to eat this meat if they do not want to eat it.

Vegetarian children

For adults, a vegetarian diet offers wide-ranging health protection benefits against diabetes, obesity, high blood pressure and bowel disease. In addition, vegetarian adults have a very significantly lower rate of heart disease and cancer than meat eaters. But should a vegetarian diet start in childhood?

The answer is that there is no reason why children should not be brought up as vegetarians. As long as they eat dairy products and eggs and their diet is planned with care, it will meet all their nutritional needs, whether they are infants

A healthy plate of food for an adult is a healthy plate of food for a child. However girls in particular can be encouraged to eat dairy foods to maintain their calcium intake as well as fortified cereals and lean meat as sources of iron. Vegetarian children should eat plenty of dark green vegetables, wholemeal bread and dried fruit in order to obtain iron that they do not get from eating meat.

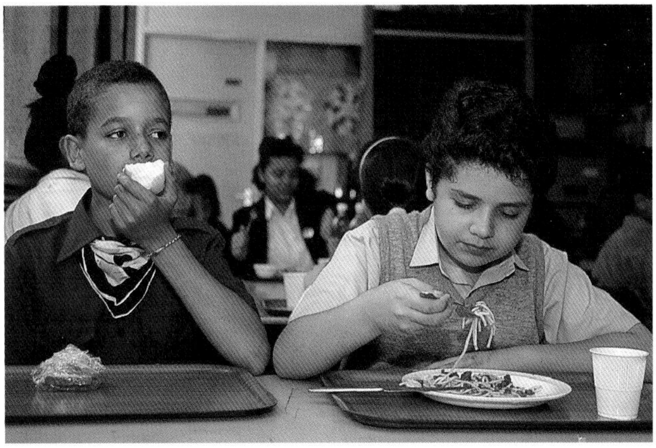

Compulsory nutritional guidelines for school meals should improve the nutrient intake for the chips-with-everything generation. However in the United Kingdom only an estimated one child in three now eats a school dinner; others rely on local shops or bring a packed lunch.

being weaned, children or teenagers. Even a vegan diet, which excludes all dairy produce and eggs as well as meat, can meet virtually all a child's nutritional needs, although it will call for greater ingenuity on the part of parents, and the child may need to take some dietary supplements.

In general, some children brought up on a strict vegetarian diet may be smaller and lighter than average in their early years. When infants are weaned on to a vegetarian diet, they may grow more slowly than meat eaters, although most catch up in the end, and many vegetarian children grow at the same rate as meat eaters. The slowed growth rate is caused by the low ratio of energy to bulk of a typical vegetarian diet, and is best handled by serving high-energy and protein foods first during a meal. This is especially important for picky eaters and children with small appetites. High-fat foods, including nut products, cheese and avocado, are important, and vegetarian children should not be given semi-skimmed or skimmed milk until it is quite certain that their diet is providing ample energy for their needs. Nor should they be given bran or very high-fibre cereals that provide bulk that is low in nutrients, and can impair the absorption of important nutrients such as iron and calcium.

Variety in vegetarian food

Vegetarian children – just like other children – need to eat a wide variety of food. Their daily diet should include food from each of the four main food groups: cereals and grains (four to five helpings); fruit (one to three helpings) and vegetables, including leafy green vegetables (two helpings); pulses, nuts and seeds (one to two helpings); and for non-vegans, milk, dairy produce and eggs (three helpings). They also need to eat a small amount of vegetable oil, margarine or butter, and a little yeast extract. Vegetarian children need to combine foods to ensure they get enough essential nutrients, particularly protein.

Protein Protein is found in a surprising range of foods, including breakfast cereals and porridge oats, and, provided these sources are combined, vegetarian children easily get enough protein. Children who do not eat eggs, milk or cheese must eat a combination of pulses, nuts, cereals and grains. Grains and cereals should be eaten together or during the same meal. Grains are incomplete proteins – they lack the essential amino acids lysine and isoleucine; pulses, which lack the amino acid tryptophan, are also incomplete proteins. When eaten together they make a complete protein. Nut creams, seed spreads, tofu and soya yoghurt are also good non-dairy sources of protein.

Calcium To ensure they get enough calcium, vegetarian children need to drink milk (600 ml/1 pint a day) or soya milk enriched with calcium. Yoghurt, cheese, tofu and a range of plant sources including treacle, broccoli, celery, soya, sesame seeds and nuts, particularly almonds, all supply calcium.

Iron and vitamin C An adequate iron intake is important, and vegetarian children need to eat plenty of non-meat foods containing iron, such as fortified breakfast cereals, wholemeal bread, dried fruit and dark green vegetables. Vegetarian diets usually provide high levels of vitamin C and it is important that they do, as vitamin C aids iron absorption, particularly when it is taken at the same time as the iron-rich food.

Zinc Zinc is another essential mineral, and is available in sunflower seeds, soya beans and doughs that contain yeast.

The vegan diet

Vegan diets tend to contain even less energy than other diets and vegan children may be both lighter and smaller than their peers. However there is no reason why they should be any less healthy, as long as plant foods are chosen carefully to provide the full range of amino acids, and the diet contains enough fat. There is a slight risk that vegan children will be deficient in calcium and vitamin B_{12}. Vitamin B_{12} is not available in plant foods, so children on vegan diets need to eat supplemented foods, such as breakfast cereals, soya milks, yeast extracts and specific vegetarian products such as veggie burgers, or they must take a supplement.

With thought and commitment, a vegetarian or vegan diet can be quite suitable for children. However what is not suitable is the diet of a child in a meat-eating family who declares unilateral vegetarianism by simply missing meat out of meals. Should your child do this, you need to discuss alternatives.

A family pet

Having a family pet is beneficial for children's emotional and mental health. Looking after a pet develops a sense of responsibility and interdependence and can help when social relationships are going through a difficult patch. Experience with pets in children's hospitals has shown that children sometimes communicate better with pets than with people, perhaps because pets are accepting and non-judgmental.

Training a pet provides a good lesson in behaviour for children, while riding a horse develops skills of balance, judgment and confidence in able-bodied children as well as those with a disability. Pet therapy has been shown to reduce aggression in disturbed youngsters, and a classroom guinea pig can bring out caring qualities in very young children. Accompanying a pet to the vet's for regular treatments, such as worming or vaccination, is an important lesson in preventive medicine for young children.

The disadvantages

While there are benefits to be gained from keeping a pet, there are also disadvantages. Pets need to be kept away from food and all areas where it is being prepared or cooked. Children should learn not to feed animals at the table, and small children must be kept away from pets' bowls. When washing up, pets' bowls should either be washed separately or after everything else.

Children need to learn to respect animals or they risk being bitten or scratched. It is natural for children to cuddle ani-

Pets play a very important role in children's emotional health. As they keep secrets so well, children can confide in them with absolute trust. Pets also frequently present children with their first personal experience of death and its healing rituals.

mals, but they should not kiss them and they should not allow an animal to lick their face.

Both dogs and cats carry fleas that can survive for months in a carpet and then jump in response to the vibration of passing feet, usually biting the legs around the upper ankle. If the animal shares a child's bed, the child can be bitten anywhere on the body.

One of the most common sources of allergen (a substance that initiates an allergic reaction) in the home is pet dander found in the fur of cats and dogs. It is so ubiquitous that it is even found in homes with no resident furry animals, but it is present in much higher quantities in homes with pets. This means that any family where an allergic tendency has already shown as asthma, eczema or hay fever should think carefully before acquiring a furry pet.

Research now suggests that it is possible that babies are sensitized to cat allergen when they are in the uterus. Highly susceptible people should therefore think hard before acquiring a cat during a pregnancy.

Infections

Cats may also carry infections, and to prevent food poisoning, children should always wash their hands after handling a pet and before cooking, handling food or eating. The organism *Toxoplasma gondii* can be carried in cats' faeces, and causes the illness toxoplasmosis, which is rather like glandular fever. It can have serious consequences if women catch it during pregnancy. A bite or scratch from a cat may cause a rare illness known as cat-scratch fever, in which a lymph node near the scratch swells, and a blister may appear near the site of the scratch. Children with the condition may also develop a fever, a rash and a headache.

Both cats and dogs also carry the roundworm toxocara (see Toxocariasis, page 102). To protect children from infection, with its occasionally very serious consequences, dogs and cats should be wormed regularly, pet owners should clear up after their animals and places where children play, such as parks, sandpits and playgrounds should be protected from dogs and other animals that might carry the infection, such as foxes.

Children should not share a bedroom with a caged bird. Close contact at a young age might increase the risk of lung cancer in adult life. Psittacosis is a risk for anyone who keeps a bird. Dusty particles from the bird's droppings can be inhaled and transmit a type of chlamydial infection, which usually appears either as an unusual type of pneumonia or a general infection. It can be treated with antibiotics.

Children can also pick up infections when visiting farms. The organism *Cryptosporidium* can pass from infected animals to children who cuddle them. It causes watery diarrhoea that can last for up to a week. An infected child can pass the organism on to other children. Children should always wash their hands after playing with farm animals.

Healthy teeth

The latest national survey shows that one pre-school child in three has tooth decay. By the time children start school, 45 per cent have some tooth decay, and by the age of nine this figure has risen to 60 per cent. Less than one-third of 15-year-olds have perfect, undecayed teeth. What is going wrong?

Children's eating habits have changed over the past generation, with much more grazing – snacking between or instead of meals. Unfortunately eating frequently is particularly damaging to teeth. After any meal, snack or drink containing sugar, the chief ingredients of enamel – calcium and phosphate – start to dissolve into the saliva in a process known as demineralization. This can last for anything up to two hours before the teeth start to reabsorb the lost minerals, but if another snack is eaten during this time, the essential process of restoration never has a chance to start.

The case against sugar

Children are also eating more sugar, which is well known to cause tooth decay. In the United Kingdom the average daily intake of sugar is 90 g/3 oz. Some of this is visible or obvious, but much of it is hidden. For example, many 'plain' and savoury foods contain sugar. Weight for weight, nearly one-tenth of plain cornflakes is sugar, while a supposedly healthy breakfast cereal such as sultana bran has a total sugar content of almost one-third. Labels saying 'reduced sugar' or 'low sugar' do not mean no sugar.

To discover what your children – and you – are eating, scan the labels on food packaging for hidden sugars; the most damaging are sucrose, glucose, fructose and maltose, but you will also find maltodextrin, invert sugar and hydrolyzed starch. Look carefully where you least expect to find added sugars. Soya milks and infant soya formula are sweetened with sugars capable of causing tooth decay.

Tooth erosion

Tooth erosion, which is caused by acid drinks and occurs regardless of the presence of sugar, is another common problem. Even a mildly acidic drink such as carbonated water can be damaging, while pure fruit juices and other carbonated drinks have a high acid content. It is not just teenagers with a three-can-a-day habit whose enamel is being etched away by these acid drinks; levels of erosion are almost as high in preschool children as they are in 13-year-olds. In some children the enamel completely dissolves to reveal the sensitive layer of dentine beneath.

Solutions

The first step is to limit snacking. Young children find this difficult, so choose tooth-friendly snacks and train your children to drink tap water. It is almost free, and it is harmless to teeth. If your child needs to take prescription drugs, ask your doctor to prescribe a sugar-free elixir.

Sugar-free chewing gum is not harmful to teeth: rather it is considered to be positively beneficial; the extra saliva it stimulates helps to neutralize the acid content of plaque (the sticky film that constantly builds up on teeth), and if it is sweetened with xylitol it may even suppress acid-producing bacteria in plaque.

Cleaning teeth

The next step is effective dental care. Parents should start cleaning their children's teeth the day the first tooth comes through (see Baby teeth, page 22). Cleaning has two purposes: the first is to spread fluoride toothpaste on to the teeth, and the second is to remove plaque. The ideal is to brush twice a day, in the morning and at bedtime, taking two to three minutes at each session. In practice your target should be a thorough brush at bedtime and as thorough a brushing as your child can manage in the morning to get the fluoride on to the teeth.

Most people brush the visible parts of the teeth better than the teeth and the parts of teeth that remain out of sight. The most neglected danger zones are the insides of the front teeth, top and bottom, and the very back teeth. Until the age of seven, parents should do the brushing. The child can then take over, but with adult supervision and help in getting at inaccessible surfaces until the age of ten. Only a small pea-sized blob of fluoride toothpaste is needed.

What does fluoride do?

Fluoride is a natural mineral that helps to restore tooth enamel. For perfect healing, however, the amount of fluoride must be just right. If there is too little, fluoride is not effective. If there is too much there is a risk that the teeth might become mottled and stained.

For maximum tooth protection the ideal level of fluoride in tap water is around one part per million; this ensures that fluoride is both incorporated into the developing teeth and stays in contact with the tooth surfaces after they have come through. However most drinking water in the United Kingdom does not contain anything like this amount. To discover the level in your area, telephone your water authority or ask your dentist.

Children who have special difficulties cleaning their teeth, or particularly vulnerable teeth, may have fluoride drops or tablets prescribed or recommended by the dentist. Most children should get enough fluoride from brushing twice a day with fluoride toothpaste.

Children under the age of six and children who cannot gargle or spit out properly may swallow toothpaste or gel. They need a low-fluoride toothpaste as long as their teeth are in good condition, they brush regularly and well, and they live in a fluoridated area. Many children's brands are low-fluoride. Infant gels have a very mild flavour and some have only tiny quantities of fluoride. Children over six who can spit out can use a medium-fluoride toothpaste, containing around 1000ppmF. to avoid your child swallowing toothpaste, work it first into the brush with a little water. High-fluoride toothpastes contain about 1500ppmF. Children have no need of such high levels.

Fluoride protection

For the best possible fluoride protection:

- Start brushing with a low-fluoride toothpaste. Some homeopathic brands contain no fluoride
- Use only a small pea-sized blob of toothpaste
- Brush twice a day – no more
- Don't wet the brush, as this causes froth, which the child tends to spit out. After cleaning, don't rinse, but spit out or brush again with a little water
- Once the child is six or more and can spit out reliably without swallowing the toothpaste, switch to a medium fluoride brand

Orthodontic treatment to move or straighten teeth produces more than a bright, even smile. It also improves the way the teeth bite and makes them much easier to clean. Without treatent, prominent front teeth are also at risk of damage.

Children with perfect teeth need to see the dentist only once a year, but the dentist will tell you if your child needs to attend more often.

Straightening teeth

Orthodontics is the branch of dentistry dedicated to straightening teeth using braces. Straight teeth not only produce a nicer, more even smile, but they are also much easier to clean. Depending on when the permanent teeth appear, orthodontic treatment can start between the ages of 11 and 13. There are two main types of brace: removable appliances that are suitable for simple corrections, and appliances that are bonded to the teeth during treatment. Some use small elastic bands that have to be changed every day. Most treatments are completed within two years and some in considerably less time.

Safety in the sun

Warnings about the dangers of exposure to sunshine can appear unnecessarily doom-laden. It is hard to believe that the most natural source of light and warmth can be so deadly that we need to protect ourselves – and especially our children – from it. Awareness that sunshine is good for you also goes against the health promotion messages that children need clothing, adequate shade and appropriate sunscreens to protect them from bright sunlight.

Yet the facts are these: to synthesize enough vitamin D (which is important for both absorbing calcium from the intestine into the bloodstream and for regulating the balance between calcium in the skeleton and in the blood) children need to spend no more than half an hour a day outside in moderate sunshine in summer; and only their lower arms, legs and face need be unclothed to synthesize the amount of vitamin D they need.

Ultraviolet rays and skin cancers

Overexposure to the harmful ultraviolet rays of sunlight during childhood is, meanwhile, taking its toll. The latest figures from Australia show that over two per cent of people who were surveyed in Queensland had the skin cancer squamous cell carcinoma and that painful sunburn in earlier life had made them more prone to the disease.

Six episodes of painful sunburn made people three times more likely to develop squamous cell carcinoma. Basal cell carcinomas, or rodent ulcers, are also on the increase.

In the United Kingdom over 4000 people a year are developing the fast-growing and most serious type of skin cancer, malignant melanoma, and 1500 a year are dying of it. There are over 40,000 new cases of skin cancer every year (malignant melanomas as well as the more easily treated squamous cell carcinoma and rodent ulcers, or basal cell carcinomas).

Sensible sun protection measures taken now by most families not only guard against potentially cancerous radiation, they also protect the skin against damage to collagen and elastin. Collagen and elastin maintain firmness and flexibility in the skin and shield it against a premature fragility and thinning of the skin.

These are preventable cancers and children and teenagers should be protected from them.

Protecting your child

On an individual basis you can easily make sure your family acts sensibly in the sun. This means wearing wide-brimmed or legionnaire-style hats, and clothing with a dense weave (one that will not allow light through when you hold it up to the sun) that covers the whole body apart from the lower arms, legs and face. It means taking to the shade between 11 am and 3 pm – even in northern latitudes. Infants under six months of age should never be exposed to the sun, and outdoor activities should be sited in the shade.

Unless there is ample shade, children should not take part in heat-of-the-day outdoor activities such as watching sports, picnics or beach trips.

Sun bathing, which is particularly prevalent among teenage girls, should be discouraged. When you cannot avoid the sun, for example on visits to the seaside, you should always use a sunscreen with a minimum sun protection factor of 15, or a higher protection factor, such as 25 or more, for children who have blue eyes and fair or freckled skin.

On a community basis you can form alliances to ensure that there are enough shaded areas in your children's school playground for all children at midday, that the design of school uniforms protects children against the sun's rays and that children are allowed to use sunscreen at school for outdoor sports and outings. You should also lobby your local council to plant trees to shade children's playgrounds.

Television, computers and videos

The flickering screen is as much a part of children's lives today as the library book was a part of yesterday's childhood. Between them, television, videos and computers offer an unrivalled round-the-clock entertainment and information service, and it is not surprising therefore that, on average, children spend two or three hours in front of the television every day. Some children spend longer watching television than they do in the classroom at school.

Effects on health

Is there a health price to pay for so much screen-watching? It appears there is. The latest national diet and nutrition survey in the United Kingdom showed that children are becoming overweight not because they are eating more, but because they are taking less exercise. One of the chief reasons for this is because they spend much of the time watching a television or computer screen.

Another finding is that a delay in language development in children across the social spectrum is often caused by excessive television viewing. Even infants exposed to too much background television are now experiencing language delay (see Speech and language, page 309).

Certain types of personality appear to be more likely to become addicted to television. The more time they spend in front of the screen, watching television or videos or playing computer games, the less time they have available to develop creative or interpersonal social skills. There is a real risk that these children may become social loners. But how long is too long? It is any time when the child is not actively engaged in what they are watching, but either are lost in their own world or positively bored.

Possible dangers

A number of medical conditions can be triggered by the flickering of the screen. In a small number (about five per cent) of children with epilepsy, flickering light can trigger seizures. Children are often first affected between the ages of six and

At an age when children find difficulty in distinguishing fact from fantasy, images of violence such as this can be harmful – although they can also be helpful in embodying, acknowledging and ultimately reconciling forceful emotions.

eighteen, and the seizure occurs when light flashes or flickers at a certain frequency. Children with photosensitive epilepsy should therefore not sit close to a television screen and should preferably stay at least 2.5 m/8 ft away. Covering (not simply closing) one eye while viewing may be beneficial, as may using a screen measuring less than 35 cm/14 in. As further protection the brightness can be turned down and children should view television in a well-lit room (although some children cope better if it is dark).

Computer screens rarely trigger photosensitive epileptic seizures, but as vulnerable children may be sensitive to sequences in certain video games they should only play using a computer monitor (not a television screen) or hand-held console, and should not play when they are tired. A good, but unfortunately expensive, solution to the problem of flickering screens is to use a television or computer that has a liquid crystal display screen.

Effects on behaviour

Many parents' concern over television centres on its effects on children's behaviour. In addition to fostering demands for advertized products, it is believed to make children aggressive. There is no doubt that children do sometimes imitate the violence they have seen recently on television and that children who are already aggressive are most affected. Large numbers of research studies have established that there is an association between television violence and levels of aggressive behaviour, but a causal link has not been established. It is also possible that television violence can exert longer-term effects, and that even after ten years, children who prefer watching violent programmes remain more aggressive than children who prefer to watch less aggressive programmes. However it is important to keep a sense of balance. Occasional viewing in a family where aggression is not used as an approach to solving problems is unlikely to harm children, while unsupervized and frequent viewing of violent films in a home where children see, enact or are the victims of aggression is likely to be very much more harmful.

Parenting for positive health

The way parents manage their children's behaviour has a significant effect on their health. Health attitudes matter, too, and are caught rather than taught. So parents who shrug off a cold or a tumble are likely to have children who have a similar matter-of-fact approach. In the same way, parents who reach for the medicine chest (whether to get orthodox or complementary remedies) or the telephone and the doctor's telephone number at the first sign of illness are likely to have children who are equally unsure of their own natural capacities for self-healing.

Computer literacy is an essential part of children's primary school education. Commonsense suggests that using computers for positive and investigative purposes helps to protect children against screen exploitation.

Parenting for good health involves attitudes that boost self-esteem and self-confidence, a trust in one's own judgement and an awareness of its limitations. How do parents breed these balanced, health promoting attitudes?

Self-esteem first develops in children from the discovery that their parents like them and spend time with them, trust them and respect them. It comes also from knowing that there are limits – bedtimes, a rejection of any aggression – and that these are applied consistently. This type of parenting, called 'authoritative', rather than its contrasting styles authoritarian or permissive, not only produces children with a high self-esteem, but also children with a high level of self-control and self-reliance, who are able to form their own judgements and have a well developed sense of right and wrong.

In early childhood parents take health decisions on behalf of their children. As their children mature and enter the upper primary school years, they take more and more of these decisions themselves. Those children who have authoritative parents are most likely to take decisions that will be to their lasting benefit.

TEENAGE HEALTH

Ask a group of teenagers what their major concerns are, and they are extremely unlikely to mention health. Adolescence is a time when young people are concerned with finding out who they are and where they fit in with the world, with achievement, getting on and enjoying themselves. Health only comes into the equation when it holds them back from what they want to do.

Surveys confirm that the vast majority of adolescents consider themselves to be in excellent health. They may take painkillers for headaches or have fillings in their teeth, but they view these as minor disturbances rather than signs of ill health. If young people do think about health, they realize by the teen years that they are responsible for themselves. In most cases they have had enough health education at school to know that the way they lead their lives has a strong influence on their future health.

Adolescence is rarely a period of unbroken serenity. Teenagers are prone to turbulent and confusing emotions, which can expose them to the risks of mental health difficulties. Depression and distress are common and in teenagers suicide is a leading cause of death. There is hardly an age when reassuring parental support is more needed.

Yet when things do go wrong who do they turn to? Reassuringly, perhaps, the evidence points to the fact that most teenagers first turn to their parents for health advice. Despite appearances, parents matter to teenagers. The way parents behave and what they believe in has a strong impact. Approval and disapproval are important. Research shows that teenage children of parents who strongly disapprove of smoking are seven times less likely to smoke themselves, and as there appear to be strong links between smoking and drug-taking, parental disapproval acts as a strong health incentive.

Of course parents are not the only reference source for health information. Teenagers also find out about health from their friends, from school, from television, and from books and magazines. But the importance that teenagers attach to their parents' attitudes puts parents on the spot. How much do parents know about the health issues that teenagers might raise? How much up-to-date information do they have? Parents need more and better information on the health risks their teenagers are likely to run – on alcohol and smoking, on illicit drugs and underage sex. When things start to go wrong – as they well may, because teenagers need to experiment just as their parents once did – parents need help recognizing the signs and knowing what to do.

Teenage eating

Teenagers, especially girls, are notorious for eating an inadequate diet. However the blame does not lie entirely with the teenagers themselves. Many school cafeterias provide what young people will buy, rather than what is necessarily nutritious; television commercials advertize what will sell. At an age when appearances and peer-group pressures are at their peak and health concerns are at their lowest, it is hardly surprising that image matters more than intrinsic healthiness. What teenagers care about is not long-term health gains or postponing the onset of chronic illnesses in old age, but weight loss, body shape, complexion and the environment. When it comes to exercising food choices, adolescents consider friendships, group identity, image and the amount of money to which they have access.

Surveys show that teenagers eat food that is high in fats and sugars, and that as they get older they drink less milk and more canned drinks, tea and coffee. By and large they get enough calories from their food, but these are likely to come from high-starch and/or high-fat foods, such as chips, milk, biscuits, meats and puddings. Three-quarters of all 10–15-year-olds eat more fat than they need. A large number of girls go short of calcium or iron, although boys, because they drink more milk, usually get more than enough calcium. Intake of some micronutrients, such as vitamin B_6, folate, magnesium and zinc, is low in both girls and boys. There is also clear evidence that teenagers do not eat enough of the non-starch polysaccharides, better known as fibre.

However in some ways at least, the situation is improving. While it is true that teenagers often go short of micronutrients, they usually get enough of the major nutrients – carbohydrate, protein and fats – and enough energy. Growing children do need extra energy, but actually not as much more than an adult as you might imagine; even at the peak of their growth spurt, it has been estimated that young people only need an extra 70–120 calories a day.

A constant media bombardment of catwalk images of unnatural thinness can seriously undermine the fragile self-esteem of a teenage girl. Schools and families have a duty to present children with a balanced image of good health at a normal weight.

With their interest in weight loss, teenage girls eat more healthy foods, such as fruit and vegetables, and drink more fruit juice than boys. This is reflected in television commercials, which are as likely to promote 'healthy' foods, such as fruit products, high-fibre cereals, wholemeal crispbreads and low-fat butter substitutes, as they are to promote high-fat burgers and ice cream.

Problem areas

A general survey of teenagers' food choices will point to a number of problem areas:

- *Weight-reducing diets that are too strict* By the age of 15, more than half of all teenage girls have tried to lose weight. Obsessive weight control can leave youngsters undernourished, and in girls this can delay the start of menstruation or make it erratic. By cutting certain foods, such as potatoes, out of their diet, young people not only lose bulk and starch, but risk upsetting their balance of vitamins and minerals as well. If they cut out milk there can be effects on bone density leading to problems with osteoporosis later in life
- *Too little calcium* Around 45 per cent of the adult skeleton is laid down during adolescence, so teenagers need a substantial calcium intake. Traditionally, boys have drunk enough milk to meet their calcium needs, but girls have not, although the wider availability of low-fat milk products may be changing this. The two periods in life when calcium requirements

are highest are, first, in infancy and young childhood, and second, in adolescence. Although adolescents absorb calcium more efficiently than adults, they still need calcium-rich foods to ensure that the skeleton is properly formed. Apart from milk, other dairy foods are the best form of easily absorbable calcium for most teenagers. For children who are vegans, calcium-enriched soya milks and vegetable sources (for example, broccoli, sesame seeds, almonds, spinach and watercress) are also important

- *Anaemia* This is common among teenagers, partly because their rate of growth means that they need more iron and partly, in girls, because of blood loss through menstruation. One-fifth of all adolescent girls are thought to be anaemic. Eating fortified breakfast cereals, red meat and green, leafy vegetables will boost iron intake
- *Poor quality, low-budget food eaten away from home* Many teenagers rarely eat family meals at home and snack instead. Food provided at school is extremely important both in terms of the nutrients it provides and the health promotion example it sets. Meals at many schools follow a cafeteria system, providing popular high-fat foods as well as fruit and salads. A recent survey found that over half the weekday intake of chips for 14–15-year-olds was eaten at school. Many schools also have vending machines offering additional unhealthy foods and drinks
- *Skipping meals* In terms of overall food intake this does not matter, provided the equivalent amount of food is eaten over the course of the day, but many girls miss breakfast and some skip lunch as well, then make up by eating less nutritious break-time snacks
- *A low folate intake, inadequate to protect a baby should a teenage girl become pregnant* Foods that naturally contain folate include dark green leafy vegetables, such as broccoli and sprouts, as well as enriched foods, such as many breads and breakfast cereals. In the United Kingdom the recently introduced symbol on food packaging that identifies folate-enriched foods should help girls to make healthier choices

Improving teenagers' diets

Healthy eating for teenagers is little different from healthy eating for other age groups. Teenagers should eat a variety of foods every day, with at least four helpings of starchy foods (some of them high-fibre); five helpings of fruit and vegetables; three helpings of meat and/or other protein alternatives, such as fish, pulses and grains (see Vegetarian children, page 27) or eggs; and three helpings of low-fat dairy foods. Whether these foods are eaten as snacks or as meals is much less important than the fact that they are eaten every day. Teenage girls should make sure they include foods that are high in calcium (low-fat yoghurt, fromage frais) and iron (fortified breakfast cereals and lean meat). Teenagers should eat enough food to maintain a healthy weight, but no more, and they should not eat too many fatty or too many sugary foods. It is also important for teenagers to enjoy their food and to establish eating habits that will have a positive influence on their future adult health.

Parents can have a considerable influence on what teenagers eat. While home economics has been removed from the curriculum in many schools in the United Kingdom, there is no reason why parents cannot teach simple cooking skills. In a society where people are becoming less and less skilled, there is every reason why they should. Shopping can be a joint undertaking, with young people taking the chance to exercise their food choices. If school meals are nutritionally inadequate, make a simple packed lunch and, if your income allows, give the teenager the cost difference as extra spending money. Share the cooking at home, so that each teenager takes responsibility for one family meal a week.

Exercise and sport

One of the biggest lifestyle changes for today's children is the lack of exercise naturally built in to their daily life. The number of parents who drive their children to school has reportedly risen by 60 per cent in the past ten years. In the 1970s, 90 per cent of junior school children walked to school; now,

Physical fitness among teenagers is a growing concern. Recently almost half the potential British army recruits had to be rejected because they were unfit. Laying emphasis on general fitness activities, such as running, instead of competitive team sports is more likely to take lasting fitness into adult life.

fewer than one in ten does. Fewer teenagers are cycling to school – although 90 per cent of children own a bicycle, only two per cent of journeys to school are made by bicycle.

In school, sport no longer commands the central position it once held in the curriculum. Over half of all children spend less than two hours a week in school on physical education and fewer children are taking part in sport outside school hours. What is more, the activities that children do pursue in school, especially competitive team games, tend not to be continued outside school or past childhood. At home, children's opportunities for free, active play are limited by parents' concerns for their safety. The result of all this is that children are less fit than they used to be.

The benefits of exercise

Regular exercise is one of the best ways of keeping healthy. It controls fat deposition and is associated with stronger bones. It not only makes the heart and lungs work more efficiently and strengthens muscles, but it keeps joints moving well and helps children to relax and sleep better. Exercise promotes a good appetite, lowers the risk of illness, and makes children livelier, more energetic and more alert. It improves a child's self-confidence and sense of well being. And children who are active are much more likely to be active adults.

For the keen and well-motivated there are organized sports activities. A recent survey has shown that nearly two-thirds of all boys aged 14 and 15 play football outside school lessons, over half of them ride a bicycle, and more than one in five plays basketball or tennis or goes jogging. The figures for girls, however, are less reassuring: almost a quarter undertake no organized sport at all outside school, and the only activity undertaken by more than one girl in five is riding a bicycle.

Exercise for non-sporty teenagers

If you have a child who can't catch a ball, can't kick straight and is always the last to be picked for the team, how can you ensure that they stay active and fit throughout their childhood years and retain an enthusiasm for activity that they will carry into adulthood?

Non-sporty teenagers need non-competitive sports. Girls can work out to fitness videos in the privacy of their homes. Many prefer aerobics and weight-training to traditional forms of activity, although the benefits of aerobic exercise in terms of fitness have been questioned. Swimming is an excellent whole-body activity of moderate intensity. Most swimming pools run their own clubs and in the early stages at least, they are not particularly competitive. Walking can be either a sociable, whole-family activity or strictly functional. Try to walk with your children at least three times a week, making each walk at least 3 km/2 miles long.

Cycling is another good form of whole-body exercise. Whether your children are able to cycle safely depends largely on your local road conditions. However, they should always have road safety training (see pages 28-29) and wear a properly fitted helmet.

Equipment and safety

Appropriate clothing and protective equipment are particularly important for children. Trainers should fit well and be shock absorbent. Headgear should be of an approved standard and correctly and regularly maintained. It is also important to make sure that sports-mad children do not overdo it and do not take up inappropriate activities, such as boxing. Although there have been no definitive studies, many adult cases of arthritis and back pain are thought to derive from excessive exercise in childhood, and not allowing enough time to recover after sports injuries. International studies show that children are sustaining more sports injuries, some of them quite serious. Some specialists believe that injuries occur more frequently after a growth spurt, and believe that children should concentrate on exercise for flexibility at these times. If a child does sustain an injury, activity levels should be minimized until they are fully recovered.

Drug and substance abuse

The use of illicit drugs among teenagers has increased in recent years and is now alarmingly common. The United Kingdom arm of a recent Europe-wide survey covering 7700 15- and 16-year-olds in 70 schools revealed that drug use in this age-group is more common than cigarette smoking. The most commonly used drug is cannabis: around four teenagers in ten had experimented with it and one in ten use it frequently. One teenager in five had sniffed glues or solvents; one in seven had used LSD; and one in eight had used amphetamines. Ecstasy was used by around one teenager in fifteen.

Drugs are part of the scenery for today's teenagers. Most will be offered them, often by friends or schoolmates. They take them because they are curious; because everyone else is doing it; because they are bored; and because they like the thrill of doing something dangerous.

Another finding of the Europe-wide survey was the link between cigarettes and cannabis. Very few non-smokers tried cannabis, while most teenagers who smoked ten or more cigarettes a day had also smoked cannabis. Most young people who use cannabis do not go on to use other illegal drugs, but it may bring them into contact with the criminal underworld.

Recognizing the signs

For parents, one of the problems with illicit drug use is that they may have no personal experience on which to draw.

All children can be tempted to experiment with drugs and solvents. School, family income or background and intelligence make no difference. Drugs are usually bought in clubs or pubs, or even on the street, so parents who want to protect their children need to know where their spend their leisure time.

Children are unlikely to volunteer the information that they have been taking drugs or sniffing glue, and it can be difficult to recognize the signs. Some of the signs are similar to normal adolescent behaviour, so it is important not to jump to conclusions. However it helps if parents are alert to a change in patterns of sleep, unexpected mood swings and unusual behaviour, secretiveness, loss of money from home, loss of appetite, irritability and aggression, loss of interest in friends and pastimes, poor memory and concentration, and a deterioration in school performance.

If you notice an accumulation of the signs listed above, bring up the subject. If your teenager is taking drugs, tell them you disapprove and explain why. For many teenagers, drug-taking is a single experiment that can be put down to youthful curiosity, but if it has been going on for some time it would be sensible to contact a family support group for advice and information.

Protection against drug dependency

The factors that protect young people from going beyond the experimentation stage are difficult to categorize, because every case is different. However a stable, happy family life is a strong protective factor. Parents need to be available to listen and talk to their teenage children, and they need to do things together – even if it is only watching television. It helps if they can meet their children's friends and invite them home. And it also helps to set a good example with their own drugs of dependence – alcohol, cigarettes and even medicines. For the teenager, it helps to have clear goals in life, and also to acquire certain social skills – knowing how to be assertive without being overbearing, how to cope with stress, how to stand up to social pressures and how to solve or at least weigh up their own problems.

In Britain it is illegal to possess, sell or give away an illicit drug, or to allow anyone to sell, give away or produce a drug in the home. A parent who finds drugs in their home can hand them over to the police or destroy them to prevent an offense being committed.

Types of drug

The following is a necessarily brief description of the main types of drug to which children may be exposed. Parents may wish to obtain further information from organizations and agencies specializing in the subject.

Street amphetamine (speed, whizz, sulphate, billy) is usually sniffed or mixed into a drink. It induces feelings of energy, exhilaration and self-confidence and reduces appetite, but these feelings are followed by a bad hangover effect. Speed can also bring on tantrums, irritability and mood swings. Long-term use causes insomnia and mental problems, as well as debilitation caused by the lack of food and sleep.

Barbiturates (barbs, downers, blues, reds) are usually taken as tablets. They are sedative drugs and although their first effect is one of relaxation, they then produce an effect like drunkenness, which is compounded by drinking alcohol. It is easy to overdose on barbiturates.

Cannabis (marijuana, dope, hash, shit, grass, weed, pot) is the most commonly used drug. Within a few minutes of smoking it, or longer after eating it, cannabis lifts the mood to a feeling of calm and well being. It also makes the user dreamy and relaxed, slows down reactions and affects coordination and concentration. These effects last for a few hours. Larger doses can provoke a state of panic or other unpleasant effects. In the longer term, heavy users can become dependent. Cannabis smoke contains more carcinogens than tobacco and because the smoker inhales more deeply, four 'joints' may well do as much damage to the lungs as 20 cigarettes will do.

Cocaine (coke, snow, charlie) is a stimulant drug and an anaesthetic that is usually sniffed, but can be injected intravenously or prepared in smokable form as freebase. Crack is a form of smokable cocaine. Cocaine makes the user feel energetic and euphoric, but it causes dependence and regular users may become excitable and paranoid.

Ecstasy (E, diamonds, doves) is often used as a party drug. It comes in tablet form and induces a feeling of calm, alertness and well being. However the hangover is unpleasant and high doses can induce panic or anxiety attacks. When combined with dancing for many hours, Ecstasy can contribute to a rise in body temperature and dehydration. Users of Ecstasy who are dancing need to take sips of water, but drinking too much water can be fatal.

Heroin (smack, H) can be smoked, sniffed or injected. It is a painkiller similar to morphine and produces an effect of warmth, drowsiness and calm. However heroin is taken, it is addictive, and sudden withdrawal triggers very unpleasant side effects. Injecting drugs is not common among schoolchildren but is particularly dangerous because of the risk of infections such as hepatitis or HIV from shared needles. Accidental overdose of heroin can be fatal.

LSD (lysergic acid diethylamide, acid, trips, tab) is an hallucinogen that is supplied on small squares or as pills that produce a 'trip'. It can trigger 'bad trips' in which the user feels panicky, agitated and may experience terrifying hallucinations. Spontaneous flashbacks can occur months or even years after the drug was taken.

Magic mushrooms (Liberty cap mushrooms) have an hallucinogenic effect which is similar to that of LSD. The mushrooms can be eaten raw, cooked or infused as a tea. Apart from the risk of causing unpleasant hallucinations, magic mushrooms may be confused with other, poisonous, species of mushroom.

Solvent sniffing is most common among groups of young teenagers. Solvents are not illegal and there are around 30 different types commonly found in the home – for example, solvent-based glues, aerosols, butane gas and nail varnish remover. Sniffing solvents quickly makes youngsters feel 'high', happy and carefree. This can be followed by a feeling similar to a hangover. They can cause heart failure if sprayed directly into the nose or mouth, and young people can hurt themselves while intoxicated or may suffocate while inhaling from a plastic bag. Youngsters who lose consciousness may die from inhaling their own vomit. Empty aerosol or glue cans in the house, spills and stains on clothes, a chemical smell on the breath or clothes, and obvious mood and behaviour swings are all signs that a teenager may be misusing solvents.

Tranquillizers (Valium, Librium, Ativan, temazepam) are commonly prescribed sedative drugs used to treat depression, anxiety and stress. At first they lessen feelings of anxiety, but in higher doses they have a sedative effect. Tranquillizers are addictive and withdrawal effects are unpleasant. In high doses tranquillizers can be fatal, especially if they are taken with alcohol.

Who can help?

Most countries have at least one organization that parents can contact for help and advice about drug abuse. They will usually also offer support and information to families and friends of drug users. See the Directory for details.

Teenage sexuality

During their adolescent years teenagers develop a growing awareness of their individual value and uniqueness, and of their sexual identity. Although they may have developed physically, their emotional development may not have prepared them to meet fully the consequences of their sexual behaviour. Schools attempt to address these issues in sex education. Pupils learn the basics of the biological processes in science lessons, while relationships, HIV and AIDS, and other sexually transmitted diseases are discussed outside the core curriculum against a background of moral considerations and the value of family life. However parents also need to address the issues of sexuality with their children.

Surveys show that far from getting all the information they need from school, young people want their parents to talk to them more about sex. They want them to talk about it early, before they need to know. Some parents worry that their children know everything already. Although this is not the case, teenagers may well know more about school-taught topics, such as HIV and AIDS, and it is up to parents to discover what is taught at school and when. What does their child think of what has been taught? Were there issues that were not covered? Talking about sex education given at school can be a good starting point for discussing it at home.

Discussing sexuality

Depending on the experience and skill of the teacher, sex education at school is likely to impart facts rather than discussing feelings, relationships and individual preferences in an intimate way, which can be more easily discussed at home.

Teenagers are often more likely to discuss their concerns and worries with their friends than they are with their parents, particularly their concerns about personal relationships and sexual matters. A social get-together with peers will usually elicit lively discussion and debate.

Talking about sex has to be balanced against the young person's need for privacy and confidentiality, and it is best to be ready to respond openly to a young person's tentative questions. Talking about sex more will not, as some parents worry, encourage young people to become involved in sexual activity at a younger age. On the contrary, evidence shows overwhelmingly that, if anything, more information tends to delay the start of sexual activity, especially for boys.

One aspect of developing sexuality that boys find particularly embarrassing is getting an erection, especially if it happens in public. It may not be easy to discuss this at home, but it can be reassuring if you do. Both girls and boys worry about masturbation, not realizing how common it is, partly because most parents feel inhibited about talking about it as well. Almost all adult men have masturbated at some time, while two in three women have done so, although people vary greatly in how often they masturbate. Knowing that masturbation is a perfectly normal and healthy activity can come as a relief to a guilt-wracked teenager.

Many young people feel attracted to members of their own sex as well as the opposite sex. For most this is a transient phase. Some young people remain bisexual, while others pass through a phase of homosexuality and eventually settle for heterosexuality or vice versa. The early teen years are frequently an uncertain time, and the parents of a teenager who thinks they may be homosexual are often the last people the child will tell. Public attitudes towards homosexuality are still largely unaccepting and these young people often find very little support; one thing they do need is their parents' continuing love.

Starting a sexual relationship

Far from being sexually precocious, many girls and boys are extremely self-conscious about their bodies around puberty, and are positively embarrassed by signs of their own sexuality. Later, many young people are uncertain about whether they are ready for sexual activity. Figures for the United Kingdom show that currently around one young person in four has had their first experience of sexual intercourse before the age of 16, with figures higher for boys than girls.

Many young people are acutely aware of peer pressure to start sexual activity. There is a lot of peer-group bragging about prowess, although only one girl in five is sexually active before the age of 16. Despite the images created by the teenage media, adolescents who do have early sexual intercourse usually have it in the context of a lasting relationship. Issues that parents can helpfully discuss with their adolescent children should include whether their child has a relationship in which they trust their partner; whether they feel under pressure and if so how they can say no; whether the couple have discussed contraception; how ready they are for the emotional experience; whether they are sure they will be completely protected from sexually transmitted diseases.

The law also protects children who may not be old enough to decide for themselves whether to enter into a sexual relationship. In England, Wales and Scotland the age of consent (when a young person can make decisions about sex for themself) is 16; in Northern Ireland it is 17. Any man or boy having sex with a girl under this age is committing a criminal offense. The age of consent in homosexual relationships is 18 throughout the United Kingdom.

Contraception

Discussing contraception can be difficult for young people, which may explain why half of all young couples having sex for the first time are unprotected. This lays them open to the risks not only of unwanted pregnancy, but also of sexually transmitted diseases. The advice and knowledge of a tactful adult can be especially valuable here. Parents' worries that, by talking about contraception, they may appear to be condoning underage sex are misplaced: teenagers who are told about contraception are more likely to be able to say no.

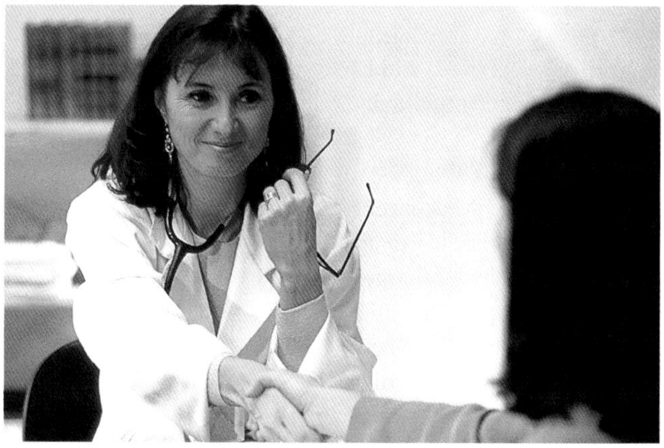

Every year in the United Kingdom around 100,000 teenagers become pregnant. While some want to, for most the pregnancy is unwanted. Free and confidential contraceptive help is available from a doctor or family planning clinic regardless of age or parental permission.

Contraception is a joint responsibility and in the young the usual options are using a condom (male or female), the pill or a diaphragm. In the United Kingdom condoms can be bought from pharmacies, supermarkets and vending machines, while other methods of contraception are available only from a family planning clinic or a doctor. If a young person under the age of 16 consults a doctor about contraception, they are entitled to free and confidential advice. Doctors are not obliged to tell the young person's parents, although they will usually encourage the teenager to tell them.

For many young people sexual intercourse is not premeditated, which helps to explain the high rates of unprotected first-time sex. To ensure a girl does not get pregnant emergency contraception (after intercourse) is available from family planning clinics or doctors. This can be a pill that is taken within 72 hours of intercourse. Alternatively, a doctor can fit an intrauterine device within five days of unprotected sex.

Despite these efforts, there are 40,000 pregnancies a year in girls who are under the age of 16, and this rate is not falling significantly. The most common reasons for hospital admission for 15–16-year-old girls are termination of pregnancy and childbirth.

Sexually transmitted diseases

HIV and other sexually transmitted diseases can be transmitted by unprotected sex, and the best way to reduce the risk is always to use a condom and to limit the number of sexual partners. The most common infections today are nonspecific urethritis, gonorrhoea and herpes, but there are many others, all of them more common in teenagers and young adults than in older people. Condoms provide the best safeguard against sexually transmitted diseases, but they do not provide 100 per cent protection. A teenager who develops any of the following symptoms should see a doctor: painful urination; itchy, burning or smelly discharge from vagina or penis; inflammation, sores, lumps or irritation in the genital area. All sexually transmitted diseases can be treated, and treatment at a clinic for sexually transmitted diseases or genito-urinary medicine clinic is free and confidential, and the service is often a walk-in one.

Who can help?

For details of organizations who can provide help and/or support, counselling and contraceptive advice for young people and parents see the Directory.

Smoking

Unlike other activities that can damage teenagers' health, smoking is harmful from the very first puff or drag. Children learn about the dangers of smoking from a young age, so why, by the age of 15 or 16, have over two-thirds of teenagers tried a cigarette, and why does one in three smoke regularly? The answer is that teenagers do not care about the long-term health risks. What does lung cancer, coronary heart disease or emphysema mean to an 11-year-old – the age at which most children start experimenting with cigarettes? Nor do the immediate health problems (shortness of breath, lack of fitness, nicotine cravings, reduced skin temperature, raised blood pressure and heart rate) matter compared with the perceived benefits of being one of the crowd and looking older than you are.

Smoking among teenage girls carries enormous health risks that transcend generations. In Scotland more women now die from lung cancer than from breast cancer. Teenage girls who smoke and who take oral contraceptives are ten times as likely to have a heart attack or a stroke.

It is only once they are smoking that teenagers realize it does not achieve this, that it may put some people off and that it costs a good deal of money. But by then many are hooked. A recent survey showed that eight out of ten teenagers do not want to be smoking by the time they are 20; but almost the same number expect that they will be. Fifteen per cent of the calls to the Quitline – the helpline in the United Kingdom for smokers who want to give up – come from people who are aged16 or under.

Prevention

What can parents do to help? Researchers have found six key factors that help to protect adolescents against smoking. First, parents' attitudes and behaviour: children in smoking households are twice as likely to smoke as those in non-smoking households, but parental disapproval (even if the parent smokes) is a strong disincentive. What is more, a recent survey found that over 80 per cent of young people thought their parents were among the best people to talk to them about smoking. Second, peer pressure: friends who do not smoke and disapprove create a non-smoking culture. Among girls in particular, smoking appears to be linked with their position in the teen hierarchy. Third, not having a brother or sister who smokes. Fourth, wanting to do well at school. Fifth, being involved in a sport, and sixth, having a good self-image and self-respect.

The anti-smoking message should start in infant school, and parents should reinforce it at home. Even if you are a smoker, make it plain that you disapprove of the habit and tell your child how difficult it is to give up. Stress a healthy life style at home. Teenagers who do not smoke often cite fitness for sport as a reason. Keep young children busy: research reveals that a key reason for taking up smoking is boredom. Accept that your child is likely to experiment with cigarettes, and when they are around the age of 11, raise the subject. If you ignore it you risk conveying to them the message that you do not care.

Talk about the associated issues – tax on cigarettes, advertizing, how easy it is for underaged children to buy tobacco products. Open up a dialogue, but do not be disappointed if your child does not feel like talking to you about is. They may think you are prying into their private, adolescent life. And they may be right. However you also have rights: a right to know where your child gets the money from to buy cigarettes; a right to know who sells them to your child, because they are breaking the law.

The facts

Smoking is now more common among teenage girls than boys, and some of the reasons they give are revealing. Smoking puts them in a better mood; they feel better socially if they have a cigarette; and they worry that if they do not smoke they will eat more.

Girls also develop a psychological dependence on smoking, which they believe makes them more socially competent. Psychological dependence is quickly followed by physical dependence. Within seven seconds of drawing on a cigarette, the effects of nicotine are felt in the brain. In habitual smokers it boosts the heart rate and raises the blood pressure, and causes the capillaries under the skin to constrict. Once the level of nicotine in the bloodstream falls, the unpleasant symptoms of withdrawal are felt: craving, irritability, anxiety and difficulties in concentrating. Smokers quickly learn to top up with another cigarette.

Cigarettes are well-known to be harmful to health. Stress the dangers, and give teenagers the facts. Of over 4000 chemicals in cigarette smoke, 43 independently cause cancer. Carbon monoxide in the smoke displaces oxygen in the blood, so there is less oxygen available to the tissues, and tar irritates the lungs. In the long term smoking is linked with coronary heart disease, atherosclerosis, bronchitis, emphysema, peptic ulcer and, possibly, infertility. The longer a person smokes, the greater are the risks.

In recent years there has been a spectacular growth in the sale of fruit-and-alcohol drinks, which have a particular appeal to teenagers and young children. Many people believe that these products have largely contributed to the rapid growth in underage drinking.

Giving up

Even if a teenager is smoking regularly, do not despair – teenagers' attitudes and behaviour are not as fixed as they appear. Stress the benefits of giving up: the smell of smoke on clothes, breath and hair will vanish; the lungs will go back to being as efficient as before; the sense of taste and smell will improve; breathing and being able to cope with sudden exertion will improve; and they will save money. Warn a teenager not to expect instant success, as giving up is a process rather than a single event, but tell them there will be a well-earned feeling of pride once they have stopped.

Alcohol

Critics say alcohol is a legalized drug, and if it was discovered today, it would probably be banned immediately. Yet 90 per cent of the population drinks alcohol, and most drink it safely as a normal social activity.

Within minutes of drinking, alcohol passes into the bloodstream and is carried around the body to the brain and other major organs. The concentration of alcohol in the blood depends on a person's body weight. Alcohol has a more pronounced effect on younger people, partly because they are usually smaller and partly because their bodies are not used to dealing with alcohol. Girls tend to be affected more than boys, again because of their smaller size and also because boys have a higher water content in the body than girls, so the alcohol is diluted further.

In the brain, alcohol acts as a depressant, slowing reactions and thoughts. Its first effects – relaxation and disinhibition – last for around an hour if just one unit (a glass of wine, single measure of spirits or half a pint of beer) is drunk. The alcohol is then broken down in the liver and its effects pass. If more is drunk, however, the toxic effects mount up, causing nausea and vomiting, dehydration, headache, lack of coordination, loss of control and sleepiness.

Because alcohol undermines judgement it can be difficult even for an experienced drinker to be sure when the early pleasant effects are starting to become unpleasant, and it is little wonder that around 1000 children under 15 are admitted to hospital every year with acute alcohol intoxication.All of them need emergency treatment and some of them need to be looked after in intensive care.

There are laws to protect young people from the harmful effects of alcohol. Children under five should have alcohol only on doctor's orders; in the United Kingdom no child under 14 may go into a bar; and no one under 18 is allowed to buy alcohol, apart from 16- and 17-year-olds who are permitted to buy beer, cider, porter or perry to drink with a meal in a restaurant or dining area.

Starting to drink alcohol

Children over five are allowed to drink alcohol at home, and all the evidence suggests that this is where many children have their first taste of alcohol. Most children have their first drink between the ages of 9 and 14; by the age of 11, 16 per cent of children have at least one drink each week. Over half of all 15–16-year-olds drink regularly, and almost all have had a drink at some time.

Many teenagers drink too much: in a recent report more than one in five 13-year-old boys and more one in eight 13-year-old girls said they had been very drunk once or more in the previous year. By the age of 15, the same report revealed, one in three boys and one in five girls had got into fights or arguments after drinking. A significant number will have drunk more than the recommended safe weekly limit of 14 units of alcohol for women or 21 units for men.

Alcohol education

Alcohol education is taught in most secondary schools; pupils learn how alcohol affects body processes and are advised about the risks of alcohol abuse. Yet for most young people the first experience of drinking alcohol is at home. It seems sensible, therefore, for parents to teach their children about alcohol when it is relevant or when the subject arises naturally. It is also a good idea to allow them to become aware of the effects of alcohol under parental guidance at home.

Parents should set a good example, and can encourage sensible drinking by teaching simple social skills, such as how to refuse a drink politely. They can explain the strengths of different drinks, so that young people are better able to make an informed choice.

Parents should also discuss the downsides of drinking too much: behaving inappropriately, talking too much, being boring, losing control and falling asleep in a social setting. Losing control and becoming unattractive to the opposite sex are potent messages to teenagers. Pointing out that alcohol is frequently involved in suicide attempts, accidents involving severe head injuries and criminal damage will also help to illustrate the dangers.

Who can help?

For organizations and agencies offering advice for children and teenagers with drinking problems see the Directory.

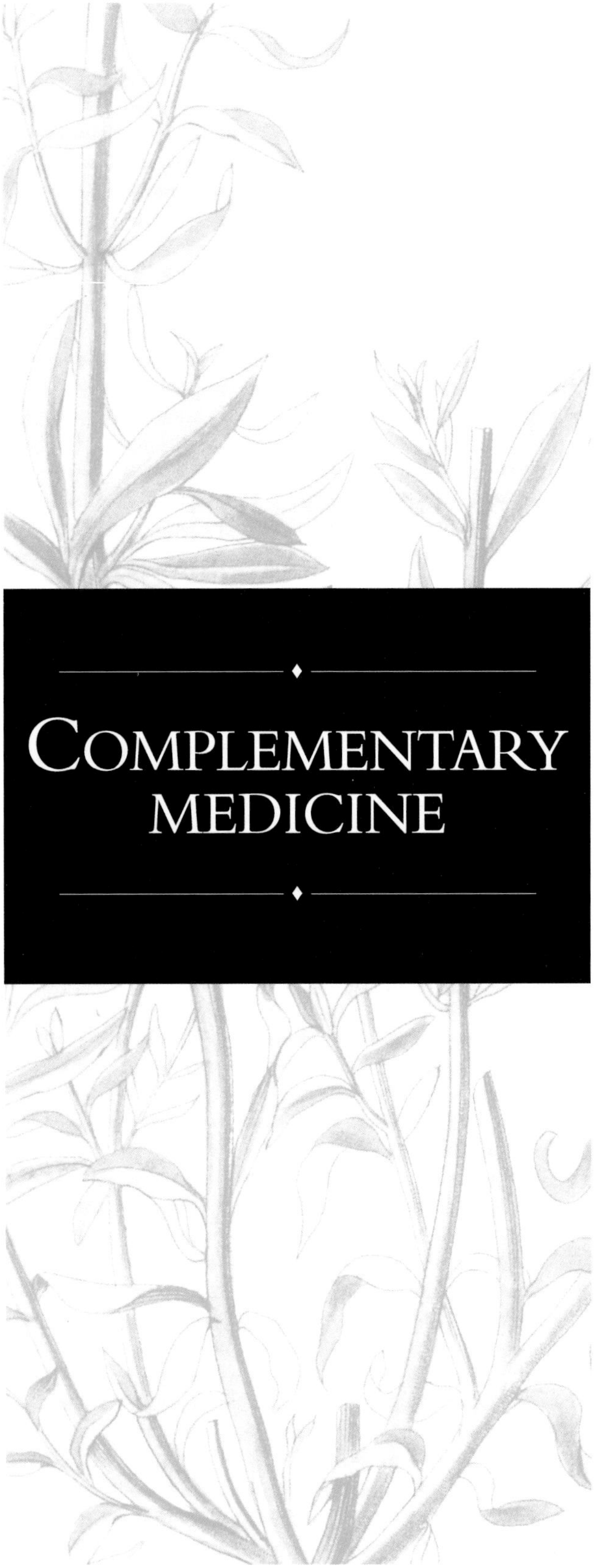

COMPLEMENTARY MEDICINE

Complementary medicine and therapies covered in this section encompass a range of diagnostic and treatment methods that are particularly suitable for most children. The purpose of their inclusion in a book in which the emphasis is on orthodox treatment is to offer parents and other primary carers a choice when taking decisions about their child's health. It is not our intention to promote one system of treatment over another, but rather to suggest alternatives that can be used in conjunction with orthodox treatment or on their own. However, it must be stressed that in cases of accidents and other emergencies, and where pathological disease is present, the first, and only, course of action is to seek help from the family doctor or the emergency services.

Safety and efficacy

The following complementary therapies are safe when practised by fully trained, qualified practitioners, and when the contraindications and other precautions given below are followed. It is the responsibility of the parent or carer to ensure that the practitioners they consult are suitably qualified, and when seeking a practitioner they should refer to the names and addresses of appropriate bodies listed in the Directory.

As with all forms of medical treatment, the effectiveness of the complementary treatment depends on the skill and experience of the practitioner, the rapport between practitioner and child, and the amount of time the child spends either receiving treatment or learning techniques.

NATURAL THERAPIES

Homeopathy

Homeopathy is one of the most widely accepted of all the natural therapies, and one of the fastest growing. The homeopathic approach is a holistic one, treating the whole person – body, mind and spirit – and not just the disease, and helping to maintain health by preventing further illness.

Homeopathy as we know it today was first developed in the 18th century by Dr Samuel Hahnemann, a German physician and chemist. It was Dr Hahnemann's belief that the body has a vital force that enables it to heal itself, and that illness results when this vital force is not in balance.

To remedy the situation Dr Hahnemann applied the ancient doctrine of 'like cures like': he prescribed small doses of substances that had characteristics in common with the symptoms of the illness in order to stimulate the body's natural healing process. In larger doses, these substances would pro-

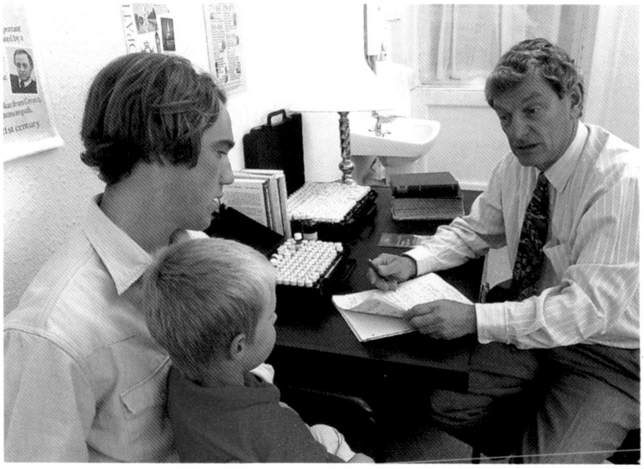

At the initial consultation the homeopath will take detailed notes about the child, including likes and dislikes. This will enable him to prescribe according to the child's unique personality, mood and temperament.

duce, in a healthy person, the same results as the symptoms shown by the ill person.

Fundamental to homeopathic practice is the idea that no two individuals are alike, and therefore that the symptoms of their illness are, in many respects, unique to themselves. Thus, two people who suffer from migraine will not necessarily exhibit the same symptoms or require the same treatment: one may feel severe throbbing pain over the left eye, another pain that begins at the back of the head and then moves and settles above one eye. For each individual, the homeopath will prescribe remedies appropriate to the symptoms and to the person's character.

Homeopathic remedies are based mainly on animal, plant or mineral substances (although some make use of human secretions or tissues, and a few, micro-organisms). The remedies are given in a dilute form, which is made by dissolving the substance in a solvent such as alcohol, and then diluting this – the mother tincture or mother solution – by a factor of 100 (1 drop of the mother tincture to 99 drops of pure alcohol). The process of dilution is repeated many times, so that each successive dilution has one-hundredth the strength of the previous one. The first dilution has a potency of one centesimal (1c), the second two centesimals (2c), and so on.* As the number of dilutions increases, the smaller the amount of the original substance that remains. A seeming contradiction of homeopathic medicine is that the higher the number of dilutions, the more potent the remedy. So, for example, a remedy of 30c is more potent than a remedy of 6c.

The remedies are usually made up as pills (pilules) with a milk-sugar (lactose) base, or as solutions. Ointments, creams, powders and granules are also available. Granules are particularly suitable for young children as they dissolve quickly.

Who may benefit?

Homeopathy can help in a wide variety of physical and emotional conditions of childhood, from colic and temper tantrums to menstrual problems. In those cases that require orthodox medical treatment, homeopathy may be able to play a supporting role.

Consultation and treatment

During the initial consultation, which may last for up to an hour, the homeopath will take a detailed medical and personal history of the child, including such matters as the constituents of the diet, amount and type of exercise taken, quality of sleep, fears and habits, and likes and dislikes. In addition, the homeopath will observe the child closely, noting such factors as posture, skin colour, gestures and so on. The homeopath will then prescribe treatment, which may include advice on nutrition, diet, exercise and other self-help measures, as well as homeopathic remedies. The homeopath may also recommend other natural therapies such as the Bach flower remedies (see page 50).

Can I treat my child myself?

Certain conditions can be treated safely at home with the common remedies (see Availability, below). The usual recommended potency is 6c, but for chronic conditions and first aid, remedies of 30c should be used. Specific remedies that can be safely used for home treatment are suggested in Parts 5 and 6, under the individual ailments and problems. For complex or chronic conditions, and for conditions that worsen or do not improve with home treatment, you should seek the advice of a homeopath.

How to administer

Pills and granules are dissolved on the tongue; solutions are given by drops directly on to the tongue. Mother tinctures are mixed with water, usually 10 drops to 300 ml/$^{1}/_{2}$ pint of cooled, boiled water. The dilute tincture can be used for gargalling and bathing.

Take care

- When giving homeopathic remedies, make sure the child avoids coffee and peppermint in all forms (including tooth-

*Some homeopathic remedies are diluted by a factor of 10 (1x) or by a factor of 1000 (1m), but in Britain the remedies are usually available in centesimals (1c, 6c, etc. as above).

paste), as these substances interfere with the healing action of the remedies. Tobacco and some other substances also act as antidotes, and the homeopath will advise

- If giving homeopathic medicines without consulting a homeopath, do not give other forms of natural therapy, such as aromatherapy (see page 51), without seeking advice, as one treatment may interfere with the other
- It is safe to take homeopathic remedies when taking prescription drugs, although some prescription drugs may interfere with homeopathic remedies. You should always tell your practitioner about any drugs, including over-the-counter drugs, that your child is taking

Availability

A number of common homeopathic remedies are available from large chemists and other suppliers of natural medicines. However, the more extensive range (some 3000 are in use worldwide) is only available from specialized retailers and manufacturers.

Finding a practitioner

Homeopathic practitioners may be medical doctors who are members or fellows of the Faculty of Homeopathy (and use the letters MFHom and FFHom respectively after their name), or practitioners who have studied at a recognized homeopathic training centre (and use the letters RSHom or FSHom). See the Directory for the names and addresses of qualified medical and other registered homeopaths.

Bach flower remedies

The Bach flower remedies were developed in the 1930s by Dr Edward Bach, a physician, bacteriologist and homeopath who held posts at University College, London, the School of Immunology and, later, at the London Homeopathic Hospital. Bach gave up orthodox, scientifically-based treatment methods and left his Harley Street practice in order to study and use natural remedies on his patients. He had an intuitive knowledge of plants and their properties, and of the 38 remedies he originated, 37 of them are based on common British plants.

Bach's work in bacteriology and pathology at the London Homeopathic Hospital brought him into contact with the principles of homeopathy (see page 48), which had an enormous impact on his thinking. He began to study the personalities of his patients and he combined the outcome of his examinations with his extensive knowledge of plants, which, he believed, contained a vital healing energy that could ultimately restore health.

Bach's view of illness was that it resulted from an emotional or mental imbalance or disharmony – which in turn was a result of a dissociation between body and soul – and that any such imbalance should be addressed in order to initiate recovery. His approach was holistic, and his aim was to 'treat the patient, not the disease'. This was to be achieved by ridding the individual of negative feelings and attitudes that had caused the physical symptoms, and by so doing, uniting body and soul and bringing the person into a state of emotional, mental and physical health.

Thirty-seven of the Bach flower remedies consist of the essences of wild plants; the other remedy, Rock Water, is pure water collected from a rocky stream. The flower remedies are prepared by steeping freshly gathered flowers in a glass bowl of pure spring water and standing the bowl in sunlight for a few hours, during which time the water is imbued with the energy of the plant through the action of the sun on the petals. This solution is the stock, which is then diluted and mixed with a small amount of brandy to preserve the liquid.

Who may benefit?

Practitioners regard the Bach flower remedies as suitable for children suffering from a wide variety of physical and emotional conditions. As Judy Howard of the Dr Edward Bach Centre has said, 'Whatever the condition or ailment, even in cases where the Bach flower remedies are not specifically indicated, they nonetheless form an excellent supportive therapy dealing with the emotional aspects, so important in the treatment of and recovery from any disease.'

Consultation and treatment

During the first consultation the practitioner will question the parent and/or child about the child's physical health and emotional and mental well being, taking into account such matters as place in the family, attitude to siblings and so on. The

The Bach flower remedies have no side effects and are perfectly safe to administer to children of all ages. It is even possible to allow the child to dilute her own remedies under the close supervision of her mother or another caring adult. With their intimate knowledge of their child, parents can often choose suitable remedies themselves, although for complex problems the advice of a registered practitoner is recommended.

appropriate remedy is found by observing closely the child's nature and assessing the state of mind. Negative aspects of the personality are generally the easiest to identify, particularly during illness, but the practitioner, parent or carer should also try to seek out the positive aspects as well in order to gain a clear picture of the child.

The 38 flower remedies are divided into 7 groups (see box), on the basis of the predominant emotional and mental symptoms exhibited by the child. The individual remedies within these groups were developed for quite specific states of mind. For example, in Group 1, fear, Rock Rose is useful for those who are terrified and panic stricken, while Aspen should be given to those with imaginary fears without real or actual cause. Detailed descriptions of the remedies are beyond the scope of this book, but there is a wide range of literature on the subject, which can be obtained from the Dr Edward Bach Centre. See the Directory for the address.

Can I treat my child myself?

Bach flower remedies are suitable both for self-treatment and for treating family members at home. Where applicable, specific remedies are suggested in Parts 5 and 6, under the individual ailments and problems. However, for complex or chronic conditions it may be advisable to see a registered practitioner before giving any home treatment.

How to administer

Instructions are given on the bottle, but the general recommendation for treating children is to dilute the remedy in the proportion of two to three drops of the stock remedy to every 30 ml/2 tbsp of spring water. Keep the diluted remedy in a small dropper bottle (dark glass bottles are available from most chemists) and administer by putting two to three drops in the child's food or drink, or placing it directly under the child's tongue. For breastfeeding babies, moisten the baby's lips with the drops of diluted remedy. Give four times a day until the condition improves, unless otherwise directed by a practitioner. Rescue cream is applied to the skin, taking it well beyond the affected area.

Take care

- No precautions are necessary. The remedies are simple to take and so safe that they can be given to babies, and also animals.

Availability

The complete range of Bach flower remedies is available from the Bach Centre, and from a large number of chemists and other suppliers of natural medicines. They can be bought as non-greasy ointments in a homeopathic base, as well as in the liquid form.

Finding a practitioner

Although there is no professional qualification for practitioners using Bach flower remedies, there are training courses, and a register of those who have completed them. Also, many of the practitioners using Bach flower remedies often practise in other areas of complementary medicine, such as homeopathy. The best way to find a suitable practitioner is to consult the governing body, association or register (see the Directory for a list of names and addresses).

The Bach Flower Remedies

- Group 1: Used to treat fear. Aspen, Cherry Plum, Mimulus, Red Chestnut, Rock Rose
- Group 2: Used to treat uncertainty. Cerato, Gentian, Gorse, Hornbeam, Scleranthus, Wild Oat
- Wild Rose
  Group 3: Used to treat disinterest. Chestnut Bud, Clematis, Honeysuckle, Mustard, Olive, White
- Chestnut
  Group 4: Used to treat loneliness. Heather,
- Impatiens, Water Violet.
  Group 5: Used to treat oversensitivity to ideas and
- influences. Agrimony, Centaury, Holly, Walnut
  Group 6: Used to treat despondency and despair. Crab Apple, Elm, Larch, Oak, Pine, Star of
- Bethlehem, Sweet Chestnut, Willow
  Group 7: Used to treat those who are too caring for the welfare of others. Beech, Chicory, Rock Water, Vervain, Vine
  In addition, Rescue Remedy – a combination of Star of Bethlehem, Clematis, Cherry Plum, Impatiens and Rock Rose – is used in first aid, to treat shock and as a preventative

Aromatherapy

Aromatherapy is one of the most popular and widely used of all the complementary therapies. The immediate and superficial effects are obvious – extremely pleasant-smelling substances that lift the spirits. However, at a deeper level, aromatherapy can be a very powerful treatment for a range of ailments and conditions associated with stress.

Although the medicinal use of plant essences is an ancient one, the term aromatherapy was not applied until the 1920s. A French chemist, René Maurice Gattefosse, accidentally discovered the healing properties of lavender oil while working in the family perfume laboratory. The experience led him to study the healing properties of essential oils and use them to treat skin complaints. In 1928 he published his findings in *Aromatherapie* – the first known use of the now familiar word. More recently, in 1964, a fellow Frenchman, Dr Jean Valnet, published his book of the same name. These two men are largely responsible for the development of the therapy as it is now practised, and today aromatherapy is studied seriously by many French doctors. In other countries, too, it is increasingly being used by nurses and trained practitioners as a complementary therapy in hospitals, hospices and other caring communities.

As with homeopathy and the Bach flower remedies, aromatherapy is holistic in its approach. It is based on the principle that the volatile nature of the essential oils can profoundly affect the mind as well as the body.

Some 200 or so essential oils are produced commercially from herbs, flowers, bark, roots and other plant material. About 60 of these oils are used by aromatherapists. The oils are usually prepared by steam or solvent distillation, which isolates the essential oils from the other plant components. Citrus oils are usually prepared by expressing, or pressing, the peel of the fruit, which contains the volatile oils.

Essential oils are absorbed into the body and eliminated quickly and efficiently in perspiration, faeces, urine and exhaled breath, without leaving any toxic substances behind.

Lavender is grown in extensive fields in the south of France (above), in England, Italy and Corsica. The flowering tips of the plant are used to prepare the essential oil, one of the most useful and safest of all the oils. With eucalyptus and tea tree, it is useful for treating children's colds, either in a diffuser or, for an older child, in a bowl of hot water used to steam the head (right).

Who may benefit?

Children of all ages, including babies and toddlers, may benefit from aromatherapy during difficult phases of normal growth and development, and when they are suffering from a physical complaint. Many of the essential oils have strong antibacterial or anti-viral properties, and are particularly beneficial in treating infections. Other essential oils are helpful for relieving stress and stress-related problems, such as headache and digestive disorders, for pain relief and for stimulating the immune system.

Consultation and treatment

The practitioner will take a detailed history of the child's development and any past ailments, as well as symptoms of the present disorder and the child's emotional and mental state, before choosing a suitable treatment. This usually consists of one or more of the essential oils, in a form most suited to the complaint.

Can I treat my child myself?

A number of oils are safe enough to be used at home, without the need to take the advice of a practitioner. However, when treating babies and toddlers who are ill, and for complex or chronic conditions in children of all ages, it is advisable to consult a trained practitioner.

Where applicable, individual essential oils, with notes on their safety, are suggested in Parts 5 and 6, under individual ailments and problems.

How to administer

Essential oils can be very potent and must first be diluted with a carrier oil, such as apricot kernel oil or grapeseed oil. The usual recommended dilution for children is 3–5 drops of essential oil to every 30 ml/2 tbsp of carrier oil, although this will vary with the age of the child. Essential oils can be applied to the skin, inhaled (for example, by using a vaporizer), added to bath water, used in compresses, ointments and other skin preparations, and given orally, but only under strict supervision by the practitioner.

Take care

- Some essential oils can be toxic if they are not prepared properly or are taken in excessive doses. Others, such as bergamot, neroli and the citrus oils, may cause skin irritation when the skin is exposed to sunlight

- Use only those oils specifically recommended for children, in the specified doses and by the specified method. Oils that can be used safely with babies and young children in blended form include rose, lavender and chamomile
- Never take or administer any essential oil by mouth unless advised by a qualified aromatherapist

Availability

Essential oils are now widely available from chemists and health shops, and from shops specializing in natural products. If you buy a reputable brand from a reputable source you can be sure you are getting only the finest oils and not an adulterated product.

Finding a practitioner

The aromatherapist should be a member of a recognized professional association and should have studied at a reputable training centre. See the Directory for how to find a registered practitioner. Make certain that the practitioner you choose is registered and that you feel confident and comfortable with them.

Nutritional therapy

Nutrition as a recognized therapy is still relatively new, but it has grown with the increasing awareness that an inadequate diet can lead to, or exacerbate, ill health, and the recognition that in order to maintain good health it is necessary to eat a healthy diet.

Nutritional therapy is based on the fact that the vital elements in food can aid the healing process, and that under certain conditions some foods are responsible for causing disease and illness. The idea is not new: it held an important place in the work of Greek physicians, such as Hippocrates in the 5th century BC, and in the doctrines of Chinese, Egyptian and Indian healers. Yet it was not until the late 19th century that some of these vital elements were identified and isolated. The first of these was a vitamin, vitamin B_1 (thiamine), which caused beriberi when it was deficient in the diet, but which cured the disease when foods containing B_1, such as fresh vegetables, were added.

By the early 1900s several other nutrients, originally called 'vitamines', had been identified, and their importance in maintaining health understood. When, in 1933, the first vitamin (vitamin C) was synthesized, the possibility of manufacturing nutrients and using them to supplement the diet became a reality.

Without doubt, the best way to give children the nutrients that maintain and promote health is to give them high quality, fresh foods, prepared in such a way that most, if not all, of the essential nutrients are retained. Fresh vegetables and fruit are ideal, especially when eaten raw in salads or simply well washed and eaten as they come.

Foods and their constituents (preferably in their natural form, but also in synthesized form) are the basis of nutritional therapy. The treatment aims to improve and maintain health by enhancing specific metabolic processes that take place in the body. In some cases certain foods may also have to be eliminated from the diet.

Who may benefit?

Nutritional therapy is suitable for everyone, particularly for providing support during other forms of treatment. It has an important role to play in the prevention and treatment of serious diseases, such as cancer and heart disease, and in the diagnosis and treatment of chronic conditions, such as eczema, asthma, PMS and migraine.

Consultation and treatment

Nutritionists will want full details of the child's present diet, past medical history, known allergies and present symptoms, as well as details of the child's life style. They may also carry out a few simple tests in order to eliminate allergies and food intolerances, and to ascertain the child's nutrient requirements. Treatment may involve a prescribed diet tailored to the child's needs.

Can I treat my child myself?

Home treatment should be restricted to providing a healthy diet. Supplements should only be given to children over the age of 12, and only to maintain health unless otherwise directed by a nutritionist or doctor. For children under the age of 12, and for all children with an ailment that has a suspected dietary cause, seek professional advice.

How to administer

Nutritional supplements are manufactured in tablet, capsule and liquid form; some, such as vitamin E, are sometimes added to creams and ointments. Follow the instructions and dosage given on the packaging*. Large doses of a supplement are usually administered as an injection by a doctor. For prescribed supplements, follow your doctor's or nutritionist's instructions on dosage.

Take care

- Supplements should only be given when the diet is a deficient in nutrients. When levels of nutrients are normal, supplements, especially in large doses, may be harmful
- Never exceed the recommended dosage of supplements
- Always seek your doctor's advice before seeing a nutritional practitioner, to rule out causes requiring orthodox treatment

Availability

Vitamins, minerals and other supplements are widely available from chemists, supermarkets and health shops.

Finding a practitioner

The nutritionist should have undertaken a recognized training course and belong to a professional association. Nutritional therapists who are qualified in other areas of complementary therapy and have a specialized knowledge of nutrition include doctors, herbalists and acupuncturists. If you do not have a personal or professional recommendation, see the Directory for how to find a qualified practitioner.

Western herbalism

Western herbalism ('Western' to distinguish it from Chinese herbalism, discussed on page 62) is one of the oldest of the natural treatments. The properties of herbs were studied by the Greeks, most notably by Theophrastus (?372–?287 BC), who described many of them in *Enquiry into Plants*, and the Greek Dioscorides, who, *circa* AD 50, recorded the medicinal properties of many herbs in *De Materia Medica*.

Western herbalism relies on the unique properties of specific plants to restore balance in the body and to actively encourage the body to heal itself. As with the majority of complementary forms of medicine the emphasis is on dealing with the whole individual, not just with the specific ailment or complaint.

In England herbalism flourished during the 16th and 17th centuries, with the works and writings of herbalists such as William Turner, John Gerard, John Parkinson and Nicholas Culpeper. However, in the 17th century, herbalism as a healing art was overshadowed by developments in science and by the rise of orthodox medicine. It was to remain in the background until the mid-20th century, but in recent years herbalism has become one of the most widely used of all the complementary therapies.

Modern Western herbalism is based on the belief that plants have a vital energy, or vibration, that can be beneficial to the body by encouraging the body's natural ability to heal itself. Plants increase and direct the body's energy, bringing the body into a state of balance. Western herbalism has this belief in common with both the Bach flower remedies and aromatherapy (see pages 50 and 51), and like them takes a holistic approach to illness, treating the whole person and not just the disease.

Herbal remedies are prepared in such a way that all the plant's energy is harnessed, and the many substances that constitute the plant work together to promote a safe and gentle cure. In contrast, conventional drugs are prepared by isolating the active property of a plant and, in some cases, synthesizing it. Medical herbalists hold that, without the benefit of all the constituents contained in the whole plant, orthodox drugs have only a limited effect, and as a consequence unwanted side effects are inevitable.

The purpose of therapy does not end with curing illness, however; it is also used to bring about a balance between the various body systems and so prevent illness.

Herbal remedies are made up in a number of ways. The flowers, stems and leaves can be used to make a herbal infusion (also known as a tea or tisane); the roots, seeds and bark of herbs are usually prepared as a decoction. Another, more time-consuming method of preparation is to make a tincture by steeping the herb in a mixture of alcohol and water for several weeks. Other herbal preparations include essential oils, syrups, poultices, creams, compresses and ointments. (For details on how to prepare infusions and decoctions, see How to administer, page 55.)

*In the United Kingdom, government guidelines on the daily requirements of foods and supplements needed to maintain health are changing. The old guidelines (recommended daily allowances, or RDAs) are being replaced by dietary reference values (DRVs), within which the reference nutrient intake (RNI) replaces the RDA. RNI is the amount of a nutrient required daily by 97% of the population. The RNI is now found on most supplements. Unlike US guidelines, UK government guidelines do not always distinguish between the requirements of males, females, pregnant women and children when stating RDAs or RNIs.

Who may benefit?

Babies and older children who are suffering from a wide variety of ailments may benefit from medical herbalism, particularly when it is used as a supportive therapy for orthodox medicine. Western medical herbalism is particularly helpful when dealing with chronic conditions.

Consultation and treatment

The medical herbalist will take the child's case history and will usually carry out a physical examination. The consultation may also include tests and diagnostic procedures, such as measuring blood pressure, taking X-rays and examining urine samples. Some herbalists may also use diagnostic tests from other branches of complementary medicine. As well as prescribing herbal remedies, the practitioner may also recommend dietary changes and exercise.

Can I treat my child myself?

A number of herbal remedies are perfectly safe when given as teas and decoctions, and used in herbal bath preparations and herb pillows. However, for serious conditions that do not require orthodox treatment you should seek the help and advice of a registered medical herbalist.

How to administer

Herbal teas are prepared by pouring about 250 ml/9 fl oz of hot water over a heaped 5 ml/1 tsp of the dried herb. If you are using fresh herbs, double the amount. Stir and leave to steep for a few minutes. Strain the liquid and drink when it has cooled slightly. Herbal teas for children (not babies) can be sweetened with honey. The recommended dosage for babies is 5 ml/1 tsp, and for children, 50 ml/2 fl oz.

Decoctions are made by placing 15 ml/1 tbsp of powdered root or bark in 600 ml/1 pint of water, simmering for 15–30 minutes in an enamel or stainless steel pan, and then straining. The dosage is the same as that for herbal teas.

Infusions and decoctions can also be added to bath water. Use 10–20 times the doses given above.

Where applicable, herbal remedies, with notes on their safety, are suggested in Parts 5 and 6, under individual ailments and problems.

Take care

- Herbs can be powerful and can have serious toxic effects. They must be treated with respect. Use only herbs specifically recommended for babies and children. All others should be used only under the strict supervision of a medical herbalist
- If your child shows any unusual reactions after taking a herbal remedy, stop giving it immediately and consult a registered medical herbalist or your family doctor

Availability

Dried and fresh herbs, herbal teas and other herbal preparations are widely available at shops specializing in natural health products. When using commercially prepared remedies, always follow the directions on the packet.

Finding a practitioner

The best way to find a medical herbalist is by personal recommendation, or on the recommendation of a qualified medical practitioner or other complementary practitioner. The medical herbalist you consult should be a member or fellow of the National Institute of Medical Herbalists and have the initials MNIMH or FNIMH, respectively, after their name. If you do not have a professional recommendation, see the Directory for how to find a qualified and registered herbalist.

MANIPULATIVE THERAPIES

Osteopathy

Osteopathy is a manipulative medicine and therapy with a holistic approach: it treats the person, not the disease. Its founder, Andrew Taylor Still, was an American country doctor practising in Virginia. Disillusioned with orthodox medicine, he began to base his treatment on the idea that if the structure of the body was sound, then the body's life force would maintain general fitness and health.

Osteopaths treat patients by manipulating misaligned bones and injured joints, working on the structure of the body – the skeletal, muscular and nervous systems – in order to relieve pain, improve mobility and restore health by bringing the whole body back into balance. Practitioners maintain that work on the body's structure will improve any mechanical disorder in the structure itself, and/or promote optimum conditions under which the body's organs can return to normal functioning. Therapy consists of a variety of movements, including stroking, twisting and stretching.

Who may benefit?

Children suffering from disorders and diseases of the muscular, nervous and skeletal systems, or from digestive and respiratory disorders, among others, may benefit from osteopathy, either as the primary therapy or therapy following orthodox treatment such as surgery.

Osteopathy is compatible with orthodox medicine, and in a large number of cases it can offer considerable support to orthodox treatment.

Osteopathic techniques promote the body's natural healing processes. An osteopathic session involves manipulation of the body's joints and muscles to correct imbalances and dysfunctions that may be causing pain, and to provide treatment for conditions that, in the long term, may lead to disease. When seeking treatment for their child, parents should ensure that they consult a qualified osteopath who specializes in children's disorders.

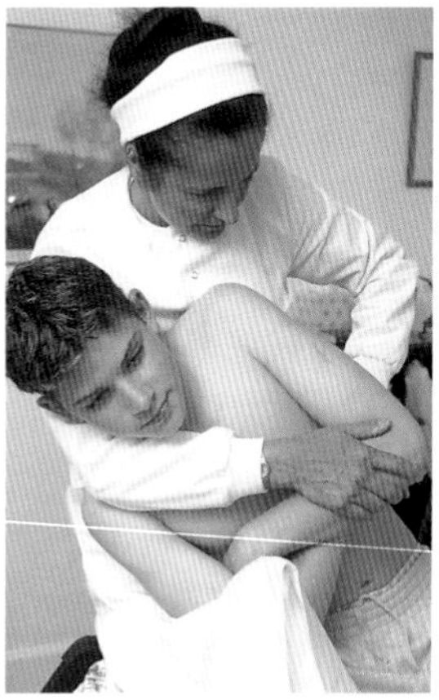

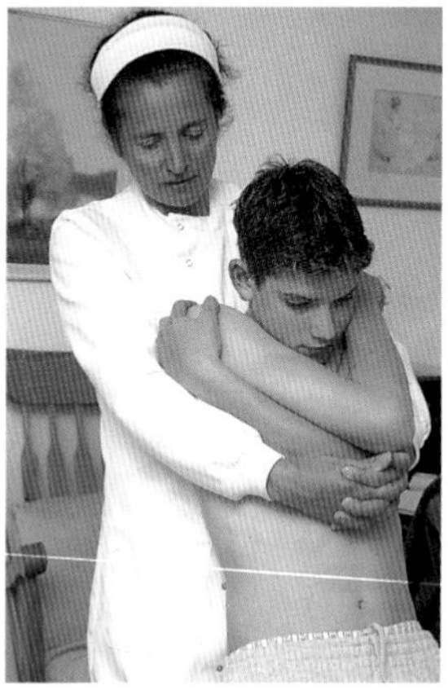

The various forms of osteopathy and chiropractic emphasize different aspects of a similar type of treatment. None is painful and a wide range of conditions can be successfully treated. Only a very few people who suffer from very weak or fragile bones or from very inflamed joints should not make use of these treatments. Under normal circumstances the patient will probably be seen by the osteopath (left) or chiropractor for at least three sessions after the initial consultation.

Consultation and treatment

To assess how well the child's body is functioning, the osteopath will take a case history, including details of past ailments, any developmental problems, habits and preoccupations. The osteopath will note the child's posture and mobility, and carry out an examination of the physical structure by palpating the joints, muscles and tissues. In some cases it will be necessary to perform blood and urine tests, or X-rays.

Treatment varies with the individual; the osteopath may restrict manipulation to soft tissue treatment, in which the tissue is gently manipulated in order to relax tense muscles and improve mobility. During treatment emphasis is placed on the psychological benefits of touch, in addition to the physical benefits of manipulation.

Can I treat my child myself?

No. Osteopathy should only be practised by a registered practitioner. Never try it yourself at home.

Take care

- There are no contraindications for paediatric osteopathy carried out by a reputable, qualified osteopath

Finding a practitioner

Osteopaths may be medical doctors who have trained in osteopathy (and use the letters MLCOM after their name), or non-medical osteopaths (who use the letters DO or BSCI [OST] after their name). For how to find a paediatric osteopath and other qualified practitioners, see the Directory.

Chiropractic

Chiropractic is a therapy that fundamentally addresses the skeletal system. It is concerned with the correct alignment of the joints and the spine, and the effects that any misalignment can produce on the nervous system and therefore on the body as a whole.

The man who developed chiropractic was David Daniel Palmer, a Canadian living in Iowa, USA, where he practised as a healer, and possibly as a practitioner of the old art of bone-setting. Palmer maintained that there were self-correcting mechanisms in the body, specifically in the skeletal and nervous systems. He developed his manipulative technique for treating symptoms that he believed originated in the structure of the body. Palmer himself invented the name chiropractic to describe his therapy, combining the Greek words *cheir*, meaning hand, and *practikos*, meaning practitioner.

Chiropractors practising today carry on Palmer's work in much the same way as he did. They diagnose and treat mechanical disorders of the joints, particularly those in the spine; they free trapped nervous tissue and thereby promote self-healing in the organs and other body structures that the nerves supply. The manipulative technique usually involves direct pressure on an area by means of thrusting movements.

Who may benefit?

Children may benefit from chiropractic; babies can be treated with more gentle techniques. It is suitable for a number of muscular and skeletal disorders. As with osteopathy, chiropractic is compatible with orthodox medicine, and in many cases can offer considerable support to orthodox treatment.

Consultation and treatment

The chiropractor will want to know about the child's medical history, present and past ailments and disorders, problems in development and other personal details. The child's posture will be carefully observed and the reflexes tested. The chiropractor may recommend X-rays and blood or urine tests to help with the diagnosis. Treatment consists of physically manipulating the bones and joints. When necessary, advice will be given on diet, exercise and improving posture.

Can I treat my child myself?

No. Chiropractic should only be practised by a reputable, qualified chiropractor.

Take care

- Chiropractic should not be undertaken if the child has recently fractured any bones, or has an inflammation or tumour in the spine

Finding a practitioner

Qualified chiropractors have undergone a five-year training course at a recognized college (and use the letters BSC after their name). A recommendation from a doctor is one way to find a registered chiropractor specializing in the treatment of children. If you do not have a professional recommendation, see the Directory for the address of organiazations from which you can obtain a list of qualified chiropractors.

Reflexology

Reflexology, also known as zone or compression therapy, is a system of diagnosis and treatment that works mainly by applying pressure to the feet. A similar type of therapy was in use thousands of years ago by the Chinese, Egyptians, Indians and native Americans. The basis of the modern practice was established early in the 20th century by William H. Fitzgerald, an American doctor who became interested in Chinese acupuncture. Fitzgerald adopted the idea that the body has numerous energy channels, or meridians, along which energy flows freely when the individual is healthy. He went on to develop the idea that illness results when these channels become blocked by tension, congestion or negative feelings, and that in order to restore health the channels must be unblocked. It was a fellow American, Eunice Ingham, who discovered that the feet were particularly responsive to the stimulus provided by zone therapy, and who is largely responsible for the therapy as it is practised today.

Reflexologists divide the body into ten vertical channels, five on each side of the body, running from the head to the tips of the fingers and down to the toes. The energy flowing through these channels terminates in the feet, which give an accurate picture of a person's state of health. To the reflexologist the feet represent a map of the whole body, with a specific part of the foot corresponding to a specific part of the body; for example, the middle of the bottom of the big toe corresponds to the pituitary gland. Massage and pressure on the feet not only invigorate the whole body, but also stimulate the nervous and circulatory systems, and therefore the body's organs and other tissues.

Who may benefit?

Young children often find reflexology extremely soothing – applying gentle pressure to a wakeful baby's feet can help to promote sleep. Children suffering from ailments, such as neck and back pain, sinusitis, hay fever and asthma, among other complaints, may obtain some benefit from reflexology. The therapy does not interfere with orthodox treatment.

Consultation and treatment

The reflexologist may only be interested in examining the feet of the child, or they may want to take a detailed case history. The examination involves searching out any tender areas and areas with granular deposits under the skin, indicating blockages in the channels. During treatment pressure is applied to various areas, or the area is massaged so that the granules are broken down and eventually excreted in the urine. In some cases the reflexologist may work on the fingers and palms of the hand rather than the feet. Several sessions may be needed in order to feel the benefits, as the effects of reflexology are often cumulative.

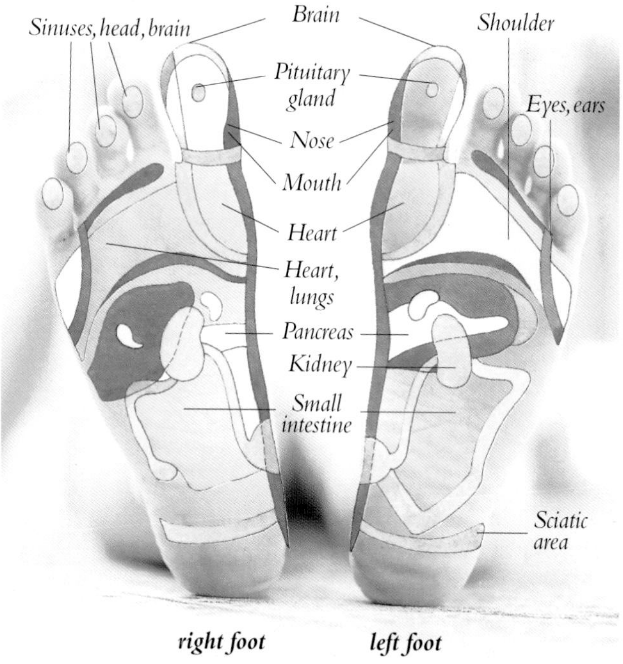

Reflexologists base their treatment on stimulating nerve endings in specific areas of the left and right foot that correspond to specific areas in the other parts of body. By so doing they attempt to influence body systems that will lead to improvement in health and well being. The above illustration gives some idea of how a foot chart is laid out.

Can I treat my child myself?
No. Reflexology should only be practised by a reputable, qualified reflexologist.

Take care
- Treatment may require deep pressure and massage, but should not be painful. A good practitioner should respond instantly to any discomfort the child feels

Finding a practitioner
Qualified reflexologists will have undergone a recognized training course and will be registered with one of the governing and regulating bodies. A recommendation from a doctor is one way to find a qualified reflexologist, but if you do not have a professional recommendation, see the Directory for where to obtain a list of qualified reflexologists.

Massage

Massage is certainly the oldest and probably the most widely accepted form of healing. It has developed from our instinct to touch, in order to give comfort, warmth and reassurance.

Massage is a complementary therapy in its own right, but it is also used by practitioners in other disciplines as an adjunct to treatment, perhaps most notably by aromatherapists (see page 51) and physiotherapists. The first records of massage as a form of healing can be found in *Nei Ching*, (translated as *The Yellow Emperor's Classic of Internal Medicine*), published in China in 2500 BC. Ancient Sanskrit texts, dating back to around 1000 BC, and the works of the Greek physician Hippocrates in the 5th century BC, also record the use of massage to treat illness. In its modern form it owes much to the work of Per Hendrik Luig, who practised in Sweden in the late 18th and early 19th centuries and developed what has become known as Swedish massage.

Practitioners take a holistic view of the individual, maintaining that, correctly done, massage has beneficial effects on the spirit and emotions as well as the physical body. They use a variety of movements and techniques, depending on the patient's condition and the desired result. Physiologically, massage stimulates the circulation of blood and lymph, and decreases blood pressure, heart rate and muscle tension, resulting in relaxation and a feeling of well being. It can also have a marked effect on self-esteem and body awareness, and may help to release suppressed emotions.

Who may benefit?
All children, even small babies, benefit emotionally and physically from massage, during both illness and health.

Consultation and treatment
The practitioner may ask the parent and/or child about any present and past problems in order to assess the reason for seeking treatment. The session begins with gliding, fanning, feathering and circular strokes (effleurage) to introduce the child to the experience of massage and to loosen the superficial muscles. Then the soft tissues – muscles, ligaments, tendons and other connective tissue – are kneaded (petrissage) to release any knots and to stretch ligaments and tendons. The practitioner may continue with work on the deeper muscles, using friction and deep pressure strokes, depending on the child's age and condition.

Can I treat my child myself?
Massage provides an excellent opportunity to strengthen the bond between parent and child. Even if you are inexperienced at massage, soft gentle strokes over the body will help to calm a fractious child and give comfort to a sick one. However, if you wish to treat your child at home, and give you and your child the full benefits massage can bring, you should learn the proper procedures and techniques. Instruction is widely available, and there are many excellent books and courses that will introduce you to the basic techniques. For chronic conditions, however, you should consult a fully trained practitioner.

Take care
- Be aware that, wrongly used, massage can cause damage to body tissues
- Never use any pressure on or around the spine or joints

Finding a practitioner
Qualified practitioners will have undergone a recognized training course in massage and will be registered. A personal recommendation from a doctor is one way to find a qualified

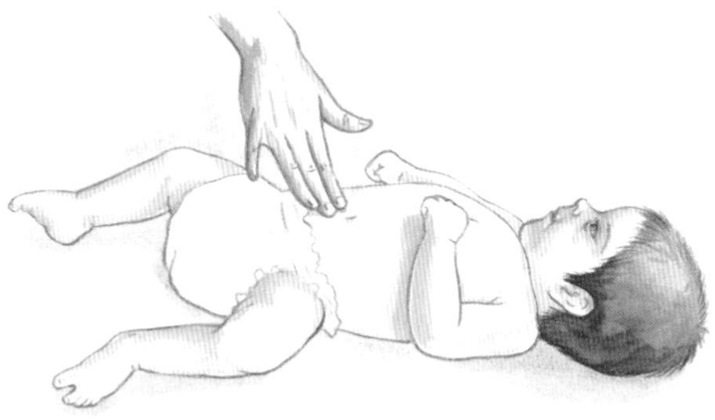

Babies are usually particularly responsive to massage, given either to soothe and calm during illness, to reinforce the bonding process or for the sheer pleasure of giving and receiving touch.

practitioner, but if you do not have a professional recommendation, see the Directory for where to obtain a list of practitioners in your area.

Applied kinesiology

Applied kinesiology is a diagnostic therapy that, like massage, is based on touch, but has features in common with acupressure and chiropractic (see pages 62 and 56). It is one of the newest of the complementary therapies, and was developed in the mid-1960s by an American chiropractor, Dr George Goodheart, initially as a diganostic tool to test muscle strength and tone in his patients. Dr Goodheart then discovered a correlation between muscle strength and tone and the state of the internal organs, such as the kidneys, heart and bladder. He accepted the acupuncturist's assertion that energy flows in channels throughout the body, and maintained that the body's natural ability to heal could be blocked by imbalances in its structure. Once these imbalances had been corrected, vital energy could flow unrestricted along the energy channels.

Who may benefit?

Applied kinesiology deals with problems of a functional nature, and is proscribed from treating pathological disorders or diseases. However, the therapy may alleviate the pain and symptoms of diseases such as chickenpox or whooping cough by improving the basic health and well being of the child, as well as relieving mental stress brought on by the illness. Applied kinesiology is particularly helpful in diagnosing allergies, such as lactose intolerance, that may trigger other symptoms and disorders.

Consultation and treatment

The practitioner will take a detailed case history, including notes on the child's diet, and will observe the child's stance and posture. Light pressure will be applied to the muscles at specific points on the body, and a diagnosis made based on the body's response. Treatment will usually involve activating the muscles by touching and gently pressing the appropriate points, so that muscle balance is restored and the flow of energy through the body is revitalized. Chiropractic or similar techniques may also be used. The practitioner will usually advise on diet, and may recommend nutritional supplements, such as vitamins and minerals.

Can I treat my child myself?

No. Applied kinesiology should only be practised by a reputable, qualified practitioner.

Take care

- There are no contraindications for therapy carried out by a trained kinesiologist

Finding a practitioner

Qualified practitioners will have undergone a recognized training programme and gained a diploma (DIPASK). They must be insured and must comply with the association's code of ethics and practice, among them that practitioners should advise their clients to seek professional medical attention if the problem lies outside their area of expertise and knowledge. The association specifies that children over the age of seven must give their consent to treatment by a kinesiologist.

A personal recommendation from a doctor is one way to find a qualified kinesiologist, but if you do not have a professional recommendation, see the Directory for where to obtain a list of qualified practitioners.

ACTIVE THERAPIES

Relaxation

Relaxation is not so much a therapy as an adjunct to other therapies and disciplines, such as yoga and hypnosis. As a learned technique for self-treatment it can produce extremely beneficial results. Many medical doctors and complementary practitioners encourage their clients to learn and practise complete relaxation as a means of counteracting stress and overcoming stress-related ailments.

There are several different methods of teaching relaxation, and the practitioner will have their own preference. Nevertheless, all these methods achieve the same result: complete relaxation of body and mind for a prescribed period of time, bringing about a release of mental and physical tension.

Who may benefit?

All children, healthy and ailing, can benefit from, and are amenable to, relaxation, a technique that relies on children's natural ability to use their imagination. However, as in many other therapeutic situations, the effectiveness of the therapy depends on the skill and experience of the practitioner, the rapport between the practitioner and the child, and the amount of time the child spends either receiving treatment or learning the techniques.

In cases where the healing process is expected to take place, but is delayed as a result of stress, relaxation reduces the output of adrenaline in the body, thereby allowing the immune system to function more effectively.

Consultation and treatment

The practitioner will want to learn something of the child's medical and emotional background. As a necessary preliminary to relaxation the practitioner will probably teach the child to breathe correctly. Many practitioners maintain that calm, deep breathing, correctly practised, brings energy into the body. On a physical level it increases oxygen intake, which is particularly beneficial to the brain and nervous system.

In addition to relaxation, the practitioner may teach the child visualization – visualizing an object or situation that has peaceful and positive associations, in order to promote healing and wholeness. Visualization can be used to overcome negative feelings and to change some aspect of life that is disruptive or disturbing.

The Fleming technique is a fairly new technique whereby the child, having fully relaxed, concentrates on parts of the body or mind that are comfortable, rather than using imaginary situations or scenes. The child is encouraged not to think of the past or the future, but to remain focused on the present. With time and practice the child will be able to use this technique whenever required, and by doing so block any unpleasant thoughts and sensations.

Can I treat my child myself?

The teaching of relaxation and visualization requires skill and expertise, and should only be carried out by an experienced practitioner. However, it is helpful if the parent also learns relaxation techniques in order to encourage the child to practise at home. The parent will also need to ensure that set times for relaxation are observed.

Finding a practitioner

Most practitioners and teachers are qualified in other areas of complementary medicine or are professionals in orthodox medicine, such as nurses and occupational therapists, who have studied the techniques. A personal recommendation from a friend or doctor is one of the best ways to find a skilled practitioner, but if you do not have a personal or professional recommendation, see the Directory for the names and addresses of associations and other bodies that keep a list of qualified practitioners.

Arts therapies

Arts therapies – drama, art, music and dance – do not directly address physical ailments, but rather they treat the individual who is in need of emotional or mental support, regardless of whether they are suffering from a physical illness. Each of these therapies has in common the object of encouraging people who are unable or unwilling to express themselves directly to express themselves through the arts – to 'talk' through painting or music, mime or dance. The therapist's aim is to help individuals achieve this end, by responding directly or indirectly, and to help them both gain insight into the problem.

John Strange, chairperson of APMT (The Association of Professional Music Therapists), in speaking of music therapy, could have been speaking for any of the arts therapies when he stated: 'As well as looking behind outward signs to inner problems, music therapy seeks out and develops inner strengths. The "means of treating the condition" cannot easily be distinguished ... between one condition and another. There is no recipe for approaching a particular problem, and the therapist often follows the patient's/client's lead in building the therapeutic musical relationship required to support change and development.'

Therapy may last for anywhere between a few months and several years, depending on such matters as the nature of the problem and the time available. During therapy there is no conscious effort to teach, as would happen in a music or dance lesson, for example. The idea is to allow the child to respond to the instruments around them as a means of communication and self-expression.

Who may benefit?

Children who are experiencing social, emotional and/or physical problems will find that the arts therapies provide an outlet for self-expression, particularly when verbal communication is difficult or non-existent – whether it is consciously

Music – even, or perhaps especially when it is spontaneous – can be a powerful expression of feelings and emotion, often communicating in a way that words cannot, something important that the child has to say. It will also help establish the relationship between therapist and child.

withheld, as occurs, for example, in elective mutes, or is a result of some form of physical disability.

Finding a practitioner

See the Directory for the appropriate body to contact for a list of practitioners.

Play therapy

Play therapy is similar in some ways to child psychotherapy, although it has a non-interpretational relationship with the child. It is suitable for all children from the age of three years onwards. The therapist does not usually direct the child, although some therapists working with children with post-traumatic stress disorder may be more directive if they feel this is necessary.

Like the arts therapies, play therapy addresses indirectly the child's unconscious by using play as a medium of communication. It is based on the principle that the child has an inherent capacity to heal and address their emotional life through play.

For details of how to find a play therapist, see the Directory.

EASTERN THERAPIES

Acupuncture

Acupuncture is part of traditional Chinese medicine (TCM), which also includes Chinese herbalism, tai chi and chi kung (see pages 62 and 63). TCM is one of the oldest forms of treatment, originating around 2500 BC, when the Emperor Huan Ti wrote *Nei Ching* (translated as *The Yellow Emperor's Classic of Internal Medicine*). Yet, with the exception of a few Chinese practitioners treating Chinese patients, acupuncture did not become well known in Britain until the 1950s. Today it is widely accepted as a beneficial complementary medicine, and is even practised by some orthodox physicians who have undertaken training in acupuncture.

Like other forms of Chinese medicine, acupuncture is centred around Tao philosophy. It is based on the idea that a vital force or energy (*chi*, or Qi) flows along invisible channels, or meridians, in the body, and that each individual is governed by the inseparable but opposing forces of yin (masculine, active, positive) and yang (female, passive, negative).

When *chi* flows freely through the meridians, and yin and yang are balanced, health results. However, when yin and yang are unbalanced and *chi* is blocked, the results become noticeable as the symptoms of illness. The purpose of acupuncture is to correct this imbalance and unblock the meridians so that *chi* will flow freely again and the patient will be restored to health.

A branch of acupuncture, called auricular therapy, is based solely on the external ear, which contains a complete set of acupuncture points. Auricular therapy is particularly useful for acute conditions.

Who may benefit?

Children with allergies, asthma, bronchitis and a number of other conditions may be helped by acupuncture (see Parts 5 and 6 on ailments for specific problems that may benefit from this therapy). Acupuncture is also helpful in relieving pain, as it releases chemical substances known as endorphins, which are found naturally in the body and have pain-relieving effects similar to morphine and other narcotics.

Successful acupuncture treatment seems to depend on the responsiveness of the individual. Some people appear to be more responsive than others, and children usually respond exceptionally well.

Consultation and treatment

Practitioners will ask questions about the child's and the parents' medical history, present complaint, life style, including diet and exercise, and emotional health. Diagnosis is made by observing such features as skin colour, the state of the nails, eyes and tongue, even body odour, and by examining the child's pulse points.

In order to treat any imbalance, the acupuncturist will stimulate the acupuncture or pressure points that occur along the meridians. (The human body contains 14 meridians and about 365 pressure points.) Stimulation may take the form of inserting fine, solid needles into the skin, applying heat –

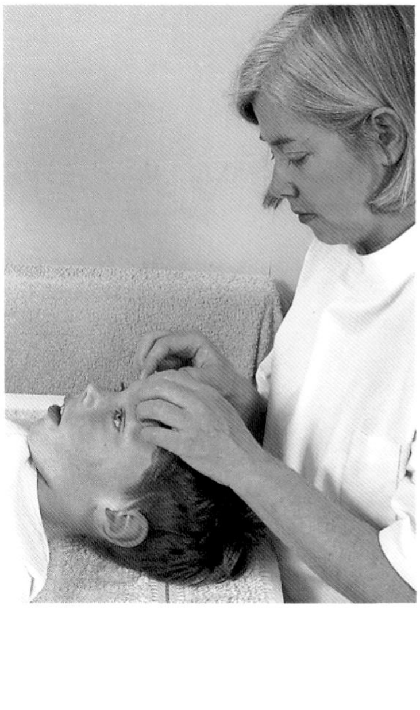

Parents should always consult an acupuncturist who has had special training in the treatment of children. In many cases the treatment will consist wholly or partly of applying finger-tip pressure (acupressure) to the relevant acupuncture points, rather than applying the more traditional needles.

called moxibustion – or applying fingertip pressure to the acupuncture points. The points usually involved are those on the forearms, hands, feet and lower legs. Sometimes all three methods may be used, and treatment may include recommendations for diet and exercise.

Note that this treatment, particularly the use of acupuncture needles, should not cause pain. In young children, fingertip pressure on the acupuncture points – known as acupressure – is generally more appropriate than the use of acupuncture needles.

Take care

- Make certain that you choose a fully trained and registered practitioner when seeking treatment (see Finding a practitioner, below)
- Orthodox drug treatment may interfere with diagnosis and treatment in acupuncture
- Acupuncture is contraindicated with some other forms of complementary therapy, but it is often used in conjunction with Chinese herbalism (see below)

Finding a practitioner

In the United Kingdom acupuncture as practised on children is a specialized form of acupuncture. See the Directory for names and addresses of organizations that have lists of qualified practitioners specializing in children's problems.

Chinese herbalism

Chinese herbalism is part of Traditional Chinese Medicine (see above) and may be used in conjunction with acupuncture and acupressure. The herbs are a potent form of medicine, and can be very effective in treating a number of disorders and in preventing ill health.

The therapeutic basis and philosophy is the same as that for acupuncture (see opposite page): the herbs restore harmony, balance and health both in the mind and the body, and are prescribed for the individual, not the illness.

Who may benefit?

Children of all ages may benefit from seeing a fully trained and qualified practitioner. A wide number of complaints respond well to treatment, including skin diseases such as psoriasis, hay fever, menstrual problems, anaemia, infections caused by viruses and disorders caused by stress.

In some parts of the world, notably China and the United States, Chinese herbalism is used to counteract the effects of chemotherapy and radiotherapy, and as a supportive treatment for patients with HIV and AIDS, by strengthening the immune system. In Britain, studies on the effects of Chinese herbs on childhood disorders has been undertaken at Great Ormond Street Hospital.

Consultation and treatment

As with acupuncture, the consultation begins with a thorough examination, much of which is carried out by the practitioner observing and touching the child. One or more herbs will be prescribed for treatment, according to the meridians and the organs* that are affected.

Take care

- Make certain that you choose a fully trained and registered practitioner when seeking treatment (see Finding a practitioner, page 63).

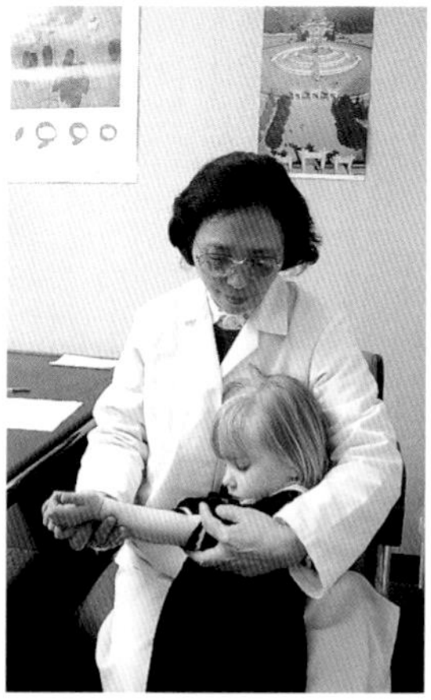

Chinese herbalism is an ancient form of healing, and a particularly potent form of complementary medicine that is highly regarded by many. Nevertheless, care should be taken to ensure that the practitioner is well-qualified and specializes in the treatment of children. Much of the diagnosis will be based on a physical examination, and on asking both parents and child detailed questions about the child.

*In the text on Chinese herbalism as a complementary treatment, where an organ name is used (liver, heart, stomach, lungs, intestines, kidneys) it refers to the energy system of the organs, and not necessarily to a pathological problem in the physical organ. Also, 'blood' is a dense form of *chi*, and includes the fluid, blood, that circulates through the body.

- Tell the herbalist if your child has suffered from jaundice, hepatitis or any other liver disorder in the past, as some herbs may have adverse effects on the liver
- Never administer a prescribed herb to anyone other than the child for whom it was prescribed

Finding a practitioner

See the Directory for the names and addresses of organizations holding lists of qualified practitioners.

Tai chi/chi kung

Tai chi and chi kung are both ancient Chinese disciplines, dating back thousands of years, and both are based around movements rooted in Taoist philosophy. Tai chi is a system of exercises that help to coordinate the body, breath and awareness; it belongs to the martial arts, albeit the soft martial arts, but is more often practised today as meditation in movement. In practice the exercises employ expressive use of gesture and the continual shifting of weight.

There are two forms, or systems, of tai chi: the long form, consisting of over 100 movements; and the short form, which has some 30–40 movements. Each movement has a specific, rather poetic name, such as 'Waving hands like clouds'.

The aims are to promote harmony with the self, initially on a physical level and later on an emotional and spiritual level, to integrate body and mind, and to reshape the body from within. By developing the inner vitality, or life force (*chi*), the individual can then use it for self-healing.

Although chi kung does not belong to the martial arts, like tai chi it is holistic in its approach. It combines breathing techniques and postures with precise movements and mental concentration, all of which help the individual to cleanse the energy channels, or meridians, to harness *chi* and to balance the complementary forces of yin (masculine, active, positive) and yang (female, passive, negative). When this has been accomplished *chi* can flow freely and the self will be in harmony with the world.

In chi kung there are four basic principles to be observed: relaxation, tranquillity, awareness and motion. The aim here is total health, well being and self-knowledge.

Who may benefit?

Tai chi has been particularly effective in helping convalescent people regain their strength and in revitalizing energy sources. It is also extremely helpful in reducing stress, as is chi kung. Teachers of chi kung maintain that, with practice and experience, chi kung can prevent and cure a wide variety of diseases, both chronic and acute.

Tai chi is meditation in movement. It consists of a system of slow, controlled movements that coordinate the body, breathing and self-awareness. Genuine practitioners insist that it should only be taught to children who have passed their 10th birthday.

Can I treat my child myself?

No. Both tai chi and chi kung need to be taught by skilled and experienced practitioners who have a sound knowledge of Eastern philosophies.

Take care

- Tai chi and chi kung are only suitable for children over 10 years of age

Finding a practitioner

See the Directory for names and addresses of organizations holding lists of qualified practitioners. Otherwise your local library may keep a list of classes teaching complementary therapies and disciplines. Make certain that the teacher has at least 10 years' experience and a diploma showing that they have studied with a master.

GUIDE TO SYMPTOMS

SYMPTOM	POSSIBLE CAUSE	PAGE
Abdomen, swollen	Coeliac disease	263
	Colic	259
Abdominal pain	Appendicitis	265
	Colic	259
	Constipation	258
	Crohn's disease	261
	Food allergies	242
	Food intolerance	241
	Food poisoning	245
	Gastroenteritis	257
	Intussusception	255
	Lactose intolerance	244
	Migraine	116
	Stomach ache	251
	Tonsillitis	224
	Ulcerative colitis	262
	Urinary tract infection	292
	(see also Feeding & digestive diagnosis)	240
Amputation		352
Anaemia		
	Leukaemia	282
	Sickle cell disorder	284
	Thalassaemia	285
	Ulcerative colitis	262
Anaphylactic shock		356
	Food allergies	242
	Insect sting	354
Ankle, painful/swollen	Arthritis	127
	Haemophilia	280
	Sprain or strain	354
Appetite loss		
gradual	Anaemia	281
	Coeliac disease	263
	Failure to thrive	71
sudden	Food fads	246
	Hepatitis	95
	Infections	80-105
	Middle ear infections	213
	Migraine	116
	Pneumonia	225
	Thrush	100
	Tonsillitis	224
Arm, broken		353
Back		
blue patches at birth	Mongolian blue spot (see Birthmarks)	167
dimple/tuft/blister at birth	Spina bifida	123
Back injury		353
Bad breath *(halitosis)*	Cold	208
	Herpes infection of mouth	103
	Tonsillitis	224
	Tooth decay	237
Baldness, *itchy patches*	Ringworm	163
Bleeding		346
gums	Gum disease	232
at teething	Haemophilia	280
at circumcision	Leukaemia	282
Blisters		357
around mouth	Cold sores	161
near mouth/nose, crusting yellow	Impetigo	160
on hands and feet	Hand, foot and mouth disease	98
small, fluid-filled	Chickenpox	87
Bloated feeling	Premenstrual syndrome *(see Menstrual problems)*	146
Blue skin *(cyanosis)*	Breath holding	117
	Convulsions	113
	Heart disease	275-279
Breathing		
child not	Pneumonia	225
	Breath holding	117
	Resuscitation	343
noisy	Croup	214
	Epiglottitis *(see HIB)*	98
problem	Asthma	218
	Bronchiolitis	204
	Bronchitis	206
	Croup	214
	Heart disease	275-279
Bruising	Haemophilia	280
	Leukaemia	282
	Meningococcal septicaemi *(see Meningitis)*	110
Burns	Chemical	347
	Electrical	347
	Sunburn	357
Catarrh		210
	Adenoids, swollen	216
Cheeks		
raw red appearance	Slapped cheek syndrome	89
red on one side only	Teething	230
Choking		348
Clumsiness	Cerebral palsy	114
	Muscular dystrophy	122
	Short sight	184
Colic	Food allergies	242
	Food intolerance	241
	Intussusception	255
	Lactose intolerance	242
Concussion		348
Confusion	Encephalitis	109
	Meningitis	110
Consciousness, altered	Convulsions	113
	Encephalitis	109
	Epilepsy	112
	Meningitis	110
	Migraine	116
Constipation		258
	Fever	83
Convulsions		349
	Breath holding	117
	Encephalitis	109
	Epilepsy	112
	Fever	83
	Infectious diseases	80-105
	Meningitis	110
Coughs		207
	Asthma	218
	Bronchiolitis	204
	Bronchitis	206
	Catarrh	210
	Choking	350
	Colds	208
	Croup	214
	Cystic fibrosis	198
	Influenza	104
	Pneumonia	225
	Tuberculosis	96
attacks of intense coughing	Whooping cough	92
Crush injury		352
Cry		
high-pitched, odd	Meningitis	110
hoarse	Croup	214
	Laryngitis	223
Crying	Colic	259
	Food allergies	242
	Middle ear infections	213
	Intussusception	255
	Nappy rash	170
	Teething	230
Cuts and grazes		353
Deafness	Adenoids	216
	Ear wax *(see Ear canal problems)*	212
	Glue ear	202
Depression	Chronic fatigue symptom	121
in teenagers		41
Diarrhoea		270
	Coeliac disease	263
	Constipation	258
	Crohn's disease	261
	Food allergies	242
	Food intolerance	241

GROWTH

Growth occurs most rapidly in the uterus and, allowing for spurts in mid childhood and during puberty, slows to a halt around the age of 15 or 16 in girls and 17 or 18 in boys. These extra years of growth in boys explain why males are generally taller than females. Until puberty boys and girls grow at more or less the same rate, sometimes following the seasons with a small growth spurt in late spring and early summer. Stretches of growth are punctuated by resting spells when children hardly grow at all. At puberty girls start their growth spurt at 9 1/2 or 10 years of age, followed by boys at 11 or 12 years. In the next three or four years, both girls and boys grow 30-45 cm/12-18 in.

Growth is chiefly determined by the pituitary gland at the base of the brain. A stimulating hormone, called growth hormone releasing factor, is produced in the hypothalamus. When this reaches the pituitary gland, growth hormone is released. The bloodstream carries growth hormone around the body to the liver and kidneys, where it is converted into a form that stimulates growth, making bones lengthen and muscle cells produce protein.

All over the developed world an upward shift in height, known as the secular trend, is visible in young people. In the United States children continue to grow taller than their parents. Researchers at the National Study of Health and Growth at St Thomas' Hospital in London have found that by 1994 English schoolchildren were one centimetre taller than in 1972, regardless of their social class. This reflects a continuing trend: in Britain five-year-olds today are on average seven or eight centimetres taller than five-year-olds in 1900.

Improved nutrition and living conditions were long considered to be responsible for the secular trend. Explanations such as smaller families and improved living conditions for the lower social classes do not appear to play a role. As the secular trend continues, its cause is more puzzling but immunization programmes resulting in fewer childhood infections provide one explanation.

Growth hormone, produced in the pituitary gland, regulates and promotes normal growth. It travels in the bloodstream to the liver and kidneys, where it is converted into a form that can be utilized by the growth plates at the ends of the long bones. This action causes the long bones to lengthen, which in turn causes the child to grow.

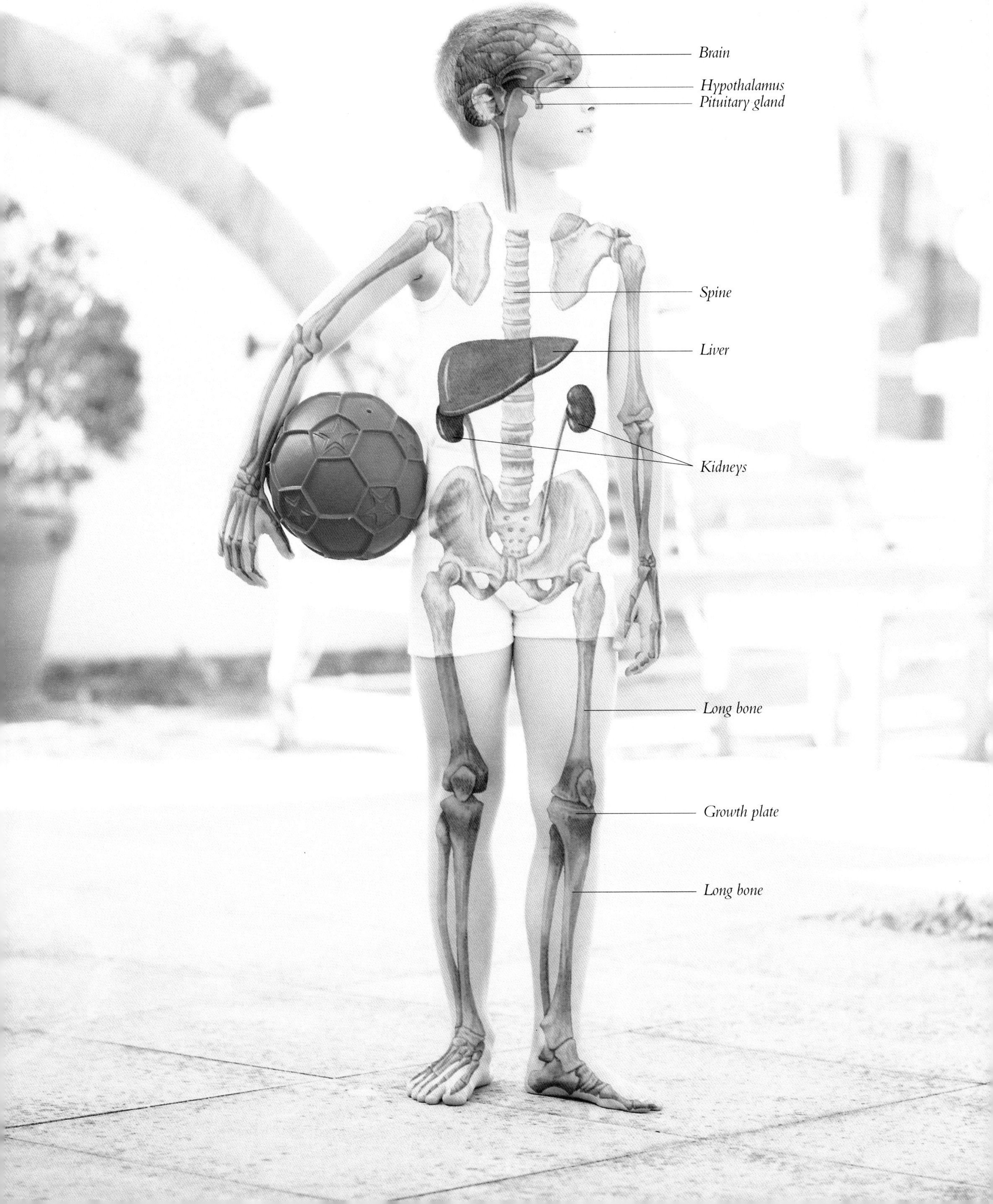
Brain
Hypothalamus
Pituitary gland
Spine
Liver
Kidneys
Long bone
Growth plate
Long bone

Growth Charts

If you want to know approximately how tall your child will be, look at yourself and your partner. Since the majority of children grow perfectly normally, as an adult your child will end up within a range of normal, determined by a factor called the mid-parental height. To calculate this, you need an accurate measure and an up-to-date growth chart (see below). For a boy, measure his father's height (in centimetres) and his mother's height. Add the two together, divide the sum by two and then add 7 cm. Plot this point with a dot on a growth chart at age 18 to see in which channel your child's mid-parental height falls. The child should grow to within 10 cm either way of this point. For girls, once you have divided the sum of her parents' height by two, subtract 7 cm. Girls can expect to grow to within 8.5 cm either way of their mid-parental height.

After the first 12 months, a child's weight matters less than their height. By itself weight loss or a slowing of weight gain is rarely a sign of a growth problem. With some disorders, such as growth hormone deficiency, the child may put on weight normally. Minor upsets, such as a slight infection, often affect weight first, then bring growth to an abrupt halt. Once the child is better a spurt of catch-up growth follows.

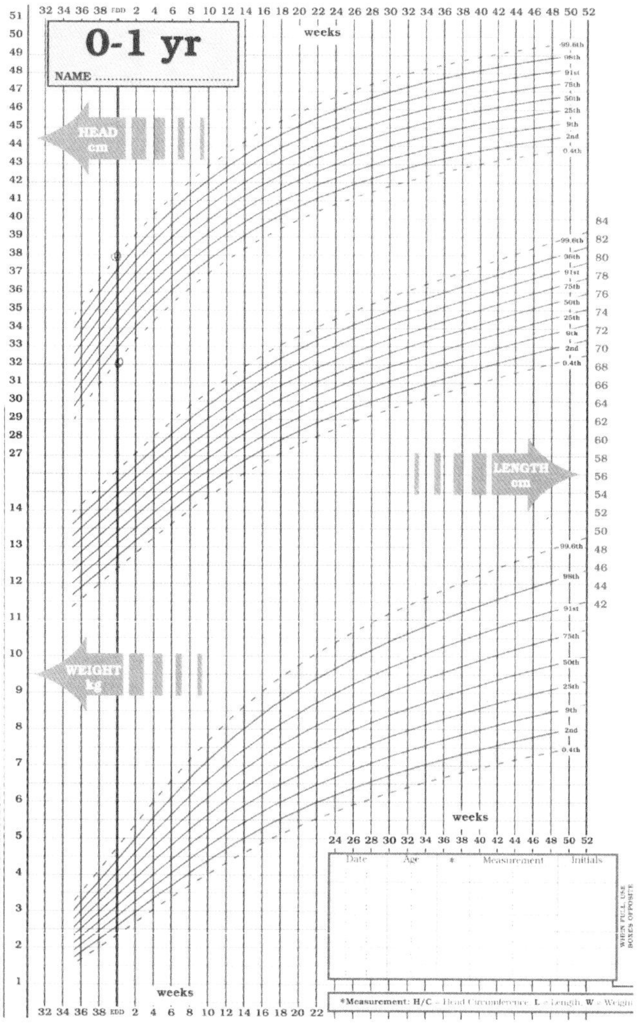

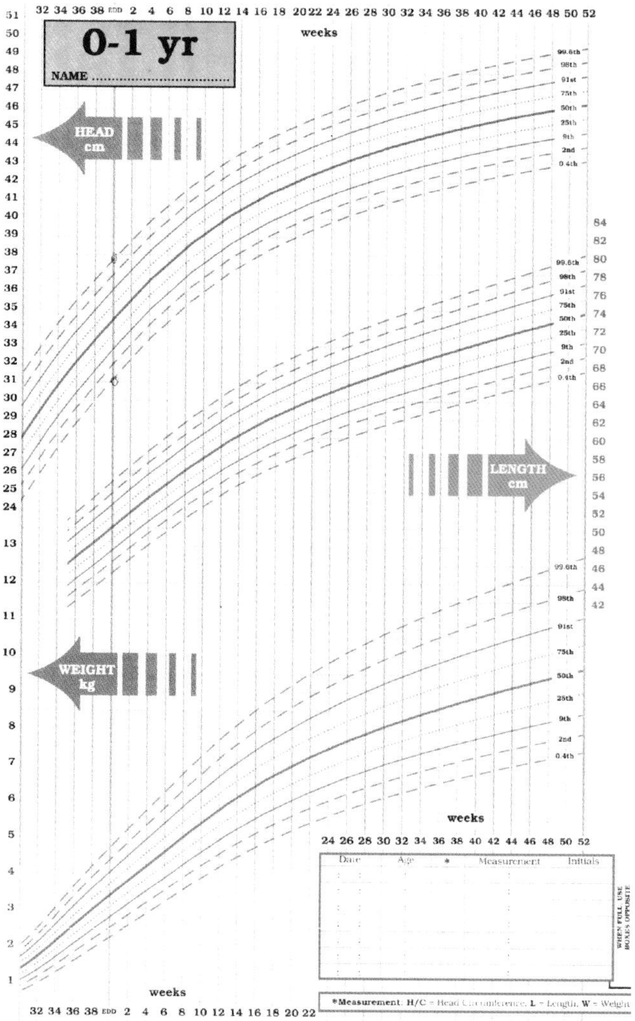

When growth charts in the United Kingdom were updated in the 1990s, they reflected the growth in the mean height of the population. The charts are divided into nine bands, known as centiles, and any child whose age-corrected height or length falls outside these centiles is unusually tall or unusually short. Regional and ethnic factors vary this picture, however, so it is important that a child's height is assessed by an experienced health professional.

Failure to Thrive

What is it?

Failure to thrive means that the baby or child is not putting on weight steadily when assessed against a standard measurement chart such as those illustrated on page 70.

Many infants and children fail to put on weight steadily or even lose weight for short periods when they are ill, if there is a problem at home or if they do not take easily to weaning. These short spells of weight loss do not matter, as the child will catch up once the problem has been overcome. However even a short spell of weight loss can be a great worry to parents. A lengthy failure to gain weight or continuing weight loss can be more serious, although the cause will probably be quite straightforward.

An inadequate intake of those foods required for health is often the main cause. In some cases children have a poor sucking reflex or uncoordinated chewing, which will give them problems swallowing and make them stop eating when they are tired rather than when they are full. Other children get enough food but vomit it back, or their bodies cannot absorb it properly, in which case there may be an underlying medical condition. It may also be that children are simply following their own natural growth pattern, with larger infants often dropping a couple of bands on the growth chart by the age of 12 to 18 months.

In many cases, early feeding difficulties can set up negative mealtime behaviour. Food refusal makes the mother tense and angry. When coaxing fails she ends the meal, leaving the child hungry. Some infants and mothers have bonding difficulties so the nurturing and feeding instinct is affected. Other mothers offer low-fat, high-fibre food, which may be too low in calories for a fast-growing toddler.

You may notice

- *The child is persistently negative about food*
- *Eats only tiny quantities*
- *May be pale and listless*
- *Seems to be losing weight*
- *Mealtimes are not enjoyable for anyone*

What to do

Tell your health visitor, who will weigh and measure the child. Seeing the results on a growth chart may reassure you that nothing is wrong. However if your child's weight drops two or more bands on the chart and stays low for a month or more, or if there is a great difference between weight and height or length on the chart, the health visitor will arrange for further investigations.

Meanwhile keep a diary for two or three days of what the child has eaten and drunk. Try to have regular meals and invite a friend if your partner cannot be with you; you need to take the emotional pressure off yourself at mealtimes, so you can ignore the child's food refusal. Stay with the child and try to praise them when they do eat something, even if they are not eating as much as you might have wanted them to eat. Agree this approach with your partner and others who care for the child.

Mealtimes can be frustrating for parents if their child consistently refuses food. When the child also fails to thrive, the matter should be investigated by medical professionals, who will be familiar with the problem.

What else?

For a child with a really low food intake, try high-energy foods such as butter, double cream, cheese and fried foods. Offer snacks as well as meals, including calorie-rich foods such as creamy yoghurts or chocolate bars. This may be enough to interest the child in food again, but a high-energy food supplement may be needed as well.

Some children need a brief hospital stay to see if they put on weight there. Blood and urine tests can be carried out to check for underlying disorders such as lactose intolerance (see page 244), coeliac disease (see page 263) or cystic fibrosis (see page 198).

Complementary Treatment

Nutritional therapy is particularly appropriate for this condition if the cause is insufficient nutrients. Advice will be given on diets and nutritional supplements. Traditional Chinese Medicine, such as **acupuncture** and **tai chi** can be helpful. **Chinese herbalism** can be of benefit, especially to infants with this condition; older children usually take a little longer to treat successfully. **Homeopathy** will treat according to the personality, temperament and mood of the child concerned (constitutional treatment). **Osteopathy** can be of benefit when there is no pathological cause.

Abnormal Head Growth

What is it?

The circumference of a newborn infant's head at birth usually measures between 31-38 cm/12½-15 in – already three-quarters of its adult size. The head is often lopsided because of pressure in the birth canal and it may be flattened as a result of the baby's sleeping position. Since mothers were advised to lay their infants to sleep on their backs or sides, the number of irregularly shaped heads has increased dramatically. This does no harm and the head eventually becomes reasonably round. To improve the shape, you can reposition your child's head while they are sleeping.

Infants may inherit a big head that grows at a normal rate. Microcephaly (a small head) may also run in the family or it can be the result of infection in the uterus, a chromosome abnormality or a development disorder.

Craniosynostosis

At birth the skull bones are not completely joined, and the larger of the two soft spot on top of the head (the fontanelles) usually remains until the middle of the baby's second year. In craniosynostosis, however, some skull bones join earlier than others, so that the head develops an odd shape as it expands unevenly. There may also be problems with the eyes, bone and joint changes and sometimes extra fingers or toes.

The condition can be inherited, with boys three times more commonly affected than girls, but the cause is unknown.

Treatment

Surgery can correct the skull shape and relieve the pressure on the brain before any damage is done.

Who can help?

For organizations and agencies offering support and advice, see the Directory.

Hydrocephalus

The brain produces a watery, straw-coloured liquid called cerebrospinal fluid (CSF) that constantly bathes the brain and spinal cord. Excess production or anything blocking the circulation of CSF can cause fluid to build up around the brain, a condition known as hydrocephalus. This puts pressure on the skull and brain and causes the skull bones to expand to accommodate the fluid. This in turn makes the baby's head large and distorted. Obstructions may be caused by blocked drainage ducts, bleeding in the brain, an infection such as meningitis (see page 110) or a tumour. Hydrocephalus may be linked with spina bifida (see page 123).

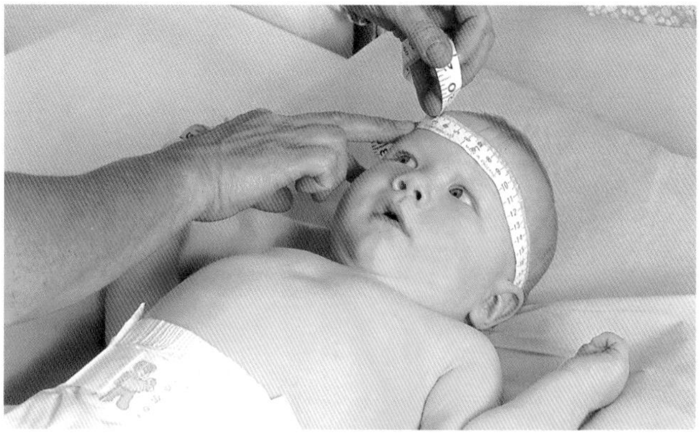

A doctor will usually measure the baby's head before the baby is discharged from hospital following birth, and again at the six-to-eight-week health check. If the head is unusually small or large, measuring the parents' heads may reveal that this is a family tendency.

You may notice

- *A large head at birth or the head grows much faster than expected because of fluid accumulation*
- *The soft spot on top of the head bulges and the blood vessels under the stretched forehead skin are visible*
- *An older child will show signs of increased pressure inside the skull, such as a headache and vomiting.*

Treatment

This depends on the cause. The infant will be given a brain scan (CT scan/MRI) to locate the obstruction. If medication will not cure the condition and the hydrocephalus is not expected to settle on its own, a 'shunt' (tube) will be inserted under the skin to drain the excess fluid into the abdominal cavity and relieve pressure on the growing brain.

Who can help?

For organizations and agencies offering help, information and support, see the Directory.

Complementary Treatment

Complementary therapies that may aid recovery following surgery include the **Bach flower remedies**, which may be helpful in alleviating fear and anxiety. **Homeopathic remedies** that can be given before surgery include Aconite 30c (*Aconitum napellus*, blue aconite) for the child who is panicking and has a great fear of surgery. These remedies should be given every half hour for up to ten doses.

Growth Hormone Deficiency

What is it?

Growth is largely controlled by growth hormone output from the pituitary gland, which is located at the base of the brain. Some children grow very slowly and on investigation are found to have a growth hormone deficiency. In the United Kingdom at present this affects around one in four thousand children. Boys are two or three times as likely to be growth hormone deficient for reasons that are still unclear, and a few families pass on an inherited tendency.

One in three children with growth hormone deficiency are overweight because of an inefficient metabolism. If the growth hormone deficiency is detected and treated early enough, the infant or toddler can reach full adult height. Without treatment a boy only grows to around 143 cm/ 4 ft 7 in and a girl to 127 cm/4 ft 2 in.

You may notice

- *Growth will tail off after the first year of normal development*
- *Children have normal intelligence and appearance, but may be overweight and have a babyish face*
- *Boys' genitals may be smaller than usual*

Treatment

At a growth clinic or specialist centre, the child will undergo tests to measure the amount of growth hormone in the blood. These may include a provocation test, in which insulin or glucagon is injected in order to provoke a surge of growth hormone, and exercise tests, measuring the hormone after the child has taken strenuous exercise, running up and down stairs or walking or running on a treadmill.

Children with a natural growth hormone deficiency can be given replacement therapy with a pure biosynthetic hormone. They need one injection a day, usually just before bed, in order to mimic nature's increased growth hormone production during sleep. During puberty the amount of growth hormone will be stepped up to track the natural growth spurt. Once the child reaches adulthood treatment may stop. Pen injectors have helped to make daily injections acceptable even to very young children. A specialist nurse can teach children how to inject themselves, and some growth clinics have a nurse attached who can visit at home.

About half of all children with growth hormone deficiency also have a failure of the sex hormones, which becomes obvious when the child reaches puberty. If at 14 years of age children show no signs of entering puberty, they can receive sex hormone replacement therapy to stimulate the secondary sexual characteristics.

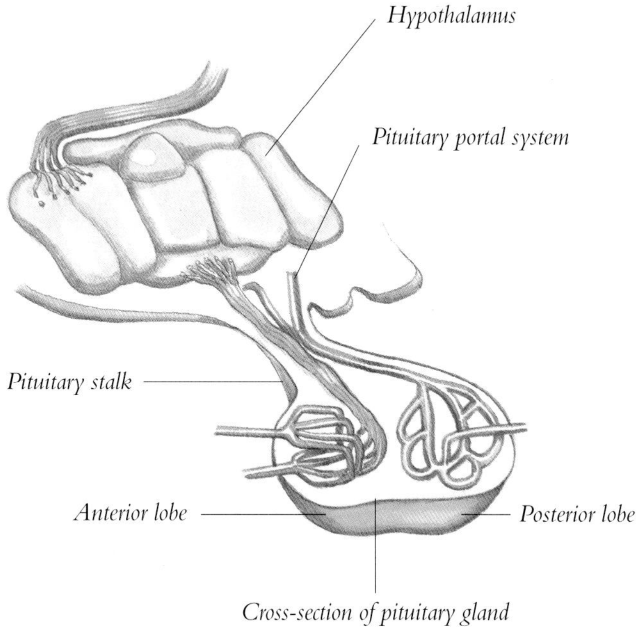

Growth hormone is produced by the pituitary gland, a pea-sized gland situated at the base of the brain. It is stimulated by the hypothalamus . Any problem with the hypothalamus, the pituitary gland or the link between the two, can lead to a deficiency of growth hormone and sometimes of other hormones. When natural growth hormone is deficient, it can be replaced with a biosynthetic one.

Who can help?

For organizations offering help and advice, see the Directory.

Complementary treatment

Complementary treatments will be supportive of orthodox treatment. **Nutritional therapists** may be able to help where the cause is a nutritional deficiency affecting the pituitary gland. The **osteopath's** aim will be to restore the natural balance of the body and body systems. **Chinese herbalists** recognize this as a deficiency disease but work first to clear any energy blockages and then to give tonic herbs. The **chiropractor** may want to keep a regular check on the development of the child's spine and extremity joints. **Bach flower remedies** may provide help with any emotional effects of the condition. **Homeopathy** and **tai chi** (for children over the age of ten) may also be beneficial.

Growing Pains

What are they?

Growing pains are burning or aching pains in the legs, which usually occur at night. The cause is uncertain, but the pains are almost certainly not caused by the fact that the child is growing. Some children are especially prone to them, with girls suffering more than boys. The peak ages are three to five years of age and again at eight to twelve years years of age. Children who suffer other recurrent pains such as migraines (see page 116) or stomach aches (see page 251) also get more growing pains. The pains are never serious and eventually disappear on their own.

You may notice

- *The child's legs ache when lying down to rest, or waking at night with a burning, cramp-like pain. The pains may specifically affect the calves, shins or thighs; they may be acute for up to ten minutes, and take an hour to fade. The following morning the legs may feel heavy and tired*
- *The pains may be much milder, just a vague, dull ache in the legs and feet after exercise*
- *The pains tend to occur in the evening or at night, especially after a day of vigorous exercise*

What to do

Check the child's legs. If one is red, swollen or looks different from the other, the cause is more likely to be an injury. See a doctor if the child is still in pain in the morning, is reluctant to use the leg, if the leg is red or swollen for no obvious reason or the child appears generally unwell.

Encourage the child to lie down. If the ache fades after a brief rest, over-tiredness may be the cause. This is especially likely if the child has had a day of vigorous activity, which can cause muscles to swell and ache.

If the pain came on suddenly, especially during or just after exercise, the child may have cramp. Gently straighten the leg out while the child is lying down, then press the toes upwards towards the shin. If it is a cramp then the acute pain will fade, but a sore ache will remain.

Treatment

If none of the above seems likely and the child is otherwise well, then this is probably growing pains. Comfort the child – the pain is frightening, especially if it awakened them during the night. Keep the legs warm under the duvet or blankets. Massage the legs gently with a pain-relieving cream or spray, checking first that it is suitable for a child. Once the acute pain has faded, prepare a warm drink to help the child get back to sleep. If the ache stops the child sleeping, then give paracetamol. If the child is prone to evening growing pains, give them a warm bath before bed and make sure their room is warm overnight.

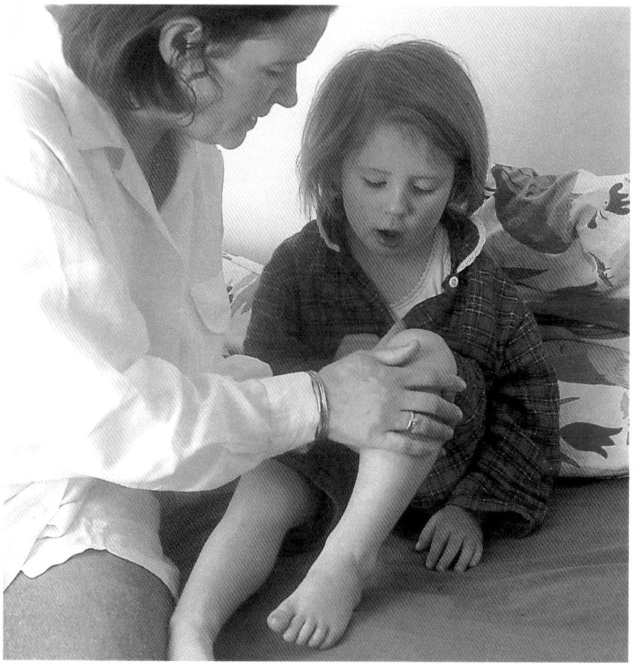

Although some doctors are doubtful about whether growing pains exist, any parent whose child has been awakened in the night by the pain is quite certain that they are not imaginary. Warmth, reassurance and a cuddle may be enough to calm the child and allow them to get back to sleep. Otherwise, paracetamol will ease the pain.

Complementary Treatment

Massage with **aromatherapy** oils can be soothing and relaxing and may help sleeplessness associated with the pain. **Bach flower remedies** may also be helpful if the child is anxious or fearful. **Homeopathic remedies** for relieving periodic pains include Guaiacum 30c (*Guaiacum officinale*, lignum vitae tree resin) for pains that get worse in cold, wet weather, and are aggravated by heat and exertion, but are soothed when pressure is applied; and Calcarea 30c (*Calcarea carbonica*, calcium carbonate) for aching pains felt in the ankles and knees, which become worse when the child is walking. The remedies should be given nightly for up to two weeks. Other appropriate treatments include **chiropractic**.

TURNER'S SYNDROME

What is it?

This disorder, which only affects females, is caused by a chromosomal abnormality. In each cell of the body children and adults normally have 23 pairs of chromosomes (strings of genetic material). However a number of children have one chromosome more or less. Children with Down's syndrome have 47 chromosomes, while children with Turner's syndrome syndrome have 45 and are missing one of the two female sex chromosomes. Some children with Turner's syndrome are a chromosome short in every body cell, but a large minority have a normal chromosome count of 46 in some cells and are one short in others. Some may have one abnormal chromosome.

Turner's syndrome affects each child very differently, but all who suffer from it have non-functioning ovaries, and therefore they are infertile. However with assisted conception many have been able to have children.

You may notice

- *At birth the infant may look normal, although sometimes the hands and feet are puffy*
- *Until the age of three or four the child will grow normally; by five or six it will become obvious she is short*
- *Extra skin folds in the neck, some bone and eye abnormalities and a broad chest with small, wide-spaced nipples*
- *By puberty the child will be very short, with an average height of 143 cm/4 ft 7 in, and have no growth spurt*
- *No sexual development takes place: the breasts do not enlarge, the body shape doesn't change, menstrual periods do not begin*

Treatment

See your doctor immediately. Turner's syndrome may be diagnosed on sight and confirmed with a blood test. Early diagnosis will mean that the child can begin treatment as soon as possible and, above all, does not have to cope with learning about her condition while going through adolescence.

The decision about how to give growth hormone treatment to raise the child's eventual adult height is complex. A child with tall parents may not need any treatment to reach normal adult height, whereas one with short parents might only reach 127 cm/4ft 2 in without treatment. Growth hormone therapy may make the child appreciably taller if started early enough. Some doctors also prescribe oxandrolene, an anabolic steroid. The child can also receive oestrogen replacement therapy from the age of eleven to stimulate the onset of puberty, including breast enlargement. Progesterone is then given in cycles to produce menstrual periods.

Girls with Turner's syndrome may have a heart defect caused by narrowing of the main artery from the heart (see Coarctation of the aorta, page 277); in some cases heart surgery may be required. Redundant skin round the neck can be removed with cosmetic surgery, which is best performed in infancy as it leaves fewer scars.

Coping with Turner's syndrome

It is always helpful to plan ahead for any problems that may occur in infancy or childhood. Some girls with Turner's syndrome need very little sleep and are very active while they are awake. Many infants have feeding difficulties both at the sucking stage and later when solids are introduced. Glue ear is especially common, so children need regular hearing checks, especially if ear infections are frequent. Short sight is another relatively common condition, so girls also require regular vision tests.

Girls with Turner's syndrome are of normal intelligence, with some excelling at school while others struggle to keep up, as in the rest of the population. Many girls with the condition go on to university and a professional life. Some, however, experience social difficulties, and such children need more understanding and support in developing their social skills. They benefit from particular attention in the areas of self-esteem and assertiveness.

Who can help?

For organizations and agencies offering support and advice, see the Directory.

Complementary Treatment

Complementary treatment will be supportive of orthodox treatment. Practitioners who may be able to help with any associated emotional problems and with improving self-image include **aromatherapy** and **relaxation.** The appropriate **Bach flower remedies** may also be useful when chosen according to the child's personality, mood and temperament.

SHORT STATURE

What is it?

There are many reasons why children are naturally short, the most obvious being that one or both parents are short. Some children are born small-for-dates, which means they did not grow well before birth because of a faulty nutrient or oxygen supply from the placenta; because the mother was ill; or because of some fault in the growing foetus. Most children catch up after birth but a few remain small and may need expert assessment.

Some otherwise perfectly normal children inherit a tendency to late development. Usually a parent or another close relative can remember being unusually short as a child. These children can be two or three years behind and as puberty is also frequently delayed by around two years such children can feel stunted as other pre-adolescents shoot up around them. This is exacerbated when a younger brother or sister overtakes the child with growth delay. Eventually, however, they should catch up completely.

In many children with a growth or thyroid hormone deficiency (see pages 73 and 142 respectively) the first sign that anything is wrong is short stature. Children who have had total body irradiation for cancer will be short for their age, as will children with untreated chronic bowel inflammation (see Crohn's disease, page 261), cystic fibrosis, coeliac disease, a chromosomal disorder, a lack of growth spurt or kidney or heart disease. A very small number of children inherit a disorder of bone growth such as achondroplasia (defect of bone growth and formation).

Treatment

If you are concerned that the child looks much shorter than other children their age, and much shorter than you would expect in your family, measure the child accurately (see page 70) and plot the result on a growth chart. Do this two or three times at six month intervals. Show this to the doctor. The growth curve of a child with growth delay may or may not appear low on the chart but the growth curve will not run parallel to the printed centiles.

The doctor may measure the child again. If the results show the growth curve is dropping away, your doctor may want to refer the child to a paediatrician or growth clinic.

At the growth clinic a bone X-ray – usually of the left hand and wrist or the legs and feet in a child under 18 months – will be taken. This will help to assess the child's bone age and estimate how much growing space remains. The child may also have a blood test in order to measure circulating hormones, chromosomes and thyroid levels.

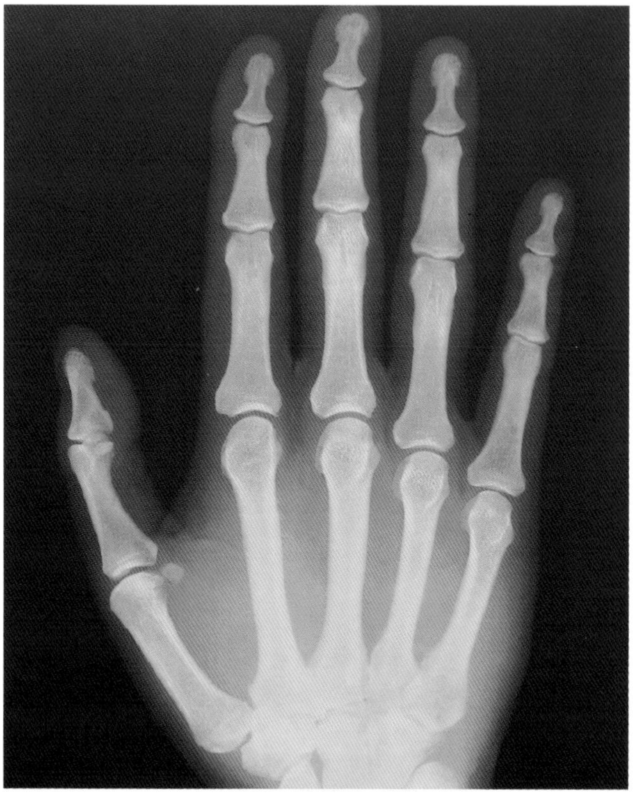

At birth a baby has gaps at the ends of long bones, allowing adequate space for growth. As the child grows the gaps become smaller; by puberty they close and the child stops growing. An X-ray of the hand can show a child's bone maturity and allow an assessment to be made of how much longer the child can expect to grow.

If being short causes social and psychological problems a boy can be given oxandrolone, an anabolic steroid that speeds up the adolescent growth spurt. Girls receive low-dose oestrogen therapy. Growth hormone may be given if the condition is caused by a pituitary gland disorder. Both treatments need careful supervision by growth experts.

Complementary Treatment

The **homeopath** will usually treat according to the personality, temperament and mood of the child concerned. **Nutritional therapists** will treat this condition if it is caused by nutritional factors and recommend additions to the diet. **Osteopathy** is beneficial when short stature is the result of delayed puberty. Both **Tai chi** and **Chinese herbalism** may help to engender a more positive mental attitude.

Excessive Height

What is it?

As a society we are getting taller, and being very tall does not usually have the social disadvantages of being too short. Adolescents enjoy the freedom that being tall gives them to start activities under age – such as getting into the cinema or a pub. All the same there are disadvantages when a child looks like an eight-year-old and behaves as if they were five – and is five. Some girls do not view with equanimity the prospect of growing to 180 cm/5 ft 9 in or more and most boys find a final height of 195 cm/6 ft 4 in quite enough.

Causes

The vast majority of very tall people are simply genetically tall, inheriting their height from their parents. Medical causes of excessive height are rarer. The true giants of the past probably had a tumour of the pituitary gland or excess growth hormone, but today this is extremely uncommon. In adults who have finished growing these disorders cause acromegaly, when the hands, feet and face grow very large.

A few rare inherited syndromes, including Sotos syndrome and Marfan syndrome, make children grow very tall. The signs of Marfan are present from birth and usually become clear before a child is ten years old. The child is very tall and thin, double-jointed and often has a deformed chest and long, spidery fingers. Heart and eye problems are common. It is important to diagnose this syndrome as the heart condition may be progressive and need surgical treatment – it is inherited, with half the children of affected adults also affected.

Sotos syndrome is extremely rare. There is no definite diagnostic test, but children often have large hands and feet and have some degree of clumsiness and slow development. They are big babies and grow fast in the pre-school years. They are often late walking and talking and are hard to feed. Children with Sotos syndrome usually stop growing earlier than other adolescents so while they end up tall they are not gigantic.

Treatment

Consult your doctor if you are concerned that the child is very much taller than their friends, especially if there are no other very tall people in the family or if there are other unusual signs. If you are worried that the child's eventual height will be excessive, ask for a prediction of final adult height. This can be calculated once the child's height, real age and bone age are known and, if possible, the recent growth rate.

In the past children who were predicted to grow excessively tall could be treated with sex hormones to accelerate puberty and end the growth spurt sooner. However, results were often disappointing and there were concerns about the side effects. Clinical trials are under way to assess the value of other treatments to reduce growth hormone secretion.

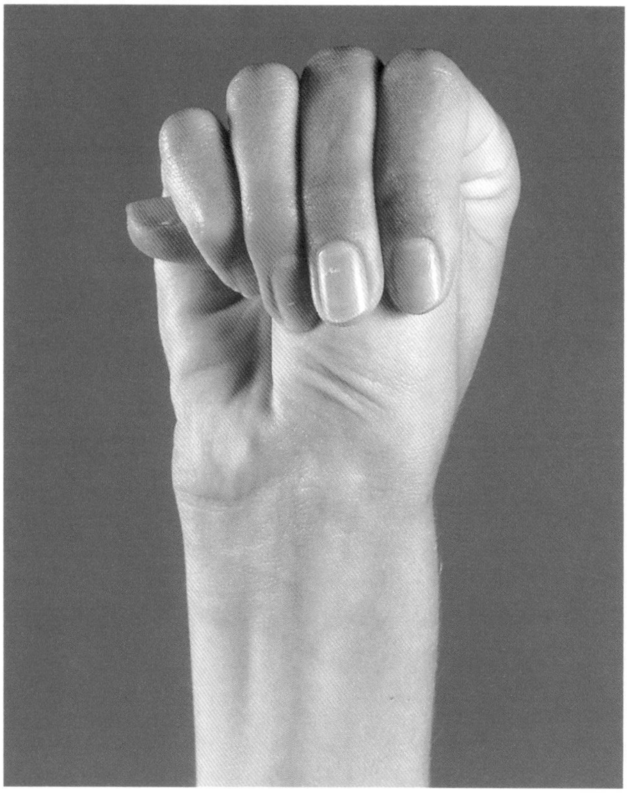

Children who have Marfan syndrome tend to have disproportionately long legs, arms and fingers, as shown here, where there is a long-fingered hand with a double-jointed thumb. Joints are loose because of weakened fibres in the connective tissues – the tendons and ligaments – throughout the whole of the child's body.

Who can help?

For organizations offering support, see the Directory.

Complementary Treatment

Complementary treatments will give support to orthodox treatment. **Chinese herbalism** may help the child develop a more positive mental attitude, and may be able to improve underlying imbalances. **Homeopathic treatment** will treat according to the personality, temperament and mood of the child concerned (constitutional treatment). **Bach flower remedies** may help with the emotional effects of the condition.

Overweight

What is it?

Overweight in children can be defined as an undesirable excess of body fat. The best time to deal with overweight is during childhood, because once established it is hard to correct. Figures show that eight out of ten fat teenagers stay that way, and that fat adults were often fat children. Yet according to recent surveys children in many industrialized countries are putting on weight. They are consuming fewer calories but eating more of the high-fat, high-sugar fast foods advertised on children's TV or viewed as integral to pre-teen and teen culture. Only a few eat even small amounts of healthy, low-calorie foods such as green leafy vegetables or salad.

Adverse effects

Critically, today's children don't get enough exercise. Fears about traffic and safety keep them indoors on the computer or watching TV. Rather than walk, they go out in a buggy or the car. Yet exercise regulates the appetite, and a quarter of the calories taken in are used for physical activity, but if they are unused they are stored as fat.

Chubbiness in babies is no cause for concern, but overweight in children is unhealthy. As a group fat children get more chest infections; if they have asthma or diabetes it is harder to control; and they take more time off school. They are less fit and are sometimes teased and rejected by their peers. There is a link between overweight, low self-esteem and depression. Most fat children have at least one overweight parent, and although it is true that fatness is partly inherited, lifestyle is more important than genes.

Substituting high-calorie drinks with low-energy or even calorie-free versions is less successful in keeping children at their normal weight than encouraging sports and physical activities. Make a point of encouraging your child to walk. Some parents justify pushing an overweight child of three or four years in a buggy because they walk too slowly.

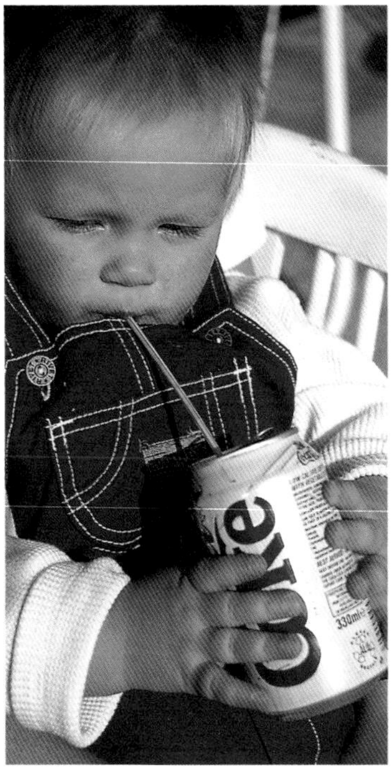

The aim in treating an overweight child is rarely to lose weight, but to stress healthy, balanced eating and activity and steady the weight gain while the child's height catches up. It is important not to stress dieting, as weight-consciousness and fussiness about food intake contribute to later eating disorders. Girls as young as six can be weight-conscious and by the pre-teen and teen years can become unhealthily hooked on thinness, partly because dieting increases a sense of control during the life change from child to adolescent.

You may notice

- *When undressed, the child looks fatter than they once were*
- *Is fatter than their friends*
- *Needs to have clothes bought in two or three sizes larger than the normal size for their age*
- *Has obvious rolls of fat. However, a bulging tummy in a child under six is caused by normally slack abdominal muscles*

What to do

If your child is under five years old, see your health visitor, or your doctor if the child is older. They will weigh and measure the child and plot the results on a growth chart as well as ruling out any medical cause. If you weigh the child yourself, always do it at the same time of day on the same scales with the child naked or wearing underwear – once a month is quite enough. As long as the child's weight curve runs roughly parallel to the centiles, and is no more than two bands higher than the height curve, most doctors will not worry too much. If the weight curve rises more steeply than the height curve, the child is putting on weight too fast.

Exercise

If the child is overweight, think about your family's lifestyle. How many of your activities involve physical exercise? Do you eat or snack a lot? The answers may give you clues about how to get started. Gradual change for the whole family has the best long-term results. Most babies and children like exercise so it is easy to encourage them with activity toys. School age children can join a club. The sports development team at your local council can give suggestions. Finding a physical activity the child is good at has the bonus of boosting self-esteem, which is important among overweight children who often feel bad about themselves.

What else?

Sorting out a weight problem is easier with professional support and some doctors employ a dietitian. Bring a food diary to the appointment, a two to three day record of what the child and the rest of the family have eaten and drunk. You may be offered group sessions for the whole family, although adolescents may be treated separately.

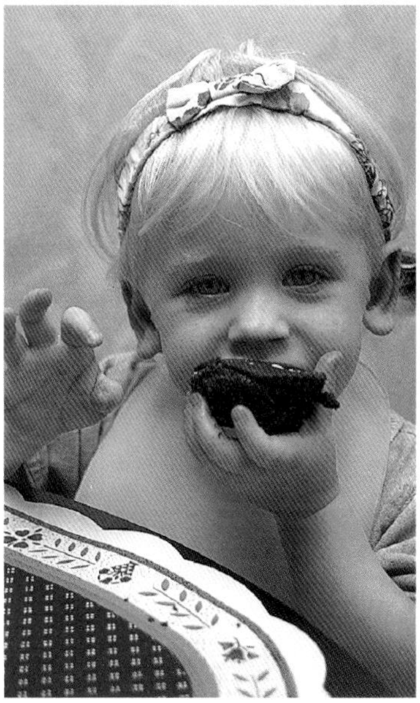

If your toddler is used to eating sugary foods, cut these foods out of the diet gradually. Children who are overweight as babies and as toddlers are more apt to be overweight when they reach adolescence. Adolescent girls are especially prone to low self-esteem when they are overweight, especially if their parents are openly critical of them.

Good dietary choices

A healthy weight for the child means a healthy diet for the whole family. School age children need to want to slim down so a cooperative approach works best. Introduce small, gradual changes, aiming for a balance – imagine a plate of food with two-fifths starchy foods such as pasta, potatoes or rice, two-fifths vegetables and fruit and one-fifth protein (meat, fish, eggs, milk and cheese).

- Don't limit bread, potatoes or pasta, but watch the butter and cheese
- Use the microwave, conventional oven or grill instead of frying
- Measure oil out carefully, allowing between half a teaspoon and a teaspoon of oil for toddlers and half a tablespoon each for older children at each meal
- Choose lean meats or remove visible fat and chicken skins before cooking. Although you should give whole milk as a drink to a child under two, semi-skimmed milk can be given between two and five and other dairy foods can be low fat. As fats are important sources of vitamins A and D, a child on a lower fat diet should take vitamin drops.
- Offer fruit for puddings. Cut sugary foods down gradually
- Halve the sugar in recipes; use reduced sugar jams and sugar-free jellies and buy fruit fresh or tinned fruit in natural juice
- Freeze low-fat yoghurt instead of ice cream.
- For snacks, try breadsticks or popcorn, both lower fat than crisps
- Take the packed lunch option at school to avoid chips and pies
- Set aside money that was used to buy sweets for rewards and treats (games, clothes, books)

Complementary Treatment

If there is an emotional cause such as unhappiness, appropriate **Bach flower remedies** may help to relieve it. **Aromatherapy** can help the child to become more confident and aware of their body. By teaching the child self-massage and bodycare using essential oils, they often become more interested in attaining a more balanced body image. The **relaxation** technique of guided imagery may help with overeating caused by stress. The **nutritional therapist** will be able to help with weight loss by devising a healthy nutritional programme. **Western herbalists** will advise on diet and nutrition while treating with herbs. Both child and therapist may need to look at factors such as anxiety. The **Chinese herbalist** may diagnose the condition as a food blockage that leads to weakness in the energy patterns of the stomach, spleen and intestines; progress is likely to be seen more quickly in children under the age of three.

INFECTIONS

Infectious microorganisms exist around us all the time. What is amazing is how well defended we are against them. Any virus, bacterium or fungal organism that tries to invade the body has to cross a series of defence lines. Early defences are the skin, the first line of defence; body fluids such as saliva and tears that contain an antibacterial agent lysozyme, which helps to destroy bacteria; and the stomach, which contains acids that kill bacteria.

If these early defences are breached, the body can mount a second line of defence, known as an inflammatory response. Chemicals such as histamine are released, which enlarge the blood vessels. This attracts special white blood cells called phagocytes to the site of infection. The phagocytes overwhelm and dispose of the invading micro-organisms. This type of response shows as swelling and redness.

The respiratory tract is also well defended.Hairs and mucus inside the nose trap germs and dust, and sneezing expels them. The cells on the air passages inside the lungs are provided with tiny hairs (cilia), which move germs and mucus upwards and out of the body, helped along by coughing.

The immune system

The immune system depends on the recognition of foreign antigens. These are often proteins on the surface of the invading micro-organism that do not occur naturally in the body. At the back of the nose and throat are clumps of tissue – the adenoids and tonsils – that are an important part of the recognition and subsequent process of destruction. The adenoids and tonsils form part of the lymphatic system, a network of channels and organs conducting lymph around the body. Lymph contains defensive white blood cells called lymphocytes, of which there are two main types. T-lymphocytes, which are in the majority, consist of killers, which release chemicals to destroy foreign bodies and helpers, which boost their activities. B-lymphocytes create antibodies and leave lasting immunity to infection.

The lymphatic system consists of a network of vessels that channel lymph from the body tissues. Along the network occur lymph nodes – clustering mainly in the armpit, neck and groin – which contain white cells produced by bone marrow, spleen and thymus. These cells destroy invading organisms.

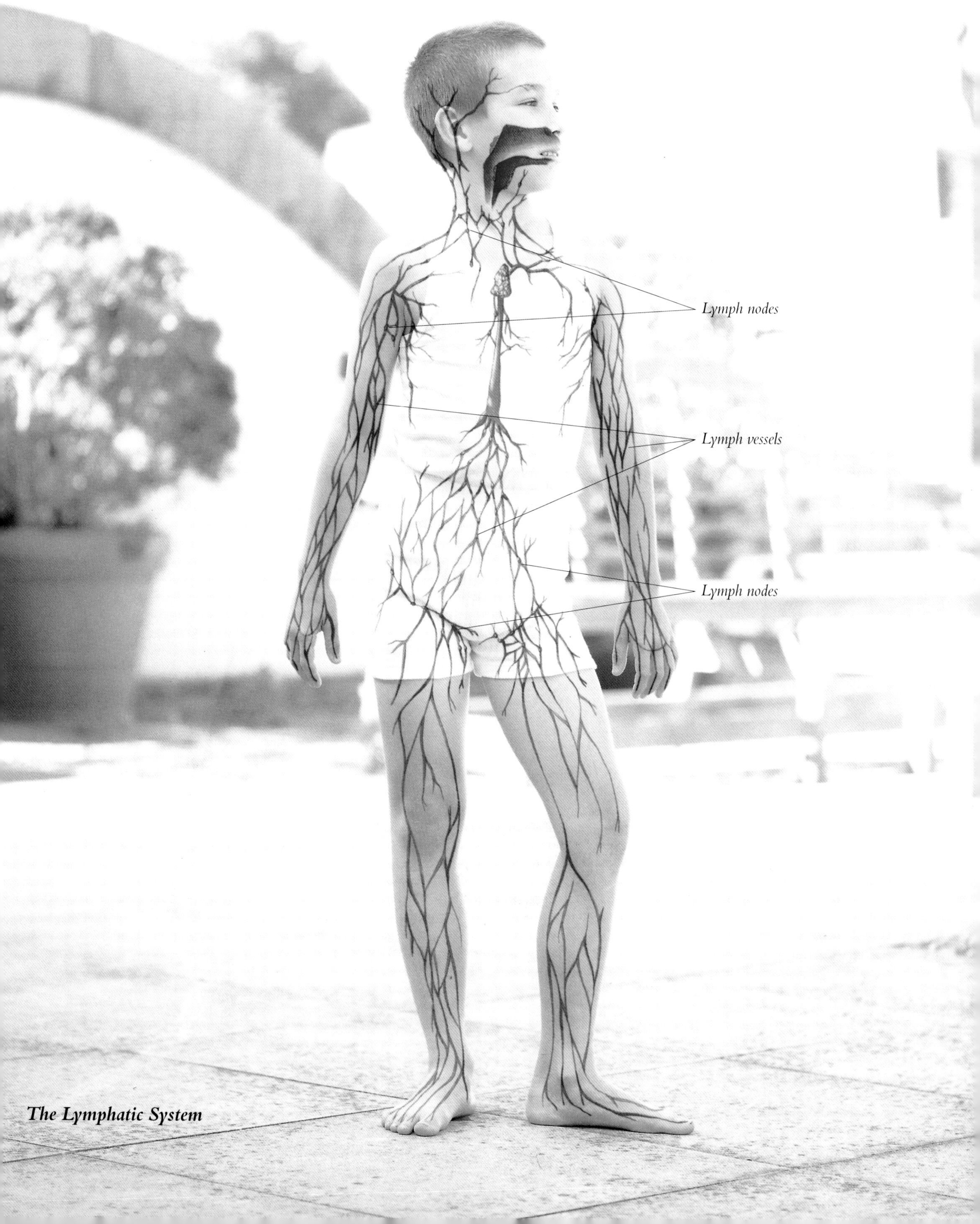

The Lymphatic System

DIAGNOSIS

With almost universal immunization, the illnesses that children commonly catch are changing. New infections have been identified, and as more families are travelling regularly by air, illnesses that used to be rare are becoming more common. Many of the infections that children catch are mild and short-lived. However any child with a high fever, especially if there is a rash, should see a doctor.

Signs	What could be wrong
Fever, appetite loss, spots turning to fluid-filled blisters	Chickenpox. Give paracetamol and contact the doctor
Generally unwell, fever, swollen glands in the neck, armpit and groin, especially in a teenager	Glandular fever. Encourage rest and contact the doctor
Unwell, fever, blisters in the mouth, and on the palms and soles	Hand, foot and mouth disease. Keep the child at home. Treat fever. Contact the doctor if you are concerned
Appetite loss, nausea, jaundice	Hepatitis. Contact the doctor. Give sips of water if the child is vomiting
Sore mouth ulcers, fever, unwell	Herpes infection of mouth. Give tempting drinks. Contact the doctor
Fever, headache, aches, cough	Influenza. Give paracetamol and frequent drinks. Contact the doctor if the child's condition worsens
High fever, rash, swollen hands, red eyes and tongue	Very uncommonly Kawasaki disease Contact the doctor immediately
Fever, flu-like symptoms within six months of travel to a country where malaria is endemic	Uncommonly, malaria. Contact the doctor immediately
Flu-like symptoms, rash spreading downwards, most often in an infant or adolescent	Rarely, measles. Give paracetamol and drinks. See the doctor to confirm the diagnosis
Fever, reluctance to eat, swelling at angle of jaw	Mumps, although this is becoming rare. Give paracetamol and liquidized foods. Confirm the diagnosis with the doctor
Sharp rise in temperature. Rash as fever drops	Roseola. Control fever. See the doctor to confirm the diagnosis
Cold-like symptoms. Pinkish rash starts on face, fades quite fast	Rubella. Give paracetamol and drinks. See the doctor to confirm the diagnosis. Keep the child away from pregnant women
Sore throat, fever, red rash spreading from body, but sparing area round mouth	Scarlet fever. Give drinks and paracetamol See the doctor to confirm the diagnosis
Unwell, fever, pink spots that start on the cheek	Slapped cheek disease. Give paracetamol. See the doctor to confirm the diagnosis if necessary
Fever, unwell, stomach ache and swollen glands and possibly symptoms in one eye	Toxocariasis. Contact the doctor
Cough that develops into acute bouts of coughing	Whooping cough in a child who has not been immunized. Contact the doctor

Fever

What is it?

Fever occurs when the body temperature rises higher than the normal range of 36-37°C/96.8-98.6°F. Fever is not an illness, but is part of the defence mechanism for controlling and killing harmful micro-organisms. In babies and young children body temperature is more sensitive than in older children, and can be temporarily upset by overheating, a hot bath or running around.

However a child whose temperature is higher than 38°C/100.4°F has a fever, the cause of which is usually an infection. It is not always necessary to measure exactly how high the temperature is – just knowing that it is raised is a clear enough sign that the child is ill. However because a fever makes a child uncomfortable, and as vulnerable children under the age of five are also prone to febrile convulsions if their temperature rises too suddenly, it is worth checking for yourself (see What to do, below).

You may notice

- *Forehead and abdomen may feel hot to the back of your hand*
- *The cheeks look flushed and sweaty and the eyes glazed*
- *The child may lose interest in food*
- *The child may be more irritable or clingy than usual*

What to do

To assess whether the child is feverish without using a thermometer, place the back of your hand on the child's chest or stomach. If the child feels warm and dry, they are probably all right. If the skin feels sweaty, the child may be too hot.

To use a fever strip, stretch it across the child's forehead for 15 seconds. Liquid crystals in the strip detect heat in the blood vessels beneath the skin and change to specific colours at specific temperatures. There are two types: in one, squares of liquid crystals change colour according to the child's temperature. In the other, a stripe lights up to mark the level of fever. The square type is easier to read.

Mercury thermometers give an accurate reading. For a child under seven years of age, or a child with a blocked nose, they are held under the arm; for a child over seven years old they are placed under the tongue. They should be left in place for 2-3 minutes. An armpit reading is 0.6°C/1.1°F lower than a mouth reading. Digital thermometers are similar to mercury thermometers but give a quicker reading and are less fragile. They bleep to let you know when it is time to read them.

An infrared thermal scanning thermometer can take an accurate temperature reading from the eardrum in just one second, and is easy to use.

Lowering a child's temperature

Take off most of your child's clothes. If the child wants to stay in bed, cover them lightly with a sheet: avoid covering them with a duvet or blanket.

Give children's paracetamol (called acetominophen in the United States) if your child is over three months of age. Paracetamol often takes 30-45 minutes to start working completely. Junifen (sugar-free ibuprofen) is a suitable alternative for a child over the age of one year. Do not give aspirin to a child under 12 years of age. Only give the dose of medicine recommended for your child's age on the container, and no more than 4 doses in 24 hours. Contact your doctor if the fever continues for more than 48 hours, or any time that excessive drowsiness or mottling of the limbs occurs; these symptoms may require the attention of a doctor, who will give a medical examination.

Offer your child their favourite clear drinks – ideally water or dilute juice. Offer a breastfed baby a feed whenever the baby wants it.

If you use a cold fan, direct it away from your child.

What else?

If your child loses their appetite for a day or so, do not worry but offer cool drinks of water, dilute juice or their favourite clear drinks. You should offer a breastfed baby a feed on demand, or every hour.

Consult your doctor if you cannot control the fever, if your baby is under six months of age, if the child's temperature rises over 39°C/102°F, remains high after 24 hours or if your child is ill in other ways.

Complementary Treatment

Chinese herbalists will use cooling herbs, which will bring the child's temperature down very quickly. Parents of children who are prone to fevers and/or to convulsions should keep the prescribed medicines handy at all times. **Homeopathic remedies** include Aconite 30c (*Aconitum napellus*, wolfsbane) given to a restless, thirsty child who has a sudden fever that becomes worse around midnight; and Ferrum phos 30c (*Ferrum phosphoricum*, iron phosphate) given for a fever that comes on gradually in a child who has a racing but weak pulse, together with red cheeks and a throbbing headache. The remedies are to be taken every 60 minutes for up to 10 doses when the condition is acute.

Glandular Fever

What is it?

Glandular fever (infectious mononucleosis) is most common in adolescents and young adults but can also affect younger children. It is caused by a herpes virus, and is frequently such a mild infection that symptoms may not be obvious. The virus appears to be spread in saliva through close contact such as kissing. The incubation period is usually ten days to two weeks but can be much longer. Glandular fever usually occurs as isolated cases, as it is not highly infectious. Once the virus enters the body the number of lymphocytes (a type of white blood cell) increases. Some of the lymphocytes assume an atypical appearance, and are known as mononucleocytes.

Glandular fever often begins insidiously. Sometimes a child will have a high fever and headache. In the early stages, if the throat is very sore, it may look like a severe case of tonsillitis.

You may notice

- *The child loses interest in food and seems generally unwell*
- *Fever*
- *Swollen, tender glands in the neck, armpits and groin*
- *Sore throat and sometimes unpleasant tonsillitis with thick white covering over the tonsils, possibly making swallowing difficult. (However a young child may not complain of a sore throat at first)*
- *Sometimes small dark red spots inside the mouth on the back of the soft palate*
- *A yellow tinge of jaundice if the liver is involved. Swollen spleen and perhaps a swollen liver*
- *A few children have a dull pink or purple blanching rash*

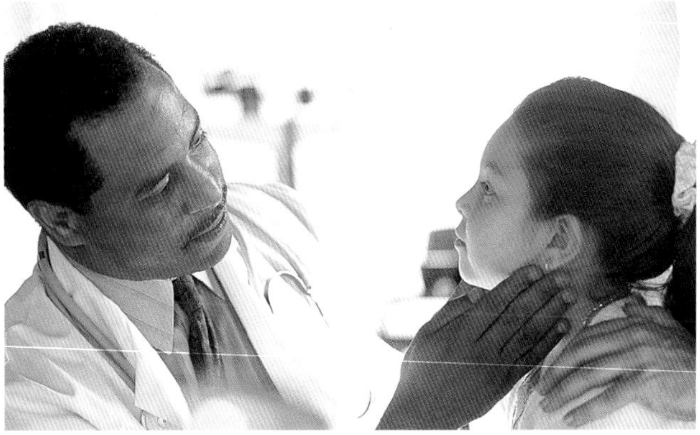

Swollen glands, most frequently those in the neck, are one of the symptoms of glandular fever, particularly when accompanied by a rise in temperature. However as these symptoms are also common to other ailments, the doctor may take a blood test to confirm his diagnosis.

Treatment

Contact your doctor, who may be able to diagnose glandular fever just from a description of the symptoms. Otherwise the doctor may take a sample of the child's blood in order to confirm the diagnosis.

There is no specific treatment for glandular fever and most children recover without the need for drugs. However they will need rest until the fever and the swollen glands have gone down. It usually takes two to four weeks for the immune system to overwhelm the virus. In a very severe case, the doctor may prescribe steroids to reduce any swelling in the throat. Steroid drugs may also inhibit the development of serious complications such as meningitis or encephalitis.

Outlook

Full recovery from glandular fever can occasionally take many months, with many young people feeling lethargic and depressed as they recover. These symptoms may be easily confused with chronic fatigue syndrome. Occasionally children become quite ill, with complications such as pneumonia or ruptured spleen. However most young people recover fully within two weeks.

Complementary Treatment

Aromatherapy helps with many of the symptoms, from pain, insomnia and lack of concentration to constipation and fatigue. The child will only be able to tolerate short sessions, otherwise their fatigue increases. **Relaxation** can be particularly beneficial for symptoms in chronic conditions of glandular fever. In the acute phase **homeopathic remedies** can be very helpful. These may include Belladonna 30c (*Atropa belladonna*, deadly nightshade) where there is a sudden onset of high fever, a red face and excitability; and Baryta carbo 6c (*Baryta carbonica*, barium carbonate) for swollen glands in a patient who is a late developer. For chronic cases the homeopath may recommend supplements of Vitamin C, B complex, zinc and evening primrose oil. **Western herbalism** is effective during the period of recovery and convalescence; the prescribed herbs will help to rebuild energy. **Acupuncture** and **Chinese herbalism** have been very effective in treating a large number of cases.

SEE ALSO CHRONIC FATIGUE SYNDROME (PAGE 123)

Measles

What is it?

Measles is caused by a highly infectious virus, which is carried in droplets and spread via the breath or by coughs and sneezes. It takes about ten days for symptoms to appear; the child is then infectious for four days after the rash comes out. After three days the rash and other symptoms start to fade.

Measles mainly affects babies under the age of one – which is too young for vaccination – and adolescents who have never been immunized. It is more often suspected than diagnosed, but diagnosis is confirmed by a saliva test. Babies are born with some immunity, but this is lost after some eight months.

You may notice

- *Fever, runny nose, sore red eyes, a cough and general ill health Tiny white spots on a rosy background inside the cheeks*
- *Fever, followed after two to four days of illness by a rash of red spots, usually on the head and neck first and spreading downwards over the body. The spots may join to form large red blotches. As the rash spreads, the fever drops. On black skin the redness does not show. Instead the surface is rough, like sandpaper. As the rash fades the skin peels much more obviously than in people with a white skin*
- *Stomach ache, diarrhoea, vomiting and swollen glands*

What to do

Give children's paracetamol to control fever and plenty of cool, clear drinks. Darken the room if light bothers the child. Keep the child away from anyone who has not been vaccinated. Watch for signs of complications; if you are at all concerned about your child's condition, contact your doctor. As measles is a viral illness, antibiotics do not cure it but they can help in the treatment of complications.

Outlook

Most children recover from measles within a week or ten days and have life-long immunity. However one person in fifteen develops serious complications such as bronchitis, ear infections and pneumonia. Convulsions may follow a high fever. Encephalitis, an inflammation of the brain, affects one child in five thousand. These complications are more common and more severe in poorly nourished and chronically ill children. Children whose immune system is suppressed by treatment for leukaemia are particularly vulnerable.

Vaccination

Measles vaccine is given as part of the MMR vaccine soon after the first birthday and before starting school. Children who have missed routine immunizations should be offered MMR with their school leaving immunizations, or when they start college. Measles vaccine is live and has a 90 per cent protection rate. A child who has recently been vaccinated is not infectious.

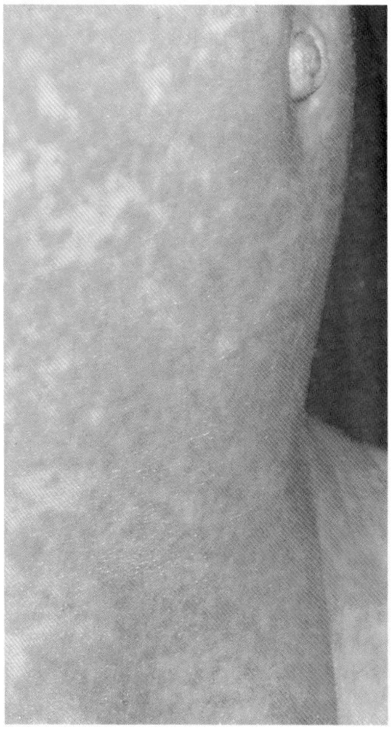

The most obvious sign of measles is the brownish-red spots on the skin. The rash usually begins on the head, particularly behind the ears, and then spreads downward to the torso, as shown here. The spots may enlarge and join up to form large blotches. Tiny white spots inside the mouth – called Koplik's spots – are also characteristic of this disease. Once quite common, measles has become much rarer because of widespread immunization programmes.

Complementary Treatment

Traditional Chinese Medicine sees measles as a useful illness because heat is expelled from the body, preventing more serious problems (including behavioural problems) in later life. **Chinese herbs** will soothe symptoms and speed recovery; tonic herbs are given in the recovery stage. This treatment may be given in conjunction with **acupuncture**, which can also be very effective. Many herbs used by **Western herbalists** can improve the immune system or reduce the body temperature. Poke root (*Phytolaccea decandra*) will help to bring out the rash. **Osteopathy** can be very helpful in enhancing health and dealing with the after effects of infectious diseases. **Nutritional therapy** may help avoid complications. **Homeopathic remedies** are given according to the stage of the illness, and include Belladonna 30c (*Atropa belladonna*, deadly nightshade) before the rash develops and Bryonia 30c (*Bryonia alba*, white bryony) when the rash appears. **Kinesiology** can help with basic health and well-being, particularly during recovery.

Rubella

What is it?

Rubella, meaning reddish, is the Latin name for German measles. It is a mild infection that was common until combined vaccination against measles, mumps and rubella (MMR) became universal. Rubella now usually crops up only in people who have not been immunized. The main groups to miss immunization are men over 20 years of age and recent immigrants. Just occasionally individuals who have been vaccinated and those who have already had rubella catch it again.

Rubella is caused by the rubella virus, which is breathed in and passed on by close contact with an infected person. Incubation takes two to three weeks and individuals are infectious for a week while incubating the virus, so transmission has usually occurred before the symptoms appear. The child with rubella remains infectious while the rash is visible and for four days afterwards.

Rubella itself is such a mild, fleeting infection that the rash has often vanished before it is confirmed. However the effects on the foetus during the first 16 weeks of pregnancy can be devastating, causing the congenital rubella syndrome, the effects of which include eye problems, deafness, heart defects, slow growth and mental handicap. In women who catch rubella during the first eight to ten weeks of pregnancy as many as nine out of ten will have affected foetuses. By 16 weeks only 10-20 per cent are affected. After 16 weeks, damage to the foetus is rare.

You may notice

- *A cold, possibly sore throat, cough, sore eyes, runny nose*
- *A rash of pinkish-red spots that starts behind the ears and on the forehead and spreads to the face and over the body within hours.*
- *As the rash spreads the child's temperature may rise slightly to 38°C/100.4°F. The rash fades quite fast and as it does so any fever drops*
- *Swollen glands, which feel like lumps at the back of the neck and below the ears. The glands may remain swollen for days or for weeks*
- *Adults occasionally develop joint pains and arthritis*

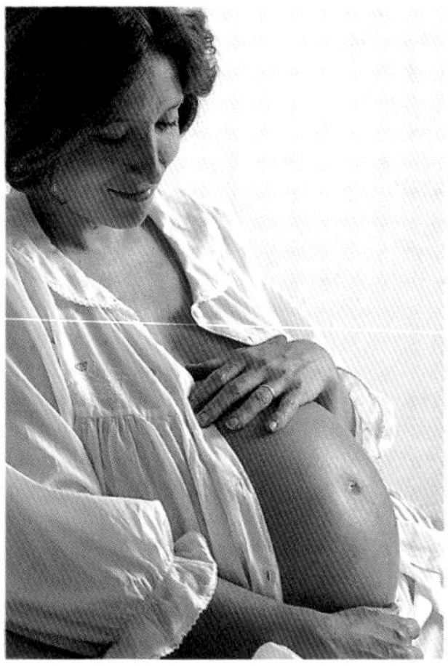

All pregnant women who have been exposed to rubella must have a blood test, even if they have already been immunized, have had rubella or had a positive blood test showing rubella antibodies. Some women may also need to have further blood tests.

What to do

A rubella rash is hard to diagnose, so take your child to the doctor, who may take samples of saliva or blood for testing. If the fever makes your child uncomfortable, give paracetamol and plenty of cool drinks. Dress the child in light clothing. If your doctor agrees that the rash is caused by rubella, keep your child away from women who might be pregnant until four days after the rash has disappeared.

Vaccination

A live vaccine is given at 12-15 months and around the age of four years at school entry. Young people should be immunized when they leave school if they have missed earlier immunization. Women who lack rubella antibodies can be immunized by their doctor; they should avoid pregnancy for one month afterwards. The vaccine takes in around 95 per cent of children and protects for at least 18 years. Children who have recently been vaccinated are not infectious to pregnant women. Pregnant women are routinely screened and immunized immediately after their baby is born if they have been found to lack rubella antibodies.

Complementary Treatment

Homeopaths may prescribe Phytolacca 6c (*Phytolacca decandra*, poke root) when there are swollen glands, ear ache on swallowing and where symptoms are relieved by cold drinks. Pulsatilla 6c (*Pulsatilla nigricans*, pasque flower) is given at the onset of the rash if the child is tearful, with red eyes and yellow catarrh. Remedies should be given every four hours for up to ten doses. Homeopathic immunization can be given during preconception care if the girl is at risk but unable to have orthodox immunization. **Chinese herbs** will soothe symptoms and speed recovery: tonic herbs are given during the recovery stage. This treatment may be given in conjunction with **acupuncture**. **Osteopathy** can also be helpful (see page 87).

Chickenpox

What is it?

Chickenpox most often affects children under ten years of age. It is caused by the virus *Varicella zoster* and is highly contagious. The infection is transmitted in the fluid that oozes from the rash or in droplets on the breath. The virus takes 10-21 days to incubate and the patient is infectious from a day or two before the rash appears until the last spots have scabs. One attack of chickenpox normally gives life-long immunity, but the virus remains dormant in the body and can cause shingles later.

Chickenpox is usually mild. However it can be more serious in children whose immune system has been affected by steroid tablets (but not inhaled steroid medications or creams) or by immunosuppressive treatment for leukaemia or a transplant. Complications from the infection are more common in adults than children, but possible signs of complication to watch for in children include coughing, drowsiness and breathing difficulties.

You may notice

- *Your child may be off-colour with fever, appetite loss and possibly a sore throat. Teenagers often feel worse than younger children*
- *Tiny spots appear first on the scalp and face, then spread to the stomach, back, arms and legs. Within hours they develop into small fluid-filled blisters. The red skin around the blisters is less obvious on a pigmented skin.*
- *In three to four days the blisters form itchy yellow scabs which fall off after ten days or so*
- *Spots may continue to appear for up to five days*

What to do

If you are confident that this is chickenpox and your child usually throws off coughs and colds easily, you can treat the infection yourself. Consult your doctor if your child feels unwell, if you are worried or if the spots redden and become sore, as they may need treating with an antibacterial cream.

Treatment

First check your child's temperature. If it is raised, give paracetamol. You may wish to inform the child's school and other contacts. Tell any of your friends who are pregnant. Stock your medicine chest with calamine lotion, an antihistamine and bicarbonate of soda.

Trim your child's nails to minimize damage by scratching. Dab on calamine or a paste made from baking soda and water, and give your child a supply with instructions to press, pat or pinch rather than scratch. Make sure the child has a daily bath in warm water in which a handful of bicarbonate of soda has been dissolved. Keep the child cool and dress in loose clothing without elastic. Leave off a baby's nappy whenever you can. If your daughter has long hair, put it up.

Your doctor can prescribe the anti-viral drug aciclovir for teenagers with a bad attack. If your child takes steroid tablets, consult your specialist, who may need to check the child's immunity to chickenpox. A protective injection of *Varicella zoster* immunoglobulin can be given if needed.

Vaccination

In some countries a live varicella vaccine can protect pregnant women but this is not currently available in the United Kingdom. A vaccine is available for children with leukaemia or those who have had organ transplants.

Complementary Treatment

Chinese herbalism and **acupuncture** can be effective in aiding recovery. **Western herbalism** can reduce the severity of the disease with appropriate herbs. An infusion made from burdock (*Arctium lappa*) and peppermint (*Mentha piperita*) and added to the bath water can soothe irritation. **Homeopathy** offers specific remedies for a variety of symptoms, including Sulphur 6c (*Sulphur*, sublimated sulphur) when there is rash and fever and the child is thirsty and hungry but nevertheless refuses food. **Osteopathy** can be very helpful in enhancing health and dealing with the after effects of infectious diseases.

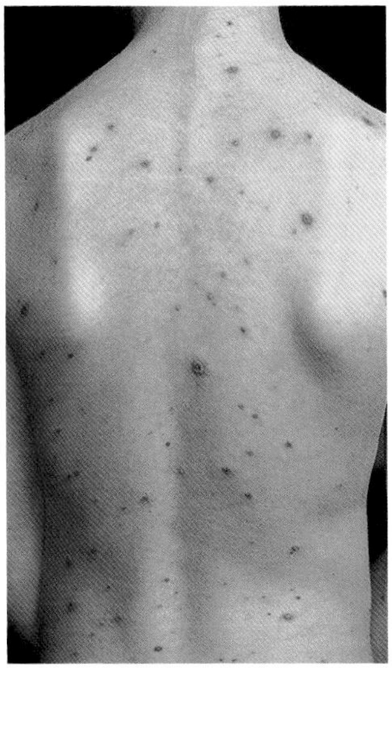

Chickenpox spots can vary from one or two to a full body rash. The rash appears in the second phase of the illness; in the first phase the child usually complains of feeling unwell and may have a slightly raised temperature. As the rash appears, the child becomes more feverish; as it fades, the fever gradually subsides.

Mumps

What is it?

Mumps (parotitis) is a viral infection that typically affects the salivary glands, although it may also affect other of the body's glands and organs. The virus spreads in droplets by coughs and sneezes. The incubation period is two to three weeks before the first symptoms show. Swelling can be on one or both sides of the face and lasts for three to seven days. Anyone who is developing mumps is infectious to other people for a few days before the jaw swells, until several days after the swelling appears.

Mumps itself is usually mild, frequently with no visible symptoms, although swallowing food or drink that stimulates the secretion of saliva can be very painful. Severe forms of the illness are more common in adolescents. Mumps can lead to complications, including meningitis, encephalitis and permanent deafness in one ear. The pancreas can also become inflamed. Adolescent boys may develop inflammation of the testes; older girls and women may develop inflamed ovaries. Despite what many people believe, there is no firm evidence that this leads to infertility.

You may notice

- *Fever, and possibly headache*
- *Reluctance to eat, swallow or even talk. The mouth feels dry and painful*
- *Swelling at the angle of the jaw. If only one side swells, the second side frequently swells as the first goes down. The swelling can be extremely painful*

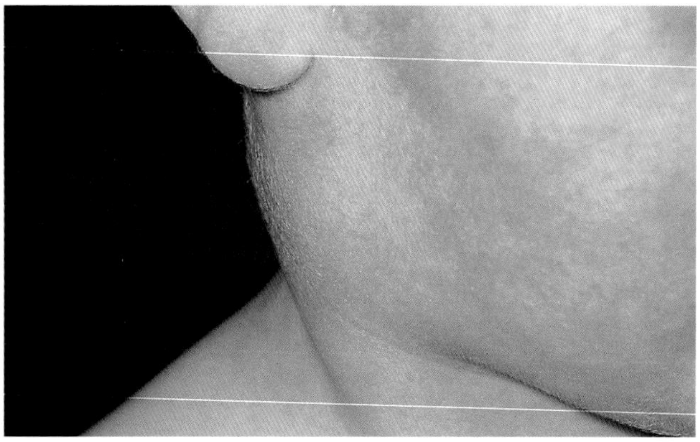

Swelling of the salivary glands under and in front of the ears causes pain on swallowing and a dry mouth. The submaxillary glands beneath the chin may also be affected. To minimize the pain which is felt on swallowing, avoid giving your child fruit juices, which will stimulate the salivary glands to produce saliva.

What to do

Keep your child at home and tell the school as soon as you have a definite diagnosis. Let the child rest if they want to. Give children's paracetamol for the pain and any fever. Rinse a face cloth in warm water and lay it over the swelling.

Offer bland, soft puréed foods to tempt the child's appetite. If necessary, give them a wide straw. Clean the teeth regularly to keep the mouth fresh. Eating and drinking are most painful first thing in the morning, so give your child drinks to sip before offering them any food.

When mumps may become an emergency

Contact your doctor if your child becomes worse when you expected them to improve. They may fully recover but develop a secondary infection a few days later. Contact your doctor immediately if your child shows any of the following symptoms:

- Change in mood – becoming irritable or drowsy
- Reluctant to bend the neck forward
- Convulsions
- Unsteadiness or confusion
- Stomach ache or vomiting

Vaccination

Mumps vaccine is given as part of the MMR vaccine soon after the first birthday and before starting school. Any children who have had only one dose of MMR should be taken to their doctor for a second dose. Mumps vaccine is live and has a 90 per cent protection rate. A child who has recently been vaccinated is not infectious.

With the very great majority of children in the United Kingdom and other Western countries now being immunized against mumps as part of their MMR immunizations, the disease is becoming rare.

Complementary Treatment

Homeopaths can help with specific remedies and dietary advice, such as the avoidance of acid foods that stimulate the salivary glands, **Osteopaths** will treat to enhance health and deal with the after effects of infectious diseases. **Western herbs** can improve the immune system, help the febrile response or lower body temperature, for example by inducing a sweat.

Slapped Cheek Disease

What is it?

Slapped cheek disease (also known as *erythema infectiosum*, or fifth disease), is a mild viral infection with rubella-like symptoms, including a bright red rash on the cheeks. It is especially prevalent during the first six months of the year and occurs in four-year cycles. For two years the peak in the first half of the year is higher than the seasonal peak in the following two years. The disease is most common among primary school children.

The disease is spread by droplets that are transmitted on the breath and by sneezes and coughs. The incubation period is four to fourteen days – occasionally as long as twenty days; once the rash has appeared a child is no longer infectious. About a quarter of the people who catch it do not show any symptoms, yet studies show that 60 per cent of the population have been affected in the past and are in all probability immune for life.

Slapped cheek disease is usually so mild in children that it resolves without treatment. In adults it can cause joint pains and a more severe illness, and can trigger a crisis in those persons suffering from sickle-cell disease or from thalassaemia. It can also occasionally cause a miscarriage, so pregnant women should avoid all contact with known infected individuals. For some months following recovery children may develop bright red cheeks again when they are exposed to sunlight or when they become overheated or excited.

You may notice

- *Your child may be unwell with a slight fever*
- *A rash of pink-red spots starts on the cheeks, which appear raw. The rash looks very like rubella. It often spreads to the back, abdomen and legs. The rash sometimes fades from the centre, giving the skin a blotchy or lacy appearance*
- *Adults may be unwell with a slight fever, swollen glands, a runny or stuffy nose and joint pains that may last for months*

What to do

If your child is unwell keep them at home and encourage them to rest. If the child is feverish, give children's paracetamol. Inform your child's nursery or school, as slapped cheek disease can occur in mini-epidemics among children. However if your child is well, there is no need to miss school, as children are no longer infectious once the rash has appeared. Contact any women your child may have had contact with who might be pregnant. They can ask their doctor for a blood test to confirm whether the infection is rubella or slapped cheek disease.

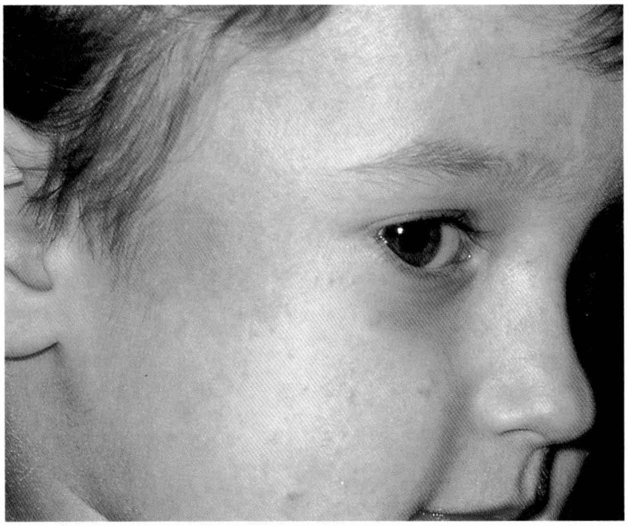

Slapped cheek disease is usually confined to children but may also occur in adults. A mild condition in childhood, it can be more serious in adulthood. Pregnant women especially should avoid contact with anyone who has the disease, as it can lead to miscarriage. Those with sickle-cell disease and thalassaemia may also be adversely affected.

Complementary Treatment

Complementary treatment will help relieve the symptoms of the disease. The **homeopath** may recommend specific remedies to reduce fever or treat swollen glands and advise on home treatment. Homeopathic remedies for fever include Ferrum phos 30c (*Ferrum phosphoricum*, iron phosphate) for a child with red cheeks, who is shivery but sweat and has a headache. **Bach flower remedies**, chosen on an individual basis, can help. If the child is fractious, a **massage** with **aromatherapy** oils, particularly geranium, lavender and chamomile, can be soothing, relaxing and calming. **Osteopathy** can be very helpful in enhancing health and dealing with the after effects of ailments. The **Western herbalist** will prescribe herbs appropriate to the condition.

Roseola

What is it?

Roseola is one of the common and mild illnesses that produces symptoms of rash and fever. Babies and young children are susceptible, especially those who are aged between six months and two years. The disease tends to occur sporadically, most often during the spring or the summer, and occasionally causes an outbreak.

Roseola is caused by an organism in the herpes family, human herpes virus-6 (HHV-VI). The disease is also known to medical professionals as *exanthem subitum,* which means no more than 'a sudden rash'. Yet another name is sixth disease, which has its origin in the 19th century Germany. At that time German doctors started to identify and number the common rashes. First was scarlet fever, second was rubella, third measles, fourth another type of scarlet fever and fifth was slapped cheek disease.

In the initial stages of the illness the child has a high temperature. As the child's temperature drops a rash appears, which may be patchy or may resemble a the rash associated with rubella or measles. Roseola is common – around one child in three will develop the infection.

The incubation period for roseola and the length of time the child stays infectious are not known, although there is some evidence to suggest that the incubation period is between five and fifteen days.

You may notice

- *A sudden high temperature. If the temperature rises very sharply the baby may be at risk of a febrile convulsion*
- *Grizzly behaviour, sore throat, going off feeds*
- *Glands swell in the neck*
- *As the fever drops after three to five days, a rash of splotchy rose spots appears over the chest, stomach and back before spreading to the arms and neck. On the thighs and bottom each spot may be surrounded by a fine halo. This rash rarely lasts more than two days*

What to do

Take your child to the doctor to make certain the illness is not rubella or measles.

The fever needs active treatment to avoid the possibility of a febrile convulsion. Give your child children's paracetamol, encouraging them to sip it with a clear drink of water or well-diluted juice. Paracetamol or Junifen takes about an hour to reduce a fever. While you are waiting for the drug to take effect, cool the child by undressing them to their nappy or underpants – you may also need to remove the vest – and cover the child with a sheet.

What else?

If your child loses their appetite for a day or so, don't worry, but offer cool drinks of water or dilute juice. Offer a breastfed baby a feed on demand, or every hour.

Complementary Treatment

Acupuncture and **Chinese herbalism** may be beneficial. **Homeopathic remedies**, which should be given every four hours for up to ten doses, are: Belladonna 30c (*Atropa belladonna*, deadly nightshade) when the child is delirious, has a high temperature and tender neck glands; Pulsatilla 6c (*Pulsatilla nigricans*, pasque flower) for a clinging, tearful child who craves fresh air and lacks thirst; and Phytolacca 6c (*Phytolacca decandra*, poke root) when there are swollen glands and ear ache on swallowing, and when these symptoms are relieved by taking cold drinks. **Osteopathy** can help to enhance health and deal with the after effects of ailments. The **Western herbalist** may be able to reduce the duration and severity of this condition with appropriate herbs.

KAWASAKI DISEASE

What is it?

This acute but uncommon illness chiefly affects young children under the age of five. It is presumed to be an unusual response by the immune system to a bacterial infection. and it does not appear to be transmitted from person to person. On its own Kawasaki disease is an unpleasant illness that can pass for an acute viral infection, but after a week or two the child appears to make a full recovery. However in around three children out of ten the disease may affect blood vessels supplying the heart. In affected children the infection inflames the lining of the blood vessels; in some children this leads to coronary heart disease.

There is no single symptom that immediately suggests Kawasaki disease. At first the illness looks like many other more common viral infections, with a high but swinging fever and a rash. Then the symptoms listed below are usually noticed. However if less than four are present the child may have a quite different illness. If four symptoms are present the diagnosis of Kawasaki disease is more likely, but at least five out of the six symptoms are needed to reach a clear diagnosis.

You may notice

- *Sudden high fever, lasting five days or more*
- *Generalized rash over the body and sometimes in the nappy area*
- *Red and/or swollen feet and hands. After some days the skin starts to peel, starting around the nails, and is eventually shed*
- *Swollen glands in the neck, usually on one side only*
- *Sore, red mouth with cracked and bleeding lips*
- *Bloodshot eyes*

What to do

Contact a doctor at the first suspicion of Kawasaki disease. This is important because it is an uncommon disease that is difficult to diagnose and the doctor may take a few days to reach a decision.

If the child is acutely ill they may be referred to hospital. There is no definitive test for Kawasaki disease but early diagnosis is important because it is possible to guard against heart damage if the disease is identified early enough. Children diagnosed within the first ten days of illness can be given intravenous gamma-globulin to reduce the risk of damage to the coronary arteries.

Children with Kawasaki disease are also treated with aspirin. Their heart and coronary arteries will be checked with an echocardiogram (see page 340). After the fever drops and the most serious phase of the illness passes, the child will make a slow recovery lasting eight to ten weeks.

Warning: Children with Kawasaki disease should not be treated with steroids except in special circumstances where gamma-globulin has not produced improvements.

Who can help?

For organizations and agencies that can provide advice and and support, see the Directory.

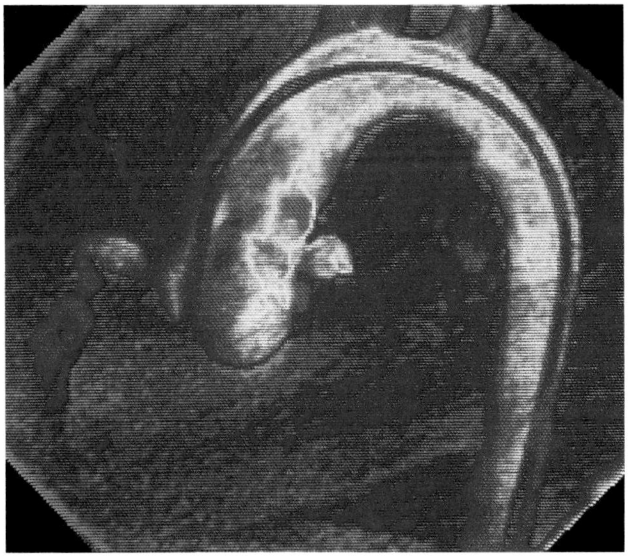

The most important complications of Kawasaki disease affect the cardiovascular system. A particular complication is shown in this coloured angiogram of an abnormal coronary artery in a child with the disease. The large aorta (yellow) forms a loop; small coronary arteries are visible coming off the aorta. These coronary arteries are abnormal in that they bulge into balloon shapes (aneurysms) along their length.

Complementary Treatment

Complementary treatment will be supportive of orthodox treatment. Where hospitalization is necessary **Bach flower remedies** and **homeopathic remedies** may help the child make emotional adjustments. The Bach flower remedies are specially indicated for emotional issues and are chosen according to the personality, temperament and mood of the child concerned. However in some cases certain remedies are commonly needed, and the following may be beneficial: Walnut to help adjustment and Mimulus for fear. Rescue Remedy can be relaxing and soothing. **Aromatherapy** combined with **massage** can have a calming effect.

Whooping Cough

What is it?

Whooping cough (pertussis) is an infection of the lungs and airways by a bacterium, and is highly infectious. Babies do not inherit an immunity so are vulnerable from birth.

The incubation period is seven to ten days. A child is most infectious while the first signs show and remains infectious for three weeks after the coughing fits begin. The cough may continue for two to three months after the infection has responded to treatment.

Whooping cough can vary from a slight cough to bouts so severe that the child can hardly catch breath and vomits as they cough. Occasionally children develop bronchopneumonia, and for very young babies there is a risk that lack of oxygen during the breathless spells will cause brain damage.

You may notice

- *In the first stage the symptoms may resemble those of an ordinary cough and cold – sneezing, runny nose, sore throat, slight fever, poor appetite*
- *A dry, irritable cough develops that may be worse at night and after eating*
- *In the second stage, which occurs after a week or two, the child has bouts of coughing. The child may appear to choke and their face may turn red or blue. When the child manages to breathe in you may hear the characteristic crowing 'whoop'*
- *Between coughing fits the child usually seems well*
- *Younger babies may not whoop, but may have spells when they stop breathing for a few seconds before spontaneously starting to breathe again*
- *Older babies may also stop breathing after a coughing fit. They may also vomit*
- *In the third and final stage the cough becomes less severe. However the child may still be weak*

What to do

Stay with your child while they are coughing. Sit the child up on your lap or put your arm around them to calm them. Hold the child still if they stop breathing – they will start again. Consult the doctor regardless of whether your child has been immunized. Tell the receptionist that you suspect whooping cough so you can be put in a separate waiting room.

The doctor will probably prescribe antibiotics for the child and for any other children in the family. The drug will not cure the cough, but it may make it less severe, and will help to protect other babies and children from catching the disease. It will also limit the chances of the child with whooping cough passing it on. Very young babies may need to be observed in hospital, where their breathing can be monitored, the airways cleared and oxygen can be given if this is necessary.

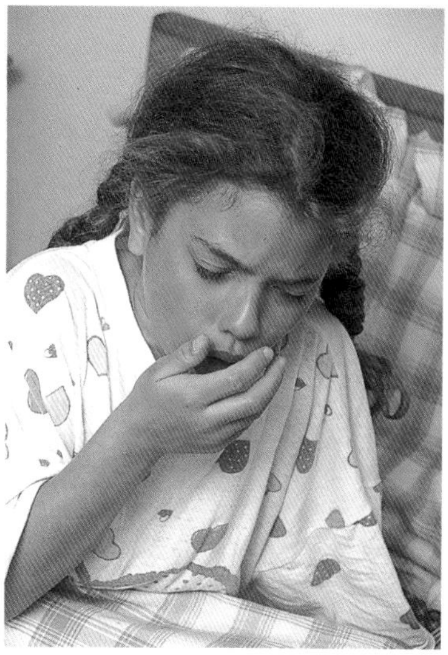

Any child or baby under six months of age with a cough so severe that she vomits or that lasts for more than a week should be seen by a doctor within a day. Children who have had whooping cough may continue to cough for several months, and they tend to cough for the next 12 months or so whenever they catch an infection .

Vaccination

Ninety-four per cent of infants are immunized. The full course of injections protects over 80 per cent of children, and in the others the illness is less severe. Babies who do not complete the full course because they develop a severe reaction to the injection can finish it with an acellular vaccine (one containing one or more of the components of the bacterium, not the whole *Bordetella pertussis*) which causes fewer reactions.

Complementary Treatment

In Traditional Chinese Medicine whooping cough is considered to be dangerous only if the child has an underlying digestive problem. **Chinese herbalism** claims to cure whooping cough if it is treated within the first one to ten days or at the first sign of a croupy cough. Children who are treated in the later stages need to continue taking their herbs until the phlegm is cleared and the digestion and lungs have been strengthened. **Acupuncture** has had extremely good results in relieving the cough. **Western herbalism** can reduce the severity of the disease with appropriate herbs and **homeopathy** offers a number of specific remedies to deal with the symptoms and aid recovery. **Bach's** Rescue Remedy diluted in water can calm a panicking child. **Tai chi**, **chi kung**, **osteopathy** and **kinesiology** can all be helpful in treating the after effects of the infection.

SCARLET FEVER

What is it?
Scarlet fever is a bacterial infection caused by the same type of micro-organism – a streptococcal bacterium – that often causes sore throats. It is quite infectious, especially among children who cough, sneeze or breathe the bacteria over each other. Some people can pass the infection on even if they develop no symptoms themselves. The incubation period is then two to four days, or more rarely as long as a week.

Scarlet fever is now a mild disease and only very rarely causes serious complications. The most common are ear infections. Kidney disease and rheumatic fever are rare, late complications that develop two to three weeks after the rash appears. Signs of rheumatic fever include aching joints and generally feeling unwell.

You may notice
- *Sore throat*
- *Fever*
- *Loss of interest in food.*
- *Vomiting*
- *After one to three days a rash of pinhead red spots appears, first on the neck, back or chest. The rash feels rough to the touch and spreads quickly over the body and face. The area around the mouth looks pale compared with the child's flushed cheeks*
- *The tongue may have a white coating with red spots. After a day or two the coating reveals a strawberry-red tongue*
- *As the rash fades, the skin turns dry and flaky and within a week can peel, especially on the hands and feet*

What to do
Keep your child at home and plan a quiet day as they may want to rest. Give children's paracetamol to control the fever. Encourage the child to drink but avoid blackcurrant or citrus drinks, which may exacerbate the sore throat.

If the fever is making the child hot, check their temperature with a fever strip or thermometer. Undress them to their underwear or a nappy and vest, which may need to be removed. Cover with a light sheet.

Consult your doctor if you are concerned about the rash. The doctor will need to decide whether treatment is needed. If necessary a throat swab may be taken and if scarlet fever is suspected the doctor may prescribe antibiotics.

Once the child has been on antibiotics for 24 hours, they will no longer be infectious. The child should start to get better within 48 hours of starting antibiotics but if they show no improvement or seem worse, you should contact the doctor again. A day after the fever subsides the child will be able to return to nursery or school.

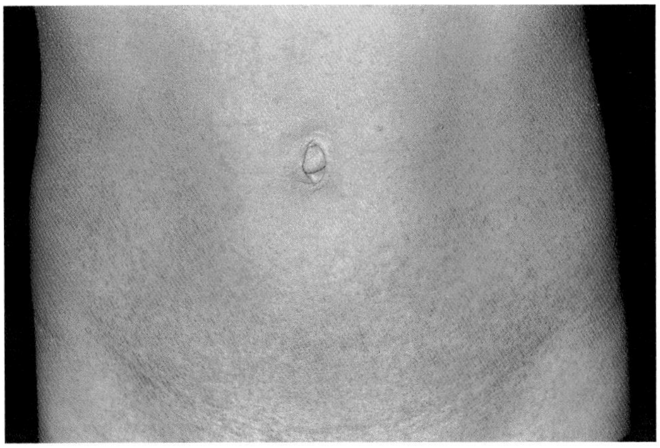

The sandpaper-like rash on the abdomen of this six-year-old boy is typical of scarlet fiver. The rash is most commonly seen on the neck, chest and in the folds of the armpits.

What else?
Offer non-acidic juices or bland milky drinks to ease the sore throat. Try giving yoghurt, melted ice cream or a milk shake to be sipped through a wide straw.

Complementary Treatment
Children who have been in contact with a person suffering from scarlet fever can be given the **homeopathic remedy** Belladonna 30c (*Atropa belladonna*, deadly nightshade) as a preventive measure. It should be given once a day for up to ten days. Belladonna 30c can also be administered every hour for up to ten doses if you suspect your child has the disease. Call your doctor is there is no improvement after this. **Acupuncture** and **Chinese herbalism** can also be helpful. Herbs would be given to clear heat and strengthen the heart. Once the child has recovered the herbalist will prescribe tonic herbs.

HIB

What is it?

Hib (*Haemophilus influenzae* B) is a bacterium that causes a wide range of serious infections, particularly in young children. It can affect the lining of the brain, causing meningitis in around six children in ten who develop the invasive infection. It also causes epiglottitis, a condition in which the epiglottis (the flap of cartilage at the back of the throat that closes off the airways while swallowing) swells dangerously and obstructs breathing. The Hib bacterium can also cause the blood infection septicaemia and infections in bones and joints such as arthritis and osteomyelitis.

Hib bacteria usually live in the nose and throat and are spread by droplets in the same way as coughs and colds. A related but much less serious strain of the bacterium can cause ear infections in young children.

Hib used to cause most illness in infants and young children up to the age of two. In infants under three months and children more than four years of age infection was rare. The peak age was 10-11 months. Since the Hib vaccination was introduced in 1992 the incidence of Hib infection has dropped dramatically in the United Kingdom.

You may notice

- *A infant developing Hib meningitis may be fretful and difficult to wake, refuse feeds, vomit and dislike being handled. Infant usually have a fever and may have an odd, staring expression and moaning cry*
- *Children may develop a headache and joint pains, shield their eyes from the light and be very drowsy. As the condition worsens the neck will stiffen and the soft spot on a baby's head may become tense or bulge*
- *Children developing Hib epiglottitis are feverish and very rapidly develop noisy breathing, have difficulty swallowing and start to drool because they cannot swallow their saliva. They tend to sit bolt upright and be very distressed*

What to do

Call the emergency services or call your doctor immediately and describe the symptoms. Follow the doctor's instructions: you may be told to take your child to hospital immediately, wait for an ambulance or wait until the doctor has called.

Treatment

Once the hospital has confirmed Hib infection, the doctor will recommend immunization for any children at home under four who have not already been vaccinated. Older children who have had vaccination need no extra protection but anyone in the household who has never had Hib immunization will be given a protective antibiotic to be taken every day for four days. This preventive measure helps to prevent Hib from developing and spreading.

Vaccination

Hib vaccination is offered to all infants in the United Kingdom at the ages of two, three and four months in a combined injection with vaccinations against diphtheria, tetanus and whooping cough. The vaccine is not live, has an excellent safety record and is effective in over 95 per cent of children. Infants sometimes develop a red swelling around the site of the injection within three or four hours, but this subsides within 24 hours.

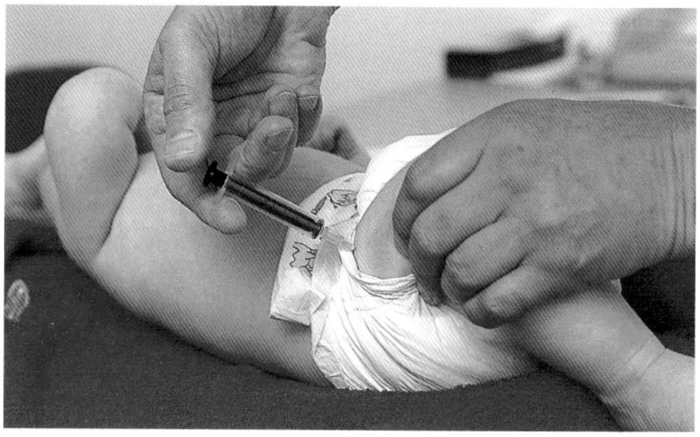

Infants who are less than 12 months of age run the greatest risk of contracting Hib infection. If they miss a routine immunization they can catch up at any time, as long as one month has passed between each dose of the vaccine. Any reactions tend to decline with later doses.

Complementary Treatment

Homeopathic remedies for suspected meningitis while waiting for help to arrive include: Bryonia 30c (*Bryonia alba*, white bryony) when the child is in great pain, quiet and unable to look into light; Aconite 30c (*Aconitum napellus*, blue aconite) when the child is restless, panicky and thirsty and the skin feels hot to the touch; and Belladonna 30c (*Atropa belladonna*, deadly nightshade) when the baby or child makes unusual noises and movements and the pupils are dilated. Remedies should be administered every five minutes. **Tai chi**, **Chinese herbalism** and **acupuncture** can help with the after effects of the disease.

HEPATITIS

What is it?

Hepatitis is an inflammation of the liver that temporarily damages cells and interferes with the formation of bile, which helps digest fats. The disease is generally caused by a virus and takes two forms: hepatitis A, or infectious hepatitis, and hepatitis B, or serum hepatitis.

In young children hepatitis A is more common and very infectious. The virus is excreted in the faeces and can be picked up by touching contaminated objects, towels or hands. It is then transferred from hand to mouth. The virus is also carried in contaminated food and drink. The symptoms usually begin two to six weeks following infection.

Children can be vaccinated against hepatitis A with a single injection into the muscle at the top of the arm. Protection lasts for about 12 months; a second injection given 6 to 12 months later protects a child for up to ten years. A child who has not been immunized but needs protection in an outbreak can be given an injection of human normal immunoglobulin (HNIG), which will protect the child for about four months.

Hepatitis B is a more serious infection transmitted by contact with an affected person's body fluids, blood or serum. A mother may pass the infection on to her baby from birth. Saliva, semen, vaginal secretions and breast milk can all contain the hepatitis B virus. All blood for transfusions and breast milk banked for donation is screened for it. Some antenatal clinics screen mothers for hepatitis while they are pregnant so their babies can be vaccinated at birth. Children adopted from parts of the world where hepatitis B is common, such as Eastern Europe, Southeast Asia or South America, can be screened for the virus. All children can be vaccinated against hepatitis B.

The symptoms for both conditions are very similar, but the symptoms of hepatitis B are generally more serious than those of hepatitis A. However most infants who are affected with hepatitis A do not show any symptoms.

You may notice

- *In children over the age of two, and in a few infants, first signs include appetite loss and vomiting with some nausea. There may be fever and the child's stomach may be tender to touch*
- *After a few days the child starts to feel better, but jaundice develops*
- *The urine is dark, while stools are pale*

What to do

Contact your doctor who may take saliva specimens and blood samples to check the diagnosis. The doctor may suggest immunization for other family members. Keep your child at home and restrict social contacts until the diagnosis has been confirmed. There is no specific treatment for viral hepatitis, but if the child is vomiting and is not hungry, give sips of a clear drink such as water or diluted fresh juice.

If you are still changing your child's nappy or helping them with the toilet, buy a pack of disposable gloves. Wash your hands meticulously after dealing with nappies and bottoms and make sure your child washes too.

A blood test will show whether a child has been infected with the hepatitis virus. (left, red blood cells from a person with hepatitis). Children are usually infectious to other people for two weeks before they become jaundiced, until about a week after onset of the disease.

Outlook

If your child has a mild case of hepatitis they will be better in days. Children with more severe cases take a month or two to recover and some who have had hepatitis B remain lethargic for weeks after an attack. The child is infectious for at least a week after the jaundice has faded and shouldn't go to school.

Complementary Treatment

Western herbalists prescribe herbs such as milk thistle (*Silybum marianus*, syn. *Carduus marianus*), which help to protect and regenerate damaged liver cells. **Homeopathy** can be effective in the acute phase but you should consult an experienced homeopath; treatment during recovery will be appropriate to the personality, temperament and mood of the child concerned (constitutional treatment). **Chinese herbalism** is supportive of orthodox treatment and will treat once tests have been carried out. **Acupuncture** can also be beneficial; **tai chi** and **chi kung** may help with after effects of the disease and **relaxation** can help, particularly with symptoms of chronic disease.

Tuberculosis

What is it?

Tuberculosis (TB) is a rare infectious illness usually caused by a type of bacteria, the tuberculosis bacillus *Mycobacterium tuberculosis*. The bacteria are breathed in and settle in the lungs, causing a cough, chest pain and fever, or (particularly in developing countries) ingested in milk that has not been tested for the bacillus. In most people tuberculosis is confined to the lungs, but in a few it spreads through the lymph system and into the blood stream. It can then affect any part of the body, including the membranes surrounding the brain (the meninges), kidneys, bones and joints. Children and teenagers are more vulnerable to tuberculosis than adults and are also more likely to develop tubercular meningitis. Around half the children who develop tuberculosis are discovered when close contacts of adults with the disease are traced. In developing countries tuberculosis is still a fatal disease. In the developed world, a child with tuberculosis who is diagnosed quickly and treated fully will recover without lasting ill-effects.

Tuberculosis is most common in children of Asian, African and Afro-Caribbean origin. The symptoms can be extremely varied but usually include those listed below.

You may notice

- *Fever*
- *Cough, possibly with chest pain*
- *Night sweats*
- *Swollen glands*
- *Possibly headache and a stiff neck*

Diagnosis and treatment

The first signs may suggest a more common illness, such as pneumonia; your child may need periodic visits to your doctor and a referral to hospital before the diagnosis is made. If the child does not improve despite treatment with antibiotics, tuberculosis will be considered. Hospital tests include a chest X-ray and a saliva test to confirm the presence of the bacillus. Children with a stiff neck may be given a lumbar puncture (see Meningitis page 110). They may also have a blood test and will be given a skin test to check the body's response to tuberculin, a protein derived from the tuberculosis bacillus. A small amount of tuberculin is injected into the skin. If the site of the injection becomes inflamed the test is positive, which means the child is infected or has been infected.

Treatment

Once diagnosed, treatment may involve a combination of antibiotics to destroy the tuberculosis bacteria but prevent drug resistance. The length of treatment varies but may certainly last for a number of months. Further treatment for at least four months with two of the same antibiotics helps to protect against a recurrence. Young children often recover from tuberculosis quickly and regain lost weight rapidly.

It is difficult for active children to be confined to the home for any period of time, but this is necessary during the treatment of TB. Parents will have to be resourceful and imaginative in order to keep their child interested and occupied.

People who have been in contact with a person with tuberculosis will have a tuberculin test and chest X-ray. Children under the age of two living in the same house as someone with tuberculosis will receive antibiotics to protect them from catching tuberculosis. They can be vaccinated later.

Vaccination

Vaccination is with a live BCG (bacillus Calmette-Guérin) vaccine, which protects 70-80 per cent of children and lasts for at least 15 years. It is available to newborn babies and in certain areas to other children. Newborn infants can have the BCG vaccine without a skin test beforehand. Other children and school children between 10 and 13 have a tuberculin skin test first and are only vaccinated if the test is negative.

Complementary Treatment

Traditional Chinese Medicine views this disease as a deficiency of lung yin. Treatment with **Chinese herbalism** is usually supportive of orthodox treatment, but it can be effective on its own. **Acupuncture**, **tai chi** and **chi kung** can be helpful. **Osteopathy** is appropriate for treating the after effects and **relaxation** can help with symptom relief, especially fatigue, pain, insomnia and even boredom. **Homeopathy** can be of benefit, particularly when the child is seen by an experienced homeopath. Specific remedies for TB include Calcarea 6c (*Calcarea carbonica*, calcium carbonate) for a child who is apprehensive and feverish with cold, clammy hands and feet and head sweats.

SEE ALSO MENINGITIS PAGE 110

Malaria

What is it?

Malaria is a serious blood disease that is endemic in many tropical and subtropical parts of the world. It is spread by the bite of the anopheles mosquito and is the greatest health hazard for families and children travelling to certain hot countries, especially in Asia and Africa. It is extremely rare to catch malaria in the world's temperate zones.

To protect yourself and your family against malaria you must take the appropriate drug a week or two prior to travelling, while you are in an affected area and for four weeks on your return. The drugs are constantly updated and you need to contact your doctor or the malaria information line for the latest advice. However the drugs do not fully protect and it is important to guard against mosquito bites as far as possible.

Mosquitoes usually bite between dusk and dawn. You should use an insect repellent containing DEET (diethyltoluamide) or a product suitable for children aged six and under. If you do not stay in a hotel with screens, you should sleep in a screened room. Cover the arms and legs in the evening and use anklets, wristbands and a mosquito net impregnated with a safe insecticide such as permethrin. An electric mat should be used to vaporize insecticides.

It usually takes a week or two between being bitten by the mosquito and the first signs of malaria appearing, but it may take much longer if the child has been taking anti-malarial drugs, which delay the onset of malaria. Therefore any fever and flu-like symptoms appearing within a year of overseas travel, and especially within six months, could be malaria.

You may notice

- *Fever is the usual symptom, which normally but not always occurs in a three-stage pattern that recurs every two or three days. Stage one is uncontrollable cold shivering; stage two fever, during which the body temperature rises rapidly; stage three sweating as the fever subsides*
- *Headache and vomiting*
- *Chills and shaking*

What to do

Contact your doctor immediately, who will probably arrange for the child to go to hospital. Blood samples are taken to reach a diagnosis. If the child is still taking preventive medicines the blood may appear clear, so blood samples may need to be taken again. Once the developing parasites have been seen under a microscope, antimalarial drugs are given according to a recommended schedule. These will clear malaria parasites from the blood. In certain types of malaria other drugs may be needed to clear parasites from the liver. Children with some types of malaria recover without treatment.

Who can help?

Some countries have a 24-hour Malaria Information line. See the Directory for details.

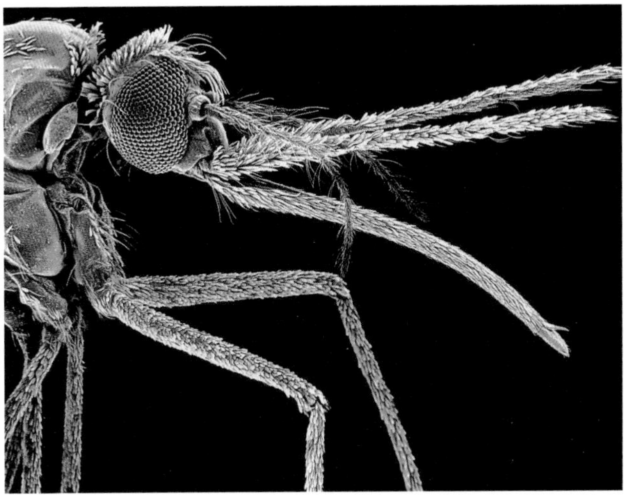

It is the female anopheles mosquito that feeds from the bloodstream, simultaneously injecting parasites into the host's body from her salivary glands. The parasites migrate to the liver, where they begin to multiply. Symptoms of the disease occur 9 to 30 days after the mosquito bite.

The ABC of malaria

A be **aware** of the risk of malaria
B don't be **bitten**
C take the appropriate **chemoprophylaxis** (preventive drug) to protect you and your family

Complementary Treatment

Western herbalists have found that sweet, or Chinese wormwood (*Artemisia annua*) is useful, possibly in combination with other herbs. **Homeopathic remedies** can be taken with orthodox drugs, and include Chininum sulph 6c (*Chininum sulphuricum*, quinine sulphate) for chills, followed by fever, sweating, pain and thirst. **Relaxation** can help by controlling symptoms such as pain, insomnia, fatigue and boredom.

HAND, FOOT AND MOUTH DISEASE

What is it?
Hand, foot and mouth disease is usually a mild viral infection in which small blisters appear on the hands, the feet and inside the the mouth. It has no connection with the foot and mouth disease that affects sheep and other animals. It is a mild infection, common in young children, that tends to occur in outbreaks, particularly in nursery schools and playgroups and most often in mild weather and in summer.

The infection is caused by a virus that is spread in droplets on the breath, especially when someone with the infection sneezes or coughs. The virus then infects the gastrointestinal tract. It can be transferred from faeces on to the hands for weeks after the infected child has recovered.

Hand, foot and mouth disease takes three to five days to develop but only causes a mild upset in most children, lasting three to seven days. Infants do not inherit immunity and the infection can, rarely, be serious for very young infants.

You may notice
- *Other children in your community have hand, foot and mouth disease*
- *Sore throat, reluctance to eat, generally unwell*
- *A fever*
- *Tiny blisters appear inside the cheeks, on the gums and on the sides of the tongue, developing into shallow grey ulcers on a red base. These blisters may not heal for seven to ten days*
- *Small, clear, sometimes itchy blisters encircled with red appear on the palms and the soles of the feet. They sometimes show on the backs of the hands, in nail folds, on the upper part of the feet and under the arms. A baby's nappy area may be affected*

What to do
When you first hear of an outbreak, watch your child carefully for the early symptoms. You can treat this infection at home but consult your doctor if you are unsure of the diagnosis. When the fever develops, keep your child away from nursery, school or playgroup until the crusts that develop from the hand and foot blisters have dropped off or until the fluid in the blisters has been reabsorbed. The child is most infectious at this stage and quite likely to pass the virus on.

Give children's paracetamol or Junifen (sugar-free ibuprofen) for the fever and encourage your child to drink – water, milk, milky drinks or milkshakes. Avoid fruit juice while the child's mouth is sore, as it can exacerbate the discomfort. Mouth ulcers often take longer to resolve than the foot and hand blisters. Most often they have gone within a week but they may occasionally take a month to clear. Cool a feverish child by undressing them to nappy or pants. Dab calamine on the blisters on the hands and feet if they are itchy. Leave a baby's nappy off when you can if the nappy area is affected.

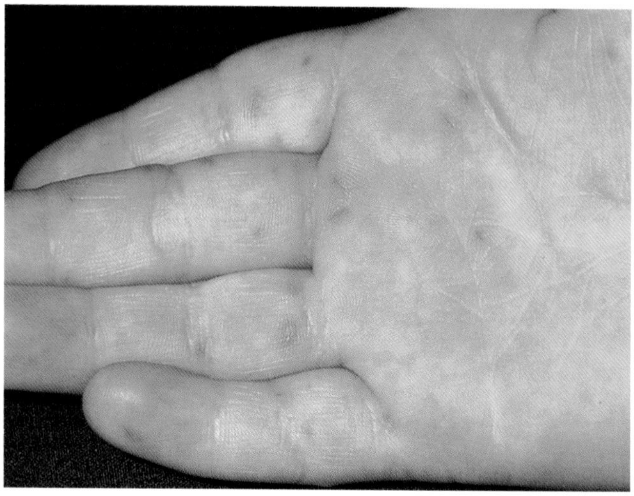

Small itchy blisters on the palms of the hand, the soles of the feet and sometimes the backs of the hands are the characteristic symptoms of hand, foot and mouth disease. The condition is caused by a virus, spread by droplets on the breath during coughing or sneezing.

What else?
You can try to limit the spread of the virus by washing any toys your child sucks and washing the hands frequently. Be extremely careful with nappy hygiene as the virus lingers in the faeces for several weeks following recovery.

Complementary Treatment

In younger children this disease responds well to **Chinese herbs** that clear the damp and heat from the digestion. It may be necessary to treat the whole family. **Homeopathy** offers specific remedies for a variety of symptoms, including Sulphur 6c (*Sulphur*, sublimated sulphur) when there is rash and fever and the child is thirsty and seems hungry but nevertheless refuses food; and Mercurius 6c (*Mercurius solubilis Hahnemanni*, quicksilver) when the child's temperature has returned to normal and the spots are healing, although some may be infected.

LYME DISEASE

What is it?

Lyme disease is a bacterial infection carried by ticks. Ticks prefer damp woodlands and mild weather. Their numbers drop after spells of hot, dry weather and in winter when the air temperature falls below 7°C/45°F. In Europe ticks may be infected with three distinct species of the *Borrelia* bacterium, and in North America usually with the *Burgdorferi* species, which they can transmit to people when they bite them to suck blood. Before feeding ticks are so tiny that it is easy to miss them; an adult tick after a meal is the size of a coffee bean. If your child is bitten by a tick, do not assume they will develop Lyme disease. Many ticks do not carry the infection and a bite does not always transmit it, especially if you catch the tick in the early stages of biting.

Lyme disease can occasionally lead to serious complications if the infection reaches the nervous system. It can cause meningitis or a paralysis of nerves on one or both sides of the face, as well as weakness and a loss of feeling in the arms and legs. The disease can also cause pain and arthritis in joints, especially the knees, which can occasionally become chronic.

You may notice

- *A circular red rash expanding from a tiny insect bite. The rash may develop two to thirty days after the bite. As the rash spreads, the centre clears*
- *Fever, headache and swollen glands, especially in the neck*
- *Some people develop none of these early signs; instead they have later symptoms such as a feverish 'flu-like illness and a rash of smaller circular red patches, followed by painful, swollen joints*

The head and mouthparts of Ixodes ricinus, *the tick most likely to carry Lyme disease in Europe. On the the continent of North America, Lyme disease is transmitted by the related ticks* I. dammini *and* I. pacificus. *The natural habitat of these ticks is damp woodland. At the centre of this picture the head, with its barbed blood-sucking mouthparts, is clearly visible.*

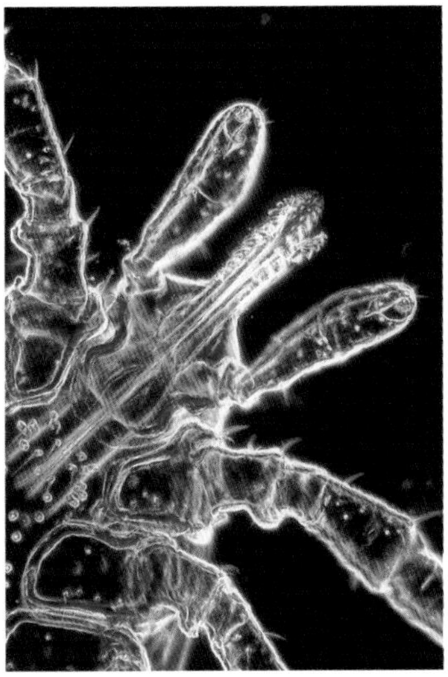

What to do

You cannot treat the symptoms of Lyme disease at home, so take your child to the doctor. Tell the doctor about any recent visits you have made to the countryside, particularly to woodland. The doctor may take a blood sample to confirm the diagnosis. If Lyme disease is suspected the doctor will prescribe an antibiotic, which should clear the infection quickly.

Prevention

Cover up when walking in grass or woodlands. Wear long trousers tucked into socks and long-sleeved tops. Spray or rub on insect repellent before going out.

Check your child regularly for ticks. If you find one, remove it gently but firmly, not squeezing it but making sure all the parts of the mouth have been removed. It is easier to remove a tick if you cover it with petroleum jelly for 15 minutes before removal.

Tick encephalitis

In the forests of Scandinavia, Central and Eastern Europe, some ticks carry a virus that can cause encephalitis. The risk is greatest in late spring and summer. Cover legs, ankles and arms and spray on insect repellent.

Travellers can be vaccinated against Lyme disease. Two doses given four to twelve weeks apart will give protection for a year.

Complementary Treatment

Relaxation is very useful for many of the symptoms associated with the disease, including pain control, headache, loss of concentration, insomnia, anxiety and so on. The Fleming technique (a type of imaging technique, see page 60) is especially helpful for loss of concentration. **Aromatherapy** and **massage** may stimulate the relaxation response. Headache, swollen glands and other symptoms may benefit from **homeopathic remedies** and **Chinese** and **Western herbalism**.

Thrush

What is it?

Thrush is a common infection in babies, children and women. It is caused by a yeast-like fungus, *Candida albicans*, which lives naturally on the skin, in the vagina, in the mouth and the bowel, in harmony with a range of natural bacteria. However when the natural harmony of the organisms that live in the intestine, in the mouth or elsewhere in the body, is upset, symptoms of thrush can occur. This is most likely to happen if the immune system is disturbed in any way, for example by a course of antibiotics, or when asthma sufferers inhale steroids. These conditions can allow the candida organism to flourish. Once it starts to flourish, candida multiplies quickly, damaging mucous membranes and triggering the typical symptoms of intense inflammation and irritation.

Although thrush is common, it is rarely serious. It usually responds quickly to treatment and will not come back if you can avoid the situations that gave rise to it in the first place. However, it can be extremely disruptive.

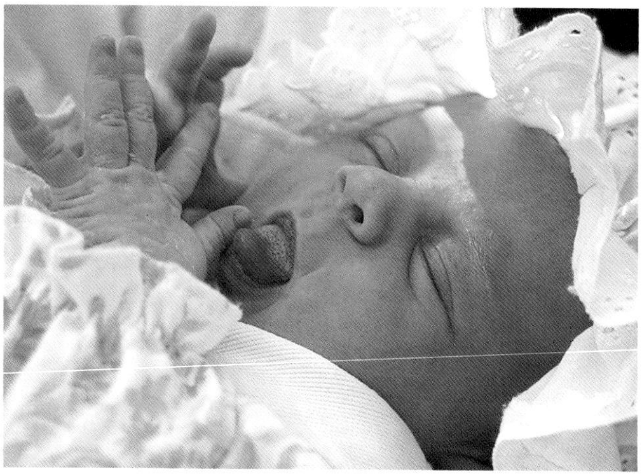

One of the most common sites in which thrush develops is the baby's mouth. The milky white spots and patches clearly visible here are evidence that the fungus Candida albicans *is present. This condition causes irritation and inflammation in the affected areas, which are exacerbated by feeding. Breastfeeding mothers, as well as their affected infants, will require treatment.*

You may notice

- *Vivid red nappy rash that does not respond to normal creams. The rash occurs in intensely sore red patches*
- *If a baby has thrush in the mouth, they will be reluctant to feed. They may start hungrily but stop before satisfying their appetite*
- *Spots inside the cheeks that look like the remains of milk. Wiped very gently with a tissue they may stay stuck or come off to reveal a sore red patch beneath*
- *Teenage girls may develop thrush around the vulva, with maddening itching, soreness and inflammation. Urinating can be intensely painful. It is especially common before menstruation, when hormone levels increase to create the right environment for candida to flourish*
- *Adolescent boys may develop penile thrush under the foreskin. It can be caused by poor hygiene; symptoms include itching and inflammation*

What to do

If you suspect oral thrush, first check inside your baby's mouth. There are many reasons for reluctance to feed, so don't jump to conclusions. If you find the characteristic white spots and sore patches, consult your doctor. If you are breastfeeding both you and your baby will need treatment.

If your baby is finding sucking from a bottle painful, try feeding with a spoon. Wash your hands scrupulously after nappy changes and before feeding.

If a child with asthma develops thrush in or around the mouth, consult the specialist asthma nurse or your doctor. It is normally helpful to inhale the steroid using a spacer, which helps the drug travel down into the lungs instead of being deposited on the inside of the mouth. After taking the asthma medication, it also helps to rinse the mouth and spit out or else clean the teeth. If a young child uses a mask as well as a spacer, rubbing a thin layer of vaseline into the skin or wiping the face afterwards with a face cloth can help to protect the skin.

If the thrush has developed during a course of antibiotics, it is important not to stop the antibiotics. Instead, continue applying the antifungal medication until the course of antibiotics has been completed.

Treatment

If you are breastfeeding a baby with thrush tell your doctor who may prescribe an antifungal cream for your nipples. As a precaution, wash your nipples before feeding. Your doctor will also prescribe an antifungal gel or liquid containing the antifungal drug nystatin or miconazole. This should be dropped on to the sore patches in your baby's mouth after every feed. The sores should start to improve within a day or two. You may also be given a cream for your baby's sore bottom if the baby has nappy rash.

When you change the nappy, make sure the baby is perfectly dry before applying the cream. It should start to work in two or three days. Leave the nappy off whenever you can. An older child may be given lozenges to suck four to eight times a day, or a mouthwash for gargling. Continue the treatment for two days after the sores have gone to help protect against re-infection.

If the prescribed creams and gels do not improve the thrush within a day or two, go back to the doctor. It is possible that a secondary bacterial infection has superimposed on the thrush. Treatment for vaginal and penile thrush includes antifungal creams or suppositories.

Coping with breastfeeding and thrush

- Wash your hands carefully before and after every feed and after changing nappies
- Try offering a spoon if sucking from the nipple is too sore. Sterilize anything that goes into your baby's mouth or boil for 20 minutes
- If your nipples become cracked and sore as well, make feeding as easy as possible for both of you. Express milk from the most sore side and feed your baby from a teat or spoon to rest the nipple
- Give split feeds of maximum ten minutes at each breast to rest your baby. You may end up feeding as often as a newborn baby just for a few days

Practical tips

- Coping with a baby with thrush is extremely tiring, especially if you have older children. Accept any offers of help and rest as much as you can to boost your own strength
- Wear loose, cotton clothes on areas affected by thrush. It thrives in a warm, moist environment
- Avoid perfumed soaps and bubble baths which can damage delicate skin
- Wash any of your baby's clothes that have been in contact with thrush at the highest possible heat. Hang in sunshine to dry completely
- Teach your daughter to wipe her bottom from front to back to avoid germs from the anus entering the vagina and causing thrush
- Two pots of live yoghurt containing *Lactobacillus acidophilus* eaten daily will help to limit the growth of the candida fungus

Natural yoghurt that contains Lactobacillus acedophilus *is a well-known home remedy for both oral and vaginal thrush. Eliminating sugars, milk products, eggs, yeast, fats, caffeine and citrus fruit from the diet for a period of time is also a recommended course of treatment that many find successful.*

Complementary Treatment

Chinese herbalism treats primarily as a digestive disorder. The diet would be considered along with herbal prescriptions. Oral thrush in infants is treated with herbal teas, given internally. In post-pubescent children heat and damp can invade the liver channel and descend to the genitals; appropriate treatment would be given, perhaps combined with **acupuncture**, which can be effective by itself. **Homeopathic remedies** for oral thrush include Borax 6c (*Borax veneta*, sodium borate) to be taken at the first sign of an outbreak, four times a day for up to five days. For penile thrush, Mercurius 6c (*Mercurius solubilus Hahnemanii*, quicksilver) should be taken four times a day for up to fourteen days. There are a number of remedies for vaginal thrush, depending on the symptoms; it would be worthwhile consulting a homeopath. Vaginal douches with Hypericum (*Hypericum perforatum*, St John's wort) and Calendula (*Calendula officinales*, pot marigold) solutions may also help. See a homeopath for advice on how to use. Adolescent boys with penile thrush may benefit too from this treatment. The **nutritional therapist** may recommend improving the diet in order to strengthen the immune system and so prevent further attacks. Using a tampon soaked in natural yoghurt may also aid recovery.

TOXOCARIASIS

What is it?

Toxocariasis is a worm infection that usually comes from dogs. Many dogs carry *Toxocara canis*, a type of roundworm that lives in animals' intestines, and almost all puppies are born with it. (Cats may carry *Toxocara cati*, a similar worm.) Eggs are excreted in the dog's faeces but are not infectious for the first two to five weeks. However they can survive for two years or more. Children playing in parks or gardens can pick up the sticky eggs on their hands and become infected when they put their hands in their mouth. The eggs settle in their intestines and hatch out. Larvae can then travel throughout the body, causing internal tissue damage in young children and, more commonly, eye damage in school-aged children. Boys are more commonly affected than girls.

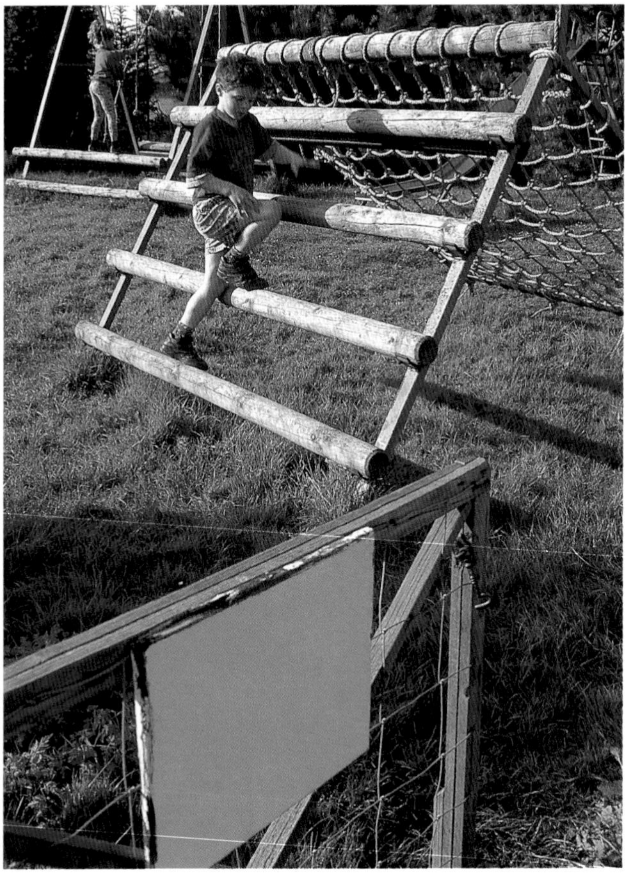

It is important to keep areas where children play well fenced so that dogs and foxes cannot enter. Studies show that in the United Kingdom as many as one school child in eight has been exposed to Toxocaria canis. *Only half the children in the United Kingdom who catch the infection have been in direct contact with dogs or puppies.*

You may notice

- *Mild fever and a general feeling of not being well, which last for a few days*
- *Coughing and signs of asthma*
- *Stomach ache*
- *Swollen glands*
- *A few children develop a squint, red eye and eventually damage to the eye*

What to do

Consult your doctor, who may reassure you that a child in contact with fresh faeces is not at risk. The doctor will probably not give any treatment even if your child has eaten contaminated soil, as they will only have swallowed a few eggs. If the child does develop toxocariasis it is usually mild and they will recover without lasting damage. If the eye is involved or the child is very unwell, the doctor may refer your child to hospital where staff will give treatment to control the symptoms, and possibly an anthelmintic worm treatment.

Children with internal tissue damage usually recover without treatment. Serious effects are rare, but as toxocariasis can cause blindness and is difficult to treat, prevention is best.

What else?

If you own a puppy or dog, a cat or a kitten, however apparently healthy, give worm treatment regularly. You can buy treatment from a veterinary surgeon or a chemist. Have a pregnant bitch specially treated to prevent the birth of infected puppies.

Scoop up your dog's faeces in a plastic bag and dispose of them carefully. Wash your hands after handling pets, before preparing food or eating.

If you notice your toddler or child eating soil that might be fouled, or playing with animal faeces, wash their hands and face very thoroughly.

Cover sandpits when they are not in use and make sure the floor your child plays on is clean.

Discourage your children from eating snacks while they play. Keep mealtimes separate from playtime and always wash hands before eating.

Complementary treatment

Orthodox treatment is essential. However the **homeopath** will give supportive treatment by helping to boost the immune system. The child concerned will be treated constitutionally – that is, accorded to their personality, temperament and mood.

HERPES INFECTIONS

What is it?

The herpes simplex virus (HSV) can cause various skin conditions, typically with small fluid-filled blisters. There are two main types of infection: herpes type 1 (HSV-I), which is spread by contact with the blisters and their fluid; and herpes type 2 (HSV-II) a genital infection that can occasionally affect newborn infants. HSV-I infections are very common but parents often do not realise their children are affected, because most do not show any symptoms. In some children, however, the first contact with HSV-I causes extremely sore mouth ulcers. The infection can then lie dormant in the nerve cells and be reactivated later as cold sores.

HSV Infections in the mouth

The first time a child catches HSV-I it can cause extremely sore ulcers on the lips and inside the mouth. The infection is called gingivostomatitis and is most common in pre-school children. The ulcers heal after seven to ten days.

You may notice

- *Intensely sore mouth: lips, gums, tongue and inside of the mouth swell, bleed and have a number of ulcers*
- *Food refusal because eating and drinking are painful*
- *Fever, swollen glands and general ill-health*

What to do

Ask your doctor to double-check the diagnosis. Drugs may not be needed for a mild attack, but if the attack is severe the doctor may prescribe the antiviral drug aciclovir. To help prevent dehydration tempt the child to drink using a straw, offering sips of cool drinks and ice cubes to suck.

Herpes in a newborn infant

HSV-II is a sexually transmitted disease that in an adult causes a painful and itchy genital rash with blisters. It is much more common in the United States than in the United Kingdom. If the mother has an active HSV-II infection at the time of birth the infant can catch it while passing through the birth canal. The infection is serious for a newborn infant, so obstetricians prefer the baby of a mother who is known to have active herpes to be born by Caesarean section. Much more rarely newborn infants catch HSV-I infection after birth if their mother has a cold sore.

Infants who are infected with the herpes virus in this way develop blisters and sores on the skin. The brain and nervous system may be affected. Because of the serious consequences of herpes infection in the newborn, infants need careful monitoring and treatment with high doses of intravenous aciclovir in a neonatal intensive care unit.

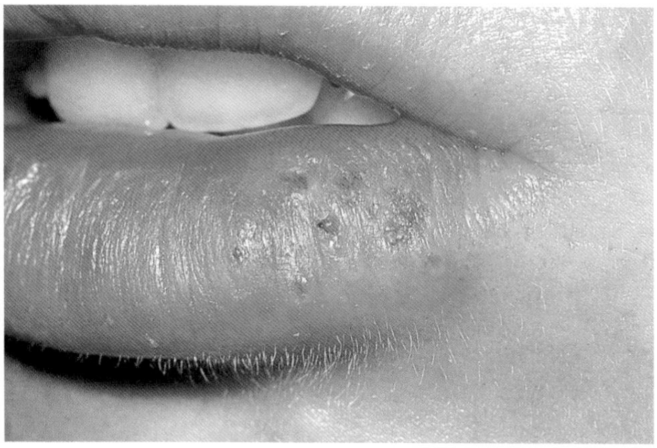

The herpes virus can remain in the body without causing symptoms until the immune system is weakened, at which time weeping blisters may appear around the mouth and the lips, as here. Medical advice and treatment should be sought in order to clear the infection.

Herpes infections of the skin

Children with eczema who come into contact with an HSV-I infection are susceptible to eczema herpeticum. This produces widespread sheets of studded blisters.

You may notice

- *Blisters giving a studded appearance, especially around the face and the neck*

What to do

Contact a doctor, who may take a sample of fluid from the blisters for laboratory analysis. The drug aciclovir will be prescribed to prevent the virus spreading. Keep children with eczema away from people with cold sores.

Complementary Treatment

Where complementary treatment is appropriate it will largely support orthodox treatment. **Nutritional therapy** will usually treat herpes simplex type 1 with supplements, particularly of vitamins A and E, and zinc. Garlic oil and vitamin E ointment can also be applied to the skin. **Homeopathic** remedies may help to relieve the symptoms.

SEE ALSO MOUTH ULCERS PAGE 233

INFLUENZA

What is it?

Influenza is an acute viral infection of the airways and upper respiratory system. There are different types of influenza virus: most outbreaks every year are caused by strains of the influenza A virus, while outbreaks caused by strains of influenza B occur at intervals of several years. Influenza is most common in winter and can occur in widespread outbreaks, involving people of all ages. It is highly infectious and spreads rapidly, especially in places such as schools and nurseries. The infection is passed on when children breathe, cough or sneeze virus-laden droplets on to other children. The first signs of illness follow quickly, in one to three days. A child who catches influenza will feel ill for two or three days but improve rapidly as the fever drops; within a week the illness has usually gone.

Although children generally get over 'flu in a few days, it can sometimes be very serious, and result in a secondary bacterial infection such as otitis media (middle ear infection). Influenza can occasionally cause convulsions in young infants.

Fit, healthy children do not need to have a 'flu injection but children with long-term diseases affecting the lungs – such as severe asthma or cystic fibrosis – and diabetics may be immunized in the autumn at the beginning of the 'flu season. Vaccines are 70-80 per cent effective.

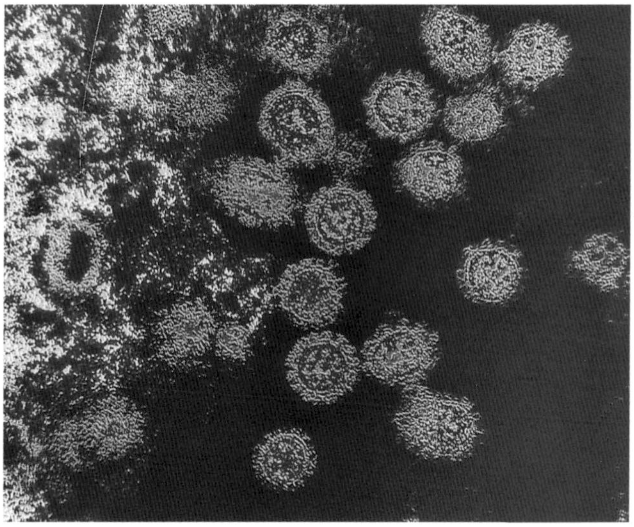

In this microscopic picture of a cell infected with an influenza virus, the round red elements are individual virus particles (virions), which the virus has stimulated the cell to produce. The influenza virus has an affinity for mucus. Spikes on the virus's surface allow it to hook on to cells in the nose, throat and upper respiratory system.

You may notice

- *Sudden fever*
- *Shivers and sweating, flushed face*
- *Headache*
- *Aching limbs and backache*
- *Dry cough and sometimes a sore throat*
- *Sore, red eyes*
- *A feeling of weakness and loss of appetite*
- *Young children may develop vomiting and diarrhoea*

What to do

Let your child lie in bed or rest on a settee downstairs if they wish. Check their temperature with a fever strip or thermometer and give children's paracetamol as required. Offer alternate warm and cold drinks; warm drinks are soothing if the throat is sore and cold drinks of water or fruit juice diluted half and half with water help to reduce the fever. Allow your child to eat if they want to, but don't force them. Contact your doctor if your child becomes worse, with a fever, of severe coughing that brings up phlegm. You should also seek medical advice if your child's breathing becomes unusual or rapid or if they develop an earache or seem unexpectedly drowsy. These signs suggest that your child may have developed a secondary infection, for which your doctor will usually consider prescribing antibiotics.

Keep your child at home from nursery or playgroup until fully recovered. During the recovery period they are vulnerable to secondary infections.

Complementary Treatment

Chinese herbalism can be effective if herbs can be given early enough, otherwise the child may have to be treated for complications such as cough, catarrh, fits, digestive problems and weakness. The **Western herbalist** will treat with herbs that reduce mucus production and inflamed membranes, fight infection and clear airways. **Nutritional therapists** would hope to strengthen the immune system and so prevent further outbreaks in the future. They may also concentrate on improving general health and strengthening the immune system. **Homeopathy** offers a number of specific remedies that may relieve 'flu symptoms. **Aromatherapy** oils, especially lavender oil, can be applied topically. Lavender oil is gentle enough to use on babies. It will be particularly useful when used as a massage oil.

HIV

What is it?

HIV (human immunodeficiency virus) is the virus that causes AIDS (acquired immune deficiency syndrome) and in children causes a chronic infection. The virus is carried in body fluids such as blood, semen and breast milk. A person who carries the virus but does not show any symptoms of AIDS is said to be HIV positive.

It is very difficult to catch the virus when normal hygiene practices are observed and, in sexually active individuals, methods of safer sex are used. The majority of children acquire HIV from their mother, most of them while they are in the uterus or during birth. As a result pregnant women who are known to be HIV positive are now offered the drug zidovudine to help protect the infant.

An infant born to a mother who is HIV positive has antibodies to the virus from birth. These are, however, antibodies to the mother's infection and do not necessarily mean that the infant has acquired HIV. The maternal antibodies remain in the infant's blood stream for 12 to 18 months, and by the age of six months infants can be tested to see whether they have been infected.

The infection is a variable disease and new drug regimes mean that some children are living much longer than in the past. A few reach adolescence and some may face choices about having their own children. Ultimately, however, HIV infection is fatal.

A quarter of the infants who are born with HIV develop symptoms of AIDS by their first birthday, and 40 per cent by the age of four years. Signs include repeated (usually bacterial) infections, persistently swollen glands, chronic diarrhoea, oral thrush, unexplained fevers and a failure to put on weight and grow at the expected rate. Children may also be slow to develop new skills.

Treatment

Treatment can bring a marked improvement. Children may reach their developmental milestones, put on weight and be more resistant to infections. However care involves frequent trips to hospital and time spent as an in-patient, as well as support in managing the social implications of the illness. The question arises of when to tell a child that they have HIV; many children have their suspicions before they are told.

Some children inevitably ask 'Will I die?' It is important to be honest but the way the answer is given depends on the child and on the stage of the disease. Planning for the immediate future is as important as dwelling on the uncertainties of the long-term outcome.

A point for debate

Increasing numbers of mothers contract HIV from heterosexual sex. Most do not realize they are at risk from HIV. Currently, 1 pregnant woman in 560 in London, England, is HIV positive. Outside London 1 woman in 10,000 is HIV positive. Should mothers be screened routinely for HIV at the antenatal clinic? Screening mothers allows effective protection to be offered during pregnancy and children who are at risk to be identified early.

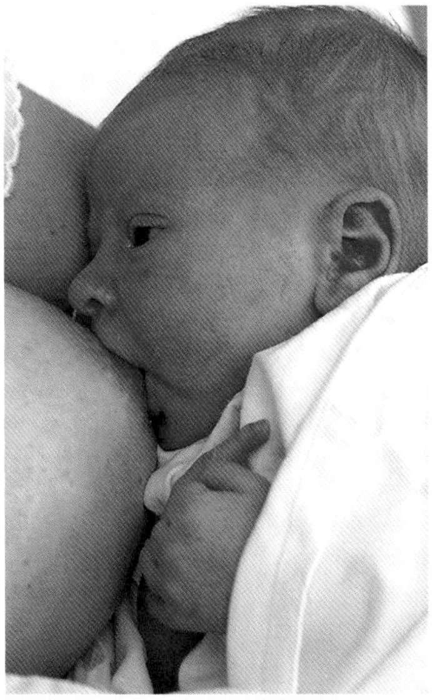

HIV positive mothers are at risk of transmitting the virus to their infants, who under normal circumstances will usually avoid getting infections when they are breastfed. When bottle feeding is safe and is culturally acceptable to the mother, it is the preferred method of feeding her newborn infant.

Complementary Treatment

Complementary treatment must be supportive of orthodox treatment. **Nutritional therapists** use individual dietary programmes to improve the body's efficiency in combating illness in general. The illness may benefit from this improved efficiency but much is dependent on how advanced the illness is, the person's constitution and other factors such as stress. **Homeopaths** treat with a holistic approach, but do consult a homeopath who has considerable experience in treating this condition.

Brain, Nerves and Muscles

The brain is the body's control centre, where all the information relayed to it from the nervous system is analysed. Together with the spinal cord, it makes up the central nervous system. The entire system is protected by three layers of tissue (the meninges) and cushioned by cerebrospinal fluid.

The brain contains two cerebral hemispheres, left, and right, which control the specialized activities on the opposite side of the body. Across the top of the central section are two strips of tissue: the motor cortex sends out messages that control movements in all parts of the body;he cerebellum, at the back and base of the brain, is concerned with muscle coordination, balance and posture. Near the base of the brain is the hypothalamus, where the endocrine systems is coordinated, and automatic activities we do not think about, such as breathing and digestion, are integrated.

The nerves and muscles

Nerves connecting different parts of the body to the central nervous system emerge from the brain at strategic points. Signals from the brain travel down the motor fibres and instruct muscles, which are bundles of elastic fibres, to move. Each muscle fibre is supplied with a nerve ending that receives impulses from the brain. When a signal arrives,the muscle to contract. Other nerve fibres register the force of the contraction and the amount of stretch. The information from these fibres is vital for limiting muscle action.

Muscle is usually kept partly contracted – this is muscle tone. Muscles that need to return to their resting position following a movement are usually pulled in the opposite direction by another muscle, which is why many muscles work in pairs. Muscle activity is also affected by chemical changes in the fluid around the muscle walls, so that a fall in the body's calcium levels, for example, can cause muscle spasm.

Sensory and motor messages from the brain are relayed from the central nervous system to the body's muscles via the peripheral nervous system. Twelve pairs of cranial nerves and thirty-one pairs of spinal nerves branch from the spinal cord to control areas of the trunk, the arms and the legs.

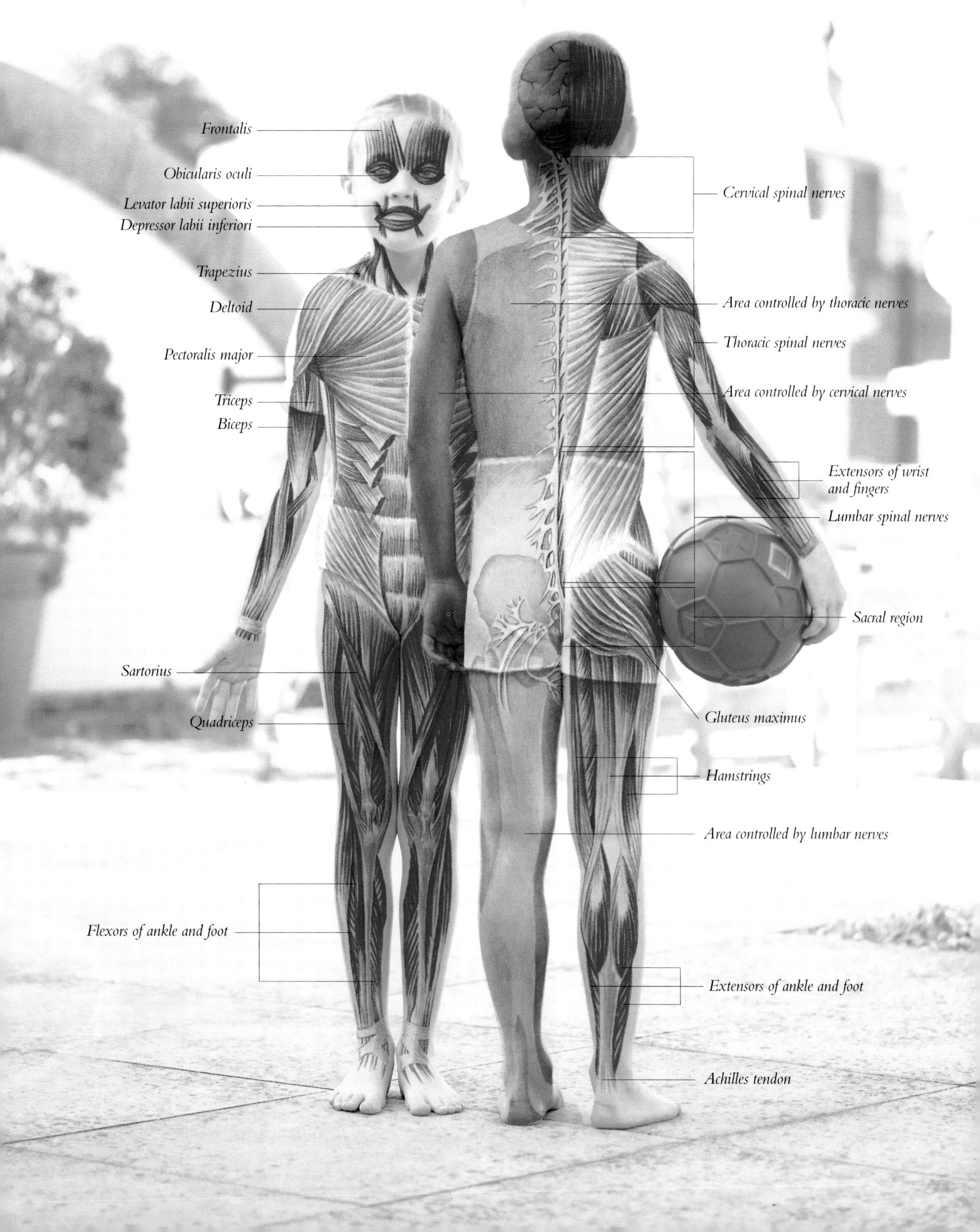
Frontalis
Obicularis oculi
Levator labii superioris
Depressor labii inferiori
Trapezius
Deltoid
Pectoralis major
Triceps
Biceps
Sartorius
Quadriceps
Flexors of ankle and foot
Cervical spinal nerves
Area controlled by thoracic nerves
Thoracic spinal nerves
Area controlled by cervical nerves
Extensors of wrist and fingers
Lumbar spinal nerves
Sacral region
Gluteus maximus
Hamstrings
Area controlled by lumbar nerves
Extensors of ankle and foot
Achilles tendon

Diagnosis

Serious disorders of the brain, nerves and muscles are rare in children. Symptoms such as clumsiness and weakness are usually a sign of a minor disorder or developmental problem, although occasionally they may be the first sign of a more serious disorder. Parents should be familiar with the symptoms of meningitis. If it is detected early treatment is usually successful.

Clumsiness

Clumsiness in children is normal, and does not usually mean that there is an underlying disease. However occasionally a clumsy child will develop more quickly with specialist support. Very occasionally, it may point to an underlying cause.

Signs	What could be wrong
Slightly clumsier than other children	Lack of opportunity to play; timid child; inherited pattern of late development; can arise while child is growing rapidly
Obviously much clumsier than other children	Could be developmental dyspraxia, which improves with encouraging stimulation and practice
Generally slow to develop	May be an early sign of learning difficulty
Clumsy and hyperactive	Never has enough time to practise skills
Behaviour problems	More common in older children; may mean child has low self-esteem and confidence
Bumps into things; has difficulty with tasks such as writing and craft	Could be a sign of short sight
Worsening difficulty walking and climbing stairs	Could be a sign of muscular dystrophy
One of a cluster of worrying signs, including poor sucking, odd reflexes and floppiness	Possible signs of cerebral palsy

Weakness

Weakness after an accident may suggest an injury such as a sprain or even a fracture. Floppiness that is longer lasting is more worrying. In hypotonia, muscles feel flabby and the child does not resist if its limbs are moved. Although most causes are not serious and the child recovers, any weakness for which there is no obvious cause should be investigated by a doctor. Weakness from birth may be a sign of brain damage.

Signs	What could be wrong
Slack muscle tone with other obvious physical signs	This is a common feature of Down's syndrome
Physical and mental exhaustion, often in an older child	Chronic fatigue syndrome; it can be progressive
Difficulty climbing stairs; late walking	Muscular dystrophy

ENCEPHALITIS

What is it?

Encephalitis is inflammation of the brain, a rare condition usually caused by a virus. It may follow an infection with the herpes simplex virus (see page 103) or, more rarely, a childhood infection such as chickenpox, mumps, measles or bronchiolitis. Yet more often it is the result of a virus attacking the brain tissues, and sometimes the membranes around the brain as well, causing meningitis. Babies under six months of age are particularly vulnerable, although encephalitis can occur at any age.

Although the majority of children with encephalitis develop only a mild form, it is always serious and needs immediate hospital treatment. Sometimes it is fatal. In other cases it can cause varying degrees of brain damage, ranging from damage with no noticeable after effects to severe learning, behavioural and movement disabilities. The long-term effects depend on the area of the brain that has been damaged.

Symptoms

The symptoms of encephalitis are very variable. They usually develop quickly, but in some cases they develop more slowly, gradually becoming worse.

You may notice

- *The child appears to recover from a virus infection but then their condition deteriorates. They may get better for a few days and then become ill again*
- *Obvious change in mood and behaviour. The child becomes very irritable or drowsy and may have a headache*
- *Unsteadiness, confusion. The child may drift into a coma*
- *Fever*
- *Convulsions*

What to do

Check that the child has not helped themself to medicines: drug poisoning can mimic the signs of encephalitis. Contact a doctor immediately. If the doctor is not available, call the accident and emergency department of your local hospital and describe the child's symptoms. Follow the instructions you are given before setting off for hospital.

Make the child comfortable by putting a pillow under the head (if the child is more than a year old) and darkening the room. In hospital, staff may set up a drip to administer fluids, nourishment and drugs. The child will be given the antiviral drug aciclovir intravenously, and another drug such as diazepam to control convulsions. There are no drugs for other viral infections.

Doctors will also investigate the cause of the infection. The child will need to have blood tests, a lumbar puncture to draw off fluid from the central nervous system, an electroencephalogram (EEG) and a brain scan.

Although many children make a complete recovery, it may be months or even years before the full effects of encephalitis become clear. While difficulties with movement and other effects of severe brain damage may be obvious immediately, more subtle learning and behaviour disorders that have occurred as a result of the condition only become apparent as academic demands on the child increase.

Who can help?

For organizations offering help and support see the Directory.

Complementary treatment

Complementary therapies will be given in support of orthodox treatment. **Homeopathic remedies** to be given while waiting for help to arrive are: Belladonna 30c (*Atropa belladonna*, deadly nightshade) if the child is delirious, with a flushed face and staring eyes; Nux mosch 6c (*Nux moschata*, nutmeg) when the child is obviously drowsy; and Gelsemium 6c (*Gelsemium sempervirens*, yellow jasmine) when the child feels weak and trembly, complains of dizziness and having a tight band around the forehead, and refuses drinks. The remedies are to be given every 15 minutes for up to ten doses. Traditional Chinese Medicine sees encephalitis as a complication of meningitis, usually after treatment with antibiotic drugs. This condition requires the attention of a skilled **Chinese herbalist**, as any number of different approaches may be used and the herbs changed on a daily basis. **Tai chi**, **chi kung** and **acupuncture** may help restore health in the convalescent stage.

MENINGITIS

What is it?

Meningitis is an inflammation of one or more of the three thin membranes that cover the brain. It can be caused by a number of microorganisms, including viruses and bacteria. Viral meningitis is usually less serious than bacterial meningitis, and although bacterial meningitis is quite rare, it develops swiftly and needs urgent treatment with antibiotics. Meningitis can occur at any time of year, although it tends to peak in the winter.

Types of meningitis

There are several different types of bacterial meningitis, including pneumococcal, tubercular and meningococcal meningitis. Haemophilus influenza meningitis was the most common form in children until the introduction of the Hib vaccine in infants in 1992.

Meningococcal meningitis is caused by the bacterium *Neisseria meningitidis*. There are two major types of meningococcal meningitis, groups B and C. Group C, which accounts for one-third of cases, is often linked with outbreaks in schools and other closed communities. Group B, which accounts for some two-thirds of cases, usually affects only one person in a community, although sometimes there is a cluster of cases. This type of meningitis is especially common in babies under the age of one year and in older teenagers. However, recently group C has shown signs of becoming more common among teenagers.

Spread of infection

The bacteria that cause bacterial meningitis do not live for any length of time outside the body, so they are not passed on in public places, such as swimming pools and parks. Many people carry the potentially causative bacteria in their nasal passages and throats, but do not develop the disease. It seems that a person's natural resistance has to be lowered for the infection to take hold. The bacteria are transmitted in nasal discharge during coughing and sneezing. When the bacteria are breathed in they reach the lining of the upper respiratory system and from there pass into the bloodstream. They are carried in the blood to the meninges, the protective membranes that cover the brain, where they cause inflammation.

In an apparently increasing number of children the infecting bacteria multiply in the blood, causing blood poisoning or meningococcal septicaemia. This is an extremely serious condition and it can develop very quickly – in a matter of a few hours. Meningococcal bacteria are the bacteria most likely to cause this form of blood poisoning.

Colds are not the only things that are passed on by coughs and sneezes. In people who carry the bacterium responsible for bacterial meningitis the microorganism, present in their throat and nasal passages, can be transmitted in exactly the same way as a cold.

You may notice

Babies show some of these signs:

- *Drowsiness and difficulty in waking*
- *Fretfulness and irritability*
- *Vomiting or food refusal*
- *A dislike of being handled*
- *Fever*
- *An odd, staring expression*
- *Neck stiffness*
- *Fontanelle may be tense or may bulge*
- *Reddish-purple spots anywhere on the skin, which grow quickly into larger marks or bruises. Pressed under an empty glass, the spots don't go white, even for a few seconds. (Almost all other rashes do)*
- *Odd shrill or moaning cry*
- *Pale or blotchy skin*

Children show some of these signs:

- *Vomiting*
- *Fever*
- *Back or joint pains*
- *Headache*
- *Off colour and listlessness*
- *Neck stiffness*
- *Dislike of bright light*
- *Drowsiness and confusion*
- *Reddish-purple marks, spots or bruises, as in babies*

What to do

Call the doctor urgently and describe your child's symptoms. Depending on where you live, you will be told either to take your child immediately to hospital or to wait until the doctor has seen the child. If the doctor suspects meningitis or meningococcal septicaemia, your child will be given an intravenous injection of penicillin (or chloramphenicol if your child is allergic to penicillin) before the journey to hospital. The doctor will probably also take a swab from the child's nose and throat to help identify the microorganism that has caused the illness.

Once a diagnosis of meningococcal meningitis has been confirmed by the hospital, tell family, friends and your child's school as soon as possible, especially during term time. The authorities will trace close contacts and offer all household and kissing contacts protective antibiotics, usually in the form of a drug called rifampicin. The incubation period for meningococcal disease is two to ten days.

Treatment

Hospital staff will probably have been alerted by the doctor to expect your child and will start treatment immediately they arrive. Depending on how ill the child is, an intravenous drip will be set up to give antibiotics to kill the bacteria, and possibly steroids to reduce the inflammation and pressure inside the skull. If drugs are needed to stop convulsions, they can be given in the same drip, as well as fluids to keep the child hydrated and analgesics for pain relief.

Your child will have blood tests and almost certainly a lumbar puncture (insertion of a hollow needle between the vertebrae into the spinal canal to draw off a small quantity of cerebrospinal fluid) to confirm the diagnosis.

It may be a few days before your child's condition starts to improve. In the meantime, they may need intensive care, with their breathing and heart supported.

Outlook

Although three-quarters of children recover completely from bacterial meningitis, some are left with permanent handicaps such as deafness and brain damage, and in one child in ten the disease is fatal. There may also be temporary damage to the nervous system, which usually clears up within a month.

Children should have a hearing check after recovery. Short-term memory may be temporarily lost, so some skills, such as potty training, may have to be taught again.

Almost all babies and children make a full recovery from viral meningitis, with no after effects.

Vaccination

Babies are offered vaccination against the bacterium Hib (*Haemophilus influenzae* B) as part of the routine immunizations, but this does not protect them against any other forms of meningitis. There is no vaccine yet against group B meningitis although trials are under way. The vaccine against group C meningitis is not effective for babies under 18 months and effects are short-lived in older children. It may be used to protect children and adults in an outbreak of group C meningitis in a school or college.

Who can help?

For organizations and agencies offering help and support see the Directory.

Complementary treatment

Complementary treatment supports orthodox treatment, particularly during the convalescent stage. In the West **Chinese herbalism** treats during recovery with cooling and then tonifying herbs. The related therapies, **tai chi**, **chi kung** and **acupuncture** can be helpful during convalescence. **Homeopathy** offers specific remedies when meningitis is suspected, to be given to the infant or child while waiting for medical help. The remedies should be administered every five minutes until the doctor arrives: Bryonia 30c (*Bryonia alba*, white bryony) when the infant or child is in great pain, unusually quiet and unable to look into light; Aconite 30c (*Aconitum napellus*, blue aconite) when the child is restless, panicky and thirsty and the skin feels hot to the touch; Arnica 30c (*Arnica montana* leopard's bane) when symptoms occur following a head injury; and Belladonna 30c (*Atropa belladonna*, deadly nightshade) when the infant or child makes unusual noises and movements and the pupils are dilated and staring.

SEE ALSO HIB (PAGE 94)

EPILEPSY

What is it?

Epilepsy includes a number of diseases in which the electrical activity of groups of brain cells temporarily gets out of control and interferes with normal brain function, leading to a seizure. There are many possible causes, including infection, head injury or birth trauma, but in many people the cause is unknown. Flickering or flashing lights, or certain visually perceived patterns such as stripes can provoke a seizure in a small number of susceptible people (photosensitive epilepsy).

Of the four main types of epilepsy, the two most common are absence epilepsy, once known as petit mal, and generalized tonic-clonic epilepsy, once known as grand mal. In the former the seizure is a brief loss of conscious awareness; in the latter seizures involve full loss of consciousness. This can be serious but is not life-threatening; the child usually regains consciousness after a few minutes. A seizure that lasts more than five minutes or is followed immediately by another is more serious and requires urgent medical attention. In a seizure the child may show one or more of the symptoms listed below, depending on the type of epilepsy.

You may notice

- *Moments of blankness lasting a few seconds, during which the child may blink rapidly*
- *Suddenly feeling unwell and/or dizzy. The muscles may twitch, they may be unaware of their surroundings or complain of blurred vision*
- *The child may lose consciousness and fall down. The body becomes rigid (tonic) and may jerk rhythmically (clonic). The child may wet themself and dribble. After a minute or two the body relaxes and the child comes to but is confused and may be irritable or feel very sleepy*
- *The child appears perfectly well between seizures*

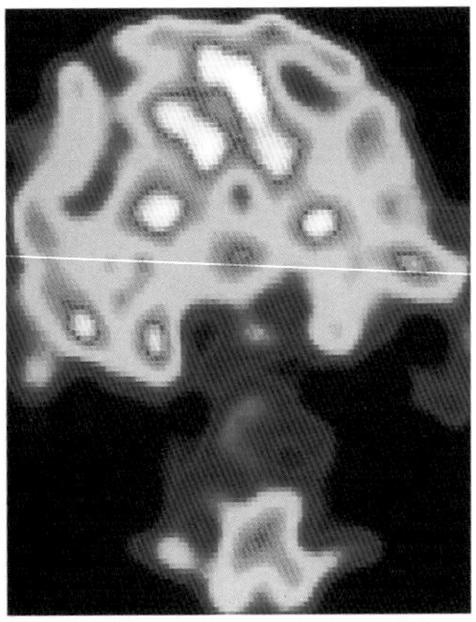

This is a brain scan of a person in the middle of an epileptic seizure. The yellow areas are those parts of the brain with high level activity. A seizure occurs when normally smooth electrical signals between the brain's neurons become disordered. During the seizure the child may lose consciousness, move uncontrollably or behave in an odd manner.

What to do

If the child has a seizure and loses consciousness, clear a space and lay them on their side with their head on something soft. Don't hold them down or give drinks. Loosen any tight clothing, and remain with your child. Once their body relaxes, lay the child in the recovery position (see page 356). Check that they are breathing. If your child is still unconscious after five minutes or another fit occurs, call the emergency services.

Diagnosis and treatment

Children with suspected epilepsy should be seen by a paediatrician. Anticonvulsant drugs taken regularly normally control seizures, but it may take a while to get the correct medication in the most suitable dosage for the child. For a few people whose epilepsy is caused by scarred brain tissue surgery may be an option, although it is not always successful. A new procedure called vagal nerve stimulation uses a tiny implant to interfere with electrical messages sent by the vagus nerve. It is used in children whose epilepsy is not controlled by medication and who, for some reason, are not suitable for surgery.

Coping with epilepsy

Don't overprotect a child with epilepsy. They need the same protection from danger all children need, plus a few added measures, such as forewarning a swimming instructor of their condition. Children with photosensitive epilepsy should sit well away from television screens. It may help if they cover one eye while watching. Special TV and VDU screens are available that minimize effects that can trigger a seizure.

Who can help?

For organizations offering help and support see the Directory.

Complementary treatment

Many herbs used by the **Western herbalist** have traditionally been given to treat epilepsy, and now are often used with orthodox drugs. **Nutritional therapists** report that epilepsy has been linked with poisoning, for example by pesticides, to food allergy and nutritional deficiencies such as magnesium. **Aromatherapy massage** has been found to reduce the incidence and severity of the seizures. **Chinese herbalism** may be an alternative to orthodox drugs, with herbs taken daily for up to one year. **Tai chi**, **chi kung** and **acupuncture** may be used in conjunction or on their own.

Febrile Convulsions

What is it?

Convulsions (fits or seizures) occur when there is a sudden increase in the strength of electrical impulses in the brain, which disrupts the surrounding nerve cells and sends uncontrolled signals throughout the body, which in some cases cause the muscles to twitch and jerk.

Convulsions in children aged between six months and five years are often brought on by a sharp rise in temperature. These fever fits, or febrile convulsions, are very common, and about a third of children who have had one febrile convulsion can be expected to have another. The tendency for fever fits runs in some families.

Fits that are not caused by a sharp rise in temperature are much less common. When convulsions occur repeatedly without fever, they may be linked to epilepsy.

A convulsion can be frightening but rarely does any harm.

The following signs are most likely in a child aged six months to around five years. The signs may last for only a few seconds or for up to ten minutes.

You may notice

- *The infant or child becomes stiff or rigid*
- *Arms and legs may tremble or twitch*
- *The eyes may roll up, fix or squint*
- *The child stops responding to you and loses consciousness.*
- *They may turn blue or become pale and limp*

What to do

Stay with your child. If you can, lay them face down over your knee, or on the ground with the head resting on something soft and turned to one side. Don't use force to turn the head.

Move toys and furniture out of reach, but don't try to put anything between the child's teeth or give anything to eat or drink. If they are sick, clear out the mouth with your finger. Gently try to remove any clothes that will come off easily. If the room is heated, turn off the heating and open a window or door to cool the air in the room

Your child will probably regain consciousness after a few seconds or minutes. Meanwhile, lay them in the recovery position (see page 356), remove any remaining clothes and speak reassuringly. Call a doctor if this is your child's first fit, particularly if it lasts more than five minutes or if it recurs.

Tepid sponging is recommended by some, but usually causes shivering, which raises the temperature, or cools the body only for a few minutes and often distresses the child. Once the child is fully conscious give them paracetamol and a small drink.

Treatment

Your doctor or the hospital staff will be able to control a fit that lasts more than a few minutes by giving the child an injection of an anticonvulsant drug. Regular doses of an anticonvulsant drug are not considered protective, but you may be shown how to prevent a fever fit, for example by squeezing an anticonvulsant into the child's rectum at the first signs of a rising temperature.

Children who have brief fever fits almost always grow out of them by the age of four or five, and do not suffer any long-term adverse effects.

Complementary treatment

Osteopathy can help to control febrile convulsions and **Chinese herbalists** prescribe cooling herbs for a child who is known to have fits and runs a temperature; they reduce the tendency and can be given when the child is stressed or overexcited. Ongoing treatment is recommended until the child is cured. For fits with fever, **homeopaths** recommend specific remedies such as Aconite 30c (*Aconitum napellus*, blue aconite) to be given every minute for up to three doses at the first sign of fitting. For other convulsions specific remedies are given every minute for up to ten doses immediately after twitching movements have stopped, and include Zinc 6c (*Zincum metallicum*, zinc) for a child in the pre-rash stage of an infectious illness.

Febrile convulsions in young children are usually caused by a sudden rise in body temperature. Once the convulsion has passed, and only when the child is fully conscious, give children's paracetamol and sips of water. Call the doctor if this is his first fit, or if you are at all worried.

Cerebral Palsy

What is it?

Cerebral palsy is a term that covers a wide range of conditions that affect movement, balance, posture and co-ordination. It is usually present at birth, although it may not become apparent until late in the infant's first year. It occurs because parts of the brain that control the muscles are injured or fail to develop, often before birth, causing individual difficulties such as weakness, clumsiness (see page 122), stiffness or paralysis.

The three main types of cerebral palsy are spastic cerebral palsy, in which the muscles stiffen and contract (shorten) so that the child has difficulty controlling their movements; athetoid cerebral palsy, which affects posture and causes unwanted movements; and ataxic cerebral palsy, which affects the child's co-ordination and balance. Cerebral palsy most often affects the arms and legs, either on one or both sides of the body.

Many children with cerebral palsy are of normal intelligence and attend mainstream schools, but some have a degree of learning disability. Others have unclear speech or a communication difficulty, and some have an additional condition, such as epilepsy (see page 112), a squint (see page 192) or hearing loss.

Cerebral palsy does not get worse, but treatment very much improves the outlook. With enough appropriate support and therapy, the majority of children with cerebral palsy should lead an active and fulfiled life. There is, however, no cure.

You may notice

- *In a young infant there is no single sign that points to a definite diagnosis of cerebral palsy. A cluster of persistent signs such as poor sucking, abnormal reflexes, floppiness or being stiff to handle is more suggestive of the condition*
- *Any circumstances before, during or soon after birth that may have led to brain damage increase cause for concern. These include infection during pregnancy that could have crossed the placenta to the foetus; extreme pre-maturity; asphyxia (lack of oxygen) during birth; a brain haemorrhage or infection such as meningitis in an infant or child*
- *Some children only show signs of cerebral palsy when they are late to crawl and walk*

Treatment

A paediatrician with an interest in cerebral palsy should take overall control of the many facets of the child's care. Physiotherapists will teach exercises to help maintain and improve the child's coordination and control. Others who may become involved include play therapists, orthopaedic surgeons, speech therapists and orthoptists (eye specialists). An early start to treatment improves the chances of success.

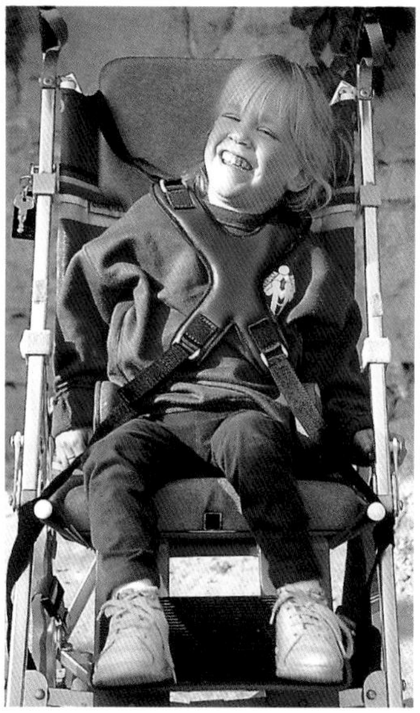

Children with cerebral palsy are frequently of normal or above intelligence, and should be treated in the same way as their peers. Many can be integrated into ordinary schools, although some may need some form of special education. Speech therapy and physiotherapy can often greatly improve their physical disabilities.

Conductive education methods designed to stimulate and awaken the senses and encourage self-awareness in the child are widely used, and are popular with children and parents.

Coping with cerebral palsy

Cerebral palsy places an emotional and financial strain on the whole family, including brothers and sisters. The divorce rate in affected families is high, so it is a good idea for parents to seek help and counselling early if they are having problems.

Who can help?

For organizations offering help and support see the Directory.

Complementary treatment

This condition may best be helped by a combination of treatments, for example **acupuncture**, **Chinese herbalism**, and **homeopathy** or **osteopathy**. Chinese herbalism would be used as an internal supportive treatment to deal with the fundamental imbalances that are seen to have caused the problem in the first place. **Chiropractic** can contribute to overall treatment, for example, by helping to restore as much mobility as possible. **Aromatherapy**, used by an experienced nurse or physiotherapist trained in aromatherapy, can reduce spasm and induce muscle relaxation when used regularly. The technique can be taught to parents so that they may use it at home.

DIZZINESS

What is it?

Dizziness (vertigo) is an unpleasant spinning feeling that may make your child feel sick and unsteady on their feet. It may be caused by the brain being temporarily starved of oxygen, which can happen when a child has not eaten for a while or has been standing still for a long time. If the brain has been starved of oxygen dizziness often occurs before the child faints. Dizziness is also a common response to amusement park rides that involve sudden changes of direction, and to car travel, when it is akin to the motion sickness. Some children can feel dizzy watching a film or video; in others dizziness may be a symptom of anxiety or a panic attack.

Dizziness usually passes off quickly, but if it does not and there is no obvious cause, such as a serious bang on the head, it could be a result of an ear infection. Occasionally the fluid-filled chambers of the inner ear that are concerned with balance can become inflamed as a result of a viral infection known as labyrinthitis.

A few children have repeated attacks of dizziness that do not end in a faint and for which no cause can be found. These attacks are usually harmless and will probably disappear by themselves in time. If dizzy spells are an indication of an emotional problem, which you feel you cannot resolve without professional help, you and your child should discuss the matter with your doctor.

You may notice

- *Your child looks pale*
- *A young child stumbles or falls*
- *Your child may complain of nausea and may vomit*
- *An older child may complain of a spinning sensation*
- *If the dizziness is linked to an ear infection, your child may be in pain or unable to hear on the affected side. There may also be a ringing noise in the ear (tinnitus)*

What to do

If your child has a sudden attack of dizziness, keep them calm and quiet. Sit them down with their head between their knees to boost the flow of oxygen to the brain. Tell them to breathe slowly in and out. If they fainted from hunger, give them a snack and a drink once they have regained consciousness.

If your child has earache or if the dizzy spells come back and there is no obvious cause, consult your doctor. If the doctor diagnoses labyrinthitis your child may be given drugs to control the nausea and vomiting; the dizziness should be better within a week. Antihistamines may help reduce any inflammation and relieve the dizzy spells.

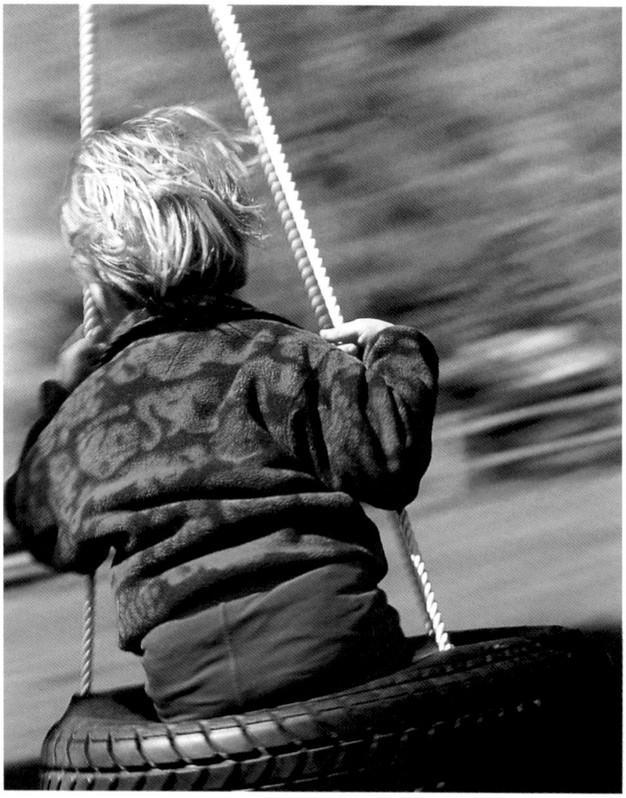

Watch the eyes of a child twirling quickly around on a circular swing and you may suddenly see them jerk from side to side. This is a sure sign that the child is no longer coordinating visual information and is feeling dizzy. The quickest way to experience this type of vertigo is to spin in one direction while moving the head in another direction. The cure is to stop spinning!

Complementary Treatment

The **chiropractor** will usually look for signs of tension in the neck and treat with manipulation. **Chinese herbalists** view this condition as a deficiency, for example of *chi*, yin or yang, or a stomach problem, and will treat accordingly. **Homeopathy** offers specific remedies to be taken when the attack first occurs. **Aromatherapy** may help if the cause is stress, but depends on whether there is associated pain. **Bach flower remedies** may help if the cause is emotional.

MIGRAINE

What is it?

Migraine is a severe headache that occurs with one or more other symptoms, such as nausea, vomiting, intolerance to light and drowsiness without fever. It is frequently heralded by an aura, or visual disturbance, such as flashing lines or lights in one eye. When the headache comes these warning symptoms usually tend to fade away.

Migraine can occur in children as young as three years, although it is diagnosed more often as children grow older and approach puberty. A quarter of a million children aged between 7 and 15 are affected, and migraine is thought to be the most common form of recurrent headaches in childhood.

Most children who suffer from migraines have a close relative who also gets migraines or regular headaches associated with nausea, and the condition seems to be more common in children who have a tendency to allergy and children who are prone to travel sickness.

The symptoms of migraine in children tend to be more acute than those experienced by adults, and children are often more violently sick than adults. However numbness or tingling of a limb is unusual, and children's migraine attacks may not last as long. In addition many children do not get an aura before a migraine.

The precise nature of what occurs during a migraine is not fully understood, although it is known that people who have migraines release abnormal quantities of the neurotrans mitter serotonin, which dilates certain blood vessels and causes the typical throbbing headache. The most common trigger in children is missed meals. Irregular sleep patterns, such as having a sequence of late nights followed by a lie-in at the weekend, are another common trigger. Foods, including chocolate, dairy foods, citrus fruits, fried and fatty food, pork or seafood, can trigger migraine in children just as they can in adults. Flashing lights may also be a causative factor. A craving for specific foods, especially sweet foods, may be an early indication of susceptibility to migraine.

You may notice

- *In a young child, spells of acute distress when the child is pale and doesn't want to eat*
- *Regular bouts of nausea and vomiting; the child is well between attacks*
- *Heavy head or headache, possibly throbbing and sometimes on one side only*
- *Stomach ache or discomfort*
- *Irritability and tiredness*
- *Possibly giddiness and a desire to avoid bright light*

What to do

Let the child lie down in a dark and quiet room. Wring out a face cloth in cold water and put it on the child's forehead. Offer sips of a sweet drink and give paracetamol.

To help prevent further attacks, check your child's eating and sleeping patterns. Regular meals and bedtimes are helpful. If you can identify a food that triggers an attack, leave it out of your child's diet.

If the above suggestions do not work for your child, or if you have any concerns about the attacks, consult the doctor. A child who has recurring migraines may be helped by a preventive medicine. However the anti-migraine drugs that are prescribed for adults to take when they recognize the early warning signs of an attack are not suitable for children under the age of ten or twelve and lifestyle changes are better than drugs.

Who can help?

For organizations and agencies offering help and support see the Directory.

Complementary treatment

Most of the complementary treatments dealt with in this book will treat migraine, often with success. Where the cause is related to a neck condition **chiropractic** manipulation works well. **Osteopathy** may give similar results. **Nutritional therapists** usually link migraine with poor liver function and food allergy. Special diets and herbs are recommended to improve liver function and help identify problem foods. **Chinese herbalism** is usually successful, although some children need to take herbs for some time, especially if the migraine is related to a food allergy, intolerance or hormonal changes during puberty. **Kinesiology** may be useful for diagnosing the cause and **reflexology** may treat with some success.

Breath Holding

What is it?

Breath holding can occur as a result of shock or pain following an injury, or during a temper tantrum. In the latter case it can be the most alarming expression of frustration in your child's repertoire. While it is upsetting for the parent, particularly if the child holds their breath for so long that they lose consciousness, the child will not come to any harm. If the oxygen level in the body falls so low that the child passes out, all the muscles in the body relax and breathing starts again spontaneously before any damage can occur. Even if the episode ends in a small fit, the child will come to no harm.

Breath holding attacks typically occur in children between 18 months and 4 years who have frenzied tantrums. White attacks are similar, caused by sudden fright or minor injury; this slows the heart long enough to lower oxygen to the brain.

You may notice

- *At a moment of high anger or frustration, the child draws in a deep breath. You wait for the scream but it does not come – the child is silent and their face turns first red, then*
- *blue. Within seconds the child may lose consciousness and start to breathe again. Seconds later the child comes round*
- *Occasionally the child has a brief fit or convulsion. The body becomes rigid, before the child regains consciousness*

What to do

The first time your child has a breath holding attack it will be all you can do to stay calm. Pull the child away from hard-edged furniture and toys so that they won't hurt themselves if they fall. If you can, lay the child on the floor, putting them in the recovery position on their side once the body is relaxed. Don't leave the child alone, but call your doctor immediately, because you must be sure that breath holding is the cause of loss of consciousness.

After the child has recovered and if they are old enough for conversation, talk the event through to see if the child can respond in a different way to whatever made them so angry. Next time you see the signs of frustration mounting, try distraction tactics. If they don't work and the child starts to hold their breath, blow on to their face. If the child does not relax, walk away. Your child is less likely to breath hold without an audience. But keep them in sight.

A child in the middle of a full-scale temper tantrum may hold his breath, and hold it for so long that eventually he loses consciousness. Although this is usually frightening for onlookers, the child will automatically begin to breath normally again and will not have done himself any harm.

Practical tips

- Don't slap or splash cold water on the face of a child about to lose consciousness. It's frightening for them and dangerous if the child passes out
- Use other ways to say 'No'. Divert attention, reach a compromise. Say 'Yes, if ...'. Postpone your decision; show you understand how they are feeling, but stick to your guns. Offer a clear choice of permitted alternatives. Express rules impersonally. 'Sticks stay outdoors', rather than 'Don't bring that stick into the house.'

Complementary treatment

Because **Bach flower remedies** deal with emotional problems they can be very helpful in cases of breath holding if no organic cause is identified. The remedies would be chosen on an individual basis depending on the needs and the temperament of the particular child. For example a child with no confidence would need Larch; a timid, nervous child would need Mimulus; and a child who demanded attention may need Chicory. **Homeopathic** remedies are Chamomilla 6c (*Chamomilla vulgaris*, German chamomile) for breath holding during a temper tantrum, and Arnica 30c (*Arnica montana*, leopard's bane) for breath holding caused by an injury. Other treatments that may prove beneficial include **osteopathy** and **acupuncture**.

Floppy Baby Syndrome

What is it?

There are many reasons why infants may be unusually floppy, or hypotonic. In most cases there is no serious underlying cause; the infant is just slow to mature and is said to have floppy baby syndrome, or benign congenital hypotonia. Medical tests do not show any reason for the floppiness in these infants, although there may be a family pattern of later-than-normal development in sitting, crawling and walking.

The infant is floppy from birth, and the floppiness does not get any worse. After a few months the infant usually starts to improve and will eventually grow out of the limpness, which leaves only signs of slight muscle weakness or extra joint mobility. Premature infants are floppier than full-term infants, but their muscle tone improves as they mature. Some infants with cerebral palsy (see page 114) are limp or stiff to handle, but there are usually other signs pointing to this disorder, such as problems in pregnancy, a difficult birth or generally slow or abnormal development. Signs of cerebral palsy are usually detected at routine development checks.

Most floppy infants eventually develop normal muscle tone, but in some the poor muscle tone is a sign of an underlying physical or mental disorder.

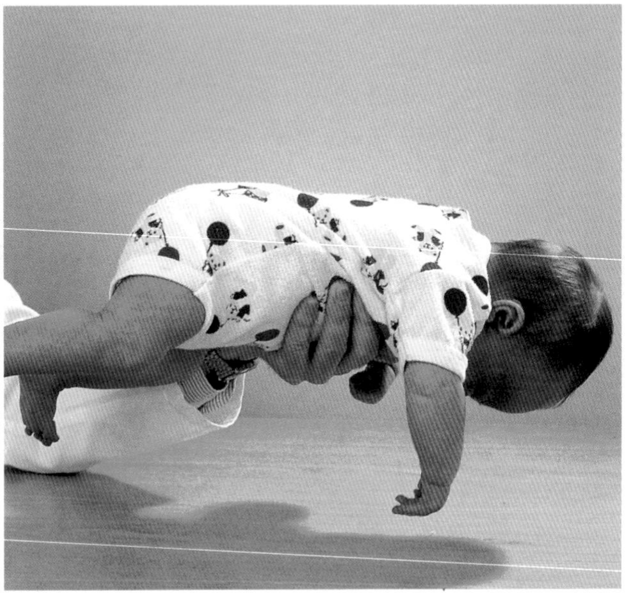

This healthy six-week-old infant is having a routine development check. The doctor is holding her under the abdomen and chest in ventral suspension. In the few weeks since her birth her muscles have already developed enough for her to keep her head in line with her body and to partially bend her hips.

You may notice

- *The foetus may not have shown much movement during pregnancy, although there are many reasons for this*
- *The infant's head control is slow to develop. At one month, an infant's head normally lags as they are pulled into the sitting position, then wobbles in the upright position before dropping forward. By three months there is little or no head lag when the infant is pulled into a sitting position. By six months the infant can sit with a firm head and a straight back as long as they are supported. All these developmental milestones arrive later than normal in a floppy infant*
- *At rest, the infant may lie with arms and legs splayed out flat. The infant tends to lie still without making many movements with their arms or legs*
- *At six months the infant is still unable to sit in an upright position, even with support, and they may not be able to take their weight on their feet*
- *An infant held upright under the arms may slip from your grasp*

What to do

Some mildly floppy infants have simply not had enough opportunity to move around and strengthen their muscles. This may be the case with infants who are frequently left in their car seats. Try to make sure that the infant has plenty of opportunities to move around and kick their arms and legs. This will help to develop muscle tone.

If your health visitor agrees that the infant is floppy, consult the doctor, who may refer you to hospital for tests. You will be taught how to do exercises with your infant to improve their muscle tone. Try not to worry – if the tests show no underlying cause your infant will develop normal muscle tone in time.

Complementary treatment

Chiropractic can be used as part of the overall treatment for this condition by improving mobility and balance. **Acupuncture** can contribute to treatment, perhaps in conjunction with **Chinese herbalism**; the latter would be used as an internal supportive treatment to deal with the fundamental imbalances that may have caused the problem in the first place. **Osteopathy** may also produce beneficial results.

Headache

What is it?

A headache is a continuous pain in the head. Headaches do not occur in the brain (it does not contain sensory nerves) but in the membranes surrounding it, or in the muscles and blood vessels beneath the scalp. Pain starts if any of these are swollen or stretched, and is often in response to a factor such as a stuffy atmosphere or hunger, but sometimes because of anxiety or stress.

A headache without other symptoms, such as fever, usually passes in a few hours and is not serious, especially if it improves after taking paracetamol and getting some loving attention. Headaches are only occasionally a symptom of an underlying disorder, but as young children don't often complain of headache, always take the complaint seriously.

You may notice

- *Young children find it hard to say exactly where a pain is and don't often complain of headache*
- *Older children nurse a sore head or say their head hurts. You have to question them to find out where the pain is felt*

What to do

Try to discover the cause of the headache. Simple triggers include missing a meal, being in a smoky room or in the hot sunshine for a long time, reading or sitting in front of a television or computer screen for a long time. If your child develops frequent headaches after close work take them to the doctor, who should arrange an eye test.

Let your child lie down in a quiet room and draw the curtains. Lay a cool damp face cloth on their forehead. Offer drinks and a snack if a meal has been missed. You can give children's paracetamol if this is appropriate.

Check your child's temperature with a fever strip or thermometer. If their temperature is 38°C /100.4°F or more, take steps to cool the child (see Fever, page 83).

Check for other symptoms, such as a stuffy or runny nose, indicating that the child has a cold. If your child is getting over a cold and the pain is around the top of the nose and eyes, and is worse when they first wake up, the cause may be sinusitis (see page 211).

If your child gets frequent headaches on one side, feels nauseous and vomits but isn't feverish, and wants to be in a dark room it could be migraine.

Consult the doctor if your child's headaches are severe and/or recur frequently, if they are worse on waking, or if your treatment doesn't give relief within four hours and your child is generally unwell.

On their own, both sitting in the sunshine on a hot day and concentrating hard on homework are enough to bring on a headache. This teenager is doing both. The headache caused by intensive study is often related to tense muscles in the neck and face and is exacerbated by worry and stress.

When a headache is an emergency

A headache is occasionally a sign that you must get immediate medical help. Get help:

- If your child has a fever, is vomiting, hides from bright light, has pain bending their chin to their chest and is drowsy or distant. The cause could be meningitis or encephalitis
- If your child has had a recent bang on the head. This can cause a serious head injury. Other signs of head injury are confused, odd behaviour, vomiting or difficulty in breathing

Complementary treatment

Most of the complementary practitioners mentioned in this book will treat headache, often successfully. **Chinese herbalists** often see headache as an exuberance of energy during the growing years, which flares to the head. Once any underlying imbalances have been solved herbs are prescribed to treat any further headaches. **Western herbalists** treat with vasodilators or vasoconstrictors, anti-inflammatory and analgesic herbs, depending on the cause. **Chiropractors** will treat headaches arising from problems in the neck.

CLUMSINESS

What is it?

All children are clumsy at times, especially when they are tired or acquiring a new skill. Many children are clumsy while they are developing particular skills, such as kicking a ball or tying shoelaces, but some children are late to develop a whole range of skills that require coordinated movement. It is not known precisely why one child in ten is notably more clumsy than others, but the reason may lie in a malfunction of the nerve pathways between the body and the brain. Clumsiness, or dyspraxia, is more common in boys than in girls, and also in infants who are born prematurely.

You may notice

- *The child may be late to sit, crawl and walk, although all get there in the end. Some children never crawl; others bottom-shuffle. Older children may dislike walking long distances and prop themselves up if they have to stand still for long*
- *The child may continue to play with manipulative toys such as activity centres at an age when most children have moved on to other toys. Later the child may use their whole hand instead of their thumb and forefinger to pick up objects. Doing up buttons, zips and laces may be a struggle*
- *A toddler or older child may not enjoy activities that need a good sense of balance, such as climbing stairs one foot at a time or riding a bike. They may appear to stumble frequently. Alternatively they may have no sense of danger*
- *They may have difficulties stopping or catching a ball*

Learning to ride a real bicycle is one of the memorable delights of childhood. At two years of age a child can sit astride a wheeled vehicle and push herself along with her feet. By three, children can pedal a tricycle, becoming expert by the age of four. Five-year-olds can usually cope with a two-wheeler with stablilizers, while by the age of six children can experiment on just two wheels.

What to do

First talk to a health or education professional – a health visitor, nursery teacher or doctor – who can view the child's difficulties in context. If they agree that there is a problem, the child will have a detailed assessment by a child development expert, which will probably include a hearing and vision test.

It is never too late to improve dyspraxia, but early treatment brings better results. For difficulties using the hands and feet, the child will have treatment from an occupational therapist. For whole body difficulties, a physiotherapist may help. An individual treatment plan will be drawn up to develop basic skills (coordination, balance, spatial awareness) as well as strategies for particular activities.

Helpful activities for manual skills include cutting, sticking and printing, as well as everyday activities such as dressing, washing, hair brushing and using a knife and fork. Action songs and gymnasium-type activities, such as catching and throwing a beanbag, help to develop body awareness. Playdough helps to tone and develop hand and arm muscles in small children; the activities involved in cooking will help older children.

Look for a nursery school and infant school with plenty of large play equipment, such as climbing frames and large building blocks, to encourage free play. Check what special support is provided at school.

Complementary treatment

Homeopathic remedies include Lycopodium 6c (*Lycopodium clavatum*, wolfsclaw club moss) for a child who is lacking in self-confidence and has poor coordination and who tries to attract attention by acting in an outrageous manner. The remedy should be given four times a day for up to two weeks. **Tai chi** and **chi kung** can help with improving coordination and confidence. The **chiropractor**'s aim will be to help the child's balance by checking the function of the spine and joints. **Aromatherapy** will make the child more aware of their body, teaching them to use the oils and massage them in.

Chronic Fatigue Syndrome

What is it?

Chronic fatigue syndrome – also known as myalgic encephalomyelitis (ME) and post-viral syndrome – is a debilitating illness that is usually preceded by a viral infection such as glandular fever. The condition is uncommon in prepubescent children. The symptoms tend to be more severe and easier to identify in teenagers; girls and high achievers appear to be more more vulnerable than other groups. Symptoms, which can vary from day to day, include extreme physical and mental exhaustion, depression, anxiety, frustration and pains in the muscles and joints. As the symptoms are similar to those in many more common illnesses, the condition can be hard to diagnose, and in fact there is still considerable doubt among members of the medical profession about the cause and precise nature of ME.

There is no single symptom that invariably points to chronic fatigue syndrome, but rather a group of persistent signs that are seen in most children with ME.

You may notice

- *Physical and mental exhaustion, which gets worse following the smallest amount of exertion*
- *Muscle or joint pains*
- *Between bouts of exhaustion the child may seem quite well*
- *Poor concentration and disturbed sleep*
- *Mood swings*
- *Headaches or migraines*
- *Sore throat*
- *Progressive weakness and pain*

What to do

Early diagnosis and correct care are vital. Don't tell your child to pull themself together because they won't be able to – the symptoms are real. Allowing a child to rest when they need to is essential, especially balancing periods of play and exercise with rest. Once the child is active again they should be paced and their activities gradually extended. With the school's agreement your child may be allowed to follow only certain parts of the curriculum.

Diagnosis and treatment

Doctors can only reach a diagnosis after ruling out other causes, such as a lingering infection. Your doctor will check your child's general health, ask about circumstances at school and at home, and may do a blood test for glandular fever. Treatment varies from bed rest to antidepressant drugs and special diets. Some doctors draw up a plan for recovery that is agreed with the whole family, including a gradual return to a normal level of activity.

It is vital to have a sympathetic doctor. If your child's doctor is sceptical or is not interested in the condition, find a more sympathetic doctor or ask for a referral to a specialist.

Mental depression, extreme fatigue and muscular aches and pains are just three of the many debilitating symptoms of chronic fatigue syndrome. Although more and more people in the medical profession now realize the seriousness of the condition and the urgent need for treatment, some are still skeptical of its authenticity. In such cases it is vital to persist in finding a sympathetic doctor or qualified therapist

Outlook

It is difficult to predict the course the condition will take in a given individual. Some children recover quickly, others improve over months or years and most are fully recovered within a year. A small number of children grow steadily worse. After recovery children often relapse following an infection or a period of stress.

Who can help?

For organizations offering help and support see the Directory.

Complementary treatment

Nutritional therapists link this condition with an individual history of antibiotics, vaccinations and environmental pollutants; the charity Action for ME found that nutritional approaches were among the most effective forms of treatment. **Homeopathy** offers treatment according to the personality, temperament and mood of the child concerned (constitutional treatment). China 30c (*China officinalis*, Peruvian bark) can be given every 12 hours for up to 3 days while awaiting treatment.

Muscular Dystrophy

What is it?

Muscular dystrophy is a group of disorders in which there is a slow, progressive breakdown of muscle fibres, leading to weak and wasted muscles. There are over 20 different forms. Some of them are very rare, and affect both boys and girls. Duchenne muscular dystrophy (DMD) is the most common form, and it is also one of the most severe forms. It affects only boys. The muscle wasting is progressive, so boys may be in a wheelchair by the age of ten. Most boys with DMD die in their late teens or early twenties, and the usual cause of death is a respiratory infection.

Most affected boys have inherited the condition, although it arises spontaneously in about one in three of those affected. Girls may be carriers of DMD. It is possible to test female relatives of boys with the disorder to see if they are carriers, and therefore at risk of passing the disorder on to their sons. Many types of muscular dystrophy can be detected in the foetus during pregnancy, either by a technique called chorionic villus sampling, which is carried out at 10–12 weeks, or by amniocentesis at 16–18 weeks.

The protein dystrophin is absent from the muscles of children with DMD and only present in small amounts in a less severe but rarer form of muscular dystrophy called Becker dystrophy. Although there is no cure for disorder at present, an exciting possibility is substituting dystrophin with a similar naturally occurring protein called utrophin, or else using gene therapy to introduce dystrophin into the muscles.

You may notice

- *The child may start walking late, after the age of 18 months. He may walk with a waddling gait and he may stumble more than other toddlers*
- *He may not learn to run*
- *He may have difficulty climbing stairs*
- *By the age of four to six, he may press his hands on his legs to take his body weight as he rises from sitting on the floor*
- *His calf muscles may look unusually swollen*

What to do

Take the child to the doctor. It is likely that the doctor will find a much more common cause for the symptoms than muscular dystrophy. The doctor may refer the child to a paediatrician or a neurologist, an expert in the nervous system. The child may have blood tests to check for high levels of particular chemicals released by degenerating muscle cells. He may also have tests on the electrical activity in his muscles, or he may have a muscle biopsy, in which a small sample of muscle is taken and examined under a microscope for signs of disease.

The aim of treatment is to keep the child active for as long as possible and to allow him and his family to enjoy his life. A sensible diet may help to prevent him becoming overweight, and as his muscles weaken, leg supports or frames can help to keep him mobile.

Families with affected sons need practical and emotional support. Muscle centres providing medical care, advice and emotional support are available. Joining a group can be a good way to gain more information and share feelings.

Who can help?

For organizations and agencies offering help and support see the Directory.

Boys with Duchenne muscular dystrophy – the most common and severe type of this muscle-wasting disease – usually need to use a wheelchair by the time they are eight or nine years of age. However being in a wheelchair does not bar children from enjoying themselves with their friends and members of the family.

Complementary treatment

Chiropractic can be an aid to the overall treatment of this condition. **Nutritional therapists** report links with deficiencies of the nutrients vitamin E and selenium. Some cases of muscular dystrophy have responded to supplements of co-enzyme Q10. Food allergy can sometimes cause symptoms similar to muscular dystrophy. **Chinese herbalism** would be used as an internal supportive treatment to improve the child's condition. **Tai chi** and **chi kung** may also prove beneficial, especially if they are used in conjunction with Chinese herbalism.

Spina Bifida

What is it?

Spina bifida is a defect in the formation of the spinal column that occurs extremely early in pregnancy, around days 14–25. The spine and the spinal cord, which contains the nerves that run between the body and the brain, are formed from a part of the developing embryo called the neural tube. Spina bifida occurs if there is a gap or split in the neural tube.

The cause of spina bifida is not yet known, but there is probably an interaction between inherited and environmental factors. Diet plays a critical role. Folic acid (one of the B vitamins) is known to have a protective effect against the development of spina bifida, and it is now recommended that all women who are trying to become pregnant and for the first three months of a pregnancy take a 400 microgram supplement of folic acid and eat foods that are rich in folates. The dose should be increased to five milligrams (only available on prescription) if the woman has a previous history of a neural tube defect, or if either she or her partner has a family history of neural tube defect.

The severity of spina bifida depends on the size of the split in the neural tube. In the mildest form, spina bifida occulta, there is a fault in one of the vertebrae (the bones of the spine), but there is no damage to the nerves. A dimple or tuft of hair may be visible in the small of the back, but most people with this form have no other symptoms. If a blister-like lump forms over the base of the spine, it is more likely that the spinal cord and nerves are involved. Nerves that control parts of the body below this area do not work properly. There is usually some paralysis and loss of sensation, which leads to problems controlling the bladder and bowels. Hydrocephalus (blockage of the fluid spaces in the brain) is commonly associated with spina bifida.

You may notice

- *Antenatal tests may indicate a problem. A blood test at 16–18 weeks of pregnancy shows the level of a protein called alpha-fetoprotein (AFP), produced by the foetus. A high level could suggest that your dates are wrong, you are carrying two or more foetuses or that there is an abnormality such as spina bifida. If a repeat test confirms a high AFP level, a foetal anomaly scan or amniocentesis is performed*
- *Tests for Down's syndrome may show raised AFP*
- *The ultrasound scan at 16–20 weeks may show spina bifida, particularly if the radiographer is looking for it*
- *At birth the infant may have a small dimple or tuft of hair in the small of the back. There may be a large blister-like lump over the base of the spine if the spinal cord is damaged*

Eating food that provides plenty of natural folates is an important step towards preventing spina bifida. Sprouts and spinach contain most folate per serving, but other vegetables such as green beans, cauliflower and potatoes provide appreciable amounts. Peas, broccoli and cabbage all make a significant contribution, as do oranges and orange juice.

What to do

While you are planning a pregnancy and for the first three months after becoming pregnant make sure that you take a 400 microgram folic acid supplement and eat plenty of foods that are rich in folates, such as green leafy vegetables, potatoes, and other vegetables, including pulses. About half of all breakfast cereals and some breads are fortified with folic acid, and yeast extracts contain folates.

Although spina bifida cannot be cured, and the defects in the formation of the spinal cord cannot be rectified, children with spina bifida benefit from treatment in specialist centres.

Who can help?

For organizations and agencies offering help and support see the Directory.

Complementary treatment

Complementary treatment is concerned with providing support for orthodox treatment. **Aromatherapy** and **relaxation** can help the child accept their body image, and help with the relief of spasm and pain. **Chiropractors** will help with the overall treatment of the condition, from improving mobility to helping balance by checking the function of the spine and joints, and restoring as much mobility as possible within the boundaries of the condition. **Osteopathy** can also offer supportive treatment.

BONES AND JOINTS

At birth, a baby's skeleton contains about 350 bones, but as the baby grows, certain bones fuse into larger units. By adulthood there are 206 bones in the skeleton. The bones not only provides the structure of the body, but parts of it (the skull, the spinal column, the pelvis and the ribcage) protect important and vulnerable organs as well. Bones also make blood cells, a particularly important function in children, most of whose bones have a core of living, red marrow that manufactures red and white blood cells as well as platelets.

When bones begin to form in the foetus, they consist of soft, pliable cartilage. Although they gradually harden during pregnancy, many bones still contain cartilage at birth. The hardening process (ossification) is not complete until the early 20s. Throughout childhood both ends of the long bones in the arms and legs contain a band of cartilage, called a growth plate. Once this cartilage has stopped responding to growth hormone, growth stops. Growth specialists can make use of this fact when examining X-rays of bones in order to assess the amount of time a child still has for growth, Traditionally, an X-ray of the hand and the wrist is used.

The joints

Most joints occur where movement is necessary at a point where two or more bones meet. There are a number of types of joint: ball and socket, as in the shoulder and hip; hinged joints, for example finger joints and the more complicated knee joint; and sliding joints, such as the spinal vertebrae or the bones in the foot between the ankle and the toes. The ends of bone within the joint are covered in super smooth cartilage and are lubricated with a fluid, the whole kept in place by a sealed capsule. Ligaments hold the bones together while at the same time allowing movement.

The proportions of the human skeleton change dramatically as the foetus grows and the child matures. The newborn's head is large relative to the body, with the midpoint at the navel. As the child grows the midpoint shifts downwards: in the adult it occurs around the genitals.

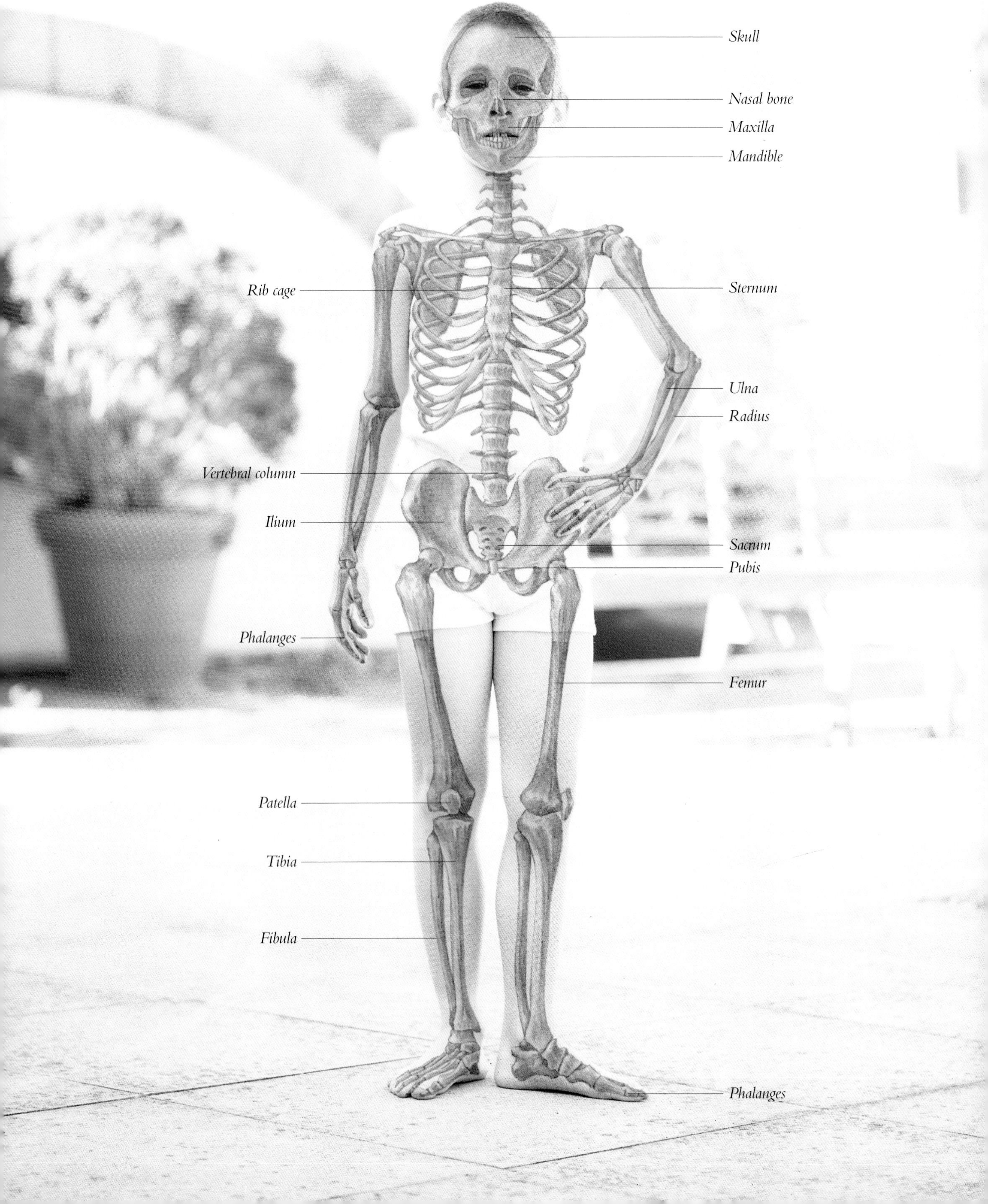
Skull
Nasal bone
Maxilla
Mandible
Rib cage
Sternum
Ulna
Radius
Vertebral column
Ilium
Sacrum
Pubis
Phalanges
Femur
Patella
Tibia
Fibula
Phalanges

Diagnosis

Serious bone and joint disorders are rare in childhood, although minor injuries affecting a bone or joint are common. If bones or joints in the legs are involved, the most obvious sign that something is wrong is often a limp, with or without pain. A child with a sudden limp for which there is no obvious cause should be seen by a doctor. If the child has persistent pain or swelling in any of the joints the cause should also be investigated by a doctor.

Signs	What could be wrong
Child limps after they have just got out of a car seat or high chair	The safety straps around the hips may be too tight. Loosen them a little
One foot or ankle (or hand or wrist) is more tender and swollen than the other	Could be a sprain or strain. Lay a cold face cloth on the affected area and rest it
Acute pain and swelling of the leg, or a lopsided look plus reluctance to bear weight	A broken bone is a possibility. Keep the leg still and call an ambulance
Limping in a toddler who has just started to walk	Congenital dislocation of the hip is occasionally first noticed in a toddler
Pain on one side only; may follow a cold or cough	Irritable hip is a possibility
Knee looks swollen and child has a fever, possibly a rash and swollen glands, followed by pain in the leg joints	Arthritis is a possibility. Contact the doctor, who may refer the child to hospital for tests
Pain around the hip, groin or possibly knee	Perthes' disease is possible. X-rays can confirm this
Tender swelling on the front of the knee in active child of school age or early adolescence	Osgood Schlatter disease. This may affect one or both knees
Child is unwell, with a fever and a tender, swollen limb	Osteomyelitis is a possibility
Swollen ankles, wrists, rash over the buttocks and the backs of the legs, and abdominal pain in an otherwise well child without fever	Allergic (anaphylactoid) purpura is likely

ARTHRITIS

What is it?

Over 14,000 children in the United Kingdom suffer from persistent disabling arthritis. The cause is not known, but it is likely that children are born with a tendency to the disease and that it is triggered by some environmental factor, possibly by an infection.

Children who suffer from arthritis have a much better outlook than adults with the disease. The most common form of arthritis in children is juvenile chronic arthritis, which affects more girls than boys. Toddlers are most vulnerable to a form of arthritis that makes them generally unwell and then causes aching and pain and swelling in the joints that bear their weight, especially the hips, knees and ankles.

Any lasting and unexplained joint pain in a child must be investigated. In some children the eyes are affected and a few children are left with permanent stiffness or disability.

You may notice

- *The child limps or refuses to walk or move part of the body. A joint, often one of the knees, looks swollen. Other joints may become painful, especially the other knee or an ankle*
- *A young child may develop a fluctuating fever. The temperature may be normal in the morning, but rises during the day to reach a peak of 39.4°C/103°F by the late afternoon or early evening. When the fever peaks you may see a red, blotchy rash. The child's glands swell and their arms and legs ache. The child may be very unwell, and this condition can last for several weeks*

Treatment

See your doctor, who will refer you to a paediatrician or a children's orthopaedic specialist. If arthritis is diagnosed the child will need regular physiotherapy to keep the joints mobile, and may need to wear splints on the affected joints. Depending on the severity of their condition, the child will be given anti-inflammatory and possibly steroid drugs. You will be shown exercises to do with your child. A few children require surgery to replace damaged joints. Arthritis is unlikely to spread beyond the affected joints in the first three months.

Outlook

Most children with juvenile chronic arthritis recover gradually, with occasional flare-ups, especially when they are overtired or have an infection. Recovery may take months or years, and in some children one or two of the joints may stay permanently stiff. However there is a one-in-two chance of a complete recovery within five years.

Treatment for young children with juvenile chronic arthritis may involve hydrotherapy. Juvenile chronic arthritis is classified as pauciarticular, affecting fewer than five joints; polyarticular, affecting five joints or more; or systemic, in which the child is generally unwell and many joints are affected.

Coping with arthritis

There are a number of things that you can do to help your child. A sheet of board placed under your child's mattress will give firm support. To make exercise more fun, encourage your child to do their exercises in a warm bath, and to use a tricycle or pedal car. If your child doesn't want to eat, give them a high-energy supplement and extra vitamins. Some children with arthritis need regular eye checks with an ophthalmologist to rule out eye disease.

Who can help?

For organizations who can provide advice and support for families, see the Directory.

Complementary Treatment

Chiropractic can help by improving mobility. **Chinese herbalism** has been very successful with this condition, and if it cannot be cured it can be successfully managed to reduce pain, increase mobility and slow or stop degeneration. The best results are achieved when herbalism is combined with **acupuncture. Western herbalism** uses anti-inflammatory, circulatory or analgesic herbs. **Aromatherapy** oils used in compresses, in bath water or during **massage** can relieve pain, improve appetite and lift depression, which is often associated with this disease. The **osteopath** can treat successfully if the disease is caused by an allergy.

Warning: Care is needed during massage, which is best carried out by a medically trained therapist.

CONGENITAL DISLOCATION OF THE HIPS

What is it?

Congenital dislocation of the hips (CDH), which in its mild form is known as unstable hips and colloquially as 'clicky hips', occurs when the hollow of the pelvis in which the head of the thigh bone sits is so shallow that the thigh can dislocate very easily. The thigh is normally held in place in this ball-and-socket-type joint by a criss-cross of ligaments, but some children are born with loose ligaments. Girls are more susceptible than boys, as are breech babies, babies who had very little room for kicking in the uterus, babies born post mature and babies in a family where other people have CDH. If CDH is detected early it can be treated successfully, but if it is only detected when a child starts to walk with a limp, it is more difficult to treat and surgery may be needed.

Clinical hip instability

In a newborn infant with CDH there is nothing to see. This is why the paediatrician who checks the infant immediately after birth always does a special hip test, opening the legs wide and then bending and unbending them. The paediatrician is feeling for a 'clunk' that indicates that one or both thigh bones are moving in or out of their sockets in the pelvis. This is called clinical hip instability. The baby feels no pain or discomfort, and four times out of five grows out of the problem without treatment.

Babies born with hip instability are often checked with an ultrasound scan when they are two weeks old. The hip test is repeated at six weeks, and the baby is checked again between six and nine months. Some babies are born with hips that appear normal in the test, but they do not develop properly. This is why some doctors now prefer to call this condition developmental dysplasia of the hip (DDH). You may be the first to notice signs, which include those listed below.

You may notice

- *One leg looks slightly shorter than the other leg*
- *There are extra skin creases on one thigh or buttock*
- *At a nappy change, when the infant has their legs apart and knees bent, one hip may not open as much as the other*
- *Very occasionally, dislocated hips are only noticed when the infant starts to walk, often with a limp and walking on their toes on the affected side*

What to do

If you suspect a congenital dislocation, or have a close relative with CDH, ask to see a children's orthopaedic surgeon or a pediatrician. Explain any family history of the condition. Your infant may be diagnosed with hip instability but the specialist may not recommend any treatment. A wait-and-see approach is sensible, because most loose hip joints get better on their own. Meanwhile, carrying a baby in a sling puts the hips in the best position. Letting your infant sleep on their tummy is also helpful, but because of the possible link with sudden infant death syndrome you must ask a doctor's advice about this first.

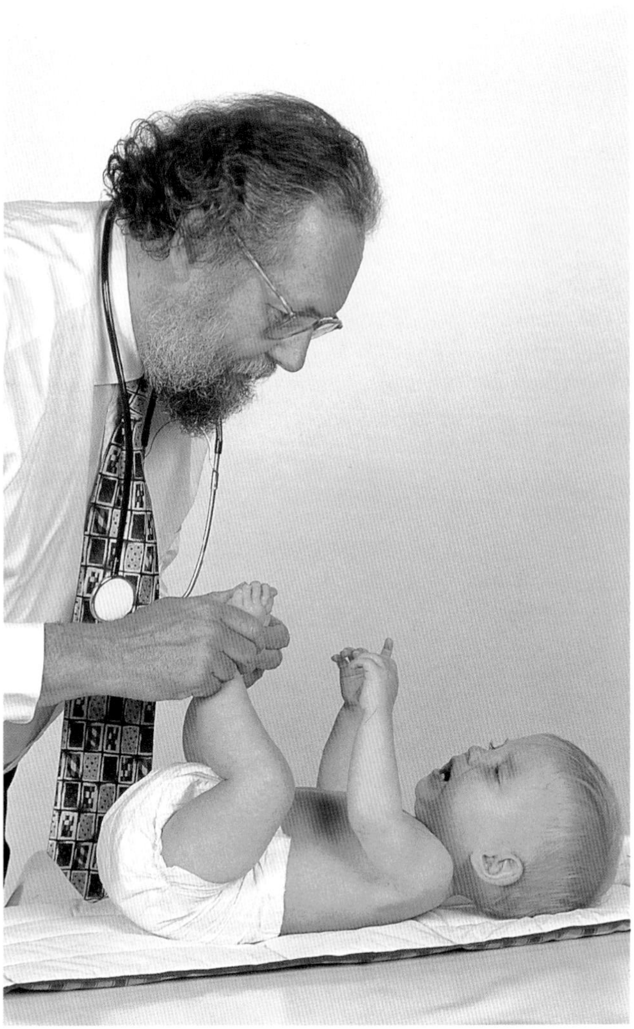

Throughout the baby's first year the doctor – or in some cases the health visitor – will examine him periodically to check his physical development. An important part of the these examinations is ensuring that the baby's legs and hips are functioning normally. The doctor checks for any dislocation of the hips by holding the legs gently by the knees, bending them and turning them outwards at the hip.

If the hip joints do not recover naturally, the diagnosis will usually be checked with an ultrasound scan and X-rays, and treatment tailored to your infant's needs. Your infant may need to wear a harness or a fixed splint, both of which are made to hold the legs apart with the hips and knees bent.

Harnesses and splints

A Pavlik harness is a soft webbing harness with straps and Velcro fastenings. It allows the baby to kick freely, in the hope that this will help deepen the socket. the baby wears the harness night and day, but it is usually adjusted weekly in hospital. A von Rosen splint, made of well-padded metal, holds the legs apart in a fixed position.

If your infant is in a splint, you may not be allowed to bath them. Wash your infant twice a day using cotton wool and water or baby lotion. Change nappies frequently to keep the harness hygienic. If the harness gets smelly, sponge it with disinfectant (avoiding skin contact) or a deodorizer. Tie-front vests can be slipped on under the harness, but other clothes go on top, so they may need to be a size too big.

If splinting doesn't work, your infant may have to wear a plaster cast, and sometimes they may have to spend time in traction in hospital first to reduce the chance of complications developing. During traction some surgeons allow babies home on a platform with an overhead frame. Following traction the baby has an operation under general anaesthetic to apply the plaster cast.

Surgery

Some babies need surgery before the plaster cast is applied. A tenotomy lengthens a tendon in the hip joint; open reduction allows the head of the thigh bone to be correctly positioned; and in femoral osteotomy the thigh bone is broken, turned and fixed into position with plates, which are removed after about a year.

Coping with a baby in a plaster cast

Life with a baby in a plaster cast is seriously disrupted. the baby is extremely heavy and hard to cuddle. Infants normally adapt to this better than their mothers. Keeping the plaster clean is expensive and time-consuming. There must be a good-sized hole in the nappy area. The plaster here should be covered with a wipeable waterproof tape. If the plaster becomes smelly or dirty, wipe it with baby cleansing solution or even shoe whitener.

During the summer a baby in plaster needs cooling with a fan. It is difficult to warm up a baby in plaster who becomes chilled, so in winter, keep your infant warm by covering their legs with long socks. To feed a baby in plaster, place them on a bean bag or wedge them securely on a seat with pillows. Wind your infant carefully, and feed little and often to reduce the risk of vomiting.

Playing with a baby in a plaster cast is not easy, but for a brief water and sand play session you can cover the plaster with a large plastic bag and sleek.

Who can help?

There may be a support group for parents of children with lower limb abnormalities in or near your area. See the Directory for details.

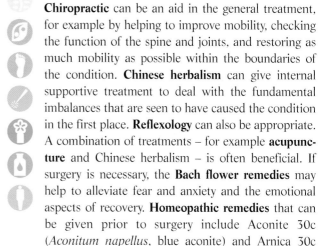

Complementary treatment

Chiropractic can be an aid in the general treatment, for example by helping to improve mobility, checking the function of the spine and joints, and restoring as much mobility as possible within the boundaries of the condition. **Chinese herbalism** can give internal supportive treatment to deal with the fundamental imbalances that are seen to have caused the condition in the first place. **Reflexology** can also be appropriate. A combination of treatments – for example **acupuncture** and Chinese herbalism – is often beneficial. If surgery is necessary, the **Bach flower remedies** may help to alleviate fear and anxiety and the emotional aspects of recovery. **Homeopathic remedies** that can be given prior to surgery include Aconite 30c (*Aconitum napellus*, blue aconite) and Arnica 30c (*Arnica montana*, leopard's bane) to relieve pain and prevent infection. Arnica should be followed by the remedy Staphisagria 6c (*Delphinium staphisagria*, stavesacre). These remedies should be given every half hour for up to ten doses. **Osteopathy** is often appropriate following surgery.

Perthes' Disease

What is it?

Perthes' disease affects the upper end of the thigh bone. In children, the long bones (in the arms and legs) have a growing area near the end. In Perthes' disease, the growing area of the thigh bone softens and, without treatment, it can be left permanently deformed. Perthes' disease can eventually lead to osteoarthritis in adult life. Usually only one thigh bone is affected, but a few children develop Perthes' disease in both of their legs. The cause is not understood, but at some time the blood supply to the bone has been restricted temporarily, and during this time the bone may have become deformed. Perthes' disease occurs in both girls and boys, but it is more common in boys, especially those who are between the ages of two and ten.

You may notice

- *The child may limp. This may start so gradually that you hardly notice it*
- *Sometimes the child has pain around the hip and groin area, or in the knee*

What to do

Take the child to the doctor. Perthes' disease is not very common and it is much more likely that the child has a condition such as irritable hip (see page 135) or a straightforward sprain. Encourage the child to rest and take the weight off their legs until a diagnosis has been made.

The doctor will refer the child to an orthopaedic specialist. The child's hips and legs may be X-rayed. Perthes' disease shows as a fragmentation and then shrinking of the head of the thigh bone. The younger the child is at diagnosis, the more likely they are to recover completely.

Treatment

Treatment depends on the child's individual case. Children under five may not even need treatment. Younger children with a mild form of the disease may not be allowed to run, jump or take part in PE at school, but do not need any other treatment. More severely affected children may need the weight taken off the growing head of the thigh bone, and this may mean that the child has to spend time in bed, possibly with the affected leg in plaster or in traction, or they may have to have the leg splinted or use crutches to protect the hip and thigh bone until the disease clears up on its own. This usually takes two to three years. Occasionally children need surgery on the hip joint, and sometimes they may need to have their leg in plaster for several weeks afterwards.

The aim of treatment in Perthes' disease is to take the weight off the head of the thigh bone while it is softened. As the blood supply naturally returns, fresh bone gradually grows and ossifies.

Coping with Perthes' disease

Encourage craft and early learning activities if your child can't be as active as their friends. Transporting a child with their leg in immobilizing plaster is a major challenge. You will need a suitable pushchair and cushions to wedge the child into a comfortable position, and you may need to hire a double buggy. Ask if your hospital operates a loan scheme.

Who can help?

For organizations offering help with mobility, information and support see the Directory.

Complementary treatment

Chiropractic can be an aid in the general treatment of the condition, for example by helping to improve mobility, checking the function of the spine and joints, and restoring as much mobility as possible within the boundaries of the condition. **Relaxation** is useful to counter irritability, pain and discomfort when the child is immobilized. **Acupuncture** can be very beneficial and supportive to orthodox treatment. A combination of treatments – for example acupuncture and **Chinese herbalism** or **osteopathy** – is often beneficial. For complementary treatments when surgery is indicated, see page 129.

Osteomyelitis

What is it?

Osteomyelitis is an infection of the bone. It is a rare condition which sometimes occurs in newborn babies who have had septicaemia (blood poisoning), but it is most common in children over two years of age who have had a minor injury or infection. It is more common in boys than it is in girls.

The disease is caused by bacteria, usually staphylococci or streptococci, that are carried in the bloodstream from the original source of the infection to the bone. The source may be something like a graze or boil, or even an infected tooth or infected tonsils. The bacteria can lie dormant for weeks before the bone infection starts, so parents may not connect the two events. In the newborn infant an infection may enter the body through the throat or the nose, the umbilical cord or the digestive system, and cause septicaemia. Under such circumstances the baby will become seriously ill before developing osteomyelitis.

Acute osteomyelitis usually affects one of the long bones in the leg or, less often, the arm. The part affected is near the growing area at the end of the bone.

You may notice

- *The child may be off-colour following an injury or accident*
- *The child develops a fever over 24 to 48 hours, and is clearly unwell, flushed and restless*
- *The child shields the affected limb or winces if you touch or squeeze it. The pain becomes markedly worse over a period of a few days, and the child will not move their arm or their leg*
- *There is slight swelling over the bone, which becomes obvious and severe*
- *The skin around the swelling may look red*
- *The child may limp if a leg is affected*

What to do

Contact the doctor immediately – prompt action increases the child's chances of a complete recovery. The doctor will check for other reasons for the fever, and will feel the limbs for any swelling and tenderness. If the doctor suspects osteomyelitis, they will refer the child to a hospital for blood tests, X-rays and bone scans. These tests will confirm the doctor's diagnosis and will identify the bacterium that is responsible for causing the infection.

Treatment

The affected limb will be immobilized with a splint, and the child will be given high doses of intravenous antibiotics to eliminate the infection. The high doses may continue for several weeks in very young children because it is important that the the infection is cleared completely. Occasionally an operation may be required to drain pus from the bone or tissues.

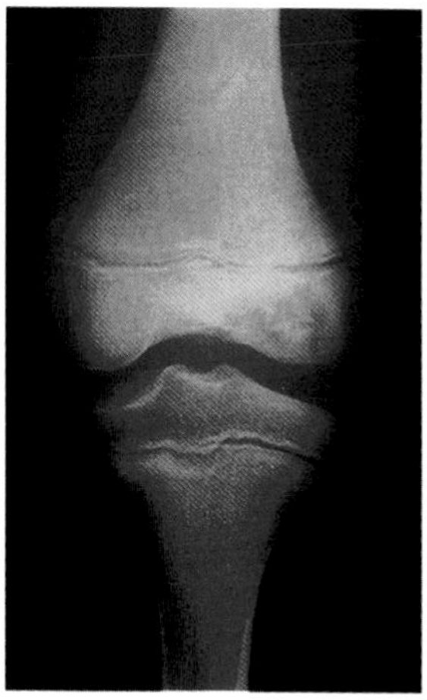

The coloured X-ray is of a lower femur (top, thicker bone) affected by osteomyelitis. The affected area can be seen centre right as a rounded shadow. Osteomyelitis can affect any bone, and is more common in children. The bacterium causing the condition is Staphylococcus aureus, *which is carried to the bone in the bloodstream. It can enter the body via a wound or an infection elsewhere in the body. The lower bone shown here is the tibia.*

Once the child starts to recover, they can take antibiotics by mouth, and they may be allowed to go home. They must continue taking the antibiotics until the X-rays, blood counts (to monitor the level of the infection) and the child's behaviour show that the child has recovered fully. This may take as long as six weeks. Once the bone has healed, it should continue to grow properly.

After a long course of the high-dose antibiotics that are needed to treat acute osteomyelitis a child may need building up for months, and perhaps a year, afterwards. Young children usually have regular check-ups to monitor the affected bone and make sure that it is growing correctly.

Complementary Treatment

Complementary treatment should be supportive of orthodox treatment. **Acupuncture** is one of the first choices in traditional Chinese medicine. **Chinese herbalism** would be used as an internal supportive treatment, dealing with the fundamental imbalances. **Homeopathy** offers Gunpowder 6c (a mixture of saltpetre, sulphur and charcoal) every two hours for up to 12 doses while waiting for orthodox treatment. **Chiropractic** can be an aid in the general treatment of the condition. If surgery is necessary, the **Bach flower remedies** may help to alleviate fear and anxiety and the emotional aspects of recovery. For other complementary treatments that can be helpful prior to and following surgery, see page 129.

SCOLIOSIS

What is it?

A slight curve to the spine is common. Scoliosis is a noticeable curvature of the spine, with a twist to one side. Depending on which part of the spine is involved, the ribcage may be twisted around. A few babies are born with this spinal twist, usually because of the way they lay in the uterus. It may first become noticeable when a toddler starts to walk. Children suffering from other illnesses that affect the muscles or nerves may develop a spinal curve as a secondary effect. However scoliosis develops most commonly in girls in the early teen years and gets worse during the rapid growth spurt.

Many babies and young children grow out of scoliosis naturally, but if a severe case is left untreated a characteristic hump develops on one side of the back. In the most severe cases the heart and lungs may not function properly and affected children may become breathless when they take exercise. Later in life scoliosis may become painful.

You may notice

- *An infant's spine does not look straight, and they may always lie on one preferred side*
- *A toddler's spine appears curved when you look at it from the back*
- *The curve of the spine does not improve when the child is sitting down*
- *When the child bends forwards to touch their toes a bulge appears on one side of the back*
- *One shoulder may look higher than the other*

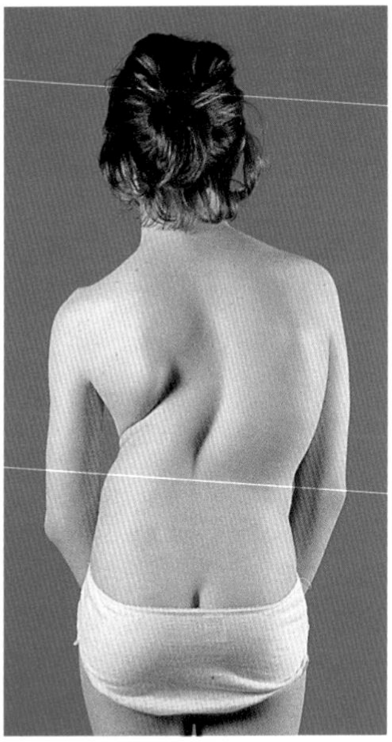

Some children are born with a skeletal asymmetry. Early referral to an orthopaedic specialist is vital, although children with a mild curve that does not deteriorate may need no treatment. The adolescent girl shown here has severe scoliosis. In most children the cause of the disease is unknown.

What to do

If you notice a curve in a newborn baby's spine, ask the hospital paediatrician or the midwife to look at it. Some babies develop the curve because they were squashed in the uterus, but they grow out of it. Nine times out of ten the baby needs no treatment, but they will be checked regularly to make sure that the curve is straightening out.

To check an older child for yourself, ask the child to stand evenly on both feet. Then ask them to bend forwards to touch their toes. If you can still see a noticeable curve in the spine or if one side of the back is noticeably higher than the other, take the child to the doctor. The doctor may monitor the child or refer them to a centre specializing in scoliosis. At first the child will probably be monitored to see if the curve is deteriorating or improving. If the curve is relatively slight, the child could have physiotherapy to improve their posture and tone up their spinal muscles. Swimming is an alternative, and is widely advised as an excellent form of exercise for toning up.

The child may have to wear a spinal brace. If the curvature is more severe, the child may need an operation to fuse and straighten the curving section of the spine. This is often done by inserting a metal rod. Occasionally children may have traction applied to their spine and must then wear a plaster jacket for two to three months afterwards.

Who can help?

For organizations and agencies that can provide more information, see the Directory .

Complementary Treatment

Chiropractors often carry out spinal checks for parents worried about this condition in their children, and scoliosis is often picked up by the chiropractor when a child is brought for an unrelated complaint. The child will be monitored and advice will be given on appropriate exercises and treatment, and/or referred to an orthopaedic specialist if necessary. **Chinese herbalism**, **acupuncture** and **tai chi** may be of benefit; **kinesiology** may help to diagnose the condition. For complementary treatments when surgery is indicated, see page 129.

KNOCK KNEES AND BOW LEGS

What are they?

Knock knees are especially common in children between the ages of two and seven, and are usually a part of normal development. Bow legs are extremely common in babies and toddlers who have just started to walk, and almost all grow out of them naturally by around the age of three.

Knock Knees

Knock knees are probably caused by a laxity in the ligaments that support the inside of the knee joints. They tend to be much more obvious in children who are seriously overweight. Many children have grown out of knock knees by the time they start school, and in almost all children the legs will have straightened out by the age of eight or nine.

You may notice

- *When the child stands with their feet placed evenly on the ground, the knees meet but the feet are splayed well apart*

What to do

You do not usually need to do anything, because the knock knees will correct themselves naturally in time. Children with a very wide separation of the feet – more than 10 cm/3 inches – or with just one bent knee may need an X-ray to establish the cause. If a child's feet continue to splay out at the age of ten, treatment may be needed. This is usually a small operation to alter the way the leg is growing.

Bow Legs

Bow legs have nothing at all to do with bulky nappies, early walking or being allowed to take the weight on the feet before the bones are strong enough to cope. In fact they are a normal part of development. Bow legs are caused by a bending and slight twisting of the shin bone, and it is possible that babies who sleep on their front with the feet turned inwards exacerbate the problem. Some plump toddlers with well-rounded calves appear to be bow legged but actually have straight legs.

Children with rickets, which is usually caused by a deficiency of vitamin D in the diet, may develop either knock knees or bow legs. However this condition is now rare in most Western countries and tends to affect mainly children with dark skin who eat an unsupplemented vegan diet.

You may notice

- *When a child is standing their ankles come close to meeting, but there is an oval space between the legs, which is widest at the knees*

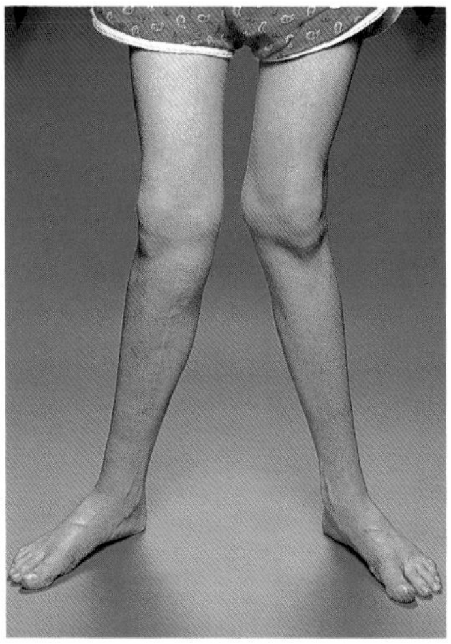

Many young children's feet splay naturally, and knock knees are a feature of normal development that requires no more than a review by the doctor from time to time. Only very occasionally do children whose feet splay out widely at the age of ten (as illustrated here) require surgery to realign the bones.

What to do

Encourage the child to sleep on their back if they don't do so already. If the bow legs are still obvious when the child has their preschool medical and you are worried about them, mention it to the doctor. An X-ray may be needed to establish the cause. Very occasionally children with severely bowed legs may need to wear special boots and splints at night that force the feet to splay outwards, or they may have an operation to alter growth or realign the shin bone.

Complementary Treatment

Chiropractic can be an aid in the general treatment of these conditions, for example by helping to improve mobility and checking the function of the spine and joints. A combination of treatments – for example **acupuncture** and **osteopathy** – is often beneficial. **Nutritional therapy** may be helpful if the child has a deficiency of calcium and vitamin D. **Kinesiology** may prove helpful, and **reflexology** can be beneficial for bow legs. **Chinese herbalism** would be used as an internal supportive treatment, dealing with the fundamental imbalances that are seen to have caused these conditions in the first place.

Osgood Schlatter Disease

What is it?

Osgood Schlatter disease typically affects active children in the years of middle childhood and early adolescence. It is a relatively common cause of pain at the front of the knee, and is more common in boys than in girls. The bony lump known as the tibial tuberosity at the knee end of the tibia (the larger of the two bones in the lower leg, also called the shinbone) becomes tender, swollen and inflamed.

The cause of Osgood Sclatter disease is not clear, but possible explanations include trauma, overgrowth of the end of the tibia or repeated pulling of the muscle at the front of the thigh (the quadriceps muscle) on the patellar tendon that attaches the tibial tuberosity to the knee. In some cases there is an extra spike of bone (called a spicule) at the site of the swelling. About half the children who develop Osgood–Schlatter disease in one knee eventually develop the same symptoms in the other knee.

You may notice

- *A tender swelling on the front of one knee below the knee cap. If both knees are involved the pain is usually worse on one side*
- *The child has a limp and is reluctant to use the affected leg*
- *There is pain above and below the knee, which gets worse during exercise and on kneeling down. The knee is tender to touch*
- *Straightening the leg out with the foot pushing on the floor or against a wall causes pain around the kneecap*
- *Symptoms may be present for many weeks or even months*

What to do

Consult your doctor, who may advise that the child takes less exercise for a while to allow the pain and swelling to subside. The amount of exercise the child can take will depend on how much pain they are in. Continuing with some exercise will not do the child any harm as long as the pain is not severe. To ease the pain, use an anaesthetic spray or rub. Wrapping the knee alternately in hot and cold cloths also soothes the pain and helps to reduce the swelling.

The swelling usually takes only a few weeks to subside, but in severe cases a full recovery may take as long as one or two years, or until the child stops growing. Sometimes the knee remains tender and swollen despite reasonable levels of rest, in which case the knee may need to be immobilized in a plaster cast for a short time. If the cause of the pain and swelling is a bony spicule, this may have to be removed by surgery. Most children with Osgood–Schlatter disease eventually recover without developing complications, although a few are left with a knobbly knee that makes kneeling difficult, and can lead to arthritis.

The cause of Osgood Schlatter disease is unknown, but may result from a sports' or other injury. During recovery the child can begin to take part in normal activities and sports such as swimming, but strenuous exercise, for example roller blading, should definitely be avoided.

Outlook

Once the swelling has subsided and the pain has gone, the child can gradually take up a moderate level of sport again, but they should be careful when taking part in competitive games and team matches. If the knee is overexerted the inflammation may return.

Complementary Treatment

Chiropractors often treat and advise for this common knee condition. **Osteopathy** can also be very effective. **Aromatherapists** can help to relieve pain with relaxing essential oils. **Tai chi**, **acupuncture** and **Chinese herbalism** can also be helpful. **Homeopathic remedies** that may aid in pain relief include Benzoic ac 6c (*Benzoicum acidum*, benzoic acid) if the knee is swollen as well as painful, and the skin over the joint is very dry and the knee cracks, the remedy to be taken every two hours for up to three days. A combination of treatments – for example acupuncture and osteo pathy or homeopathy – is often beneficial.

IRRITABLE HIP

What is it?

Irritable hip is the name given to a common condition in children for which there is no known cause. It is also known as transient synovitis. Irritable hip causes the muscles around one hip to go into painful spasm. There are no other abnormal signs and, apart from a limp, the child is well. Irritable hip can last for a few days or for a week or more. Most children recover without treatment and have no further trouble, but others have repeated attacks. It is more common in boys than in girls.

Irritable hip is not a serious condition, but the symptoms could suggest a range of other less common but more serious conditions, including arthritis (see page 127) and Perthes' disease (see page 130). The child will therefore need to be carefully investigated, but it is most likely that no serious underlying disorder will be found.

You may notice

- *The child starts to limp*
- *The child may complain of pain affecting one hip only. The pain improves when the child rests*
- *Pain and a limp may be preceded by a mild cough and cold*

Diagnosis and treatment

If a child has pain in the hip and a limp, encourage them to rest as much as possible. Consult the doctor, who may refer the child to a paediatrician or an orthopaedic specialist, or ask you to take your child to the accident and emergency department of a hospital. The child will have a range of tests to discover the cause of the pain, including: blood tests to check for infection; an X-ray of the pelvis to look for lumps, swellings or fractures; and possibly bone scans or ultrasound scans. A small quantity of fluid may be drawn off from the hip joint to check for infectious organisms.

The tests can usually all be done in one day, without the need for an overnight stay, and the child may then go home to rest. In some cases the child may be admitted to hospital for further tests, and possibly for traction on the affected leg to relieve the pain. A hospital stay for irritable hip may last a few days. Once the hip is better most children have no further trouble, although one child in ten may have further attacks and the tests may need to be repeated.

Coping with irritable hip

Many children get bored if they have to rest for any length of time, so it is a good idea to keep a special toy and activity box for when your child is resting, and be prepared to spend more time with them if at all possible. Once the child is allowed to get up, limit strenuous activities such as gymnastics, football and karate for at least another week. Non-competitive swimming provides good exercise for the muscles without straining the hip joint.

Complementary Treatment

Osteopathy can often treat this condition successfully using manipulative techniques. The **chiropractor** will check the child for any pelvic or spinal imbalance that may be causing the condition, and then treat appropriately. In most cases treatment is very effective. **Chinese herbalism** would be used as an internal supportive treatment, dealing with the fundamental imbalances that are seen to have caused the condition in the first place. **Tai chi** and **acupuncture** may aid recovery. A combination of treatments – for example, **acupuncture** and **osteopathy** or **homeopathy** – is often beneficial.

Activities such as ballet and gymnastics should be avoided for a week after an attack of transient synovitis, in order to allow the inflammation to settle. The child can then go back to her normal activities. However, any return of limping or pain in the thigh, the knee or the hip should be reported to the doctor as soon as possible. It is only sensible to discontinue strenuous activity until the doctor has seen the child.

Club Foot and Curly Toes

What are they?

Children's feet are quite different from adult's feet. They have a different shape, splaying out from the heel with the widest part across the toes. The big toe sticks out and there is often no visible arch. The bones in a newborn infant's feet consist mainly of cartilage. They ossify gradually, usually by the age of 12 in girls and 14 in boys. It is thought that, before the bones have hardened, the feet can be easily deformed by tight socks or by shoes that do not fit properly. Some foot conditions are present at birth.

Club foot

In club foot, or *talipes equinovarus*, one or both of the baby's feet are bent inwards from birth, with the soles pointing towards each other. Some babies develop the condition because their feet were squashed into this position in the uterus – a condition called postural talipes. As long as the foot and ankle joints are supple rather than stiff when the baby kicks or has their feet moved, all that is needed is regular stretching exercises and possibly strapping to correct the position. A physiotherapist will show you how to do this.

If the joint is stiff and the foot cannot be stretched gently into a normal position the baby has a true club foot. This is more common in boys and tends to run in families. It is one of the conditions tested for immediately after birth.

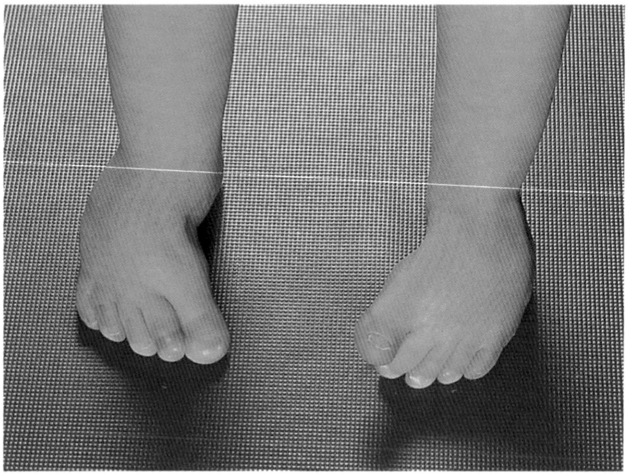

Club foot occurs quite commonly, affecting approximately one child in every thousand. Feet that have been partially corrected may be drawn back to their original position, particularly when the child has a growth spurt. The orthopaedic specialist will therefore continue to monitor the child until the foot has stopped developing, which usually occurs when the child is around 12 years of age.

Treatment

The paediatrician will test the baby's foot and ankle joints, and if they find a true club foot the affected joints will be gently and gradually manipulated. A splint or sticking plaster strapping or a plaster cast will be used to support the new position. Treatment continues until the baby is walking. The child can then wear special boots to support the feet in the pre-school years. Tight ligaments and tendons may need to be cut to loosen the position of the foot. After treatment, a child who was born with a club foot should be able to walk normally, run, play games and wear normal shoes, although the affected foot will usually be smaller than a normal one.

Curly toes

Babies whose feet were squeezed in the uterus or who have inherited a family tendency may be born with toes that curl up or under the adjacent toes. The third toe is often curled like the fourth and fifth toes, and the second toe lies over it, and is twisted sideways.

Treatment

Try moving the toe back into position. If it moves easily (even if it slips out of place immediately) the outlook is good. When your child starts walking it is very likely that this toe will correct its own position. Try holding it in place for a minute at every nappy change. If the toe is so stiff that it does not move into place, if the toes cross over or if the curly toe does not touch the ground, ask a podiatrist or doctor for advice. A podiatrist may suggest strapping the toes straight or fitting a silicone toe splint, which is worn for about 18 months. However orthopaedic surgeons are sceptical about this. They may suggest that the child has a simple operation to straighten the toes once the feet have stopped growing.

Complementary Treatment

Chiropractic can improve mobility. Osteopathy may also prove beneficial. In those rare cases where surgery is necessary, **Bach flower** remedies may help to alleviate fear and anxiety and the emotional aspects of recovery. **Homeopathic remedies** that can be given prior to surgery include Aconite 30c (*Aconitum napellus*, blue aconite) and Arnica 30c (*Arnica montana*, leopard's bane) to relieve pain and prevent infection. Arnica should be followed by Staphisagria 6c (*Delphinium staphisagria*, stavesacre). Both of these remedies should be given every half hour for no more than ten doses.

Flat Feet and Intoeing

What are they?

Flat feet and intoeing are common conditions in infancy and childhood. They are not serious and may or may not need professional attention.

Flat Feet

Flat feet in infants are usually an illusion: infant's feet are fat rather than flat. By the time most children start school, their feet have a visible arch. By the age of ten only four per cent of children still have genuinely flat feet. These children are likely to have a parent with flat feet as well.

If your child's feet appear flat you can check them as follows. For an infant, pull back the big toe. You should see a slight arch appear in he instep. For a toddler, hold their hands and help them to stand on tiptoe. there should be a slight arch in the instep. For older children, you can also check for an arch when they stand on tiptoe. Abnormal shoe wear may be a sign of flat feet. If the child has knock knees and flat feet, you should notice that the feet develop an arch as the knees straighten.

What to do

If you notice any of the above signs, be patient. Flat feet like these are very rarely a problem. The vast majority of flat feet need no treatment, unless they cause fatigue or cramp. You can buy special shoes to encourage the arch to develop, but they are not usually necessary. If you want to help, encourage your child to skip, and to stand on one leg at a time and go up and down on to the tiptoes.

If you are worried about your child's feet, see a doctor or podiatrist, who will check the feet, legs, knees and hips. They may fit an insole into the shoe if the child's shoes are being damaged, or if the child has aches or cramp in their feet.

Intoeing

Young children commonly point their toes inwards, mainly because as toddlers their hips are angled inwards and the feet follow the same pattern. This is part of normal development, and the child outgrows intoeing by the age of three or four, as the legs straighten. Some children have straight legs and heels, but the front of the foot skews inwards. This is called banana foot (metatarsus adductus), and may be caused by squeezing in the uterus.

What to do

Sleeping on the back helps to stop the foot pointing inwards, so encourage this once your child is old enough to choose their own sleeping position. The child will be most comfortable sitting on their feet or between their feet in the 'W' position – with their thighs flat on the floor and facing more or less in front of them, and their lower legs bent outward from the knees. Sitting cross-legged can also be encouraged, but some children may find this uncomfortable. Play games that encourage the child to stick their feet out. Ballet can help, as the child has to turn their feet out in the different positions.

A podiatrist or doctor will examine banana feet and see how easily they can be manipulated. A foot that can be manipulated may be massaged gently back into its correct position. In the rare cases where the foot is rigidly pointing inwards, a few weeks in plaster, usually soon after birth, will correct the angle.

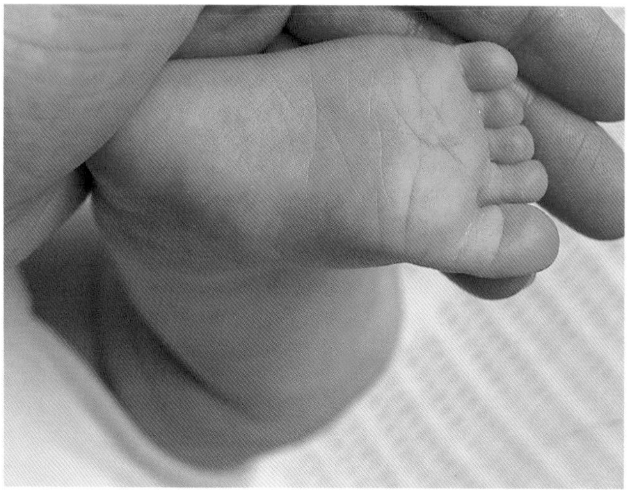

The instep on this infant's foot is already visibly developing. Once the child is walking the instep develops fully. One survey carried out in the United Kingdom showed that 97 per cent of infants under the age of 18 months appears to be flat-footed. By the age of 10 years, only 4 per cent of the children still had flat feet.

Complementary Treatment

Chiropractic can be used as an aid in the general treatment of these conditions, for example, by checking the function of the spine and joints and advising on exercises to improve the condition. **Osteopathy** and **Tai chi** may also give some success. **Nutritional therapists** may recommend supplements of calcium and vitamins or foods rich in these nutrients. Massage with **aromatherapy** oils may help to relieve pain in the calves and thighs that is often associated with flat feet.

HORMONES AND GLANDS

Physical functions such as digesting food, producing energy and, in children, growing and developing through puberty are controlled by specialised parts of the body. To work in a balanced way these parts need to be coordinated, and this is the main role of the endocrine system.

The endocrine system consists of a number of glands in various parts of the body, each producing hormones (chemical messengers) and releasing them into the bloodstream. On the whole, hormones have a gradual effect on the parts of the body they influence, with the exception of the two 'fight or flight' hormones, adrenaline and noradrenaline, that act instantly and are produced by the adrenal glands, which lie above the kidneys.

The major glands

The two controlling glands of the endocrine system are the hypothalamus and the pituitary gland, both placed at the base of the brain. The hypothalamus interacts with other body systems, such as the nervous system, and transmits messages to the pituitary gland (called by some the conductor of the hormone orchestra) which then produces hormones. The hormones in their turn stimulate other glands. For example, one of the hormones produced by the pituitary – thyroid stimulating hormone (TSH) – activates the thyroid gland at the front of the neck to produce hormones that keep the body's energy level in balance. (See page 140 for the specific roles that other hormones have in the body.)

The entire system of hormone production is carefully monitored and governed within the body by a delicate feedback mechanism. This ensures that when levels rise to a particular point, output automatically drops. When levels of a particular hormone rise too high in the blood, the hypothalamus detects the rise and prompts the pituitary to lower production.

The control centre of the endocrine system is situated at the base of the brain, where the hypothalamus influences the pituitary gland to produce stimulating (trophic) hormones, which then act on a variety of glands around the body.

Hypothalamus
Pituitary gland
Thyroid gland
Parathyroids
Thymus gland
Heart
Adrenal glands
Kidneys
Ovaries
Uterus

DIAGNOSIS

Hormones are chemical messengers produced by a gland or another body part. They are carried in the bloodstream to other parts of the body, where they act to produce particular and specific effects.

Gland or organ	Hormone	Effect
Pituitary gland	Growth hormone	Stimulates growth and development
	ACTH*	Stimulates adrenal cortex to produce hormones, e.g. hydrocortisone
	TSH+	Stimulates thyroid gland to produce thyroid hormones, including thyroxine
	FSH†	Stimulate the gonads – the ovaries and testes
	LH††	
	MSH⁂	Stimulates activity of skin pigment cells
Thyroid gland	Thyroid hormones including thyroxine	Regulates metabolism; vital for growth and mental development
Adrenal glands	Adrenaline Noradrenalin	Fight and flight hormones; increase blood supply to active muscles and decrease blood supply to internal organs under stress
	Hydrocortisone	Important for the way the body uses carbohydrates. Plays a role in suppressing inflammatory reactions
	Androgens	Stimulate development of male sex characteristics
Kidneys	Renin	Enzyme that is important in blood pressure control
	Erythropoietin	Stimulates production of erythrocytes
Pancreas	Insulin and glucagon	Control level of sugar in blood
Testes	Testosterone	Male sex hormone, stimulates growth and sexual development
Ovaries	Oestrogens and progesterone	Important for female sexual development and normal menstrual cycle

* adrenocorticotrophic hormone
\+ thyroid-stimulating hormone
† follicle-stimulating hormone
†† luteinising hormone
⁂ melanocyte-stimulating hormone

THYROID PROBLEMS

What are they?

The thyroid gland regulates the general rate of growth and development of the body. It is butterfly-shaped, and it lies across the larynx (voice box) in the throat. One of the hormones it produces is thyroxine, which has multiple effects all over the body, including the regulation of metabolism, growth rate and sexual development. A low level or absence of thyroxine produces symptoms of hypothyroidism (see page 143), and an excess produces hyperthyroidism. In newborn infants a temporary, rare, but severe, form of hyperthyroidism may be a result of the mother having too much thyroxine circulating in her blood. Antibodies cross the placenta and overstimulate the thyroid in the foetus. By the age of three months the antibodies have disappeared from the infant, and they make a spontaneous recovery.

Hyperthyroidism (Graves disease)

In this condition there is too much thyroxine circulating in the blood. It is more common in girls than in boys, but it is uncommon in children under seven. It is usually caused by an auto-immune process in which the body produces antibodies that inflame and destroy its own tissues, leading to complex changes and excess thyroxine production.

You may notice

- *The toddler is irritable, with moist, flushed skin, a rapid heartbeat and increased appetite, but fails to put on weight*
- *Unusually moodiness, irritability and excitement by turns; a good appetite but loss of weight; the eyes may protrude; they may grow unusually fast; the skin may be sweaty. If the child stretches out their hands they may shake slightly*
- *Difficulties at school because of poor concentration and restlessness*

What to do

The doctor will check the level of thyroxine in the child's blood. If it is high, the child will be treated with antithyroid drugs that control the activity of the thyroid gland. Treatment will be continued until the activity of the thyroid has been normal for at least two years. Around-one third of children will have recovered spontaneously by then. In some children surgery to remove at least part of the overactive thyroid gland may be considered. The advantage of surgery is that drugs (and their side effects) are no longer needed. Treatment with radioactive iodine is becoming more common. The iodine is taken up by the thyroid, where it destroys some of the tissue and reduces the amount of thyroxine produced.

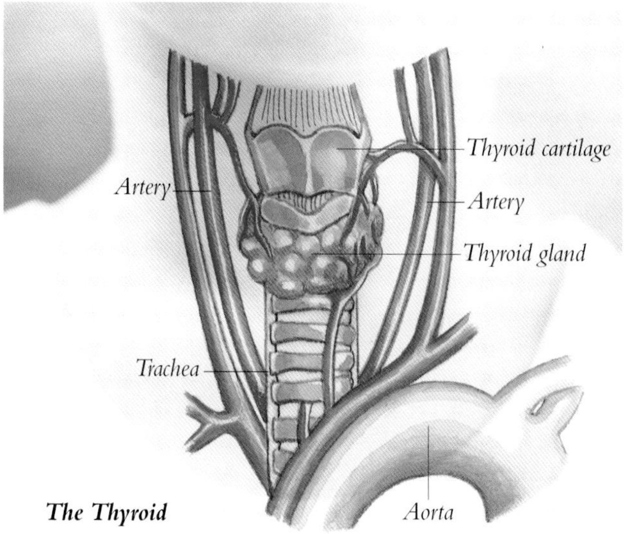

The Thyroid

Goitre

Goitre is a swelling of the thyroid gland. It does not usually affect thyroxine levels, but a goitre may develop in hyperthyroidism. It is more common in girls than in boys. There are many possible causes, the most important being inadequate iodine in the diet. Iodine is found mainly in sea fish and other seafoods, and may be added to table salt as potassium iodide.

You may notice

- *There may be swelling in the front of the neck*
- *In adolescence signs of hyperthyroidism are more common*

What to do

Take the child to the doctor, who may refer them to a paediatric endocrinologist. Depending on the cause of the goitre, thyroxine replacement therapy may be needed. Girls who develop goitre around puberty may grow out of it.

Complementary Treatment

The **Chinese herbalist** will usually treat with tonic herbs after clearing phlegm from the channels of the neck. **Western herbalism** may offer help if a single deficiency is the cause. There are specific **homeopathic remedies** for acute conditions, but you should consult a homeopath before treating children. If the homeopathic remedy does not control the symptoms within 12 hours, you should consult your doctor. **Acupuncture** and **reflexology** may provide useful support to other treatment.

Hypothyroidism

What is it?

Hypothyroidism is the name for underactivity of the thyroid gland. Thyroxine, the hormone produced by the thyroid gland, is critical for normal mental and physical development. It is produced by the foetal thyroid gland during pregnancy, and continues to be produced throughout life. Its role in mental development is critical in the first two years of childhood. Some babies are born without a thyroid gland, and in others it is small or does not function normally. Although a baby with a defective thyroid gland may develop normally in the early weeks or months, they will soon use up their supply of thyroxine and develop hypothyroidism (or cretinism).

You may notice

In newborn infants (although many show no symptoms)

- *Unusually dry, cold skin, especially on the face, hands, feet*
- *A hoarse cry, but the infant actually cries little*
- *The infant is floppy, with sluggish movements*
- *A protruding tongue, affecting feeding and maybe breathing*
- *A distended stomach, sometimes with an umbilical hernia*
- *The hair is thin, dry and brittle*
- *The infant is constipated*
- *Jaundice lasting longer than two weeks after birth*

In an older infant or child

- *Faltering growth, and the legs look especially short*
- *There is delayed bone age, so the fontanelles are unusually large and stay open for longer than normal*

What to do

As soon as hypothyroidism is identified, babies are given thyroxine by mouth. Ideally replacement therapy should start before the age of two months and it has to be continued for life. In the early days of treatment it is normal for babies to lose weight and to be unusually restless. With treatment the infant thrives, and should achieve their full intellectual potential, provided replacement therapy starts early enough and that the thyroxine shortage in pregnancy was not too severe.

Occasionally older children develop hypothyroidism. Often these children have been model pupils, but once thyroxine treatment starts they may have concentration problems as they become more aware of events around them. They lose weight initially, but then have a growth spurt, and become more interested in their surroundings. All children on thyroxine replacement therapy should have regular growth checks.

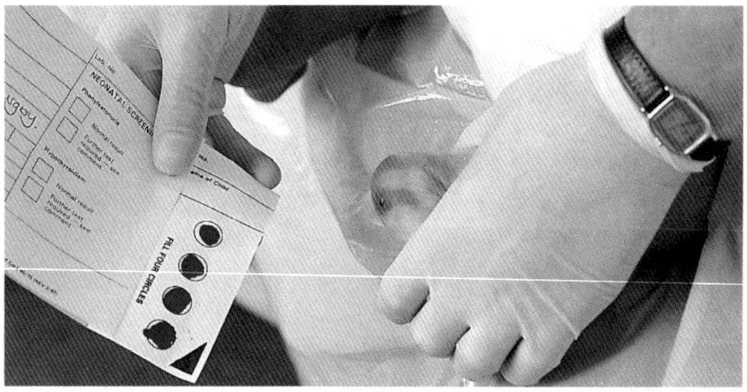

A small sample of blood is being taken from a baby's heel. Two drops of the blood are used to check the level of thyroid activity, either by measuring the level of thyroxine or the level of TSH.

The Guthrie test

Six days after birth all babies are tested for hypothyroidism and a condition called phenylketonuria (PKU), in which the infant lacks the enzyme needed to break down an amino acid called phenylalanine.A small sample of blood is taken from the side of the infant's heel. Four drops of blood are placed on a card (see illustration) and allowed to dry. Two drops of blood are used to check the level of thyroid stimulating hormone. A high level suggests that the infant is hypothyroid. If there is any doubt about the result, the test should be repeated. The other two drops of blood are used to test for PKU. If the test shows positive the infant will have more sensitive tests. If PKU is diagnosed, the baby is likely to need a diet low in phenylalanine to prevent brain damage.

Complementary Treatment

Homeopathic treatment should be carried out in conjunction with orthodox treatment; the homeopath will treat the whole individual with a view to maintaining general health. The **Chinese herbalist** will usually treat with tonic herbs after clearing phlegm from the channels of the neck.

DIABETES

What is it?

Diabetes mellitus is a condition where there is an abnormally high level of the sugar glucose in the blood. It is caused by a deficiency or total lack of the hormone insulin, which is normally produced in the pancreas, a small gland tucked behind the stomach (see Diagnosis, page 140). The carbohydrates in starchy foods such as bread and potatoes are broken down in the body to produce glucose, which is the body's main source of energy. Glucose travels around the body in the bloodstream to wherever it is needed. To convert it into energy, the body needs insulin. Because children with diabetes make little or no insulin, excess glucose accumulates in the blood.

Diabetes in children is becoming more common, for reasons that are not understood. The causes of diabetes are also not completely understood, but in certain children exposure to a virus – possibly a Coxsackie B virus – or other environmental factor may trigger off a sequence of events that eventually leads to diabetes.

Diabetes is not infectious. It can develop at any age, but in childhood there are two peak ages: the early years of primary school and the early years of secondary school. Almost all affected children have Type 1 or insulin-dependent diabetes mellitus (IDDM). They must have daily injections of insulin because their pancreases produce very little or none at all.

The symptoms develop rapidly, and the condition is usually diagnosed only weeks or days after the symptoms first appear.

You may notice

- *The child passes enormous amounts of urine*
- *Unusual thirst and tiredness*
- *Weight loss*
- *Blurred vision*

If these signs are not picked up, more serious ones appear:

- *Tummy ache and possible vomiting*
- *Heavy, deep breathing*
- *Smell of nail varnish remover (acetone) on the breath*
- *A child may go into a coma. This needs urgent medical attention*

What to do

The doctor will check the glucose level in your child's urine or blood. If it is unusually high, the child may be admitted to hospital. Usually, twice-daily injections of insulin are needed to bring the diabetes under control. You and your child will be taught how to give the injections at home; by the age of five some children can manage them alone. Make sure that more than one person in the family knows how to give injections, how to recognize the signs of low blood sugar (hypoglycaemia) and how to treat it with a fast-acting carbohydrate. The child should be given sugary drinks or food such as honey, soft sweets or glucose tablets. If the child's blood sugar falls too fast and they do not take a fast-acting carbohydrate, they should be given Hypo Stop or an injection of glucagon. Blood glucose levels need to be monitored four times a day. This is easy to do at home on fingerprick samples of blood. Urine tests give a rough estimate of glucose levels.

Children with diabetes do not need to eat a special diet, although they should eat regular meals, with sufficient starchy carbohydrates and fibre and not too much fat or sugar. Control of diabetes depends on a careful balance between food intake, exercise and insulin; this is often hardest to achieve in the teenage years.

Who can help?

For organizations offering help and support see the Directory.

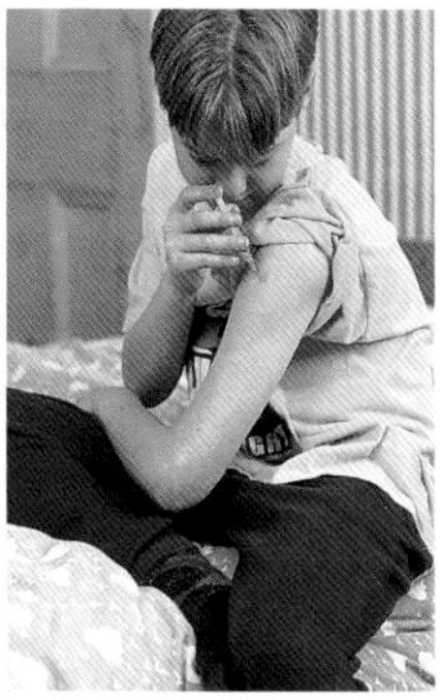

A child with diabetes usually needs twice-daily injections, one before breakfast and one before the evening meal, using either a pen injector or a conventional syringe. The injections rapidly become a routine part of the child's daily life. The child rotates the injection site between arms, legs and abdomen, thus avoiding a build-up of fatty deposits.

Complementary Treatment

Western herbalism can provide supportive treatment, using herbs to maintain low levels of blood sugar. **Homeopaths** will look at the individual and their symptoms and prescribe accordingly (constitutional treatment). **Nutritional therapists** may recommend a wholefood vegan diet and supplements of vitamin E, and/or an increase in the intake of carbohydrates and a lower fat intake, all of which may help reduce the diabetic's insulin requirement. **Aromatherapists** can teach the diabetic to gently **massage** their hands and feet using a specific method similar to lymphatic drainage. Massage with recommended essential oils should be carried out daily to maintain circulation. **Chinese herbs** are supportive for children who are insulin-dependent, and may help to relieve symptoms.

Early and Late Puberty

What are they?

Puberty is the term used to describe the time when a child begins to mature both physically and emotionally into adulthood. It is a gradual and individual process, involving changes in height, body shape, sexual development and outlook. Puberty usually takes place between the ages of ten and fifteen, but in some children changes can begin earlier or later than these ages.

The onset of puberty begins when the hypothalamus gland manufactures a trigger hormone (gonadotrophin-releasing hormone). This stimulates the pituitary gland, located at the base of the brain, to produce other hormones. These include the growth hormone, which causes the growth spurt; follicle stimulating-hormone (FSH), which controls the release of the hormone oestrogen by the ovaries; and luteinizing hormone (LH), which triggers the release of testosterone in boys and progesterone in girls.

In most girls the first sign of puberty is breast buds, which start to grow between the ages of eight and thirteen. (Many Afro-Caribbeans develop pubic hair as the first sign.) The growth spurt, which has started earlier, is almost complete by the time the first menstrual period begins, which can be anywhere between the ages of 11 and 16. During this time underarm and pubic hair are growing, the pelvis is widening and fat is being distributed in a typical female pattern around the breasts, hips and thighs. By the age of 15 periods are usually regular and predictable (see page 146).

In most boys puberty starts between the ages of nine and thirteen; this is usually later than girls, and is most obvious in the delay in the growth spurt. During this time there is a broadening of the torso, the development of muscles rather than fat and a thickening and lengthening of the vocal cords, resulting in a deepened voice. Hair begins to grow in the pubic area, under the arms and on the upper lip and chin. In terms of sexual changes, the penis enlarges and becomes more erectile, and the testes also enlarge. Hormones will trigger sperm production, and semen will be produced during wet dreams.

Early puberty

Early puberty can affect both sexes but it is about ten times as common in girls, especially in Afro-Caribbean girls, where there may be a family history. Early puberty, usually beginning in girls under eight, is rarely linked to any disorder. In boys, where there are signs of early puberty under the age of nine, the cause is frequently unknown, but occasionally a brain cyst or tumour may be responsible (also a possibility in girls).

Puberty follows a predictable sequence, but the age at which it starts and finishes and the pace of change are both very variable. All in all, puberty takes about three years to complete. An early start can have serious social consequences, as early adolescents become preoccupied with a desire for normality but feel they cannot identify with their peers.

You may notice

- *In girls, signs of puberty start before the age of eight*
- *In boys, signs of puberty start before the age of nine*

What to do

If you notice signs of early puberty in your child, consult the doctor, who should refer the child to a paediatric endocrinologist for further investigations. These will include blood tests to determine if there are any hormone or chromosome abnormalities, X-rays of the left hand to determine the child's bone age and, particularly in boys, a brain scan to investigate the possibility of a tumour.

Most girls require no treatment for early puberty – just patience until their friends catch up. However, the production of sex hormones by the ovaries or testes can be halted with a drug called a GNRH analogue, which interrupts the natural hormone production of the hypothalamus.

The GNRH analogue can be given as a spray in the nose, by daily injection or as a monthly depot injection. It is usually given until the child reaches the normal age for puberty or starts secondary school. Puberty can then go ahead at the normal rate and the child's final height is unaffected.

Early puberty may cause the child a great deal of social and psychological distress. Parental care and tolerance are particularly important during this time.

Late puberty

Puberty that begins later than the age of 14 in a girl, or 14 ½ in a boy is frequently a family characteristic.

You may notice

- *In girls, a total absence of growth spurt and any sexual changes by the age of 14*
- *In boys, a total absence of growth spurt and any sexual changes by the age of 14 ½ or more*

What to do

If your child shows no signs of puberty, and there is no obvious cause that you can think of, such as an inherited pattern of late development, then you should consult your doctor, who will refer the child to a paediatric endocrinologist for further investigations.

Treatment

As with early puberty, your child may need blood tests to determine if there are any hormonal or chromosome abnormalities, X-rays of the left hand to determine bone age and an X-ray of the pituitary gland. They may also have hormone tests to check for a shortage of gonadotrophin, and to determine whether there is a failure by the ovaries or testes to manufacture the sex hormones that produce the secondary sexual characteristics.

Treatment for girls with delayed puberty is with a low dose of oestrogen, which stimulates breast development and the growth spurt. Usually the girl's own body takes over the production of oestrogen after six to twelve months, so the administered oestrogen can be stopped.

Boys in whom puberty is delayed who are mainly concerned about their short height can be given a low dose of oxandrolone, an anabolic steroid, to be taken for three to four months. If they are more concerned about their lack of secondary sexual characteristics, they can be given testosterone. This is usually given as a long-acting injection every month for six months. The boy will then develop to the height he would have achieved without treatment, but he does so much faster and earlier.

Teenagers with gonadotrophin deficiency can receive hormone treatment to stimulate the ovaries and testes.

Like early puberty, delayed puberty will cause a child a great deal of distress. Parents need to show moral support and patience, and to give reassurance that puberty will eventually start and that everything else – fertility, adult height and sexual function – will be normal.

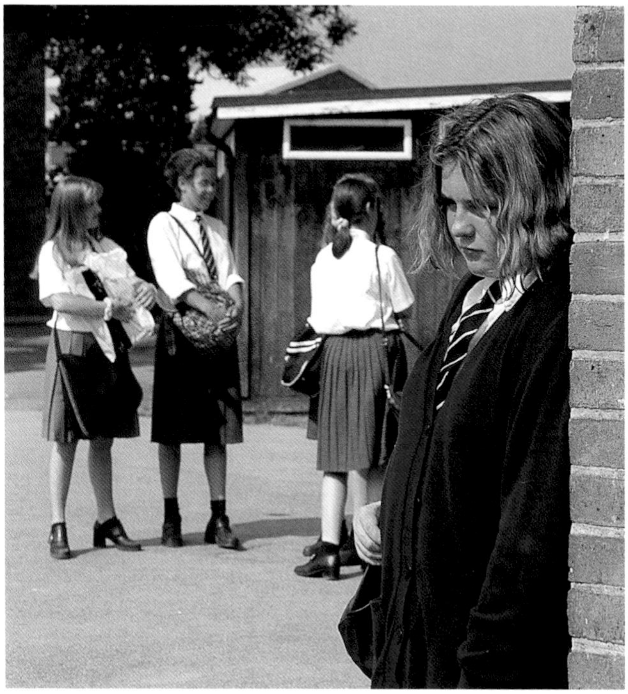

Reassurance that they will eventually catch up is sufficient for some late developers, while others suffer isolation and a sense of inadequacy. At first concerns centre on height; later, worries over sexual development overtake concerns about being short. As small teenagers are an obvious target for bullying and teasing a pattern of low self esteem can be set. Early intervention and sensitive support go a long way in preventing these psychological side effects of delayed puberty.

Complementary Treatment

The Bach flower remedy Walnut can be useful during puberty as it helps during those times when important life changes are taking place. Pubescent girls may also benefit from Willow, for self-pity, Mimulus or Rock Rose, for fear of pain, or Gentian, for despondency. Crab Apple may help during menstruation if the child feels bloated, unclean or ugly.

Menstrual Problems

What are they?

Menstruation usually starts around the age of thirteen, although onset between the ages of ten and sixteen is perfectly normal. In the first year or so menstruation may not be regular or predictable, and bleeding may stop altogether for a few months. The menstrual period can last from two to eight days, but normally lasts around four or five. By the time a girl is 16 years old, her periods will usually have become regular, with a cycle lasting between 24 and 35 days.

Irregular Periods

In the early months and years of menstruation the ovaries produce large quantities of oestrogen, which develops and thickens the endometrium (the lining of the uterus). However ovulation does not occur, and when an egg is released from the ovaries the timing of the onset of menstruation is irregular. Once ovulation starts menstruation usually becomes more regular, but may still vary for several months.

Regular periods require a balanced supply of the hormones oestrogen and progesterone. This balance is easily upset by stress; by dieting that results in rapid weight loss of more than 4 kg/8½ lb; by anorexia nervosa (see Eating disorders, page 248), or sustained strenuous exercise. Irregular periods can also be caused by polycystic ovaries, the other symptoms of which are unnatural hairiness and overweight.

What to do

Be patient. Periods eventually become more regular by the late teens. However, if the problem is caused by vigorous exercise, the amount and duration of exercise should be reduced. If weight is a problem, you should get advice from a doctor or nutritionist.

Period Pains

With ovulation, some girls have cramp-like pains (dysmenorrhoea) in the abdomen or pain in the lower back when they menstruate. This is common and quite usual, but sometimes the pain becomes much worse , or is so severe that it interferes with everyday life. The pain is often worse in the teenage years and eases off in the 20s or after the first child has been born (primary dysmenorrhoea).

Period pains usually start once ovulation becomes regular and so are undoubtedly linked with underlying hormonal changes. However the precise cause is still not perfectly understood. a possible explanation is an unusual sensitivity to prostaglandins, which stimulate the muscles of the uterus to contract and go into spasm.

Teenagers are especially vulnerable to the emotional symptoms of premenstrual syndrome. Mood disturbances associated with PMS are occasionally seen soon after the first menstrual period. Rarely, cyclical mood changes may even begin before the onset of menstruation. However teenage PMS usually begins a year or two after the menstrual cycle has become well established.

What to do

There are several home remedies worth trying that may help to ease the pain. Make up a hot water bottle, which your daughter can hold against her stomach or lower back, or have her take a warm bath or shower. Regular, relaxing exercise, especially swimming or yoga, can relieve tension in the abdominal area. Drinking lots of water and eating fresh fruit and vegetables will help guard against constipation, a condition that is often associated with menstruation. Mild painkillers such as aspirin or paracetamol will usually help to relieve the pain temporarily.

If the pain is severe you should consult your doctor, who may prescribe ibuprofen, stronger painkillers or oral contraceptives to suppress ovulation. The doctor may also prescribe drugs such as naproxen that inhibit prostaglandin activity.

Premenstrual Syndrome

Despite the view that teenagers rarely suffer from premenstrual syndrome, some girls are affected quite severely. They feel a variety of unwelcome symptoms in the days preceding menstruation. Tension, irritability, headaches, carbohydrate cravings and bloating, especially in the abdomen and breasts, are common symptoms of premenstrual syndrome (PMS).

Many of the physical symptoms of PMS are caused by fluid retention, while others, such as breast tenderness, are thought to be the result of hormonal changes. Some girls only experience mood disturbances such as depression or irritability, and need to keep a diary to be certain that they are linked with their menstrual cycle. PMS can affect girls who still have an irregular menstrual cycle, sometimes occurring only every two or three months.

What to do

There is no single remedy for PMS, so it is best to try several different approaches in order to find the one that is most suitable. Increasing the amount of exercise can relieve stress and irritability. Swimming is a particularly beneficial all-round form of exercise. Some women benefit from taking vitamin B_6 (pyridoxine), vitamin E or evening primrose oil capsules several days before the symptoms are expected. Cutting out certain foods can help, especially coffee, chocolate, and foods high in salt, such as crisps and burgers. Eating small, frequent, high-carbohydrate snacks and including healthy raw foods in the diet can also be beneficial. The doctor might suggest diuretics for severe bloating caused by fluid retention. Some doctors may advise using an oral contraceptive.

Heavy Periods

For most girls menstruation lasts about five days, with the heaviest flow during the first three days. The average blood loss is four to six tablespoons. Some girls bleed longer than this or bleed very heavily (menorrhagia) – often because the lining of the uterus is thicker than usual. This does not matter, but if the blood flow is so heavy that ordinary towels or tampons are not enough, there is a risk of anaemia.

What to do

Eat foods high in iron, such as eggs, red meat, liver, and wholemeal bread.

Consult your doctor if you are concerned, but serious causes are unusual in the early years of menstruation. If there is a tendency to anaemia the doctor may prescribe iron tablets. He may also consider one of the drug treatments that are available, which can reduce the amount of blood loss by as much as 50 to 60 per cent.

Complementary Treatment

Western herbalists use a number of herbs to regulate the menstrual cycle, ease pain and improve blood flow. These include a muscle relaxant, cramp bark (*Viburnum opulus*), and anti-spasmodic blue cohosh (*Caulophyllum thalictroides*). **Homeopathic** treatment will depend on the individual and her symptoms. Remedies might include Calcarea 30c (*Calcarea carbonica*, calcium carbonate), useful for heavy periods in young girls where other symptoms include cramping abdominal pain, weight problems and head congestion; and Viburnum 30c (*Viburnum opulus*, bark elder) for painful periods that are scanty, with pain extending to the thighs. **Aromatherapy** may be particularly beneficial in relieving pain and fatigue, PMS and depression associated with menstruation. Geranium and common chamomile (*Anthemis nobilis*) may have a positive effect on PMS; rose is helpful for painful and irregular periods and lavender for scanty and painful menstruation. Low back pain can be a contributing factor to painful periods, and the **chiropractor** would check the child for any loss of function or mobility of the spine in the lumbar area, and correct it using manipulation. **Osteopathy** may help teenagers with heavy menstrual flow, and those who have PMS, particularly if there is a structural or nutritional cause. **Nutritional therapists** have found that painful periods are often caused by deficiencies such as magnesium and essential fatty acids, and heavy periods are sometimes a result of weak capillary walls. **Acupuncture** can be helpful for irregular and painful periods.

SEE ALSO EARLY AND LATE PUBERTY (PAGE 144)

SKIN, HAIR AND NAILS

The skin, the largest organ in the body, protects the underlying tissues from damage and infection and helps to moderate changes in temperature and fluid levels. It is subject to wear and tear more than any other organ of the body. A modified form of skin, mucous membrane, even continues inside the body openings.

Skin grows in layers a few millimetres thick: the visible part is the epidermis, and beneath it is the dermis, then a layer of fat. The epidermis constantly renews itself, with skin cells gradually moving up to the surface, where they are flattened and shed as skin scales.

The dermis is tough and elastic. It is rich in nerve receptors sensitive to pain, touch and temperature and in sebaceous glands that produce sebum to lightly oil the skin. The dermis also contains the hair follicles and some three million sweat glands, which help to keep the skin cool. Apocrine glands develop at puberty; they are located around the armpits, breasts and genitals, where they secrete a thick, milky substance that smells offensive when left on the skin.

Hair and nails

Hair consists mainly of a protein called keratin. It grows from follicles rooted in the dermis, and grows in phases. Hair grows at approximately 12 mm/½ in a month for two to four years (the anagen phase); then after a period of approximately four months when it rests and stops growing (telogen and catagen phases), it loosens and falls out. Tiny glands around the hair shaft secrete sebum, the oily substance that provides the skin with its natural waterproofing. The colour of hair is determined by the presence of melanocytes at the follicles and the shape of the melanocytes.

Nails are plates of dead cells; like hair, they contain keratin. A finger nail takes about six months to grow from the nail bed to the tip of the finger, and a toenail about twice as long.

The skin is a waterproof organ consisting of two major parts: the epidermis and dermis. The dermis contains sweat, apocrine and sebaceous glands, hair follicles, blood vessels and nerves. Hair and nails are dead structures composed mainly of keratin.

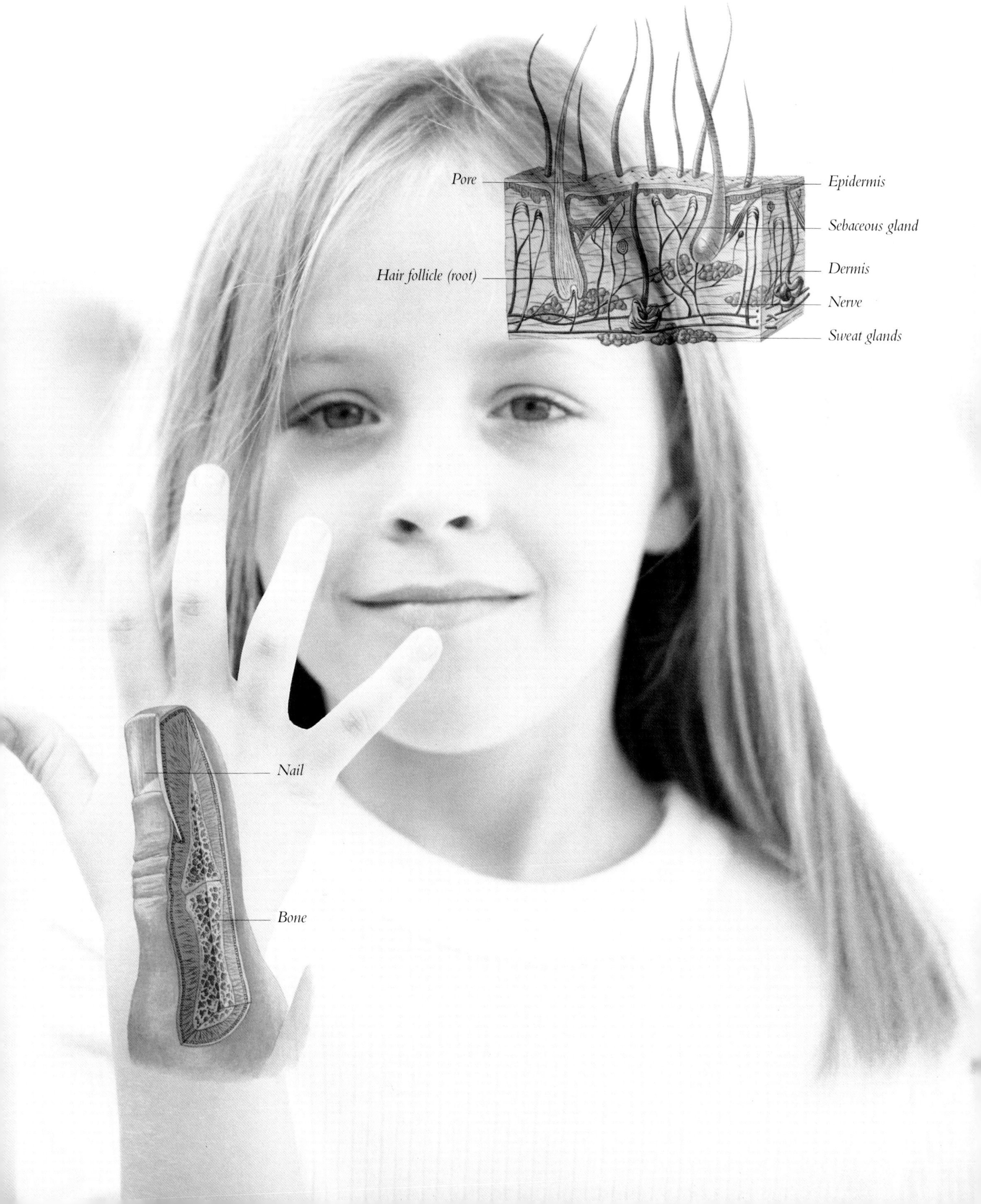
Pore
Epidermis
Sebaceous gland
Hair follicle (root)
Dermis
Nerve
Sweat glands
Nail
Bone

DIAGNOSIS

Rashes and skin reactions are extremely common in young children. In deciding what could be wrong, the first questions to ask are whether the child seems ill or has a fever. If either or both of these is the case, an infectious cause is likely.

Sign	What could be wrong
Isolated red or infected-looking spots or blackheads in a child approaching puberty	Acne is the most likely cause
Bald patches	Some children grow hair late, others twiddle their hair. A taut hairstyle may pull hair out. Occasionally a fungal scalp infection may be the cause
Sore red swelling with infected centre	Boils. Most common where skin is under pressure
Sore, slightly itchy blister near mouth or nose	Cold sores. These affect many children
Itchy red rash where the child has been in contact with an allergen, such as rubber or nickel	Contact dermatitis. Occurs near the point of contact and does not spread
Flecks of white skin near the hair roots and on the shoulders. Flecks easily removable	Dandruff is the most likely cause
Patches of rough, red, itchy skin on the face and arms, and in the skin creases	Eczema. This is becoming more common in young children
Immovable white flecks on the child's hair at the scalp	These could be the nits of headlice
In an infant, a rash of red or tiny fluid-filled bumps on the parts of the body that sweat most	Heat rash. This is common in hot weather or if the infant is too warmly clothed
Blisters around the nose or mouth that dry to a crust	Impetigo, which is highly contagious
Tiny white or yellow spots on the skin of a newborn infant	Milia. This is a harmless condition that disappears without treatment
Single oval patch of red skin, followed days later by smaller red patches	Pityriasis rosea. This is fairly common in children
Red patches with clear edges and coarse, silvery scales first on the trunk, then on the arms, elbows and legs	Psoriasis. It may be triggered by a sore throat
Round or oval, red and sometimes scaly patches on the face, scalp and body. Bald patches in the hair	Ringworm. A fungal infection that is common in young children
Itching skin, especially at night. Small itchy bumps, most commonly on the hands between the fingers	Scabies is a possibility
Sore, scaling, but non-itching rash in a young infant	May be seborrhoeic dermatitis. It is linked to cradle cap

CONTACT DERMATITIS

What is it?

Dermatitis is an inflammation of the skin that can be caused by either an irritant or an allergic reaction. Irritant contact dermatitis is much more common and can affect anyone. The irritant may be something that is mild but frequently in contact with the skin, or something strong, such as ammonia. Ammonia released in a wet nappy can cause the type of contact dermatitis that is better known as nappy rash (see page 170). Allergic contact dermatitis affects children or teenagers who develop an allergic response to a particular substance. The substances that initiate the reaction are called sensitizers or allergens. Allergic reactions may take a long time to develop (sometimes years) and are usually lifelong. Certain plants (particularly poison ivy, which is common in the United States) can start an allergic reaction; other common sensitizers include aftershave, hand lotions, make-up, deodorants and nickel (found in jeans buttons, zips, cheap earrings and watchstraps). Nickel sensitivity appears to be increasing in the United Kingdom.

Rubber can also provoke a reaction in some children, as can elastic at the waists and wrists of clothing, and stretchy crepe bandages. In some extremely sensitive children balloons can cause a reaction. Some children have quite specific and unusual reactions, for example, to poster paints. Lanolin (wool fat) used to cause skin reactions in many children, because it was frequently contaminated with pesticides used in sheep dips. The use of the most harmful pesticides has now been restricted and wool-cleaning processes have become more thorough, resulting in high-grade lanolin that does not cause allergic reactions.

Certain plants can trigger severe dermatitis when substances they contain are exposed to sunlight. In the United Kingdom the sap of the giant hogweed, cow parsley and the herb, rue, are the chief culprits.

You may notice

- *An itchy, red rash at the point of contact with the irritant or the allergen*
- *Flaking or blistering of the skin. The blisters break or are scratched open and form crusts*

What to do

Identify the source of the trouble and, if at all possible, avoid it. If this is not possible, make sure the irritant does not come into direct contact with your child's skin. Encourage a young child to wear an all-in-one, or an older girl to wear a body under jeans. Use a non-biological washing powder or one made specially for sensitive skins. Avoid any products that are likely to irritate the skin even more, especially bubble baths and highly scented soaps. While the rash is clearing up do not use soap on the affected area; use an aqueous or emollient cream instead, or just use plain tap water. The rash will clear and should not spread, although a complete recovery may take some weeks. Recovery can take longer if contact with the irritant or allergen has continued for some time.

If the rash continues for a week after you are certain you have removed all sources of contact with the irritant or allergen, take your child to the doctor. The doctor may prescribe a mild corticosteroid cream to be used sparingly. The cream will ease the itching, and also reduce the inflammation and soothe the irritated skin.

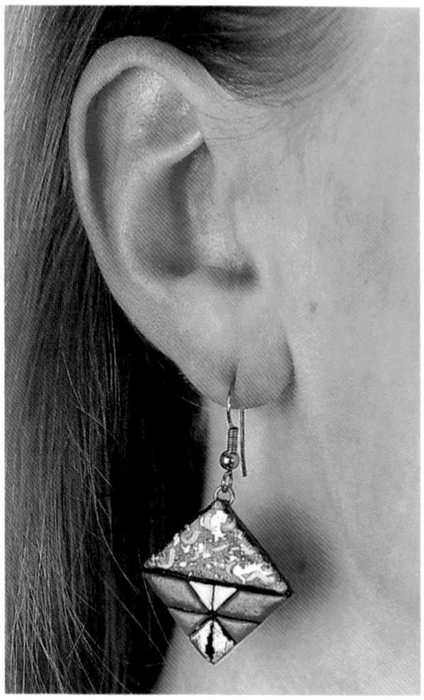

Nickel is a common component in metal alloys used in jewellery. Easily absorbed through the skin, it causes dermatitis in sensitized individuals. Worldwide, sensitivity is on the increase. Children who develop this form of dermatitis should wear sterling silver or gold earrings instead of those made from metal alloys.

Complementary Treatment

Crab Apple – **a Bach flower remedy** – diluted in water and applied topically may be helpful in reducing itchiness, as may Rescue Cream. Itching associated with urticaria caused by nettle stings or other plants may be relieved by the **homeopathic remedy** Urtica 6c (*Urtica urens*, nettle) or by Urtica ointment. Geranium is one of the essential oils used in **aromatherapy** to relieve itching, and is safe to use for self-treatment. Other oils with antibiotic properties can be used to treat secondary infections caused by scratching. An aromatherapist will be able to advise specific oils.

SEE ALSO SKIN ALLERGY (PAGE 173)

HEAT RASH

What is it?

Heat rash (also known as prickly heat or *miliaria rubra*) is the most common rash seen in young babies. It develops because babies' sweat glands are not yet working efficiently and so they are not able to cool down if they become overheated – perhaps because they are dressed too warmly in hot weather or their room is too hot, or because they are in an incubator or receiving phototherapy for neonatal jaundice. The sweat glands leak sweat under the skin, and this causes a mild inflammation, which usually disappears within a few days. If you examine the rash with a magnifying glass, you will see a tiny sweat pore at the centre of each red spot. Children and babies with fair skin are most likely to suffer from heat rash.

Heat rash is not serious, but if the rash is still clearly visible several hours after the baby has cooled down, you should contact the doctor.

You may notice

- *The infant develops a rash of red or pink bumps. You can sometimes see tiny fluid-filled blisters*
- *The rash is on parts of the body that sweat most – in the skin folds in the nappy area and the trunk; on the face, neck and shoulders; and under the arms*
- *If the rash is extensive the infant will be restless and irritable*
- *The infant's cheeks look hot and pink*

What to do

Cool the baby by undressing them and bathing them in tepid (not cold) water. If it is not possible to bathe them, wipe them all over with a damp sponge or face cloth, leaving the skin moist. Pat the baby gently dry and replace their nappy. Dress them in just a cotton vest or a T-shirt. Continue the cooling process by wiping the baby's forehead with a face cloth that you have wrung out in tepid water.

Check the temperature of the baby's room. It should be between 16 and 20°C/60 and 68°F, comfortable for you wearing light clothing. If the room is too hot, turn the heating down or off. Cool the air by turning on an electric fan, but do not direct this straight at the baby.

Offer the baby drinks. If you are still breastfeeding the baby, frequent feeds will help to keep their fluid levels up. If the baby has been weaned, offer them boiled, cooled water or very dilute juice.

If the baby has a rash, bathe them in water without any added bath oil or bubble bath until the rash has gone. And do not use calamine or a solution of bicarbonate of soda to ease the itching. They are likely to cake on the baby's skin. Talcum powder can also be irritating if it cakes with sweat.

Warning: Never leave a baby in a stationary car on a hot day. The temperature inside can rise dangerously fast. Not only can this cause heat rash, it can also cause severe dehydration and heatstroke.

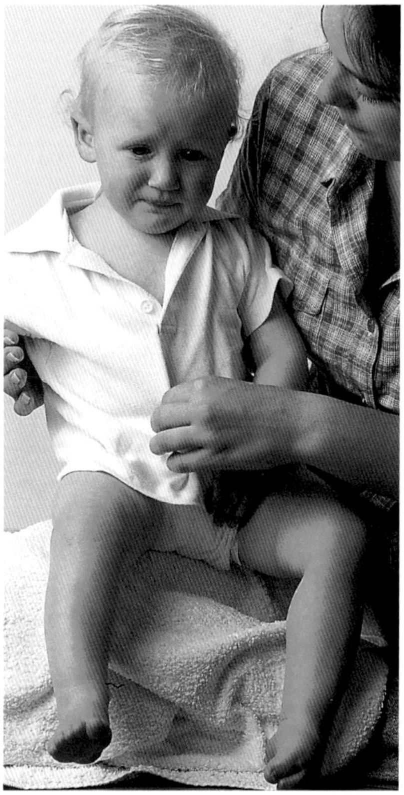

Once you have cooled the baby down by sponging, dress him in loose, cotton clothing such as a vest or T-shirt. Babies are particularly susceptible to heat rash because their sweat glands are not fully developed. To prevent further incidents, make sure that rooms are not overheated, protect him from strong sunlight, and dress him appropriately during spells of dry, hot weather.

Complementary Treatment

Western herbalism offers numerous soothing herbs, including common or Roman chamomile (*Anthemis nobilis*) and echinacea (*Echinacea purpurea*, rudbeckia), which should be applied directly to the skin as ointments, lotions or compresses. **Chinese herbalists** would expect an instantaneous cure from chrysanthemum tea. **Homeopaths** may recommend Urtica 6c (*Urtica urens*, nettle) or Urtica ointment. The **Bach flower remedy** Crab Apple can be diluted with water and applied topically; alternatively, Rescue Cream may help soothe the itchiness and make the child more comfortable. Topical applications of some **aromatherapy** oils will reduce any swelling and will have a cooling effect on the skin.

CHILBLAINS

What is it?

Chilblains are itchy, red swellings that occur in very cold, damp weather. Any part of the body can be affected, but the hands and feet, especially the toes, heels and fingers, are most vulnerable. The body defends itself against the cold by boosting the circulation to the major organs – the heart, brain and lungs – partly at the expense of the circulation to the extremities. In cold conditions the tiny blood vessels just beneath the surface of the skin narrow, and the blood becomes thicker. If the circulation to the toes and fingers is restricted, the skin turns bluish-purple and feels numb. Waste products that are normally carried away by the circulation stay in the extremities, temporarily damaging the tissues. It is this tissue damage that causes chilblains to develop as the skin warms up. Some people, especially children, are particularly susceptible, and wearing tight socks or gloves that restrict circulation can make the problem worse. Chilblains can be prevented by keeping the hands and feet well wrapped and warm in winter.

Children who play outside in wintry conditions should wear lined mittens and boots to keep their extremities warm. However any situation in which cold damp weather and tight clothing are combined is liable to provoke sore and itchy chilblains. So, for example, children who go horse riding and wear tight trousers are also at risk.

You may notice

- *Sore, red and slightly swollen patches on the hands or feet*
- *The child complains of itchiness in the hands or feet*
- *The child may limp*

What to do

If the child's hands or feet have become very cold, fill a basin with tepid water and encourage them to hold their hands or feet in the water until they warm up. Gradually increase the temperature by adding warm water to the basin. Once the skin has turned pink all over, gently dry the hands or feet. If it is the feet that are affected, put on soft, warm socks.

The itchiness may last for a day or two. To relieve it, sprinkle a little talcum powder in the child's slippers or over the feet, or dab on calamine lotion.

The chilblains will disappear on their own in a few days as long as the child's hands and feet are kept warm at all times.

What else?

Prevention is better than cure. Make sure your child does not wear gloves or footwear that are too tight and will restrict circulation. Socks and tights should be comfortably loose, and in cold weather two or three thin layers will keep feet warmer than one thick layer. In very cold weather children should wear padded boots, particularly if they have to stand still outside for a long time. Babies and toddlers sitting in pushchairs are particularly vulnerable, and need the extra protection of a lined foot and knee warmer.

A child who gets frequent chilblains should not stand around in the cold. If children do have to spend any length of time in low temperatures – in the school playground, for example – they should be encouraged to keep moving by playing active games. Regularly exercising the feet may improve the circulation and help to keep chilblains at bay.

Complementary Treatment

Western herbalists usually suggest powerful circulatory stimulants, such as chilli pepper, which can be very effective. **Chinese herbalists** also treat by stimulating the circulation with herbs used topically and internally. **Homeopaths** will prescribe specific remedies, which should be taken every half hour for up to six doses: for example, Agaricus 6c (*Agaricus muscarius*, fly agaric) for chilblains that are burning and itchy, with red, swollen skin; Petroleum 6c (*Petroleum Oleum petrae*, coal oil) for individuals prone to rough skin, with chilblains that are burning and itchy, with weepy and watery skin, and worse in damp conditions. **Aromatherapy** concentrates on improving circulation and therapists recommend soaking the feet in warm water to which one or two warmth-inducing essential oils have been added.

Milia and other Newborn Rashes

What is it?

Newborn babies often develop spots or rashes. Many are caused by glands in the infant's skin adapting to independent life, and they soon clear up without treatment. However as new mothers are in regular contact with health professionals, it is best to show any skin problems that concern you to the doctor, health visitor or midwife.

Milia

Milia are tiny white or yellow spots on a baby's face. There are three types. Swathes of yellow pin-prick spots over the baby's nose, forehead and face are caused by minute glands in the skin producing an excess of an oily substance called sebum, which acts as a natural lubricant for the skin. The overproduction of sebum is stimulated by hormones produced by the mother in late pregnancy, which cross the placenta. As the effect of the hormones lessens over the first few weeks after birth, so the milia disappear. Meanwhile, resist any temptation to squeeze milia, as this can leave a scar.

Blocked sweat glands can produce a rash of tiny blisters on pinkish-red skin. The blisters may look infected and the rash is most obvious where the baby's skin gets too hot, such as in skin creases or in the groin. the baby may be quite restless if the rash spreads over the body (see Heat rash, page 152).

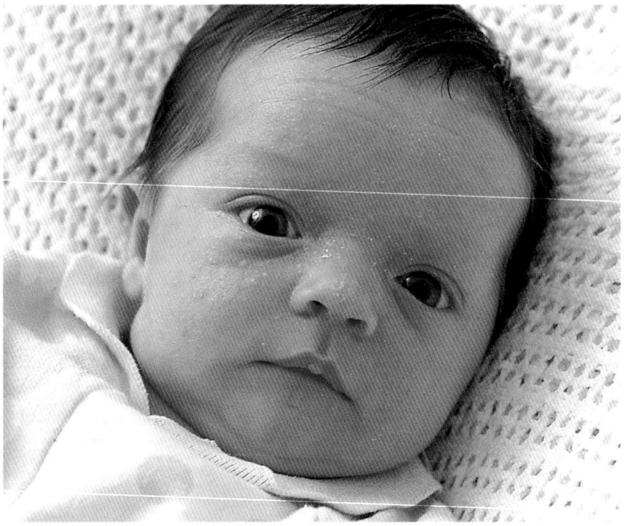

Babies are rarely born with a perfect peaches-and-cream complexion. As the sweat and sebum glands adapt to their new environment a variety of rashes may occur. In full-term babies the skin is mature at birth, but babies born before 30 weeks have fragile skin, which is very easily damaged and is vulnerable to infection.

Remove a layer of the baby's clothes or covers to cool them down, or if they are very overheated bathe them in cool water. The rash fades within a couple of days, but it may come back.

A light sprinkling of creamy-white spots on a baby's face or sometimes on other parts of the body may be tiny cysts containing keratin, the protein component of skin. These milia pop open, and clear up within six weeks.

Erythema toxicum

Around half of all babies develop uneven red patches over the skin, especially on the back, chest and stomach, in the first two to four days after birth. At the centre of each patch there may be a little blister, which can sometimes look infected. Within two or three days the blisters and red patches fade naturally. This rash, known as erythema toxicum, is rare in preterm babies.

Other skin conditions

Sometimes the unusual appearance of a newborn infant's skin is the result of their blood flow adjusting to independent life. Some babies have greyish-blue hands and feet in the first day or two of life as the circulation to the extremities improves. Provided they are kept warm, the hands and feet soon turn pink. A blotchy red rash is very common in the first couple of days. It is most likely to be caused by a higher than normal volume of blood flowing through the tiny capillaries beneath the skin as the circulation adjusts.

A dramatic phenomenon that is seen occasionally is the baby who is pink down one side of their body and quite pale down the other. The sharp demarcation disappears rapidly and causes no further problems.

Peeling skin is common in newborn babies, especially those born past their due date. It is most obvious at the wrists and ankles and on the palms and soles, but it does not cause the baby any pain and it does not mean that they will have skin problems later. Rub baby oil or olive oil into these areas.

Complementary Treatment

Irritable infant rashes may be soothed with Rescue Cream, a **Bach flower remedy**. Topical applications of the **aromatherapy** essential oil, lavender, will be both safe and soothing. **Chinese herbs** used topically are often effective.

Seborrhoeic Dermatitis

What is it?

Seborrhoeic dermatitis is an eczema-like skin rash that appears in the first weeks of life. The most obvious difference from atopic eczema (see page 156) is that the baby is not bothered by the rash, as there is no itchiness. The rash is most obvious on the face and the scalp (where it is known as cradle cap, see page 158), and in the folds of the skin. The cause of seborrhoeic dermatitis in babies is not well understood, but it is known to be different from the seborrhoeic dermatitis that affects adults, which is caused – like dandruff – by an overreaction to the organism *Pityrosporum ovale*. Sometimes seborrhoeic dermatitis in babies can be triggered by nappy rash, which starts in the groin and works its way up the body.

Although seborrhoeic dermatitis sounds as if it has a link with the sebaceous glands, which produce the oily substance called sebum that lubricates the skin (overproduction of which produces a milia rash, see opposite), there is no connection. The rash caused by seborrhoeic dermatitis normally clears within a few weeks, although it may be more stubborn in the nappy area. Babies with black skin may be left with lighter skin patches after the rash clears. However these patches will gradually darken.

You may notice

- *Thick, greasy yellow scales on the infant's head*
- *Red patches with a fine yellowish scaling elsewhere, especially on the face, cheeks and eyebrows, and behind the ears, which become redder when the infant cries or gets hot*
- *Moist, reddened skin in other skin folds, especially the neck and under the arms*
- *Raw nappy rash that is obvious in the skin creases as well as the surfaces that touch the nappy*
- *The red patches may become soggy and ooze yellowish fluid*

What to do

Consult the doctor to be sure of the diagnosis. If the rash has no secondary infection, the doctor will usually prescribe a mild hydrocortisone ointment that should clear it in two to three weeks. If there is a secondary infection or a colonization by the yeast-like fungus *Candida*, which is particularly likely in the nappy area, the doctor may prescribe a combination cream with an antifungal or an antibacterial agent.

If the baby's scalp is affected, wash the hair regularly with a mild cradle cap or medicated shampoo. You can also lightly rub baby or olive oil into the patches on the scalp at bedtime. After shampooing the hair in the morning and towelling it roughly dry, try to gently lift off the scales with a brush or comb. If the flakes are stuck firmly to the scalp, then leave them alone. Repeat this treatment every day until the scalp clears. If the cradle cap is particularly stubborn, or if the patches spread on to the face from the scalp, your doctor can prescribe a mild antifungal shampoo. You can soothe the inflamed patches on the child's skin with a mild emollient, such as an aqueous cream.

Ointments and creams containing borage oil have recently been found to be effective in treating seborrhoeic dermatitis. Borage oil is rich in gamma-linoleic acid.

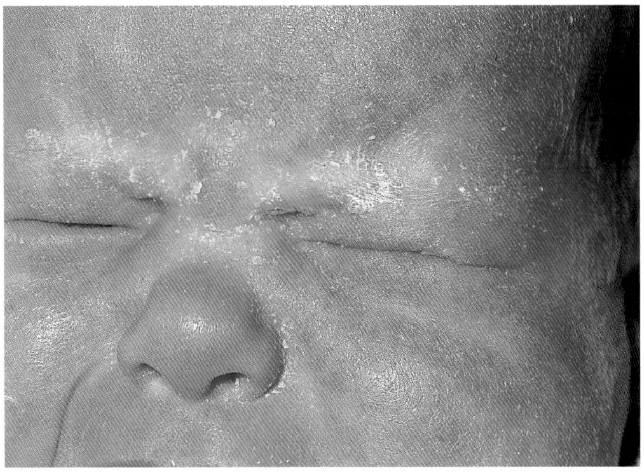

Seborrhoeic dermatitis often starts in infants aged two to six weeks – certainly before the age of six months. The rash can look quite dramatic but usually clears within weeks. It may, however, return, particularly in the nappy area. Children who have seborrhoeic dermatitis seem to have a somewhat higher risk of developing psoriasis later on.

Complementary Treatment

Homeopathic remedies include frequent applications of Calendula ointment (*Calendula officinalis*, pot marigold) to the affected areas. The homeopath may also prescribe specific remedies to be given every four hours for up to 14 days: for example, Graphites 6c (*Graphites*, black lead) where the affected skin is weepy, encrusted and easily infected; Lycopodium 6c (*Lycopodium clavatum*, wolfsclaw club moss) where Calendula ointment does not appear to be effective; or Viola 6c (*Viola tricolor*, heartsease) where the condition mainly affects the scalp and face, with thickly encrusted lesions accompanied by swollen glands. **Chinese herbalism** recommends a herbal tea. **Western herbalism** and **aromatherapy** may also be helpful.

ECZEMA

What is it?

Eczema is the most common skin problem in young children, affecting at least one child in eight, regardless of the colour of their skin. It can be very mild, consisting of just one or two red, scaly patches, or it can cover the entire body with an intensely itchy rash. Eczema is one of the allergic or atopic conditions to which an infant may have inherited a susceptibility (see Skin allergy, page 173), and, like other allergic conditions, it is becoming more common. Seven out of ten children with eczema have a relative with an allergy-related disorder, such as hay fever or asthma , and half of all babies with eczema go on to develop asthma.

It is usually impossible to pinpoint the specific trigger that initiates eczema in an infant, but it may be contact with house dust, animal fur, pollen or all of these. Overheating, dry air and cold weather make eczema worse, as do teething, colds and other infections. Because the spots are so itchy, children often scratch them. Eczematous skin is prone to infection. The skin may become weepy and crusted. Infection is now known to be an important trigger factor for eczema.

There is no cure for eczema, but in almost all affected children it goes into remission, in 40 per cent by the age of two and 90 per cent by their teens. Teenagers, many of whom are especially sensitive about their appearance, may find it difficult to cope with the physical effects of eczema, and the itching can have a disruptive effect on their studies.

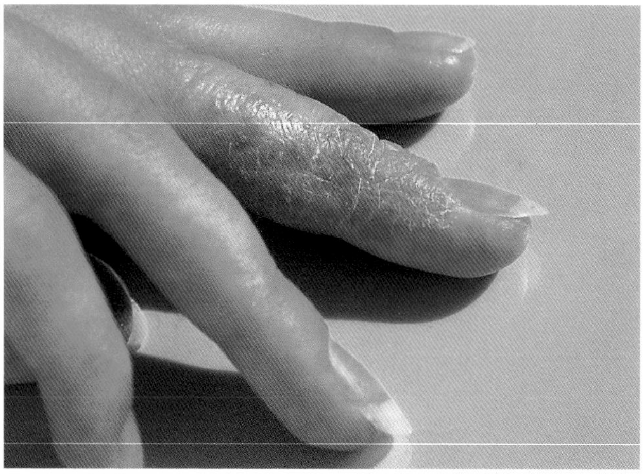

Teenagers and children with eczema are particularly sensitive to external irritants, which can initiate a local form of dermatitis. They should wear protective gloves to avoid contact with detergents and hot water, which can dry their hands, particularly during the winter when the weather is cold and dry.

You may notice

- *An infant may become restless, sleeping poorly and rubbing their face*
- *There may be small scratches on the baby's face and arms where they have rubbed or scratched the skin*
- *There may be patches of rough, red itchy skin on the face and arms. These may spread, affecting the skin creases at the wrists, elbows and knees. Sometimes skin all over the body becomes dry and rough*
- *In black children, the patches of eczema may look paler than the surrounding skin*
- *Small red pimples, blisters or cracks may appear on the affected areas*

What to do

Keep the affected skin smooth and supple by moisturizing it regularly with an emollient cream that you can buy from the pharmacist. Do not use soap, baby lotion or bubble bath, all of which can irritate the skin. Some (but not all) children get relief from a daily bath in tepid – not hot – water with a capful of moisturizing bath oil added. For young children, choose a children's non-slippery bath oil. Alternatively, apply emulsifying ointment to the child's skin before they have a bath. You may find it easier to rub the oil or emulsifying ointment into damp skin or to massage bath oil into the skin as the child is in the shower. Encourage the child to stay in the water for 20 minutes by providing bath toys. After bathing, pat the child gently dry with their own towel and leave the skin slightly moist. Spread emollient cream thickly over the skin. To avoid any risk of contamination do not dip your fingers into the pot – use a spoon or spatula instead.

Medical treatment

The doctor can prescribe soothing skin preparations, and if eczema keeps the child awake at night, the doctor may also prescribe a sedating antihistamine drug to be taken an hour before bedtime. A mild steroid cream, such as one per cent hydrocortisone, can speed up the healing of skin that has been badly damaged by severe eczema. This should be used on areas of red, inflamed skin only, and in small quantities – the doctor can show you how much to apply. If the child's skin is raw and weeping from scratching the doctor can prescribe antibiotics to combat infection.

Evening primrose oil can sometimes improve eczema in the long term, although its effectiveness is controversial. The doctor can prescribe capsules to be added to the feeds of a baby over 12 months old.

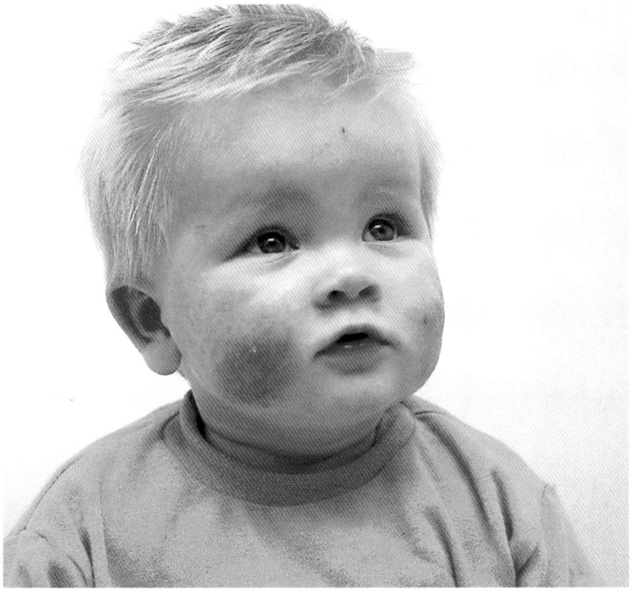

The cheeks are often the first place where eczema occurs in young children. Once the baby starts teething or thumb sucking, dry patches of eczema may appear around the mouth, usually as a result of local skin irritation. Frequent, liberal applications of emollient creams help to prevent the skin from drying out and becoming irritated.

Your doctor can also advise you about whether you should change your child's diet. If eczema develops as a sign of allergy to cows' milk, the doctor can prescribe a low-allergen milk substitute. However you should never remove milk – or any other food you suspect, such as eggs, fish, vegetables, wheat, colourings or preservatives – from a child's diet without checking first with a health professional.

Children with very severe eczema often get much better with wet wrapping, a technique that initially involves a health professional – and after instruction, a parent – coating the child's skin thickly with moisturizers before wrapping the child in layers of moist bandage. Steroid cream may be applied to any patches of inflamed eczema. Some children benefit from short spells of continuous wet wrapping, while others need it only during the night. However this treatment is also controversial.

Coping with eczema

To stop the child scratching, keep their nails short and, if necessary, sew cotton mittens on to their sleepsuit, or buy styles with mittens attached. Keeping the temperature of the bedroom at no more than 18°C/64°F will also help.

Restrict the access of furry or feathered pets to a limited part of the house, such as the kitchen, and try to keep the house dust mite at bay. This is, however, an almost impossible task that involves wet-wiping the bedroom and vacuuming frequently throughout the house, ideally with a high-filtration vacuum cleaner.

Keep soft toys, soft furnishings and carpets to a minimum. A weekly overnight spell in the freezer will help to kill any mites in soft toys.

Choose absorbent, non-irritating material such as cotton for clothes, and avoid wool. Avoid white clothes, which will show up stains from creams and ointments, and dark clothes, which show skin flakes. Choose long, baggy styles with long sleeves and legs, and seams that do not rub. Use pure cotton towels and bedding.

Try out non-biological or sensitive-skin washing powders until you find one that suits your child's skin, and wash new clothes before use to remove fabric finishes that may be irritants. Always wash and cream your child's hands after they have played with sand, playdough or water, and teach them to do this themselves.

Who can help?

For organizations and agencies who can provide information and advice, see the Directory.

Complementary Treatment

Nutritional therapists will look for food allergies as the main cause of this condition, and recommend eliminating from the diet those foods that are responsible. The condition may also be linked to poor liver function, and may be exacerbated by deficiencies of zinc, essential fatty acids or vitamin A. Steps will be taken to improve liver function or treat any deficiencies. **Homeopathy** has proved to be helpful in many cases, but treatment should be sought from a qualified homeopath who will prescribe constitutionally (taking the child's mood, personality, temperament and symptoms into account). **Chinese herbalists** expect good results from herbal treatment, particularly when treatment begins at or near the onset of the condition. **Western herbalists** usually concentrate on trying to find and treat the cause of the disease. Rescue Cream, from the **Bach flower remedies**, can produce good results, and is useful while seeking other treatment. Applied **kinesiology** may help identify allergies that trigger the condition.

Cradle Cap

What is it?

Cradle cap is a very common scalp condition in babies and it can occasionally affect children up to the age of five. It has nothing to do with poor hygiene and does not mean that your child will go on to develop eczema (see page 156). It is probably caused by overproduction of sebum, the oily substance secreted by the sebaceous glands in the skin. These glands normally produce just enough sebum to keep the skin oiled and in a healthy condition. When cradle cap spreads beyond the scalp it is part of the skin condition called seborrhoeic dermatitis (see page 155).

Cradle cap is quite harmless and it is easy to treat at home. It usually clears up within a few days or weeks at the most. It may well recur, but once the baby's hair has grown and thickened you will no longer notice the cradle cap. The following signs may be present in both infants and toddlers, but they are most common in infants who are aged between three and nine months.

You may notice

- *There may be thick scales of skin on the baby's head. The scales may be yellowy-brown in colour, or they may just look like dead skin compared with the rest of the head*
- *There may be red, sore – but not itchy – skin on the infant's forehead and over the eyebrows, behind and on the ears, in the armpits, or in the nappy area*

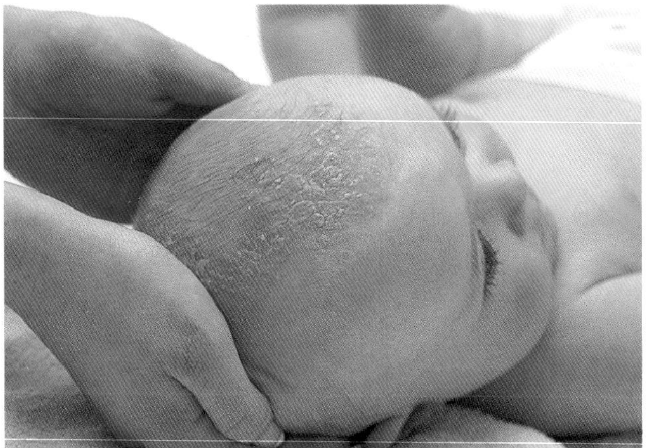

Cradle cap is one of the most common skin disorders in young babies, and frequently covers the areas on the top of the head that are occupied by the soft fontanelles. Shampooing the scalp and lifting the skin scales will not, however, damage the baby's head, as the membranes that cover the fontanelles are very tough.

What to do

After your infant's evening bath, rub a pure oil, petroleum jelly or soft paraffin gently but thoroughly into the scalp. Baby oil, grapeseed oil or pure virgin olive oil can also be used, but do not use any nut oils if anyone in the family has a nut allergy. This is just a precaution, because it is not yet known whether applying nut oils to a baby's skin can sensitize them and cause nut allergies later in life. Protect the cot sheet with a cover.

In the morning, shampoo your infant's hair using a specially formulated cradle cap shampoo. You can buy this from any pharmacist, but stop using it if you notice that the baby's skin is becoming red or irritated. While shampooing the infant's hair, protect their eyes with a shampoo shield. Towel the hair roughly dry, then brush or comb it with a soft-bristled brush or round-toothed comb, gently lifting off the scales. Leave the scales alone if they are still firmly stuck to the scalp. Repeat this treatment every day until all the scales have gone.

If the cradle cap is very stubborn, take your infant to see the doctor. The doctor may prescribe a mild hydrocortisone ointment, possibly with an antifungal or antibacterial ingredient as well if there are any signs of infection.

Complementary Treatment

The base oils and creams used in **aromatherapy** can be effective when used on their own; however, the addition of essential oils makes the treatment more pleasant. **Nutritional therapy** would hope to prevent the condition, which may be caused by a deficiency of zinc and/or essential fatty acids, by attention to the mother's diet during pregnancy. **Chinese herbalists** will prescribe herbs to be taken internally. **Homeopathic remedies** include frequent applications of Calendula ointment (*Calendula officinalis*, pot marigold) to the affected areas. The homeopath may also prescribe specific remedies to be given every four hours for up to 14 days: for example, Graphites 6c (*Graphites*, black lead) where the affected skin is weepy, encrusted and easily infected; Lycopodium 6c (*Lycopodium clavatum*, wolfsclaw club moss) where Calendula ointment does not appear to be effective; or Viola 6c (*Viola tricolor*, heartsease).

DANDRUFF

What is it?

The skin is constantly growing and renewing itself, and as it grows the top layer flattens, hardens and is rubbed off as tiny dust-like particles. In fact a high proportion of house dust is made up of these minute skin scales. The normal growth cycle of skin lasts around 30 days, but on the scalp it is slightly shorter.

Everybody sheds some skin scales from the scalp, but when so many are shed that they become noticeable they are called dandruff. This happens when the growth cycle of the skin on the scalp is speeded up so that more skin flakes are shed than normal. Dandruff is not particularly common in young children, but around puberty it can become more of a problem. The rapid growth cycle of skin on the scalp is probably caused by an overreaction to a fungus-like organism called *Pityrosporum ovale*. This lives naturally on the scalp and only causes difficulties when the body overreacts to it.

You may notice

- *Tiny flecks of white skin around the roots of the hair. Unlike the nits left behind by headlice, these flecks are easily moved and can be gently combed or brushed out*
- *A dusting of white flecks on a dark pillow or sheet, or on the shoulders if your child wears plain, dark clothes*
- *Your child may scratch their head as dandruff can be itchy*

What to do

Wash your child's hair with a mild medicated or anti-dandruff shampoo. Mild shampoos often contain tar, sulphur or salicylic acid, which help to soften and loosen the scales. Shampoos for more serious dandruff may contain selenium sulphide, which slows down the growth of skin cells and so reduces dandruff. These shampoos usually need to be left in contact with the scalp for a few minutes, and a shampoo shield can be useful for young children to stop them getting shampoo in their eyes.

There is an effective fungicidal shampoo containing ketoconazole, which is available on prescription. This not only treats dandruff effectively, but it can also prevent its return. You should always double-check with your doctor before using it for younger children. To be most effective you should shampoo your child's hair with the prescribed shampoo twice a week for two to four weeks, depending on the severity of the dandruff. Then use it once a week or once a fortnight. You shouldn't use it more than once every three days.

These measures are very likely to keep your child's dandruff under control, but if they are not effective, your doctor can prescribe a mild corticosteroid cream, which will control the flaking and soothe any inflammation of the scalp.

Dandruff causes social embarrassment in older children and teenagers. Among the plethora of available remedies, a shampoo containing the antifungal ketoconazole is the most effective remedy. It is available over the counter from a pharmacist or with a doctor's prescription.

Coping with dandruff

As dandruff is likely to be a long-term problem, encourage your child to wear light-coloured clothes and to avoid plain, dark tops. If they wear a dark-coloured school blazer, they should comb their hair before they put it on.

Complementary Treatment

Nutritional therapists have linked dandruff with deficiencies of the B vitamins, zinc and essential fatty acids. Increasing the amounts of these nutrients in the diet or taking supplements may eliminate the problem. Flaking and scaling skin may be relieved by topical applications of suitable **aromatherapy** oils. **Homeopathic treatment** can be helpful in both chronic and acute cases. The homeopath will prescribe appropriate remedies, as well as advising the individual on self-help treatments. These may include taking the tissue salt Kali sulph (*Kali sulphuricum*, potassium sulphate) three times a day for up to a month, then three times a day for five days out of seven until there is an improvement. The **Chinese herbalist** will prescribe herbal shampoos, and herbs to be taken orally.

IMPETIGO

What is it?

Impetigo is a bacterial infection of the skin that is most commonly seen on the face. It is usually caused by bacteria infecting the skin through a cut, a patch of eczema or a cold sore, and it is extremely contagious. Impetigo is very common in schoolchildren, probably because young children do not produce much sebum, the oily fluid secreted by the sebaceous glands in the skin, which not only lubricates the skin but also has antimicrobial properties. Children spread impetigo by touching the scabs and then transferring the bacteria to toys, clothes or towels.

The bacterium that causes most cases of impetigo is *Staphylococcus aureus*, which lives on the skin and in the noses of many children. It causes impetigo only if the skin is damaged in any way. Less commonly a streptococcus may be to blame. Impetigo is rarely serious, but the child will have to stay away from nursery or school until the scabs have dropped off, which takes about five days.

You may notice

- *The child has tiny blisters, especially on the face around the nose and mouth. The blisters sometimes appear on the neck or hands*
- *The blisters break very easily, exposing a moist, weepy patch that oozes a cloudy yellow liquid, and dries to form a thick, golden crust*
- *The blisters appear on circles of reddened skin, 1.25-2.5 cm/½-1 in in diameter. Occasionally they join up to form unsightly clusters*
- *The patch of impetigo may spread from the edges, or a separate patch may form*
- *As the patches heal from the middle, they leave rings of reddened skin*

What to do

If you suspect that your child has impetigo consult your doctor, who can confirm the diagnosis. A small patch of impetigo near the mouth can sometimes be mistaken for a cold sore. The doctor may prescribe an antibiotic ointment that will clear the infection and also help to soften and remove the crusts. They may also give the child a course of antibiotics, usually penicillin or erythromycin, to be taken by mouth. The antibiotics should clear the infection within five days.

At home, be scrupulous about hygiene. Make sure the child's hands are washed frequently. If you bathe the child's sores, wash your hands before and after you do this. To bathe the sores, sprinkle salt into warm water to make a saline solution, then dip some cotton wool into it and wipe off the crusts. Alternatively, you can use soap and warm water. Dab the sores dry with soft kitchen paper. The crusts can be softened with warm (never hot) cooking oil. Keep the child's face cloth and towel separate from the rest of the family's, and wash them daily on the hottest wash cycle to kill any bacteria. To prevent the child from picking or rubbing at the crusts, give them lots of craft, playdough and constructional toys to keep their hands busy. Trim their nails short so that they cannot pick at the scabs.

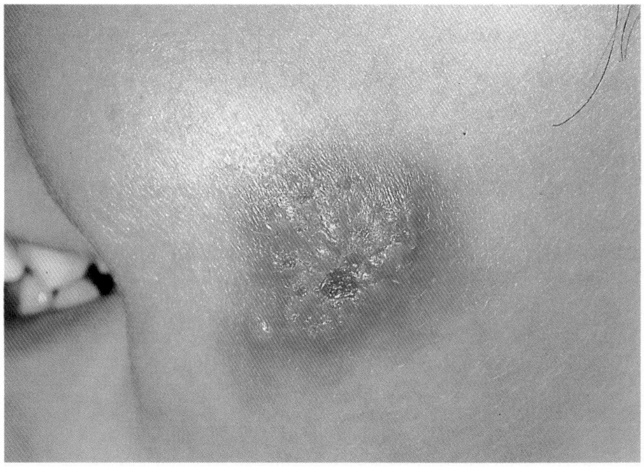

Impetigo (here, a lesion on a child's cheek) used to be such a common infection in school children that it was known colloquially as 'school sores'. It was more commonly seen among the poorer sectors of society and today is still particularly frequent in developing countries, especially in the countryside. It begins as a red patch and develops into soft pustules that join together. These eventually form crusty yellow blisters.

Complementary Treatment

Homeopathic remedies include Antimonium 6c (*Antimonium crudum*, black sulphide of antimony) for blisters surrounding the mouth and the nose; Mezereum 6c (*Daphne mezereum*, spurge olive) for encrusted blisters that mainly affect the scalp, producing oozing pus; Arsenicum 6c (*Arsenicum album*, arsenic trioxide) where the infection is accompanied by physical exhaustion and mental restlessness; and Croton 6c (*Croton tiglium*) when the child has inflamed and pus-filled blisters on the scrotum. These remedies should be taken every hour for up to ten doses. You should take the child to the doctor if they do not clear the infection.

Cold Sores

What is it?

Cold sores are caused by the herpes simplex virus (HSV), which can cause various skin conditions, and usually produces small, fluid filled blisters. There are two main types of infection: herpes type 1 (HSV-I), which is spread by contact with the blisters and their fluid; and herpes type 2 (HSV-II) a genital infection that can occasionally affect newborn babies.

HSV-I infections are very common. Parents are the usual source of infection for small children, while teenagers can catch the virus from skin-to-skin contact. The first time the virus attacks, usually between the ages of two and five, it does not cause cold sores. In fact, the first attack is usually so mild that it passes unnoticed; occasionally it brings on an influenza-like illness with painful mouth and lip ulcers. Once in the body, the virus lies dormant until it is re-awakened, often by hot sun, a biting wind or a cold.

Cold sores are more likely to develop when a child is run down. Overstretching the mouth – for example, at the dentist – can also bring them on, and girls are more prone around the time of their periods.

Cold sores appear on and around the mouth and nose, and anyone who has a cold sore is extremely contagious. The blister itself, the fluid that is inside it and the child's saliva all carry the infection.

You may notice

- *The child complains of a sore, itchy area near the mouth. This phase lasts for around a day*
- *A clear blister appears on a red patch. Sometimes you will see a cluster of tiny blisters*
- *The blister crusts over after a day or two, and the scab falls off within a week or ten days*

What to do

If you are unsure whether your child has a cold sore, the doctor or pharmacist will be able to distinguish it from similar conditions, such as impetigo.

At the first tingly cold sore sensation, apply cold sore cream, lotion or vaseline. To ease the tingle, hold a piece of wetted, frozen cotton wool to the sore. If your child gets repeated attacks or seems run down take them to the doctor. The doctor can prescribe antibiotics if the sore becomes infected, and may prescribe the antiviral cream aciclovir to apply as soon as you notice the first symptoms.

You should also take your child to the doctor if they have eczema and develop a cold sore, because the herpes virus can produce an extremely unpleasant rash consisting of sheets of individual blisters. Your doctor will treat this rash with the antiviral aciclovir.

To prevent your child's lips from cracking in the cold, apply vaseline or lip balm before they go outside. In sunny weather, apply factor 25 or 30 sunblock.

Avoid kissing your child's mouth and do not let them kiss others. Always wash your hands after touching the sore.

Coping with cold sores

A child with a sore on the mouth will find it hard to eat. Give them soft foods such as ice cream, yoghurt, mushy vegetables or even baby food. If drinking is uncomfortable, the child may find it easier if they use a straw.

Sterilize everything that goes into the child's mouth, and keep their face cloth and towel separate from the rest of the family's. Keep a child with a cold sore well away from anyone with eczema.

Complementary Treatment

Nutritional therapists will usually recommend vitamins A and E and zinc supplements. Vitamin E oil and garlic oil can be applied directly to the sores. **Homeopaths** will look at the individual and their symptoms and prescribe accordingly (constitutional treatment). Remedies to be used during outbreaks include Rhus tox. 6c (*Rhus toxicodendron*, poison ivy) when the chin and mouth are affected and ulcers appear at the corners of the mouth. **Western** and **Chinese herbalists** usually treat with topical applications of herbs, and may give constitutional treatment as backup. **Aromatherapists** have found that many essential oils, including tea tree, are beneficial and help to heal the skin. They can be applied neat or diluted with a carrier oil. Children who have recurrent cold sores may benefit from seeing an **acupuncturist**.

Bald Patches and Baldness

What is it?

The most common reason for a baby to be bald is an inherited tendency to grow hair at a later-than-average age. Some babies are born with a thick head of hair, while others still have wispy hair at the age of five. Anything between the two is normal, and the age at which a child grows hair is not linked in any way with adult baldness.

Patchy baldness may be caused by rubbing or pulling hair as it grows, an infection of the scalp such as ringworm (see page 163), a recent illness or certain drugs. A few children develop bald patches for no known reason, although this condition, called alopecia areata, is more common in children who have a tendency to allergies. Eventually the hair regrows, but your child may feel embarrassed about the baldness until it does. Baldness is almost never serious, although it may need to be treated by a doctor.

What you might notice and what to do

- *The infant is bald.* Most babies lose their newborn hair within a few weeks of birth. It can be months before the hair grows back, and sometimes the regrowth is a completely different colour and type of hair. Many babies have 'comb-able' hair by their first birthday. If your child still has wispy hair at the age of three, keep what hair there is trimmed short so that it will look thicker.
- *The infant develops a bald patch on the top/back of the head.* The bald patch may have fuzzy, baby hair. The bald patch is caused by the baby rubbing their head on the cot sheet or baby seat. The baby's hair will grow properly once your child is up and walking.
- *The child has odd, small bald patches and constantly twiddles/pulls their hair.* Constant twiddling and twisting – a condition called trichotillomania – breaks the hair shafts. If your child twiddles when they are bored, concentrating or nervous, train them to sit on their hands or give them something else to fiddle with. A related type of hair loss, known as traction alopecia, is obvious at the edges of the scalp in children with tightly combed back hairstyles, especially some Afro-Caribbean hairstyles. The hair normally grows back again in a few weeks.
- *The child has itchy round red patches where the hair has come out.* This could be ringworm (see page 163). Consult your doctor.
- *The child has a number of bald patches or the hair is thin after an illness or drug treatment.* Some drugs, including anti-cancer drugs, and a few illnesses that cause a high fever, can upset the hair roots, although it may be two or three months before the effects become noticeable. If this happens, consult your doctor. Your child's hair will almost certainly grow back again within a matter of weeks.

Coping with bald patches

Children should always wear a hat when they are out in the sun, but this is even more important if their hair is thin or if they have bald patches.

If your child's hair is thin and slow to grow, choose a short hairstyle. Do not tie it back with rubber bands, which will snap the hairs, and always use a soft nylon or bristle brush when grooming the hair.

Complementary Treatment

Where the condition is the result of emotional trauma, therapists using **Bach flower remedies** will treat the reaction to the trauma and allow the physical effect – the hair loss – to take its course and correct itself. Rescue Cream or Rescue Remedy applied directly to the scalp may also help. **Aromatherapy** can be supportive to orthodox treatment, helping the child to relax and accept their altered body image. Essential oils may be used to reduce the enlargement of the hair follicles sometimes found in this condition. **Western herbalists** usually treat with topical applications of herbs, and may give constitutional treatment as backup. **Homeopathy** may also provide an effective treatment. Homeopathic remedies that may be prescribed include Phosphorus 6c (*Phosphorus*) when the child's hair falls out by the handful, and Kali carb 6c (*Kali carbonicum*, potassium carbonate) for hair loss that is associated with dandruff. These remedies should be taken every 12 hours for up to 30 days. In general, the homeopath will treat the child constitutionally – that is, according to their personality, mood and temperament.

RINGWORM

What is it?

Despite the name, ringworm (tinea) is not caused by a worm, but by a fungus called tinea. It can affect the skin of various parts of the body, including the trunk (*tinea corporis*), the scalp (*tinea capitis*), the groin and the feet (see Athlete's foot, page 179). Ringworm is usually passed on by direct contact with an infected person, but children also often catch it through cuddling or stroking a pet – most often a kitten or puppy – that is carrying ringworm spores on its skin or in its fur. It can also be passed on indirectly, for example, from skin flakes that have fallen on to the floor or furniture, or by using the towels or face cloths of someone with ringworm infection. Cattle ringworm can be spread on barbed wire, and children with shaved hairstyles may catch ringworm when their heads are shaven with unsterilized razors.

Ringworm is not usually serious, but it is unsightly and embarrassing. Because it is contagious, you should keep your child off school until treatment has started. Scalp ringworm (especially the cattle type) can be more serious than ringworm on the trunk, and it needs prompt treatment to avoid the possibility of permanent bald patches.

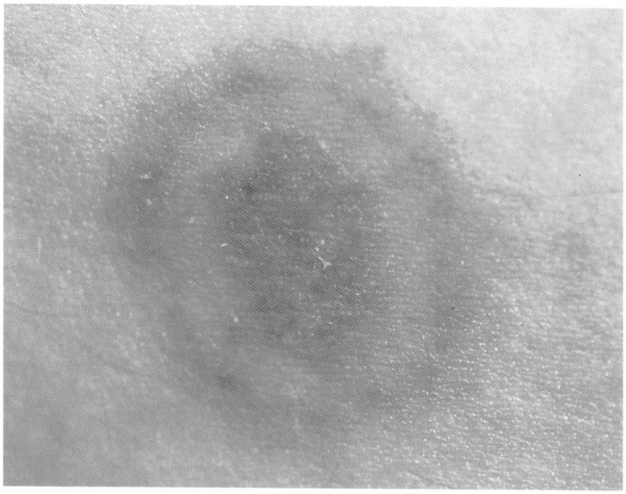

A tinea corporis *lesion, showing the characteristic raised and inflamed edges and clearing patch in the centre. The most common causes of ringworm in the United Kingdom are* Microsporum canis, *usually acquired from puppies or kittens, or* Trichophyton rubrum, *which is caught from other people. Zoöphyllic infections passing from animals to humans are especially inflammatory.*

You may notice

- *On the head: small round patches of scaly skin, which can become inflamed and swollen. As the patches spread, the centre heals and the hairs snap off to leave stubble. The result is a moth-eaten appearance to the hair*
- *On the body: round or oval red patches, which spread slowly outwards leaving pale, healed skin in the centre. Sometimes the patches are scaly. They are most common on the face, although they also appear on the body, arms and legs*
- *Wherever they appear, ringworm sores can be itchy as well as red and inflamed*

What to do

Keep your child away from nursery or school until they have been seen by a doctor and the diagnosis has been confirmed. The doctor may take a sample of brushed hair or a small scraping from the scalp. The doctor will prescribe the antifungal drug griseofulvin, as tablets or syrup, which the child needs to take for four to eight weeks to completely eradicate the infection. If the child completes the full course of treatment, ringworm of the trunk and scalp will usually be cured and is unlikely to recur.

To keep the child's scalp clean, wash their hair daily with a mild shampoo. You do not need to have the child's hair cut short, but brush their hair gently every day to stop it becoming matted. The doctor may give you cream to put on the ringworm patches after washing the hair. For ringworm on the body, treatment is antifungal cream applied twice a day for two to four weeks.

Always wash your hands after touching the child's ringworm patches and make sure the child does this too. Keep the child's towel and face cloth separate from the rest of the family's, and wash them daily. Buy the child a new hairbrush and comb, and dispose of the old ones, along with any hats the child has worn. If a household pet is the source of infection, make sure the pet also receives treatment.

Complementary Treatment

Homeopathy and **Chinese herbalism** are the most relevant treatments. For an infected scalp, give the remedy Sulphur 6c (*Sulphur*, sublimated sulphur), followed by Sepia 6c (*Sepia officinalis*, cuttlefish ink) if there is no sign of improvement. When the infection affects and is confined to the trunk, give Tellurium 6c (the element tellurium). Remedies should be taken every four hours for up to ten doses. Chinese herbalists will prescribe herbs steeped in Chinese vinegar for topical application; these may be taken internally if there is a digestive problem as well.

HEAD LICE

What are they?

Head lice are extremely common, especially among primary school and nursery children. As they like warmth, these insects, the size of a match head, live close to the scalp and cling to the hairs. When two children have their heads together the lice move rapidly from head to head. They make no distinction between clean and dirty hair, and live only on humans. The only way they can move is by crawling – they cannot fly, jump or hop through the air.

Lice lay their eggs (the empty shells of which are known as nits) close to the scalp, and they glue them to the base of the hairs. You are unlikely to see an egg before it hatches as it is well camouflaged, reflecting the colour of the host's hair. However you may see the hard, pearly white shell of a hatched louse stuck firmly to a hair.

Sometimes a child who has nits does not have lice, because the lice have all hatched and moved on to another person's head. The eggs take seven to ten days to hatch. The new baby louse, the size of a pinhead, leaves the pearly white shell, and grows by moulting its skin three times over the next seven to fourteen days.

Children with head lice may scratch their heads, but apart from the irritant effect lice are not harmful, and they do not carry any particular diseases. In very large numbers, lice can make a child feel unwell, but this is extremely rare and most children who get lice have only a few. However they are unpleasant and you should keep your family free of them.

The first warning of head lice for many families is a letter from the playgroup, nursery or school, informing parents that other children have them. Other possible signs are as follows.

Examine the teeth of the comb carefully after each stroke to check for head lice. At first you may find flecks of dust, fluff or flaky skin between the teeth and as thoroughly wettened lice do not move, you may find identification difficult. Compare what you find with this picture and, if any doubt remains, use a magnifying glass.

You may notice

- *The child has an itchy scalp. However people can have lice for several weeks before they start to itch*
- *You may see immovable white flecks on your child's hair. Unlike dandruff, which brushes out easily, the nits cling firmly to the hair*
- *The child has a red rash on the back of the neck, which is caused by an allergy to the louse droppings*

What to do

If you receive a letter from your child's nursery, playgroup or school, or you notice any of the above signs, check your child's hair thoroughly. First, wash the hair with a normal shampoo and apply lots of conditioner. Second, untangle the hair with an ordinary comb. Then run a fine-toothed detector comb (available from the chemist) through the hair, starting at the roots and angling the teeth towards the scalp. Comb even really long hair right to the tips. Make small partings and comb the locks of hair separately. Check the comb for lice after each stroke, and wipe it on kitchen paper. If you are not sure whether what you see is a louse, place the suspect object on a tissue, touching a hair. Once it has dried out, a louse will grasp the hair.

Bug busting

The insecticide-free method of clearing lice in the United Kingdom is called bug busting. This requires a special bug buster comb, available with a full kit. To carry out the procedure, first shampoo your child's hair as normal and apply a generous amount of conditioner. Then, without rinsing out the conditioner, comb out the tangles with a normal comb. Once the comb moves freely through the hair, divide the hair into sections and slot the bug buster comb into one section at at time – keeping the teeth in contact with the scalp for as long as possible. Then comb right down to the hair tips. After each stroke, check the comb for lice, and rinse away in the washbasin any lice you find.

When you have combed the entire head, rinse off the conditioner. Leaving the hair as wet as possible, sit the child

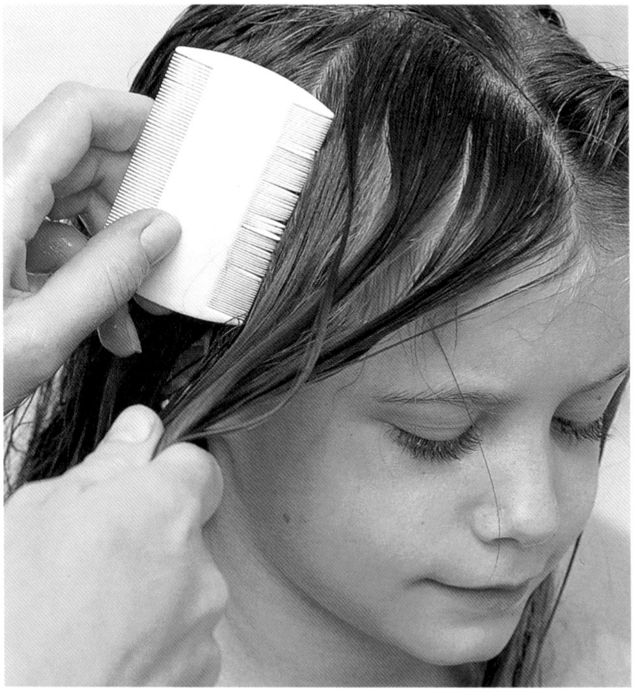

During wet combing, wettened lice lose their grip and are combed out of the hair. Wet combing is an effective and pesticide-free way of clearing lice from a child's hair; it also acts as a preventive by removing new lice before they are old enough to mate and lay their eggs.

upright with a towel around their shoulders. Repeat the section-by-section combing process, clearing any lice off the comb as you find them. If you do find lice, repeat the bug busting process every three or four days for the next two weeks, so that any lice emerging from eggs are removed before they spread.

Using an insecticide

If you prefer to use an insecticide treatment, ask your pharmacist, doctor or health clinic which lotion or rinse they are currently recommending. Do not use shampoos, as they do not come into contact with the eggs for a long enough period to work properly.

Lice and nits can become resistant to some treatments, and within local areas different treatments are used in rotation to try and prevent the lice developing a resistance. Lotions containing carbaryl are available only on prescription from a doctor. Children with asthma, eczema, dry skin or cradle cap must be treated with a water-based lotion, not an alcohol-based one.

Follow the manufacturer's instructions very carefully, leaving the lotion in contact with the hair for the recommended length of time. Do not exceed the number of doses stipulated by the manufacturer. If eggs continue to hatch out, use the bug busting method instead. The presence of chlorine in the hair may reduce the effectiveness of some head louse treatments, so if your child swims regularly, wash their hair with an anti-chlorine swimmer's shampoo and allow it to dry completely before starting treatment.

Check the heads of the whole family, and inform everyone your child has regular contact with. There is no shame in head lice, and warning all contacts is the only way to interrupt the spread. All babies, pregnant and breastfeeding mothers should be treated using the bug busting method, not the insecticide method.

Prevention

To protect your child during an outbreak at school, wet-comb their hair twice weekly (or more) with a detector comb to remove stray lice and damage others that are not removed. Combing the hair when it is wet makes it easier to detect lice because wet lice move slowly. Conditioner makes the hair slippery so the lice lose their grip on the hairs.

Who can help?

An increasing number of schools now have a bug busting day once or twice a year when every family checks for nits and lice at the same time. For where to get more information about the schools' pack or the family Bug Buster kit see the Directory.

Complementary Treatment

Orthodox treatment must be the first course of action for this problem. Once this is underway the **homeopath** may offer constitutional treatment (prescribing according to the individual and their symptoms) to render the child less attractive to infestation. **Western herbalism** may also be supportive. **Chinese herbalism** gives similar results to orthodox treatment, but is much smellier.

Scabies

What is it?

Scabies is an infestation by a parasite, *Sarcoptes scabiei*, that burrows into the skin to lay its eggs. The eggs hatch and more mites emerge. The result is intense, but relatively harmless, irritation. The mites are so tiny that even the very largest of them are scarcely visible.

Scabies is caught by skin-to-skin contact. This may be through sharing a bed with someone who has the infestation, or by holding hands or other close physical contact. Spread of the mite is encouraged by factors such as overcrowding and poor hygiene. A child will become contagious as soon as they are infested with the mite, even though it can take a month or more before they show the first signs of scabies. Although scabies is a nuisance and is contagious, it will not make a child ill. However the intense itch that is caused by an allergic reaction to the saliva or droppings of the scabies mite will make the child scratch, and this will frequently result in a secondary skin infection.

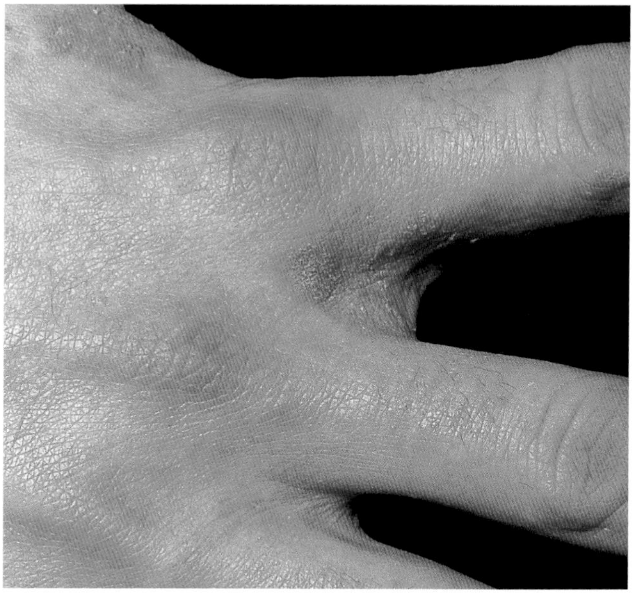

Surface burrows under the skin between the fingers show where the female scabies mite, Sarcoptes scabiei, *lays her numerous eggs. When intense itching starts after about a month, the skin may be covered with sores and spots that mingle with the burrows and obscure them.*

You may notice

- *The child rubs or scratches the insides of the arms and thighs, the waist, groin and armpits, especially in bed at night or after a bath. The child may rub the soles of their feet together to gain some relief*
- *There may be small, itchy bumps on the skin that look infected. The bumps can appear anywhere on the body, but they are most common between the fingers, on the hands and wrists, on the feet, and in the armpits and groin. Scabies rarely occurs on the head or face of older children, but it can affect these areas in babies*
- *Occasionally, fine meandering lines are visible on the skin in the same areas as the spots*

What to do

Keep the child off nursery or school, and take them to see the doctor. The doctor will prescribe an insecticide lotion that must be applied to the entire body, and especially around and under the fingernails, the soles of the feet, between the fingers and behind the ears. You do not need to apply it to the head of a child, but a baby's head must be covered in the lotion, leaving space round the eyes, and also around the mouth so that the baby cannot lick it off. The lotion needs to stay in contact with the skin for at least eight hours, so it is best to apply it just before bed. If the child washes their hands during treatment, reapply the lotion. The lotion should be rinsed off with soap and water, usually after 24 hours. One treatment is usually enough, although the doctor may recommend a second treatment seven to ten days later. All members of the family and the child's close friends will need treatment, even if they have no signs of scabies, because they may well have the infestation.

The itching can go on for up to three weeks after treatment. You can apply calamine or antihistamine cream to soothe it. It will also help to keep the child cool.

Before applying the lotion note exactly where the child's spots are. This is because treatment may take more than a week to work, and to be sure that it has been effective, you must notice if any new spots appear after this time.

Wash clothes, bedlinen and towels on a hot wash, dry in a dryer or in hot sunlight and iron them. This should ensure that all the mites are killed.

Complementary Treatment

Homeopathic treatment consists of administering Sulphur 30c (*Sulphur*, sublimated sulphur) to all members of the family every 12 hours for up to three days. If this remedy does not result in improvement within seven days, see your doctor.

Warning: Individuals suffering from eczema should not take Sulphur 30c.

BIRTHMARKS

What are they?
Many babies are born with birthmarks somewhere on their body; they are usually harmless concentrations of one of the components of normal skin.

Salmon patches (angel's kisses or stork marks)
These are often found on the eyelids, the forehead and at the back of the neck. They are dull red patches that become more obvious when the baby cries. They are caused by tiny dilated blood vessels beneath the skin, and they gradually disappear. Marks on the face are usually almost invisible by the child's first birthday, except when they strain or cry. Marks on the neck may be visible until the child is four or even older.

Mongolian blue spots
These are slate-blue patches over the lower back and bottom that can look like bruises. They are common in Asian and Afro-Caribbean children and occasionally occur in Caucasian children. They are caused by large numbers of pigment cells collecting in the deep layers of the skin before birth. In the first few days of life the blue patches may get darker, but then they gradually fade and disappear during childhood.

Port wine stains (naevus flammeus)
At birth port wine stains appear as irregular patches of slightly flushed skin, often on one side of the face or neck. They are caused by dilated blood vessels in the skin, and they are permanent. They do not change size, but the colour deepens, eventually becoming a shade between pale pink and dark purple. Port wine stains can be treated with pulsed dye lasers, which make the stain paler and sometimes scarcely visible. Treatment sessions usually start in early childhood so that the child does not have to cope with the social effects of going to school with an obvious birthmark.

Strawberry marks (capillary haemangiomas)
Strawberry marks are often invisible at birth, but they develop within a few days or weeks into a soft, raised lump with a bright red speckled surface. They continue to grow until the baby is six to nine months old, and then they gradually shrink and get paler. They are most common on the face, neck and the nappy area. As most strawberry marks disappear before school age, they are usually left alone. However if a strawberry mark threatens to interfere with a vital body part, such as an eye or ear, it can be treated with the cortico steroid prednisolone, which shrinks it. A strawberry mark that has not started to shrink by the time a child is' five or six can be treated with laser therapy. In older children, plastic surgery can tidy up any remaining signs.

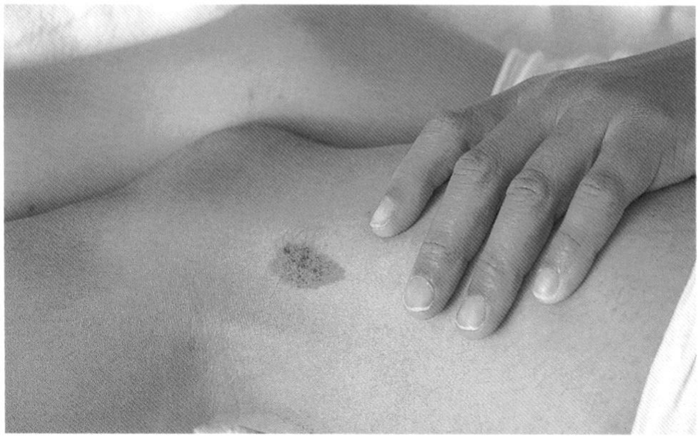

Birthmarks are caused by an accumulation of tiny blood vessels called naevi, which lie close to the skin's surface, or by localized pigmentation of the skin. Local pigmentation causes moles – which can be flat, as shown here, or raised – and Mongolian blue spots. Birthmarks that are unsightly can often be removed by plastic surgery or laser treatment, or camouflaged with specially formulated cosmetics.

Moles (melanocytic naevi)
Moles appear in various guises; they may be flat or raised, smooth or hairy. They consist of large numbers of pigment cells within the skin. If they are present at birth they tend to be larger and darker than the moles that appear gradually throughout childhood. Moles that are very unsightly or in positions where they will be difficult to shade from the sun may be removed by plastic surgery. Various techniques are used including dermabrasion (gradually scraping the skin surface away), skin grafts and laser therapy.

Who can help?
For organizations offering support and information on birthmarks see the Directory.

Complementary Treatment
Orthodox treatment is the first course of action for dealing with birthmarks generally, but a consultation with a **homeopath** can be helpful for strawberry marks. The recommended homeopathic first aid for strawberry marks that bleed is to apply pressure and administer Phosphorus 6c (phosphorus) every five minutes until the bleeding stops. Thereafter give three doses of Phosphorus 30c, at intervals of 12 hours.

PSORIASIS

What is it?

Psoriasis is a common non-infectious skin disorder. It is rare in babies, but it can affect older children, with an average age of onset of between ten and twenty years. The exact cause is unknown, but children with psoriasis have an inherited tendency to produce skin cells about seven times faster than normal. The top layer of the skin is constantly being replaced by new cells produced beneath the surface. Normally, each skin cell has a life of between three and four weeks; the cells die as they reach the surface, and are rubbed off as scales. In psoriasis this process is speeded up, and the replacement cycle lasts only two to three days. Psoriasis tends to fluctuate periodically. The child will have periods of clear skin, interspersed with episodes of psoriasis. In a child with an inherited tendency to the disease an episode of psoriasis is often triggered initially by a throat infection. Other common triggers include injury, cold weather and stress.

You may notice

- *The child may have clearly edged red patches of skin covered with coarse, silvery scales. The patches may be itchy and may first appear on the trunk, arms, elbows, legs, knees or scalp*
- *There may be a spray of raindrop-like round red spots over the body, especially on the chest and back, two to three weeks after the child has had a bacterial (streptococcal) throat infection or tonsillitis. This type of 'raindrop' (guttate) psoriasis clears on its own, though it may take months to do so*

What to do

Take the child to the doctor, who may take a throat swab or prescribe an antibiotic such as penicillin to clear the throat infection, if this is the trigger. The doctor can then prescribe emollients and moisturizers to stop the skin from drying out. To clear the psoriasis, the doctor may suggest an ointment containing dithranol, which is left on for 30–60 minutes or overnight, depending on the strength. However, dithranol is messy to use and it temporarily stains the skin brown. The doctor may also prescribe a shampoo or a bath additive containing coal tar, which is an anti-inflammatory and helps to clear scale. Adolescents with stubborn psoriasis may have treatment with ultraviolet light, or be prescribed a cream or ointment called calcipotriol, which is related to vitamin D.

When applying emollients, use a spatula rather than putting your fingers into the tub, and ask your pharmacist to dispense large quantities of emollient in several small tubs rather than one large one. This will ensure that you do not have one tub open for a long time.

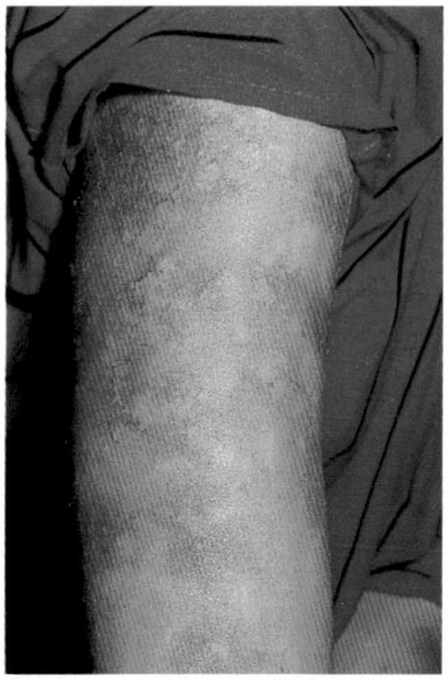

Children with mild psoriasis may be prescribed a coal tar or steroid cream or ointment. If the psoriasis is widespread, however, an ointment or cream containing dithranol may be prescribed. Dithranol has to be applied and washed off carefully to avoid damage to the skin. It can leave a purple-brown stain, clearly visible here, which fades two or three weeks after the treatment has been completed.

Clothing should be soft and loose, and made of pure cotton or pure new wool. Choose light coloured tops if the scalp is involved, because skin flakes look unsightly on dark materials. If the skin is very sensitive, the child should wear their nightclothes inside out to prevent the seams from rubbing on the sore skin.

Sunlight helps to clear the rash, so psoriasis is usually better in the summer.

Who can help?

For organizations who can give information and advice, see the Directory.

Complementary Treatment

Treatment for psoriasis with any complementary therapy – as with orthodox treatment – may be prolonged because of its complex nature . Treatment with an **osteopath** may include working on the nervous system to stimulate the eliminative capacities of the liver, kidneys, skin and bowels. **Western herbalists** will usually expect good results from relieving stress factors and improving liver function. **Nutritional therapists** maintain that the condition is caused mainly by toxins and therefore concentrate on diets that enhance liver detoxification. They may also recommend increasing the daily intake of zinc and/or essential fatty acids. **Chinese herbalists** regard psoriasis as a blood deficiency, which needs time to cure. Treatment usually includes floradex. Reports suggest that Rescue Cream, a **Bach flower remedy**, is extremely successful. **Acupuncture** may also produce beneficial results.

PITYRIASIS ROSEA

What is it?

Pityriasis rosea is a skin rash that is fairly common in children and young adults, but rare in babies. It begins as a single oval patch of red skin, known as the herald patch, which is usually somewhere on the child's trunk. A few days later lots of smaller patches appear on the trunk, upper arms and upper legs. The cause is unknown, but it is thought that a virus is probably responsible because the condition occasionally occurs in clusters, and it is more frequent in spring and autumn. If the cause is a virus, it is not a very infectious one, because a child who is affected only rarely passes it on to other members of the family.

You may notice

- *Occasionally the child may feel under the weather and have a slight fever, as if they were developing a cold*
- *The herald patch, which usually measures 2.5-5 cm/1-2 in across, is red and scaly, but not particularly itchy. It is usually on the child's back or chest, but occasionally it may be on the upper arm. It is followed a few days later by a sudden rash of smaller oval pink patches, mostly on the trunk. Sometimes the patches spread to the upper arms and thighs. The patches start as a little spot, which spreads outwards to form a pink or copper-coloured circle with a fine scaly outer edge. On the child's back the patches follow the lines of the ribs, sweeping down from the spine to give a Christmas tree effect*
- *In black children it is difficult to see the redness at first, but the patches become obviously darker than the surrounding skin, with noticeable scaling at the edges*
- *The patches may spread to the face in black-skinned children, although the face is only rarely affected by the rash in white-skinned children*
- *Each patch tends to peel from the centre to the outer edge*

What to do

Take the child to the doctor for a definite diagnosis. Other than that there is usually no need to treat pityriasis because in most cases it is not itchy or sore, and it clears on its own over three to eight weeks. Ask the doctor for a letter for your child's school or nursery to explain what the rash is, that your child is not infectious, and that they can take part in all sporting activities. If the patches are itchy, the doctor can prescribe a mild steroid cream to soothe them. If the itching is severe, the doctor may prescribe antihistamine tablets or syrup. You can also rub in emollient moisturizer or use a bath oil to keep the child's skin soft and supple. It is very unusual for a child to have more than one attack of pityriasis rosea.

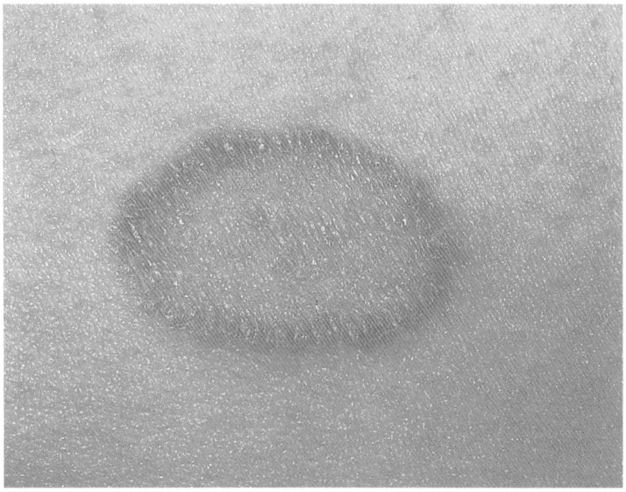

The characteristic clear oval shape of the 'herald patch' of pityriasis rosea usually appears between three and ten days before a rash of smaller, oval and scaly red patches breaks out. The rash appears predominantly on the trunk, where there is a tendency for the patches to be arranged parallel to the lines of the ribs.

Complementary Treatment

Homeopathy may give good results with this condition and is generally more gentle than orthodox treatment, although you should get advice from your doctor if homeopathic remedies do not improve the condition after seven to fourteen days. Arsenicum 6c (*Arsenicum album*, arsenic trioxide) is useful where pityriasis is accompanied by restlessness, anxiety and the constant desire for sips of water; Natrum mur 6c (*Natrum muriaticum*, salt) may be used for red spots overlain with white scales, where exercise and warmth make itching worse; and Radium brom 6c (*Radium bromatum*, radium bromide) where fiery red spots are burning and painful. The remedy should be administered four times a day for up to three weeks. Rescue Cream, a **Bach flower remedy**, may also help. Crab Apple, diluted in water and applied to the skin with a cotton wool pad, may help to relieve any itchiness.

NAPPY RASH

What is it?

Nappy rash is an extremely common condition, affecting as many as one infant in every three at any given time. The use of disposable nappies has made severe nappy rash much less of a problem, but mild nappy rash is still the most common skin condition in babies. Nappy rash may last for only a day, and most rashes clear within ten days. Over the age of 12 months a baby urinates less frequently and is therefore less likely to develop nappy rash.

Of the various types of nappy rash, irritant dermatitis is the most common. It occurs when a baby's bottom is sealed in a urine-soaked environment. Friction from the nappy or tight clothes makes the baby's moist skin more vulnerable to irritation. If a baby is left in a wet nappy for long time – overnight, for example – ammonia is produced as a result of the reaction between the urine and bacteria in the faeces. The ammonia, which has a characteristic fishy smell, dissolves in the warm surrounding moisture to produce an intensely irritating alkaline solution. Bacteria from the faeces can set up further chemical reactions that make the nappy rash worse.

Causes of nappy rash

Nappy rash is more common in bottle-fed babies than breast-fed babies, and during weaning on to solids. Some babies develop acute nappy rash when they are teething or when they have an infection, such as a cold. Diarrhoea is another common cause, because the loose stools are often highly acidic and can damage the upper layers of skin. Stubborn nappy rash may be caused by thrush (see page 100), an infection caused by the fungus *Candida albicans*, and this is especially likely if the baby has recently had a course of antibiotics. If the rash is red, moist and glistening, and affects the skin folds as well as the area in contact with the nappy, and the baby also has cradle cap (see page 158), the rash may be seborrhoeic dermatitis (see page 155).

Although nappy rash looks extremely sore, the baby is usually completely untroubled by it. It can almost always be treated simply at home. Occasionally it needs to be seen by a doctor, but it is never a serious condition.

You may notice

- *The infant may have red patches or spots in the nappy area. The patches mostly affect the parts of the bottom that come into direct contact with the nappy. The patches may look shiny and glazed*
- *There may be a rash of bright red pimples that spreads out from the anus*
- *There may be red patches spreading beyond the nappy area to the chest and back*
- *The infant may have raw nappy rash that is obvious in the skin creases as well as the surfaces that touch the nappy*
- *There may be redness just in the skin folds*
- *There may be a strong fishy smell when changing the nappy*

What to do

Change the baby's nappy frequently, making sure that you clean the bottom extremely carefully. Wash your hands first and then clean the surface area gently but thoroughly with cotton wool and warm water or baby lotion. Baby wipes are not necessary, but if you want to use them, choose wipes that are hypoallergenic, pH-balanced and alcohol-free, and do not wipe too vigorously. Pat the area gently but thoroughly dry, and leave the baby to kick with the nappy off. Then wash your hands again. This is the simplest and most effective way to cure nappy rash.

What else?

Heat makes the rash worse, so in the summer leave nappies off whenever you can. If the baby's bottom is exposed to sunlight, use a zinc oxide barrier cream. When you must use a nappy, smear on a protective nappy rash or zinc and castor oil cream first, making sure thta the cream gets into all of the skin creases.

A cream containing a mild antiseptic will protect against bacterial infection. If you can, use disposable nappies, It is

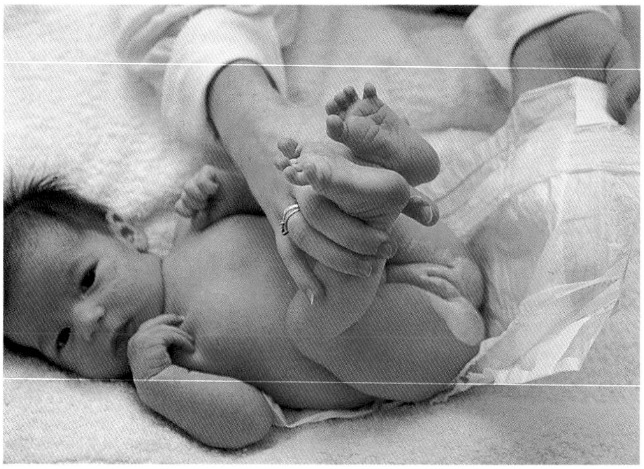

Babies with nappy rash are usually not bothered by the condition – it often looks much sorer than it actually is. However it should always be treated, and this can be done simply and effectively at home

also important to change the baby's nappy as soon as you suspect that it has become wet or dirty.

If you are still feeding your baby during the night, change their nappy after they have been fed while they have nappy rash. When you dress the baby avoid clothes that hug the groin, and do not use a sling or a baby carrier that has tight straps while the baby has nappy rash.

Aggravating irritants

If you have recently changed the type of nappy you use and your baby has developed nappy rash, try another type. Try buying really cheap nappies and changing them more frequently than usual, or try superabsorbent nappies.

Although it is uncommon, it is thought to be possible for babies to react to chemicals used in the manufacture of nappies. If you are using terry towel nappies the baby may be reacting to enzymes in biological washing powder. Use a non-biological powder or one that is made especially for sensitive skins instead.

If the baby has just been weaned on to solids, check if what they are eating could be causing the nappy rash. Some babies develop a rash after eating acidic fruits, such as satsumas, or food that goes straight through the digestive system, such as peas or raisins.

Consult your health visitor or doctor if the rash does not improve in two or three days, if the rash is spreading or if the baby seems ill in other ways.

Secondary infection

Severe nappy rash is very often associated with a secondary thrush infection and can be bright red, shiny and itchy. The rash may spread beyond the nappy area, and you may see the skin peeling at the edges of the rash. Check for white patches that look like flecks of milk inside the baby's mouth. These are signs of oral thrush. You can buy an antifungal cream from the pharmacist, but it is better to let a doctor see the rash. The doctor can prescribe a stronger antifungal cream or one containing a mild corticosteroid, such as hydrocortisone, which will help both thrush and seborrhoeic dermatitis, or a combination cream with an antibacterial agent if there is secondary infection.

If the rash becomes itchy and the baby has rough skin patches elsewhere on their body, they may have eczema (see page 156). The doctor can prescribe creams to moisturize and soften the skin, as well as barrier creams for the bottom. The doctor can also prescribe a mild antiseptic cream if the skin has become infected.

Complementary Treatment

Many **aromatherapy** oils can help to heal, but they must be very dilute; the nappy should be changed as soon as the child is wet or has soiled. **Homeopathy** can be very helpful. Specific remedies include Sulphur 6c (*Sulphur*, sublimated sulphur) where there is a red, scaly, dry rash; Calcarea 6c (*Calcerea carbonica*, calcium carbonate) for nappy rash in a fat infant who has profuse head sweats during the night; Rhus tox 6c (*Rhus toxicodendron*, poison ivy) for itchy skin with tiny blisters; and Mercurius 6c (*Mercurius solubilis Hahnemanni*, quick silver) when the area is very moist and sweaty and the baby produces an unusual amount of saliva. Remedies should be applied four times a day for no more than five days. If there is no improvement after this, consult a homeopath. The **nutritional therapist** may suggest a vitamin C supplement, which may be helpful, and emphasize the importance of normal hygiene. For rashes generally, the **Chinese herbalist** usually prescribes herbs to be taken internally, as well as a soothing wash.

Do's and Don'ts

Do

- Leave your infant nappy-free whenever possible
- Use a barrier cream – even if you use a cream for thrush as well
- Find a brand of nappy that suits your infant
- Avoid foods that provoke toddler diarrhoea
- Use a stay-dry nappy liner
- Wash and rinse terry nappies thoroughly in softened water, sterilizing them first and using non-biological powder or powder for sensitive skins.
- Soften them by tumble-drying briefly or using fabric conditioner. Alternatively, use a nappy laundering service

Don't

- Leave a baby in a wet or dirty nappy for longer than you have to
- Use plastic plants
- Use soap and water if it dries your infant's skin or baby lotion if it stings. Try aqueous cream instead
- Dress the baby in tight clothing

ACNE

What is it?

Acne is an extremely common condition in adolescence. It affects as many as nine out of ten teenagers, although in most it is only mild. It occurs because the level of sex hormones in the body rises at puberty and causes the sebaceous glands in the skin to produce too much of an oily substance called sebum. There is also overproduction of the top layer of skin cells, and the pores that lead to the sebaceous glands can become blocked by plugs of keratin (the protein part of the skin). This causes blackheads, and it allows the bacteria that thrive on sebum to multiply. The surrounding skin then becomes inflamed as the blood vessels expand to bring more infection-fighting cells to the blocked pore. The inflammation is usually accompanied by the production of pus.

As girls start puberty earlier than boys, they are prone to develop acne earlier, but the condition is usually worse in boys. Hereditary factors also play a role, and severe acne often runs in families.

You may notice

- *Isolated red spots or papules on the face, neck, back, chest or shoulders. Spots may develop into pustules with a white or yellowy head and can be painful. Whiteheads and blackheads are common*
- *Small pitted scars may develop where spots have healed. In darker skin types there may be obvious, but temporary, changes in skin colour around the scars*

Adolescent boys and girls can suffer severe psychological effects from even mild cases of acne, so all episodes should be taken seriously. Treatment is successful in the most severe cases but it is fruitless to expect instant results. Perseverance with treatment, combined with a good deal of patience, will produce results eventually.

What to do

Modern methods of treatment are effective, even for severe acne. However recovery is not instant, and even cases of mild acne can take as long as two months to show an improvement.Without treatment, the individual spots of acne do heal. However because new spots continue to appear all the time, the teenager's skin is never clear and the resulting complexion can be very distressing. The first step is self-medication with over-the-counter preparations. These contain substances that dry the skin, and they may also have antibacterial properties.

If these do not work the pharmacist will be able to suggest a range of creams, gels or lotions containing benzoyl peroxide or nicotinamide. Benzoyl peroxide treatments tend to dry and redden the skin, so it is best to start with a mild (2.5 per cent) preparation, and work up gradually to the highest strength (10 per cent) only if necessary. It is important that all skin treatments are applied over the entire affected area and not just to the spots.

If scars develop or if the acne is on the back, where it is difficult to apply skin preparations, see the doctor, who may prescribe a course of antibiotics to be used with benzoyl peroxide or an antibiotic cream or lotion. The doctor may also prescribe tretinoin, in cream, gel or lotion form. It is important to persist with treatment, but if there is no improvement after two months, discuss other options with the doctor. If acne persists, or if the teenager is very distressed by their appearance, the doctor may refer them to a dermatologist, who can prescribe a highly effective form of tretinoin in tablet form.

Who can help?

For organizations and agencies offering support and information. see the Directory.

Complementary Treatment

Nutritional therapists maintain that acne vulgaris is linked to diet, including excess fat intake, intolerance to certain foods and nutritional deficiencies, particularly zinc and vitamin A. It may also be a result of liver congestion. **Aromatherapists** recommend a regime including diet, massage, steaming and good hygiene. Essential oils have antiseptic properties and in low dilution will reduce bacteria on the skin. A **homeopathic consultation** will give advice on diet, nutrition, cleansing and exercise, as well as prescriptions for specific remedies. **Chinese herbalists** treat acne by clearing phlegm, heat and poisons from the body, and may recommend dietary changes.

Skin Allergy

What is it?

An allergic reaction is an inappropriate response by the body's immune system to a substance that does most people no harm, such as pollen, house-dust mite faeces, animal fur or certain foods. The substances that trigger the allergic reaction are called allergens. When allergens first enter the body of susceptible, or atopic, people, white blood cells called lymphocytes recognize the allergens and produce antibodies called immunoglobulin E (IgE), which are directed towards the allergens. The antibodies attach themselves to cells in the body called mast cells, which contain a substance called histamine. When more allergens enter the body they join on to the antibodies, causing the mast cells to release the histamine. Histamine causes an inflammatory response in many parts of the body, including the lungs (see Asthma, page 218); nose, eyes and throat (see Hay fever, page 221); and skin (see Eczema and Urticaria, pages 156 and 174).

The skin is frequently the first part of the body to show an allergic reaction, with eczema common in children under the age of one. Some skin allergies are not confined to atopic children; they can affect anyone. Contact dermatitis is a specific reaction in the skin to a particular substance, as happens, for example, when a nickel stud on a pair of jeans produces inflammation on bare skin.

You cannot completely protect your child against allergic reactions, but you can delay their start by not exposing your child at too young an age to well-known allergens such as eggs, peanuts or cows' milk. Fortunately most children grow out of acute allergic reactions that affect the skin, particularly eczema, and breastfeeding can help to protect against the these conditions or can certainly delay their onset.

You may notice

- *Red, scaly, itchy patches where the skin has been in contact with a chemical. For example, on the ears of girls who wear earrings (nickel), or the waist or wrists of a baby (rubber elastic in a babygro). This suggests contact dermatitis*
- *Itchy white and red patches that look like nettle stings all over the body. These can be caused by foods (seafoods, berry fruit, nuts, eggs, chocolate and drugs), plants or animals – a lick from a cat or dog is enough to bring up a nasty weal in a sensitive child. This is urticaria*
- *Red, scaly, itchy patches on the face and in the skin folds caused by atopic eczema*

What to do

If it is obvious what is causing the reaction, make sure the child avoids that substance. Contact the doctor for confirmation of

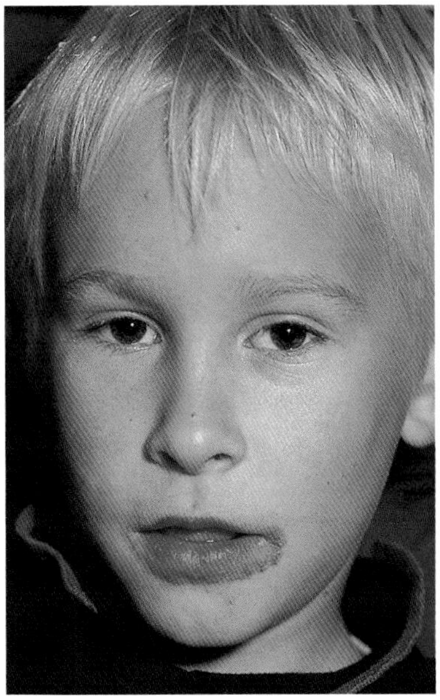

Lip eczema, also known as lip-licking dermatitis, is common in young children with the nervous habit of running their tongue around their lips. The lips become dry, rough and reddened, with the worst effect on the upper lip. Occasionally a similar effect can be seen in a child with a contact sensitivity to a particular brand of toothpaste.

your diagnosis. If your description of the child's symptoms does not give enough information, the doctor may refer the child to hospital for allergy tests. These may include: skin prick tests, in which a small amount of allergen is placed on the skin and a prick made through it (an itchy weal shows that the child is allergic to the chosen substance); patch tests that check for dermatitis, in which small patches are taped to the back for 48 hours; and RAST (radioallergosorbent) tests to measure the quantity of IgE antibody to a specific substance in a small blood sample. These tests do not provide a definite diagnosis on their own, but they can help to confirm a diagnosis suspected from your description of the child's symptoms.

General treatments for allergy include antihistamine drugs and steroid ointments to reduce the inflammation.

Complementary Treatment

Osteopathy would treat the whole person, not the allergy, by bringing the body back into balance. **Nutritional therapy** can help to identify any food allergy that may be the cause and advise on elimination diets if the allergen is difficult to identify. The **homeopath** may also be of help in this respect. **Acupuncture** can be effective when the cause is an underlying disharmony preventing the uninterrupted flow of *chi*. **Kinesiology** is particularly helpful in diagnosing allergies that may trigger other symptoms and disorders.

SEE ALSO CONTACT DERMATITIS (PAGE 151)

URTICARIA

What is it?

Urticaria (hives) is an allergic skin reaction that brings the child out in itchy red weals with white bumps, just like nettle stings. It is caused by the sudden release of the chemical histamine – from cells called mast cells – which inflames the tissues, making them swell, redden and itch. Urticaria is very common in children and may appear soon after they have eaten a particular food – strawberries, fish, nuts, eggs and chocolate are common triggers – a drug such as penicillin or a food colouring, such as tartrazine. The weals appear suddenly and fade within hours, but may recur for the next few days. Children with urticaria that lasts for more than six weeks are more likely to have another atopic (hypersensitivity) condition, such as eczema, asthma, or hay fever. Teenagers can develop a type of urticaria brought on by exercise, in which there is a rash of small itchy red weals.

Newborn babies may develop a form of urticaria on the second day after birth. This is a blotchy rash with white or yellow lumps surrounded by inflamed patches of skin, usually on the face, chest, arms and thighs. The rash normally disappears on its own within a few days.

You may notice

- *Small and large raised pink or red patches with a clear red edge, often circular, appear soon after the child eats a food to which they are sensitive*
- *The weals have a white or yellow lump in the middle and they may be itchy*
- *After a few hours the weals fade, but they recur for a few days*
- *There may be swelling under the rash, especially when it occurs on the child's face*

What to do

If the rash does not cause any swelling on the face, just observe it carefully and dab on calamine lotion to ease the itching. The cause of most urticaria is never found, but try to remember what your child has eaten recently.

If the rash is making the child's face swell, contact your doctor urgently. If the doctor is not available take the child to the nearest accident and emergency department. Although most face swelling goes down quickly, very occasionally the rash spreads to the throat and restricts the airways, causing the child to wheeze.

The doctor may prescribe an antihistamine drug, usually chlorpheniramine (Piriton) or loratidine (Clarityn), a newer, less sedating antihistamine. Your doctor or pharmacist will advise you, but do tell them if your child is taking other medication. A child with throat swelling may be given an injection of adrenaline. Urticaria may very occasionally be part of an anaphylactic reaction, in which the face, mouth and throat swell up. Call the emergency services or your doctor if a child develops signs of anaphylaxis.

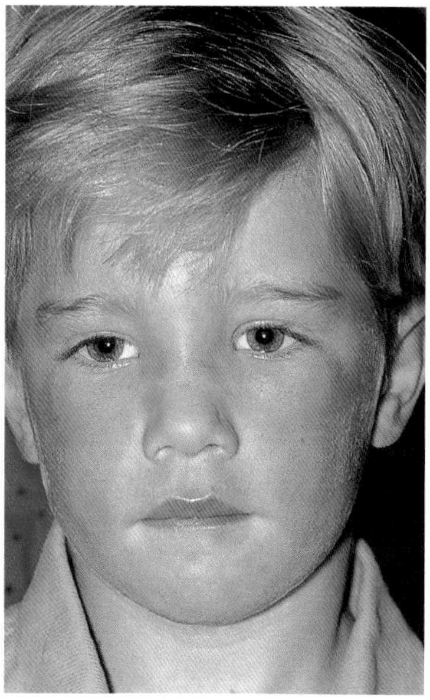

The cause of an urticarial reaction is more commonly discovered in children than in adults. In babies under six months of age a food allergy is the most common cause, while in an older child, such as this boy, reactions to medications are relatively frequent. In the majority of children, urticaria clears up fairly quickly.

Complementary Treatment

Homeopathy offers a number of specific remedies, including Apis 30c (*Apis mellifica*, honey bee or venom from sting) where burning and swollen lips and eyelids are made worse by warmth; and Rhus tox. (*Rhus toxicodendron*, poison ivy) for a burning, itching rash that develops into blisters, and the child is very restless. Conditions that recur should be referred to a homeopath, who will look at the individual and their symptoms and prescribe accordingly (constitutional treatment). When urticaria is linked to food allergy, **nutritional therapists** may be of help in identifying the problem food, and advising on its elimination from the diet. **Applied kinesiology** may also help in identifying the culprit. **Acupuncture** and **osteopathy** – both usually combined with advice on diet – **Chinese herbalism**, **aromatherapy** and the **Bach flower remedy** Rescue Cream, can all be effective in treating the complaint.

SEE ALSO ECZEMA (PAGE 156) SKIN ALLERGY (PAGE 173) ASTHMA (PAGE 218) AND HAY FEVER (PAGE 221)

Boils

What are they?

A boil is a bacterial infection of the hair follicle (the pore from which the hair grows). The most common cause is the bacterium called *Staphylococcus aureus*. Boils are most often seen either where the skin is under pressure, such as under a tight collar, or where it is moist, such as under the armpits.

If a hair follicle becomes infected a large, red and very tender lump develops. The tender lump gradually develops a whitish-yellow centre as the follicle fills up with pus. Covering the skin – with an airtight plaster, for example – makes boils more likely to develop, and so may using steroid ointments. Occasional boils are not serious, but they can be excruciatingly painful.

You may notice

- *A large, painful red swelling. The middle of the spot turns yellowy-white and then comes to a point when ready to burst*
- *Small yellow pimples that look infected. On white skin you can see a reddened patch around the infected spot, but on black skin only the spot is clearly visible*

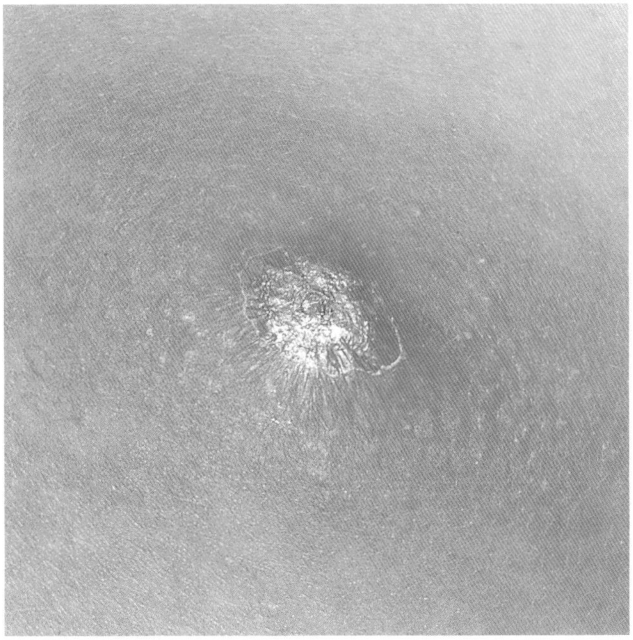

The boil on this individual is surrounded by an area of cellulitis – an inflammation of the cellular tissue. To encourage a painful boil such as this one to come to a head, you can apply magnesium sulphate paste and cover the boil with a plaster. Magnesium sulphate paste is available from chemists. Once the boil has burst, clean the area thoroughly, apply antiseptic cream and cover the area with a fresh plaster.

What to do

To ease the pain, lay a hot face cloth over the boil. This may make it swell, burst and start to ooze pus. Be prepared for this. Have some tissues and salt water solution ready to clean and disinfect the area. Clean away the pus by wiping away from the centre and press very gently around the boil to be sure that all the pus has come out. Do not squeeze the boil or you may spread the infection. Clean the area around the boil with hot water, pat it thoroughly dry with a paper towel and smear on some antiseptic cream. Burn all the tissues and paper towels that have been in contact with the boil, or seal them in a plastic bag and throw the bag away, then wash your hands very thoroughly. Carefully cover the boil with an open-sided sterile dressing.

If your child develops a very large or painful boil, or gets more than one or two, contact your doctor. The doctor may swab the area to identify the bacteria responsible and give your child antibiotics, usually penicillin or erythromycin. If the boil is large and reaching a head, your doctor may lance it – open it with a sterile needle to allow the pus out. It does not hurt and immediately reduces the pain, although the area will be sore for a day or two.

If your child gets a succession of boils, the whole family may be carrying the bacteria that is responsible. Checking for this involves taking swabs of the places that are most likely to harbour bacteria, including the nose and fingernails. While your child has a boil, the whole family should take showers instead of baths to reduce the risk of spreading the infection.

Complementary Treatment

Acupuncture may be effective in stimulating the body's healing processes. The **Bach flower remedy**, Crab Apple, may be useful as a cleanser when taken by mouth. **Western herbalists** will use cleansing and immune-enhancing herbs, and will advise on alterations in life style to prevent further eruptions. **Aromatherapists** will advise on the use of essential oils for compresses, bathing, soaking and massage, or neat topical applications. **Homeopathic remedies** to reduce pain and swelling include Belladonna 30c (*Atropa belladonna*, deadly nightshade) for the early stages, taken every hour for up to ten doses; otherwise constitutional treatment (prescribing according to the individual and their symptoms) will be given. **Nutritional therapists** offer dietary advice to improve a poor immune system, which they believe to be the cause of the problem.

INGROWING TOENAILS

What are they?

When toenails curve over at the sides and cut into the flesh of the toe they are called ingrowing toenails. This is not the same as a nail that has been allowed to grow too long, and has then cut into the skin at the end of the toe. Some children are born with curved nails that tend to dig into the soft flesh at the sides, particularly of the big toe. Nails that are trimmed in a curve instead of straight across are more likely to ingrow. Tight socks and footwear make ingrowing toenails worse. At first an ingrowing toenail causes only mild soreness and swelling, but there is a risk of it becoming infected and extremely painful.

You may notice

- *The child has a red, painful swelling at one corner of a toenail, especially on a big toe*
- *There may be yellowy pus if the nail corner becomes infected*
- *The child may limp*

What to do

If you notice a slight redness at the corner of your child's nail, check how straight the nail is trimmed. If it looks curved, trim it straight and leave the corners alone. Do not trim it too short. Make a mildly antiseptic solution by adding one teaspoon of cooking salt to 600 ml/1 pint of warm water, and bathe your child's foot in it. Use a cotton bud to push the skin back from the nail extremely gently, then wipe the area with surgical spirit to toughen any soft, moist skin. If you wish, you can dab on some antiseptic cream. Repeat this every day at bathtime until the swelling has gone down. In summer, encourage your child to go barefoot whenever possible, and to wear open-toed sandals, to allow fresh air to circulate around the toes. In winter, let children go barefoot indoors. When your child is wearing shoes, fold a small handkerchief or a piece of lint and use it as padding over the toe in case they stub it. These measures may be enough to reduce the inflammation.

What else?

If the toe becomes redder or more inflamed, or if when you push the skin back very gently you reveal a sharp edge of nail, take the child to the doctor. Do not attempt to cut the sharp edge of nail off yourself. The doctor may prescribe antibiotics for the infection and surgical spirit to toughen the skin. They may also refer the child to a podiatrist or chiropodist, who will gently push the skin back from the nail, working from the root to the cutting edge. If they find a spike of nail digging into the flesh of the toe, they will trim it off.

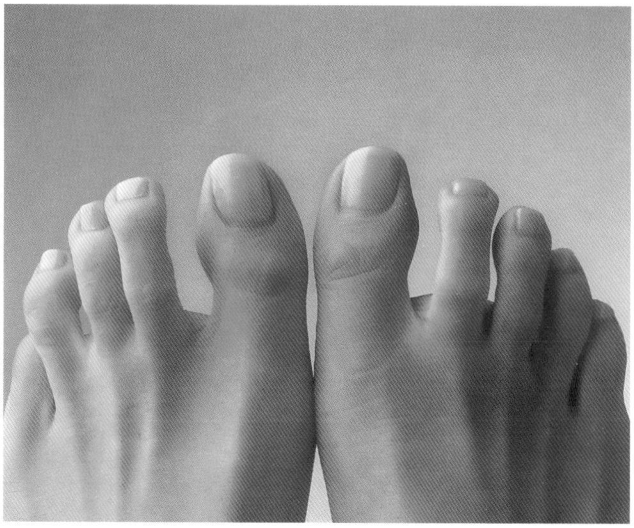

Good nail care helps to prevent ingrowing toenails and subsequent infection. At birth a baby's nails are tiny and soft; one of the few effective ways to trim them safely in the early weeks is to nibble them. A young child's nails should be cut with nail scissors, while the tougher nails of an older child are best cut with clippers, making a straight line across, then curving the corners but leaving them visible.

Prevention

To prevent ingrowing toenails, make sure you always trim your child's toenails straight across, leaving the corners visible. Then curve the corners slightly so they do not catch on socks or tights. Make sure the child always has enough space in their socks and shoes to wriggle the toes freely.

Complementary Treatment

Homeopathy is the most useful complementary treatment for ingrowing toenails, and is mainly preventative. Magnetis austr 6c (*Magnetis polus australis*, south pole of magnet) is recommended for strengthening nails that repeatedly ingrow, and Thuja 6c (*Thuja occidentalis*, white cedar) for nails that are very brittle. The remedies should be taken every 12 hours for up to 30 days. For infected nails, take Belladonna 30c (*Atropa belladonna*, deadly nightshade) or Hepar sulp. 6c (*Hepar sulphuris calcareum*. Calcium sulphide) may be effective where pus appears in the nail bed when the nail is pressed, and skin surrounding the nail is very tender.

VERRUCAS

What are they?

A verruca is a wart (see page 178) on the sole of the foot, and it is one of the most common foot infections in children. It is caused by a virus, which enters a skin cell, multiplies and spreads to adjacent cells. The hard, horny swelling that it produces usually gets pushed under the skin by the weight of the body pressing down as the child stands or walks. Verrucas (also called plantar warts) look like small white or brown circles level with the surface of the skin. Sometimes there are tiny black dots visible, and these are the ends of capillaries (small blood vessels). Verrucas do not always hurt and they are not serious, but they are infectious by contact.

You may notice

- *There may be one or more small round white, flesh-coloured or brown lumps or circles on the sole of the foot, sometimes with one or two minute black dots visible*
- *The circles may appear in clusters, giving a floret-like appearance. This is a mosaic verruca, especially difficult to treat*

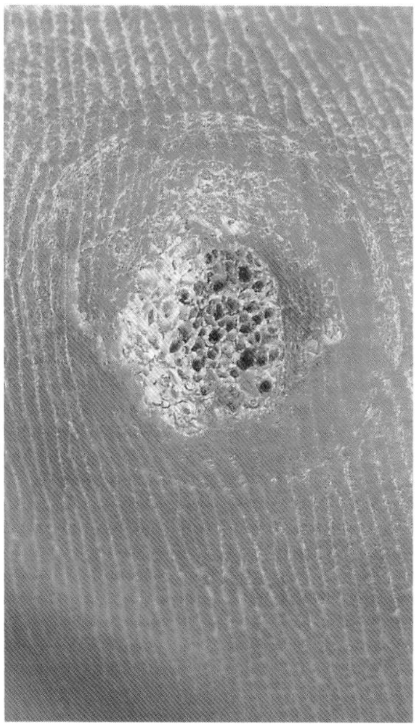

Verrucas are particularly common in older children and adolescents and can be distinguished from corns by the dark ends of blood vessels, which are clearly visible here. A single verruca may be no bigger than a pinprick, while others may grow together to form a mosaic that can be more than 25 mm/1 in across. The mosaic type is particularly stubborn and may be present for years.

What to do

If you are sure the growth is a verruca, you can treat it at home. Otherwise, let the doctor or a chiropodist look at it first. However, as most verrucas disappear without treatment within six to eight months, many health professionals suggest that you do nothing. Some believe they should be treated to avoid spreading on the child's own feet or to other people. Treatment may also be recommended if the verruca is painful. Because the virus is easily spread, the verruca should be covered with a waterproof plaster when the child goes barefoot. This is especially important in school changing rooms and at swimming pools, because the virus finds it easier to enter the skin cells when they are wet.

Verrucas often hurt at the end of the day, but if a verruca hurts all the time you can try home treatment. Treatments are either irritant, drying or caustic. The most effective is salicylic acid, in the form of an impregnated plaster, a paint or a gel. The child's foot should first be soaked in warm water for two or three minutes to soften the verruca, then the top of the verruca should be rubbed with a nailfile or wet and dry sandpaper. Apply one or two drops of paint or gel to each verruca, being careful to avoid the surrounding skin, and allow it to dry. Finally, cover the verruca with a waterproof plaster. Repeat the treatment every day for the next 12 weeks or until the verruca disappears.

If home treatment does not work consult the doctor, who may refer the child to a chiropodist who can freeze the verruca with liquid nitrogen. This can be extremely painful, and is rarely used on very young children, although an anaesthetic cream helps to ease the pain. After about ten days a blister forms over the verruca, lifting it off.

A last resort is to use electrocautery or surgical curettage, where the verruca is burnt or scraped out. These methods can leave scarring.

Complementary Treatment

The **Bach flower remedy**, Rescue Remedy, can be applied externally to the area to help reduce any pain. **Homeopathic** treatment for painful verrucas is Causticum 6c (*Causticum Hahnemanni*, potassium hydrate) taken every 12 hours for up to 21 days. If this does not produce an improvement, see the homeopath, who will usually prescribe according to the individual and their symptoms (constitutional treatment). **Chinese herbalists** usually prescribe herbs to be used topically. **Aromatherapists** generally treat with neat applications of recommended essential oils, such as lemon, tea tree and lavender.

Warning: The essential oil lemon may cause a skin reaction when treated skin is exposed to sunlight. Tea tree oil may also result in sensitivity.

Warts

What are they?

Warts are much easier to recognize than they are to treat. They are firm, painless lumps with a rough surface, and they are found most frequently on the backs of the hands and fingers, the soles of the feet and the knees. They consist of a surface of dead skin cells covering live skin cells that are infected with the human papilloma virus. The virus can be passed on by touch or by contact with the shed skin of a wart. Warts do not have roots and they are completely harmless. However they are often unsightly, and their position may cause the child some discomfort. Sometimes warts appear singly, but they can spread at an alarming rate.

Babies under two rarely catch the virus that causes warts, but warts are common in children and particularly in teenagers. Eventually the body's immune system engulfs the virus and the wart disappears, leaving the child with lifelong immunity. However warts usually take a long time to clear naturally – only half of all warts disappear spontaneously within a year, and it takes two years for most of the rest to go – and home treatment is common.

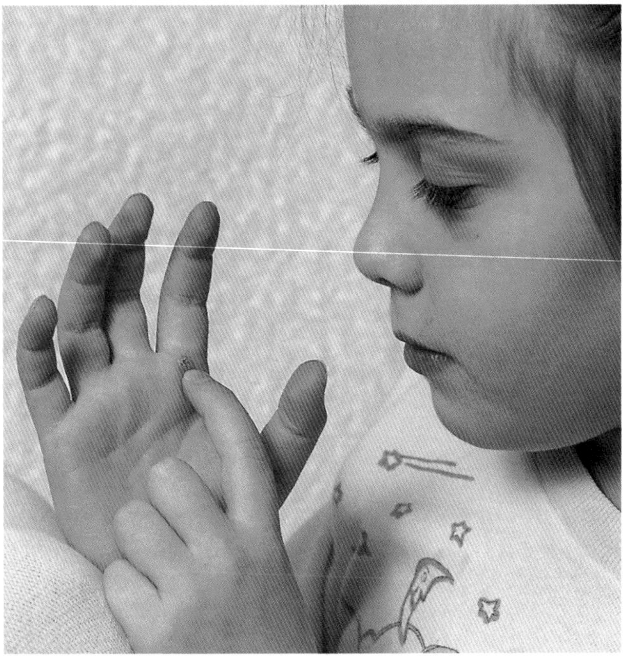

Warts commonly appear on the hands, where they can be a source of intense embarrassment to children such as this young girl. It is usually best to leave warts alone; they will disappear on their own. Otherwise, simple home treatments are often successful, although home treatment should not be tried on a wart on the face or the mouth.

You may notice

- *Thickened spots with a rough, horny surface that grow until they are several millimetres across*
- *The warts may be joined together in clumps so that they look like hardened cauliflower florets*
- *There may be tiny black spots in the centre of the lump. These are blood vessels, and they indicate that the growth is a wart rather than a corn*

What to do

It is usually easy to recognize a wart, but show it to the doctor to confirm your diagnosis. It is best to wait for the wart to disappear on its own, but if you want to treat it, you can ask your pharmacist for a lotion, gel or impregnated plaster. Salicylic acid is the most successful home treatment, but you must be careful to put it only on the wart as it makes surrounding skin sting. Rub down the wart first with an emery board or wet and dry sandpaper, then soak the skin in warm water for two to three minutes and pat dry. Apply the lotion, gel or plaster and let it dry. If you use a lotion, cover the surrounding skin with a corn plaster or an ordinary plaster with a hole punched through it. Rub down the surface of the wart every day, and repeat the treatment.

If home treatment has not worked after 12 weeks, take the child to the doctor. The wart can be frozen with liquid nitrogen (cryotherapy) , but this treatment is too painful for most young children. For older children an anaesthetic cream applied before treatment can help to relieve the pain. After about ten days a blister forms and lifts the wart straight off. However, warts may come back after cryotherapy.

While a child has warts, they should have their own sponge, face cloth and towel to prevent spreading the virus.

Complementary Treatment

Aromatherapy treats warts with some success with neat applications of essential oils. **Homeopathic** remedies include Thuja 6c (*Thuja occidentalis*, white cedar) for fleshy, cauliflower-like warts that ooze and bleed easily; and Dulcamara 6c (*Solanum dulcamara*, bittersweet) for hard, fleshy, smooth warts that appear mainly on the backs of the hands. Constitutional treatment (prescribing according to the individual and their symptoms) may be necessary if specific remedies fail to produce a result. **Chinese herbalists** usually prescribe herbs to be used topically and internally; results can be very quick or frustratingly slow. **Western herbalism** may also prove beneficial.

ATHLETE'S FOOT

What is it?

Athlete's foot, also called *tinea pedis*, is a common skin infection in which the skin under and between the toes cracks, peels and then becomes sore and itchy. It is caused by a very common fungal organism that thrives in warm, wet conditions. Athlete's foot is contagious and it is often found in public places where people go barefoot, such as swimming pools and changing rooms. It is most common in adolescents, although children with sweaty feet do catch it.

You may notice

- *The child's feet tend to get hot and sweaty. At the end of the day the skin between the toes becomes soft and white, or it is soggy and red*
- *The child rubs and scratches their feet*
- *The skin between the toes is red, scaly and intensely itchy.*
- *The infection often starts between the little and fourth toes*
- *If the child scratches the skin it may crack open, bleed and become infected*

What to do

Wash the child's feet carefully in tepid water and pat them gently dry, being especially careful to dry between the toes. Examine the sore area. If you can see redness between just two toes, you can treat it yourself. Soreness and peeling that has spread further, or that has started to scale or ooze, should be seen by a doctor.

Ask your pharmacist for an antifungal cream, which you should apply night and morning. First wash and dry the feet thoroughly, making sure that the face cloth11, sponge and towel are used only for the child with the infection. Rub the cream into the sore areas; you can also sprinkle antifungal powder into your child's socks or shoes. Athlete's foot should start to improve in a day or two, but continue to apply the cream for three or four weeks until all signs of infection have gone. During treatment your child should not go barefoot.

If you cannot see any improvement after four or five days your child may need a stronger antifungal, which you can buy from the chemist. Alternatively, take your child to the doctor, who may want to check the diagnosis by taking a tiny sample of skin. The doctor can prescribe stronger antifungal treatments or antibiotics if the sore areas on the foot have cracked and become infected.

Coping with athlete's foot

Cool your child's feet by dipping them in cold water after a wash in tepid water. If their feet get very hot and sweaty, hold face cloths – previously frozen for two or three hours – under the toes. This helps relieve the itching.

Some children have naturally sweaty feet, which encourages athlete's foot. To prevent it developing, make sure your child's feet get plenty of air by letting them go barefoot whenever possible. Your child should wear clean socks every day; open sandals will keep feet cool. If your child's shoes have rubber or synthetic soles, insert a leather insole. Check that shoes are not too tight and make sure your child alternates between at least two pairs, so that they always put on perfectly dry shoes.

Make sure your child wears flip-flops in changing rooms at the swimming pool and sports centre.

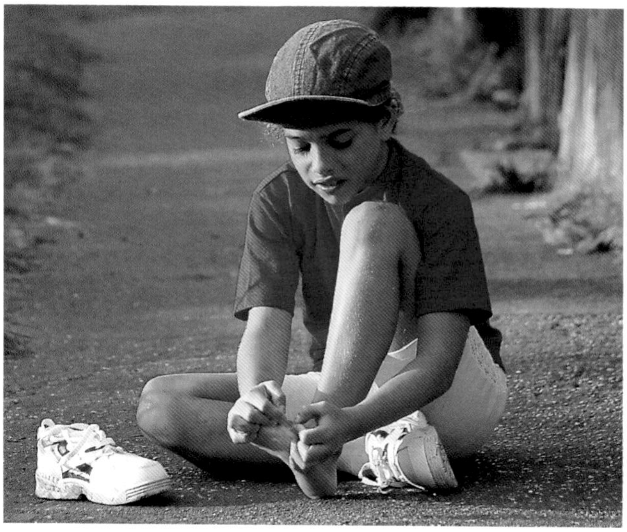

The hot, sweaty environment encouraged by wearing trainers is particularly likely to lead to athlete's foot. If your child wears trainers frequently, make sure they have two pairs, so that damp trainers need never be worn. Before putting them on, sprinkle in antifungal powder.

Complementary Treatment

Western herbalists and **aromatherapists** have found that antifungal herbs and essential oils, respectively, may be beneficial. They will also give advice on hygiene and footwear. The **homeopath** will prescribe according to the individual and their symptoms (constitutional treatment) in order to boost the immune system. **Chinese herbalists** will prescribe herbs to be used in a herbal bath; the feet should be bathed daily in the liquid, which should be kept in the refrigerator and boiled up every day. This is smelly, and it is time-consuming, but it is usually very effective.

EYES

The eye is the most delicate and complex of the five sense organs. It is therefore well protected in its bony socket, with lids and a blinking reflex to ensure the lids close at sight or sound of danger. Tears containing a natural antiseptic, lysozome, keep the eyes moist and free from pollutants, dust and micro-organisms. The tears are produced in glands above the eye and constantly wash across the eyeball; they then drain into the nose through tear ducts at the eye's inner corner. The lids are lined with moist conjunctiva, membranes that extend over the eyeball as far as the cornea.

Viewed from the front, the central black dot is the pupil, the opening through which light rays enter the eye. Surrounding the pupil is the coloured, muscular iris, which constantly adjusts the size of the pupil to allow in the right amount of light. Around the iris you can see the eye's tough outer white coat (the sclera).

Structure of the eye

Viewed in cross section, the eye is constructed in layers. At the front is the transparent, tough and slightly protruding cornea, which is the eye's outer lens. The cornea helps to focus light rays on the retina at the back of the eye. Behind it is the iris and immediately next the crystalline lens, a transparent, elastic organ that can change shape to adjust focus. Behind the lens lies a transparent gel, the vitreous humour, which fills the main interior chamber of the eye. Lining the back of the eye is a light-sensitive coating, or layer, which is the all-important retina.

·Light rays entering through the pupil fall on to the two types of light-sensitive cells of the retina, called rods and cones. This stimulates a stream of impulses that are transmitted along the optic nerve to the brain. In the centre of the retina, where the optic nerve is situated, is the blind spot. The blind spot contains neither rods nor cones. A doctor examining a child's eye with an ophthalmoscope can see this blind spot as a bright, whitish-yellow circle.

To see clearly, both eyes must be pointing at the object. The correct alignment of the eyes depends on delicate muscles attached to the socket bones, which hold the eyeball in position and allow the eyes to move about without moving the head.

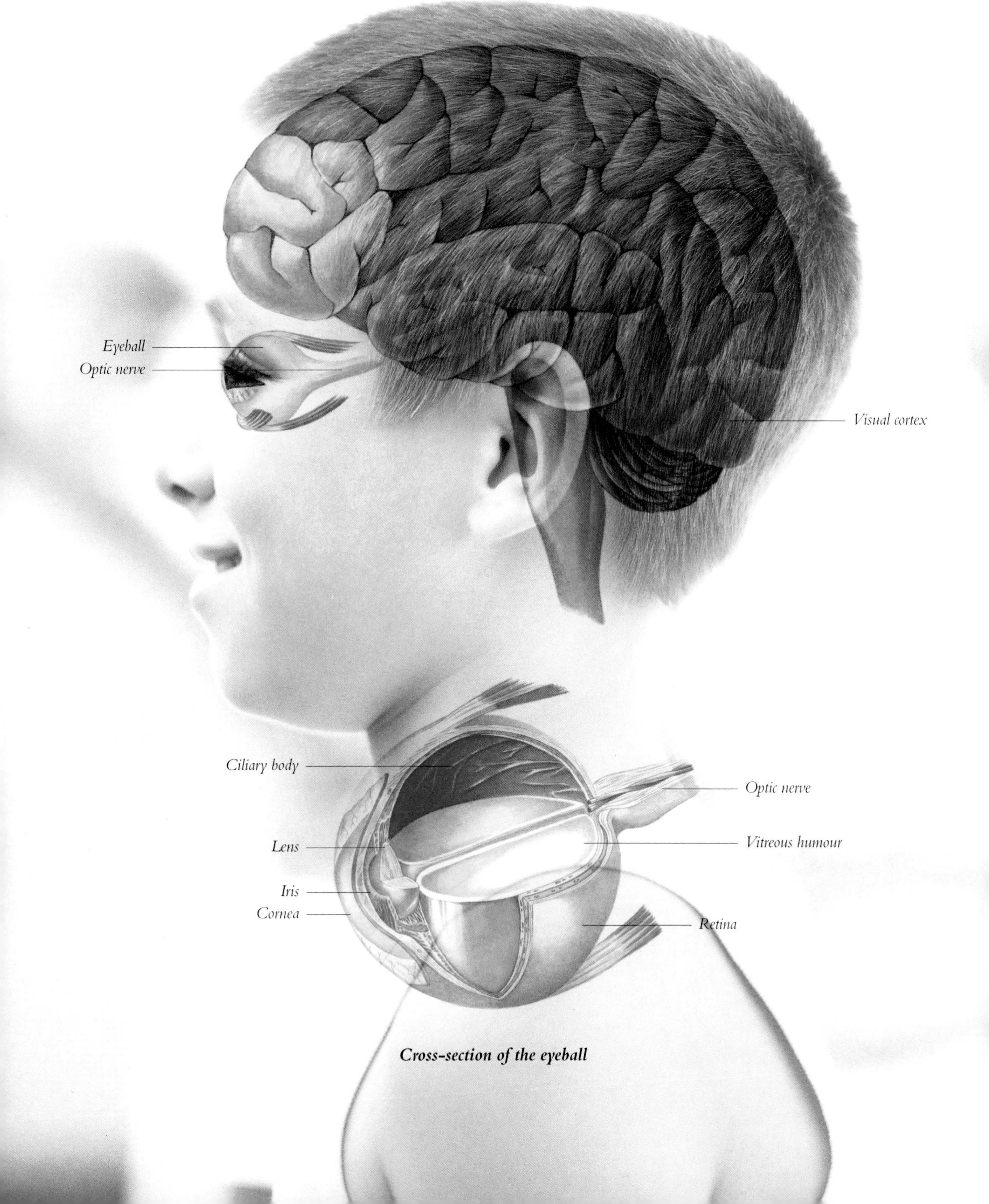

Cross-section of the eyeball

DIAGNOSIS

Symptoms that affect the eyes can affect either the eye itself or the eyelids surrounding it. In general, conditions that concern the eye itself are more serious, but any infection near the eye should be taken seriously.

Sign	What could be wrong
Affecting the area around the eye	
Eyelids are sore and red, and may be itchy. In the morning they may be crusted together	Blepharitis, an inflammation of the eyelids. It can be caused by an infection, an allergy or by irritation by skin scales
The whites of the eyes look bloodshot and may feel gritty and sore. The eyes may water or you may notice a thick white or yellow discharge, and in the morning the lids may be stuck together	These signs suggest conjunctivitis, which, if in one eye, can be caused by an eyelash, speck of dirt or grit, but if the symptoms occur in both eyes, there may be an allergic or infective cause. If the child is generally unwell with a fever, it could be measles, pharyngo-conjunctival fever (a viral infection) or, rarely, Kawasaki disease (see page 91).
Sore red swelling on the rim of the eye. Comes to a head as an infected point	A stye, or infection in the follicle of an eyelash
Persistently watery eye in a young infant. The watery discharge may thicken and the eyelids may stick together	Blocked tear duct is most likely. One or both eyes can be affected
Affecting the eye itself	
An opaque white area in front of the pupil of the eye	This can be a sign of a cataract, which is usually congenital
The child may look at close work from very close to and may develop a squint	These are possible signs of long sight
The child may hold books close to the eyes or view a screen from very close	Possible signs of short sight. This is unusual in young children, but often emerges in the teens
The eyes do not appear to be looking in the same direction	A squint (strabismus) is the most likely cause

Short Sight

What is it?

Short sight (myopia) and long sight (see page 184) are refractive errors, in which there is a mismatch between the size of the eyeball and the focusing power of the eye. In normal circumstances, light rays enter the eye and come to meet exactly on the retina, the light-sensitive membrane at the back of the eye. In short-sighted children the eye focuses too strongly or the eyeball is too long, so the light rays meet in front of the retina. The result is usually blurred vision. Short-sighted children usually see close objects in crisp focus while anything in the distance – for example a cinema screen – is blurred.

Short sight is rare in a new baby and is relatively uncommon in very young children. As the eyeball grows the problem often emerges around the age of seven or eight, or later in the teenage years, and progresses to a variable extent until the early twenties. Short sight is frequently inherited.

You may notice

- *An infant with extremely short sight may not focus on you while feeding or may be late to smile*
- *An older child may hold pictures or books very close to their face or sit too close to the computer or television screen*
- *Short sight may be detected at a routine vision test at school*

What to do

Take the child for an eye test if you are concerned about their vision. This should be done every six to twelve months if either you or your partner wears glasses. During the eye test, young children may be asked to match pictures, shapes or capital Es pointing in different directions; once they can read they may be asked to match pairs of capital letters. The child may be given a picture book to check their close vision.

Children who have 6/6 vision can see what anyone with normal vision can see at a distance of 6 m/20 ft. If they can only read the largest, top line of the chart, their sight is recorded as 6/60, which means that they can only see at 2.1 m/6 ft what other people can see at 18 m/60 ft. This would mean they were very short-sighted.

Short-sighted children may need to wear glasses to help the normal development of the eyes. They will also probably be worn at school for blackboard or whiteboard work and for playing ball games but not necessarily for reading.

Warning Laser treatment has recently become an option for short-sighted adults who do not want to wear glasses or contact lenses. Laser therapy for short sight should not, however, be used on anyone younger than their early to mid-twenties, as their eyes may still be growing.

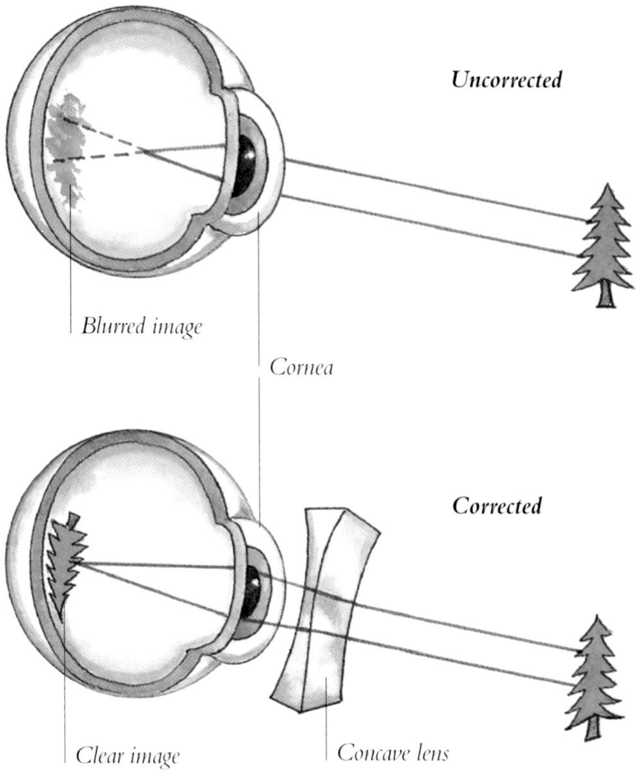

In short sight the eyeball may be too long, so that the light rays do not reach the retina and the image forms in front of it, producing a blurred image of things in the distance. Close objects may be seen very clearly. Short sight is corrected by wearing glasses with a concave lens, which focuses a clear image on the retina.

Complementary Treatment

Osteopaths will treat this condition in young children. **Homeopathic treatment** is constitutional (according to the personality, temperament and mood of the child concerned) but specific remedies may help while seeking treatment. These include Phosphorus 6c (phosphorus) where the sight becomes worse with nervous exhaustion, and Physostigma 6c (*Physostigma venenosum*, Calabar bean) when the sight seems to be deteriorating. The remedies are to be taken four times a day for up to two weeks. **Chinese herbalism** combined with **acupuncture** may help in the short term; **reflexology** and **kinesiology** may also be beneficial.

LONG SIGHT

What is it?

Long sight (hypermetropia) and short sight (see page 183) are both refractive errors, which means that images do not focus precisely on the retina, the light-sensitive membrane at the back of the eye. Most babies have naturally long sight. This is because their eyeballs are relatively small – at birth they are only three-quarters of the eventual size they will become in adolescence.

Children cope with their natural long sight by automatically focusing, making the flexible internal crystalline lens thicker or thinner, until they see clearly. Focusing, also known as accommodation, is easier for the young, who have elastic eye muscles, than for middle-aged people, who gradually lose the muscular power to thicken or thin the crystalline lens.

Children who have very long sight and cannot focus images precisely on the retina can have their vision corrected with glasses. Glasses can also be prescribed for children who have one eye that is markedly more long sighted than the other. The brain tends to ignore the image that arrives blurred and this can lead to a convergent strabismus, or squint (see page 192), where one eye points in towards the other.

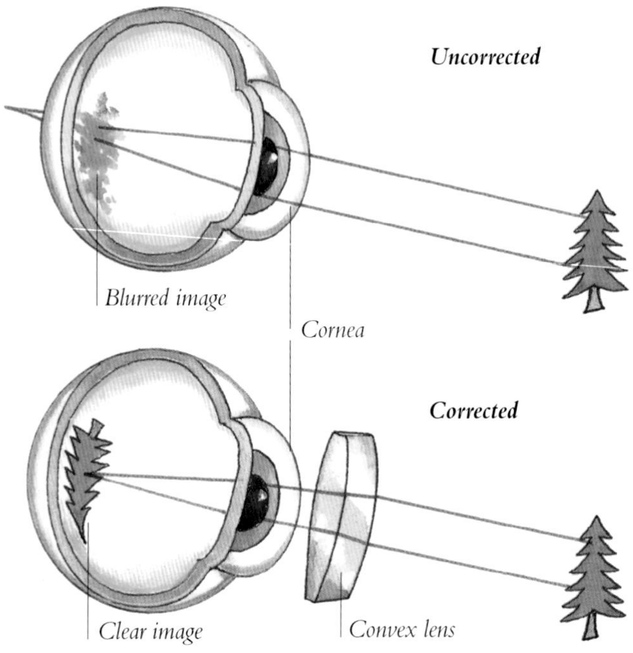

In long sight the eyeball may be too short, so that the light rays pass beyond the retina and the image forms behind it. In children who are very long sighted, this produces a blurred image of things that are seen close to. Long sight may be corrected by wearing glasses with a convex lens, which focuses a clear image on the retina.

Long sight often runs in families: if one parent is affected, each child has a one in two chance of also having long sight; with two affected parents, the risk rises to three in four. If long sightedness is not diagnosed and treated early, eventually clear distance vision will be affected.

You may notice

- *The first sign of long sight may be a squint*
- *Children with long sight may have quite good close vision because they are able to accommodate. If they are markedly long sighted, however, they may not enjoy leafing through picture books and may lose interest quickly in activities that require close visual concentration, such as craftwork, fine drawing and writing*

What to do

If you notice problems, take the child for an eye test. If either parent wears glasses the child should have eye tests every six to twelve months. Young children may be asked to match pictures, shapes, capital Es pointing in different directions and, once they can read, pairs of capital letters. The eyes of children under six will be examined with a retinoscope, a torch-like instrument, which will show what happens to light reflected back from the retina. In a child with long sight the returning light rays diverge. For older children, a variety of different lenses are used to identify the degree of abnormality. Other tests check the internal structure of the eye and any degree of squint.

Many long-sighted children do not need glasses because of their natural powers of accommodation. However, children who cannot focus on close work without squinting, or have to make such an effort that they get a headache or eyestrain, will need to wear glasses. Children with long sight and a squint need to wear their glasses all the time, while other long-sighted children can remove their glasses for activities such as playing football.

Complementary Treatment

Osteopaths will treat this condition in young children. **Homeopathic treatment** is constitutional (according to the personality, temperament and mood of the child concerned) but specific remedies such as Ruta 6c (*Ruta graveolens*, rue) may help while seeking treatment. **Chinese herbalism**, **acupuncture** and **reflexology** may also prove beneficial.

SEE ALSO SHORT SIGHT (PAGE 183)

Visual Impairment

What is it?

Minor vision problems are quite common among children, while defects severe enough to interfere with education and everyday life are fortunately rare.

Most visually impaired children have some useful vision and what they can see is quite individual. Some can tell the difference between light and dark, others have either central vision or can only see out of the side of the eye. Still others see blurs or blank patches within crisply focused areas. If the child is partially sighted, this means that with glasses or lenses the child's better eye can see at 6 m/20 ft what people with normal vision can see at 24 m/80 ft. A child who can only see at 3 metres/10 ft what other people can see at a distance of 60 m/200 ft will be registered as blind. More than one youngster in three with a visual impairment has an additional learning or physical disability.

The most common causes of visual impairment are defects in the development of the eye before birth, congenital cataracts (see page 186) and severe short sight (see page 183). Injuries and diseases that affect the eye or nerve pathways within the brain are other possibilities. There is often an underlying genetic cause, which makes it important for parents to get genetic counselling.

Children should receive repeated tests of vision throughout childhood partly because visual defects are extremely difficult to diagnose accurately and partly because as the eye develops and extra demands are made – such as reading small print at school – defects may emerge.

You may notice

- *At birth the infant may not fix their gaze on you as they feed*
- *An infant may not follow a large colourful object moved across their field of vision*
- *Wandering eye movements (nystagmus) may develop*
- *There may be a dislike of bright light*

What to do

Contact your health visitor or doctor as soon as you notice any signs that concern you. Even very young baby's can have their vision tested to show how much information is being perceived and processed in the brain. It is very important to detect problems early in order to preserve and develop the vision that remains.

Children with a visual impairment need wide-ranging support. They should be treated by an ophthalmologist for the eye disorder. The ophthalmologist will arrange for any aids needed to maximize vision. They will need the support of the local child health team to minimize the effects of blindness on other areas of development. Finally, children with a visual impairment will need assessment for general and special education and the family will probably need support.

A few visually impaired children have no vision, but most have some. They may be able to tell the difference between light and dark or see at the sides or just the centre of their visual field. It is important to encourage children to use whatever vision they have and to associate it with the other senses, as this mother is teaching her child to do by feeling and discovering the shape and texture of things.

Who can help?

For organizations and agencies who can offer help, advice and information, see the Directory.

Complementary Treatment

Children with visual impairment may benefit from therapies that offer emotional support, such as the **arts therapies** and **play therapy**. The **Bach flower remedies** may be helpful while the child is undergoing investigation and treatment. **Homeopathic remedies** may also help with emotional problems associated with the condition.

CATARACTS

What are they?

The crystalline lens of the eye (as opposed to the eye's outer lens) is located behind the coloured iris and the pupil. As light rays come in through the pupil this lens helps to bend them to focus on the retina, the light-sensitive membrane at the back of the eye. In order to have perfectly clear vision the lens must be completely transparent. Cataracts occur when there are opaque areas in the lens, which are caused by changes in its protein structure. Although most cataracts occur in old people or develop after birth, babies can be born with congenital cataracts.

Causes of infantile cataract include an infection in the early weeks of pregnancy that damages the developing eye, such as rubella (German measles) during the first eight weeks of pregnancy. Babies with metabolic diseases – such as the rare disease galactosaemia (an inability to convert the sugar galactose into glucose) – or with Down's syndrome (see page 316), may have cataracts, and in some rare instances they are an inherited disorder.

If they are identified early, cataracts in babies with galactosaemia can be corrected by following an appropriate diet. Older children who develop cataracts may have sustained an injury to the eyes. Sometimes doctors are unable to find a cause for the disorder.

A child who has had cataracts removed needs to wear contact lenses or glasses at least until his eyes have stopped growing. He will then enjoy excellent vision as long as he has no other visual defect. In families affected by hereditary cataracts, this can mean that an affected parent is functionally blind while an affected child has excellent vision because surgery was undertaken promptly.

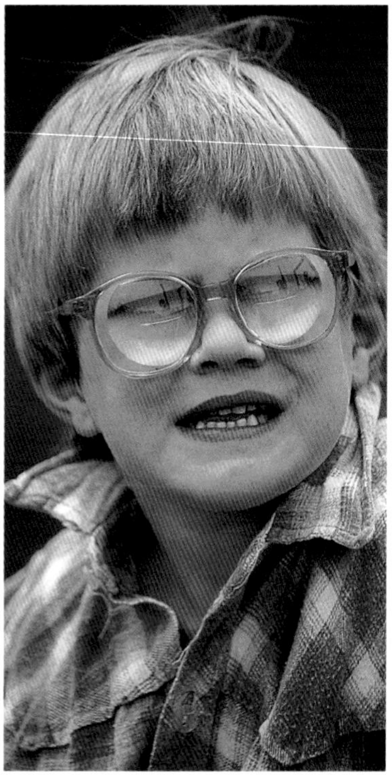

You may notice

- *An opaque area in the front of the eye. This may vary in size from a tiny white dot to an area covering the whole pupil*

Treatment

The paediatrician who examines the newborn child in hospital will shine a fine beam of light into the eye with an ophthalmoscope. This will enable the doctor to see the lens clearly and diagnose whether an opacity exists.

Each child will be treated individually. Small cataracts that do not interfere with vision may need no treatment. A cataract in only one eye will interfere with the brain's ability to develop binocular vision and so needs to be removed surgically. Surgery is usually performed in the first few weeks of life to avoid the affected eye losing its power to see altogether. Some infants who are born with total cataracts on both eyes, which would leave them functionally blind if not removed, will need surgery in the first month of life.

During surgery the entire crystalline lens will be removed and contact lenses fitted to compensate. Later on these children will need to wear glasses as a substitute for their missing lens. When an adult has a cataract removed, a intraocular lens (a plastic lens implant) is often inserted in place of the original lens. These lenses are not used in children because it is not yet known how long they last, and also because a child's eye is still growing and developing. Intraocular lenses can be fitted in children who are in their mid-teens after their eyes have stopped growing.

Complementary Treatment

Complementary treatment will be supportive of orthodox treatment. Those that may be appropriate include the **Bach flower remedies** and homeopathic remedies to deal with the emotional aspects in older children requiring surgery. **Homeopathic remedies** that can be given before surgery include Aconite 30c (*Aconitum napellus*, blue aconite) for the child who is panicking and has a great fear of surgery, and Gelsemium 6c (*Gelsemium sempervirens*, yellow jasmine) if the child is very apprehensive, weak and trembling. Phosphorus 6c (phosphorus) can be given to relieve vomiting following surgery; and Arnica 30c (*Arnica montana*, leopard's bane) to relieve pain and prevent infection. Arnica should be followed by Staphisagria 6c (*Delphinium staphisagria*, stavesacre). These should be given every half hour for up to ten doses.

Colour Blindness

What is it?

Colour blindness, or colour vision deficiency, is characterized by an inability to distinguish between certain colours. There are a number of types and degrees of severity.

Colour vision deficiency is usually caused by a defect in the light-sensitive pigments in cone cells in the retina, a reduced number of cone cells or, more rarely, an optic nerve disease or injury. In normal colour vision, as light enters the eye it falls on to the retina, the film-like, light-sensitive membrane lining the inside of the back of the eye. Within the retina are millions of specialized nerve cells that convert light into nerve impulses for transmission to the brain. These cells are called cones and rods because of their shape and it is the cones that are involved in colour vision.

Colour vision

Light travels in varying wavelengths and when it arrives at the retina the different wavelengths create colour sensations by stimulating three different types of cone. Light with a long wavelength stimulates more cones sensitive to red, medium wavelength light stimulates more green-sensitive cones and short wavelength light stimulates more blue-sensitive cones. The light changes pigments inside the cone which then emits an electrical impulse.

An inherited disorder

Most children who have a colour vision deficiency have inherited a pigment abnormality or a defect in the cones. The two most common problems involve the green and red pigments. Children with a marked deficiency in red vision (protans) see all shades of red as dark. Children with a marked deficiency in green vision (deutans) may find that shades of green, brown, orange and red all look the same. Blue vision abnormalities are rare, as is monochrome vision, which is true colour blindness. The majority of children with a colour vision defect have a mild abnormality, frequently affecting their green vision.

All colour vision defects are more common in boys and tend to run in families. About eight per cent of boys have some type of red/green deficiency, compared with less than half a per cent of girls.

You may notice

- *The child may have difficulty picking out subtle differences in shades of colour*
- *The child may persistently paint in inappropriate colours – a purple sky or brown grass*

A simple test can reveal whether or not a child is colour blind. It consists of a series of cards printed with coloured dots, some of which make the shape of a number. The child names the number and traces it with her finger. Colour blind children are unable to see the numbers.

What to do

If you notice any of the above symptoms, take the child to your doctor who will refer you to an ophthalmologist for testing. Alternatively you can wait until the child starts secondary school when a vision test will be carried out. This usually includes a test for colour vision called the Ishihara test, and involves distinguishing a concealed number from a background of coloured dots. A secondary test in which the child chooses one of four dots most similar in colour to a central dot shows how severe the colour deficiency is.

Coping with colour blindness

While a minor deficiency isn't a problem, a serious defect will severely restrict the choice of a career. Someone who cannot discriminate colours accurately will have difficulties driving a public service vehicle, piloting an aeroplane, working in electronics or as an electrician or in some grades in the armed forces. Teenagers with a colour vision defect should take expert advice from an optometrist, an ophthalmologist or a colour vision clinic before deciding on a career.

Complementary Treatment

Complementary treatments are not appropriate for the condition of colour blindness.

STYES

What are they?

A stye, or hordeolum, is an abscess that has formed in the follicle out of which an eyelash grows. It is caused by a bacterial infection, usually staphylococcal, which gets into the follicle, and often occurs when a child whose hands are dirty rubs their eyes. Ordinarily, staphylococci live quite harmlessly on the skin, in the nose and in the throat, but once they are inside the skin they can cause such an infection. The pus that results, which contains live white blood cells and bacteria as well as dead matter, will continue to accumulate until the stye subsides; or until it becomes so large that it bursts.

Some children are prone to styes, especially if they are run down or their immune system is not fighting fit. Styes are not serious, but they can become very sore.

You may notice

- *A painful red swelling on the child's eyelid*
- *The swelling grows and comes to a taut, yellowish point over two or three days*

Treatment

If the stye does not clear up on its own, then try to discharge the pus. Never squeeze the stye to burst it. Soak pads or balls of cotton wool in hand-hot water and lay them over the stye for up to 20 minutes at a time. Repeat as often as needed. If the stye is very painful, give children's paracetamol.

When the stye bursts, gently wipe away the pus and blood with sterile wipes. Wipe as thoroughly as you can to avoid re-infecting another eyelash root with the pus. Wash the area around the eye with water and then apply antibiotic drops or ointment prescribed by your doctor. Afterwards, wash your hands well.

See your doctor if the stye is very large or if the child gets recurrent styes. The doctor can take swabs from the child's nose and throat to discover if the bacteria are originating there.

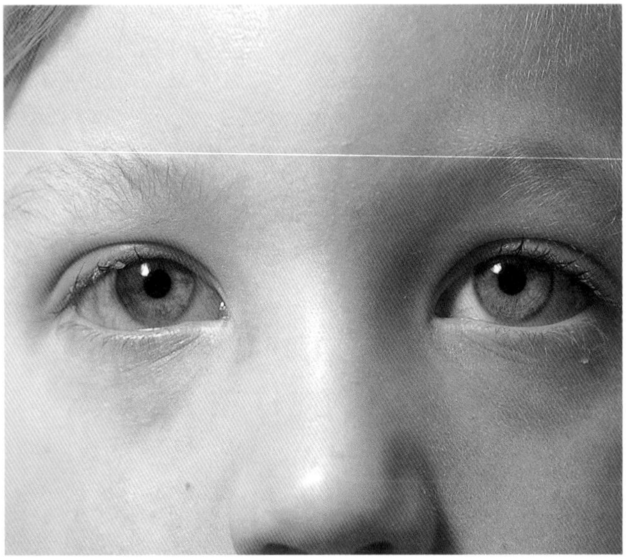

The best way to relieve the soreness and pain that is caused by a stye is to rinse a cloth or pad of cotton wool in hot water and lay it over the affected area. This will also encourage the stye to come to a head and burst. Once the stye has burst the acute pain subsides but the area around the eye will remain sore for a day or two.

Preventing styes

- Get children into the habit of frequently washing their hands
- Discourage them from picking their nose. Make sure they always have tissues to wipe a runny nose
- If they get a series of styes and seem run down, add more fresh foods and juices to their diet
- Encourage children to wear protective goggles while cycling to avoid irritating already sore eyes
- Tell them to avoid smoky atmospheres, which can irritate a stye. Ask smokers to smoke outdoors

Complementary Treatment

In Traditional Chinese Medicine the eyes are seen as the sense organ of the liver, and work would focus on liver energy; **Chinese herbalism**, used with **acupuncture**, may be helpful, particularly in the short term. The **Western herbalist's** view is that styes are often a sign of reduced immunity needing internal treatment, with anti-inflammatory herbs, among others. The **nutritional therapist** will also concentrate on strengthening the immune system and advise on diet in order to prevent further occurrences. **Kinesiologists** may take a similar approach. **Homeopaths** will treat recurrent styes according to the personality, temperament and mood of the child concerned (constitutional treatment). Specific remedies for acute conditions are Pulsatilla 6c (*Pulsatilla nigricans*, pasque flower), taken every hour for up to ten doses, and, if this is not effective, Staphisagria 6c (*Delphinium staphisagria*, stavesacre), given as Pulsatilla dosage.

Blocked Tear Duct

What is it?

Tears keep the eyes clean, moist and healthy. They bathe the eye constantly so that the view from the cornea is always clear and the eyelids can slide up and down easily. Tears are salty and contain a natural antiseptic that helps to prevent eye infections.

Located at the inner corner of the eye is a tiny drainage channel; tears that have already bathed the surface of the eyes flow into this channel and from there into the nose. At birth this channel may have only just established a clear passage and in quite a few babies it is still blocked. Tears gather, the eyes water and may become infected.

In about half of all affected children the blocked tear ducts open up naturally before the child is six months old. Only a very few children need surgery to open the drainage channel.

You may notice

- *The child has a persistently watery eye on one or both sides – even when not crying. The fluid is usually clear*
- *Discharge may collect in the eye, and the eyelashes will stick together after the child has a sleep*
- *The discharge may appear infected*

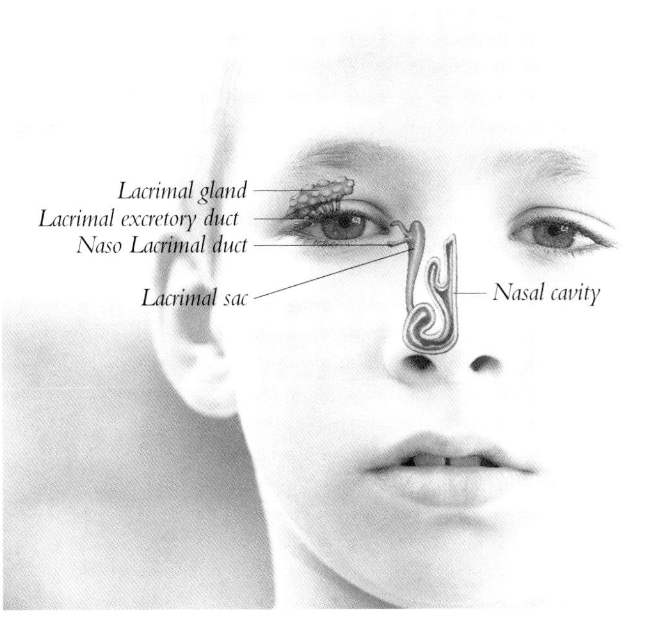

You can gently massage a blocked tear duct to allow tears to flow away. The correct place to do this is just beneath the lacrimal sac at the inner corner of the eye, where the duct drains into the nose. Before starting the massage, make sure that your hands are perfectly clean.

What to do

Speak to your health visitor or doctor who will be able to show you the method for opening the tear ducts so that the tears flow away. This is: using your fingertips, gently massage the tear ducts between the inner corner of the eye and the bridge of the nose.Repeat twice a day. You also need to bathe the child's eyes regularly by wiping from the outer corner to the inner corner with a cotton wool pad dipped in warm, boiled water. If the discharge looks infected your doctor may take swabs to discover its source, and then prescribe eye drops or ointments to clear it.

If the watering continues because the blockage remains, the doctor may recommend a tiny operation by an ophthalmic surgeon to open up the ducts. The surgery, which is done under a general anaesthetic, entails easing a fine probe into the tear ducts and stretching them. The system is then washed through with saline solution. The operation is usually carried out around the infant's first birthday, but if the eyes water a lot it may be performed earlier.

Administering eye medication

Giving eye drops This is easiest if done with two people: one person to hold the child's head steady while the other person holds the dropper in one hand and steadies it on the child's forehead. Using the index finger of the other hand, pull down the lower lid and drop in the eye drops between the eye and the eyelid. Never let the dropper come into contact with the eye. *Giving eye ointment* Steady your hand on the child's forehead with the tube ready squeezed, then pull down the lower lid and squeeze a tiny amount of ointment on the inside of the eyelid. Blinking spreads the ointment over the surface of the eye.

Complementary Treatment

Chinese herbalism may have some effect, but this treatment is most effective when it is combined with **acupuncture**, although parents may find this an inappropriate treatment for infants. **Osteopathy** will often treat infants successfully. For an infected tear duct causing the blockage, the homeopathic remedy Silicea 6c (*Silicea terra*, flint), taken four times a day for up to one week, may relieve the condition.

CONJUNCTIVITIS

What is it?

Conjunctivitis is an inflammation of the transparent membrane (the conjunctiva) that covers the eyeball and the inside of the eyelids. When dust or a piece of grit inflames the conjunctiva, it usually only produces a pink patch on the white of one eye. However if the whole eye is affected then an infection by a bacterium or a virus is more likely to be the cause, especially in children. A bacterial infection produces a thick discharge, whereas a viral infection often makes the eye more watery; children may also have a cold or sore throat. Some children react to allergens such as pollen with red, watery eyes, but this is more common in adults. Occasionally newborn babies catch a conjunctival eye infection during birth, for example if the mother has a chlamydia infection, or they may have an underdeveloped or blocked tear duct (see page 189). Conjunctivitis is more serious in the newborn baby, and the baby will need immediate treatment, as their sight can be affected.

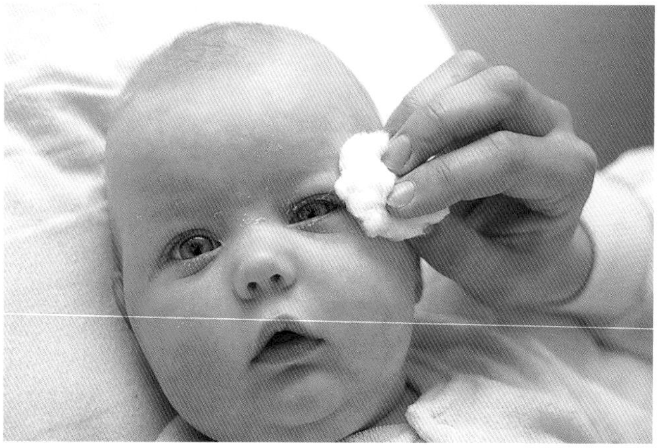

When a baby with conjunctivitis wakes in the morning the eyelashes may be gummed and crusted together. Wipe the eyes with a pad of clean cotton wool dipped in boiled water, which has been left to cool and to which you have added a sprinkle of salt. A folk alternative is to wipe the baby's eyes with breastmilk.

You may notice

- *The whites of one or both of the eyes look pink*
- *The eyes may water or there may be a thick white or yellow discharge causing blurred vision*
- *In the morning the eyelids may be stuck together*
- *The eyelids may swell up, nearly closing the eyes*
- *The child may rub the eyes if they feel itchy*
- *Apart from the watering, the child can see normally*

What to do

If only one eye is affected, check for a foreign object such as an eyelash or speck of dust or grit on the inner eyelid. If you find one, wipe it away with a corner of clean tissue or ask a child over three years old to blink ten times. To clean crust or discharge from the eyes, wipe from the inner corner outwards with a piece of cotton wool dipped in warm salted water .

If both eyes are affected, consult your doctor, who can prescribe antibiotic drops or ointment or, in the case of allergic conjunctivitis, an antihistamine drug. These should continue to be be used until 24 hours have elapsed since the child's eyes have cleared. The eyes should improve within a day, but if they are no better in two or three days take your child to the doctor again.

Coping with conjunctivitis

Lay an baby on the side with the affected eye down to stop tears infecting the other eye. Wash your hands and children's hands with soap and water frequently and whenever they rub or touch their eyes. Keep the family's face cloths and towels separate, and if the children are over 12 months old, change their pillowcase every day.

If children's eyes are sore, protect them from dust with dark glasses or a hat with a plastic shade. Some children are allergic to the preservatives in eye drops. Ask your doctor for a prescription for preservative-free drops.

Complementary Treatment

A dilution of Crab apple, a **Bach flower remedy**, added to the bathing solution, may help to relieve pain and clear the eyes. **Western herbalism** will treat with herbal compresses, which will considerably reduce inflammation: **Chinese herbalism** treats with herbs applied topically and taken internally and can be very effective when combined with **acupuncture**. Chinese green tea is said to clear wind-heat from the eyes and is used by computer kids of all ages. **Homeopathic remedies** include Argentum nit 6c (*Argentum nitricum*, silver nitrate) for copious discharge; and Euphrasia 6c (*Euphrasia officinalis*, common eyebright) where there is very little or no discharge. Give these remedies every hour for up to ten doses. Euphrasia mother tincture can also be used to bathe the eyes. Put 10 drops of tincture and 1 level tsp salt into 300 ml/1/2 pint of warm water. Use every four hours, no more than four times a day. See your homeopath or doctor if there is no improvement.

Blepharitis

What is it?

Blepharitis is a common inflammation of the edges of the eyelids. It can be caused by an infection, by irritation from flakes of cradle cap or dandruff, or by an allergic reaction to substances such as eye make-up or ointments. It more frequently affects children suffering from eczema and is often seen in adolescents. Although it is not a serious condition, blepharitis can be infectious, so the child will need to be treated immediately. Unfortunately it has a tendency to persist or to return following treatment.

You may notice

- *The eyelids will look red and sore and may be itchy*
- *On waking in the morning, the child's eyes may be crusted together*
- *There may be white flakes of skin between the eyelashes*
- *The eyes may look pink, as if the child has conjunctivitis*

What to do

If the eyes are crusted over first thing in the morning, hold a warm, wet tissue, a piece of sterile non-fluffy lint or a handkerchief over each eye in turn. Rinse the cloth regularly and dip it in warm water until the crusts have softened enough to enable the child to open their eyes. Then wash the cloth and your hands thoroughly.

To clean the eyes of scales, use a piece of cotton wool dipped in boiled and cooled water and wipe the eyes, one at a time, from the inner corner outwards. For extra antiseptic effect you can use a weak saline solution made by dissolving a teaspoon of cooking salt in 600 ml/1 pint of warm water, or you can use half-strength baby shampoo, but wipe the eyelids afterwards with fresh water. Repeat the bathing procedure two or three times a day – and be sure to wash your hands afterwards each time.

If the condition has been caused by dandruff, treat it with an anti-dandruff shampoo. If eczema is the cause, use an emollient such as petroleum jelly.

See your doctor for treatment. This may entail an antibiotic ointment or, in the case of an allergic reaction, a mild steroid ointment. Persistent dandruff may be cleared with a special antifungal shampoo.

What else?

It is vital to keep the child's towels and face cloth separate from the rest of the family's until the eyes are better.

To keep the eyes from crusting together overnight, lightly apply soft white paraffin or aqueous cream to the child's eyelids at bedtime. Keep the child away from any unnecessary irritants such as smoke. If the child has to go out in a dusty atmosphere, sunglasses should be worn.

Schools frequently exclude pupils with conjunctivitis until they have recovered. As it is easy to confuse blepharitis with conjunctivitis, you may need a doctor's note to inform the school that it is appropriate for the child to attend.

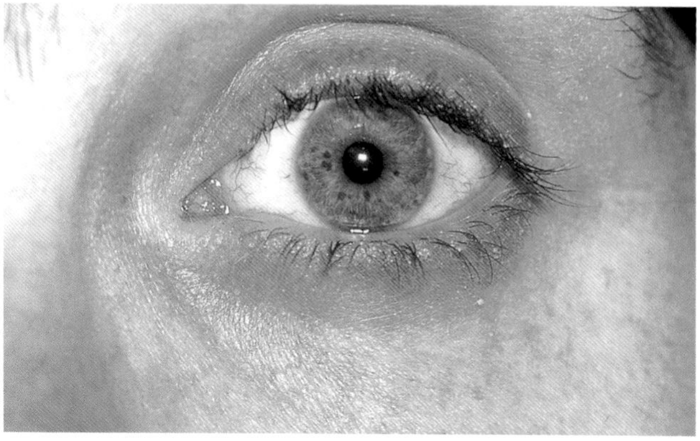

The child's sore and somewhat swollen eyelids are typical of blepharitis. Regular applications of antibiotic ointment after removing crusting and scales should clear bacterial blepharitis within 14 days, although the treatment should be continued for a further two weeks.

Complementary Treatment

Traditional Chinese Medicine thinks of the eyes as sense organs of the liver and both **Chinese herbalism** and **acupuncture** treat accordingly. Chinese herbalists treat blepharitis with internal herbs to clear damp and heat from the liver and the yang channels, which may result in a sense of brightness and clarity of vision. **Western herbalism** may also be effective in reducing inflammation. **Homeopathic remedies** are Hepar sulph 6c (*Hepar sulphuris calcareum*, calcium sulphide) for red and gummy eyelids; Sulphur 6c (*Sulphur*, sublimated sulphur) when the lids are sore, burning and ulcerated and made worse by bathing in water; and Calcarea 6c (*Calcarea carbonica*, calcium carbonate) for red, swollen eyelids that are gummy on awakening. Remedies should be given every four hours for up to two weeks. Bathing eyelids at night with saline solution and then applying Calendula ointment (*Calendula officinalis*, pot marigold) can also help.

SEE ALSO CONJUNCTIVITIS (PAGE 190)

Squint

What is it?

A squint, or strabismus, occurs when the eyes do not look in exactly the same direction, and it may be linked with short or long sight (see pages 183 and 184). Convergent squint, the most common type, arises when one eye looks inwards towards the nose. It is often caused by a long-sighted child straining to focus when looking at an object at close range. In divergent squint, one eye looks outwards. This occurs because the muscles attached to the eyeball are not properly balanced. In both instances double vision may result because the eyes are out of alignment.

Squint is common, affecting one in twenty children. It may show soon after birth, or become more obvious when the child starts doing detailed work at nursery or school. Squint tends to run in families and may appear for the first time after a viral illness.

Children who have better sight in one eye can develop a squint if the weaker eye is left untreated. In a condition called amblyopia, or lazy eye, the brain suppresses the weaker image from the eye with the poorer vision. This eye then becomes lazy, its direction may wander and eventually the child may even become blind in that eye.

Very young babies cannot always coordinate their eye muscles and an eye may turn occasionally. By around three to four months, however, the eye muscles will have strengthened and the baby's eyes should look straight. Many older children only have a squint when they are tired or ill – but this symptom still deserves investigation. Around the age of five, children's eyes should have normal vision, and if any defects arise they must be dealt with quickly in order not to jeopardize the child's sight.

There are a number of forms of treatment for squint, including eye patching, glasses, eye exercises (or a combination of these) and, if necessary, surgery. The majority of squints can now be successfully corrected.

You may notice

- *The eyes do not always look in the same direction*
- *When a light is shone in the child's eyes, the reflection back from the pupils is not symmetrical*
- *The child may sit oddly, twisting around to focus on something*
- *The child may close or cover one eye, especially when they are in bright light*
- *If the child has a vision problem as well, as is common, they may often bump into things or hold objects very close to their face*

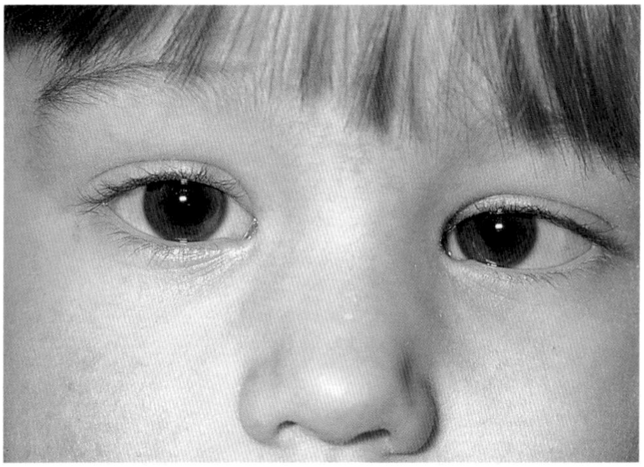

A convergent squint such as this one can be caused when a child with long sight tries hard to focus on objects at close range. If normal vision is to be retained in the squinting eye, the sooner the squint is treated the better. Without treatment, the brain suppresses the image that is received from the squinting eye.

What to do

If you suspect the child has a squint, double-check your impressions. When the baby is awake and alert, hold a bright toy about 20 cm/8 in from the face and move it slowly from side to side. A baby of four months should follow with both eyes. One eye that flickers or drifts suggests a squint. With an older child, play a game of pirates. If they strongly prefer one eye to be covered rather than the other, they may have a lazy eye. If you are still unsure, ask other people who care for the child or see the child regularly if they have noticed a squint.

Even if the squint is only occasional, see your doctor, who should refer you to an optometrist for tests. These will include a test to observe symmetry in vision, and a cover test, in which eye movements are watched when one eye is covered. If the squint cannot be corrected with glasses or exercises the child will be referred to an eye surgeon.

Treatment

There are a number of ways to treat a squint. Children may be given a patch to wear over the good eye for a certain amount of time every day. The patch may cover the eye completely or adhere to glasses, and is designed to force children to use their weaker eye. Children may well have to wear glasses to correct unequal vision between the eyes or to improve long sight. They will probably have to wear the glasses all the time at first, but they may be able to leave them the glasses off later except for close work. Older children may be expected to do exercises to tone up the eye muscles. Such exercises might involve reading using filters, or using a bar to help the child to use both eyes together.

Surgery

In some cases surgery to move the eye to a new position by realigning the eye muscles may be required. Sometimes the surgeon will operate on both eyes.

Just after the operation the eye will be bloodshot and swollen, there will be a scarred area and perhaps even a squint. Healing will be gradual, and the full effect of surgery may take some weeks to assess. Children who wore glasses

A patch that is worn over the right eye forces the child to use his left eye. If treatment starts soon enough, even surprisingly poor vision can be enormously improved by wearing a patch. However if this treatment begins too late, there may be little or no improvement, particularly if the child is over ten years of age.

before surgery usually need to wear them afterwards, as will children with a second visual defect. About one-third of children who have undergone surgery will need another operation to fully correct the squint. However once the eye is fully corrected, only an expert will be able to tell that the child ever had a squint.

Coping with squint

Many children feel very self-conscious about wearing an eye patch or glasses. Give children as much support as possible, which they will undoubtedly need when they have to deal with less sympathetic children at school.

Try to keep a child who wears a patch busy, as this will distract their attention from the patch and will help to stimulate the weaker eye. Make sure the child does not peep around the patch.

Encourage children to wear their glasses according to their schedule, and to do their eye exercises regularly at home.

Complementary Treatment

Osteopathy may help, but the results are variable. **Homeopathy** will support orthodox treatment but specific remedies are available that should be taken three times a day for up to three weeks during orthodox treatment. Give Gelsemium 6c (*Gelsemium sempervirens*, yellow jasmine) first, and, if this does not resolve the problem, Alumina 6c (Alumina, aluminium oxide). If these do not have any effect, you should consult a homeopath. Traditional Chinese Medicine thinks of the eyes as sense organs of the liver, and all treatment would be directed to this part of the body. **Chinese herbalism** may be helpful when combined with **acupuncture**, although it will probably be effective only in the short term. **Reflexology** may also be of some benefit.

Ears, Nose, Throat and Respiration

Viewed from the outside, it might seem unusual that the ear is part of the same body system as the nose and throat, although it is connected The visible parts – the pinna, which receives soundwaves, and the ear canal, which funnels them to the eardrum, a membrane that vibrates in response – are only the start of the system. Behind the eardrum is the middle ear, connected to the back of the throat by the Eustachian tube. Inside the middle ear are three tiny bones, the malleus, incus and stapes, which transmit and amplify sound vibrations through a second membrane into the cochlea of the inner ear. Nerve endings pick up sounds and turn them into electrical impulses, which are transmitted along an auditory nerve to a hearing centre in the brain.

The respiratory tract

The spaces and passageways above the larynx (voice box) – the mouth, throat, nose and sinuses – make up the upper respiratory tract. At the back of the throat are the tonsils and at the back of the nose the adenoids. Both are lumps of lymph tissue that form part of the body's immune system (see page 138). In front of the entrance to the larynx is the epiglottis, a flap of tissue that prevents food entering the respiratory tract. Air passes through the larynx and down the bronchi to the lungs, protected by the ribcage. Inside the lungs the bronchi divide repeatedly until they become tiny bronchioles, which themselves divide into tinier structures, the alveoli. Here oxygen crosses into the bloodstream, while carbon dioxide passes back into the air in the lungs. Any dust, viruses or bacteria that reach the lungs are caught in mucus and swept out by the waving action of hair-like cilia lining the airways.

The respiratory system facilitates the uptake of oxygen from the air into the bloodstream and the expulsion of waste carbon dioxide, together with germs, dust and foreign particles that are trapped by hairs and cilia and are carried out in excess mucus.

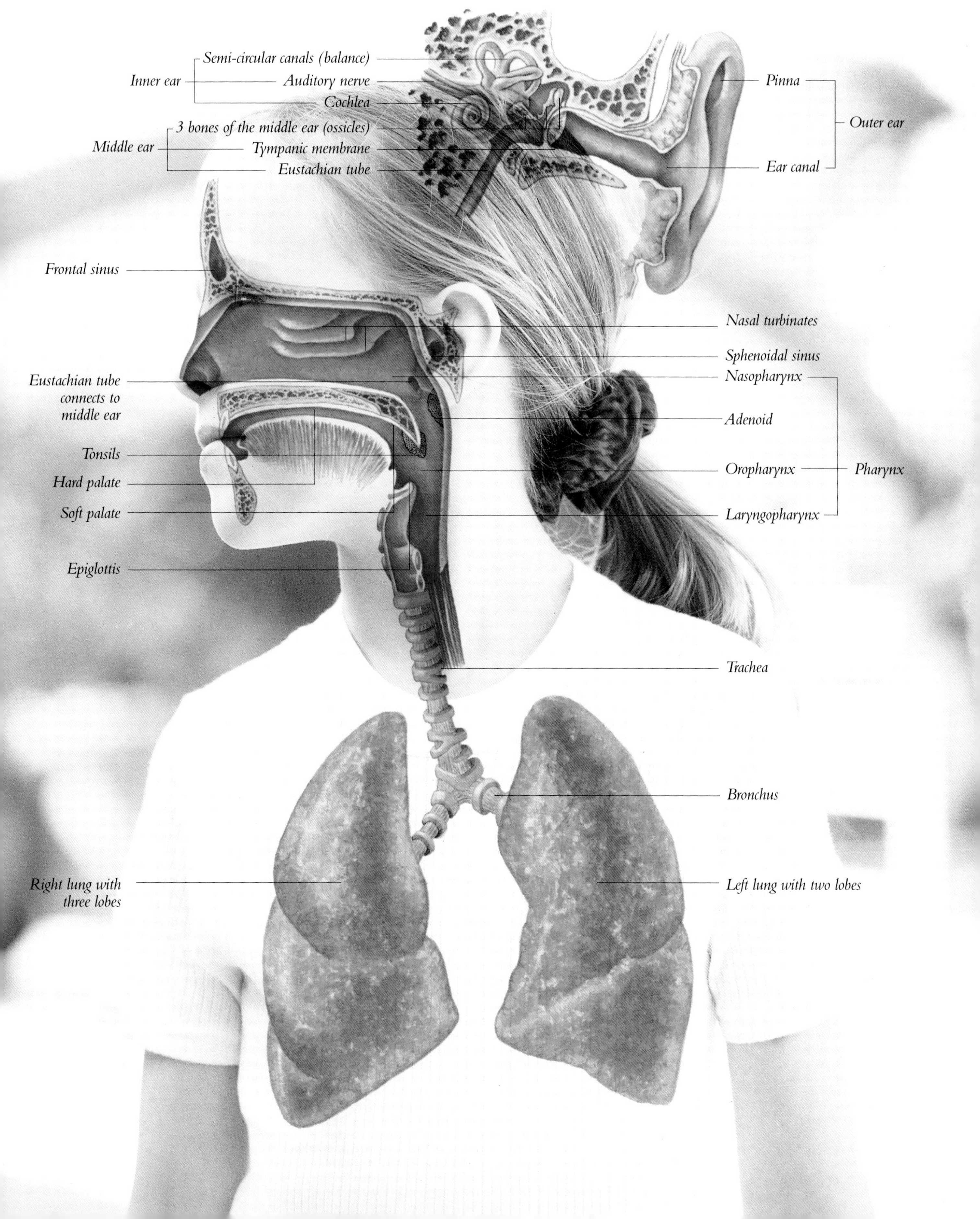
Semi-circular canals (balance)
Inner ear
Auditory nerve
Cochlea
3 bones of the middle ear (ossicles)
Middle ear
Tympanic membrane
Eustachian tube
Pinna
Outer ear
Ear canal
Frontal sinus
Nasal turbinates
Sphenoidal sinus
Eustachian tube connects to middle ear
Nasopharynx
Adenoid
Tonsils
Oropharynx
Pharynx
Hard palate
Soft palate
Laryngopharynx
Epiglottis
Trachea
Bronchus
Right lung with three lobes
Left lung with two lobes

DIAGNOSIS

Minor respiratory ailments are common in childhood. Most young children are frequently affected by coughs and colds caused by viral infections. Most clear quickly, but occasionally further infections of the breathing passages or lungs develop. Many other infections start with the symptoms of a cough or cold. Some children have breathing passages that are sensitive to allergic triggers. Much less commonly, breathing problems can be a sign of an underlying condition.

Sign	What could be wrong
Mouth breathing, catarrhal, runny nose, possibly recurrent ear infections	Possibly swollen adenoids. Symptoms common up to the age of five
Runny nose and sneezing all year round	Quite possibly allergic rhinitis
Persistent cough at night, and possibly on exercise, as well as wheezing	Asthma is a possibility
Cold, followed by a cough and breathlessness in an infant	Bronchiolitis is a possibility. Contact the doctor
After a cold, a child develops a cough, fever and possibly rapid breathing	This could be bronchitis. It affects toddlers and older children more often than infants
A sudden, harsh, barking cough, usually at night	This could be croup. Contact the doctor immediately
Frequent colds that go to the chest, with a gradually worsening cough	Occasionally this is the first sign noticed in cystic fibrosis
Sneezing and runny nose in spring/early summer	If there is no fever, hayfever is the most likely diagnosis
Hoarse voice, sore throat, possibly fever	Laryngitis. This can develop on its own or after a cold
Unwell, breathless, possibly cough and fever	Pneumonia. Contact the doctor immediately if the child is breathless. This may also be the presentation of heart failure
Cold, followed by tenderness around the nose, forehead and eyes	Sinusitis is a distinct possibility in an older child
Unwell, sore throat, fever, possibly stomach ache	Tonsillitis is a likely cause

FOR OTHER POSSIBLE REASONS FOR: RUNNY NOSE, SEE RUNNY NOSE (PAGE 197); COUGH, SEE COUGH; (PAGE 207) WHEEZING, SEE WHEEZING (PAGE 220)

Runny Nose

What is it?

When the lining of the nose becomes inflamed or irritated, it produces extra mucus. Most of the mucus trickles unnoticed down the back of the throat, but when there is too much, some of it emerges as a runny nose. Most runny noses are the result of a cold (see page 208) or other viral infection. They are not serious, except in young infants who need to suck to feed, and who may be unable to do this if their nose is blocked with mucus.

In the early summer a runny nose, sneezing and sore eyes could suggest hay fever. Children who have these symptoms all year round may have an allergy to a substance such as house dust mite or pet fur (see Allergic rhinitis, page 217). A runny nose on one side only could mean that a an object such as a bean (foreign body) has been pushed up the nostril.

What to do

Check for other signs of illness. A child who has a fever should be given children's paracetamol and clear drinks. As these symptoms herald many other childhood infections, keep a watchful eye.

If an infant develops a runny nose, keep them warm and moisten the air by laying a damp towel over a radiator. Offer extra feeds on demand to a breastfed infant, or drinks of freshly boiled, cooled water to an infant on formula.

Infection with a rhinovirus (shown here is a group of rhinoviruses magnified 70,000 times) is one of the most common causes of a runny nose. There are over 100 strains at large in a community. In addition to causing colds, rhinoviruses cause wheezing in asthma and have been found in children with viral pneumonia.

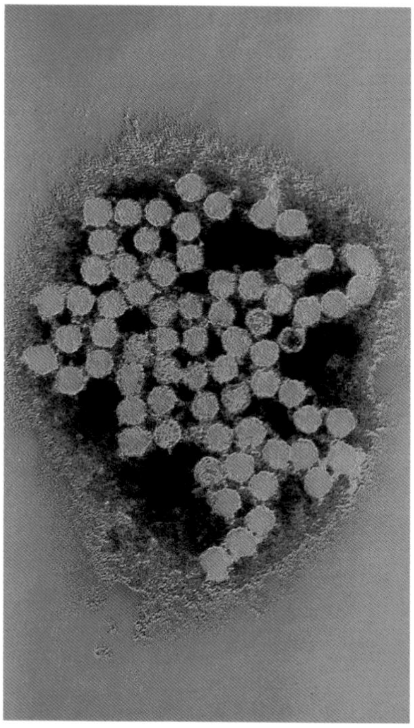

When medical attention is needed

Take an infant to the doctor if:

- They have difficulty sucking. The doctor can prescribe nose drops to be given before feeds. Use nose drops for a maximum of seven days only, to avoid making the problem worse (rebound congestion) when they are stopped
- This is the baby's first cold and you are worried. Coping with colds is a matter of experience and no doctor minds a consultation for the first one
- Children's paracetamol and extra drinks do not control the fever
- Other signs of illness develop. For example, if the child seems really unwell, if breathing becomes noisy or rapid, or if the discharge from the nose turns a thick yellowy-green
- The signs suggest hay fever. The doctor can prescribe drugs to help relieve the symptoms
- The nose is runny on one side only, and when you look inside you can see a foreign body. Don't even attempt to remove it. It is too easy to push it to the back of the nose where the child could inhale it. If the mucus coming from the nose is smelly and infected, take the child to an accident and emergency department

Coping with a runny nose

A warm drink first thing in the morning helps to clear the nose. Exercise also helps to clear the nose, so encourage your child to be up and about as soon as they feel ready.

Teach a toddler to blow their nose one nostril at a time, while you press the other nostril shut. Cloth handkerchiefs harbour germs, so use paper tissues or wipe an infant's nose with cotton wool moistened in warm water. Smear petroleum jelly under the nose and around the mouth to stop chapping.

Complementary Treatment

Nutritional therapy may be useful but this depends on the cause. **Aromatherapy** oils inhaled from a paper tissue or in steam can reduce irritation. **Western herbalists** can prescribe herbs with anti-catarrhal effects. The **homeopath** will prescribe for this condition as for catarrh (see page 210).

CYSTIC FIBROSIS

What is it?

Cystic fibrosis (CF) is an inherited condition that causes abnormally sticky secretions in the lungs and intestines, resulting in chronic respiratory and digestive problems. Underlying this condition is a defect caused by the way tin which water and salts pass in and out of body cells. One effect of this is that the sweat of people with cystic fibrosis contains twice as much sodium and chloride as you would expect – so infants taste salty when kissed.

In cystic fibrosis the normally liquid mucus inside the lungs thickens and becomes so sticky that a glutinous phlegm clogs the airways, making the child cough and wheeze. Bacteria take hold, causing chest infections which eventually lead to lung damage. When that occurs, more destructive bacteria, such as *Staphylococcus aureus* and *Pseudomonas*, invade the lung, resulting in more serious infection.

At the same time, in the digestive system, the pancreas is unable to secrete the enzymes that are vital for absorbing the nutrients from food. Because of this deficiency, infants become undernourished despite eating hungrily. Eventually the liver and pancreas themselves become damaged.

Almost all boys with cystic fibrosis are infertile because the tubes that carry sperm from the testes are blocked. Girls are usually fertile.

Cystic fibrosis may be obvious at or soon after birth, but some children only show signs after months or even years have passed. Ten to fifteen per cent of infants become very ill soon after birth. In some areas up to 20 per cent of newborn infants are screened and diagnosed from a routine blood test after birth. The early signs can be vague and confused with more common illnesses such as colic (see page 259), milk intolerance (see page 244) or asthma (see page 218).

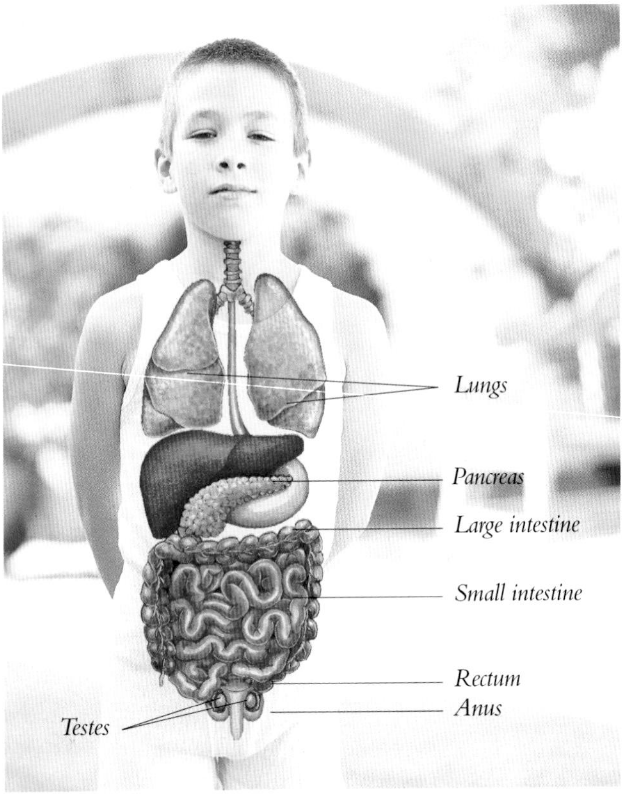

Cystic fibrosis affects many quite different parts of the body, including the lungs – in which abnormally sticky secretions gather – the pancreas, which is unable to secret vital digestive enzymes into the intestines, and in boys, the reproductive system, when tubes carrying sperm from the testes become blocked.

In the genes

Children inherit cystic fibrosis from their parents who are perfectly healthy, but who each carry a fault on a particular gene, known as the cystic fibrosis transmembrane regulator gene (CFTR). The genes of someone with cystic fibrosis, or a carrier, have a tiny gap in the genetic instructions. If both mother and father pass this gene defect on, the child will have two matching defective genes and will develop classic cystic fibrosis. The majority of northern Europeans affected have one or two of six common mutations. Scientists have now found that there are 450 different mutations that cause the condition, and the number is still rising.

Most carriers do not know they are carriers. The majority of the one in twenty-five northern Europeans – two million people in the United Kingdom alone – who are carriers can be identified by a simple mouthwash test. This currently has an accuracy rate of 80 to 90 per cent. If both parents are carriers, the foetus can be tested by chorionic villus sampling after ten weeks, or amniocentesis at 16 to 18 weeks. It may soon be possible to test the foetus from a sample of the mother's blood.

Affected parents, children and unaffected siblings (who are carriers) can have genetic counselling, which can predict with certainty the chances of giving birth to a child with the condition.

You may notice

- *The infant doesn't pass meconium, the first dark green, sticky stools, and the abdomen becomes swollen*
- *An older infant may feed well, but put on very little weight and pass pale, foul-smelling, oily diarrhoea*
- *The child may catch a lot of colds, which go to their chest*
- *Their cough gradually gets worse*

Treatment

Consult your doctor, who can refer you to hospital where tests will be carried out. These include a sweat test (a test of the level of salt in the sweat), together with genetic testing (see In the genes, opposite).

Once the diagnosis has been confirmed, the child will be referred to a specialist centre where parents are shown how to give physiotherapy to clear sticky phlegm from the lungs. Children will need between one and three sessions a day and arrangements for sessions may need to be made at school.

Children with the condition are prone to lung infections and antibiotic treatment is extremely important to protect the lungs. If the child requires frequent intravenous antibiotics, a fine tube can be put into a vein so that treatment can be given whenever it is needed. In some centres children are given a 14-day course of antibiotics every three months to protect their lungs. Children will also need immunization against influenza as well as the routine immunizations. A relatively new drug, known as DNase, may be inhaled to thin the mucus in the lungs.

In addition to physiotherapy, young children will need exercise to keep their lungs clear and strengthen their chest muscles. Swimming, sit-ups and blowing games, trips to the playground and toddler gym are all good options. Older children with cystic fibrosis should take part in normal school sport and social activities.

Enzyme supplements during every meal and snack will help the absorption of nutrients from food. However because not all of the food is digested, children will need extra calories and large meals, and also supplements of vitamins A, D, E and, sometimes, K to replace lost vitamins.

Infection can reduce appetite and maintaining an adequate weight is considered so important that a small feeding tube is sometimes inserted through the stomach wall (a gastrostomy) to give special feeds overnight.

Outlook

Cystic fibrosis is always serious and although it shortens life, it need no longer be thought of as life-threatening in childhood. Many children who are born today with this debilitating condition can expect to live more than 40 years. Heart-lung transplants have revolutionized life for a few. Early trials of gene replacement therapy have shown that it is possible to insert a normal gene into cells in the nose to mask the faulty CFTR gene (cystic fibrosis transmembrane regulator gene), and clinical trials are under way to introduce the gene into the cells of the lung. With those affected now and in the future, this will lead to much safer, less demanding and much more effective treatment.

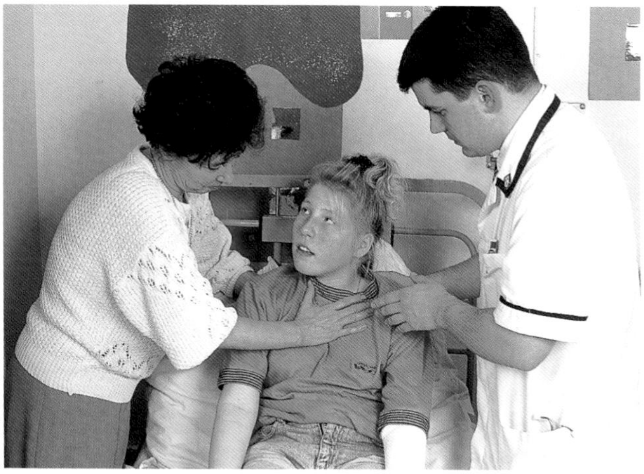

Children who have cystic fibrosis need regular chest physiotherapy, usually twice a day and even more frequently when they fall ill. Physiotherapy helps to loosen the sticky secretions that accumulate in the lungs, so that the child can cough them up and spit them out. A physiotherapist teaches parents how to give physiotherapy and then stays in touch as parents take over the daily routine.

Who can help?

See the Directory for details of organizations and agencies who can give support and help.

Complementary Treatment

This will be supportive of orthodox treatment. **Massage** may help to clear the lungs. **Homeopaths** can often advise on diet, including supplements of vitamins, zinc and selenium, which may be beneficial. Constitutional treatment (according to the personality, temperament and mood of the child) may also help. The **Bach flower remedies** can provide an excellent supportive therapy for the emotional aspects of the condition.

Hearing Impairment

What is it?

Each ear consists of three main parts: the outer ear, the middle ear and the inner ear. The outer ear is made up of the part we see, which is called the pinna, and is made of skin and cartilage, and the outer ear canal. These parts catch and funnel sound inwards to the middle ear and inner ear beyond the eardrum, where sound vibrations are converted into nerve impulses and transmitted to the brain.

Children are rarely totally deaf, and most children with a hearing impairment have what is called a conductive hearing loss. This occurs because there is a mechanical defect in the outer or middle ear that prevents sounds from being conducted to the inner ear. For example, it can be caused by wax blockage in the outer ear canal, glue ear (see page 202) or damage to one of the small bones in the middle ear. Depending on the cause, many young children grow out of conductive hearing loss by the age of ten or eleven. In children with a sensorineural (perceptive) hearing loss there is damage in the inner ear. Sounds received from the middle ear are not passed on to the brain. Some children have both types of hearing loss, and one or both ears may be affected.

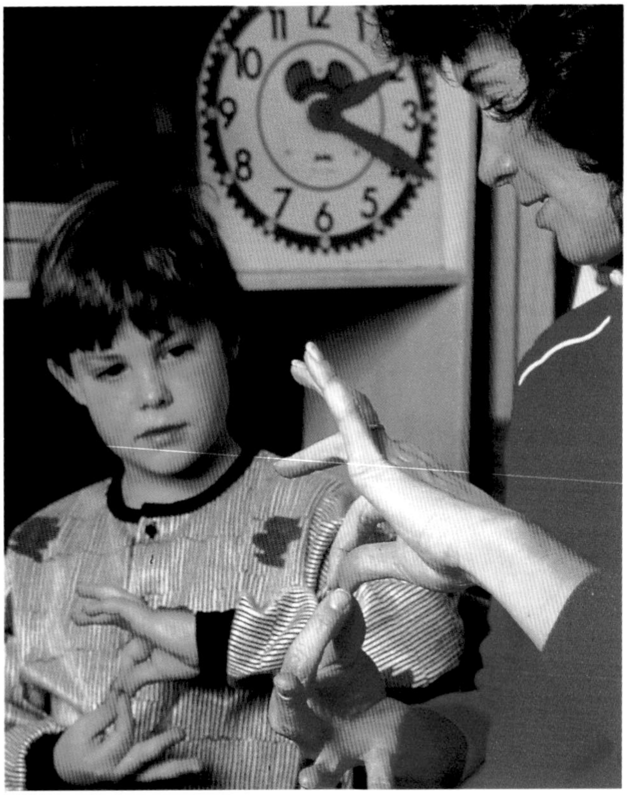

A child learns to communicate by using sign language. This can be helpful, but many parents want a child with diminished hearing to learn to speak as well. If the child gives no indication that they can hear, even when wearing aids, it can be stressful for the parents. With special training parents learn to notice when their child is listening and to talk to and play with them. Talking to the child and playing with them is even more important then with hearing children.

Monitoring children's hearing

Even a temporary or fluctuating hearing loss should never be ignored, because it can have long-term effects on a child's speech and learning ability. Infants who run a particular risk of hearing loss should be monitored regularly. This includes low birthweight infants, premature infants born before 32 weeks and infants who needed longer than a very short stay in neonatal intensive care; infants who have had meningitis, encephalitis or mumps, or whose mothers caught rubella or cytomegalovirus during pregnancy; and infants with a relative who needed a hearing aid before the age of five.

In some areas infants' hearing is checked soon after birth in an 'auditory response cradle', which detects changes in movement in response to sounds. Other tests involve analysing electrical signals in the brain in response to a series of clicks (brainstem evoked response audiometry) or responses in the inner ear (evoked otoacoustic emissions). Elsewhere infants have a hearing test at six to eight months. Parents may be the first to suspect a hearing loss in their child.

You may notice

- *Shortly after birth, the infant doesn't startle, blink or open their eyes wide in response to a sudden, loud noise*
- *At one month the infant doesn't become still if you make a sudden, continuing sound*
- *At three months the infant doesn't quieten to your voice*
- *At six months the infant doesn't turn immediately to your voice coming from across a room, or to very quiet noises made on each side*
- *At nine months the infant doesn't search for sounds made out of sight, and doesn't babble*
- *At 12 months the infant shows no response to their name or other familiar words*
- *The child is late learning to speak, shouts and is inattentive, especially in a group at story time.*

What to do

If you suspect a child is not hearing properly, seek advice from a health visitor or doctor. The child can be referred to a

children's audiology centre. Tests may include the following.
Co-operative testing The tester gives simple instructions in a quiet voice, such as 'Give it to teddy'. This is suitable for children aged between 18 and 30 months with reasonable language skills.
Performance tests The child performs a task, such as putting a brick in a basket, at a signal made by the tester behind a screen. The signal may be a word, a 'ss' sound or a warble tone. This test is suitable for children who are aged between 24 and 30 months.
Speech discrimination The child identifies simple objects or pictures by name, such as plate, plane, fish, chick.
Pure tone audiometry Sounds at a set level are played to the child through headphones. The child performs a simple task, such as putting pegs in a board, when they hear the sound. This test is often used for the four to six year age group.
Tympanometry This tests for problems in the middle ear, but doesn't check hearing. Relative air pressure on each side of the eardrum is measured, because hearing is best when air pressure is equal on both sides. It can be used at any age.

Treatment

The results of testing may be reassuring (see Glue ear, page 202). If the child is found to have a hearing impairment a hearing aid can be fitted. This will improve the child's hearing, although it will never make it completely normal. Radio aids, where the parent's voice is fed into a microphone and linked to the aid, are useful at home to allow a parent to keep in touch with a young child who is out of sight. They can also be used at school.

Children with a hearing impairment may be taught by a total communication method, including speech, signing, lip reading, gesture and body language. The aim is to allow the child to communicate and use as much speech as possible. Some deaf children attend a mainstream school; others attend a special unit attached to a school, or a school for the deaf.

Deaf children should sit at the front of the classroom with the better ear (if there is one) turned towards the teacher. From here they will be able to watch the teacher's face, and they will also be able to turn and watch other children's faces as they speak.

Coping with hearing loss

Children with hearing loss manage one-to-one situations better than group situations. When choosing pre-school education, look for somewhere with a small group size, which will usually be better for the child.

This child is having his hearing tested with pure tone audiometry. When the machine makes a noise, the child responds in a way he has already agreed with the tester. The pitch and volume of the sounds made by the machine gradually decrease until they become inaudible.

Make sure that you always get a child's attention before speaking to them, and make sure that they can see your face. Talk through new situations and experiences, even everyday experiences, with your child, telling them what to expect. This helps a child to make sense of their environment.

It can be helpful to use a camera to record events, so that you can talk about them afterwards with a visual aid.

You should be prepared for bad behaviour when your child's lack of understanding frustrates them.

Who can help?

See the Directory for organizations who can give support.

Complementary Treatment

The complementary therapies that deal mainly with emotional and behavioural problems, such as problems of adjustment, are most appropriate. The **Bach flower remedies**, arts therapies and play therapy may help the child gain in confidence and deal with emotions such as anger and frustration. However, **nutritional therapists** believe that some cases of deafness are caused by food allergy and would attempt to find the allergen and treat accordingly.

Glue Ear

What is it?

Glue ear, which is also known as otitis media with effusion (OME), is a form of fluctuating deafness that is extremely common in young children. It is usually caused when, in response to an infection, the lining of the middle ear produces excess mucus. Mucus in the middle ear normally drains away down the Eustachian tube to the back of the throat. However in young children these tubes frequently do not work efficiently because they are short and do not slope downwards as steeply as in adults. This makes it easy for bacteria and viruses to travel from the throat and nose into the middle ear cavity. Repeated infections can leave the Eustachian tubes blocked, and the problem may be made worse if the adenoids (see page 216) are also swollen, because this can block the entrance to the Eustachian tubes. If the tubes are blocked the mucus collects in the middle ear, thickens and becomes gluey, leaving the child's hearing muffled.

Who is most vulnerable?

Bouts of glue ear can start in early infancy. The two peak ages are around one to two years and again at five, when children start school and are exposed to a large number of bacteria and viruses. Most children recover within six months, and the deafness always clears on its own eventually, but some children can be affected off and on until they are ten or eleven. By then speech, behaviour and reading may have been affected. Children vary in how much they are affected by glue ear. Some can disguise a major hearing loss by picking up visual and other clues, while others are disorientated by even a minor loss. The effects of glue ear vary from day to day, so many parents wonder if their children 'hear when they want to'. In fact, they hear when they can.

A child who can cope in a one-to-one situation with a fluctuating hearing loss that is caused by glue ear may show a marked inability to concentrate when expected to listen in a group. Children with glue ear may also find it difficult to cope with background noise.

You may notice

- *An infant of four months with glue ear may not quieten or smile at your voice. They may not turn to a noise made out of sight by seven months, and may fail the seven-to-nine month hearing test*
- *By nine months of age the infant may become very distressed when you go out of sight or they may jump when you appear suddenly*
- *They may be unusually clingy and difficult. Sleep may be disrupted and the infant may frequently catch a cold*
- *A child or toddler may have the TV volume too loud or may sit very close to watch*
- *The child may find it hard to sit still and concentrate in a group, and may wander off or daydream instead*
- *Some children watch intently as they lipread or observe your gestures. In a few children the most obvious sign of glue ear is bad behaviour and poor concentration*
- *Glue ear is not usually painful, but some older children complain of a stuffy feeling in the ear. The condition is worse for a few weeks after the child has recovered from a cold and it is usually more continuous in winter.*

What to do

If you suspect a child is deaf, even intermittently, see the doctor. The doctor will probably do a hearing test and may then refer you to an audiology department, either immediately or after a repeat hearing check. A member of staff will examine the child's ears with an instrument called an otoscope to see if there is glue behind the eardrum and may prescribe antibiotics if the eardrum is inflamed. Antibiotics will usually clear the glue, but eventually it returns, so some doctors prescribe mild steroids as well, which will reduce any inflammation and stimulate the Eustachian tubes to open and so that air pressure on either side of the eardrum is equalized.

Allergy-prone children seem to suffer more from glue ear than other children, so if the doctor thinks the cause is allergic, they may suggest ways to reduce the child's exposure to certain allergens (the substances that cause the allergy). Some doctors also recommend antihistamine drugs, which will dampen the allergic reaction.

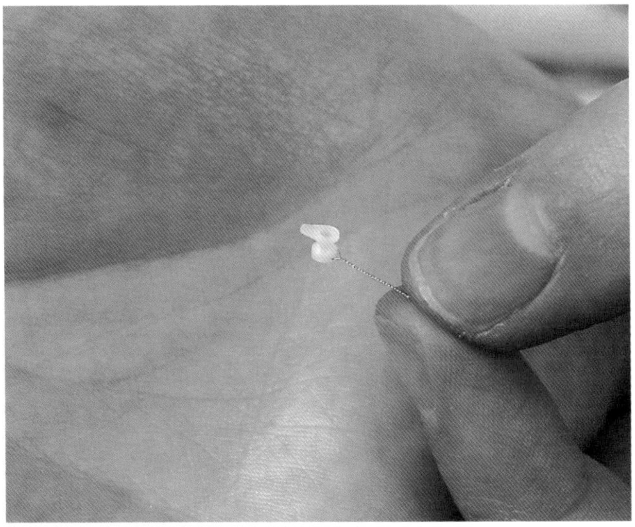

Grommets are minute plastic tubes inserted into a tiny slit in the eardrum to allow air to flow freely and to normalize air pressure inside the middle ear. Grommets usually fall out into the ear canal after a few months, leaving only a slight scar on the eardrum. Children who are expected to need this treatment repeatedly or over a long period may have a special type of grommet fitted that remains in place much longer.

At the audiology clinic the child will have a hearing test. Between the ages of six and eighteen months infants have a distraction test. The baby is distracted by a person holding a toy in front of them while a second person makes noises from behind to check how the baby responds. From 18 months to around 2½ years, some clinics do a performance test, giving the child simple instructions from behind a screen. Over the age of two-and-a-half, children are tested with a range of sounds played through headphones.

The result of a hearing test is given as decibels of hearing loss or as a percentage. A normal speaking voice measured from about 1 m/3 ft away is 60–70 decibels; a shout is 80 decibels; and a whisper just 30. At 140 decibels, sound is painfully loud. Children with a 50–60 decibel loss in both ears will not hear normal speech. A child with a loss of 25–30 decibels in both ears for three months or more is likely to require treatment.

Treatment

The child may need a straightforward operation under general anaesthetic to cut a slit in the eardrum, drain the glue and maintain an open airflow into the middle ear. Some children have their adenoids removed in the same operation to help prevent glue ear returning. Many children have a grommet inserted in one or both eardrums. Grommets are minute tubes shaped like mini cotton reels, which allow air to flow in and out of the middle ear. They often produce a dramatic improvement in hearing. Most grommets stay in place for about six months before falling out. The hole in the eardrum heals up quickly, but if the glue returns, the grommet may be replaced. A child with grommets needs watertight earplugs for hairwashing. The doctor may allow swimming, but jumping or diving into the pool won't be permitted.

Coping with glue ear

To communicate with a child with glue ear talk to the child face-to-face. Give simple, clear instructions and be ready to repeat them. Turn off the radio or television while talking, so there is only one source of sound. Choose a playgroup or nursery with small groups and structured activities.

Read to the child, sing songs and teach rhymes to build up speech. If the child's speech is affected, ask the doctor to refer the child for a speech therapy assessment.

Teach a child of three or more to blow their nose one nostril at a time to help keep the middle ear aerated.

Complementary Treatment

A **Chinese herbalist** may treat glue ear as a chronic stage of otitis media with catarrh. The child will often be weak from illness or overwork. **Acupuncture** will often be of help, as will **Western herbalism**. **Nutritional therapists** hold that glue ear is often linked to food allergy and will treat accordingly (see page 242). Topical applications of **aromatherapy** essential oils in the external canal can help. **Homeopathy** will treat persistent conditions constitutionally (according to the personality, temperament and mood of the child concerned) and/or support orthodox treatment, prescribing specific remedies prior to and following grommet insertion. **Kinesiology** may also prove helpful in some cases.

SEE ALSO HEARING IMPAIRMENT (PAGE 200)

BRONCHIOLITIS

What is it?

Bronchiolitis is a chest infection in which the bronchioles, the tiny airways in the lungs, become inflamed and blocked. It is usually caused by the respiratory syncytial virus (RSV). RSV is most common between November and March, when it can cause mini epidemics.

The condition mainly affects infants and toddlers whose bronchioles are quite small – only one-tenth of a millimetre across – and can therefore become obstructed relatively easily. Younger infants are more severely affected than older infants, in whom the virus may only cause a nasty cold (see page 208) or no symptoms at all. Bronchiolitis is contagious as well as infectious, and as the virus survives for 30 minutes or more on unwashed hands it can easily be passed by direct contact from person to person.

All adults have antibodies to RSV so mothers should in theory pass them on to their infants across the placenta during pregnancy. However these antibodies do not give much protection to a new baby who can occasionally develop a severe infection soon after birth. RSV bronchiolitis is still uncommon under the age of four weeks, becoming most common in infants between the age of two and five months. Most frequently an older brother or sister or an adult with a cold passes the virus on to the baby.

Certain infants are more susceptible to bronchiolitis than others. These include infants who come from very large families, especially if they are living in cold, damp housing conditions; those who live in households where people smoke; and those who were born prematurely and who had breathing difficulties after birth.

You may notice

- *The illness usually starts with a cold. Over the next day or two the child develops an irritating dry cough*
- *There is difficulty feeding*
- *Breathlessness*
- *Moderate fever, which is rarely higher than 38°-38.5°C/ 100.4°-101.3°F*
- *Wheezing – a high pitched whistling or rustling noise*
- *Restlessness*
- *In a severe case, rapid, laboured breathing so the child seems to struggle or pull in their chest as they breathe*

What to do

Contact the doctor immediately. While you are waiting for the doctor's arrival, keep the baby warm, comfortable and as calm as possible – crying makes it even harder for them to breathe. Cuddle the baby on your shoulder or prop them in their carry seat, because they will breathe more easily if they are sitting in an upright position.

Encourage the baby to drink, even if it is just small amounts. Offer the breast or bottle twice as often as usual and boiled, cooled water as well. Check for a fever. If the baby's temperature is over 38°C/100.4°F and the baby is more than three months old, give them children's paracetamol. Do not give them any cough medicines.

Keep the air in the room warm and moist by laying a damp towel over the radiator or by placing a bowl of water near it to vaporize. Alternatively, use a vaporizer or humidifier.

In an emergency

Call an ambulance if:

- The infant's breathing becomes laboured or difficult
- The lips, tongue or area around the mouth look blue
- The infant becomes lethargic and drowsy

Treatment

The doctor will examine the baby and listen to the chest. Infants who have mild symptoms can be nursed at home as above, but those who need help with breathing or feeding will be admitted to hospital.

If your doctor recommends that you look after your infant at home, try to find a way to help them to sleep propped up at night. Try letting them sleep in their car seat or raise the head end of the cot by placing a pillow under the mattress or large books under the legs.

To loosen mucus from the baby's lungs, ask your doctor to show you how. You should lay the baby across your knees, stomach down, and pat their back sharply with the flat of your hand.

In hospital, staff will carry out a number of tests. A sample of the virus may be taken from the back of the nose through a fine tube – probably the most uncomfortable procedure of the whole stay – and a probe on the finger will painlessly measure the amount of oxygen circulating in the blood.

The baby may be put in an individual cubicle to prevent the spread of infection to other infants. If necessary, extra oxygen will be given through a headbox (a see-through perspex box placed over the baby's head). If the baby is too restless for a headbox, a tube may be taped under the nose to carry extra

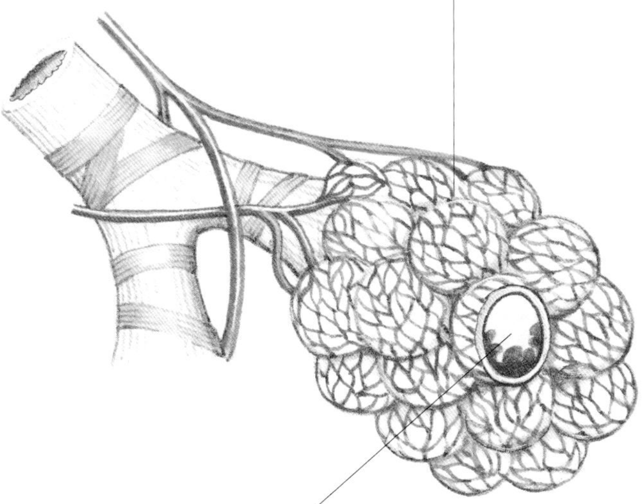

In response to viral attack, the tiny bronchioles near the end of the bronchial tree become swollen and pour out extra mucus. The cilia, structures that normally help to keep the airways clear, fail to operate. Mucus gathers, eventually causing a blockage, so that air is trapped in the alveoli at the tops of the bronchia tree.

oxygen into the lungs. If feeding problems arise, a soft tube will be passed through the child's nose and down into the stomach to allow the baby to feed without making special efforts to breathe.

In some hospitals infants with bronchiolitis are also given drugs through a nebulizer or direct into the headbox. (However the use of drugs is controversial and many hospitals do not use any.) Ipratropium bromide, a drug that is also given to infants with asthma, may be used to relax and widen the airways. Some hospitals also give the antiviral drug ribavirin, together with moist, oxygen-rich air administered through the headbox if the baby is premature, less than six weeks old, or has an additional underlying problem.

What else?

Infants with bronchiolitis are often tired by the extra effort they have to make breathing and feeding, so they may not feel like being stroked or played with. The baby may be happiest just to sit propped up with someone familiar in sight.

Most infants will stay in hospital for three to five days. While your infant is in hospital, check that it is safe for you to enter other cubicles, because it is likely that you too are carrying the virus – it is highly infectious and can be passed on by touch as well as by breathing. Washing your hands regularly will help to prevent the spread of infection.

Outlook

The next few times the baby catches a cold they will tend to cough and wheeze more than before, but these symptoms lessen with time. In the first two years after the illness, half to three-quarters of infants who have had bronchiolitis will have further episodes of wheezing. However by the age of five most infants who have had bronchiolitis will have no further respiratory problems.

Complementary Treatment

Complementary treatments mainly provide support for orthodox treatment. They include **Chinese herbalism** and **acupuncture**, **Western herbalism** and **kinesiology**. **Homeopathic remedies** while waiting for professional help to arrive are: Carbo veg 30c (*Carbo vegetabilis*, vegetable charcoal) for a infant who is hoarse and wheezy and blue in the face, the breath exhaled feels cold and the attack begins in the evening; and Antimonium tart 30c (*Antimonium tartaricum*, ammonium chloride) for a infant who is exhausted with attempting to breathe, is too weak to cough up phlegm, vomits, with nostrils that are sucked in with the effort of breathing.

BRONCHITIS

What is it?

Bronchitis is a chest infection that is caused by a virus or a bacterium. It affects the larger airways (the bronchi) inside the lungs, which then become swollen and produce extra mucus or phlegm. Bronchitis tends to affect toddlers and older children rather than infants, and may develop when a viral infection spreads down the airways. It is more common in a cold, damp climate and when air pollution levels are high enough to irritate a child's airways. It is not uncommon in measles and chickenpox infection.

You may notice

- *A normal cold, during which new symptoms develop*
- *There is a dry, hacking cough, which turns chesty and rattles after a day or two*
- *Phlegm, which may be yellow. The child may swallow the phlegm or they may cough so much that they vomit*
- *Rapid breathing – over 40 breaths a minute – which may be wheezy*
- *Fever and appetite loss*

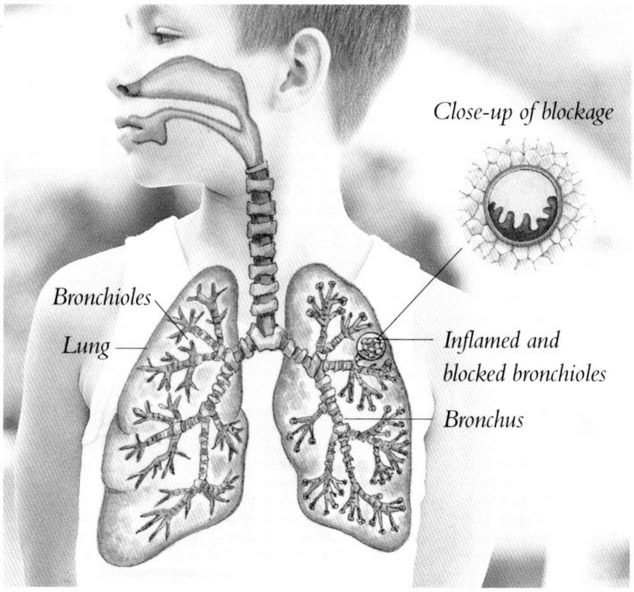

The typical chesty cough of a child with bronchitis is a reflex action designed to clear the airways of the extra mucus that is produced when the bronchi become inflamed and swollen.

What to do

Contact your doctor. Meanwhile, keep the child warm and prop them up to sleep if that eases the breathing. If the child is running a temperature of 38°C/100.4°F and is more than three months old, give children's paracetamol. To ease coughing, offer soothing warm drinks such as honey and lemon, warmed lemon barley or blackcurrant, and give them frequently. (Only give honey to infants over 12 months of age.) Do not give a child with bronchitis a cough medicine; it may make matters worse, because suppressing the cough may allow phlegm to collect in the airways.

Keeping the air in the room warm and moist may to help the child's breathing. Lay a damp towel over the radiator, place a bowl near it or use a vaporizer. Alternatively, use a humidifier. Make sure that nobody smokes in the house.

Treatment

The doctor will examine the child and listen to the chest. If the symptoms are mild the child can be nursed at home. Antibiotics will only be given if the doctor concludes the bronchitis is caused by bacteria, or a secondary invasion by bacteria after a primary virus infection. The cough usually fades gradually and the child is well within a week or two. However a child who has repeated attacks should be seen by a specialist, as there may be an underlying cause.

Wheezy bronchitis

This is the name given to the tendency of young children to wheeze and cough regularly after a cold. It is now considered to be a form of asthma (see page 218). The child may be prescribed a bronchodilator such as salbutamol to relax the airways and, if the wheezing continues, a drug to soothe any underlying inflammation in the airways. These are the same drugs that are used to treat asthma.

Complementary Treatment

Osteopathy can help and may prevent recurrence by strengthening the respiratory system. The osteopath will advise on self-help, such as deep breathing and exercise. **Chiropractic** techniques may aid breathing. **Chinese herbalism** and **acupuncture** can be beneficial. **Aromatherapy** oils can help control symptoms, especially pain, when inhaled, applied to the thorax or used in compresses and massage. **Homeopathic treatment** can also be very effective.

Coughs

What are they?

Coughing is an extremely efficient reflex action that keeps the airways and lungs clear of dust, foreign matter and excess natural secretions. There are two types of cough – a dry cough, when nothing comes or is brought up, and a productive cough, when phlegm or mucus is brought up. Healthy children cough on average 10 times a day but coughing at night is more unusual. Most coughs are healthy or a symptom of a passing cold, but a cough in a very young infant could be linked to feeding difficulties, and if the cough occurs with other signs of illness a chest infection may be the cause. A persistent cough in a teenager may signal the start of smoking.

You may notice

- *The child has a dry cough that brings nothing up. After two or three days the cough becomes loose and rattly*
- *The child also has a cold*
- *The cough is worse at night*
- *The child becomes sick, either coughing violently in spasms that end in being sick or producing a lot of phlegm which they swallow, eventually making themselves sick*
- *There may be other signs such as wheezing, breathing difficulties or fever*

What to do

If the child has a cold, wipe or help them blow their nose regularly to limit the mucus dripping down and irritating the throat. For an irritating night cough with a cold, raise the head end of the mattress either by putting a pillow under it or putting books under the bed legs. Alternatively, you can give the child an extra pillow or put a baby in their seat to sleep.

Give the child warm, soothing drinks, for instance hot honey and lemon or water, to loosen mucus, and avoid any cough medicine unless prescribed by the doctor. (Only give honey to children over 12 months of age.) A cough that is bad enough for medicine is bad enough to be seen by a doctor.

Make sure that the air is warm but moist. Lay a damp towel over the radiator, keep the child in a moist kitchen or use a vaporizer – and keep children away from smoky atmospheres.

Complementary Treatment

In Traditional Chinese Medicine coughs are seen as a weakness of chi and weakness in lung energy, a complication of another illness (causing a deficiency in the spleen) or the result of inoculation. Both **Chinese herbalism** and **acupuncture** will give specific treatment once the cause has been identified. **Aromatherapy** oils can help control symptoms when the oils are inhaled, applied to the thorax or used in compresses and during massage. **Western herbs** can make the cough more productive, reduce irritation and fight infection. **Osteopathy** can also have a positive effect and **homeopathy** offers a large number of remedies suited to individual symptoms.

Be on the alert

Contact a doctor if the cough doesn't settle down in 24-48 hours or if any of the following symptoms occur.

Symptom	Possible cause
A cough develops in a baby under six months	This could suggest bronchiolitis (see page 204). In a very young infant it could mean that the milk is going down the wrong way
The cough turns chesty and the child's breathing becomes fast, noisy or difficult	The child may have developed a chest infection. This may occasionally be the first sign of cystic fibrosis (see page 198)
The cough is accompanied by fever, chills and by a runny nose	This could be influenza
The child coughs persistently at night, and possibly wheezes as well as coughs	Asthma is a possibility
A sudden barking cough comes on at night	This could be croup
A previously well child suddenly starts to cough	A small toy, nut or object may have been inhaled (see First Aid)
A cold followed by persistent coughing spasms, especially at night, often resulting in vomiting	Whooping cough. A baby, or vaccinated child may not 'whoop' but cough, with occasional vomiting, for 2-3 months. The Chinese name is 'the hundred day cough'

COLDS

What are they?

The common cold is caused by an infection that inflames the mucous membrane lining the nose and throat. Among its many symptoms are a runny nose, sneezing, sore throat, catarrh, headache, raised temperature and a feeling of being unwell. There are many different viruses that can cause a cold, with over 100 different strains of the most common type. Most toddlers and pre-school children catch six to eight colds a year, but some children suffer from serial colds, with one overlapping the next. Children are more susceptible because their immune system has not yet come into contact with a wide enough range of viruses, but the good news is that the more colds children have, the more they build up their immunity, which will protect them in future.

On the whole, young children's colds are light and last only a few days, but they may sometimes herald other infections such as tonsillitis, ear infections or chest infections.

Children catch colds on average six to eight times a year. Most infections occur in winter, so close proximity helps viruses travel from one child to another through coughs, sneezes and talking. It is therefore important to teach children to sneeze and cough into a handkerchief.

You may notice

In an infant

- *A snuffly nose and going off their feed because they can't suck and breathe through a blocked nose at the same time*

In an older child

- *A runny or blocked nose, with or without sneezing*
- *Coughing, especially at night, as mucus from the nose tickles the back of the throat*
- *Loss of appetite*
- *A moderate fever of 38°C/100.4° F. This will drop as the cold develops*

What to do

If infants or children just have a runny nose but are otherwise sleeping and feeding normally, breathing easily and aren't too hot, you can treat them yourself. Dab the nose with cotton wool or tissues, dipped first in warm water if the mucus has turned crusty. Prevent the skin around the nose from becoming sore by dabbing on vaseline or petroleum jelly. Give an older child a stick of lip balm to prevent their lips from chapping.

Teach children who are about three years old how to blow their nose by pressing one nostril closed while they snort through the other. If children blow through both nostrils together they may force secretions into the Eustachian tubes that lead to their ears, causing an ear infection.

A warm, steamy atmosphere eases a blocked nose, so give children warm baths and warm drinks. Slip an inhalant tissue under the cot sheet or, for an older child, inside the pillowcase. Alternatively add a drop or two of decongestant oil to a cloth handkerchief and tie it well out of your child's reach. You can also add a drop or two of decongestant oil to a bowl of steamy water and put it in the child's room safely away from the bed or cot.

Coughing helps clear virus-laden mucus from the airways and prevents it reaching the lungs. To ease the cough, keep the air in the bedroom warm and moist and give warm drinks, such as honey and lemon, to a child over 12 months. But don't give any medicines to suppress the cough. You can help children breathe more easily by raising the head end of the mattress, either by slipping a pillow underneath it or by putting books under the bed legs.

What else?

Check the child's forehead and the back of the neck for fever. If the skin feels hot, double check your child's temperature with a feverstrip or thermometer. If the temperature is raised, cool the child by giving them the correct amount of children's paracetamol for their age. Offer children water or juice or give them ice cubes or lollies made from fresh fruit juice. If their temperature is over 38°C/100.4°F, strip them down to a vest and nappy. When put to bed, cover them with a sheet.

Infants with a cold won't be able to feed easily as their nose may be blocked, their throat may be sore and they may have lost their appetite. Sit them up in their chair or prop them up on pillows to feed. Feed little and often and don't expect them to suck for long. While breastfeeding, break open a decongestant capsule and empty the contents on to a tissue or handkerchief and put it by the breast. Offer a bottle-fed baby extra drinks of boiled, cooled water.

Medical treatment

You can usually look after a child with a cold yourself, but in some cases it is necessary to consult your doctor. A child whose nose is so blocked that they can't suck or comfort themselves with a dummy, thumb or fingers may be prescribed paediatric nose drops to be given 10-20 minutes before a feed. Decongestant nose drops can be used for infants over three months for up to five days, but if they're given for longer they might cause rebound congestion – swelling inside the nose – when you stop giving them. You can also buy a nasal aspirator from a pharmacy to suck secretions out of a baby's nose before feeding.

If children are coughing then the cold virus may have made the airways sensitive or caused a chest infection. Infants under six months of age must always be seen by a doctor, as most infants who have a cough may have stopped drinking and eating, and may have become dehydrated.

Children who grunt as they cough or whose ribcage is sucked in between coughs, need urgent hospital admission. If their breathing becomes fast, noisy or difficult, then they may have developed a chest infection, for which antibiotics may be required.

Finally, consult your doctor if the child develops other signs such as earache, drowsiness and irritability, or if the cold is recurrent or doesn't get better.

Extra help for colds

In infants

- Infants are prone to nappy rash when they have colds. Use extra barrier cream, leave the nappy off or change it more frequently
- Infants who have a cold can have their immunizations on time, but if you are worried or the child has a fever, then check with your doctor first

In children

- Children with colds are often extra clingy. Keep them with you and give them lots of attention,
- Keep your child well away from a smoky atmosphere. Smokers' children develop more colds

Fresh air, even when the temperature outside is low, will not do a child with a cold any harm and may even be beneficial, as long as the child is well wrapped up. Contrary to belief, cold weather does not cause colds, either. They are caused by a virus.

Complementary Treatment

There are a number of **homeopathic remedies** for colds, specific remedies depending on the symptoms. Aconite 30c (*Aconitum napellus*, blue aconite) is useful for the first stages and Dulcamara 6c (*Solanum dulcamara*, bittersweet) for a cold that appears when the child has been hot and then becomes wet or damp. **Nutritional therapists** recommend high doses of Vitamin C at the first signs of cold and a daily vitamin C tablet as a supplement to a healthy diet in order to prevent colds. **Western herbalists** will have a wide range of herbs, and prescribe on the basis of the individual and their symptoms. Herbs may include elecampane (*Inula helenium*), useful to clear phlegm from the lungs. **Aromatherapy** oils can help control symptoms when inhaled with steam, applied topically to the thorax, or used in compresses and in massage. Fretful babies of all ages can be massaged with chamomile or lavender oil, and will benefit from lavender or tea tree burned in a vaporizer. The recommended blend for massage is 1-3 drops of essential oil in 2 tablespoons of vegetable carrier oil. For the vaporizer, add the drops to water.

Catarrh

What is it?

The mucous membrane lining the nose secretes a thick lubricating fluid called mucus, which also helps to trap dust and germs. The mucus produced in the nose usually trickles unnoticed down the back of the throat. However if the mucous membrane is inflamed it swells and produces much more mucus than it would normally. Catarrh is simply an excess of mucus in the nose.

In young children inflammation of the mucous membrane is usually caused by a viral infection, but it can also be caused by an allergy (see Allergic rhinitis, page 217). Repeated infections often leave the adenoids at the back of the throat permanently swollen (see Adenoids, page 216). Swollen adenoids can then block the drainage channels from the middle ear, causing infection page 213) or glue ear (see page 202).

Catarrh is extremely common in pre-school children, but almost all of them grow out of it by the age of seven or eight at the latest. Catarrh is a nuisance, but it is not harmful.

You may notice

- *A toddler is snotty or an infant is snuffly. An infant may also have difficulty feeding*
- *A child breathes through the mouth*
- *Some catarrhal children are prone to sore throats, earache or deafness*
- *The symptoms are often particularly obvious in a child's first year at nursery or school*

What to do

Check your child for signs of infection. If the child is hot to the touch, lethargic, has suddenly lost their appetite or you are worried about them, make an appointment with your doctor. If your child has catarrh but seems otherwise well, you can treat them yourself.

Try to keep your child's nose clear, particularly before meals or feeds. Wipe an infant's nose with a wisp of cotton wool dipped in warm water. Teach an older child to blow their nose one nostril at a time. Consider using a nasal aspirator.

What else?

To help your child sleep, prepare an inhalation in a large flat-bottomed bowl. Pour in warm to hot (but not boiling) water and add herbal decongestant drops. Sit your child with their face over the bowl for five to ten minutes so that they can breathe in the steam. Stay with them while they are doing this. Alternatively, a warm bath before bed can help to clear a child's nose, and a vaporizer will help to keep the nose clear at night. Decongestant drops on a child's bedclothes or nightclothes, or on a handkerchief or on cloth tied out of a baby's reach, can ease catarrh at night.

If a baby is having difficulty feeding your doctor can prescribe paediatric nose drops for a few days. Give them to your child about ten minutes before a feed.

A child who seems constantly catarrhal and develops long-standing glue ear may need to have their adenoids removed in order to help keep the Eustachian tubes open.

Coping with catarrh

If your child has catarrh, smear petroleum jelly on the nose and upper lip to prevent chapping, and make sure they always have plenty of tissues so that they do not wipe their nose on the back of their hand or their sleeve.

Don't allow anyone to smoke near your child as this can make catarrh worse.

Complementary Treatment

Traditional Chinese medicine can be very effective, particularly **acupuncture**; **Chinese herbalists** usually recommend garlic for this condition. (Garlic can be given in odourless capsule form.) **Western herbalists** will have a wide range of herbs to reduce production of excess mucus and fight infection. **Homeopathic remedies** in acute cases include Sanguinaria 6c (*Sanguinaria canadensis*, bloodroot) for profuse, offensive, yellow catarrh, where the nose feels dry and hot and there is frequent sneezing. Chronic cases require the advice of an experienced homeopath. Other appropriate therapies include **aromatherapy**. Essential oils can reduce irritation, allow the child to sleep and control the production of mucus. Fretful babies will benefit from lavender or tea tree oil burned in a vaporizer.

SINUSITIS

What is it?

Sinusitis is inflammation or infection of the membrane lining the sinuses, and it is a common condition in older children. The sinuses are the air-filled spaces in the bones of the face and skull, the purpose of which is to filter and pre-warm air before it goes down to the lungs. The sinuses that most commonly become infected are the ones in the forehead between the eyes, and in the cheekbones on either side of the nose. Sinusitis usually follows a cold, and it develops because the drainage holes that lead from the sinuses into the back of the nose become blocked. The virus that caused the cold may also cause sinusitis, or it may develop as a secondary bacterial infection. They may also become infected as a complication of the swelling of the mucous membranes associated with allergic rhinitis (see page 217). Some children get an attack of sinusitis with every cold, while others are never affected. Sinusitis is extremely unusual in young children because they have no air in the sinuses, but is much more common in children over the age of ten.

Sinusitis may be serious enough to need antibiotics, but it almost never leads to complications.

You may notice

- *First the child has a cold with a blocked or runny nose. The discharge may be thick and white or yellow-green*
- *The child complains of pain or tenderness around the forehead, nose and eyes*
- *The child has a fever*
- *Chronic sinusitis may develop. The child may have repeated attacks of sinusitis and may also complain of a blocked or runny nose and a cough at night*

What to do

To ease the pain of sinusitis, lie the child down, wring out a face cloth in hot water and lay it over the tender area. Check the child's temperature with a fever strip or thermometer. If it is raised, give children's paracetamol and a drink. If the child's temperature is over 39°C/103°F consult the doctor. The doctor may prescribe antibiotics and decongestant nose drops to reduce the inflammation and allow the sinuses to drain. For how to give nose drops, see page 334.

If you have a vaporizer, switch it on. Otherwise, prepare a wide-bottomed bowl of warm water and let the child breathe in the steam. You can add herbal decongestant drops if you wish to make the steam more fragrant. Sit the child at a table and drape a towel over their head to direct the steam towards the face. Stay with your child while they are doing this.

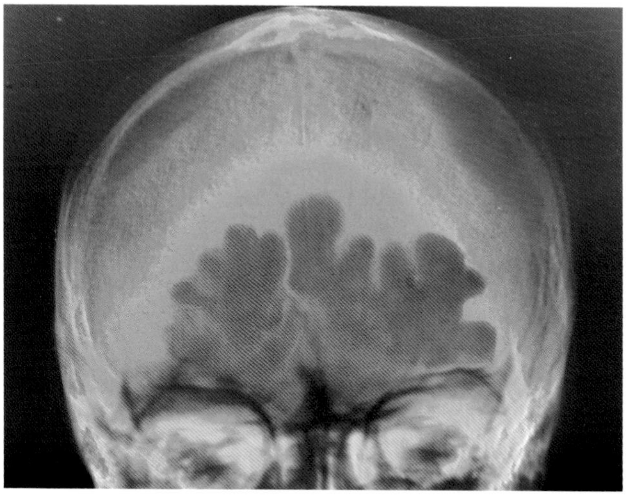

The X-ray above shows the extent of inflamed sinuses in a person with sinusitis. The sinuses shown are the frontal sinuses in the forehead, the sphenoidal sinuses, and the many spaces of the ethmoidal sinuses. The cheekbones contain maxillary sinuses.

To try and prevent sinusitis in a child who is prone to the condition, use a vaporizer or give regular steam inhalations whenever they get a cold, and teach children to pinch their nose as they jump into a swimming pool so that water is not forced up into the sinuses.

Complementary Treatment

Osteopathy can have a pronounced effect, and **chiropractic** techniques can be very effective in helping to ease congestion in the sinuses. **Nutritional therapists** will usually look for a food allergy as the main cause and treat the child accordingly. **Chinese herbalism** will treat topically and internally with herbs; the results can be remarkably quick or frustratingly slow. For recurrent sinus problems the **homeopath** will treat according to the personality, temperament and mood of the child concerned (constitutional treatment). Homeopathic remedies for this condition include Silicea 6c (*Silicea terra*, flint) when the child complains of throbbing, tearing pain that is felt deep within the bones of the face, and reports that the tip of their nose is itchy. The remedy is to be administered every two hours for up to two days. Other appropriate and possibly effective therapies include **acupuncture** and **Western herbalism**, which can be of considerable help, and **kinesiology**.

Ear Canal Problems

What are they?

The ear canal links the external part of the ear (the fleshy part called the pinna) with the middle ear. It is a passage less than 25 mm/1 in long that ends at the eardrum, which is air and watertight. The only time the eardrum is not watertight is when it is perforated. In children perforation of the eardrum usually occurs because of a build-up of pus in the middle ear caused by a middle ear infection.

The ear canal can also become infected (a condition called otitis externa), or it can become obstructed with wax.

Outer ear infection

Children who swim frequently are particularly prone to infections of the ear canal. Damp skin is susceptible to any bacterial infection that may be present in the water, and fungal infections may then make the problem worse.

You may notice

- *The ear canal looks sore, red and swollen*
- *There may be a red scaly area around the opening of the ear*
- *There may be a discharge from the ear*
- *The ear may be itchy*
- *The child may complain of fullness in the ear, or slight deafness*
- *Sometimes the pain can be excruciating*

What to do

Do not let your child go swimming, and try to protect the infected ear from direct contact with water – for example by giving the child earplugs or a shower cap to wear when taking a bath or shower. Try to stop the child from touching or scratching the ear. Wipe away any discharge from the outside, but leave the ear canal alone.

If the child is in pain, give them children's paracetamol. Take the child to the doctor, who may clean out the ear and then prescribe antibiotic and/or steroid eardrops to clear up the infection and relieve itching and inflammation. If the infection is caused by a fungus the doctor will prescribe an antifungal cream.

Ear wax

Ear wax, also known as cerumen, is a yellowy-brown secretion produced by glands in the ear canal to clean and moisten the canal. Most children produce only small amounts of wax, but some children make so much that it blocks the canal. The sudden appearance of runny wax in the canal may be a sign of a middle ear infection.

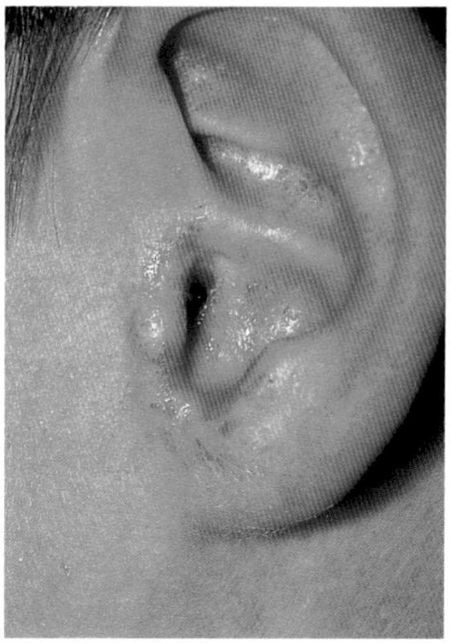

The pus oozing out of this child's ear has come from behind the eardrum, which has perforated under pressure as a result of a middle ear infection. Once the eardrum has burst, the child's pain is usually dramatically relieved. The hole in the ear will normally heal in around a week. In the meantime the child should avoid swimming and cover the ear when washing.

You may notice

- *Small amounts of brown, hardened fluid in the canal, or little flecks of crusty material. The child's hearing is patchy*
- *An older child may complain of a feeling of fullness in the ear*
- *After swimming, hair-washing or a bath the symptoms get worse because water makes the wax swell*

What to do

Leave the ear canal alone. Gently wipe wax off the earlobe with a piece of cotton wool and warm water. Never try to remove wax from the canal with a cotton bud; this can impact the wax and make the condition worse. Take your child to the doctor, who may put drops into the ear to soften the wax, or wash out the child's ear with warm water and a syringe. You can also get sodium bicarbonate drops to loosen the wax from a pharmacy.

Complementary Treatment

Traditional Chinese medicine, such as **Chinese herbalism** and **acupuncture**, can be of great benefit treating a blockage. They will also be supportive of orthodox treatment. The **nutritional therapist** will concentrate on preventive measures to ensure good health and a healthy immune system. A consultation with an **aromatherapist** can help. The **homeopath** will treat chronic conditions according to the personality, temperament and mood of the child concerned (constitutional treatment). For copious production of wax and intermittent hearing loss, give Causticum 6c (*Causticum Hahnemanni*, potassium hydrate) four times a day for up to one week.

MIDDLE EAR INFECTIONS

What are they?
Middle ear infections, in which the space behind the eardrum fills with pus, are very common in infants and young children. This is because their narrow Eustachian tubes, which connect the ears with the back of the throat, and their large adenoids are susceptible to infection. Also, their Eustachian tubes are shorter than in adults, so bacteria and viruses travel more easily from the nose and throat to the middle ear. Children with allergies are particularly susceptible to ear problems, as are infants and children in group daycare, because they are exposed to so many infections. Earache in young children should always be taken seriously as an infection that causes the eardrum to rupture can affect hearing in later life.

You may notice
- *An infant will be miserable and may go off their feeds. They may be feverish, sleep badly and rub or scratch the side of the face. They may have vomiting and diarrhoea*
- *An older child will complain of earache. Typically it is a throbbing ache or a sharp, stabbing pain. The pain may follow a cold or cough. The child will be feverish*
- *If the pain stops suddenly the eardrum may have ruptured. You may see pus, sometimes streaked with blood, oozing out of the ear*

What to do
Gently wash off any sticky or crusted discharge on the ear lobe with warm water and cotton wool. Don't wash inside the ear. Check the child's temperature. If it is raised, give children's paracetamol and consult the doctor.

To relieve pain, warm a soft cloth on a radiator and place it on the baby's sheet or child's pillow for them to lay their head on, with the affected ear against the cloth. Alternatively, rest the child's cheek against a thickly covered hot-water bottle.

Most ear infections are caused by viruses. However the doctor may prescribe an antibiotic (which will only be effective against bacteria), especially if the child is under the age of two or if they can see the eardrum bulging. As most children get over earache within 24 hours, with or without treatment, the doctor may give you a prescription for antibiotics but suggest that you wait to see if the pain subsides. The doctor will usually want to check that the ear infection has cleared and that hearing is normal after the course of antibiotics is finished.

Coping with earache
Wait until the ear infection has cleared before letting the child go swimming. It is better not to wash the child's hair while they have an ear infection, but if you have to, cover the ear to stop any water or shampoo getting in.

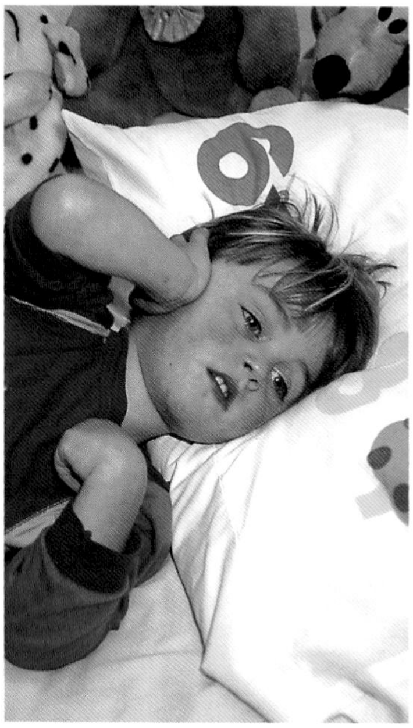

The acute throbbing or even stabbing pain of an earache caused by a middle ear infection is enough to wake a sleeping child and make it very difficult for him to get back to sleep again. Give the appropriate dose of children's paracetamol and a warm cloth or covered hot water bottle, but resist the temptation to bring the child into bed with you if he has a fever.

A young child with earache may not want a doctor to examine their ear with an otoscope (an instrument for examining the ear). It may help if the doctor examines the good ear first, and suggests that the child looks through the otoscope, perhaps at a teddy's ear.

Flying or travelling through a deep tunnel can give a child intense earache, especially if they have a cold, because of the change in air pressure. Give the child a sweet to suck or a straw to drink through on take-off and landing or while travelling through a tunnel, or let a baby feed.

Complementary Treatment

Experienced complementary practitioners will take great care when treating this condition, and recommend orthodox treatment when appropriate. Topical applications of **aromatherapy** essential oils can help, but this must be carried out by an experienced aromatherapist, preferably one who is medically trained. For acute and chronic ear infections consult the **homeopath** for treatment. Traditional Chinese medicine such as **Chinese herbalism** and **acupuncture** can be of great benefit, treating phlegm and blockage, which can help to prevent further problems. They will also be supportive of orthodox treatment. Both **Western herbalism** and **osteopathy** may also aid recovery.

CROUP

What is it?

Croup (laryngotracheobronchitis) is an infection of the larynx (the voice box) and the trachea (the windpipe) that is especially common in young children in the winter and spring. It is caused by a virus or bacteria that inflames the airways and makes them swell. As a baby's and toddler's airways are narrow, very little air can get through. In older children the airways are wider so the effects of the inflammation and swelling are less obvious.

Croup mainly affects infants over six months old and young children, and is usually first noticed at night. Some children have just one attack although many have repeated bouts.

Before an attack of croup the child may have had a cold for a day or two.

You may notice

- *A harsh, barking cough like that of a seal*
- *Breath coming in noisy, rasping gasps, particularly when breathing in. The child may also wheeze (see page 220). If the rasping is obvious both on breathing out and in, the croup may be getting worse*
- *The child is struggling to breathe, and you can see the child's chest sucking in*

What to do

Act fast but don't panic, as your child will breathe more easily if you stay calm. Ask another adult in the house to telephone the doctor or hospital immediately. Pick up the child, cuddle them on your shoulder and go straight to the bathroom. Close all the windows and doors and turn on all the hot water taps. Allow the child to breathe in the steamy atmosphere. Within approximately ten minutes the breathing should start to become silent and the cough should stop. Perhaps surprisingly, this treatment which many believe works, has not been confirmed to be effective when scientifically tested.

When the child is breathing easily again, prop them up in their carry seat, in bed on pillows or in the sitting room on cushions. If the breathing becomes more laboured, take them back to the steam-filled bathroom.

The doctor may prescribe a steroid drug to inhale from a nebulizer or to take by mouth. If the child doesn't respond quickly, they may have to be taken to hospital.

Protect children by never allowing smoking in the house. Cold air can trigger attacks so keep children who have had previous attacks indoors in the warm on cold evenings. If the child is getting a cold or starting to lose their voice, steam up the bedroom with a humidifier at bedtime.

Emergency signs

If the child shows any of the following signs, call your doctor immediately.

- Breathing and coughing are no better after ten minutes in a steamy atmosphere
- Breathing becomes laboured; the child struggles for breath or you can see their chest heaving in and out as they try to breathe
- They become drowsy or restless
- Their face turns grey or blue

A steamy atmosphere helps to soothe croup. In many homes the easiest room to steam up is the bathroom. Alternatively, try boiling pans of water in your kitchen or leaving an electric kettle on with the lid off to discourage cut-out, but watch that it does not boil dry.

Complementary Treatment

Chinese herbalists view this as a digestive problem and treat it as such, and also resolve the phlegm. Garlic is particularly recommended. **Western herbs** can reduce excess mucus production and relax airways. **Homeopathic remedies** include Aconite 30c (*Aconitum napellus*, blue aconite) for a child who wakes in the night coughing and breathless. Repeat if the child is not asleep in an hour. If the child does not respond or gets worse give Spongia 6c (*Spongia tosta*, roasted common sponge) and Hepar sulp 6c (*Hepar sulphuris calcareum*, calcium sulphide) alternately every hour for up to three doses each.

Nose Bleeds

What are they?

Nose bleeds occur when capillaries (tiny blood vessels) in the lining of the nose are broken. The capillaries usually break either right at the front of the nose, just inside the nostril, or near the back, not far from the throat, and usually only one nostril is affected. An injury to the nose, pushing a small object or toy up the nose, picking the nose or overenthusiastic noseblowing can all break the delicate surface of the capillaries. Nose bleeds often look more serious than they are, but a nose bleed that continues for more than 30 minutes needs medical attention. A child should also see the doctor if the nose starts bleeding after an injury.

Repeated nose bleeds may occur during an infection (such as a cold) that causes a runny nose and associated crusting that can damage the lining, or when a child becomes overheated, especially if the air is very dry.

What to do

Sit the child down with the head tilted forward over a basin or sink. Tell the child to breathe through their mouth and not to sniff, and meanwhile pinch the soft part of the nose just below the bone. Lay a face cloth that has been rinsed in cold water, and possibly containing some crushed ice (or a half-full packet of frozen peas), over the bridge of the nose. Tell the child to spit out any blood into the basin. After ten minutes check if the bleeding has stopped. Don't look any earlier than this or a clot that has formed may be removed. Once the bleeding has stopped, wipe away any blood from the face with cotton wool or kitchen paper and warm water. Tell the child to sit quietly for a while, and to resist the urge to sniff, pick at their nose or blow it for the next few hours, or the bleeding may start again.

What else?

If the nose is still bleeding after half an hour, or if it starts bleeding after a head injury, take the child to hospital. If the child has got a small object lodged in the nostril there may well be a nasty smell and discharge with the bleeding. If this is the case, take the child to the accident and emergency department of the nearest hospital.

Children who get repeated nose bleeds may be referred to an ear, nose and throat surgeon. If the cause is a particularly fragile blood vessel inside the nose, it can be cauterized under local anaesthetic. Silver nitrate on a cotton tip applicator is used to seal off the blood vessel. If the surgeon uses electric cauterization, which seals the vessel using heat, the child may need a light general anaesthetic.

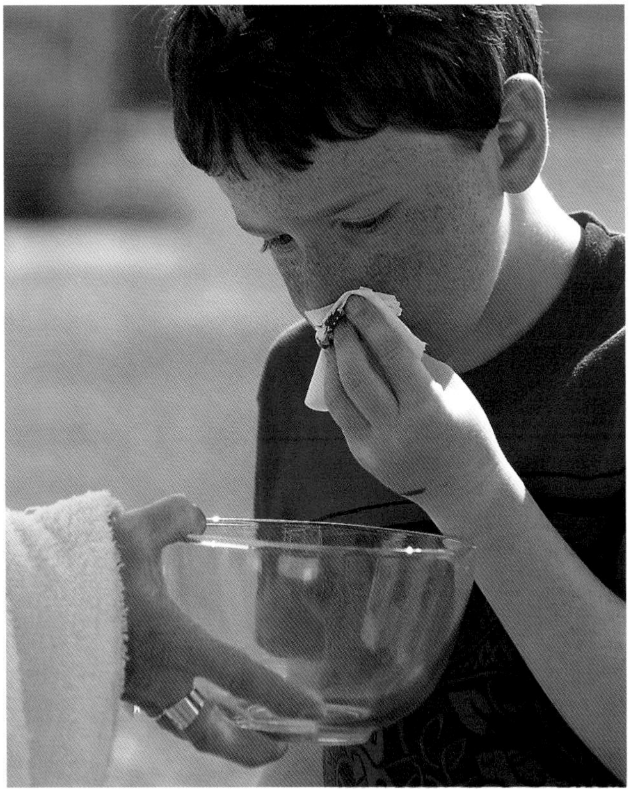

Keeping the head tipped forward during a nosebleed avoids having to swallow blood before clotting starts. Apply a cold compress over the bridge of the nose to speed the clotting process and tell the child to breathe through the mouth. Dissuade him from blowing his nose for half an hour after the bleeding has stopped. Children who inadvertently swallow blood may vomit it back up.

Complementary Treatment

Chinese herbalism treats acute conditions with pseudoginseng, inserting it into the nose. Treatment of chronic conditions involves resolving heat in the lung or heart channels. **Homeopathic** first aid remedies include Arnica 6c (*Arnica montana*, leopard's bane) when the bleed follows an injury; Ipecac 6c (*Cephaelis ipecacuanha*, ipecacuanha) when the blood is coloured bright red; and Phosphorus 6c (phosphorus) when bleeding results from violent nose blowing. **Nutritional therapists** may advise increasing the intake of fruit and vegetables, a deficiency of which can promote nose bleeds caused by weakening of the blood vessels.

ADENOIDS

What are they?

The adenoids are two glandular swellings at the back of the nose and throat. They contain lymphocytes, the white cells that help to fight infection by trapping and destroying germs as they enter the body through the nose and mouth. The adenoids are important in early childhood, when children catch an average of six to eight colds a year and are exposed to many more respiratory infections. However, by the age of five the adenoids have started to shrink, and by puberty they have usually disappeared altogether.

The adenoids respond to infection by swelling. In some children they swell so much that they obstruct the passages at the back of the throat, causing a variety of symptoms. As the infection subsides and the adenoids shrink, the symptoms disappear. However, in a few children the adenoids grow even larger from the age of five, and if the symptoms are troublesome the adenoids can be removed in a simple operation by an ear, nose and throat surgeon.

You may notice

If the adenoids are obstructing the passage from the nose to the throat

- *Breathing through the mouth*
- *The child seems 'catarrhal'*
- *Frequent sore throats*
- *Snoring*
- *A nasal tone to the child's voice*

If the adenoids are obstructing the flow of secretions from the nose down the throat

- *A persistently runny nose*
- *Middle ear infections*
- *Sinusitis*

If the adenoids are obstructing the ends of the Eustachian tubes leading to the back of the throat

- *Repeated ear infections*
- *Glue ear, presenting as hearing impairment*

What to do

Describe your child's symptoms to the doctor, who will examine the adenoids and the back of the throat using a lighted mirror. If the adenoids are enlarged, the doctor may prescribe antibiotics. However antibiotics are only effective against bacteria, and because most respiratory infections are caused by viruses antibiotics will not be of any use.

Aromatic oils can help with a chronically blocked nose., although they do not affect the swollen adenoids. Menthol and eucalyptus are available as rubs or in capsules that are broken open and dabbed on to clothing, hankies or bedclothes. You can also add a few drops of oil to a bowl of warm water, but place this well out of the child's reach, and always follow the manufacturer's instructions on minimum age.

Inhaling from a large bowl of steam can help to clear a blocked nose. Stay with the child and use comfortably hot, never boiling, water.

If the adenoids are causing the child repeated problems, particularly glue ear, ear infections, obstruction of the nose or unclear speech, they can be removed in a straightforward operation called an adenoidectomy.

Removing the adenoids

The adenoids are removed in a simple 15-minute operation. Children are given a general anaesthetic, but if the adenoidectomy is being performed on its own, the operation is almost always carried out as day surgery. The child will have a sore throat afterwards, but can eat normal food by the next day.

Complementary Treatment

The traditional Chinese therapies of **herbalism** and **acupuncture** may be beneficial, particularly the latter. **Western herbs** can help to fight infections, and **nutritional therapists** will usually recommend foods that promote a healthy immune system to fight infection. The **kinesiologist** may address the health of the child with energy balancing and with nutritional supplements. **Osteopathy** can often treat successfully if the adenoids are not too obstructive. The **homeopath** will treat according to the personality, temperament and mood of the child (constitutional treatment) when the condition is chronic but does not require surgery. For homeopathic remedies where surgery is indicated, see Complementary Treatment, page 276.

ALLERGIC RHINITIS

What is it?

Rhinitis is inflammation of the mucous membrane that lines the inside of the nose, and it makes the nose run. It can be caused by a number of complaints, including colds. When it is caused by an allergy it is known as allergic rhinitis. This can be either seasonal, when it is better known as hay fever (see page 221), or perennial, occurring all year round. In children under the age of ten, allergic rhinitis is much more likely to be perennial than seasonal. However as the incidence of hayfever in the population is increasing, this may change.

Perennial rhinitis is triggered by an allergen (a substance that produces an allergic reaction) that is present throughout the year. The most common allergens that trigger allergic rhinitis are pet allergen and house dust mite. Pet allergen is a protein found in cat fur, skin scales (dander) and saliva. In people whose asthma (see page 218) is triggered by pet allergen, it is dander floating in the air that causes them to wheeze as soon as they enter a room with high levels of cat allergen. Cat hairs on the clothing of a pet owner are usually enough to trigger symptoms in susceptible individuals. House dust mites are present in all homes and it is their faeces that act as an allergen. Some children with perennial rhinitis react to moulds that grow on damp walls and windows.

You may notice

- *The child's nose runs with clear mucus. They appear always to have a cold*
- *Sneezing, especially on waking in the morning*
- *Difficulty sucking*
- *The child may complain that their nose feels blocked*
- *Mouth breathing and snoring*
- *A typical upwards rub of the nose using the back of the hand*

What to do

Check first whether the child has a fever or other symptoms of a common cold (see page 208). If they appear well apart from the symptoms in the nose, take them to the doctor. The doctor may take a sample of mucus for laboratory analysis. This will show whether there is any sign of infection, or if there is a raised level of mast cells, which would indicate that the child has an allergy. Mast cells contain a substance called histamine, which is released when an allergic person is exposed to the allergen; it causes inflammation.

If the child has an allergy the doctor may prescribe children's saline nose drops for younger children, to be given three or four times a day. (For advice on giving nose drops, see page 334.) For an older child the doctor may prescribe a steroid nasal spray and a nasal decongestant to be used first if the nose is blocked. However, decongestants should only be used for three or four days at a time because overuse can make the problem worse – this is called 'rebound congestion'.

Coping with allergic rhinitis

Take reasonable steps to reduce the child's exposure to allergens. If pet allergen is the trigger, keep cats out of bedrooms and rooms with soft furnishings, vacuum floors and settees regularly, and wash the cat weekly.

To keep house dust mite under control vacuum and damp dust daily, use a high filtration cleaner, use anti-allergy bedding once the child is over a year old, put soft toys in the freezer overnight once a week and do not let an allergic child sleep in a bottom bunk.

Seasonal allergic rhinitis is increasing among young people, and by the age of 15 half the children who will develop symptoms have already done so. An early symptom is an itchy nose, which you can help to ease by smearing vaseline inside the nostrils to stop spores and pollen from settling in the nose.

Complementary Treatment

Aromatherapy oils can control symptoms when oils are inhaled, applied to the thorax, or used in compresses or during massage. **Western herbs** can soothe inflamed membranes and relax airways. **Nutritional therapy** may be able to identify any food allergen and treat accordingly. **Kinesiology** can also be helpful in identifying the allergen(s). **Chinese herbalism** can give good results, although the length of treatment depends on how long the child has been suffering, and **acupuncture** is often successful. **Homeopaths** have numerous specific remedies and will treat according to the personality, temperament and mood of the child concerned. Again, treatment may be lengthy.

SEE ALSO SKIN ALLERGY PAGE 173

ASTHMA

What is it?

This common illness, which often begins in childhood, occurs when the small airways (the bronchioles) in the lungs become inflamed. As a result the lining of the airways swell and produce more mucus than usual, while the muscles in the walls of the airway tighten. The result is the characteristic asthmatic gasping and wheezing when trying to breathe in and out through narrowed airways and, sometimes, a persistent cough to clear the excess mucus.

Asthma, which can range from mild to severe and even life-threatening, can be brought on by a variety of different causes. In most infants and toddlers the symptoms are triggered by virus infections such as the common cold, but between colds the child is usually well. Asthma often runs in families, especially in those with a predisposition to allergies. Symptoms can also start when the child comes into contact with allergic substances such as house dust, pollen, furry animals and feathers. Once the child's airways are inflamed, many other factors can trigger a bout of coughing or an asthma attack: car fumes, cigarette smoke, breathing in cold air, taking exercise, laughing and crying can all lead to an attack of breathlessness.

You may notice

- *The child sleeps restlessly and wakes at night, coughing*
- *A whistling, rustling or squeaky sound (wheezing) when breathing. It may be so bad at night that the child wakes up. The child may make the same sound after running around*
- *Coughing so much when taking exercise that the child has to stop. This is usually a dry, irritating cough*
- *Wheezing when the child catches a cold or develops a cough they can't shake off*
- *Your child seems perfectly well when they aren't coughing or wheezing*

Treatment

Take the child to the doctor. Asthma can be difficult to diagnose in young children, especially if they recover by the time they get to the surgery. Diagnosis is easier in school age children because they are able to use a peak flow meter, a device that shows the maximum rate at which air can be forced out of the lungs. A diagnosis of asthma is more likely if the peak flow measurements are low, or if they vary a great deal from one day to the next.

If asthma is diagnosed, the doctor will draw up a management plan and arrange for you to see a specialist nurse. The nurse will show you how to administer the child's medicine most effectively.

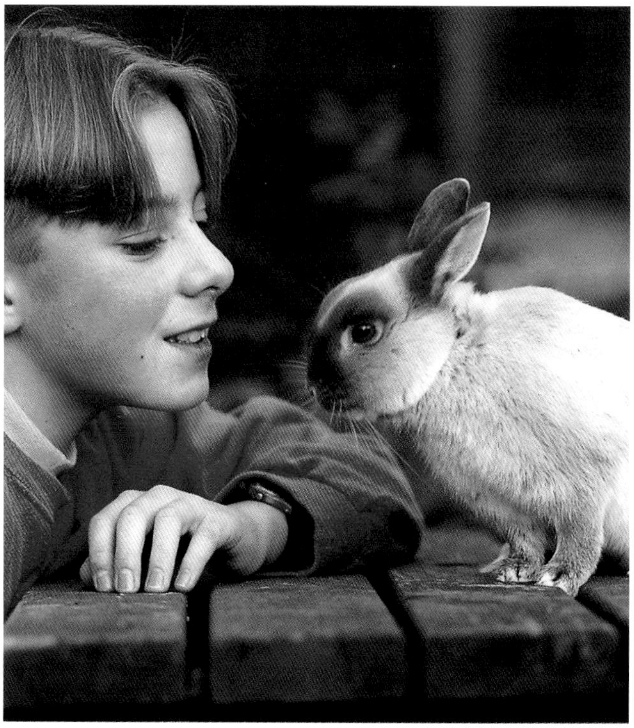

Families of children who start to wheeze when they are near furry animals often wonder if they should get rid of the offending pet. But parting with a loved family pet can make a child so upset that his asthma temporarily becomes worse. It also takes months for the allergen – especially cat allergen – to be cleared from the house, and there is some evidence that houses are almost never clear.

Drugs for asthma are designed to be breathed in, so they work where they are needed, deep in the lungs. There are two main types: reliever inhalers and preventer drugs. Reliever inhalers (bronchodilators) relax the muscles in the airway walls; they usually come in blue inhalers to be used when an attack is coming on or if one is expected – before sports, for example. Every child with asthma should always have access to their blue reliever inhaler.

Preventer drugs come in white or brown inhalers and are taken every day, even when the child is well. There are two types of preventer drugs: sodium cromoglycate or inhaled steroids. Both of these damp down the inflammation of the airways and make the child less likely to over-react to allergens that are breathed in. In case of confusion, you should label these puffers reliever and preventer.

Children who do not like taking preventer drugs regularly can inhale them through a mask while they are sleeping. Young children will need an attachment to the inhaler – called a spacer (see opposite) – with a face mask for the very young, so that they are able to inhale the medicine properly. For older children an inhaler is available that dispenses dry powder as the child breathes in.

Outlook

Two-thirds of young children outgrow their asthma, although some have renewed symptoms as adults. The outlook is best for those children who only wheeze when they have a cold and for children with mild asthma. But regardless of whether the asthma is mild or severe, all children need appropriate treatment. Insufficient treatment can cause sleep disturbance and, in severe cases, slow growth, poor performance at school and acute attacks of asthma that sometimes require admission to hospital.

What to do in case of an attack

A child having an attack of asthma finds breathing difficult and may be too breathless to talk or feed, or may breathe very fast. Stay calm and follow the steps below. If this is the child's first asthma attack, go straight to step 4.

1 Stay calm and follow the emergency plan agreed with your doctor
2 Give the bronchodilators immediately, using a spacer if available. Wait for five to ten minutes. If the breathing is no better, repeat the dose
3 Hold the child, sitting upright if they are comfortable in this position
4 If the two doses of medication have no effect, contact your doctor, ambulance/accident and emergency department urgently

Preventing asthma

Colds in children are, perhaps, unavoidable, but you can avoid irritants and keep exposure to allergens to a minimum.

- Don't allow anyone to smoke near your asthmatic child. If you are planning another baby, don't smoke when you are pregnant as this makes it more likely that the baby will have asthma
- Don't allow the child to walk or cycle on busy main roads. Nitrogen oxides in car fumes and high ozone concentrations at ground level can make attacks worse in some children
- Try to find another home for the family cat or any other furry creature. If that is impossible, restrict the parts of the house to which furry animals have access. There is a theory, as yet unproven, that cats can sensitize infants even before they are born
- Try to pinpoint the individual triggers for the child. If you can't, the house dust mite is a likely culprit. Damp dust your home regularly, particularly the child's bedroom; use synthetic or easy-wash bedding, or special protective mattress, duvet and pillow covers; and freeze cuddly toys overnight

Who can help?

For organizations offering help and advice, see the Directory.

Complementary Treatment

A combination of therapies is usually most helpful, but see pages 52-65 for any possible contraindications. **Chiropractic treatment** can relieve restriction in the movement and expansion of the chest and thereby aid breathing. **Chinese herbalism** can be very effective, especially if combined with **acupuncture,** diet and breathing exercises. **Nutritional therapists** link asthma with nutritional deficiency, food and other allergies, and excessive amounts of toxins in the body. The **kinesiologist** may be helpful in identifying any underlying allergy as the cause and recommending further treatment. Herbs prescribed by the **Western herbalist** may help to relax the airways. For **homeopathic treatment** it is best to consult a homeopath to find the most suitable remedy (ie) for the child, including remedies for use in acute attacks. The **aromatherapist** will recommend oils that may control the symptoms, reducing irritation and mucus production and allowing sleep. **Osteopathy** may also be helpful. The **Bach flower remedies** can be useful when emotional issues cause or aggravate the problem. **Tai chi** and **chi kung** may help breathing.

WHEEZING

What is it?

Wheezing is very common in young children but the majority grow out of it by the age of six. Over half the children under three whose airways are still small and who wheeze because of chest infections are likely to outgrow the tendency. Children who do not outgrow the tendency or children who start wheezing over the age of three are more likely to have an allergic cause for their condition. In all groups, children who have mothers who smoke are more likely to wheeze.

You may notice

- *A high-pitched, musical whistling sound that is obvious when the child breathes out*
- *Breathing may become laboured*

What to do

Contact your doctor if the child develops any sort of noisy breathing. Treatment will depend on the cause. Meanwhile, keep the air in the child's room warm and moist by laying a well wrung-out towel over the radiator, or using a humidifier. Stay calm, as children are sensitive to parents' feelings and this will help to ease their breathing. Sit children with breathing difficulties upright: infants can sit in their seat or be held upright against an adult's shoulder, and older children can sit at a table, leaning slightly forwards and resting their arms on the table.

Young children who wheeze when they catch a cold or other viral infection are often treated with drugs inhaled through a large device called a spacer. This makes it easier for the child to breathe in the drug and also improves the amount of medication reaching the airways.

Why children wheeze

In an infant under twelve months

- Obvious wheezing and breathlessness in a baby are often caused by the respiratory syncytial virus (RSV), which brings regular winter epidemics of bronchiolitis (see page 204)
- Asthma is a possibility (see page 218).
- Infants born very premature who needed ventilation may develop a chronic lung disease known as bronchopulmonary dysplasia. They are likely to cough and wheeze as young babies and are prone to chest infections

In a toddler or pre-school child

- By the age of six, almost half of all children have experienced at least one episode of wheezing. This probably means that some are more likely to develop asthma, particularly if there are other signs of allergy-related illnesses in the family

Inhaling an object at this age is rare, but serious.

- The child may inhale a nut (especially a peanut), a small toy, a leaf or even a seed (see First Aid, page 000). Wheezing can start suddenly and the child may choke and cough as well

In a school-age child

- Asthma is by far the most common cause of wheezing. Many children with asthma at this age have signs of other allergic diseases, such as allergic rhinitis (see page 217), hay fever (see page 221) or eczema (see page 156)
- A chest infection is a possible cause and if recurrant may be caused by cystic fibrosis (page 198) or, rarely, a deficiency in the immune system for fighting infection.

Complementary Treatment

Osteopathy can be helpful in clearing the airways. **Aromatherapy** may control symptoms, reducing irritation and mucus production and allowing sleep. **Chinese herbalism** views wheezing as an attack of wind and cold, and will prescribe accordingly, usually with cinnamon and ginger as the base of the prescription. **Acupuncture** can be beneficial and may be used in conjunction with other therapies.

HAY FEVER

What is it?

Hay fever is an allergic reaction to grass or tree pollen, causing a runny nose, sneezing and itchy, watering eyes. It was traditionally thought of as a condition affecting teenagers and adults, but in fact it is quite common in younger children.

Hay fever, which runs in families, often affects people who tend to suffer from allergy-related disorders. In such people the immune system has a tendency to over-react to harmless substances and to produce particular antibodies (IgE antibodies) against them. These antibodies trigger a chain of events, resulting in the release of a range of inflammatory chemicals, including histamines, that cause the symptoms of hay fever.

In spring hay fever is caused by pollen from trees such as oak, plane or birch; in the summer it is caused by grass (and nettle) pollen. The season usually starts at the beginning of May, but it can be as early as March, and lasts until July, although some children have symptoms until October.

You may notice

- *Every spring or summer the child develops an itchy nose, mouth and throat and a stuffy nose*
- *The child sneezes clear or discoloured mucus*
- *Itchy, pink and watery eyes, sometimes with conjunctivitis. Older children may describe the feeling as gritty*

What to do

Check with a feverstrip or thermometer that the child's temperature is not raised. A fever is a sign that your child is more likely to have a cold or has an infection.

Lay a cool, damp face cloth over the child's eyes to ease the itch and help prevent the child from rubbing them. Give an older child a box of tissues and a pot of vaseline to smear around the nose to prevent it becoming sore.

Note when the sneezing is worst to help pinpoint the trigger. You cannot completely avoid allergens, but you can limit exposure to pollen by keeping the bedroom windows closed at night, and not letting the child play outdoors at peak pollen times – first thing in the morning and mid to late afternoon. When pollen counts are high avoid grassy and leafy areas and keep the car windows and air vents shut.

Treatment

Your doctor can prescribe treatments to ease the symptoms by reducing the underlying inflammation. These include eye drops and nasal sprays containing sodium cromoglycate, or a steroid drug. Antihistamines can be helpful in easing the itch and the discharge.

Anyone who suffers significantly from hay fever can have preventive treatment. The doctor can prescribe the cromoglycate or steroid nasal spray and eye drops. They can be used up to four times a day starting two to four weeks before the child's personal pollen season begins.

Coping with hay fever

Consider seaside holidays – there's less chance of exposure to trees and grasses. For outings, prepare a hay fever kit, including a moist face cloth in a plastic bag to cool the eyes, tissues, eye drops and any hay fever medication the child is taking. Have the child wear wrap-around glasses to protect the eyes from pollen.

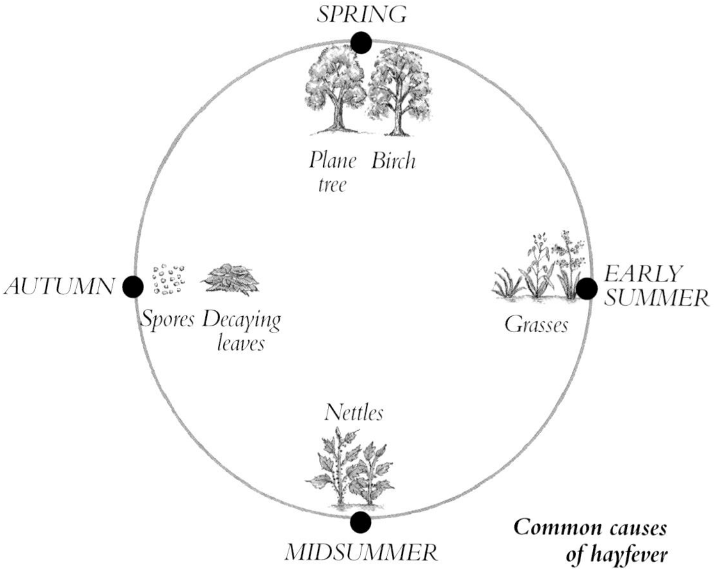

Common causes of hayfever

Complementary Treatment

Chinese herbalism can give very effective results if the child is seen soon after onset of symptoms and the lungs can be strengthened. When the condition is chronic the child will be treated with herbs to keep the hay fever under control. **Western herbs** can reduce excess mucus production and have an astringent effect on inflamed membranes. **Aromatherapy** oils can reduce irritation and allow sleep; any psychological causes or effects can be helped if the child learns to carry out their own treatment. There are a large number of **homeopathic remedies**; consultation with a homeopath is advisable. Other appropriate therapies include **acupuncture** and **Bach flower remedies**.

SORE THROAT

What is it?

Sore throats are extremely common in children. They occur all year round, but especially in winter. A pre-school child in regular contact with other children will catch up to four throat infections a year, most caused by a virus, but some as a result of infection with the streptococcus bacterium.

A sore throat is inflammation of the pharynx, the area that stretches from the back of the nose down to the larynx (voice box), and sore throats are also known as pharyngitis. An infection that spreads from the pharynx into the Eustachian tubes can cause a middle ear infection (see page 213). If the infection causes inflammation of the tonsils it is called tonsillitis (see page 224). Very occasionally a streptococcal sore throat may lead to a kidney inflammation (acute glomerulonephritis). A child with a streptococcal sore throat and a rash may have scarlet fever (see page 93). A persistent sore throat with swollen glands in the neck, armpits and groin could be glandular fever (see page 84).

Most sore throats get better in two or three days. It is difficult even for a doctor to distinguish between viral (the majority) and bacterial (the minority) sore throats. Some doctors prescribe antibiotics, which will be effective only for bacterial infections, and others recommend paracetamol. Some give antibiotics only if a sore throat has lasted for four or five days, or if the child is generally unwell.

You may notice

- *A toddler may refuse food and be generally unwell*
- *An older child may tell you that their throat hurts, and possibly their head and stomach as well*
- *The child may have a fever of 38°C/100°F or more*
- *The glands on either side of the jaw may be swollen. They feel like broad beans under the skin*
- *A young child may have bad breath (see page 234)*

What to do

Give regular doses of children's paracetamol and offer warm soothing drinks. Choose favourite drinks and don't worry if the child takes sips. Warm lemon and honey (for children over 12 months of age) or milky drinks ease discomfort, especially if alternated with cool drinks. If the child doesn't want to drink, give ice cream, yoghurts or ice lollies.

If you wish, you can examine the child's throat yourself. Sit them under a good light and get them to mouth 'Aah' or 'Baa baa' while you gently hold down the tongue with the handle of a fork or spoon. The back of the mouth may be bright red and the tonsils may be obviously red and swollen.

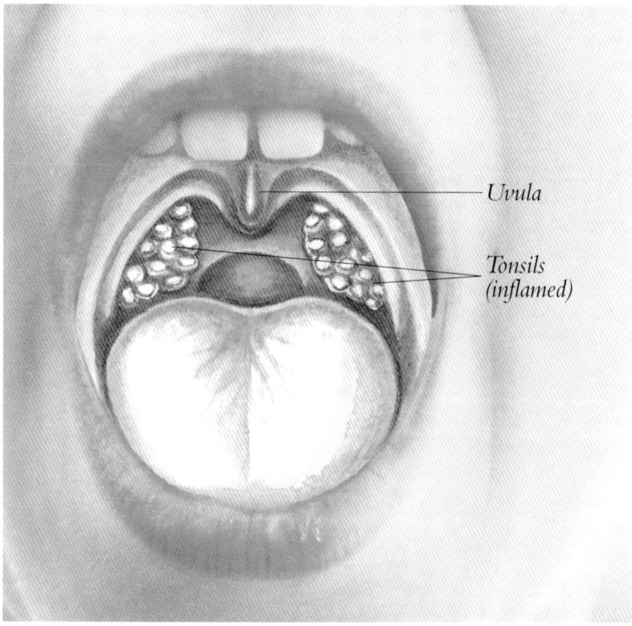

In a child with a sore throat the throat will be inflamed from the back of the nose down to the larynx, the area known as the pharynx. The tonsils also be inflamed and swollen, and the child may have a fever.

Don't expect your child to eat for a day or two, but consult your doctor if your child stops drinking or if a baby misses more than one feed; if a child develops breathing difficulties; or if the sore throat isn't better in three or four days. The doctor may take a throat swab to identify the cause of the infection. The doctor may wait for the results, which can take 24–48 hours or may prescribe antibiotics immediately, especially if the child is generally unwell.

Complementary Treatment

Chiropractors have found that recurrent sore throats in children are frequently accompanied by restrictions in the normal functioning of the neck, and treatment is used to help boost the immune system. **Chinese herbalism** can treat successfully with sage gargle, raspberry syrup and strengthening herbs; **acupuncture** can also give successful results. **Nutritional therapists** can recommend foods that will help to strengthen the immune system and may also suggest vitamin C supplements. **Homeopaths** will treat recurrent sore throats according to the child's personality, temperament and mood. **Osteopathy** and **kinesiology** may help recurrent conditions.

LARYNGITIS

What is it?

Laryngitis is inflammation of the larynx (voice box), which is positioned at the top of the trachea (windpipe). It is caused by either a bacterial or, more usually, a viral infection of the larynx, and it is most common in winter. Sometimes laryngitis develops after a sore throat, cold or flu. As bacteria only rarely cause laryngitis, antibiotics do not usually help. The inflammation, which also affects the vocal cords, usually clears up without treatment in four or five days, but occasionally the infection may spread from the larynx to other parts of the airways, the chest or even the middle ear. In young children swelling of the larynx can obstruct the air passages and cause croup (see page 214), which is a serious complication. This is much less likely in children of school age.

You may notice

- *The child's voice becomes cracked and hoarse, and speaking may be painful. In a severe case the child may lose their voice altogether*
- *The child complains of a sore throat, especially when swallowing*
- *The child may have a fever*
- *There may be a dry, barking cough like croup*
- *The child's breathing may be noisy*

What to do

If the child's voice is hoarse, but they seem otherwise well, give them warm, soothing drinks, such as honey and lemon, (if the child is over 12 months of age) and encourage them to speak as little as possible. Check whether the child is hot and feverish, and give them paracetamol to soothe the pain of the sore throat and to help lower the temperature if it rises to 38°C/100°F or above.

Humidify the air in the child's room. If you don't have a humidifier, the simplest way to do this is to lay a damp towel over a hot radiator. Alternatively you can place a bowl of water near the radiator. For a more intensive supply of moisture, encourage your child to take a warm bath or shower and breathe in the steam. A younger child can sit in the bathroom while you run the hot taps to steam up the room.

If the child has any difficulty in breathing, or if their breathing becomes noisy, contact your doctor right away. It means that the larynx has swollen and could partially block the trachea. Don't under any circumstances try to to look down the child's throat. The voice box is not visible and you could block the trachea completely. If you are can't contact the doctor, call an ambulance immediately.

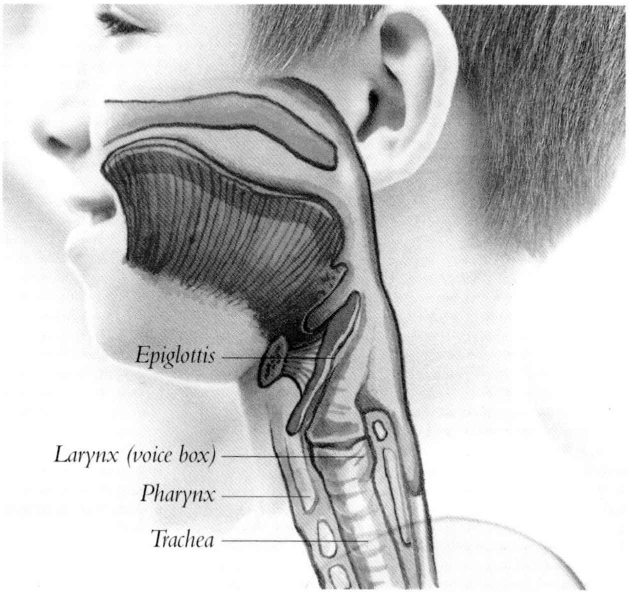

Complementary Treatment

Homeopaths have a number of specific remedies for acute conditions, to be taken according to symptoms. In chronic conditions the homeopath will treat according to the personality, temperament and mood of the child (constitutional treatment). For chronic conditions, **Chinese herbalism** will treat the stomach and lung energy systems. **Acupuncture** can also treat successfully. **Western herbalists** will usually prescribe herbs that fight infection, soothe inflamed membranes and relax airways.

Emergency

If the child shows any of the following symptoms, call the doctor immediately. If you are unable to contact the doctor, call the emergency services and ask for an ambulance.

- The child's breathing and cough are no better after ten minutes in a steamy atmosphere
- The child's breathing becomes laboured or they struggle for breath, or you can see the chest heaving in and out as the child tries to breathe
- The child becomes drowsy or restless
- The child's face turns grey or blue
- The child's rasping, noisy breathing has become continuous

TONSILLITIS

What is it?

Tonsillitis is an infection of the tonsils, the two glandular swellings at either side of the throat that help to trap and destroy invading micro-organisms (viruses and bacteria). When people breathe in viruses or bacteria, the tonsils swell as they produce antibodies to try and fight off the infection . Sometimes the micro-organisms overwhelm the tonsils, and they become infected, red and swollen. In children, the tonsils may become chronically swollen as they become exposed to a range of infections for the first time. Tonsillitis usually clears up within a week or ten days, but it can be linked with middle ear infections (see page 213).

You may notice

- *The child has a fever*
- *The child is obviously unwell and miserable*
- *The child may lose interest in food because swallowing is painful. A child over the age of five or six may complain of a sore throat*
- *The child may have stomach ache, because glands in the abdomen can swell as part of the immune system's defence action. The child may vomit*
- *The glands in the neck below and in front of the ears become swollen*
- *The child may have bad breath*

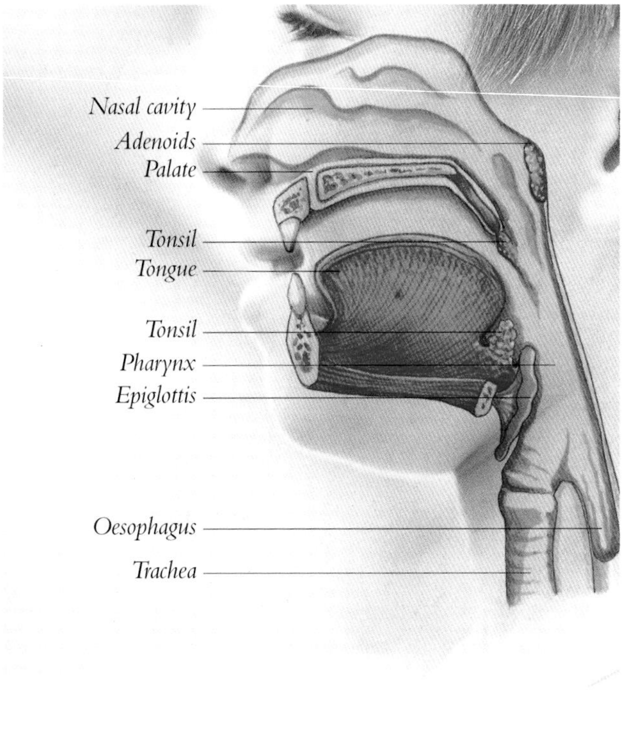

What to do

If you look into the child's mouth you may be able to see two large red swollen masses at the back of the throat – the inflamed tonsils, which may be flecked with pus. Give paracetamol for the discomfort and to lower the fever.

Tempt your child with a variety of drinks, especially chilled ones, but don't necessarily expect him to eat for a few days. Keep the child at home away from other children.

If your child is very unwell or has a series of attacks of tonsillitis, consult the doctor. If the doctor believes that it is being caused by bacteria, they will prescribe antibiotics. These work quickly, so the child should feel much better within 24 hours. The doctor may also take a swab from the child's throat and send it for analysis.

Tonsils are not often removed nowadays, especially in preschool children, because they are a useful part of the defence system until the child is seven or eight. They are usually only removed if they have become the focus of chronic infection in the child's throat, or if the child gets frequent sore throats with ear infections. Frequent means four or more attacks of tonsillitis a year for a year or two.

Tonsillectomy

If the child's tonsils are taken out, the adenoids at the back of the nose are often removed at the same time. The operation usually means at least one overnight stay in hospital. The tonsils are levered gently away from the back of the throat and cut out under a general anaesthetic. Immediately after the operation the child's throat will be very sore, and they will not feel like eating for at least 24 hours.

Complementary Treatment

Western herbalists will treat with herbs that fight infection, reduce excess mucus production, and relieve swollen and inflamed tissues. **Chiropractors** have found that recurrent tonsillitis in children is frequently accompanied by restrictions in the normal functioning of the neck, and treatment is used to help boost the immune system. **Nutritional therapy** will concentrate mainly on preventing recurrence; during a bout of tonsillitis the condition is treated with vitamin C supplements, which help to speed recovery.

Pneumonia

What is it?

Pneumonia is an inflammation of the lungs that is usually caused by infection. Most cases are caused by a virus, commonly the respiratory syncytial virus (RSV) that causes bronchiolitis (see page 204), an infection that particularly affects young babies. Bacterial pneumonia is less common. In some cases pneumonia is caused by a mixture of viruses and bacteria. The infection affects the medium-sized and small airways (the bronchi) in the lungs as well as the alveoli, the tiny air sacs at the end of the bronchial tree. The virus or bacterium causing the pneumonia can be cultured from a sample of the sputum, but as the infection is deep in the lungs and children with pneumonia often don't cough up sputum, a blood test may be needed instead.

Pneumonia varies in severity from a mild illness to a severe infection needing hospital treatment. Pneumonia can also be a consequence of inhaling food or drink into the lungs, or as a result of inhaling an object such as a toy, coin or pen cap (see First Aid, page 348).

Depending on how severe the infection is, pneumonia may start with a cold and develop gradually over a few days or the child may quickly become very unwell.

You may notice

- *The child loses interest in food*
- *Breathlessness – rapid, shallow breathing even when resting (see box below), possibly with grunting noises. You may notice the child's ribs suck in as they breathe*
- *Possibly a cough, sometimes so severe it makes the child vomit*
- *Fever and/or headache*

What to do

Contact your doctor immediately. Meanwhile keep the child comfortable and offer drinks if they can keep them down. Children may find it easier to breathe if they are propped up or if infants are sat in their carry seat. Give children's paracetamol if the temperature is over 38°C/100.4°F, they are not vomiting and they are over three months old. Keep the air moist and humid, with a humidifier if possible. Do not give the child cough medicine.

The doctor will examine the child and listen to the lungs. For a milder case of bacterial pneumonia, antibiotics, to be taken for seven to ten days, will be prescribed. It is important to finish the course, even if the child gets better before completing the treatment. Keep the child at home until they are clearly better – drinking, eating and playing normally.

However if the child is very young or is finding breathing or feeding difficult, they may need to be admitted to hospital to be given extra oxygen or assistance with feeding. In hospital their lungs will be X-rayed and they may have a blood test to discover the cause of the pneumonia.

Complementary Treatment

Complementary treatment will be supportive of orthodox treatment. **Western herbalism** can be effective in fighting infection. **Acupuncture** and **Chinese herbalism** can be supportive of orthodox treatment in the recovery stages. As most children will be fairly weak, time will be spent toning the body. **Osteopathy** can also be useful for treating the after effects of pneumonia. The **aromatherapist** will recommend oils – to be inhaled, applied to the thorax, or used in compresses and during massage – which relieve pain by relaxing the muscles. **Homeopathic remedies** to give in the acute phase while waiting for help to arrive include Belladonna 30c (*Atropa belladonna*, deadly nightshade) for stabbing pains around the rib cage made worse by breathing in, being delirious with high fever and the eyes wide and staring.

What is the normal breathing rate in a young child? Use these guidelines to check the child's breathing.

At birth	40–50 breaths a minute	Upper limit 60 breaths
2 months–1 year	30–40 breaths a minute	Upper limit 50 breaths
1–5 years	20–30 breaths a minute	Upper limit 40 breaths
5–16 years	12–20 breaths a minute	Upper limit 30 breaths
Adult	0–14 breaths a minute	Upper limit 20 breaths

Mouth and Teeth

The mouth forms both the first part of the digestive tract, and an important part of the respiratory and speech systems. The upper and lower jaws provide the bony surrounding structure, with a bridge of bone under the hard palate. The palate separates the mouth from the nose and consists of a firm front section, and a soft, fleshy section that is the soft palate; this presses against the back of the throat during swallowing to prevent food from entering the nose.

The tongue, an organ of criss-crossing muscle fibres, takes up most of the bottom of the mouth. Its upper surface is covered in tiny papillae surrounded by sense cells known as taste buds, capable of distinguishing between sweet, sour, salty and bitter tastes. Lips encircled by a ring of muscles seal the front of the mouth. The mucous membrane that lines the mouth is kept moist by saliva, a watery, alkaline fluid secreted by three pairs of salivary glands.

The teeth

The visible part of a tooth is the crown. It is covered with an extremely hard enamel shell that cannot register pain and protects the dentine underneath. Dentine is more like hard bone and produces twinges of sensitivity to both heat and chemicals. Inside the dentine is the exquisitely sensitive pulp, threaded through with blood vessels and nerves. Beneath the crown of the tooth is the root, embedded in the jaw bone, and usually longer than the crown. The root is covered with cementum, similar in composition to dentine, which helps to keep the tooth firm in its socket.

There are three types of deciduous teeth: incisors, canines (eye teeth) and molars. The adult teeth also have pre-molars between the canines and the molars. Incisors have a narrow blade-like edge for shearing food. Canines are good at tearing food and molars at grinding it.

As well as being concerned with digestion and breathing the mouth is also concerned with speech. The top of the mouth, at the front, contains the hard palate, with the soft palate lying behind it. Both tongue and palate influence clarity of speech.

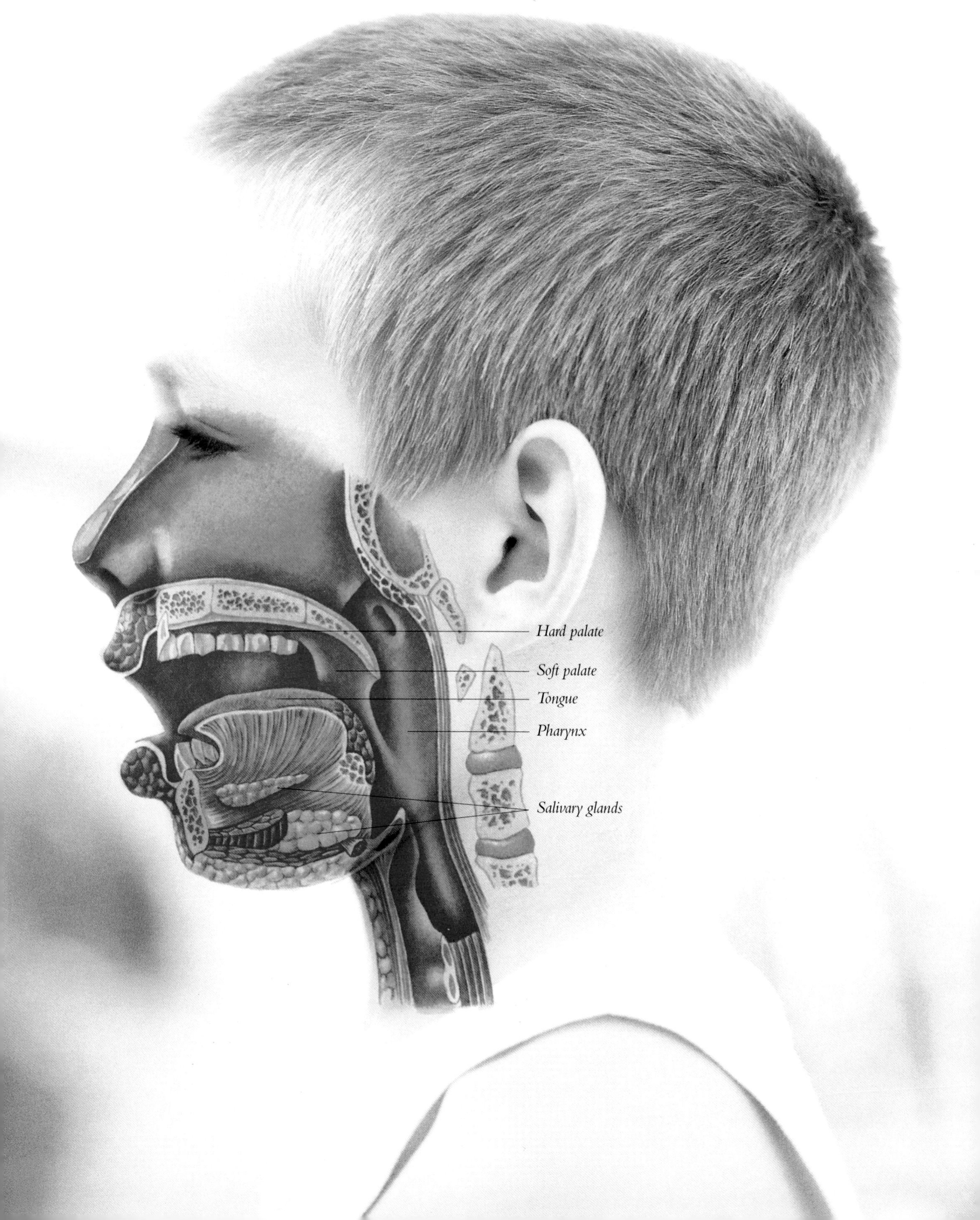
Hard palate
Soft palate
Tongue
Pharynx
Salivary glands

Diagnosis

A child who refuses food and seems generally off colour or ill in any other way should always be seen by a doctor. But if the child seems quite well apart from a sore mouth, it is worth taking a look inside the mouth. There are a number of minor ailments that may make a child reluctant to open the mouth or feed.

Sign	What could be wrong
Dribbling, restless at night. May have one flushed cheek. You may see a tense blister on one gum or a sharp edge of tooth	Teething, especially when molars come through at 10–14 months, then again at 2–2½ years
Refuses food and acid juices such as orange or black-currant. May dribble. Shallow white-grey spots with red edges on gums or inside the cheeks or lips	Mouth ulcers
Dry lips with fine cracks and sometimes peeling skin. More common in cold wet weather	Chapped lips. Use a lip salve or balm when the child goes out, especially in a buggy
Circle of dry, reddened skin around the mouth. Sore, may crack open	Lick eczema, caused by the child running their tongue around the mouth. Cover with vaseline at night
Sore, slightly itchy area on lips or near mouth. Small, clear blister emerges on a reddened base	Cold sore is likely, especially if the child is getting over a cold, or if the weather is sunny or cold
Starts to feed, but gives up quickly, or refuses feeds. White spots like milk remains inside the cheeks that don't come off easily when wiped with tissue, and leave raw, red patch	Oral thrush, which may be linked with a severe nappy rash
Painless blisters on the upper lip of a breast- or bottle-fed infant	Sucking blisters in a hungry infant. As long as they don't put the infant off feeds, they don't matter
Bleeding when the teeth are brushed	Infrequent or inadequate brushing. This could be an early sign of gum disease
Toothache	Most likely cause is tooth decay but sinusitis can cause toothache in the upper back teeth
Pain only when eating something sweet or cold	May be sensitive teeth, caused by tooth erosion or decay under an existing filling

Cleft Lip and Palate

What are they?
A cleft (or hare) lip and/or palate occurs early in foetal development when the two halves of the lip or palate fail to unite. The lip is left with anything from a small notch to a gap up to the nose on one or both sides. With a cleft palate, there may be a slit or hole in the roof of the mouth. Cleft lip and palate are common and some babies have both, while in others only the lip or the palate is affected. Other abnormalities occur in a third of children and there are over 350 associated conditions, so careful assessment is necessary. The exact cause is uncertain and most cases are wholly unexpected, although a tendency towards this condition runs in some families. It is very likely that a gene or a number of genes are involved.

A cleft lip or palate is often distressing to the parents of the newborn, but they are not life-threatening. The infant does not usually need special care and can stay on the postnatal ward. However, a cleft palate can sometimes cause feeding difficulties, including breastfeeding problems, because milk goes directly up into the nostrils. Later on a child with a cleft palate may need special dental treatment and speech therapy.

You may notice
- *A cleft lip is obvious at birth. The midwife or paediatrician should always check the infant's mouth for a cleft palate immediately after birth*
- *Just occasionally, a small hole in the palate may first become evident as a feeding difficulty, when milk comes out through the infant's nose*

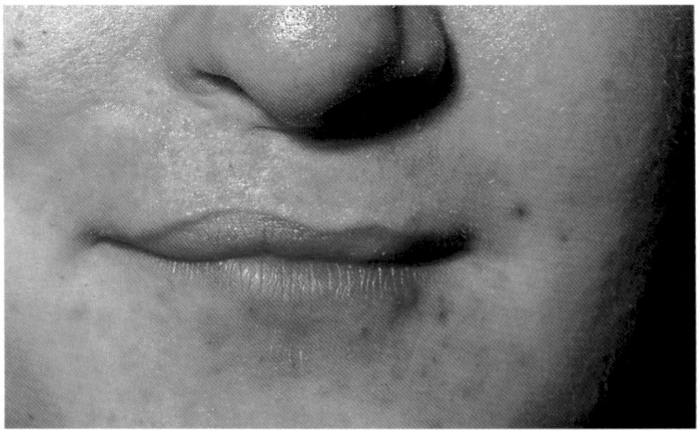

The aim of surgical treatment for cleft lip is to achieve a normal appearance, with a normal set of teeth as well as good hearing and speech. The repair can be almost invisible, as shown above. If both the lip and the palate are affected the lip is usually repaired first, although the exact timing depends on the individual child.

Treatment
Babies with cleft lips usually have surgery within a few months of birth, and those with cleft palates when they are between six months and two years old. The timing of the surgery is a decision you should make together with the surgeon, who should be able to reassure you with before-and-after photographs. (If none are shown, ask to see some.) Before surgery is carried out, you may need to use a range of adapted bottles and teats to help with feeding, or a breastfeeding counsellor can help you start breastfeeding. An orthodontist may make a plastic plate, called an abturator, to help the infant with feeding and speech and to encourage the palate to grow properly.

Children with cleft lips and palates need to pay special attention to their teeth, so it is important to limit their consumption of sugary drinks and food.

Later on an audiologist will check the child's hearing, because glue ear is common in children with this condition. The child may have to have a grommet (a small tube) inserted in the ear if glue ear is a problem. When the child starts to talk, a speech therapist can help with any speech difficulties. As children grow, some with a repaired cleft lip and palate may develop a concave profile. Further surgery may be needed to correct this.

Who can help?
For details of organizations and agencies offering help and support see the Directory.

Complementary treatment
Osteopathy can be beneficial following surgery. **Homeopathic remedies** that can be given prior to surgery include Aconite 30c (*Aconitum napellus*, blue aconite) and Arnica 30c (*Arnica montana*, leopard's bane) to relieve pain and prevent infection. Arnica should be followed by Staphisagria 6c (*Delphinium staphisagria*, stavesacre). These remedies should be given every half hour for up to ten doses. The **Bach flower remedies** may help to alleviate fear and anxiety and the emotional aspects of recovery.

Teething

What is it?

The process of teething lasts for several years, until all of the milk (deciduous) teeth have come through. These are followed by permanent teeth, which include the wisdom teeth.

Milk teeth

The first teeth appear when the child is around six months old, although they have been forming since early pregnancy. The exact time when teeth emerge depends mainly on inherited tendencies. Some babies teethe early and a few are born with a tooth already through. Late teething, where infants are still toothless on their first birthday, also runs in families.

Teething is much more painful for some babies than others. The first teeth to come through (erupt), the top and bottom incisors, do not usually appear to cause much pain. The first molars that appear at 12–15 months may be markedly more painful; they are followed by the canines at 16–18 months and the second molars at 20–24 months. By the age of three, most children have all 20 of their milk teeth.

You may notice

- *From about three months, infants will put everything in their mouths*
- *They will start biting longer and sucking harder*
- *Dribbling will increase dramatically*
- *They may become more restless at night and more irritable during the day*
- *The gums may be red and swollen, sometimes with a tiny white mark resembling a mouth ulcer*
- *They may have a bright red cheek on the teething side*
- *Some children may get a sore bottom, run a slight fever and develop mild diarrhoea*

What to do

Try rubbing the infant's gums gently with your finger. Let them chew – it both soothes and helps to toughen the gums. They may enjoy chewing on fingers (theirs or yours), a conventional teething ring or a soft, chewable teether. Avoid giving them objects with sharp edges. If they find sucking painful, let them take their time over feeds. Offer the breast frequently or extra drinks of boiled, cooled water if they are on bottles. Dribbling can mean they lose a lot of fluid. Rub a little teething gel on to the sore gums with a pad of cloth or your little finger just before a feed. This has a numbing effect that lasts for about 20 minutes. Don't use teething gel more than six times a day. Chill a water or gel-filled teether and let them bite it – the cold helps to numb any painful sensations.

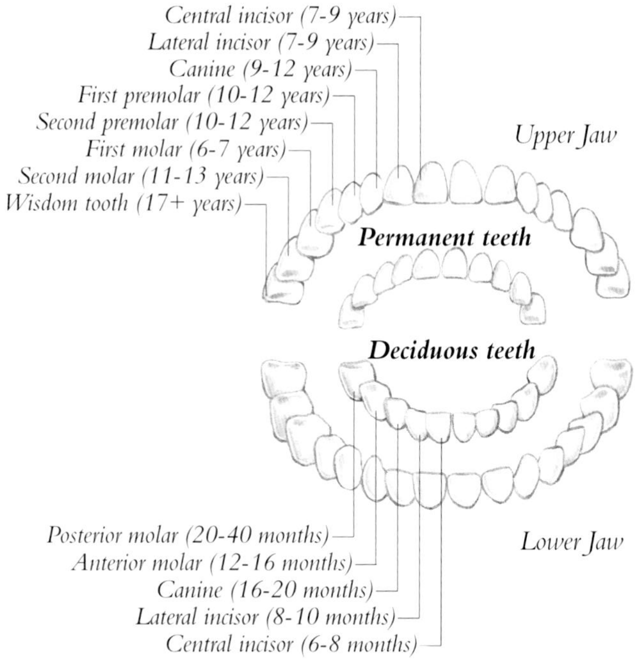

There are three types of deciduous teeth: incisors, canines (eye teeth) and molars. The adult teeth also have pre-molars between the canines and the molars. Incisors have a narrow blade-like edge for shearing food. Canines are good at tearing food and molars at grinding it Teeth begin to erupt on average when infants are six months of age, although some infants have no teeth until the age of one year.

Offer babies over six months of age finger foods such as toast, cucumber, carrot or celery sticks, cooked green beans and slices of fruit, such as pear or apple. Stay with them while they chew the food. Protect the skin around the mouth and chin from the effects of dribbling with petroleum jelly or aqueous cream, especially at bedtime.

If you are unsure whether your child's discomfort is caused by teething or by being unwell, check with your health visitor or doctor. Consult your doctor or dentist if the infant still has no teeth at 18 months.

Permanent teeth

At about the age of six, the lower front incisors loosen, followed by the upper incisors, the lower canine teeth and the primary first and second molars. The last milk teeth to go are frequently the upper canines at the front corner of the jaw. The first permanent molars come through behind the existing molars at the age of six, and the second molars at the age of twelve. The permanent premolars come through at ten to twelve years. Wisdom teeth or third molars usually appear in the late teens and are frequently crowded out by other teeth.

Developing permanent teeth is not painful, but in a few children the replacement of milk teeth with permanent teeth does not happen in an orderly way.

You may notice

- *Many children look as though their permanent teeth are too big and are crowding their jaw. Once the infant molars have fallen out there will be more room in their mouths*
- *There may be a space between the front permanent teeth, but this usually closes up as the canines emerge*
- *Some children keep their milk teeth while the permanent teeth grow through*
- *Some children do not develop a full set of permanent teeth. Others have extra teeth*
- *Some children have faults in the enamel covering of their permanent teeth and need protective treatments such as fissure sealing. Most often affected are those who were born premature, had a difficult birth or were ill immediately after birth. Some children inherit enamel problems*
- *A few children have discoloured teeth, particularly if they have been given excessive amounts of fluoride*

What to do

Children whose permanent teeth come through crooked, spaced or protruding can wear an orthodontic appliance or brace to correct them. This is rarely needed before all the permanent teeth come through unless there is such serious misalignment that the child is teased at school.

Thumb sucking

This very common habit in babies and young children usually stops by the age of three. Light sucking of the thumb or fingers may have no effect on tooth alignment, but vigorous sucking can produce a thumb-sized gap or teeth that do not close over each other properly (malocclusion). As long as the child stops thumb sucking by the time the permanent front teeth come through then no lasting harm will be done. If the child cannot stop they may well need a corrective brace later – and that may be all they need to break the habit.

A cooled teething ring brings instant and drug-free relief to a teething baby. Giving rusks or oven-baked breadcrusts that have been stored in the refrigerator works in the same way, as does the round end of a cold plastic spoon. Don't chill teethers in the freezer, however, and don't give a baby ice, as the cold can be more painful than the teething pain.

Complementary treatment

Cooling **Chinese herbs** can be given to relieve soreness and help the family to sleep. Rescue Remedy, a **Bach flower remedy**, rubbed on the gums or given orally (diluted in cooled boiled water for infants) can help reduce the emotional upset caused by pain. **Acupuncture** can be effective and **homeopathy** offers a number of specific remedies. They include Belladonna 30c (*Atropa belladonna*, deadly nightshade) for a flushed, hot child with wide staring pupils; Actaea 6c (*Actaea spicata*, baneberry) for a nervous, restless child; and Kreosotum 6c (*Kreosotum*, creosote) for teeth with poor enamel that decay easily and quickly. Remedies should be given every 30 minutes, or more frequently if the pain is bad, for up to ten doses. The homeopath may also recommend the tissue salts Calc. phos. (*Calcium phosphate*) and Calc. fluor. (*Calcium fluoride*) to be given during the child's teething period.

Gum Disease

What is it?

Although gum disease (periodontal disease) is thought of as a condition that affects adults, it often begins in childhood as gingivitis. This is an inflammation of the gums, when the edges of the gums are swollen and red and often bleed during brushing. Gingivitis can be halted at this stage with regular and careful brushing. If this does not occur, then the bacteria in the plaque will release toxins and chronic gum disease will develop, progressively damaging the support structure of the teeth. Eventually this can lead to teeth loosening and falling out in adulthood.

Gum disease is caused by plaque, the soft layer of bacteria that forms on all teeth. If plaque remains for too long, for example because of poor dental hygiene or difficulties in brushing irregular teeth, it will harden and calcify to form tartar (calculus), which in turn encourages more plaque to stick to the teeth. If calculus is not cleaned or brushed off regularly, gum disease will worsen and a pocket will form between the gums and the teeth where more plaque and calculus can gather. The supporting bone is then affected and the tooth will loosen. Calculus should be removed by scaling, which is carried out by the dental hygienist or dentist.

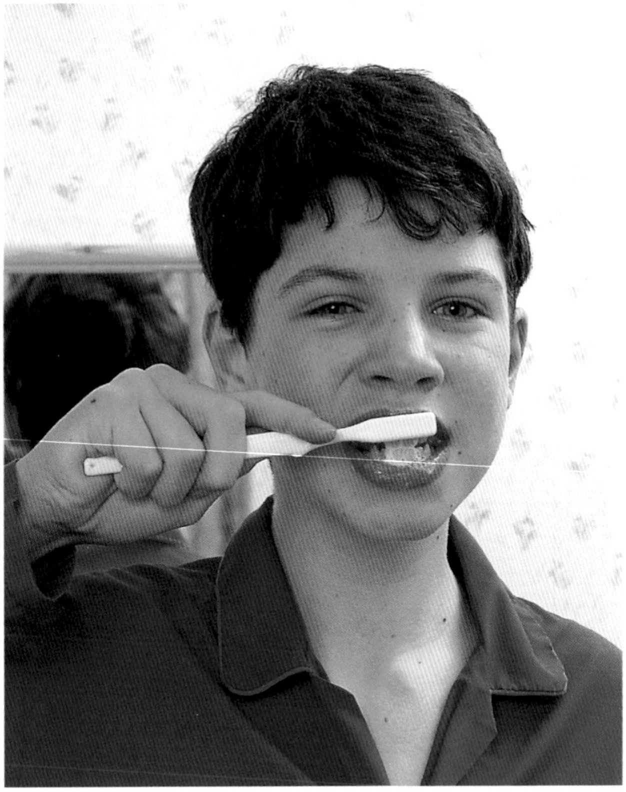

Gum disease frequently begins during childhood. It occurs when the margins of the gums become swollen and inflamed, mainly as a reaction to accumulating plaque. The best way to prevent gum disease is to teach children to brush their teeth twice daily. A gentle scrubbing technique usually works best, with the child holding the toothbrush like a pen to avoid too much force and using short horizontal movements to dislodge the plaque.

Preventing gum disease

The best way to prevent gum disease is to start children brushing their teeth regularly and carefully from an early age. Up to the age of seven, you may need to brush their teeth for them. Choose a child's toothbrush or a brush with a small head and medium hardness synthetic filaments. Place the filaments at the gum edge of the tooth and make horizontal movements to remove plaque from the edges. Then use a circular scrub technique over the boundary where the tooth and gum meet. Only apply gentle pressure and take your time until the teeth feel silky smooth. Scrubbing the teeth wears the surface down. Replace the toothbrush every two or three months or when the filaments start to curl.

From the age of seven children should be able to brush their teeth on their own, but they may need supervision at first. Plaque disclosing tablets will help them to see how effective their efforts have been.

An antiseptic mouthwash also helps to keep plaque under control. These are most useful for children over the age of six or seven who can reliably rinse without swallowing. However, they are no substitute for brushing.

Take children to the dentist once a year. Dentists can detect problems early on, and if calculus gathers on a child's teeth, either the dentist or the hygienist can clean or scale it off so the teeth are smooth again.

Complementary treatment

Aromatherapy oils made up as mouthwashes can soothe and aid the healing process. The **homeopath** may recommend rinsing the mouth with Hypericum and Calendula solution four times daily when the gums are infected. The dosage is five drops of mother tincture of each to 300 ml / ½ pint cooled boiled water. Specific remedies include Phosphorus 6c (phosphorus) for gums that bleed when they are touched and where gaps exist between the gums and the teeth; this remedy should be taken every four hours for up to three days. **Acupuncture** can also be effective.

Mouth Ulcers

What are they?

Mouth ulcers, also called aphthous ulcers or canker sores, are intensely painful sores inside the mouth. Although they are not infectious, they are very common, and at any one time one person in five has a mouth ulcer. Toddlers and children – especially girls – in the primary school years suffer most.

Mouth ulcers run in some families, but the exact cause – whether a bacterium, virus or an over-reaction by the body to stress or certain foods – is unknown. Often the cause is quite innocent; for example, an accidental injury to the mucous membrane inside the mouth by a sharp new tooth, a toothbrush or spoon, nervously chewing the cheek, or drinking and eating something that is too hot.

Ulcers may appear singly or in crops and usually heal within a few days. Some children get a succession of mouth ulcers, but however badly affected a child is, they tend to suffer less as they get older. Mouth ulcers are not serious unless the child gets so many that the mouth and gums become inflamed. Occasionally the cold sore virus is responsible during a first infection, when the child may be quite unwell and needs hospitalization because they can't swallow anything.

You may notice

- *Toddlers may dribble more than usual*
- *Younger children don't want to eat because their mouths are sore, and they may complain that drinking orange or blackcurrant juice hurts*
- *Older children with experience of mouth ulcers may recognize a burning or tingling sensation inside their mouths before the ulcer appears*
- *On the gums, tongue or the inside of the lip or cheek, one or more shallow whitish-grey sores with an irregular shape and a red, inflamed edge. They have a crater-like appearance, filled with whitish-grey slough*

What to do

Check that the ulcers don't appear after children have eaten a certain food. Chocolate, salty crisps, acidic fruit or vinegar can all trigger them. Also check that the ulcers are not thrush (see page 100), which leaves white, curd-like spots inside the cheeks. Thrush wipes off, leaving a raw spot, but ulcers do not. Look at children's hands and feet. If there are blisters there as well, children may have hand, foot and mouth disease (see page 98).

If you do find mouth ulcers, dab on teething gel or a liquid or gel mouth ulcer treatment using a clean fingertip or cotton wool pad. This will anaesthetize the ulcer long enough for children to eat or to clean their teeth. An antiseptic mouthwash or salt water after a meal may help the relieve the discomfort and keep the mouth clean. If there is any pain, lay a chilled face cloth over the ulcer.

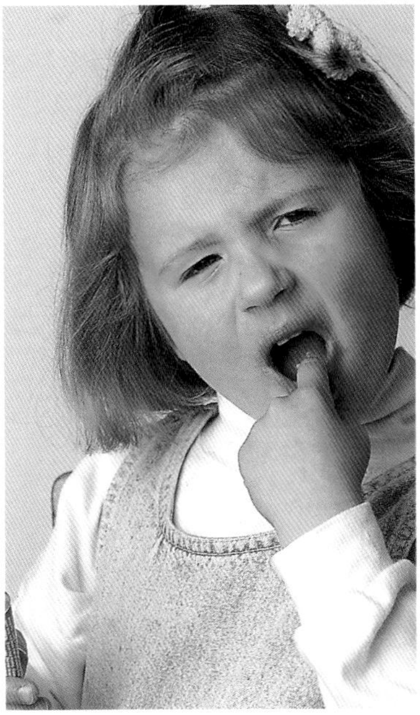

If your child develops a painful mouth ulcer, consult your pharmacist who can suggest an anaesthetic gel or mouthwash to relieve the soreness at least long enough for your child to eat or to brush their teeth. As an alternative, try a chlorhexidine mouthwash or one made with half a teaspoon of salt and 200ml/ ⅓ pint of warm water.

If the child doesn't want to eat, you may be able to encourage them to drink. Give the child a straw to bypass the ulcers, and offer chilled water, milk or non-acidic fruit juices or sugar-free squash. Once the child can eat, start them on bland foods such as yoghurt, custard or ice cream.

If the ulcer is not better in three days or if the sores keep recurring, your doctor can prescribe a pain-relieving anti-inflammatory cream or hydrocortisone lozenges.

Complementary treatment

Both **Chinese herbalism** and **acupuncture** can be very successful in treating mouth ulcers. **Nutritional therapists** link many mouth ulcers with an intolerance to foods such as citrus fruit, which are a common cause. Therapists using **Bach flower remedies** recommend a mouthwash containing Rescue Remedy and Crab Apple. **Relaxation** and **aromatherapy massage** can help improve physical health generally by relieving stress, which is often a cause of mouth ulcers. The **Western herbalist** may use powerful astringent and antiseptic herbs such as myrrh to clear the ulcers and improve resistance to infection.

Bad Breath

What is it?

Young children only occasionally have bad breath (halitosis), but older children who don't brush their teeth, brush their teeth badly, or have dental problems, are as liable to bad breath as adults.

Most cases of bad breath are caused by a build-up of micro-organisms in the mouth, which may happen overnight. Saliva is a natural mouthwash, helping to keep the mouth free from debris and bacteria during the day. At night, however, the salivary glands produce less saliva and therefore the mouth is washed less often. This causes the thick smell of the breath in the morning. When the teeth and gums are poorly brushed, food and bacteria decompose between the teeth. The bacteria give off sulphide compounds, which have the unmistakable smell of rotting eggs.

A smell on the breath may be linked with a particular medical condition; for instance, the smell of acetone (nail varnish remover) is one sign of diabetes, and a foul smell may be one sign of appendicitis. In liver or kidney failure, the breath may smell of fish or ammonia.

Bad breath on its own is rarely sufficient cause to see the doctor. However, if regular cleaning doesn't remedy the problem, then seek medical attention if your child has any of the symptoms described right.

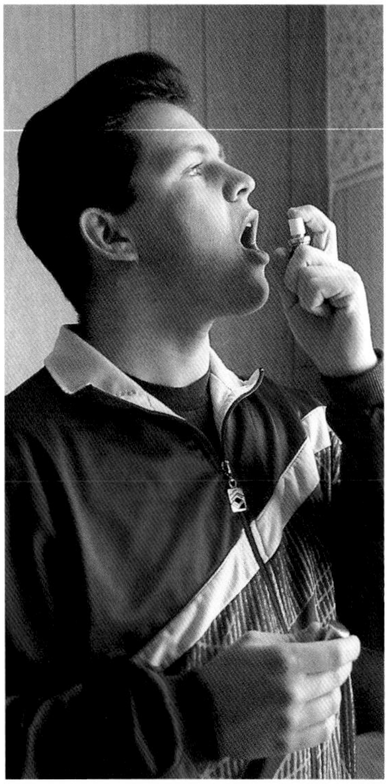

Around two-thirds of people are estimated to have bad breath at some time, caused by volatile sulphur compounds produced by bacterial activity in the mouth. Once a child is old enough to gargle and spit out rather than swallow mouthwash, regular use of an antibacterial rinse containing chlorhexidine gluconate is a simple answer. Breath sprays are useful for masking offensive odours short-term in social situations.

You may notice

- *You suspect the child has put something up the nose – there may be a thick whitish or blood-stained discharge from one nostril*
- *The child seems ill*
- *The breath smells especially foul*

What to do

If the breath smells of rotting eggs, check if the child is brushing their teeth and gums properly. It may be necessary to supervise or take over teeth-cleaning for a few days and see whether the breath improves. Use disclosing tablets to see if the child is cleaning plaque off thoroughly. Children under seven cannot usually gargle properly. If you want a younger child to use a mouthwash, choose one that is harmless if swallowed. An older child can use a mouthwash, a chlorhexidine gluconate spray or a special children's mouthrinse.

An empty stomach can give a child's breath a stale odour, which is obvious first thing in the morning or when they have missed a meal. Give the child something bland, such as hot chocolate with toast or a bowl of breakfast cereal, make them thoroughly clean their teeth and then check the breath.

Infected tonsils (see page 224) or an infection in the mouth or nose, especially if combined with heavy catarrh (see page 210), can turn breath foul. Some children get bad breath as they develop a cold. Make the child blow their nose and give them warm drinks to loosen any mucus. If the smell is still strong, they should clean their teeth before and after eating.

Make an appointment with the dentist, especially if the child has not had a check-up for six months; tooth decay or gum disease may be causing the problem.

Complementary treatment

In traditional Chinese medicine bad breath is usually treated as a dysfunction of stomach and spleen energy, combined with a heat or lung yin deficiency. **Chinese herbalism** and **acupuncture** will treat accordingly. Both **tai chi** and **chi kung** can help to improve breathing and cleanse the breath. **Western herbalism** can help once the cause has been identified. **Homeopathic remedies** include Aurum 6c (*Aurum metallicum*, gold) for pubescent children with putrid- or bitter-smelling breath. **Nutritional therapists** often consider bad breath to be a result of constipation. Toxins in the bowel are absorbed into the bloodstream and released in the breath when they reach the lungs, causing an offensive odour. Treatment is to make dietary changes.

CHAPPED OR CRACKED LIPS

What are they?

Cold, wintry weather, hot sunshine or a fever can dry out the skin, which may then become chapped and cracked. The lips are especially liable to chapping and cracking because they are among the most exposed parts of the skin. Some children have particularly dry lips, which are prone to cracking.

The glands in the skin around the mouth secrete a protective film of oil, which keeps lips moist. However, in cold weather the glands produce less oil, and this causes the lips to become flaky and dry out. Some children may make matters worse by chewing pieces of skin from the lips. Small cracks develop, which can be extremely sore and so deep that they bleed. Once these cracks have appeared in the lips it is easier for other infections to take hold, such as the herpes simplex virus that causes cold sores (see page 161).

You may notice

- *The lips may become inflamed, red and sore*
- *The lips may become dry and flaky. They may then crack, especially in the corners*
- *The lips may bleed*

What to do

Cold weather, spending too much time in the sun without protection, a mouth infection or an allergy to cosmetics can often cause cracking of the lips, producing a condition called cheilitis. The lips look dry, cracked and inflamed, and feel very sore. In cold, windy weather make sure children's lips are protected with lip balm; in sunshine, their lips should be protected with a high factor sunblock.

If a child has a fever or a cold that has caused painful cracked lips that bleed, it is important to keep the lips dry and to avoid reopening the deep cracks. Give children soft, mushy food so that they don't have to open their mouths too wide to eat, and let them drink through a straw. When a child has a cold, make sure that their lips are protected with liberal quantities of lip balm.

Children who habitually run their tongue around their lips will cause them to become dry, chapped and raw because of the repeated chafing and irritation. (Yeast extract can cause a similar reaction around the mouth.) You can help children to stop licking their lips by applying an aqueous cream or other emollient around the mouth to protect the skin and give it an unpleasant taste.

Lip biting is a nervous habit that is common among children. It makes the lips scale and crack, and even when flakes of skin peel off children usually keep on chewing the lips.

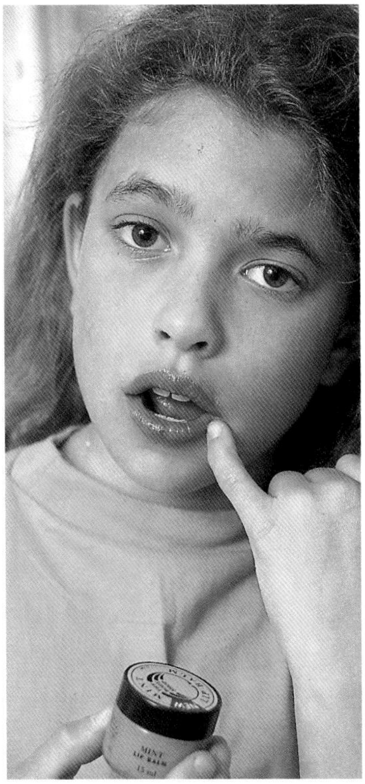

Applying a salve, chapstick or lip balm is the best way to protect lips against cold or the drying effects of bright sunshine. Balms are available in a wide variety of child-friendly flavours. Make sure that your child keeps her pot to herself to avoid spreading infection.

Children who chew their lips should apply lip balm morning and night, and should be encouraged to use a chapstick whenever they feel like chewing their lips.

Complementary treatment

Rescue Cream, a **Bach flower remedy**, is soothing and will aid healing of chapped, cracked lips. Some **aromatherapy** oils help regenerate healthy skin, possibly (and largely) because of the cream or oil base in which the essential oils are diluted. For chapped lips, **Western herbalists** may recommend topical applications of a cream or oil containing aloe vera, an anti-inflammatory herb, which is both soothing and healing.

Damaged Teeth

What are they?

Children's teeth, both milk (deciduous) and permanent, can be damaged in a variety of ways. In young children, milk teeth are frequently knocked out or pushed out of place when the child is learning to walk or crawl. This usually happens when the child falls or bangs into something while they are holding an object in their mouth.

The upper incisors are most frequently affected, especially in boys, and it has been estimated that 15 per cent of preschool children sustain some dental injury. Most often it is only the surface enamel that is cracked or chipped, but quite a few children sustain damage to the dentine. In very young children damage right into the central pulp is rare.

Tooth damage in older children usually occurs during contact sports, when teeth may be knocked out or chipped. Such damage can often be avoided by wearing a mouthguard.

Knocked-out teeth

Children's teeth can be knocked out at any age. The problem is less serious with milk teeth than with permanent teeth, as all the milk teeth will be shed naturally.

What to do

First find the tooth. A young child may have inhaled or swallowed it, and may choke (see First aid, page 350).

Milk teeth

To stop bleeding and keep the site clean, place a pad of clean lint or a clean cloth or handkerchief over the socket and slightly higher than the neighbouring teeth. Young children may need help holding the pad in place, while older children can simply bite down hard. Take the child to the dentist or the accident and emergency department immediately.

A knocked-out milk tooth is rarely replaced by the dentist, who will simply clean out the socket. Any resulting gap in the teeth will not normally affect the way the permanent teeth come through.

Permanent teeth

If a permanent tooth has been knocked out, the child needs to have it replaced quickly, ideally within ten minutes, although the chances of saving the tooth are still good if it is replaced within an hour. Take the child to the dentist or the accident and emergency department immediately.

You can first try to replace the tooth yourself. If the tooth is dirty or bloodied, rinse it in milk – not tap water. Then pick it up by the crown and quickly press it back into its socket, making sure that it is the right way round. Squeeze the gum around the tooth, then hold the tooth in place.

Alternatively, place the tooth in milk to keep the root moist and seek immediate dental treatment. The dentist will rinse it in saline or milk, clean out the socket and then hold the tooth in position with a flexible splint for a week, until it has become firm. To prevent infection, the child may be given a tetanus booster as well as antibiotics.

Chipped permanent tooth

The damage can be minor or more extensive, depending on which part of the tooth is affected.

What to do

Take the child and the chip of tooth to the dentist. If only the enamel is affected the chip can be bonded back, but if the dentist suspects that there has been damage to the root, then the tooth will be X-rayed. If the tooth has not completely come through yet, the dentist will monitor its growth to ensure that there is healthy root development. A badly damaged tooth will also be monitored, perhaps for as long as 18 months. If the tooth turns grey, it usually indicates that it is dying and will need to be removed.

Complementary treatment

Complementary treatment will be supportive to orthodox treatment. When the child is distressed and in shock, Rescue Remedy, a **Bach flower remedy**, may be helpful. Where the socket has been bleeding but has stopped, the **homeopathic** solution Hypericum and Calendula can be used to rinse the mouth every 30 minutes. Hypericum 6c (*Hypericum perforatum*, St John's wort) can be taken every five minutes for up to ten doses following treatment when the child is in much pain, followed by Staphisagria 6c (*Delphinium staphisagria*, stavesacre) if Hypericum does not help.

Tooth Decay and Erosion

What are they?

Most children start to experience decay (dental caries) in their permanent teeth between the ages of eight and twelve. The cause is plaque, a yellow-white deposit all over the surface of the teeth. Plaque affects two of the three layers of teeth: the dentine, which is calcified tissue; and the enamel, which is the hard protective layer.

Plaque contains, which act on the sugars in food and drink to produce a mild acid. The acid etches into the enamel, dissolving out calcium and phosphates into the saliva for 45–60 minutes after eating or drinking. Saliva then dilutes and washes away this acid, and some calcium and phosphate return to the tooth. If more sugar comes into the mouth during this time, more calcium and phosphate leach out and decay sets in. Tooth enamel can also be eroded by acidic drinks. This process starts in the pre-school years, and by the time children become teenagers, 30 per cent will have tooth erosion caused by their consumption of canned, carbonated and juice drinks.

Preventing tooth decay and erosion

The most important way to prevent tooth decay is to restrict children's intake of sugar. Never add sugar to a baby's drinks and dilute juices to at least half-strength. At bedtime and during the night give only water. If possible, avoid soya baby milk, which contains damaging sugars. Because drinks bathe every surface of the tooth, encourage babies to drink from a cup rather than a bottle from six months onwards, and aim to give up bottle feeding by 12 months. Encourage older children to drink sugar-free drinks and to vary fizzy drinks with still drinks or tap water.

Read labels carefully for hidden sugars. The most damaging are sucrose, glucose, fructose and maltose, but maltodextrin, invert sugar and hydrolyzed starch all cause decay. Avoid giving children between-meal snacks that contain sugar, and offer instead tooth-friendly alternatives, such as fruit and vegetables, cheese, savoury biscuits, oatcakes, breadsticks and plain yoghurt.

Brushing

It is also vital for children to learn to brush their teeth regularly and correctly (see Gum disease, page 232). This will help remove plaque and will spread the mineral fluoride, present in many toothpastes, over the teeth, strengthening the tooth enamel against decay. (Other sources of fluoride are water, and drops or tablets, available from your dentist.) Up to the age of seven, you need to brush children's teeth for them or they may brush under your supervision. Use a low fluoride toothpaste for children under seven and a medium fluoride for older children.

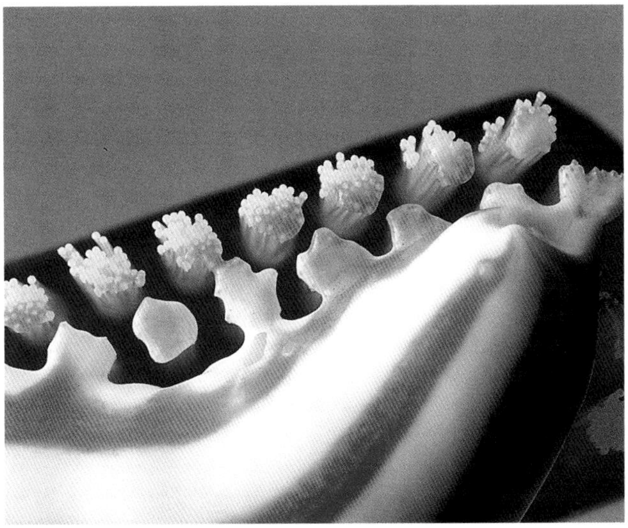

Fluoride is known to be responsible for the dramatic improvements in children's dental health over the past 30 years. Children living in an area where fluoride is not added to the drinking water should use a medium-fluoride toothpaste containing around 100ppm; those living in a fluoridated area should use a low-fluoride paste .Only a small pea-sized amount is needed and should be spat out after brushing.

You should take children to the dentist from an early age so that they get into the habit of a yearly check-up. The dentist can detect problems early on. For decay in milk or permanent teeth, the dentist will recommend an amalgam filling (strong and hard-wearing) or a white composite filling, which looks better and is more suitable for front teeth.

Complementary treatment

Aconite 6c (*Aconitum napellus*, blue aconite) is a **homeopathic remedy** for children who are fearful and panicky at the prospect of going to the dentist. Gelsemium 6c (*Gelsemium sempervirens*, yellow jasmine) is for children who are apprehensive and feel weak and wobbly at the knees. Chamomilla 6c (*Chamomilla* vulgaris, German chamomile) is useful for a child who has a temper tantrum at the thought of dental treatment, or is extremely sensitive to pain. Arnica 30c (*Arnica montana*, leopard's bane) can be given after any dental treatment, every hour for up to ten doses. For toothache, **Western herbalists** frequently recommend oil of cloves, a standard local analgesic.

FEEDING AND DIGESTION

The digestive system starts in the mouth, where chewing breaks food into pieces that are mixed with saliva for easier swallowing. A digestive enzyme from the salivary glands begins to break down starch. Food is then swallowed into the oesophagus and enters the stomach.

As food enters the stomach it passes through a muscular ring (sphincter), which prevents it returning up the oesophagus. The food now stays in the stomach for a few hours, where it is broken down further and mixed with mucus and fluids. Glands in the stomach lining produce enzymes to continue the digestive process, and hydrochloric acid, as enzymes work best in an acid environment.

The intestines

Semi-digested food is then squeezed in small amounts through the pylorus into the small intestine (bowel), a very long tube with muscular walls which contract in waves to push it along. A small tube enters the first section, the duodenum, bringing bile (to act as a natural detergent and emulsify fats) from the gall bladder and pancreatic juices (to digest fats, carbohydrates and proteins) from the pancreas. Food travels next into the jejunum, where nutrients are absorbed into the bloodstream.

Nutrient-rich blood is taken from the intestine in the portal vein to the liver. In the liver glucose is removed and any unneeded amino acids converted into urea, to be passed out later in urine (see page 286). After passing through the ileum, the food moves into the colon (large intestine). As digestive matter travels along the colon, large numbers of bacteria complete the digestion of carbohydrates. Water is absorbed from the paste-like waste matter, turning it gradually into more solid faeces. Once they reach the rectum, the faeces are excreted through the anus.

In the digestive system food is converted into a form that the body can use. Some nutrients, such as vitamins, can be absorbed as they are; others, such as fats, have larger molecules that need breaking down before they can be absorbed.

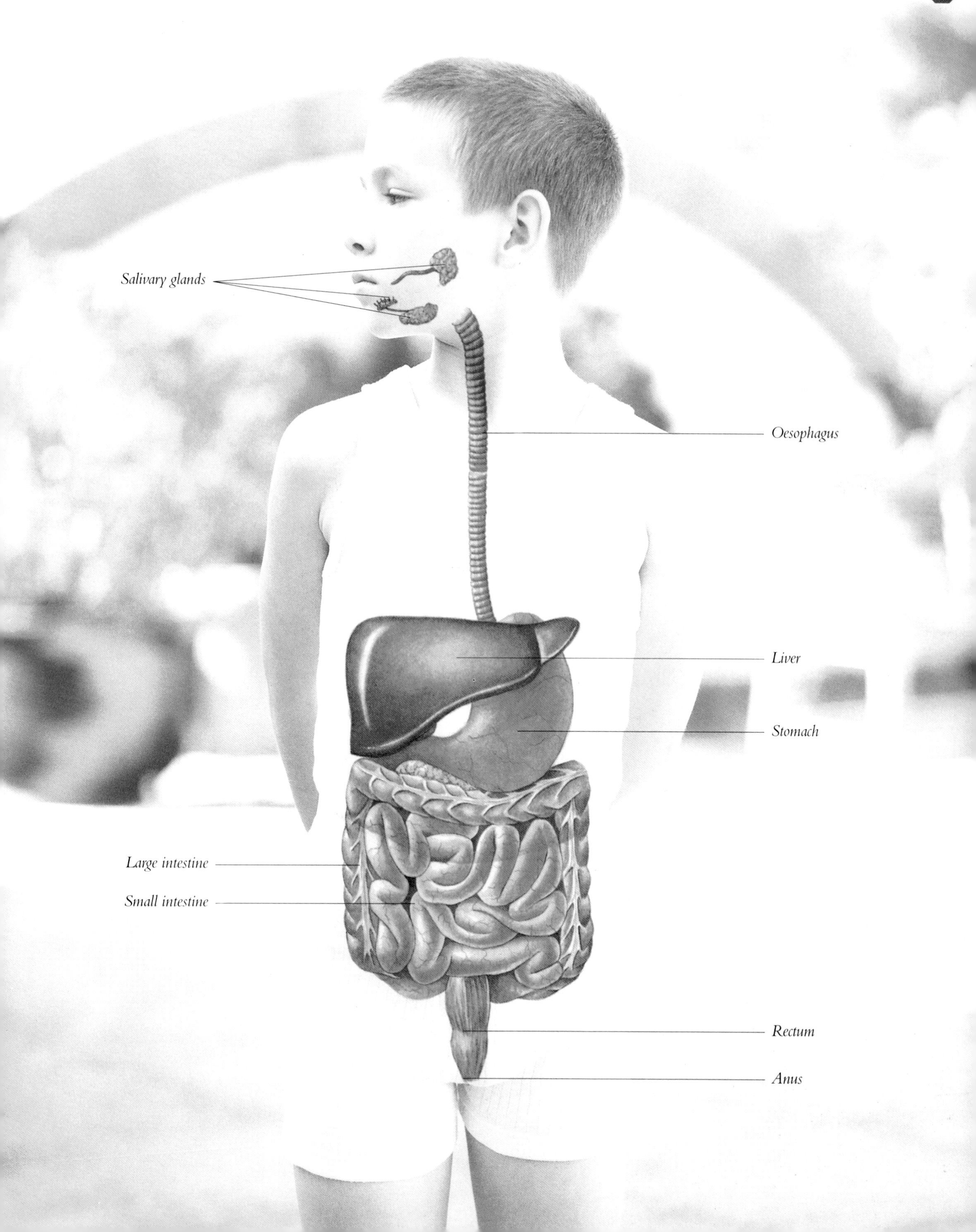
Salivary glands
Oesophagus
Liver
Stomach
Large intestine
Small intestine
Rectum
Anus

Diagnosis

Minor feeding and digestive disorders are common in childhood, and are usually nothing to worry about. However symptoms such as stomach ache and vomiting can be a sign of a more serious underlying disorder and should never be ignored.

Sign	What could be wrong
Relentless crying in an infant under three months,	Three-month colic is a possibility
Cramping pain on one side during upright exercise, worse if, the child ate or drank before exercising	A stitch. This is common in activities such as running
Vomiting, loose and frequent motions, fever	Gastroenteritis or food poisoning. Give sips of clear liquids. Contact the doctor if there is diarrhoea and vomiting, especially in an infant
Cramping pain after eating and before passing a motion; hard, large motions; poor appetite; lethargy	Constipation. Give extra fluids, fruit and more high fibre foods
Urinary symptoms (pain, frequent urination) and fever	Urinary tract infection
Pain in the abdomen lasting for more than six hours; it may start near the navel and move to the lower right abdomen, but the child cannot easily localize the pain. The child may not let you press the stomach. Rare under the age of three	Appendicitis. Call the doctor. Do not give the child anything to eat or drink while waiting for the doctor
Pain in the abdomen starting within an hour or two of eating a particular food	Food intolerance is possible. Try withdrawing the food (if it isn't an essential item)
Repeated stomach ache, possibly with vomiting and visual symptoms; the child is pale and not hungry	Abdominal migraine. Allow the child to lie down in quiet, dark room. Give sips of sweetened drinks
Severe colicky pain, pallor, unusual screaming in an infant who is calm and well between screaming bouts	Intussusception. Contact the doctor immediately
Frequent diarrhoea, possibly containing mucus and/or blood, in an older child or teenager	Colitis. This is rare in younger children

FOR OTHER CAUSES OF STOMACH ACHE, SEE STOMACH ACHE (PAGE 251)

Warning: Any child who has an attack of acute stomach ache that lasts for more than three hours should be seen immediately by the doctor or taken to the Accident and Emergency Department of your local hospital

FOOD INTOLERANCE

What is it?

A food intolerance is a reaction to a specific food or ingredient. A food allergy (see page 242) is just one type of food intolerance, but there are many more. They include a reaction to an irritant ingredient such as curry powder, which can produce diarrhoea; a reaction to large amounts of particular foods such as fruit; and an inability to digest a particular food because the body lacks a certain enzyme or chemical. A common example of such an enzyme deficiency is lactose (milk sugar) intolerance, which is caused by a lack of the enzyme lactase. Research suggests that other disorders may be linked with enzyme deficiencies.

Food intolerance can be inborn or acquired. In susceptible people, eating certain foods can produce the symptoms of allergy. This is because the foods themselves contain histamine, the chemical that lies behind many of the inflammatory symptoms of allergy. Cheeses, salami, pepperoni and sauerkraut may all contain histamine.

You may notice

- *Digestive symptoms. Colic and diarrhoea are the most common symptoms*
- *Rashes*
- *A wide range of different physical and emotional symptoms, depending on the offending food*

What to do

If it is obvious that the child is reacting to a particular food and it is not an essential part of a child's healthy diet, try avoiding it for two weeks. If the food is essential – milk, for example – consult a doctor or dietitian first for advice about a milk substitute. If you cannot see any clear link between he symptoms and any suspect food, keep a food diary; for a few days, noting down all the symptoms and what the child has eaten. This may reveal connections you had not considered. If it does not, ask your doctor to refer your child to an allergy specialist who may be able to pinpoint the cause.

Enzyme deficiencies

Apart from the shortage of lactase that underlies lactose intolerance, enzyme deficiencies causing metabolic disorders are quite rare. They do, however, have serious effects, which are usually caused by a build-up in the tissues of a particular chemical. Such deficiencies are inherited and some of the more common include those listed below.

Complementary Treatment

Complementary treatment consists mainly of giving support to orthodox treatment, depending on the cause. For certain conditions the **Western herbalist** may treat with herbs that improve digestion and lessen irritability of the gastrointestinal tract. Treatment by an **acupuncturist** and/or **Chinese herbalist** may also be effective. The **homeopath** will treat according to the personality, temperament and mood of the child concerned. **Relaxation** may help with some of the emotional factors, such as pain, fear and anxiety, as may the appropriate **Bach flower remedy**.

Food Intolerance and Enzyme Deficiencies

Disorder	Defect	Treatment
Phenylketonuria (PKU)	Inability to metabolize amino acid phenylalaline	Low-protein diet and milk substitutes
Galactosaemia	Inability to convert galactose into glucose	Lactose and galactose-free diet
Glycogen storage disease	An inability to break down glycogen	High carbohydrate diet
Porphyria	Blockage in the production of haem, a component of haemoglobin	Depends on type. Usually essential to avoid sunlight
Fructose intolerance	Inability to break down fructose	Fructose/sorbitol-free diet
Maple syrup urine disease	Inability to break down certain amino acids	Life-long diet low in these amino acids

Food Allergy

What is it?

A food allergy is a hypersensitive reaction to a normally harmless substance in food. Allergic reactions are either immediate and unmistakable or they develop insidiously and have less clear-cut symptoms. Immediate reactions are quite common, especially in babies and young children, whereas a delayed reaction occurs less frequently.

Causes and symptoms

When children eat or drink the harmless substance, called the allergen, their immune system mistakes it for a harmful antigen, a substance that triggers an immune response. Specifically it makes antibodies, called immunoglobulins, to the allergen, which remain in the immune system long after the food has been digested and waste eliminated. Therefore the next time the child eats that food, the antibodies will attach themselves to cells in the tissues called mast cells and trigger the release of a cocktail of chemicals, including histamine. These chemicals are responsible for the main symptoms of the allergy, which can be extremely varied. They include: redness, swelling, an itchy rash, vomiting, runny nose and wheezing. The most severe reaction is anaphylactic shock (see box , page 243 and First Aid, page 358).

These reactions are more common in families with an inherited tendency to allergies. As they can occur when the baby is first exposed to a food, it has been suggested that the child has already been sensitized through breastmilk or even before birth. Whether children can be sensitized initially to a food product by skin contact – nut oils used in massage, for example – is an open question. To avoid this problem it is recommended that you use an alternative oil such as grapeseed, or one of the vegetable oils.

Common allergens

Food allergies appear more often in children than they do in adults. Cows' milk protein and eggs are the most common food allergens, but most children outgrow these allergies by the age of three or four years. Peanuts cause the strongest reaction of all, and a child allergic to peanuts may react to other nuts. This allergy is usually lifelong. As it has recently been shown that very young babies have developed nut allergies, some people believe that women with a history of allergic illness should avoid eating peanuts while they are pregnant or breastfeeding. Other nuts involved in food allergies include brazil, cashew, hazelnut, walnut and pecan. Wheat, fish, shellfish and legumes also frequently cause adverse reactions.

Peanuts are frequently the culprit that triggers a nut allergy. Other nuts that can cause an allergic response include almonds, brazil nuts, cashews, hazelnuts, walnuts and pecans. Parents of children with a nut allergy should be extra diligent when buying prepared foods and examine the list of ingredients very carefully. Nuts are often the hidden ingredients in a number of foods, including savoury varieties.

You may notice

An infant who has not yet been weaned

- *May have colic*
- *Develop diarrhoea*
- *Fail to put on weight steadily*

After weaning a child may show a variety of symptoms, including

- *Diarrhoea and failure to thrive*
- *Eczema*
- *Urticaria – patches of itchy yellow/white lumps surrounded by red, inflamed skin*
- *Sneezing and runny nose*
- *Red, swollen rashes*
- *Vomiting*
- *Stomach ache*
- *Wheezing*
- *Glue ear*

Symptoms such as urticaria and vomiting can come on immediately after eating a food that triggers the allergic reaction. Other symptoms such as eczema or glue ear develop more slowly.

What to do

If you or others in your immediate family have allergies, there is a possibility that your child will have one. To prevent such an allergy developing, you should breastfeed for at least four to six months and ideally for a year. While you are breastfeeding and possibly also while you are pregnant, avoid foods that are common allergens, or foods to which you know you are allergic. If you cannot breastfeed, ask your doctor for advice. You may be prescribed a hydrolyzed protein formula milk.

Delay giving babies foods that are common allergens, for example, eggs, nuts, wheat, fish, shellfish and legumes, until six months, and only give ordinary cows' milk after a year. Some specialists now recommend that allergy-prone children avoid peanut products until they are three years old and possibly as old as seven.

If you suspect a particular food is causing a problem, keep a diary of food and symptoms for a few days. Introduce new weaning foods one at a time every two or three days. This makes it easier to pinpoint a problem. Only withhold a suspect food on your doctor's advice.

What else?

The majority of children will outgrow most food allergies. However before you put your child back on a food, always check with your doctor first. On rare occasions, your doctor may suggest that the child tries the food first in hospital in case there is a sudden severe reaction.

Allergic babies can have their immunizations as normal. Current research shows that those who are allergic to eggs can be given the measles/mumps/rubella (MMR) vaccine safely. If you are still concerned, you can have the child immunized in hospital under careful observation.

Anaphylactic shock

The most serious reaction to food starts within seconds or minutes of a child swallowing a food to which they are allergic. Symptoms often include:

- Burning, irritation or itching in the mouth or throat
- Itching anywhere on the body
- A flushed skin
- Sore red eyes
- Swollen mouth and throat, which can make swallowing and breathing very difficult

YOU MUST DIAL THE EMERGENCY SERVICES IMMEDIATELY. ANAPHYLACTIC SHOCK IS LIFE THREATENING.

Children who have had one anaphylactic shock are often prescribed a syringe ready loaded with adrenaline in case this happens again.

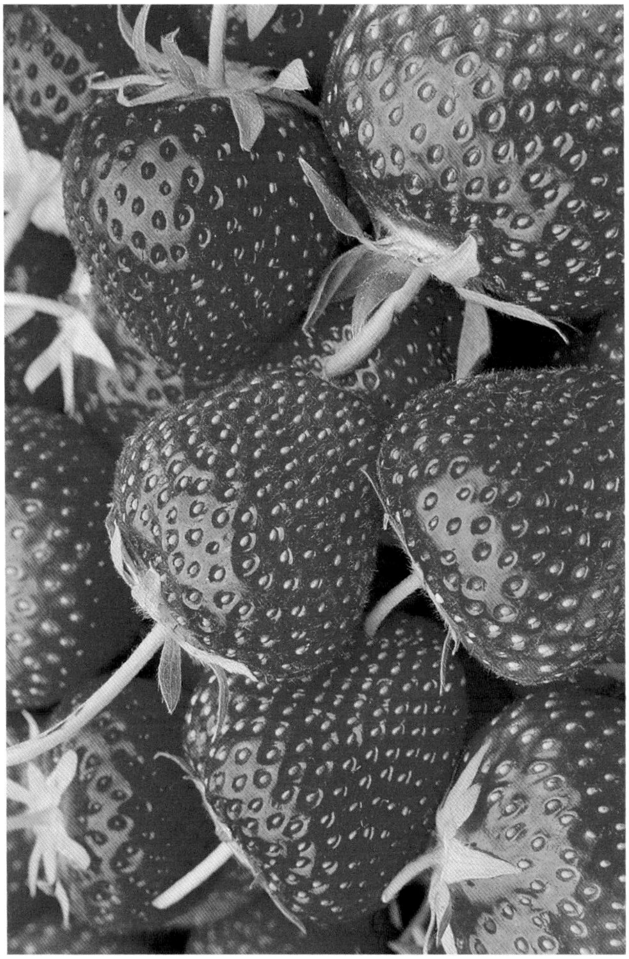

Strawberries are a common allergen, particularly in children. The symptoms of an allergic reaction to this fruit include hives, an upset stomach, facial swellings, particularly of the eyelids and lips, and symptoms resembling those of hay fever, such as itchy eyes and nose. Any child suffering from these symptoms should be seen by a doctor.

Complementary Treatment

Osteopathy would treat the whole person, not the allergy, by bringing the body back into balance. **Nutritional therapy** can help to identify the allergy and advise on elimination diets if the allergen is difficult to identify. The **homeopath** may also be of help in this respect. **Acupuncture** can be effective when the cause is an underlying disharmony preventing the uninterrupted flow of *chi*. **Kinesiology** is particularly helpful in diagnosing allergies that may trigger other symptoms and disorders.

Lactose Intolerance

What is it?

Intolerance of cows' milk is different from cows' milk allergy. The latter is caused by a hypersensitive reaction by the body's immune system to proteins in the milk, while lactose (milk sugar) intolerance is caused by an enzyme deficiency in the small intestine.

Lactose is normally broken down in the small intestine into glucose and galactose by the enzyme lactase. If there is insufficient lactase for this to take place, then undigested lactose passes into the large intestine and ferments, producing watery loose stools and wind.

Lactose intolerance can be temporary or permanent, and as lactose is present in human as well as cows' milk, the symptoms are the same whether a baby is breast- or bottle fed. The most common temporary cause is gastroenteritis, in which the mucous lining of the intestine has been damaged by the infection. Newborn babies, especially those who were premature, may also have a shortage of lactase because of a delay in the development of enzyme production.

The most common reason for permanent milk intolerance is an inherited shortage of the enzyme lactase. This occurs in up to 90 per cent of people of Asian and African extraction, whereas only 5 to 15 per cent of Caucasians have the condition. Children with coeliac disease (see page 263) may also develop milk intolerance.

Cows' milk supplies reasonable quantities of a wide range of essential nutrients. While it is easy to find these nutrients in other foods, there are not many foods apart from milk, cheese and other dairy products that are rich in calcium. This is an important reason for consulting a dietician or doctor before putting a child on a milk-free diet.

Symptoms may only become obvious in children after the age of two or three

You may notice

- *After a bout of gastroenteritis, the child may have a recurrence of diarrhoea when they go back on to milk. The diarrhoea is explosive, frothy, watery and often produces a dramatic nappy rash. The child may also be colicky and produce large amounts of gas*
- *Chronic diarrhoea from birth*
- *Failure to put on weight*
- *Colic*
- *Abdominal cramps and bloating*

What to do

Contact your doctor immediately. Diarrhoea in a baby or young child is always serious and the correct cause needs to be identified. The doctor may need to test a liquid stool for sugar and will tell you how to collect it. If sugars are found in the stool, the doctor will prescribe a milk substitute such as soya formula for four to six weeks, to allow the intestines time to recover. After this you should try the child on a small amount of milk or dairy produce and watch for any recurring symptoms. If symptoms do return, then a further four weeks on a milk substitute may be necessary.

Outlook

Children diagnosed with the condition may have to follow a lactose-free diet. However they can still eat yoghurt, as the lactose has been converted into lactic acid, and cheese, which contains very low levels of lactose. Many children can take small amounts of milk but they will develop symptoms if given too much. Knowing how much can be tolerated will come after trial and error.

Complementary Treatment

Complementary treatment will consist mainly of supporting orthodox treatment. **Kinesiologists** can be of help in identifying the problem and often find that lactose intolerance lies at the root of many other childhood ailments. Supportive treatment by an **acupuncturist** and/or **Chinese herbalist** may also be effective. **Relaxation** may help with some of the emotional factors, such as pain, fear and anxiety, as may the appropriate **Bach flower remedy**.

See also DIARRHOEA (page 265)

FOOD POISONING

What is it?

Food poisoning is a form of gastroenteritis that is caused by contaminated food or water. Bacteria are one of the primary contaminants, and these include *Campylobacter*, found in poultry and unpasteurized milk; *Salmonella*, found especially in milk, eggs and poultry products; *E-coli*, found especially in meat products but also on unwashed vegetables; and *Shigella*, which causes a type of dysentery. Food poisoning can also be caused by viruses, poisoned mushrooms and chemicals. Symptoms appear between two and six hours after eating, and the condition is more common in the summer and on holidays abroad. Because food poisoning causes diarrhoea and, frequently, vomiting it is always serious for babies and young children. Food poisoning is rare in breastfed babies but it can affect children of any other age. Recently babies have been infected by *Salmonella anatum* in baby milk and children by *E-coli* 0157 in prepared meat products.

Preventing food poisoning

- Wash your hands before preparing or eating food and after changing nappies, wiping bottoms and handling pets. Teach children to do the same. Cutting boards and utensils must be rinsed before use. Defrost frozen poultry completely before cooking and ensure that it is fully cooked before eating. Cover any cuts on your hand with a waterproof plaster
- If you can, make up fresh formula for each feed. If you make formula in advance, keep it in the fridge in a covered, sterilized container. Never store warm milk in a vacuum flask
- If you heat ready-made meals, make sure you heat them through thoroughly
- Wrap or cover prepared food and keep it in the fridge away from raw food
- Freeze home-cooked food as soon as it has cooled
- Throw away partly eaten food
- Use a thermometer to make sure the temperature of your refrigerator is below 5°C/41°F. Cook food to at least 70°C/158°F to kill harmful bacteria such as *Salmonella* and *Campylobacter*. Use a temperature probe in a microwave

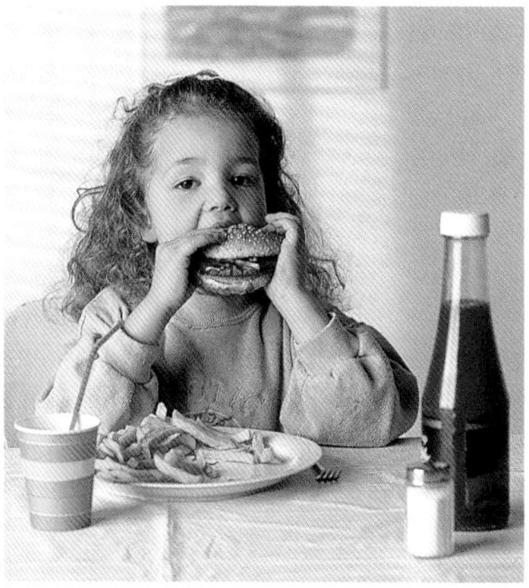

Meat products are a common source of food poisoning caused by the bacterium E-coli. *As cooking destroys* E-coli *it is vital that burgers and other products made from meat are thoroughly cooked all the way through so that no pink meat remains.*

You may notice

- *Stomach pain, nausea and vomiting*
- *Diarrhoea or odd-smelling stools*
- *A flushed face and feverishness*

What to do

Contact your doctor immediately if the child is vomiting and has diarrhoea, especially if the child is under three years of age, as there is a risk of dehydration (see page 252). Note how much the child drinks and when they vomit, and show these notes to the doctor. The doctor will probably suggest a rehydration drink. These come as powders to mix with water. Follow the instructions on the packet precisely. Boil and cool tap water for a baby, but an older child can be given tap water and may prefer the effervescent rehydration tablets. If the baby cannot manage the whole drink, keep the rest in the refrigerator for up to 24 hours.

If the baby is being breastfed, feed as often as they will drink, then offer a rehydration drink from a syringe or spoon. Give a bottle-fed baby boiled, cooled water in addition to the rehydration drink. Flat cola or dilute apple or pineapple juice can be a temporary drink for children until the doctor has seen them. Once the diarrhoea begins to ease and vomiting has stopped, offer a weaned baby or child bland foods such as toast, rice, mashed potatoes and plain biscuits.

Complementary Treatment

In most cases this condition requires orthodox treatment, but complementary therapies such as **Western herbalism** may be appropriate for dealing with the after effects. There are several **homeopathic remedies** for food poisoning in which the symptoms are similar to those of gastroenteritis.

Food Fads

What are they?

Food fads usually involve a strong and lasting dislike of certain foods or categories of food. They are quite normal in pre-school children, many of whom grow out of them by school age. There are several sorts of pre-school faddy eater: the selective eater, who eats very few foods but still grows healthily; the underweight child who eats tiny quantities; the child who accepts purées but nothing with lumps; and the child who has missed out on learning about diet and appetite because of illness.

Infant feeding habits

Many young children stick to a small number of favourite foods, but as long as their diet has a reasonable variety, food fads are unimportant. Many young children also eat variable quantities – much more one day than the next – but this does not mean they are faddy. Rather it is because a young child's appetite is more precisely geared to their energy output than an adult's appetite.

Babies' appetites vary. Some show diminishing interest in feeding once they are weaned, or prefer sloppy foods or foods with a smooth texture they don't need to chew. Other babies, once they begin crawling, find food less interesting than exploring. Babies around the age of one develop more effective ways of saying 'No' to food: they learn to purse their lips and turn their heads firmly away when offered a food they don't want, and they can also spit food out and shake their head. In such a situation it is advisable to stop and try again later.

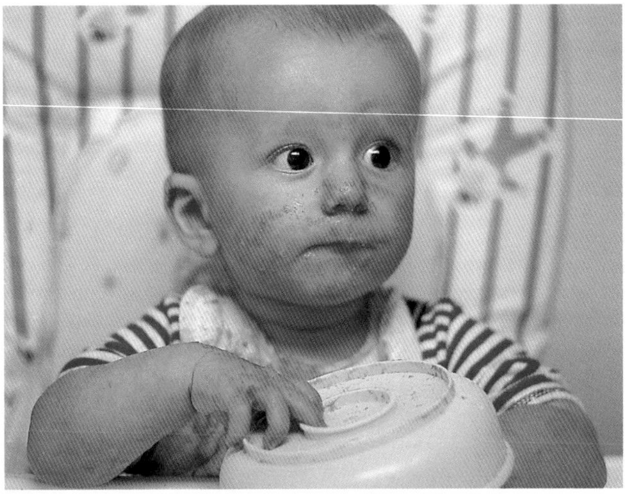

Play is the way all young children learn most effectively, exploring both with their hands and their mouths. Stopping them from playing with food denies them the opportunity to learn about texture, which is an important facet of food. However it is sensible to limit the damage that older babies and young toddlers inevitably inflict on their environment by offering semi-solid foods in preference to liquid ones.

Real food battles often start in the second year when children realize they have complete control over what they accept to eat and refusal becomes a means of self-assertion. If food fads are handled in a matter-of-fact unemotional way or ignored altogether, they often fade by the time the child is three or four years old.

Food fads can also start if children lose their appetite when they are unwell (see Appetite loss, page 250). They may enjoy a return to baby foods or the extra attention you give them to persuade them to eat. However you will usually be able to distinguish between children who have lost their appetite because they are unwell and children who are perfectly healthy.

Food refusal

Refusing a particular food is almost always unimportant. Suddenly refusing an entire meal may be the first sign of illness, so you should observe children carefully and ensure they are getting enough to drink. Children who consistently refuse food and are light in weight for their age or who are not growing as well as expected should be examined by a health visitor or doctor. There is a very small group of young children with severe feeding and eating difficulties. Recent research suggests that unpleasant early feeding experiences such as repeated vomiting may be linked with later feeding difficulties.

What to do

When the child refuses food, just take it away without commenting. Don't leave them sitting a long time in front of uneaten food. Don't bribe or persuade them to eat and never force them to eat.

If they make a habit of refusing food, give them smaller portions on a tiny plate. Always include something they definitely like. You'll both feel better if they finish the plateful.

If the child doesn't like eating alone, eat with them. Talk about something more interesting than food. But don't hover or fret if they are dawdling as this will take away their appetite. The child may also eat better if they have a friend who has a good appetite to visit. They may also eat better when they are away from home.

If you really think your child is not getting enough to eat, write down everything they eat and drink in one day. If you

People who believe that food is only to be eaten have not yet met the average toddler. Although some young children are fastidiously clean, most pass through a temporary stage of messy exploration. Early experiences such as squidging food through the fingers give way to more imaginative exploration, as with this toddler who is splodging his bottle in his food /While your child is going through this stage, protect every nearby kitchen surface.

find the child is snacking, that is normal. Small children often eat six times a day, so just make certain the snacks are reasonably healthy. Prepare snacks such as fruit, cheese cubes, fromage frais or salad vegetables, but don't give too many high-fibre foods to young children with tiny appetites, as this often bloats the stomach. 'Healthy diets' high in fibre, the so-called 'muesli belt syndrome' may actually cause children to be under-nourished and fail to thrive. High fibre foods contain high levels of phyatates, naturally occurring chemicals that combine with important nutritive minerals such as calcium, iron or zinc. This process reduces the availability of the minerals to the child.

If your child is drinking large quantities of fluids, try to make them cut down; although fluids fill them up they contain less energy and nutrition than the same volume of solid foods. However do make sure they drink 500 ml/18 fl oz of milk a day: larger quantities will depress their appetite.

What else?

To raise your child's interest in mealtimes, you can let them help you prepare the food; if they are old enough, let them help plan the menus for the week. Make their meals look colourful and attractive, but don't invest too much energy in preparation in case they refuse them. Children may eat more if you prepare a dish for the whole family, from which they can help themselves.

Keep mealtimes regular and let children have their drink at the end of the meal.

Make sure a young child gets baby vitamin drops, containing vitamins A, C and D. You may be able to buy these cheaply from a health centre, or from a clinic if your child is under five years of age.

Even if you are worried about your child's eating habits, don't talk about them in front of the child.

Getting professional advice

Health visitors can weigh and measure your child and plot their growth on a chart, which can be reassuring (see page 70). They will probably reassure you that the child's food fads are normal, but they may also refer you to a dietitian for advice and practical suggestions. If, however, the child only eats tiny quantities and appears pale and lethargic, consult your doctor to ensure there is not an underlying ailment causing the problem.

Complementary Treatment

Bach flower remedies may help where an emotional or traumatic experience such as choking is at the root of the problem, and appropriate remedies can be chosen to suit the child's needs. Mimulus and or Rock Rose, for example, would address any fear of eating. Traditional Chinese Medicine – **acupuncture, tai chi**, **chi kung** and **Chinese herbalism** – holds that stomach and spleen energy is mainly responsible for eating and digestive problems, and where there are emotional issues, there is usually a link with liver energy; treatment would therefore concentrate on these areas. The **homeopath** will usually be able to advise parents on how to deal with feeding problems. The condition might also be helped by **reflexology**.

SEE ALSO FAILURE TO THRIVE (PAGE 71)

Eating Disorders

What are they?

Eating disorders are an expression of hidden, uncomfortable and sometimes painful feelings. By exerting extreme self-discipline sufferers find they can take control over their bodies and believe they can also block out the painful feelings. Eating disorders involving starvation, such as anorexia and bulimia, induce a temporary physical high, which feeds the sufferers' false sense of elation that they are in control.

In reality, they are not. People with eating disorders are trapped in a world of self-delusion in which thinness equates with success, happiness, popularity and a high self-esteem.

Causes

Eating disorders can affect anyone from any background at any age, but they tend to develop during adolescence, a time of intense preoccupation with independent identity and body image. At this age some teenagers may find the emotional demands of growing up overwhelming and see control of food as a way of making time stand still for them. Girls are more prone to eating disorders than boys, but many boys still suffer. Apart from a psychological vulnerability imposed by society's expectations of women, girls are more susceptible than boys because of their greater concern with slimness.

Studies show that girls as young as five or six are becoming preoccupied with body image, dieting and weight control. Around half of girls under eleven say they would like to lose weight and be thinner and even six-year-olds know which are the fattening foods to cut out. Girls of this age are affected both by parental attitudes about slimness and a wider culture in which thin is good and fat is bad.

The typical picture of someone with anorexia is a conscientious, even perfectionist girl – but with a disastrously low self-esteem. Making a teenager feel good about themselves rather than their achievements is an important step towards treating an eating disorder.

Recognizing the problem

However, recognizing an eating disorder can be difficult unless it is advanced anorexia where the signs are painfully obvious. The sufferer usually skillfully hides the symptoms. Yet recognizing the signs and asking for help is important because early recognition improves the outlook. Forty per cent of sufferers recover completely; 30 per cent improve a great deal. Early recognition is especially important in children, because eating disorders can become severe more quickly than they do in adults.

The first step in overcoming the disorder is getting the person to realize there is a problem. They next step is to balance their wish to solve the problem against the illusory feelings of control on which they have depended. At this stage sufferers need someone in whom can confide. They may very well not want to talk to their parents but may be willing to talk to a relative stranger. Telephoning an eating-disorder helpline can be the first stage in accepting the problem and asking for help.

The ultimate aim of treatment is for the sufferer to feel in purposeful, balanced control of their life without expressing their emotions through food. Expert counselling can be very helpful in the early stages of anorexia. Responsibility for medical care needs to be taken by a doctor.

Where a child or teenager is concerned, both parents and frequently other family members need to be involved in the therapy so they can be consistent and cooperative in their approach and support each other.

Anorexia

Mild forms of anorexia affect one in twenty adolescent girls and young women. More severe forms needing professional treatment affect one young woman in two hundred. Anorexia starting in childhood almost always needs professional treatment to correct what has gone wrong and to support changes in behaviour.

You may notice

- *An intense fear of getting fat even when the person is obviously underweight*
- *Disturbance of body image – claiming fatness when actually skinny*

- *Strict calorie control to keep weight down. Very little fat or carbohydrate is eaten*
- *Constant preoccupation with food and calorie-counting*
- *Periods stop*
- *Avoidance of family meals and the invention of plausible reasons for not eating*
- *Initially, boundless energy, even restlessness. As more weight is lost, fatigue, weakness and an inability to concentrate set in*
- *Noticeably cold hands and feet*
- *Excessive exercising, often alone*

Bulimia

Bulimia involves three elements – bouts of overeating, action to make up for the bingeing (fasting/vomiting/laxatives) and a distorted body image. It is often a development of anorexia and typically affects older teenagers. Bingeing is a response to feelings that seem unbearable and involves eating very large quantities of food, frequently high fat and high carbohydrate, sometimes uncooked or direct from the freezer. Guilt and self-disgust naturally follow. Purging the system makes up for the guilt and prepares the body for the next cycle. Externally, people with bulimia may be happy and popular. Inside they believe they are a sham and are terrified of being found out.

You may notice

- *Preoccupation with food, bouts of gross overeating and a sense of loss of control*
- *Intense fear of fatness and overvaluation of body shape as a source of self- esteem*
- *Weight fluctuates around normal*
- *Smell of vomit in the toilet after meals*
- *Erosion of the teeth by gastric acids*

What to do

In either case, ask your doctor for help. Children should be assessed, treated and supported by a team of professionals from child and adolescent mental health services, including a paediatrician. With anorexia, an early aim is to boost the child's calorie intake. The child who is dehydrated or who loses a lot of weight may need to go into hospital – preferably to a specialist eating disorders unit. Addressing the underlying psychological issues is important for longer-term recovery. Children may need help to talk about their emotions, as well as more mundane matters such as eating patterns. The whole family should be involved in treatment. Families themselves may need support in helping a child with an eating

Learning to cook is an important part of developing a healthy attitude towards food and eating. It can also play a vital role in helping children overcome eating disorders by re-awakening an interest in food. However anorexic children may cook for the family without themselves eating. They should not only cook and prepare food; they should also eat with the family at mealtimes that are relaxed and enjoyable.

disorder and in learning what to do for the best. Parents and children may need counselling. Self-help groups can support families by sharing feelings, experiences and solutions.

Who can help?

For organizations offering help, see the Directory.

Complementary Treatment

Complementary treatments generally focus on providing support to orthodox treatment. **Chinese herbalism**, **tai chi**, **chi kung** and **acupuncture** – can offer supportive treatment to counselling or psychotherapy. **Western herbalists** may treat anorexia with bitters to enhance the appetite and improve digestion. For both anorexia and bulimia, **relaxation** and **aromatherapy** can help young people become more confident and aware of their body; self-massage using relaxing essential oils can sometimes encourage a return to a normal body image. The **homeopath** can often provide supportive treatment through a holistic approach. Specific remedies for bulimia, which may control the urge to binge, include Pulsatilla 30c (*Pulsatilla nigricans*, pasque flower) and Calcarea 30c (*Calcarea carbonica*), every 12 hours for up to 7 days when the urge to binge is strong.

APPETITE LOSS

What is it?

In children, appetite loss (anorexia) is usually temporary and caused by an emotional upset or feverish illness. Longer lasting appetite loss could suggest a more serious underlying condition and deserves investigation by a doctor.

Young children's appetites are closely geared to their energy output, so the amount they eat or drink varies from meal to meal. When a child's growth rate drops the appetite drops as well. This is most obvious between six and twelve months of age and from the age of two years. Personality also has an influence: placid babies usually eat more than determined, active ones.

From the age of five or six children – particularly girls – become consciousness of their body shape and this may become an issue. In this case the reason for not eating is easy to identify, as it usually leads to pickiness about food rather than total appetite loss. In older children and adolescents loss of interest in food may be caused by stress at home or at school or even drug abuse.

Appetite loss is not a feature of the eating disorder anorexia nervosa; on the contrary, anorexics are preoccupied with food and body weight and consciously suppress their appetite.

There may be many other reasons why a child stops eating. For example, a weaned baby who is drinking more than 600 ml/1 pint of milk a day will not want solids (500 ml/18 fl oz of milk is sufficient). Toddlers prefer grazing to eating meals, and snacks and drinks may make them feel full. In addition, a refusal to eat may indicate that the child is using food to assert their independence; this is quite common from the second year onwards.

If none of the above factors is applicable to your child, then it is possible that a baby who was perfectly well and now suddenly refuses a feed may be suffering from an illness. Check to see whether any of the symptoms listed below apply to your child.

You may notice

- *A fever (this may be a sign of infection)*
- *An upset in your family's or child's routine*
- *A blocked nose, which prevents sucking*
- *The child is teething and is finding sucking painful*
- *The child has a sore throat and is unable to drink*
- *White flecks inside the mouth, which may indicate the child has thrush*
- *Loss of weight, or weight gain is slower than usual*
- *Foul-smelling, light-coloured stools*
- *Bed-wetting or passing urine more often then normal*

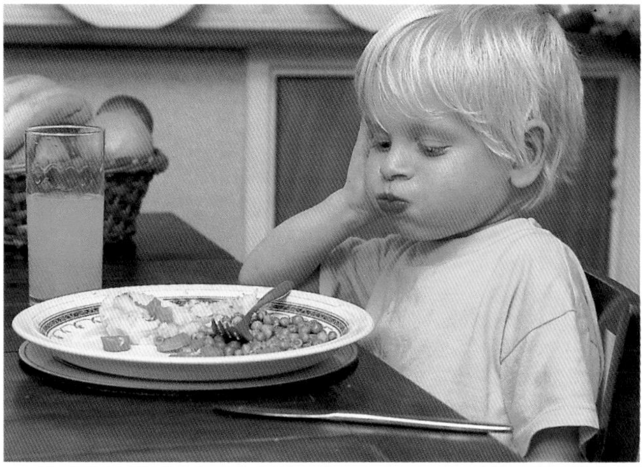

Loss of interest in food is one of the commonest early signs that a child is unwell. Forcing a child to stay at the table when he clearly has no interest in eating is almost always counterproductive, and can even lead to eating difficulties later in life. Ten minutes in front of a plate of food that is not wanted is more than enough. Just take it away without comment and try to find out why your child has lost his appetite.

What to do

If the child's appetite does not return within a few days or they are still displaying one or more of the above symptoms, see your doctor.

Complementary treatment

Aromatherapy oils can encourage salivation and peristalsis and therefore appetite. Essential oils are particularly useful for appetite loss following chemotherapy or surgery. If the cause is emotional, an appropriate **Bach flower remedy** may be effective, and **massage** can aid relaxation and increase self-esteem. **Kinesiology** may help by improving the child's general health. In Traditional Chinese Medicine appetite loss is viewed as a weakness of spleen energy, therefore **Chinese herbalism** and **acupuncture** will treat accordingly. The **homeopath** has a large number of remedies for this condition and will prescribe according to the personality, temperament and mood of the child concerned (constitutional treatment). Specific remedies include Argentum nit 6c (*Argentum nitricum*, silver nitrate) where there is also a lack of thirst.

SEE ALSO EATING DISORDERS (PAGE 248) FAILURE TO THRIVE (PAGE 71)

Stomach Ache

What is it?

A stomach ache, a pain that occurs anywhere between the bottom of the ribcage and the groin, is often referred to as abdominal pain. Stomach ache is common in children, although a child under two is unlikely to complain of it. The causes may be physical or emotional, and as a symptom on its own a stomach ache usually disappears without any treatment. Sometimes you can guess the cause – for example, a child has overeaten or eaten too quickly, causing indigestion. Often the cause is never discovered, but as stomach ache can occasionally be a sign of a serious illness, you should carefully observe children for any other signs of illness or for any worsening of the pain.

Quite a number of children of primary school age have repeated attacks of stomach ache, sometimes with vomiting, a headache, pallor and possibly sleepiness afterwards. Recurrent abdominal pain may have a link with migraine and sick headaches in adults, but many children grow out of the tendency and have no further problems. Young children will often complain of stomach ache when they have an ear ache.

You may notice

- *A child under two years of age is unable to tell you that they are in pain. The signs are crying and pulling up the legs*
- *A child over two will be able to tell you roughly where the pain is but may not be able to be very specific*
- *A child may have repeated bouts of stomach ache when they are also very pale, possibly vomiting and may have a headache*

What to do

If the child has none of the symptoms listed in the box above right, and the pain is not severe or getting any worse, let them lie down if that is what they want. Do not give the child any food or milk, but place a glass of water within reach. Give the child a covered hot-water bottle, which may help ease the pain, but never leave a young child alone with one.

If the child does not feel like drinking, just give sips of the water or gently moisten their lips. If you think the child might vomit, give them a towel to cover their clothes or the bedclothes, a basin, a face cloth, a jug of water and a glass.

Consult your doctor if you suspect that a baby or toddler under two has a stomach ache, if the child is still unwell the next day, if the pain is so bad that it stops the child in his tracks, if any vomiting continues for more than an hour or so, or if the stomach ache keeps recurring. See FEEDING & DIGESTION diagnosis (page 240) for other possible causes.

In an emergency

Contact your doctor immediately if your child develops any of the following symptoms:

- The pain continues for six hours or more without any improvement
- You notice any swelling in the groin or in a boy's testicles
- There is any pain or tenderness in the groin or in the testicles
- The child vomits but the pain still continues for three hours or more

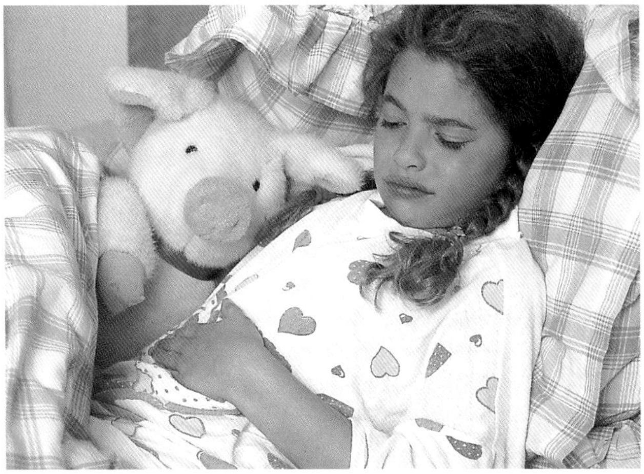

Stomach ache is a common complaint of childhood. In most cases it disappears gradually, within a few hours if it is caused by something the child has eaten. Bed rest may be the only treatment needed.

Complementary Treatment

Complementary treatments for stomach ache that is not symptomatic of a more serious condition include special **massage** techniques such as stomach channel massage, in which the leg is massaged. **Aromatherapy** oils used as a compress can be very comforting, as can a soothing herb tea such as chamomile. If the cause is emotional, an appropriate **Bach flower** remedy may be effective. **Homeopathic** first aid for stomach ache awaiting emergency treatment is Bryonia 30c (*Bryonia alba*, white or common bryony) to be given every five minutes until help arrives.

DEHYDRATION

What is it?

Dehydration occurs when the amount of water in the body drops significantly. A baby's body consists of about 75 per cent water and this proportion tapers off gradually throughout childhood to reach 60 per cent in adulthood. In mild dehydration the child loses five per cent of body weight; moderate dehydration means a loss of 10 per cent; severe dehydration means a loss of 15 per cent.

Food and drink provide a daily water input which is normally balanced by an output in urine, sweat and evaporation through the skin. In a healthy child thirst regulates fluid intake and a simple biofeedback mechanism regulates output. But if for any reason a child does not get enough fluid, or if more water leaves the body than enters it, they can become dehydrated. This is a particular problem in vomiting with diarrhoea, or if a baby has a very high temperature and cannot drink. Dehydration in a baby or a young child is always serious and needs urgent treatment. The most common cause of the condition is gastroenteritis (see page 257) or infections accompanied by a fever.

It can be difficult to see the signs of dehydration in a normally well-fed infant or toddler, but watch out for any of the symptoms listed below.

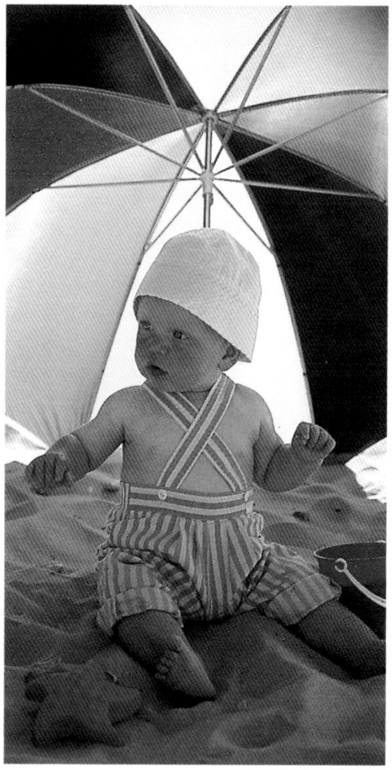

A baby outside in hot sunshine rapidly loses body fluid through sweating because of his high water turnover in relation to body weight. Protect him from dehydration by shading him from direct sun, offering frequent breastfeeds or safe, clear fluids. On holiday in a hot climate, water for babies should be pre-boiled or drinks only accepted from sealed cans or bottles.

You may notice

- *Diarrhoea and possibly vomiting as well*
- *Refusing drinks*
- *A dry nappy after several hours or not producing any urine.*
- *Any small amount of urine may be very dark*
- *Restlessness, an anxious look*

As dehydration worsens, other signs will be:

- *When you pinch the skin it takes a few seconds to become smooth again*
- *The soft spot (fontanelle) on the top of the infant's head may dip slightly*
- *The eyes look sunken and there are no tears*
- *The mouth and lips seem dry*
- *The child is thirsty, restless and irritable at first but becomes quiet and still*

What to do

Contact your doctor immediately. If the symptoms seem mild and the baby or child is still drinking, the doctor will probably prescribe an oral rehydration drink These come as powders to mix with water. Follow the instructions on the packet precisely when you make up the drink. Boil and cool tap water for babies. For older children the powder can be mixed with tap water, and they may prefer the effervescent rehydration tablets. If the baby cannot manage the whole drink, you can keep the rest in the refrigerator for up to 24 hours.

Give breastfed babies breast feeds as often as they will drink, then offer a rehydration drink from a syringe or from a cup or spoon. Offer a bottle-fed infant boiled, cooled water in addition to the rehydration drink. Flat cola or dilute apple or pineapple juice can be a temporary drink for children until the doctor has seen them.

Give children fluids every 30-60 minutes. a baby under two should drink one to one-and-a-half times their normal volume of feeds or drinks as a rehydration drink, while a child over two years of age should take 1 litre/1¾ pints of fluid every 24 hours.

Complementary Treatment

This condition requires urgent orthodox treatment, but complementary therapies may be appropriate for dealing with the after effects of dehydration. The **osteopath's** aim will be to bring the whole body back into balance; the **Chinese herbalist** will usually prescribe tonic herbs. **Kinesiology** and **Western herbalism** may also be helpful.

VOMITING

What is it?

All children vomit occasionally, and as long as this is an isolated incident and the child is otherwise well, it is not a cause for concern. However any child who vomits repeatedly risks dehydration (see page 252) especially if there is diarrhoea (see page 270) as well. Sometimes vomiting is preceded by nausea or there may be bouts of nausea on their own. These should be monitored carefully, for although they might be a symptom of an emotional problem, they may also be indicative of a more serious condition.

Always contact your doctor immediately if you note any of the symptoms listed below.

You may notice

- *The infant has lost all feeds for six hours*
- *Nappies are dry for three hours or more or a child doesn't urinate for six hours*
- *The child has vomited for 12 hours*
- *The vomiting is accompanied by a stomach ache that has lasted for three hours*
- *The child stops drinking*
- *The lips and mouth become dry*
- *The vomit is greeny-yellow*

Complementary Treatment

Chinese herbalism may prove helpful where vomiting is caused by a food blockage or digestive weakness. **Western herbalism** can also be effective: for example, for vomiting brought on by over-excitement, melissa (*Melissa officinalis*) or chamomile (*Anthemis nobilis*) tea may settle the stomach. **Homeopathic remedies** include Ipecac 6c (*Cephaelis ipecacuanha*, ipecacuanha) for vomiting generally. Remedies are to be given every hour, or every 15 minutes in severe cases, for up to 10 doses. **Relaxation** can help control the vomiting reflex following chemotherapy, radiotherapy and surgery, reducing the need to rely on anti-emetics, but the child must be taught the techniques prior to orthodox therapy. For recurrent vomiting with no known cause, the **chiropractor** would check for spinal irritation in the thoracic area. Manipulation to reduce and control the irritation would be given.

Diagnosing vomiting

Check for other signs that could be a possible cause

Infants	**What could be wrong**
Bring back a small amount of milk or curds during or after a feed	Posseting
Regularly bring back part of feeds. Otherwise well and gaining weight	Gastro-oesophageal reflux
Pallor, then violent vomiting that shoots out over 30-90cm/1-3ft	Pyloric stenosis
Diarrhoea, fever, stomach ache watery stools	Food poisoning or gastroenteritis
Stomach ache in spasms during which the child is pale and lethargic	Intussusception

Children	**What could be wrong**
Many of the following can also affect infants	
Unwell, flushed, feverish	Infection, e.g. in the urinary tract
Vomits during or immediately after coughing fit, fever, runny nose	Cough, whooping cough
Drowsiness, fever, crying, headache, stiff neck, dislikes bright light, drowsiness, reddish-purple rash	Meningitis
Severe headache, visual disturbance	Migraine
Serious stomach ache from navel to groin for four to six hours	Appendicitis
Nausea, vomiting, injury to head within the past few days	Head injury (see First Aid, page 353)
Makes a conscious effort to vomit after eating	Eating disorders

Posseting and Reflux

What is it?

Posseting occurs when a well and thriving infant brings back part of a milk feed as curds or milk, often when being winded during a feed or at the end. Some children are prone to posseting, especially if they get very hungry before a feed or swallow more air than normal as they feed. Once children are weaned on to solid foods posseting usually disappears.

Gastro-oesophageal reflux is a more severe type of vomiting (see page 253) that starts a few weeks after birth. Apart from regularly bringing back part of the feeds the baby is perfectly well. Reflux occurs because the gullet (oesophagus) is short, the ring of muscles around the entrance to the stomach is slack and the waves of muscular activity, which help the milk down into the stomach, are not strong or efficient enough. Most babies grow out of reflux naturally by their first birthday.

You may notice

Posseting

- *The infant effortlessly brings up small quantities of milk or curds with wind, but is well afterwards. The child still puts on weight and behaves normally between feeds*

Gastro-oesophageal reflux

- *The infant brings back milk at every feed. Vomiting may be quite forceful and the quantity can be so large that you wonder if any milk has stayed down*
- *The child is more likely to bring milk back if they cry*
- *Between vomiting, the child is perfectly well and usually puts on weight*
- *In a few babies there are traces of blood in the curds and milk. This is caused by the acid stomach contents damaging the lining of the gullet*

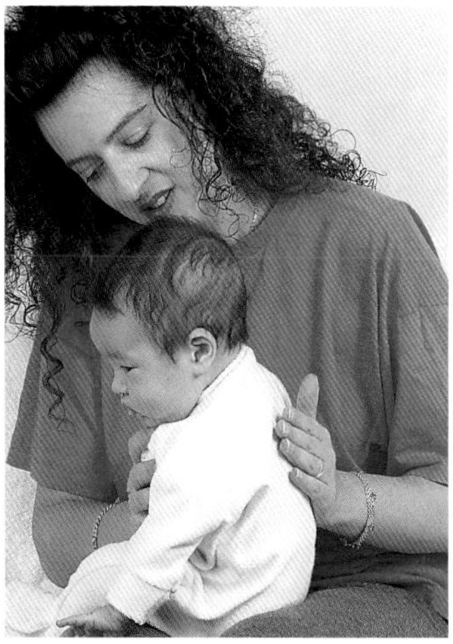

Careful feeding and winding of babies who are still being given a full milk diet can substantially reduce the frequency and the volume of the posseting. For bottle-fed babies, using a teat with a smaller hole can prevent the baby from being overwhelmed by the flow of milk into his mouth.

What to do

Feed children very carefully, making sure they swallow as little air as possible. Do not let them cry for very long before a feed. Always tilt the bottle so the teat is full. Wind gently during the feed and afterwards. If these steps do not work or you are worried about the quantities of milk the child brings back, consult your doctor.

Treatment

The doctor will examine the child, ask about feeding and order tests. These may include a barium swallow, in which the child is tilted upright and given a feed containing barium sulphate, which shows up on X-ray film. The radiographer will observe whether any of the feed goes down the wrong way into the lungs and whether it comes back up the oesophagus out of the stomach. In some hospitals the acidity of the contents of the gullet is also monitored.

The doctor may prescribe a special feed thickener which may contain an antacid (you should never thicken the child's feeds yourself, even if they are bringing back a lot of milk). To help keep milk down after a feed, seat the baby tilted at an angle of 30 degrees, and let them sleep on their side with their head raised above the level of their feet.

Complementary Treatment

Chinese herbalism links posseting and reflux to a food blockage or weakness in stomach energy, both of which are easily treated. Parents are encouraged to leave sufficient time between feeds to allow the digestion to mature. **Acupuncture**, **homeopathy** and **osteopathy** may also be helpful for these conditions, again working on strengthening the digestion. **Western herbalists** usually recommend fresh ginger root (*Zingiber officinale*), which can be added to milk for a young bottle-fed infant. Breastfeeding mothers would be advised to drink ginger tea.

Warning: Do not use ginger if there is inflammation in the digestive tract.

INTUSSUSCEPTION

What is it?

Intussusception occurs when part of the intestine telescopes in on itself. It is not common – affecting only two babies in one thousand – and it is rare in babies under one month. Most babies develop it between one month and one year, and three-quarters of all cases occur in children under two.

Intussusception most commonly arises at the junction of the small intestine and the large intestine, when a part of the small intestine collapses into the large intestine, leaving little room for waste matter to get past. If the signs are ignored or misinterpreted – as three-month colic, for example – the telescoped part of the intestine may swell and cause a blockage, resulting in a serious obstruction. The cause of the condition is not fully understood, although in many children there is an association with an infection, and the first signs often follow a cough or cold or similar infection.

You may notice

- *Severe, colicky pains – enough to make an infant scream and draw up their legs in agony*
- *The infant turns very pale and becomes limp*
- *The attack lasts a few minutes, after which the infant calms down, appears perfectly well and may fall peacefully asleep. More attacks of screaming and pallor follow within minutes or hours. The intervals between screaming bouts get shorter*
- *Possibly vomiting*
- *Possibly blood and mucus in the faeces*
- *The signs in older children are less dramatic. They may suffer from stomach ache and lose interest in food*

Treatment

Contact your doctor immediately. The child will need to be admitted to hospital, where they will be checked for signs of shock and given extra fluids. An X-ray, which will show the blockage in the intestine, or an ultrasound scan of the abdomen, showing the section of the intestine that has collapsed in on itself, will be performed. The child may be given a gas enema, in which a fine tube is inserted into the rectum and oxygen or air is introduced under pressure to force the doubled back section of intestine to straighten out. Alternatively they may be given a barium enema, in which liquid barium is used under pressure instead of oxygen or air. The child will then stay in hospital for a day to check that the intestine doesn't telescope again.

If these measures do not correct the telescoped intestine, the child will need an operation to straighten or cut out the collapsed section. In the majority of children who have this treatment the problem never returns.

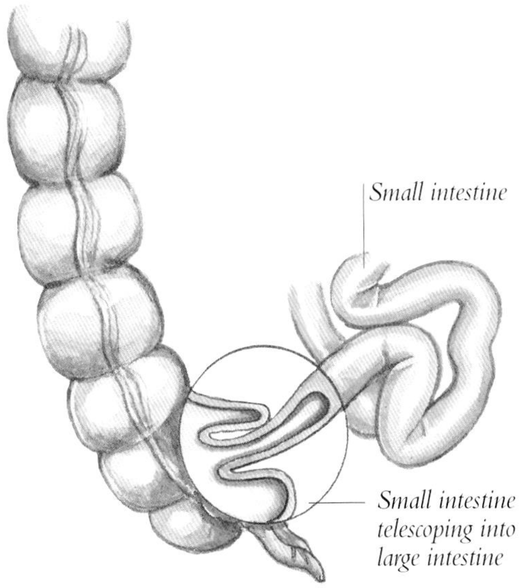

When one end of the small intestine telescopes into the large intestine, muscular spasms follow. The spasms are the body's attempt to correct the condition. When these fail, the intestine remains collapsed and partially obstructed. Continued spasm causes the typical colicky pain that is associated with intussusception.

Complementary Treatment

Complementary therapy will be restricted to alleviating negative emotions that arise from the condition and from orthodox treatment. The safe and gentle **Bach flower remedies** can be effective in dealing with anger and frustration that often accompanies physical pain. Rescue Remedy may be appropriate following surgery in dealing with emotional trauma. **Homeopathic remedies** that can be helpful when given every 15 minutes while waiting for help to arrive include: Belladonna 30c (*Atropa belladonna*, deadly nightshade); Colocynth 6c (*Citrullus colocynthis*, bitter apple) for pain that is relieved by bending the child double; and Nux 6c (*Strychnos nux vomica*, poison nut tree) for pain that is not relieved by bending the child double. (See page 276 for remedies that help before and following surgery.)

Soiling and Encopresis

What are they?

Soiling occurs when a child regularly passes liquid or part liquid faeces into clothing. Encopresis means passing a stool not in the toilet or pot but somewhere socially unacceptable instead. A minority of children with these problems have never learned to control their bowels, but the majority have previously achieved control. Over a quarter of the children affected also wet the bed (see page 302).

Soiling and encopresis are not the same as acquiring bowel control later than normal, that is, over the age of three. Nor are they the same as having the occasional accident, which happens to all children.

Chronic constipation often underlies both soiling and encopresis, but serious medical causes of soiling and encopresis are rare. Although encopresis is unusual after the age of ten, the social consequences – distaste from adults and rejection by other children – are very serious. Because there may be an emotional problem that needs resolving, the child should be given immediate and sensitive support.

You may notice

- *Solid or liquid faeces in the child's underpants. This is not the same as 'streaking', when the child's underpants are dirty because they have not been careful enough about wiping themselves after using the toilet*
- *Dirty pants may be hidden*
- *A smell of faeces*
- *Stomach ache, loss of appetite and energy*

Dozens of nappies on a washing line are perfectly normal when there is a baby in the house: having to hang out dozens of pairs of underpants because an older child is soiling is quite another matter: both child and parents with need expert and sensitive help and advice.

What to do

Keep a week's diary of when the child soils, where and how soon after a meal. Have reasonably regular meals and take the child to the toilet 20–30 minutes afterwards. Give a warm drink with the meal to stimulate the gastrocolic reflex – this is especially important after breakfast.

Make going to the toilet a relaxing experience. Tell the child to take a book, hand-held computer game or tape with them and encourage them to sit there for five to ten minutes. Some children soil because they don't go to the toilet regularly or dash out too quickly. They then get into the habit of holding on for too long until they are caught out. Make sure the child takes regular exercise as this helps get the bowels moving.

Put a nappy bucket half-filled with nappy sterilizing fluid next to the toilet for accidentally soiled pants. Check that the nursery/school toilets don't frighten or put the child off going. Some young children hang on to avoid using school toilets.

If the child stains their pants and has a mixture of old, hard faeces with fresh stools, the cause may be constipation. Increase the intake of drinks, fibre (wheat cereals, brown bread, baked beans) and fruit (unpeeled apples and pears are rich in fibre, bananas have little, orange juice none) and talk to the health professional you find most approachable.

If these steps do not work or your soiling is severe, consult your doctor, who will be able to prescribe a drug to clear constipation and may check for any underlying cause.

Praise the child whenever they make even a small amount of clear progress. Be prepared for treatment to take weeks or even months.

Who can help?

For organizations who can help, see the Directory.

Complementary Treatment

The **arts therapies** and the **Bach flower remedies** can play a helpful role where there is an emotional cause. Walnut is a beneficial remedy whenever a life change has taken place, and it helps the child to settle down again. Other remedies would be chosen according to individual needs and the issues involved. **Aromatherapy**, **massage** and **relaxation** can be helpful where the problem is related to stress. Vaporized oils and/or massage before bed will help to relax the child. **Homeopathy** will treat according to the personality, temperament and mood of the child concerned (constitutional treatment) if the cause is emotional. Otherwise it will be treated as constipation.

GASTROENTERITIS

What is it?

Gastroenteritis is inflammation of the stomach and intestines. It is extremely common in babies and young children. Most attacks are caused by a rotavirus, a highly infectious organism that is most prevalent in the winter and early spring. The condition can also be caused by other infectious organisms – adenoviruses, parvo-like viruses, astroviruses and caliciviruses. The first symptom may be a respiratory infection.

Gastroenteritis can be easily passed from one child to another, either by droplet spread or when children with unwashed hands touch food that is then eaten by another child. A significant number of cases of gastroenteritis are caused by food poisoning, particularly during the summer.

You may notice

- *Fever and vomiting that lasts for one to three days*
- *Diarrhoea, which is more copious, frequent (between six and ten times a day), watery and smellier than usual faeces. Diarrhoea can last from four to seven days*

What to do

Consult a doctor immediately, especially if any of the following apply: a baby under six months misses two feeds or is vomiting and also has diarrhoea; a child under three has diarrhoea and is vomiting; a child of any age cannot keep fluids down. A baby who is keeping nothing down and has diarrhoea risks becoming dehydrated (see page 252).

To treat the diarrhoea and vomiting, breastfeeding mothers should continue breastfeeding; all mothers should stop giving cows' milk and other foods, and offer instead flat cola drinks, diluted apple or pineapple juice and diluted fruit juice drinks. Rehydration drinks, available as powders to mix with water, should also be given. Follow the packet instructions precisely.

For babies, boil and cool tap water, but for an older child use straight tap water and perhaps the effervescent rehydration tablets. If the baby cannot manage the whole drink, keep the rest in the refrigerator for up to 24 hours. Give the child fluid every 30-60 minutes or between breastfeeds to avoid more vomiting. If vomiting persists after a feed, drinking fluids little and often – a 5 ml/1 teaspoon every five minutes – helps absorption and reduces vomiting.

Once the diarrhoea and vomiting have stopped, offer the child drinks of half-milk, half-water, or make up bottle feed to half strength. After a day on these fluids, graduate to full strength milk and then to solids, using bland foods or puréed vegetables first. Older children can be given food such as plain biscuits or toast.

Outlook

Breastfeeding protects babies against rotavirus infections as breast milk contains antibodies (IgA antibodies) specific to the virus. A significant number of younger children and babies develop a temporary lactose intolerance after recovering from gastroenteritis. When they start to drink milk again, watery, frothy, acid diarrhoea (see page 270) is produced. Such children will need to have a lactose-free formula for a few weeks.

Regular handwashing using warm water and soap after using the lavatory and before cooking, preparing food or eating, is one of the most effective ways in which you can help to protect your child against gastroenteritis. This takes on an added importance when your child is recovering from a gastrointestinal infection.

Complementary Treatment

Chinese herbalism may be particularly useful for toning the body and rehydrating and supporting the stomach after a bout of gastroenteritis. **Acupuncture** can be effective for both acute and chronic cases. For children other than babies, **nutritional therapists** may advise fasting during an attack, as food is thought to prolong the complaint. Astringent herbal teas such as blackberry and peppermint may be taken. Other complementary therapies that offer help for this condition include **homeopathy**, **kinesiology** and **osteopathy**.

Warning: Do not allow children to fast without first obtaining the advice of a qualified practitioner.

CONSTIPATION

What is it?

Constipation in children can develop for a variety of reasons, many of them quite harmless. For example, if children are short of fluids or fibre in the diet, or they have had a feverish illness, then constipation may be a short-term difficulty. Toddlers under pressure to be potty-trained can be vulnerable to developing constipation, as can children who become engrossed in play and forget to go to the toilet. (Breastfed babies may not move their bowels for days, but this does not mean they are constipated.) In rare cases constipation may be a sign of a more serious disorder. It is best to deal with constipation immediately because waste matter that has built up in the rectum dries out quickly, making it more difficult and more painful to pass.

A high fluid and high fibre diet can be helpful in preventing the onset of constipation as well as in treating it. Children who dislike high fibre cereals such as muesli can be encouraged to drink fruit juice and to eat extra fruit.

You may notice

- *The child goes longer than normal without passing a motion. When they do, it's hard and rough or very large*
- *Poor appetite, stomach ache*
- *Smelly soiling, with lumps of old stools mixed in with fresh faeces*
- *Streaks of blood in pants, nappy or on the stools*
- *Wetting the bed at night again*
- *Lethargy*

What to do

Note when the child passes a motion, what it is like, their behaviour at the time and what they have eaten or drunk. Don't get too upset, however, if the child doesn't have a bowel movement every day; for some children (and adults) the normal rhythm is every few days.

Boost fluid intake with home-made ice lollies and extra drinks. Establish a regular pattern of daily meals. Give more wholemeal foods and whole breakfast cereals such as wheat biscuits or porridge. Start gradually with a mixture of white and wholemeal flour, pasta, cereals and rice.

Offer more fresh fruit and vegetables. Dried fruits such as raisins, apricots and figs help, as do peas and beans, sweetcorn, baked beans and jacket potatoes.

Massage the abdomen of a constipated child in a circular motion using baby lotion,

You can encourage toddlers to move their bowels by putting a toddler step by the toilet, and showing them how to push with their feet. If a toddler does become constipated while potty training, put them back in nappies for a month. When you re-start, make training fun with rewards for performance – such as a hug or quality time – and make no comments on accidents.

Don't give the child any laxatives, drugs or suppositories except on medical advice.

Treatment

Consult your doctor if the above doesn't work or if you notice any blood on the stools. Don't delay in asking for help as the sooner constipation is addressed the easier it is to rectify. The doctor may examine the child's anus to check the muscle tone and see if there are any tears, and may suggest a mild softening laxative such as lactulose or docusate sodium. This should be taken with six to eight cups of water a day and will help clear the bowels within 24 hours. Some children need to take laxatives for months and some also need senna, a bowel stimulant laxative (see below) to help establish regular habits. If these don't work, the doctor may refer the child to hospital for further investigation.

Complementary Treatment

Chinese herbalists believe the condition is usually caused by a food blockage in babies, and weakness in liver energy in older children, but there may also be an emotional problem. It should be treated until cured to avoid problems later in life. **Nutritional therapists** point to lack of fibre in the diet as the main cause, although it can also be a result of magnesium deficiency, food allergy or slack abdominal muscles. **Reflexology** is most effective for stool retention and constipation after surgery and radiotherapy. **Western herbalists** have a range of laxatives, such as the stimulant senna (*Senna alexandrina*) and the soothing bulk laxative psyllium seed (*Plantago psyllium*). Other appropriate therapies include **acupuncture**, **osteopathy**, **aromatherapy massage**, and **relaxation**.

Colic

What is it?

Colic is more than just crying. It is an unsoothable attack of misery and apparent pain that usually starts in the evening and lasts for hours. During a bout of colic intense crying gives way to fussing, when the baby can be soothed temporarily but will quickly start crying again. Colic is very common – at least one infant in five develops it, often starting in the first weeks of life, reaching a peak around six weeks and tailing off after the age of three months (this is known as three-month colic). In the past, explanations for colic have centred on digestive tract problems, but the view is gaining ground that colic is not a separate illness, rather it is actually an extreme form of normal crying.

Strategies for dealing with a colicky baby

- Offer breast or bottle even if it is only an hour since the last feed. Some babies like to suck longer than feed. Small, frequent feeds suit some colicky babies better
- Wind the baby over your shoulder. Crying makes them swallow air
- Change the nappy
- Give a cuddly joggle. Warm, rhythmic movement works wonders. Some babies prefer a gentle rock in a warm bath
- Put the baby in a sling – if your back will take it
- Take the baby for a bumpy walk or drive
- Distract the baby with a tape of your favourite music (they may have heard it in the womb) or a womb noise tape. These work best if started in the first month. Beyond a month, try something louder, such as a vacuum cleaner
- Swaddle the baby firmly but not tightly in their cot blanket or shawl, arms and legs inside
- Lay the baby tummy down on a well-wrapped hot-water bottle on your knees
- Give a dummy or colic drops
- Leave the baby swaddled in the cot with the lights dim or off for up to 15 minutes. Check every few minutes
- Turn the baby alarm around so he can hear you, not you him

You may notice

- *The infant screams on and off after feeds, especially in the evening. The screaming may start during the feed*
- *The crying continues for hours. The infant then falls asleep exhausted*
- *Unmistakable signs of pain: red face, clenched fists, tense tummy, knees pulled up*
- *Between the bouts of crying, the infant is healthy and*
- *happy and develops normally*

What to do

Contact the doctor if there are other signs of ill-health such as vomiting or diarrhoea, or if the crying is different from normal crying. Once the baby is pronounced healthy, work out a colic strategy based on what works. If you need support, join a baby-sitting circle, explaining the problem when you join, so you can get out one evening a week with your partner.

Who can help?

For organizations offering help and advice, see the Directory.

Complementary Treatment

The **Western herbalist** will usually treat with antispasmodic and other herbs, which can be very effective. **Chiropractors** frequently treat this condition, and babies can respond very well to gentle work on the spine. Some **aromatherapy** oils can reduce spasm and pain when used in a warm, comforting compress. Both **acupuncture** and **Chinese herbalism** offer treatment, Chinese herbalism in the form of soothing prepared medicines. Rescue Remedy, a **Bach flower remedy**, applied to the temples, fontenelles, wrists and stomach can be soothing and aid relaxation. Rescue Remedy diluted in cooled, boiled water can also be given by mouth. Treatment by an **osteopath** can be very helpful but will depend on the cause. **Reflexology** may also prove beneficial. **Homeopathic remedies** include Byronia 30c (*Bryonia alba*, white or common bryony), given every five minutes for up to ten doses, for a infant who is very irritable and screams at the slightest movement.

PYLORIC STENOSIS

What is it?

Pyloric stenosis is a thickening and narrowing of the ring of muscle (the pylorus) that links the stomach with the small intestine. A blockage results, which means that when milk reaches the stomach it can get no further, and when the stomach contracts it is vomited back. Pyloric stenosis is more common in boys and may run in families. It usually develops two or three weeks after birth, when there is repeated, forceful vomiting. However signs may not show until the child is six weeks old, or, more rarely, even three months old.

Pyloric stenosis is serious because dehydration will occur if milk cannot be kept down. A simple operation can correct the condition so eliminating further feeding problems.

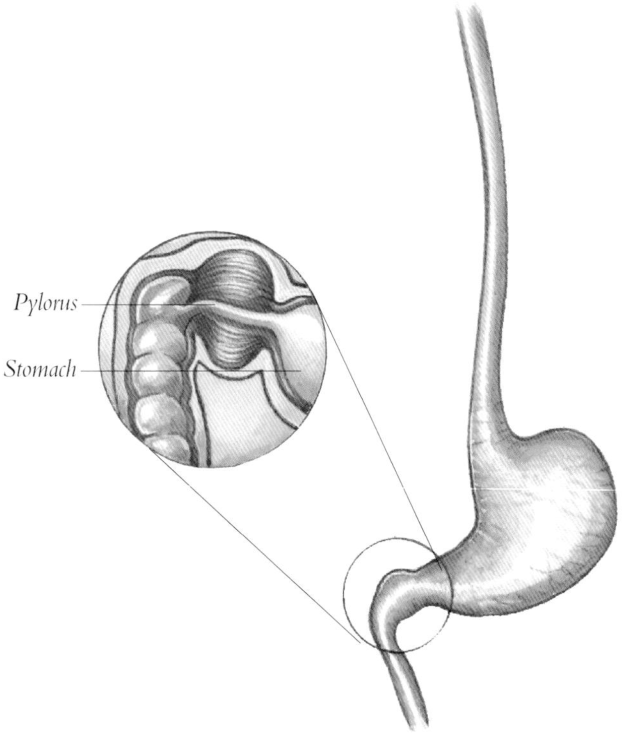

In pyloric stenosis, the muscular wall at the outlet of the stomach into the intestine is thickened. When milk cannot get through at the proper rate, the stomach's attempts to force it out project it through the mouth.

You may notice

- *An otherwise well infant starts to vomit after feeds. The force of the vomiting (called projectile vomiting) increases, and it becomes so violent that milk curds are spurted 30-90cm/1-3ft away*
- *The infant is hungry and wants to feed soon after vomiting*
- *Very little urine is passed. Nappies may stay dry*
- *There may be constipation or no bowel movements*
- *Weight gain slows down, then stops, and the infant may start to lose weight*
- *If the vomiting continues, the baby will develop symptoms of dehydration*

Treatment

Contact your doctor if the child vomits forcefully after two consecutive feeds or if a pattern of repeated and forceful vomiting after feeds develops in a baby under three months of age. Meanwhile, offer the baby sips of boiled and cooled water or short and frequent breastfeeds.

The doctor will observe the child's abdomen during feeding to see if there are muscle contractions, which show that the stomach is not emptying, and also feel for the thickened outlet on the right between the rib cage and the navel. If pyloric stenosis is immediately diagnosed, the child will be referred to a paediatric surgeon, but if there still is doubt, the doctor will order tests. These may include an ultrasound scan, which would show thickening and narrowing at the outlet from the stomach. Less commonly, a barium meal will be given in the form of a feed containing barium sulphate, which shows up on X-ray film. The radiographer will observe whether the feed goes down the oesophagus, into the stomach and towards the outlet.

If the condition is diagnosed a simple operation to cut open a thickened section of the tube will be performed. Before surgery the child will be given fluids to correct the effects of dehydration. The operation will be carried out under a local or general anaesthetic. Within hours the child will be able to take feeds again, and within two days will be back to normal.

Complementary Treatment

Acupuncture and **osteopathy** may give support to orthodox treatment. China 6c (*China officinalis*, Peruvian bark) is a **homeopathic** remedy to be given prior to surgery – four doses at two-hourly intervals. (For useful homeopathic remedies following surgery see page 76.) **Bach flower remedies** may help to alleviate fear and anxiety prior to surgery and emotional adjustment during recovery. **Aromatherapy**, **massage** and **relaxation** may also be beneficial while the child is convalescing.

SEE ALSO VOMITING (PAGE 252) POSSETING AND REFLUX (PAGE 254)

Crohn's Disease

What is it?

Crohn's disease is one of the two inflammatory bowel diseases, the other being ulcerative colitis. The condition can affect any part of the digestive tract, but the primary sites are the large intestine (or colon), the small intestine, the rectum and the anus. The most common site is the section of bowel where the small intestine joins the large intestine (the ileum). The intestinal wall reacts to the inflammation by thickening and developing patches of deep, penetrating ulcers, resulting in abdominal pain, urgent and persistent diarrhoea, and sometimes rectal bleeding.

Crohn's disease is not common but it appears to be on the increase. It can affect people of any age, but one of the peak periods of development is late childhood and adolescence. It often runs in families and is slightly more prevalent in females. The cause is not known, although one theory points to exposure very early in life to the measles virus in genetically susceptible people. There is no cure, rather periods of remission, but the worst of the symptoms can be controlled.

You may notice

- *Repeated bouts of severe abdominal pain*
- *Persistent diarrhoea*
- *Weight loss*
- *Slowing down of growth, which may stop altogether, and sexual development*
- *Mouth ulcers*
- *Fever*
- *Rashes*
- *Joint pains*
- *Appetite loss*

Treatment

Contact your doctor, who will refer the child to the hospital for tests. These may include a colonoscopy, in which a flexible fibre-optic tube will be used to examine the lower end of the intestine, and a biopsy of the intestinal lining. The child will be sedated before the tests are carried out. A barium enema may also be given so that any intestinal abnormalities can be clearly seen on X-ray.

Treatment consists of keeping symptoms under control with drugs while making sure the diet is as nutritious as possible. During a flare-up, steroids, which control the inflammation, are given by mouth or as an enema, or as a special liquid diet, which is either drunk or given through an intragastric tube. High doses are used initially and then reduced, and may be given on alternate days to achieve a balance between allowing the child to grow normally and controlling the inflammation. An anti-inflammatory drug such as mesalazine is also given.

During a serious flare-up the intestines will need to be rested, and the child may be fed intravenously or given liquid feeds. Sometimes the child has overnight drip feeds that are rich in nutrients and calories, and are designed to help the child catch up growth if this was retarded prior to diagnosis. Once the child starts eating normally again the diet should remain nutrient-rich and varied.

A few children still fail to thrive despite this treatment and for them surgery to remove the inflamed or obstructed parts of the digestive tract – a colectomy – can make a dramatic improvement in their lives. In the long term, however, symptoms tend to return.

Coping with Crohn's disease

Children will need a great deal of parental support as they may feel embarrassed by their condition, and by their slow physical and sexual development. They will always need ready access to a toilet.

Who can help?

For organizations offering help, advice and information, see the Directory.

Complementary Treatment

In many cases **nutritional therapy** links this disease to food allergy, and therapists use a range of nutritional products to aid healing and reduce permeability of the gut. Individual dietary programmes will be worked out to provide nutrients that are lacking as a result of the disease. **Homeopathy** may be very helpful in relieving symptoms, but consulting an experienced homeopath is strongly advised. Treatment will be according to the personality, temperament and mood of the child concerned (constitutional treatment). **Western herbalism** may also be helpful in treating some of the symptoms and any related stress.

Ulcerative Colitis

What is it?

Ulcerative colitis is one of the two inflammatory bowel diseases, the other being Crohn's disease. In ulcerative colitis the colon and/or the rectum become swollen, inflamed and ulcerated, resulting in severe left-sided abdominal pain, diarrhoea, weight loss and tiredness.

Although ulcerative colitis is not common in children, it often starts in the teens and remains as a life-long illness. Symptoms are not continuous but come and go with a frequency that varies considerably from child to child. Only one affected child in ten will ever have one attack of colitis. Around 20 per cent of affected children have symptoms every few months but are well at other times. Relatively frequent flare-ups are not uncommon in many of the others.

Cause

Colitis in babies may be caused by an allergy to cows' milk protein (see Lactose intolerance, page 244) and around ten per cent of people with colitis find that milk makes their colitis worse. In older children and adults the cause is not clear.

Inflammatory bowel diseases can be difficult to diagnose in children because they occur so infrequently. The symptoms are also similar to those of much commoner conditions. Some children show a marked delay in growth but once treatment starts they are able to catch up.

You may notice

- *Frequent diarrhoea, worse in the early morning and sometimes occurring at night*
- *Mucus and blood mixed in with the faeces*
- *Stomach aches*
- *Weight loss and failure to grow*
- *Mild anaemia, caused by loss of blood*

Treatment

Contact your doctor, who may want to check a specimen of the child's stool for infection. The child may then be referred to hospital for tests. These will include a colonoscopy – in which a flexible fibre-optic tube will be used to examine the lower end of the intestine from the inside – and a biopsy of the intestinal lining. These procedures are carried out under sedation. A barium enema may be also be given so that any intestinal abnormalities can be clearly seen on X-ray.

The treatment involves both diet and medication. Any foods that make the diarrhoea worse can be avoided. These may include cows' milk – which causes symptoms in about one-tenth of sufferers – but discuss this with your doctor before trying out a milk-free diet. Other foods which commonly upset colitis sufferers include peas, nuts and wheat-based products. Resting the bowel during a flare-up can help it recover more quickly. Children can be given intravenous feeds or put on a liquid diet (known as enteral feeding) of fluids containing pre-digested nutrients.

The drug sulphasalazine or mesalazine can help to prevent colitis if taken even when the child is well. In addition, children need steroids to soothe the inflammation during a flare-up. Some drugs are given by mouth, others as an enema. Children may also be given drugs to control diarrhoea, to see them through the school day.

Most people never need surgery for colitis, but a colectomy – the removal of the diseased section of colon – produces a great improvement in health.

Coping with colitis

Children will need a great deal of parental support as they will feel embarrassed by their condition. They will need ready access to a toilet.

Who can help?

For organizations offering help and support, see the Directory

Complementary Treatment

Acupuncture can be effective for both chronic and acute phases, particularly if children are seen in the early stages of the disease. **Osteopathy** may help, but this will very much depend on the cause. The **nutritional therapist** will be able to advise parents and child on necessary dietary changes, and probably the need for vitamin, mineral and other supplements. **Relaxation** will help to reduce stress that is related to the condition.

COELIAC DISEASE

What is it?

Coeliac disease (also known as gluten enteropathy) is a disorder of the upper part of the small intestine, the lining cells of which become damaged by gluten, the protein found in wheat, rye, barley and possibly oats. Once damaged the intestine is unable to absorb the fats, calcium and other nutrients from food, which then pass through the digestive system and emerge as diarrhoea or bulky, foul smelling stools, or become lodged in the digestive tract, causing constipation. Although the symptoms – such as weight loss, bloated stomach, anaemia and listlessness – usually appear gradually, occasionally babies with coeliac disease can become seriously ill with acute diarrhoea and vomiting leading to dehydration.

The cause of the condition is unknown, but it might be a result of an allergic reaction, a lack of an enzyme that breaks down gluten or an intestinal membrane abnormality. It has also been suggested that babies who are breastfed or who are not introduced early in life to foods containing gluten may avoid the condition. Yet coeliac disease does tend to run in families. Some babies develop a temporary gluten intolerance but true coeliac disease is a life-long condition that requires a life-long diet. However it is completely manageable and the child will remain healthy as long as foods containing gluten are avoided (but see Complementary Treatment, below).

You may notice

- *An infant who was previously completely healthy develops symptoms after starting to eat gluten-containing foods such as rusks or bread*
- *The infant stops gaining weight and loses their appetite.*
- *They may start to lose weight*
- *The infant may pass frequent large, pale, porridgy stools that smell foul, float in the toilet and are hard to flush away*
- *The infant may become miserable and listless*
- *The infant may vomit and develop watery diarrhoea*
- *Eventually the infant's stomach looks swollen, compared with his wasted bottom and thighs*

What to do

Don't assume that your child has this condition, as coeliac disease can mimic other digestive disorders. Also, don't change the child's diet, because it is essential for correct diagnosis that the child is on a diet containing gluten when tests are carried out.

If necessary, contact your doctor, who will refer the child to hospital for tests. These will include a blood sample to be tested for general abnormalities suggesting anaemia, and for particular antibodies (known as endomysial antibodies) that are created by the immune system in response to gluten. There may also be tests on the urine and faeces. The child will also have a biopsy of the intestinal lining, initially while they are still eating a diet that contains gluten. Another biopsy will be performed in babies under 18 months of age when foods containing gluten have been reintroduced.

If the diagnosis is confirmed a dietitian will provide a gluten-free diet and, once followed, the child should improve dramatically. They will be happier, start to gain weight and grow faster, and their stools will be of normal size, smell and colour. The child may need vitamin D supplements and possibly iron and folic acid to deal with deficiencies.

Weaning foods for babies usually include rusks. However in susceptible babies rusks made with wheat flour can trigger inflammation of the gastro-intestinal tract, known as coeliac disease . Delay giving wheat-based rusks until a baby is at least six months old.

Who can help?

For organizations offering support, see the Directory.

Complementary Treatment

Consultation with an experienced **homeopath**, may make the avoidance of gluten unnecessary. The homeopath and **acupuncturist** will treat according to the personality, temperament and mood of the child concerned, and include essential dietary changes. **Chinese herbalism** will concentrate on supportive treatment and take measures to prevent further problems later in life. **Nutritional therapists** will be able to advise on a gluten-free diet. **Kinesiology** may aid in the diagnosis.

Travel Sickness

What is it?

Travel (or motion) sickness starts around the age of two (before that age the brain is not sufficiently developed), and many children learn to compensate for it or overcome it. It is caused by confused and conflicting messages to the balance organs in the brain concerned with movement. For example, if a child is reading a book in a car, the balance organs tell the brain the vehicle is moving but the eyes tell the brain it is still.

Certain types of movement are more liable to provoke travel sickness – rhythmically jerking up and down, moving forwards to a jolting halt or suddenly changing direction. Travel sickness is usually worse on boats and in cars, but fast, tilting trains can also produce it. It can even affect children playing in playgrounds or fun parks. Once a child has been travel sick, even thinking about a journey can often bring on waves of nausea.

Travel sickness is usually worse in the morning, and girls seem to be more susceptible to it than boys.

You may notice

- *The child goes very quiet*
- *The child turns pale and sweaty*
- *The child becomes drowsy or sleepy*
- *The child feels nauseated and within minutes they may become sick*

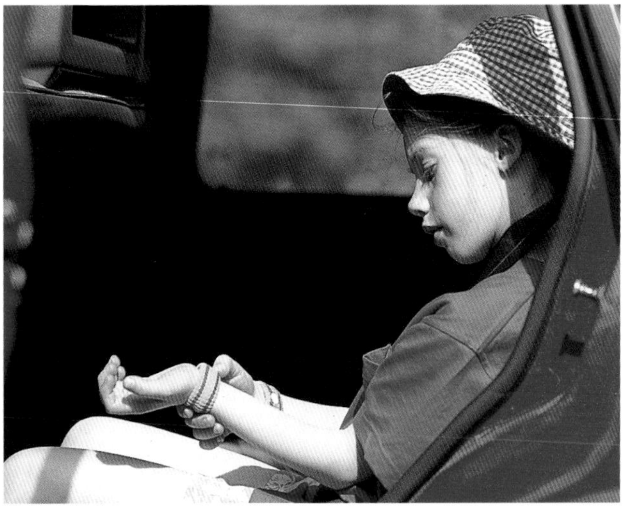

The child is using an elasticated wristband incorporating a plastic button, which controls nausea without the use of drugs. It is worn over the pericardium 6 acupressure point (the Nei-Kuan point) above the wrist. This point lies three finger widths above the upper wrist crease on the inside of the arm, and between the two tendons.

What to do

On a car journey, place the child where they can see out of the window. The best position is the middle of the back seat, as long as you have a three-point seat belt fitted. Keep the child's head still with a travel pillow or a children's head rest. Do not let them read if they are prone to sickness; let them listen to tapes instead. If the child becomes sick, stop the car. Let the child sit outside until they feel better or have been sick. Give sips of cold water. In a plane, avoid the tail section; on a bus avoid seats over the wheels. If you are on a boat, let the child lie down flat on their back near the centre of the ship or lean over the side and watch the horizon.

Preventing travel sickness

The solutions are often individual, but you can try these

- Give the child a light snack before setting off. Both hunger and a full stomach make travel sickness worse
- Keep a supply of barley sugar, boiled sweets or ginger biscuits in the car. A flask of iced water helps
- Take antihistamine tablets or elixir 30 minutes before setting off
- Try travel sickness tablets containing hyoscine. A children's version is suitable from the age of three. The tablets are best taken half an hour before the journey. Hyoscine impregnated skin patches may become available for use by children who are more than ten years of age
- Keep an emergency kit: a lidded plastic box, with a shake of bicarbonate of soda to neutralize the smell of vomit; a flask of cold water and a face cloth

Complementary Treatment

In **Western herbalism**, herbs such as ginger (*Zingiber officinale*), can be very helpful when taken before and during the journey. Ginger is also the first choice in **Chinese herbalism**, which also offers pochai pills as an effective treatment. An **acupressure** device worn around the wrist (see caption, left), can be very effective for all types of sickness.

Warning: Do not use ginger if there is inflammation in the digestive tract.

Appendicitis

What is it?

Appendicitis is an acute bacterial infection of the appendix, the finger-shaped tube of gut located at the end of the large intestine and attached to the caecum on the right-hand side of the abdomen. Although the cause is not always known, appendicitis often results from a build-up of faeces in the appendix which causes a blockage. Appendicitis is not common in children under two, but it becomes more frequent in older children and teenagers. In young children appendicitis can worsen very rapidly. The infected appendix can burst, causing a more widespread peritonitis – an inflammation of the membrane that lines the abdomen and covers the abdominal organs.

You may notice

- *Severe but intermittent stomach ache near the navel, moving down to the right groin. Young children cannot localize the pain accurately*
- *Nausea, sometimes vomiting, and diarrhoea. The child will not want anything to eat*
- *The child stays still because moving or walking around makes the pain worse, as do sneezing or coughing. They may try to prevent anyone touching the lower right part of their abdomen because it is so tender*
- *Slight fever (37-38.5°C/98.6-101.3°F). To help with diagnosis, put a feverstrip on the child's right groin for 15 seconds. Repeat on the left groin. In appendicitis, the right groin is likely to be a little warmer*
- *The vomiting and diarrhoea may at first suggest gastroenteritis or another abdominal disorder*

The appendix – a closed finger-like tube sticking out from the intestine – is situated at the caecum, the beginning of the small intestine. A swollen appendix is painful and needs immediate medical attention.

Treatment

Call the doctor immediately. Do not give the child any food or drink in case surgery is necessary. Do not even give paracetamol for the pain and fever. Cool the face and lips with a damp face cloth. Let the child lie still.

If the doctor suspects appendicitis, the child should go to hospital immediately for observation and tests, including urine tests, ultrasound scans and possibly a chest X-ray. Once diagnosed an appendectomy will be performed. The surgery takes about ten minutes and is done under a general anaesthetic. Speed is essential, because the appendix may perforate, causing peritonitis. The treatment will then also entail washing the affected area, inserting a tube to drain off pus and giving the child antibiotics. The operation leaves a small scar above the right groin.

The child will be able to eat and drink the day after the operation. Drainage tubes will be removed after two days and the child will be allowed to go home within two to three days. Seven to ten days after the operation the stitches will be removed, and within two weeks the child will usually be fit enough to return to school. For the first two weeks children should avoid playing any games that might knock the operation site.

Complementary Treatment

Chinese herbalism may be helpful for cases of 'grumbling' appendix by clearing abdominal stagnation. For surgical procedures, **Bach flower remedies** may calm the child prior to surgery and help with the emotional aspects of convalescence. Rescue Remedy can be particularly beneficial. **Homeopathic remedies** can help prior to and following surgery (see page 276). **Relaxation** can help control the vomiting reflex that often occurs after a general anaesthetic, thereby reducing the need to rely on anti-emetics. However the child must be taught the techniques before they have surgery.

LIVER DISEASE

What is it?

The liver performs vital functions in the body, including making and processing chemicals in the blood and disposing of wastes, but it can become damaged in a number of ways. In children these are: through metabolic disorders, congenital defects, poisons and infection.

Metabolic disorders are caused by inherited enzyme deficiencies and are quite rare. They can lead to faulty chemical processes inside the liver which eventually damage the organ. For example, in the condition called kernicterus, which affects mainly premature babies, a deficiency of enzymes in the liver will cause a build-up of bile, resulting in severe jaundice (see page 267). Or there may be a deficiency in the enzymes that convert galactose, derived from milk, into glucose, resulting in a rapid fall in the level of blood sugar.

The liver may also be damaged by a congenital defect such as an obstruction, which blocks the flow of bile out of the liver to the gall bladder. Drugs – for example too much paracetamol – poisons and a poor blood supply can all damage the organ. In older children liver disease is more likely to be caused by an infection such as hepatitis.

Children with liver disease usually show only a few of the symptoms that are listed below. Sometimes a baby appears to be perfectly healthy, but the doctor notices a problem at the six-week health check or later, such as an enlarged liver or enlarged spleen.

You may notice

- *In young infants, the first sign of liver disease is usually jaundice that lasts more than two weeks after birth and is not breastmilk jaundice (see page 267). The whites of the eyes look yellow and the skin sun-tanned*
- *Pale, fatty or offensive stools*
- *Deep yellow urine. It is never watery or colourless*
- *Poor or possibly excessive feeding and possibly slow growth*
- *Tendency to bleed or bruise because the blood is slow to clot*
- *Swollen stomach*
- *Nausea, vomiting, appetite loss*
- *Stomach ache*
- *Tiredness*
- *Vomiting blood or passing it in the stools*

Treatment

Contact your doctor. Liver disease is very rare and there is probably a harmless explanation for the signs you have noticed. However, spotting liver disease early greatly improves the chances of successful treatment. Such treatment will depend upon the underlying cause. Some conditions get better on their own. For others, the child will need drugs or a special diet. Babies born with an obstruction to the bile outflow from the liver can have an early operation called portoenterostomy. If diagnosis or the operation are delayed, the child may need to have a full or partial liver transplant, sometimes using a segment of liver from an adult relative.

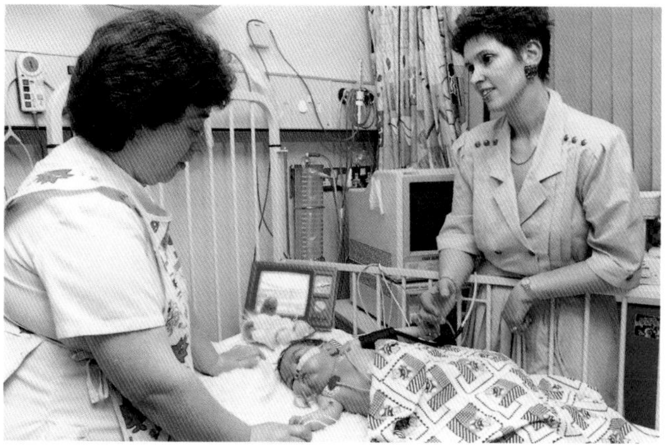

This baby is receiving treatment in a hospital liver unit. Fortunately liver disease in children is rare, and only infrequently requires surgical intervention. In many cases special diets or drugs may be the only treatment required.

Who can help?

For organizations offering help and support, see the Directory.

Complementary Treatment

Western herbalists may prescribe herbs such as milk thistle (*Silybum marianum*), which help to protect and regenerate damaged liver cells. In **nutritional therapy** attention is paid to any excess saturated fat in the diet, which puts the liver under stress. Therapists use foods and herbs such as dandelion and beetroot to help drain toxins from the liver and gallbladder, which will help the liver regenerate. **Reflexology** can be helpful during recovery. Both **Tai chi** and **chi kung** may help during convalescence, particularly in chronic cases, by renewing energy and restoring strength. **Homeopathic remedies** can be beneficial and are prescribed according to the underlying cause.

SEE ALSO HEPATITIS (PAGE 97)

Jaundice

What is it?

Jaundice is caused by an excess of the yellow bile pigment bilirubin in the blood and body tissues. The yellow coloration of the skin and the whites of the eyes that are characteristic of the condition are the most obvious sign of liver disease. Jaundice is normal in newborn babies, whose immature livers cannot process bilirubin quickly enough. As the foetus needs more red blood cells than a newborn infant, the excess is broken down in the liver and the haemoglobin converted to bilirubin. This goes to the bowel to be excreted, but if there is too much it spills into the bloodstream, causing jaundice. When it is at extremely high levels it can cause a condition called kernicterus.

More than half of all babies develop jaundice three to five days after birth. There is a rapid improvement over the next two to three days and a slower fading over the next week. Two weeks after birth most babies are clear of jaundice. If they are not, they should have urine and blood tests to check their liver function.

Breastfed babies may remain jaundiced for longer than bottle-fed babies. This type of jaundice causes the child no problems and should not affect the decision to continue breastfeeding.

Liver disease very occasionally causes jaundice in babies. This type of jaundice does not improve within two weeks of birth and there may be other signs of illness (see page 266).

Blood group incompatibility between mother and baby, and infections, may also be looked for if the level is high enough to need treatment.

You may notice

- *A faint yellow tinge in the newborn infant's skin, which shows first a day or two after birth. The colour deepens gradually*
- *The whites of the newborn's eyes may turn yellow. This is a useful check in infants with a pigmented skin*
- *The baby may become listless and arch their back and neck backwards, a symptom of kernicterus*

Treatment

It is important for newborns with jaundice to feed well and have extra fluids. Sunlight can help to reduce the amount of bilirubin in the blood, which is why you may be advised to place the child's cot near a window for ten to twenty minute spells, out of the glare of the sun.

If there is any concern about the newborn's bilirubin level it will be checked from a blood sample taken from the heel or hand. The level will be recorded daily until it steadies or starts to fall. If the level does not fall as quickly as expected the newborn may need phototherapy. For this treatment, the child is undressed and their eyes shielded. They are put under blue fluorescent lamps, the light from which will break down the bilirubin, which the baby will excrete. Sometimes babies are placed on fibre-optic blankets to increase the amount of absorbed light. Treatment is usually given intermittently, for example for one hour in four.

With very severe jaundice, such as jaundice that occurs with kernicterus, prompt treatment is vital in the first few days after birth to avoid brain damage or permanent weight loss. In this case the newborn will need an exchange-transfusion of fresh blood to remove bilirubin from the circulation.

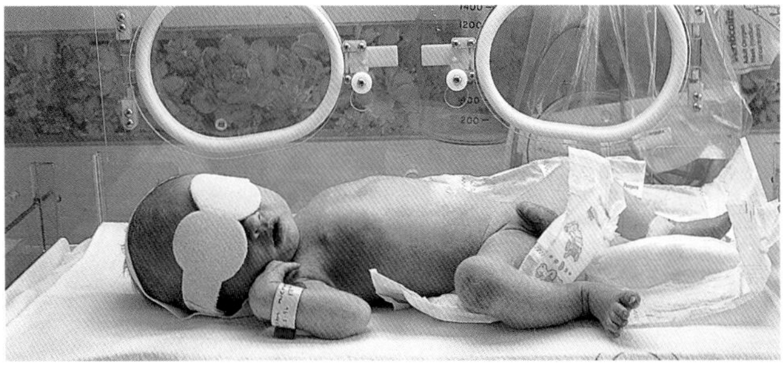

Newborn babies suffering from jaundice whose bilirubin levels do not fall quickly enough will usually be given phototherapy, which involves lying under blue fluorescent lamps. The baby's eyes are shielded from the light.

Complementary Treatment

Homeopathy is supportive of orthodox treatment in most cases. Remedies for neonatal jaundice, to be given when symptoms are first noticed, include Chamomilla 6c (*Chamomilla vulgaris*, German chamomile), and Mercurius 6c (*Mercurius solubilus Hahnemanii*, quicksilver) if Chamomilla proves ineffectual. The remedies are to be administered every two hours for up to ten doses. Jaundice in older children is treated according to the underlying cause. Treatment for older children includes **nutritional therapy**, where therapists are concerned that any excess saturated fat in the diet will put the liver under stress. Therapists use foods and herbs such as dandelion and beetroot to help drain toxins from the liver and gallbladder. **Reflexology** can be helpful during recovery. Other appropriate treatments include **Western herbalism** and **acupuncture**.

THREADWORMS

What are they?

Threadworms are tiny parasites that look like fine threads of white cotton and are up to 1 cm/½ in long. They are extremely common, especially in children. At any one time an estimated 40 per cent of children under the age of ten years are infected, many without realizing it.

Threadworms live in the dark, airless spaces of the intestine, and the female comes out of the anus to lay eggs. The eggs are coated with an sticky, irritating substance and are transferred by scratching and rubbing on to the hands and then into the mouth, on objects or clothing, setting up a cycle of re-infection. The stickiness wears off and the eggs shower down into toilet areas and bedrooms when the affected child undresses. They can then float into the air. When the eggs are swallowed, they hatch into worms in the intestine. In cool, moist conditions the eggs remain infectious for six or eight weeks. Fortunately they are easy to treat and to keep at bay in the future.

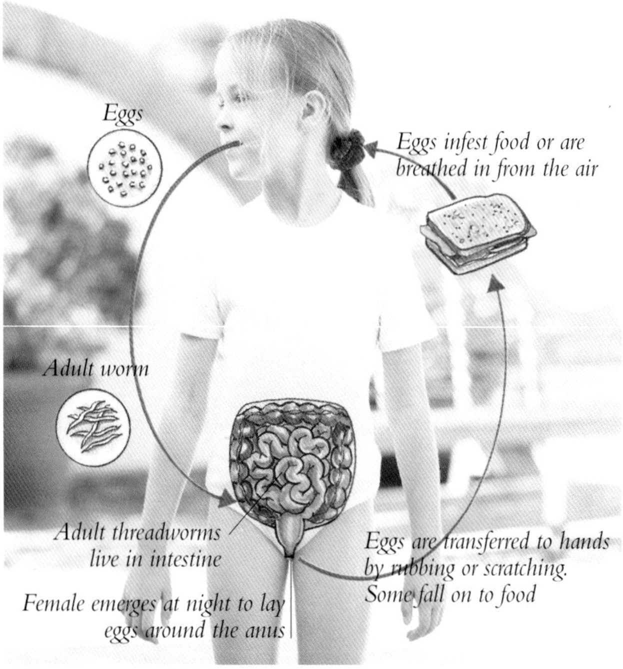
Eggs
Eggs infest food or are breathed in from the air
Adult worm
Adult threadworms live in intestine
Eggs are transferred to hands by rubbing or scratching. Some fall on to food
Female emerges at night to lay eggs around the anus

You may notice

- *Sleep disturbed by itching, so the child is irritable and restless the next day*
- *Scratching or rubbing the bottom, especially when in bed or when curled up for a rest. The area around the bottom may look red and sore*
- *Thin white threads in the child's motions or on toilet paper.*
- *Anything that moves is probably a threadworm*
- *Possibly bed-wetting after being previously dry*
- *Pain when urinating caused by a urinary tract infection*

Treatment

First check whether your child really has worms. Put them to bed in a T-shirt rather than pyjamas. About an hour after bedtime, examine their bottom with a torch. This is not pleasant, but you may see direct evidence. For a child under two inspect the faeces daily.

The whole family must be treated even if they have no symptoms; this may need to be repeated seven to fourteen days later to catch any newly-hatched worms. Treatment is with mebendazole or piperazine, which come as a syrup, as a powder to dissolve in water, milk or juice and as a tablet. During treatment, see that everyone bathes or showers every morning.

Thoroughly vacuum play areas, bedrooms, bathroom and pets on the day treatment begins. Wipe down high-risk areas (toilet seats and handles, door handles, toys and taps) with a piece of damp kitchen paper, then throw the paper away.

Warning: Pregnant or breastfeeding mothers and parents of children under two should consult their doctor for advice on alternative methods of treatment.

Preventing threadworms

- Insist on scrupulous hand-washing after going to the toilet and wash your own hands carefully after changing nappies. Hands should always be washed before cooking or eating
- Keep the child's nails short and well-scrubbed.
- Everyone should wear underwear or pyjamas at night and they should be washed daily
- To get rid of eggs in the home, thoroughly wash all bedding and clothes. Check that bedding is bone dry

Complementary Treatment

Chinese herbalists prescribe the safe and gentle remedy pumpkin seeds and advise on hygiene to prevent recurrence. **Homeopathic remedies**, to be given three times a day for up to 14 days, include Cina 6c (*Cina artemisia maritima*, sea southernwood) and Teucrium 6c (*Teucrium marum verum*, cat thyme).

Umbilical Hernia

What is it?

A hernia is a weakness in a muscle wall that allows an organ or body tissues to protrude through it. In newborn babies and young children hernias are most often found near the umbilicus (navel), when part of the intestine bulges out. One infant in five has some degree of umbilical hernia. It is more common in girls, and in Afro-Caribbean and premature babies. Although an umbilical hernia may look worrying, it is almost never serious, and the complications that can occur with inguinal hernias (see page 296) are virtually unknown. For this reason most umbilical hernias are left to heal naturally. Many disappear by the time of the child's first or, at the latest, second birthday.

You may notice

- *A soft round swelling with a firm edge approximately the size of a penny in the centre of the infant's navel. This is different from the protruding navel which is common in most infants*
- *When the child cries, strains or coughs the swelling may become more pronounced*
- *When the child is relaxed and lying down, the swelling may disappear completely*
- *More rarely, there will be a cone-shaped protrusion, which is usually situated just above the umbilicus. This is a para-umbilical hernia*

What to do

Most umbilical hernias disappear on their own, although the less common para-umbilical hernias are more likely to need surgery. Consult your doctor, but expect a wait-and-see approach to be adopted. Check the hernia regularly at bath-time to make sure it is not getting larger. When the baby is relaxed and calm – just after a feed or a bath – gently press the hernia back. It should flatten. Never pad or strap anything over an umbilical hernia as the will do nothing useful. However if the hernia has a tendency to bulge when the baby coughs or cries, press it gently with your thumb to check that it is not obstructed.

Treatment

Your doctor will want to check the child regularly and will tell you to watch for signs that the hernia is not healing naturally. If the hernia is still obvious by the time the child is three years of age, surgery to seal the muscle wall is an option. The child will need a general anaesthetic, but the operation is quick and very straightforward. It is is usually performed as day surgery.

Take care

See your doctor if

- The swelling becomes hard or will not subside if you press it gently
- The child is in pain, crying or starts vomiting – don't assume the cause is the hernia
- The swelling gradually increases
- There is a swelling in the groin or in the testicles. This could may be a hernia and is more likely to cause problems.

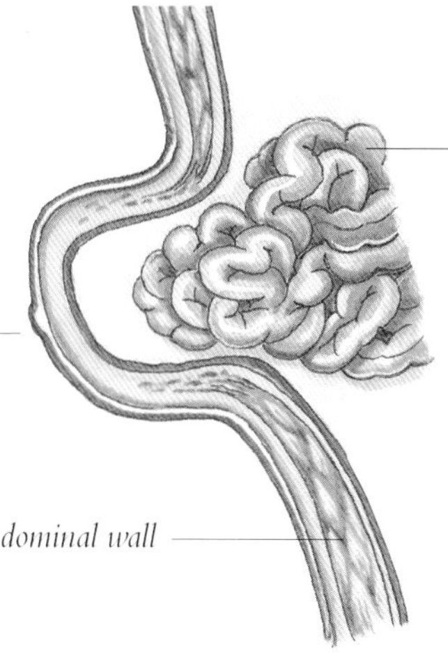

An umbilical hernia can be pushed backed into place when the baby is relaxed, but will probably reappear again when the baby becomes upset. Most disappear on their own by the time the child is a year old. Surgery is rarely needed, but if necessary is performed at 3-4 years.

Complementary Treatment

Homeopathic remedies can be helpful, but if there is no improvement within two months, see your doctor. Specific remedies include Silicea 6c (*Silicea terra*, flint) for a baby or toddler who is thin and weedy, with a large head and sweaty feet; Calcarea 6c (*Calcarea carbonica*, calcium carbonate) for an overweight infant or toddler who is very quiet and prone to head sweats in the night, especially if the child likes to eat earth or worms; and Nux 6c (*Strychnos nux vomica*, poison nut tree) for all other cases. Remedies are to be given three times a day for up to three weeks.

DIARRHOEA

What is it?

Diarrhoea means that the body is getting rid of waste matter too quickly. Normally, as food passes through the large intestine, much of the liquid waste matter is absorbed, and by the time the remaining undigested waste matter reaches the rectum it will be firm. However if the lining of the large intestine is irritated or it is inflamed, the waste matter will rush through, taking liquid material with it. In severe cases diarrhoea draws water out of the body, so that the waste matter emerges as a liquid.

Babies who are exclusively breastfed usually produce runny yellow faeces, but these are normal and not an indication of diarrhoea. Nor are the thicker faeces of a bottle-fed infant. Toddlers and young children may frequently pass liquid stools in which there is undigested food, such as raisins, peas, sweetcorn or pieces of carrot. This is likely to be toddler diarrhoea, a completely harmless condition that clears up on its own by the time the child is three or four years of age. In the meanwhile, you can mash these foods with a fork prior to feeding your child.

Acute and chronic conditions

Diarrhoea can either be acute, marking an abrupt change from the child's normal motions, or chronic. In the case of acute diarrhoea there are often other symptoms. The more common causes of acute diarrhoea are gastroenteritis and food poisoning, when the child is likely to have a stomach ache, may also be vomiting and possibly have a fever. Children who are on antibiotics may develop diarrhoea, as may children who are newly weaned – the latter because their colon is not yet used to solid food. Another possible cause of a sudden bout in older children may be stress brought on by nervousness – for example, before giving a performance or taking an examination.

Causes

Children who drink quite large quantities of fruit juice or squash may develop diarrhoea as part of a condition called squash-drinking syndrome, which may be caused by the concentration of sugar in the liquid. This can be prevented by progressively diluting squash or fruit juice until you are giving the child water with only a hint of juice.

Some children who have just recovered from gastroenteritis may develop a temporary lactose intolerance (see page 244), where the mucous lining of the intestine has been damaged. They will need a milk-free diet until the intestine has recovered.

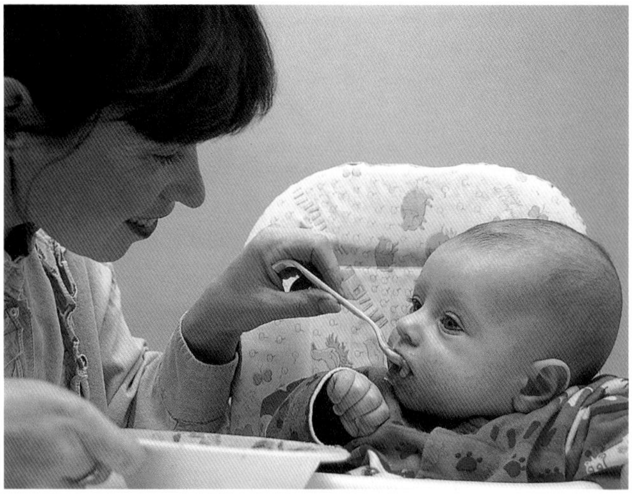

Diarrhoea in babies may occasionally be caused by too much sugar in puréed foods or fruit drinks. Babies who are being weaned are best fed on sugar-free foods, which will also protect their newly formed teeth.

Babies and children with chronic diarrhoea can seem perfectly well apart from the fact that they have runny stools, but some may have additional symptoms. Chronic diarrhoea may be caused, oddly enough, by constipation; if solid stools are blocking the child's rectum, liquid faeces may be seeping out past the solid matter. If the diarrhoea appears soon after the child has eaten a particular food, the presence of a food intolerance is a possibility.

More uncommon causes of chronic diarrhoea include coeliac disease, where symptoms start soon after a baby is started on foods that contain gluten – such as rusks or bread – and cystic fibrosis, when the diarrhoea produces pale, foul-smelling faeces; other symptoms are likely to include failure to thrive and a cough. In older children, Crohn's disease may give rise to repeated bouts of colicky stomach ache, diarrhoea and other symptoms. Children with ulcerative colitis may have blood and mucus mixed in with the faeces and they may also have stomach aches. Liver disease may also be a causative factor in diarrhoea.

Serious cases

Diarrhoea in babies is always serious because in a few hours a great deal of fluid can be lost and the child can become dehydrated (see page 252). Diarrhoea is not as serious in children who are still able to drink fluids, but you should always consult your doctor if your child stops drinking or if they start to vomit.

A breastfed baby suffering from diarrhoea is given plain water or rehydration drinks between feeds in order to replace the fluid that is lost with the faeces. Dehydration is a serious side-effect of diarrhoea.

You may notice

- *Diarrhoea marks a change in the child's faeces, which may become more fluid*
- *They may be copious, or there may be a change in their consistency*
- *The faeces may be completely liquid or contain little bits of solid waste, undigested food or mucus*
- *They may be blood-stained*
- *The faeces may arrive explosively and smell different*

What to do

If a baby has been sick or is refusing feeds as well as having diarrhoea, then consult your doctor immediately. Do not give the child any bottled milk. You should continue to offer the breast to a baby who is still on milk feeds, or else give sips of boiled and cooled water. Check for symptoms of dehydration or for other signs of illness, such as a fever of 38°C/100.4°F. If you notice any other symptoms, consult your doctor without delay.

What else?

Do not give the child any milk; instead offer plain water or oral rehydration drinks. Such drinks replace the lost fluids and contain essential nutrients and minerals as well. Be sure to follow the packet instructions when making up these drinks. It is best to give small quantities of liquid frequently – every 30-60 minutes or between breastfeeds – so you do not provoke any more vomiting. A child who will not accept an oral rehydration drink may take it if it is flavoured with a dash of fruit juice or squash.

If the child is bright, happy and feeding well despite the diarrhoea, consider recent changes in their food. If you are still breastfeeding, the cause could be something you have eaten or, in a few rare cases, cows' milk in your diet. If the diarrhoea disappears but then returns, discuss with a health professional the possibility of leaving out the suspect foods for a few days to see if there is any improvement. If you suspect the problem is caused by milk intolerance, consult your doctor who can arrange tests for levels of acid and sugars in the faeces.

Complementary Treatment

Where diarrhoea is caused by food intolerance or allergy, the **nutritional therapist** and **kinesiologist** will want to identify the culprit and advise on future avoidance. **Chinese herbalists** prescribe herbs to strengthen weakness in stomach and spleen energy. **Acupuncture** is the more effective treatment in the acute phase, and, when used together with Chinese herbalism, has been known to give excellent results. **Western herbalists** have many herbs at their disposal that can be used to treat diarrhoea and will choose from these appropriate astringent, anti-inflammatory herbs. **Aromatherapy** oils can often reduce pain caused by a distressed gut or abdominal muscles. **Homeopathic remedies** include Chamomilla 6c (*Chamomilla vulgaris*, German chamomile) for diarrhoea associated with teething, where the baby passes greenish stools and is irritable and difficult to please, the remedy to be taken every hour for up to ten doses. Remedies for older children include Argentum nit 6c (*Argentum nitricum*, silver nitrate) where there is anxiety and apprehension, belching and a craving for salt and sweet things, the remedies to be taken every half hour for up to ten doses. **Reflexology** may also be beneficial.

SEE ALSO COELIAC DISEASE (PAGE 263) CROHN'S DISEASE (PAGE 261) DEHYDRATION (PAGE 252) FOOD ALLERGY (PAGE 242) GASTROENTERITIS (PAGE 257) ULCERATIVE COLITIS (PAGE 262) VOMITING (PAGE 253)

HEART, BLOOD AND CIRCULATION

The blood is the body's major transport system. It carries oxygen, glucose, hormones, antibodies and other essential substances to sites where they are needed, and transports waste products to the kidneys for disposal. Blood consists of a fluid, plasma, as well as red blood cells, white blood cells and platelets. The red blood cells, of which there are millions in every drop of blood, contain a protein, haemoglobin, which gives blood its characteristic colour and carries oxygen from the lungs to the muscles and organs. The main task of white blood cells is to resist infection, whether it is a general infection, such as chickenpox, or local, such as an infected cut. When a child is confronted by an infection, the body manufactures extra white blood cells that produce antibodies to overwhelm and kill bacteria and viruses. Platelets are the smallest type of cell in the blood and are essential for clotting. When blood vessels are damaged, platelets clump together and release chemicals that cause the blood to coagulate.

The heart

Blood enters the heart in the right atrium and flows down into the right ventricle. It then travels to the lungs to pick up oxygen, returns to the left atrium and down into the left ventricle, from where it is pumped forcefully out into the arteries through the aorta, the body's main artery.

On leaving the heart, blood travels first through muscular arteries that branch into thin capillaries, which allow oxygen out and waste carbon dioxide in. Capillaries also help to regulate the body's temperature by expanding or narrowing in response to heat and cold. The blood, now de-oxygenated, then flows from capillaries to the veins, which carry the blood back to the heart.

The heart is placed centrally in the chest and is protected by the ribs. It works like a twin-action pump, receiving de-oxygenated blood from the veins and sending oxygenated blood around the body in the arteries and then into the capillaries.

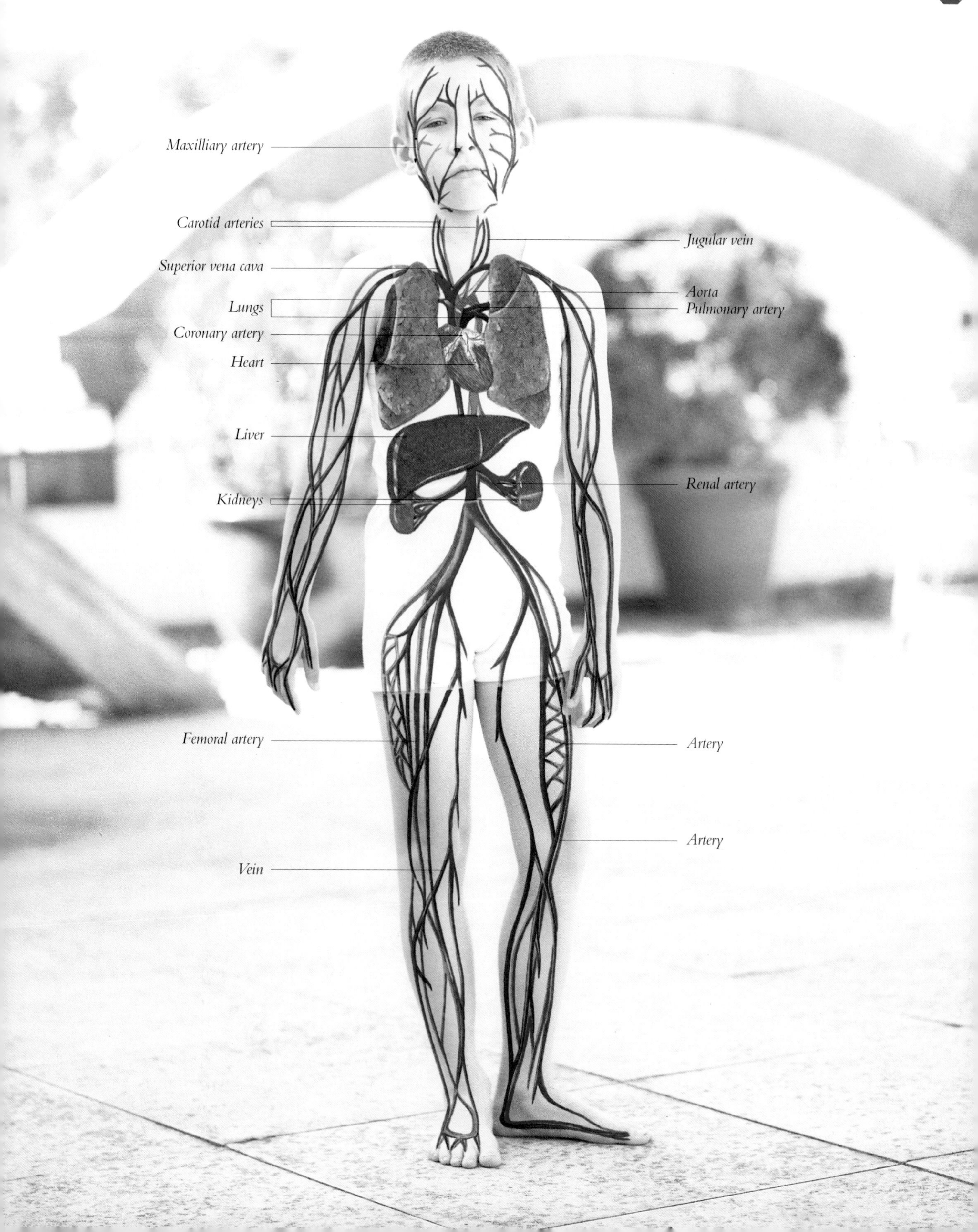
Maxilliary artery
Carotid arteries
Jugular vein
Superior vena cava
Aorta
Lungs
Pulmonary artery
Coronary artery
Heart
Liver
Renal artery
Kidneys
Femoral artery
Artery
Artery
Vein

Diagnosis

With the exception of iron deficiency anaemia, the disorders of the heart, blood and circulation that can occur in childhood are rare. Many of the heart conditions that occur are some form of congenital anomaly, that is, a condition that was present at birth. Most of these are minor. There are also a number of inherited conditions that affect the blood.

Sign	What could be wrong
Listless behaviour, possibly faddy eating and pale skin	Iron-deficiency anaemia. This is extremely common in toddlers and pre-school children
An older infant or toddler bruises easily and may bleed when a tooth comes through	Haemophilia is a possibility in a boy
Unusual pallor; tendency to catch infections; child bruises and bleeds easily	There are many common causes of these symptoms. Leukaemia is rare
In babies over six months, pain and sometimes swelling in the hands and feet; anaemia; susceptible to infections	A sickle cell disorder is possible, especially in a child of African or Afro-Caribbean origin
Anaemia, failure to thrive and appetite loss around 3–18 months	Thalassaemia is a possibility in a child from Asia or the Mediterranean

Congenital heart disease

Heart disease requires special diagnostic tests. The only signs that parents may notice are general signs that the heart is not working efficiently. All these signs can have a perfectly innocent interpretation and can also suggest other conditions.

Heart murmurs

Most heart murmurs in infants and young children are perfectly normal. Tests are only needed if the doctor who hears the murmur is in any doubt about the cause or if the child shows any other signs of heart disease.

Breathlessness

Children with heart problems may have enough oxygen-rich blood flowing around the body, or too much blood may be flowing to the lungs, which become congested. The child then gets breathless or appears to tire more quickly than other children when exercising. In babies, breathlessness can also cause problems with feeding, leading to slow weight gain.

Blue skin

Many babies have a pale tinge to their skin. Children with a heart condition may have a more obvious bluish tinge to the lips and tongue. Babies with 'wind' are often bluish around the mouth, but their lips remain pink.

Brief unconsciousness

A child can appear to faint briefly. It may be difficult to distinguish a faint from a convulsion. A faint can be caused by a change in the heart rhythm or an interruption in the flow of blood from the heart.

Heart Murmurs

What is it?

The normal heart produces two main sounds, audible only with a stethoscope. The first is like a 'lubb' and means the lower heart chambers (the ventricles) are contracting or squeezing in readiness to pump blood out of the heart. The second sound is like a higher-pitched 'dubb' and means that the valves have closed behind the blood that has been pumped out of the lower chambers. After each 'lubb-dubb' there is a pause. However in some children the heart produces murmurs – sounds over and above the normal sounds the doctor would expect to hear.

The majority of heart murmurs in young babies are perfectly normal and are caused by the turbulent flow of blood through the heart. In the first few days of life the heart works hard to meet the newborn's extra needs, and may beat more than 100 times a minute. Such heart murmurs – known as functional heart murmurs – are so common that eight out of ten babies are affected. They tend to be louder and easier to pick up when a child is feverish or is stressed.

Many heart murmurs disappear in infancy as the baby matures and adapts to independent life. Others disappear later in childhood, usually before school age. Even in those cases where they persist into the teenage years the child may still be completely healthy, with a heart that is working normally. Around half of all school children and teenagers have a functional heart murmur.

Other heart murmurs – known as organic heart murmurs – may be a symptom of a structural problem, such as a defective valve or hole in the heart (see page 276).

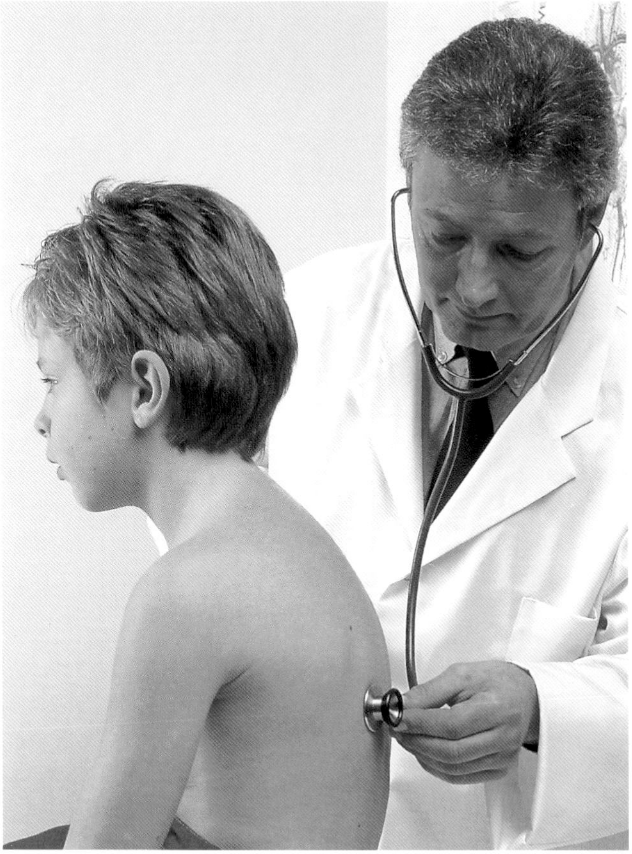

A doctor listening to a child's heart with a stethoscope can tell if the heart sounds he hears are normal or not. When the murmur is not a sign of heart disease it is called innocent, benign or functional. Innocent murmurs are heard in half of all healthy school-age children. A soft heart murmur can probably be heard in eight out of ten young infants.

Diagnosis

The paediatrician will listen to the newborn's heart just after birth, and further examinations are carried out regularly at the child health clinic. If a heart murmur is detected and there is any doubt about its cause, or if the child has any other symptoms of heart disease, tests will be performed. These may include an echocardiogram, an electrocardiogram (ECG) and possibly a chest X-ray (see pages 339 and 340). If the murmur is functional then the results of the tests will be perfectly normal and there should be no need for further investigation or treatment. However if the murmur is a symptom of a structural problem such as a hole in the heart or a defective valve, then treatment may be necessary.

Complementary Treatment

Functional heart murmurs fall within the range of normal, and therefore do not require orthodox or complementary treatment. For complementary therapies that may offer supportive treatment to children who have been diagnosed with a heart condition, see page 276.

Hole in the Heart

What is it?

It has been estimated that one per cent of babies are born with a congenital heart disease, and fifty per cent of these involve a hole in the muscle wall, or septum, which separates the left and right sides of the heart. A hole in the ventricles, the partition between the two pumping chambers, is called a ventricular septal defect (VSD). A hole between the atria, the two upper filling chambers, is called an atrial septal defect. When such a defect occurs, blood may flow the wrong way through the hole and gradually damage the heart muscle or make it work much too hard. Not all babies need surgery, as small ventricular septal defects may close on their own. Large ones may also get smaller, and in the meantime a baby may be given drugs to regulate the heart.

You may notice

- *Children with a small hole don't show any symptoms*
- *Holes in the dividing wall between the atria often only show in adulthood when a routine examination reveals a heart murmur*
- *Infants with large holes in the dividing wall between the ventricles are often breathless, exhausted, difficult to feed and do not gain weight as fast as expected (see page 71)*

Normal

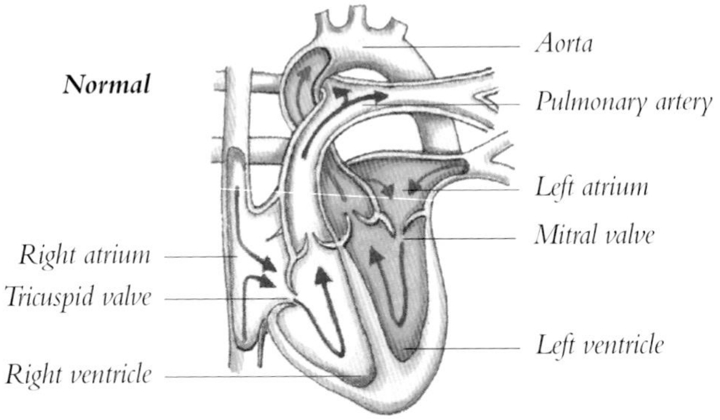

Ventricular Septal Defect

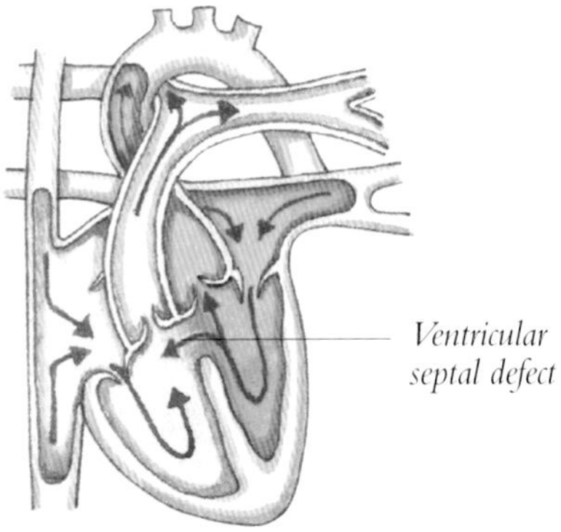

Diagnosis

Your paediatrician will listen to the newborn's heart just after birth, and if symptoms are found the child will be referred to a cardiologist. To confirm a suspected hole in the heart the child will have a chest X-ray and an echocardiogram (an ultrasound scan). A Doppler echocardiogram may be used to confirm the diagnosis (see page 340).

Treatment

Small ventricular septal defects don't need treatment, but large ones do. Initially the child will be given drugs to help the heart cope with its extra work. Following this, the child will have an operation to repair the hole. This procedure can transform a pale, breathless baby into a pink, active one. During the operation, the surgeon will correct the fault by closing the hole with a patch, while a heart-lung machine takes over the child's circulation and breathing.

Surgery lasts between two and five hours, and the child will spend time afterwards in intensive care, attached to a ventilator and monitors. The equipment will be removed after a day or two and recovery will be very fast. The child will have a scar down the middle of the chest or below one breast, depending on the position of the hole. To prepare yourself for the operation, and give you confidence to reassure the child, you should try to see a child of the same age in intensive care.

Coping with heart problems

To protect against endocarditis, an infection of the heart, children with heart conditions will need to have antibiotics for any procedure that involves penetrating the skin, and before having a tooth filled or extracted. Children with heart conditions also need to brush their teeth regularly and thoroughly. A child who has had an atrial septal defect repaired will have an electrocardiogram (ECG) every three or four years.

Complementary Treatment

Osteopathy may aid recovery following surgery, and **Bach flower remedies** may help to alleviate fear and anxiety and the emotional aspects of recovery. **Homeopathic remedies** to be given prior to surgery include Aconite 30c (*Aconitum napellus*, blue aconite) if the child is panicking and is very afraid, and Gelsemium 6c (*Gelsemium sempervirens*, yellow jasmine) if the child is very apprehensive, weak and trembling. Phosphorus 6c (phosphorus) can be given to relieve vomiting after surgery. Give remedies every half hour for up to ten doses.

COARCTATION OF THE AORTA

What is it?
About seven-and-a half per cent of babies with congenital heart disease are born with a narrowed aorta, which is the main blood vessel taking oxygenated blood from the heart to the rest of the body. This means that although the left side of the heart is pumping harder than normal, not enough fresh blood and oxygen reaches the tissues in the lower part of the body. The cause of the condition is unknown. It is a feature of Turner's syndrome (see page 75). Coarctation of the aorta is sometimes diagnosed soon after birth, but may not become apparent until the child is older, by which time increasing strain will have been put on the heart.

You may notice
In infants
- *The child is breathless*
- *Feeding becomes too much effort*
- *The skin looks pale. The feet may feel cold*
- *The child may go into shock*

In children
- *There may be no symptoms*
- *Sometimes the child gets tired easily and has headaches and dizziness*
- *They may also develop cramps in their legs*

Diagnosis
If a baby develops any of the above symptoms either in hospital or after you have gone home, you should contact your doctor immediately. The baby will be brought back to hospital as a matter of urgency.

For children, the defect may be found by a doctor listening to the heart during a routine check-up. A heart murmur (see page 275) may be noticed and there may also be high blood pressure in the arms and low blood pressure and weak pulses in the legs.

To diagnose the condition, hospital staff will carry out tests, including an echocardiogram (see page 340) to show where the problem lies and the extent of the narrowing. In an older child other tests such as a chest X-ray or cardiac catheterization may be carried out. An echocardiogram and chest X-ray can be done as an outpatient, but the catheterization will involves a hospital stay of a night or two. This entails inserting and inflating a balloon attached to a catheter to stretch the aorta.

Treatment
Very slightly narrowed arteries may not need treatment, but the child will be seen regularly as an outpatient. In babies, if the narrowing is severe, it will be corrected immediately. Either the narrowed section of the aorta can be removed and the two ends joined together or balloon dilatation during cardiac catheterization may be tried. Sometimes, however, the aorta narrows again after this operation, so the procedure is repeated.

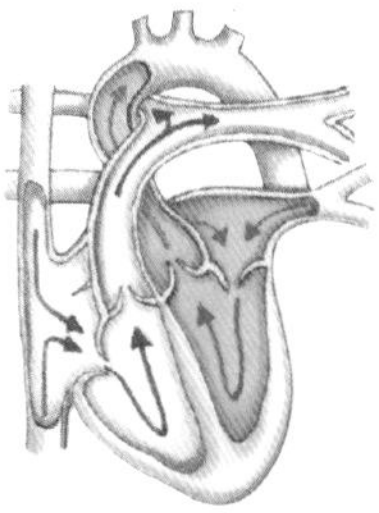

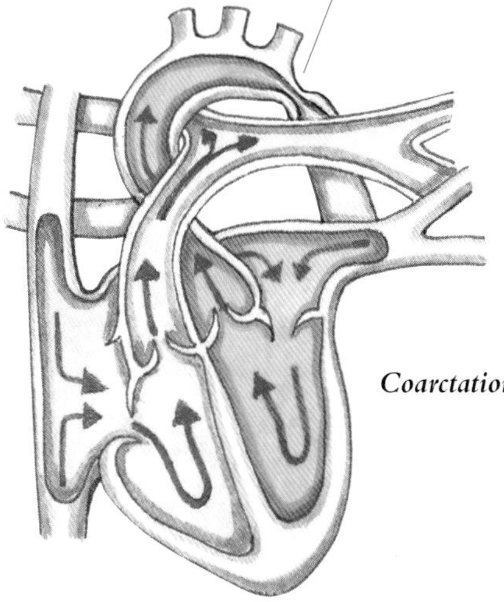

Coarctation of the Aorta

In older children, coarctation of the aorta involves a narrowing of the aorta, the body's main artery, which carries oxygenated blood. The problem is corrected either by making an incision in the left side of the chest or by introducing a balloon catheter through the artery in the groin. The balloon is inflated to stretch the aorta where it narrows.

Coping with heart problems
After surgery children will be seen regularly as an outpatient. All babies with congenital heart disease are given antibiotics before an operation to protect the heart from the bacterial infection endocarditis. Antibiotic protection will need to be continued afterwards for medical and dental procedures, and tooth brushing should be carried out regularly.

Complementary Treatment
Complementary therapies that may aid recovery following surgery include **osteopathy**. The **Bach flower remedies** may help to alleviate fear and anxiety and the emotional aspects of recovery. For appropriate homeopathic remedies see page 276.

Tetralogy of Fallot

What is it?

One out of every two thousand newborn babies suffer from this condition, in which there are a number of major heart defects. In the first, the pulmonary artery, the artery taking blood from the heart to the lungs, has an unusually narrow entrance. This condition is called pulmonary stenosis and can occur on its own. In the second, affected children will have a hole in the heart (see page 276), specifically in the muscular wall between the heart's two pumping chambers, the right and left ventricles. This is called a ventricular septal defect (VSD) and can also occur on its own.

Additionally, the right ventricle also becomes thickened because it has to pump harder through the narrowed pulmonary artery. In normal circumstances the pulmonary artery would take blood from the heart to the lungs to pick up oxygen, but if the entrance to this artery is narrow, not enough blood will pick up oxygen. The result is that too much blood will circulate to the body without having been oxygenated in the lungs. Some of the blood may also flow directly into the other pumping chambers so that the blue, deoxygenated blood will be pumped around the body.

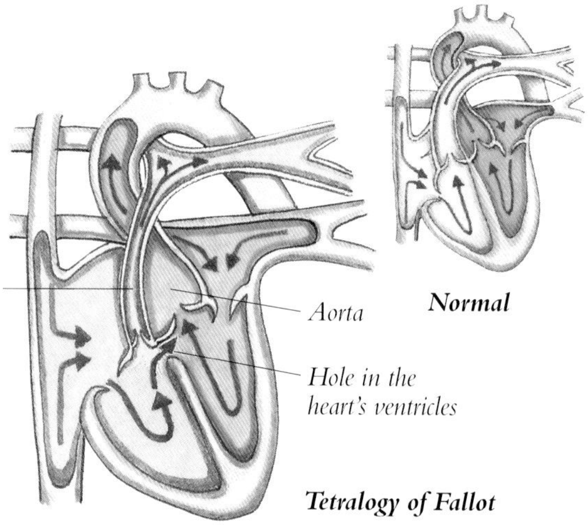

Children with this heart condition have an abnormally narrow entrance to the artery taking blood to the lungs, and a hole in the septum, the muscular partition separating the heart's two chambers. Surgery is necessary to correct the defect, either with a balloon catheter or by making an incision in the middle of the chest.

You may notice

- *The infant will gradually become more breathless and blue and deteriorate over weeks or months. The blueness may first be noticed when the infant strains their heart by crying or when the child becomes active*
- *Between the ages of three and nine months the infant will suddenly turn blue and breathless and pass out for a minute or two. These attacks often happen in the morning, usually after breakfast*
- *When the child is older and starts to be physically active they will become breathless.*

Diagnosis

Your paediatrician will listen to the newborn's heart just after birth, and if symptoms are found, the child will be referred to a cardiologist for tests. These will include an electrocardiogram (ECG), a chest X-ray and an echocardiogram (see page 274). The paediatrician may also perform a cardiac catheterization (see page 277).

Treatment

The type of operation that will be needed will depend upon the child's age and the extent of the narrowing in the pulmonary artery. One option is a temporary shunt, consisting of a fine plastic tube that links the aorta with the pulmonary artery. This operation is usually performed on younger children to improve blood flow to the lungs until a full operation can be carried out.

Full correction involves open heart surgery to close the hole between the two ventricles and to permanently widen the entrance to the pulmonary artery. After the operation the child will be in intensive care for a short time and will have a scar down the middle of the chest.

Coping with heart problems

Children who have made a successful recovery can be as active as any other child. They will need outpatient checks at first, but at increasing intervals, and like children with other heart defects, they will need antibiotic protection when having a tooth filled or extracted and for any procedure that penetrates the skin. They will also have to brush their teeth regularly and thoroughly to ensure that the teeth remain healthy and do not require dental treatment.

Complementary Treatment

Complementary therapies that may aid recovery following surgery include **osteopathy**. The **Bach flower remedies** may help to alleviate fear and anxiety prior to surgery and the emotional aspects of recovery. For suitable **homeopathic remedies,** see page 276.

Persistent Ductus Arteriosus

What is it?

Just after birth some important changes take place in a baby's circulation. In persistent (also called patent) ductus arteriosus, one of these changes fails to occur. While in the uterus, the foetus gets its oxygen from its mother, via the placenta. After birth, when the baby starts to breathe, they get their oxygen from the lungs. As part of this changeover, a small channel called the ductus arteriosus closes off. Before birth the ductus arteriosus allows blood full of oxygen to flow from the body's main blood vessel – the aorta – into the lungs. If the spontaneous closure of the ductus arteriosus doesn't take place, there is an increased flow of oxygen-rich blood to the lungs and a decreased flow of oxygen-rich blood to the rest of the body. In many premature babies the ductus arteriosus doesn't close for a few weeks after birth.

You may notice

- *An infant with a small open duct may have no symptoms at first. After a while, or if the open duct is large, the infant will become increasingly breathless and difficult to feed*
- *The infant may be slow to gain weight*
- *Older children may become more tired and breathless than other children*

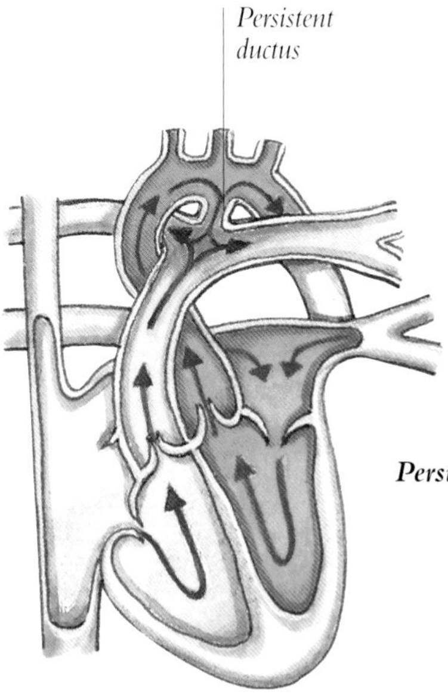

Persistent Ductus Arteriosus

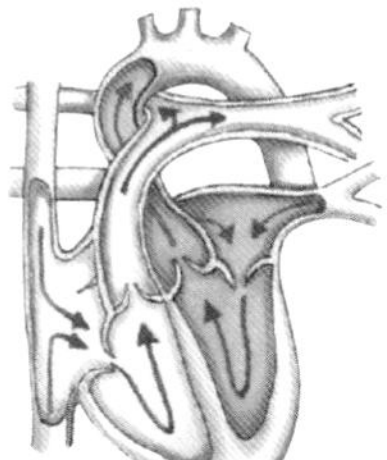

Normal

In this condition the ductus arteriosus, the blood vessel between the aorta and pulmonary artery, stays open, instead of closing just after birth. This allows blood to flow from the aorta to the lungs, making the heart work harder. The condition is usually corrected around the age of four or five, most often by inserting a catheter attached to a miniature umbrella into a vein in the groin, or, rarely, by surgery.

What to do

Ask the doctor to examine the baby. If the doctor suspects persistent ductus arteriosus, they will refer the baby to hospital for an echocardiogram (EEG, an ultrasound scan of the heart). This allows the doctor to visualize the structure of the heart to get an accurate view of its activity. The baby has to lie still for some time – between 15 and 60 minutes – but the test is completely painless.

If the duct is still open three months after birth it is unlikely to close on its own. It will then need to be closed surgically, preferably before the child starts school. There are two ways to do this.

The child may have a long, fine tube (called a catheter) passed into a vein in the groin, and this will then be manoeuvred into the heart. The procedure is monitored using echocardiography, and the surgeon can see the catheter on a screen. At the tip of the catheter is a pair of miniature 'umbrellas', in a closed position. The doctor positions the umbrellas across the duct and then snaps them open to close the duct. The catheter is then removed, leaving the umbrellas in place. This procedure requires two or three days hospitalization. If the umbrellas don't fully close the duct, a second pair may be inserted in the same way 6 or 12 months later.

Some babies are too small for this procedure and some ducts are too large to be closed using this method. In such cases the baby will have a traditional operation, involving a stay of less than a week in hospital. A cut is made under the left arm and the duct is tied or clipped shut. As soon as the duct has been closed the child's circulation becomes normal.

Coping with persistent ductus arteriosus

Children with heart conditions need antibiotics to protect them against an infection of the heart called endocarditis. Antibiotics are given an hour before any procedure that involves penetrating the skin and before having a tooth filled or extracted. Children with heart conditions also need to brush their teeth regularly and thoroughly, to prevent an infection getting into the bloodstream.

Complementary Treatment

Complementary therapies that may aid recovery following surgery include **osteopathy**. The **Bach flower remedies** may help to alleviate fear and anxiety prior to surgery and the emotional aspects of recovery. For **homeopathic** remedies that are suitable for surgery see page 276.

HAEMOPHILIA

What is it?

The blood contains substances called clotting factors that are essential for normal blood clotting. Haemophilia is an inherited disorder caused by a shortage or absence of one of these factors. In haemophilia A (the most common type) the deficient or absent factor is factor VIII, and in haemophilia B it is factor IX. People with haemophilia bleed for longer than normal. Bleeding from cuts and grazes can usually be controlled with light pressure and a plaster, but a knock or bump can cause internal bleeding, often into a joint. The bleeding causes severe pain, and in the long term it damages the joints and causes arthritis. How much and how often a child bleeds varies enormously – they may have only one or two attacks a year or they may have attacks every week.

Haemophilia mainly affects boys, although it is passed on by women. If a woman carrier becomes pregnant there is a 50 per cent chance of a male child inheriting haemophilia and a 50 per cent chance of a female child being a carrier. In 95 per cent of families female carriers can be identified by a blood test. Chorionic villus sampling early in pregnancy (around ten weeks) can show if the child is affected.

In normal circumstances a tumble that results in a cut or graze requires only a plaster and some tender loving care from mum. However for a haemophiliac minor accidents usually necessitate medical care.

You may notice

- *A crawling infant or toddler bruises for no obvious reason*
- *A joint, often an ankle or knee, becomes stiff, painful, red and swollen*
- *An infant may bleed for a long time when a tooth comes through, following a cut in the mouth or circumcision*

What to do

Take the child to the doctor, who will refer them to a haemophilia centre, often linked with a hospital department of haematology. The child will have blood tests to diagnose the disorder.

Treatment

Haemophilia is treated by injections of the missing clotting factor. Some children need two or three injections a week to prevent bleeding, whereas others need an injection only after an injury or accident.

To begin with a nurse or doctor will give the injections, but parents are taught how to give them, and when the child is old enough they will be taught how to give the injections themselves. Concentrates of factor VIII and factor IX are prepared from donated blood, and in the late 1970s and early 1980s many haemophiliacs were given concentrates contaminated with the human immunodeficiency virus (HIV). All donated blood is now screened for HIV and the hepatitis virus, and concentrates are treated to destroy viruses. Recently synthetic factor VIII and factor IX have been produced and may become the treatment of the future.

Coping with haemophilia

Toddlers need to be watched to try and prevent them from injuring themselves, and also to spot injuries that do occur as early as possible. Older children should not be overprotected – they learn to recognize the symptoms of a bleed and can tell parents so that treatment can be given as soon as possible.

Babysitters and relatives who look after the child should be aware of the child's condition, and should know what to do in the event of a bleed. But don't let worry stop you from leaving your child with a reliable adult and going out.

Sport helps to prevent arthritis in haemophiliacs, but sports with a high risk of head injury, such as rugby or boxing, are not advised.

Who can help?

For organizations offering support, see the Directory

Complementary Treatment

Haemophilia can be helped by **relaxation** and **aromatherapy**. Essential oils used in massage, in bath water and as compresses aid pain control, insomnia and nausea. Relaxation techniques also help relieve the child's symptoms and help the child deal with the emotional effects of the condition, such as anxiety.

Anaemia

What is it?

Anaemia is a deficiency in the number of red blood cells or a deficiency in haemoglobin – the substance in the blood that transports oxygen to the brain and muscles. It has many causes. In the United Kingdom iron-deficiency anaemia is the most commonly reported nutritional disorder among young children. Iron is a vital component of haemoglobin: if the body has a deficiency of iron it does not produce enough haemoglobin, and this in turn leads to anaemia.

Children who are severely anaemic for a long time risk catching repeated infections, lagging behind in speech and mental development, and doing badly at school. However it is not clear what effect mild iron deficiency has on children.

Babies are born with a store of iron that they gradually use up over the first four to six months of life. Premature babies and twins are born with smaller reserves and they are often given iron supplements. After weaning, children get the iron they need from food and drink. This is when iron deficiency becomes common, because many young children do not eat a wide range of foods. Some also drink a lot of cows' milk, which contains little iron, whereas formula milks are fortified with iron, and the iron in breastmilk is exceptionally well-absorbed. A small number of children may have an underlying illness that means they do not absorb iron efficiently, and they develop severe long-term anaemia.

Some children who are anaemic appear quite normal, but you may notice one or more of the following signs.

You may notice

- *The child is unusual listlessness and apathy*
- *Has a poor appetite and becomes a faddy eater*
- *Is prone to infections*
- *Has pale skin; membranes inside the eyelids may look pale*

What to do

Give your child more foods that are rich in iron, such as meat, liver, eggs and fortified bread and cereals. If your child does not show any improvement, take them to the doctor, who will take a blood sample for analysis. If the haemoglobin concentration is below a certain level the doctor will diagnose anaemia, and may prescribe an iron-containing syrup to correct it.

Prevention

It is better to prevent anaemia from developing than have to treat it. You can do this by starting your child on solids between the age of four and six months, and introducing red meat three times a week soon after six months. Babies on a meatless diet should have iron-rich vegetables such as broccoli, lentils, peas and beans, as well as foods rich in vitamin C, to boost iron absorption. Broccoli, spinach and leeks provide iron and vitamin C. Introduce a varied diet as soon as possible, and make sure it includes foods rich in iron, such as red meat, fortified bread and breakfast cereals, dark chicken meat, fish, pulses, dried fruits and nuts (well ground), and dark green leafy vegetables.

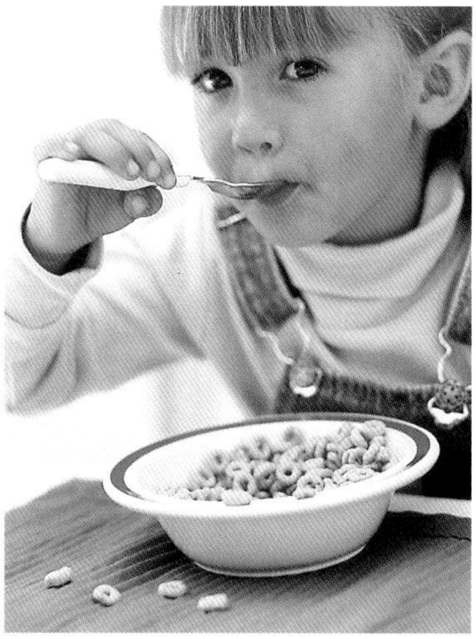

A recent study has shown that children who eat breakfast cereals – which are usually fortified with vitamins and iron – are generally better nourished than other children. Girls who don't eat breakfast cereals on a regular basis are particularly likely to have an iron shortage.

If you stop breastfeeding your infant before they are 12 months old, give them formula or follow-on milk. Don't give breast- or bottlefed babies ordinary cows' milk until they are at least 12 months old. If you give your infant commercial baby food, use iron-enriched varieties. The labels will tell you if iron has been added.

Cereals should be a mixture of whole (high fibre) and refined varieties. Too much high-fibre food is not good for a young child because it contains a substance that interferes with the way iron is absorbed. Do not give young children tea: it contains tannin, which also interferes with iron absorption.

Complementary Treatment

For iron-deficiency anaemia the **nutritional therapist** may recommend iron-rich foods (see orthodox treatment, above) in preference to supplements. For anaemia caused by deficiencies in vitamin B_6, B_{12}, folic acid or zinc, supplements are recommended, and/or foods containing good supplies. **Western herbalism** can help to restore strength. **Chinese herbalists** may prescribe blood tonics, such as floradex, followed by prescriptions containing rehmannia, angelica, peony, ginseng and licorice.

LEUKAEMIA

What is it?

Leukaemia is a cancer that affects the white blood cells. It is the most common cancer of childhood. In the United Kingdom around 420 children a year develop leukaemia, most commonly children who are aged between two and five years old.

Although childhood leukaemia is no more common today than it was 40 years ago, advances in treatment mean that more than two in three children who develop leukaemia now recover. In children, the most common type of leukaemia is acute lymphoblastic leukaemia (ALL), with acute myeloid leukaemia (AML) less common.

Development

Leukaemia begins in the bone marrow, which produces three main types of blood cells: red oxygen-carrying cells (erythrocytes), white infection-fighting cells (leucocytes, of which there are three types) and platelets, which are needed for clotting. In leukaemia the bone marrow makes huge quantities of one type of abnormal white cell. (The type of abnormal cell that is produced depends on the specific condition; for example in myeloid leukaemia leucocytes are affected.) These spill out into the blood, the lymph system, the liver, spleen and sometimes into the cerebrospinal fluid, which circulates around the brain and spine. In the bone marrow, the leukaemic cells interfere with the production of red cells, platelets and the other white blood cells.

Causes

It is not yet known what triggers childhood leukaemia, although genetic make-up is more important in childhood leukaemia than it is in adult leukaemia, and some children with fragile links between particular genes are vulnerable to the disease. However it is exceptionally rare for a second child in a family to develop the disease unless they are an identical twin, when the risk is 25 per cent. The children of parents who have had leukaemia at some time in their life do not inherit the disease.

One or more environmental triggers may be needed for leukaemia to develop. Viruses, chemicals such as benzene, high voltage cables and both 'natural' and leaked radiation have all been suggested as possible causes, but because the incidence of childhood leukaemia is low, it has proved difficult to pinpoint the triggers.

If you notice any of the common signs of leukaemia (listed below) in your child, don't jump to conclusions. It is far more likely to be a common childhood illness. Doctors only consider leukaemia when they see a cluster of symptoms that don't respond to treatment as fast as expected.

You may notice

- *The child is unusually tired and pale, catching repeated infections, particularly sore throats, ear infections and sometimes skin infections, such as boils*
- *Bruises or dark red blotchy spots may appear for no reason*
- *The child may have a lot of nosebleeds and you may notice that the gums bleed easily during tooth brushing*
- *The child may limp because their bones ache*
- *The neck, armpits and groin may feel puffy as a result of swollen glands.*

What to do

Most children develop the symptoms over a week or two, but a few show them over weeks or months. If you are worried that your child may have leukaemia, take them to the doctor. The doctor will examine the child carefully and take a blood sample, which will be processed within a day. If this shows leukaemic cells you will be told immediately, and the doctor will arrange for the child to go immediately into hospital in order to have more tests.

Tests for leukaemia

A biopsy of the bone marrow will show which type of leukaemia is present. The biopsy involves inserting a fine needle into the hip under general anaesthetic and sucking out a small amount of marrow. The child may also have a lumbar puncture to take a sample of cerebrospinal fluid. This will show if there are any leukaemic cells in the cerebrospinal fluid. Some children will also have a chest X-ray and a scan of the abdomen.

The initial treatment

Children with leukaemia are usually treated at a specialist centre, and the treatment depends on the type of leukaemia. Treatment for AML is very different from treatment for ALL. Before treatment starts the child may be given one or more blood transfusions and sometimes antibiotics as well to clear up any infections. Treatment for ALL follows these stages. First, a fine tube, or catheter, is inserted into a large vein under general anaesthetic. A combination of drugs is given to target cancer cells at different stages of development. The child may be in hospital for a few days or weeks. Once all the leukaemic cells in the blood and bone marrow have been destroyed, the child is said to be in remission. They will also have to take some drugs by mouth and will need regular mouthcare to help prevent ulcers.

Secondary treatment

About a month after the first course of treatment the child has a top-up dose of different anti-cancer drugs. Injections of anti-cancer drugs into the cerebrospinal fluid and sometimes into the bloodstream will kill off any lurking leukaemic cells. A few children also have radiotherapy to their head and spine. A second and sometimes a third top-up dose of anti-cancer drugs are given.

Once initial treatment has been completed the child can go home. They will need to keep taking low-dose anti-cancer drugs and protective antibiotics. This stage lasts two years and the child is usually well enough to go back to school while still receiving treatment. Apart from hair loss just after treatment (the hair grows back), the child will appear perfectly well to other people.

When the child is back home it is important that they lead as normal a life as possible. Children may show some changes in behaviour, such as unusual moodiness or a variable appetite, but these can be side effects of the drugs the child continues to take. At this stage the child will still make regular visits to the hospital, and the doctors will warn the parents of any symptoms to watch for which might suggest a relapse. Children on maintenance therapy are susceptible to certain infections and if they are themselves not immune to measles and chickenpox they should avoid contact with other people who have these illnesses.

Children who are still well after two years have a series of final tests to check for leukaemic cells in the cerebrospinal fluid and the bone marrow. If all the test results are clear the drugs can be stopped.

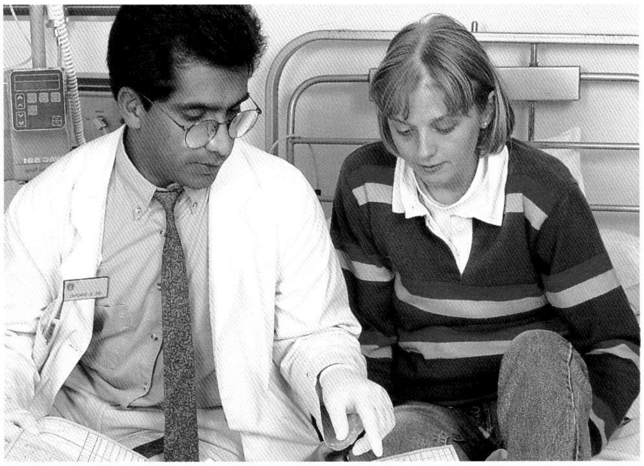

Teenagers with leukaemia may be able to stay in hospital in a special teenage unit, so the practical and emotional problems of having a rare but long-term illness can be shared, not only with other teenagers in a similar situation, but also with staff who have a very special expertise.

Other forms of treatment for leukaemia

Some children with leukaemia will need additional forms of treatment.

Bone marrow transplants The diseased bone marrow is destroyed with anti-cancer drugs and sometimes radiotherapy. Bone marrow from a healthy brother or sister, or from an unrelated donor, is introduced into the circulation via a drip. The marrow cells find their way into the child's bones and rapidly multiply to form new bone marrow throughout the body.

Peripheral blood stem cells This is an alternative to a bone marrow transplant, and involves taking blood from a matched donor or relative. Stem cells, which are 'all-purpose' blood cells that can develop into other types of white blood cell, are separated off and transfused into the patient, while the rest of the blood is returned to the donor.

Cord blood transfusion This is a transfusion of cells from a baby brother or sister's umbilical cord. Cord blood is especially rich in stem cells.

Complementary Treatment

The complementary therapies concentrate on providing support for orthodox treatment. **Aromatherapy** can aid pain control, insomnia and nausea. Essential oils may be applied during **massage**, added to bath water or used in compresses. **Relaxation** may bring some relief from symptoms and help the child to deal with the emotional effects of the disease, such as anger, anxiety and fear. **Osteopathy** may be beneficial in minimizing the effects of chemotherapy. **Tai chi** and **chi kung** may help to restore strength following treatment.

SICKLE-CELL DISORDERS

What are they?

Sickle-cell disorders are a group of blood conditions in which the haemoglobin (substances in the red blood cells that carry oxygen) has a faulty structure. They include sickle-cell anaemia, haemoglobin C sickle-cell disease and sickle beta thalassaemia. The red blood cells – which are normally round but the shape of which can easily be altered – become rigid and crescent-shaped. These abnormal cells block smaller blood vessels and the tissues become starved of oxygen. The abnormal cells die sooner than normal red blood cells, so anaemia develops.

Sickle-cell anaemia is an inherited disease that is most common in people of African and Afro-Caribbean descent, but it can occur in people from the Indian subcontinent, the Middle East or the eastern Mediterranean. An affected child inherits a sickle-cell gene from each parent. If a child inherits only one sickle-cell gene, they will have a condition called sickle-cell trait, which does not usually affect their health, but means that they will be carriers of the disease and may pass it on to any children they have in later life.

Carriers can be tested, and in some areas screening in pregnancy is routine. If both parents are carriers, there is a one-in-four chance that each of their children will have sickle-cell anaemia. Tests on the foetus can be carried out by chorionic villus sampling or amniocentesis. Newborn babies can be diagnosed on the basis of a blood sample.

Although being a carrier makes no difference to the general routines of life, it becomes an important factor in conditions where oxygen levels are low, such as scuba diving or having a general anaesthetic. Sickle cell anaemia is a serious condition that needs medical supervision.

Symptoms do not usually start before a baby is six months old.

You may notice

- *The child has pain, sometimes with swelling of the hands and feet*
- *The child suffers from serious infections, such as pneumonia or meningitis*
- *The child's stomach is unusually swollen*
- *The child may show signs of anaemia*

What to do

If you are worried, take your child to the doctor. If a blood sample shows sickle-cell disease, the child will be referred to a hospital with a specialist haemoglobinopathy department or special centres in the community. The aim of treatment is to keep children as healthy as possible. They will have to take penicillin twice a day to protect them from infections and must eat a well-balanced, nutritious diet with extra folic acid and lots of fluids to avoid dehydration. They need to stay warm and dry and should avoid overexertion. They should have all their normal childhood immunizations and also be immunized against flu and pneumococcus.

Despite treatment, children are prone to sickle-cell crises – bouts of pain, infections, anaemia and jaundice. Crises can be brought on by getting cold and wet, taking exercise outdoors in cold weather or being dehydrated. Signs of a crisis are suddenly feeling severe pain and becoming unwell, with a headache, neck stiffness or drowsiness. Children in crisis need to go to hospital. Meanwhile you should keep them comfortable and, if they cannot drink, place a damp face cloth over their lips.

Coping with sickle-cell disease

Children with sickle-cell disease should not go out in the cold and wet. Sports such as long distance running, hiking or sprinting are not suitable, and they should only swim in warm water. They will also need extra time to dry and warm up afterwards. Bedwetting is common.

Children with this condition should have regular eye tests from the age of ten.

Who can help?

For organizations offering support see the Directory.

Complementary Treatment

The **nutritional therapist** will be able to devise a dietary programme suited to the individual's needs, to improve the body's ability to combat illness. Orthodox treatment can be supported by **relaxation**, **aromatherapy** and **massage**, all of which may help to alleviate symptoms and have a positive effect on negative emotions associated with the condition. Both **Tai chi** and **chi kung** may help to restore the child's strength following treatment.

SEE ALSO WETTING (PAGE 302) DEHYDRATION (PAGE 252) JAUNDICE (PAGE 267)

THALASSAEMIA

What is it?

Thalassaemia is an inherited blood disorder that is most common in people from the Mediterranean countries, the Middle East, the Indian subcontinent and Southeast Asia. A genetic defect causes faulty production of red blood cells in the bone marrow. Red blood cells normally carry oxygen around the body to the tissues, but in thalassaemia there are not enough red cells to fulfil this function and the signs of anaemia develop (see Anaemia, page 281).

There are two main types of thalassaemia, known as beta and alpha thalassaemia, and many different varieties. Beta thalassaemia is the most common type. Individuals who have one faulty gene for thalassaemia are carriers of the disease. This is called a thalassaemia trait, thalassaemia minor or silent carriers.

Carriers can be identified from a simple blood test. They are perfectly healthy, although their blood has unusually small red blood cells, and they may develop slight anaemia. If two carriers have children, each child has a one-in-four chance of being born with two faulty genes, which gives rise to the condition known as thalassaemia major. Thalassaemia major can be detected during pregnancy by taking a small sample of blood from the foetus or by chorionic villus sampling.

Thalassaemia major is a serious illness and, if left untreated, it can be fatal. However with modern treatment many children now live to become healthy adults and have their own children.

People with thalassaemia tend to come from those parts of the world in which malaria is a common disease. In some countries, such as Indonesia and parts of India, it is thought that as many as ten per cent of the population may carry the gene for this condition. One reason for this may very well be that those people who carry thalassaemia are also more resistant to malaria.

You may notice

- *When an infant is between three and eighteen months old, they may develop signs of serious anaemia, including pale skin and lack of energy*
- *The infant may have a poor appetite and fail to thrive*

What to do

If your infant develops signs of anaemia, and you or your partner have thalassaemia trait, take the baby to the doctor. The doctor will take a blood sample for testing and if it shows thalassaemia major the child will be referred to a specialist treatment centre.

Treatment

Treatment usually involves children receiving a blood transfusion every three to four weeks to boost the number of healthy red blood cells. They must also be given a drug called desferrioxamine, which removes the build-up of excess iron caused by regular transfusions. The drug has to be given by injection, and is pumped continuously for ten hours into a site under the skin, five nights a week.

Children may need to take extra vitamin C to enhance the effect of desferrioxamine. Iron-removing drugs that can be taken by mouth are now being developed. Many children also have their spleen removed in later childhood. With these treatments, children are able to lead an almost normal, healthy life.

Some children with thalassaemia have a bone marrow transplant. This is usually performed in infancy, and the marrow is donated by a close relative with compatible bone marrow. Although it is a major operation, it may achieve a complete cure.

Who can help?

For organizations that offer support, advice and information, see the Directory.

Complementary Treatment

The complementary therapies concentrate on providing support for orthodox treatment. **Aromatherapy** can aid pain control, insomnia and nausea. Essential oils may be applied during **massage**, added to bath water or used in compresses. **Relaxation** may bring some relief from symptoms and help the child deal with the emotional effects of the disease, such as anger, anxiety and fear. Both **Tai chi** and **chi kung** may help restore strength following treatment.

GENITALS, URINARY TRACT AND KIDNEYS

Liquid waste from the body is disposed of through the kidneys and urinary system. The key players are the kidneys, two bean-shaped organs situated either side of the spine at the top of the abdomen and well protected from harm by the ribcage. The rest of the urinary tract consists of two long ureters that lead down from the kidneys; the bladder; and the urethra, which takes urine down to the outside world. They all have a comparatively simple storage and drainage function.

Kidneys

One-fifth of the blood in the body flows through the massive renal artery from the heart into the kidneys, where it is filtered. Water, sugars and salts are extracted and a weak solution left to flow through the long tubules that drain eventually into the ureter. Essential substances such as glucose, amino acids and calcium are extracted, leaving urine, almost all of which is water. The kidneys also allow the body to keep its fluid levels and their composition constant, whatever the intake. When we take in more fluid and food than we need, they dispose of excess water and salts.

Bladder and urethra

Urine travels through the ureters to the bladder, an elastic, muscular bag. Once it is full, contractions squeeze urine out past the sphincter at the top of the outlet tube – the urethra – where it exits the body. In a boy the urethra is five times as long as in it is in a girl. It not only transports urine, but beginning with puberty carries sperm from the testes and seminal vesicles near the bladder. In a girl the opening of the urethra is enclosed in the vulva but is separate from the vagina.

The reproductive system of a young girl (right) is similar to that of a woman, with a few exceptions: the vaginal wall is thinner and the vagina itself smaller. In a boy (top and far right) the testes have usually descended before birth, although this may not always happen.

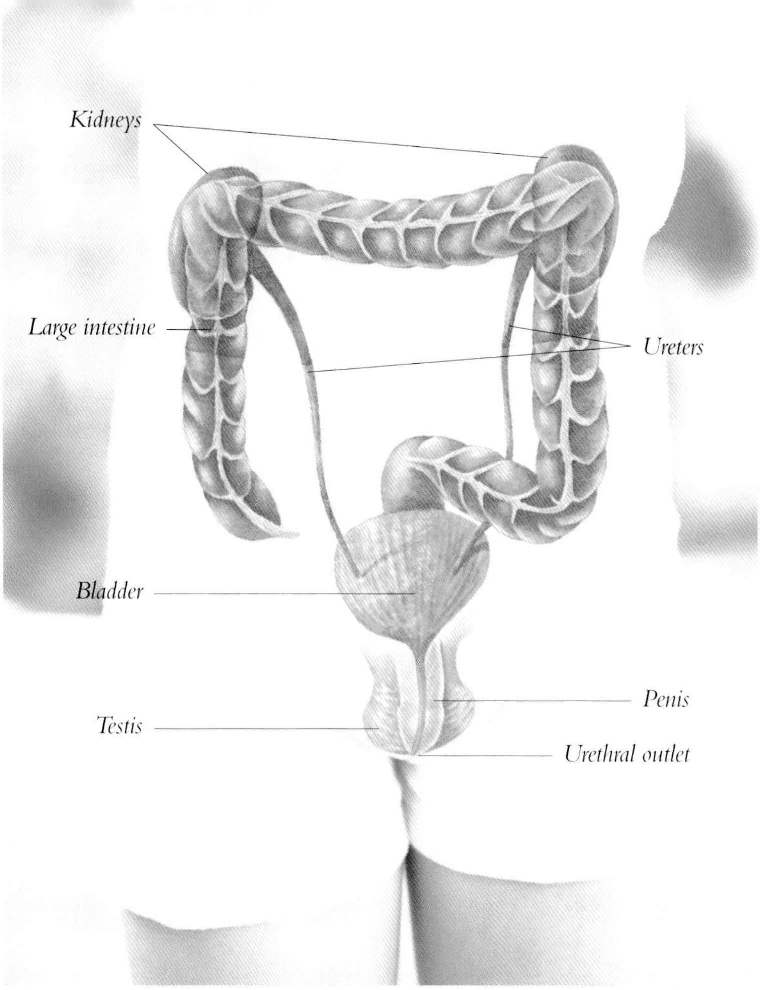
Kidneys
Large intestine
Ureters
Bladder
Penis
Testis
Urethral outlet

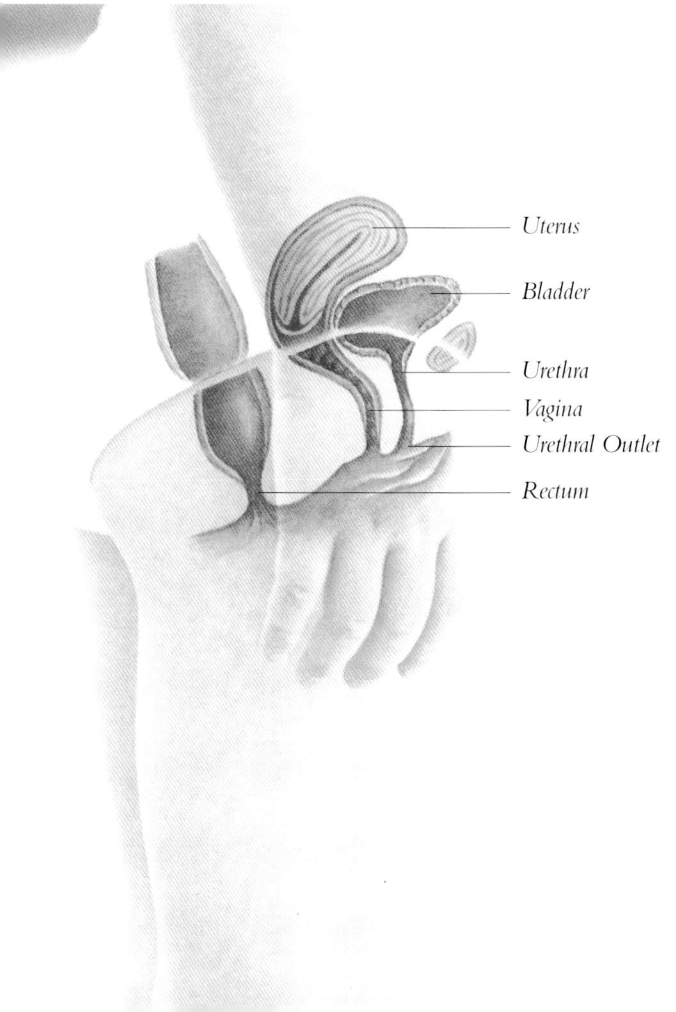
Uterus
Bladder
Urethra
Vagina
Urethral Outlet
Rectum

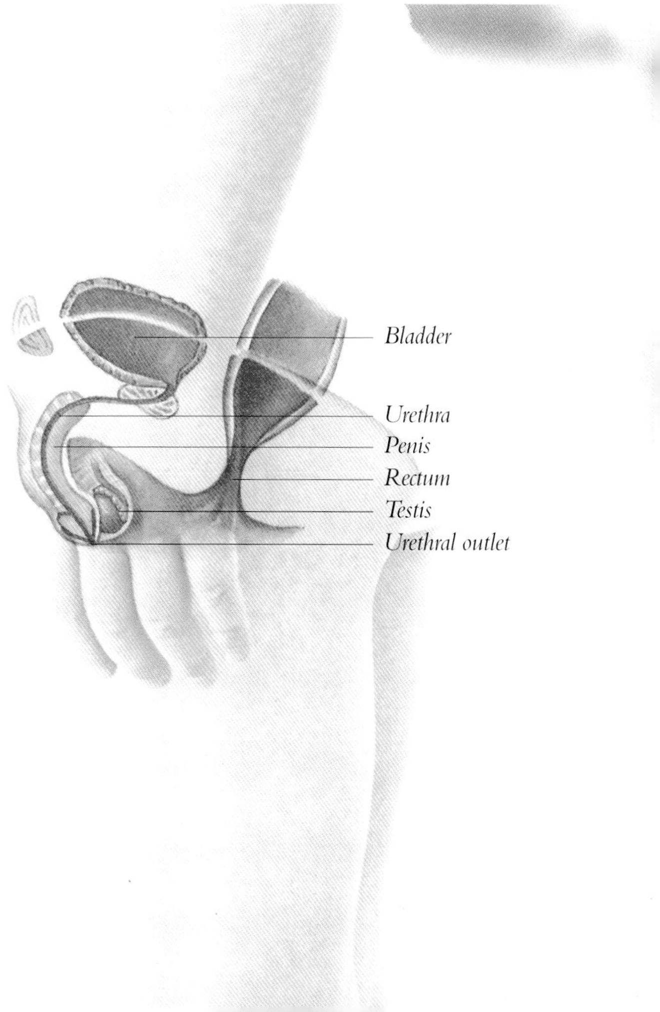
Bladder
Urethra
Penis
Rectum
Testis
Urethral outlet

Diagnosis

There are a number of common conditions that affect the genital and urinary systems of children. Developmental problems mainly affect boys, and can usually be corrected fairly easily. Urinary infections can develop into more serious conditions if they are left untreated, so should never be ignored.

Sign	What could be wrong
Swelling in the scrotum of an infant boy, which may enlarge and shrink or stay the same size	Hydrocele. Consult the doctor
The opening that is normally at the end of the penis is on the underside	Hypospadias. Consult the doctor
Diarrhoea (blood-stained), vomiting and stomach pain, and the child passes very little urine	Haemolytic uraemic syndrome. Consult the doctor
Child first passes large quantities of urine, then very little; energy and appetite loss	Possibly kidney failure. Consult the doctor as soon as possible
Dribbling stream of urine, ballooning and possibly infections of the tip of the penis	Phimosis. Consult the doctor
Sore, red penis tip	Balanitis. Consult the doctor
One or both sides of the scrotum in an infant boy feel slack and empty	Undescended testes. Consult the doctor
Pain on urination	Any condition that makes the genital area sore, such as nappy rash, a sore vagina, or balanitis
Painful, frequent urination, more common in children over the age of two	Urinary tract infection. Consult the doctor
Deep, concentrated yellow urine	Hot weather; little to drink, possibly fever; child has been eating orange/yellow food (e.g. carrots, satsumas, sweetcorn) or has taken rifampicin, an antibiotic given to protect against meningitis
Red or 'smoky' darkened urine	Blood in the urine from infection (may smell 'fishy'). Acute glomerulonephritis, uncommon in developed countries
Passing large quantities of urine	Drinking too much, diabetes or a kidney disease
Passing small quantities of urine	Drinking very little, especially in hot weather or, much more rarely, haemolytic uraemic syndrome

Sore Penis

What is it ?

Penis problems are quite common in boys and vary in degree of seriousness. Slightly sore, red skin at the end of the penis may mean no more than that the final drips of urine have not been shaken off at the end of urination, and the dampness has chafed the skin. A baby in nappies may also have a rash from contact with urine. If the soreness has spread to the glans (the tip of the penis) the foreskin may become slightly swollen and obstruct the opening, making it difficult to urinate. This is a sign of balanitis, inflammation of the foreskin and glans.

If the baby or boy has been circumcised the penis will remain sore for about one week.

You may notice

- *The tip of the penis is sore, red and may be slightly swollen*
- *The boy may cry or complain that it hurts when he urinates*
- *There may be sores on the uncovered tip of a penis that has been circumcised*

What to do

Most causes of a sore penis are not serious and can be dealt with easily at home. However if there is any redness that does not clear up within two days or keeps returning you should take the child to your doctor. If the child shows symptoms of balanitis you should take him to the doctor immediately.

Most causes of a sore penis are straightforward and can be treated simply at home. In infants, irritation from a wet nappy is quite common and leaving the infant nappy-free for as long as possible can speed healing. Sometimes a thread or hair can wind itself around the glans, causing swelling and inflammation. Check before putting on a new nappy.

Never try to force the foreskin back. If the end of the foreskin becomes red, wash the penis very carefully, ideally in the bath, pulling the foreskin back gently only as far as it will easily go. Pat dry carefully and dab on antiseptic cream. If the child is in pain, give paracetamol liquid. Frequent baths, perhaps as often as four or five times a day, may help.

What else?

If the child is still in nappies, let him go nappy-free for as long as possible. When you do use a nappy, change it as soon as it becomes wet.

If a baby is already circumcised and sores develop on the tip of the penis, keep him out of nappies as much as possible. When you put nappies on again, protect the glans with petroleum jelly.

If the penis remains sore, consult your doctor who can prescribe an antibiotic cream which should clear up any infection. Most infections clear quickly, although some boys have recurrent attacks.

Boys who get repeated and painful attacks of balanitis may benefit from circumcision.

Prevention

Teach a child aged seven or older to draw back the foreskin (if he can) and wash the end of the penis and around the foreskin carefully every day.

Complementary Treatment

The **homeopathic remedy** Mercurius 6c (*Mercurius solubilis Hahnemani*, quicksilver) may help. Give every four hours for up to five days. The foreskin and head of the penis can be bathed with Hypericum and Calendula solution every four hours. Dilute 5 drops of the mother tincture in 0.25 litres/½ pint of cooled, boiled water.

SEE ALSO CIRCUMCISION (PAGE 291)

UNDESCENDED TESTES

What is it ?

The testes are formed inside the abdomen before birth, and normally make their way down to the scrotum by the 36th week of pregnancy. In approximately six per cent of infants – and many more premature babies – one or both testes have not yet reached their final destination at birth. Undescended testes are therefore a perfectly normal finding in premature babies and are only abnormal in babies who are born full term. In some boys, the testes can be felt within the scrotum but have not dropped right down; moreover they cannot be moved down. In others a gentle downwards massage can bring them into place at the bottom of the scrotum. In a minority of boys whose testes have definitely not descended, one or more testes has stopped in its descent, while in the majority the testes has taken a wrong turning and ended up in the wrong place, a condition known as maldescended testes.

In many cases where the testes can be felt within the scrotum or gently massaged downwards, they will descend properly within three months of birth. After this age they are unlikely to descend any further without treatment.

Babies with undescended testes are not adversely affected. Later, however, the testes do not develop normally, and in adult life fail to produce normal sperm. Testes that are not properly descended are also more likely to become twisted, cutting off the blood supply and causing severe pain.

You may notice

- *The doctor who carries out the neonatal examination on a male infant may notice that one or both sides of the scrotum feel slack and empty*

Treatment

If the problem is noticed first at the neonatal examination, nothing needs to be done immediately. The baby will be checked again at six to eight weeks of age. If you want to check for yourself, ask the doctor to show you how. It is easiest to check in the bath or while you are changing a nappy, as long as your hands are warm. The testes are sensitive to cold and may retract and apparently disappear if handled with cold hands. Once the testes are emerging into the scrotum, they feel firm and round to the touch.

If there is any doubt about the descent of the testes at the age of six to eight weeks, you or your doctor should ask the opinion of a paediatric surgeon. If the testes still do not descend, a small operation (orchidopexy) is needed to bring them down into the scrotum. After manoeuvring the testes into the scrotum, they are usually fixed with a few stitches to prevent them springing back. Orchidopexy is usually carried out as day surgery and performed around the age of one to three years. Performing the operation in early childhood is likely to improve fertility later, which is usually normal.

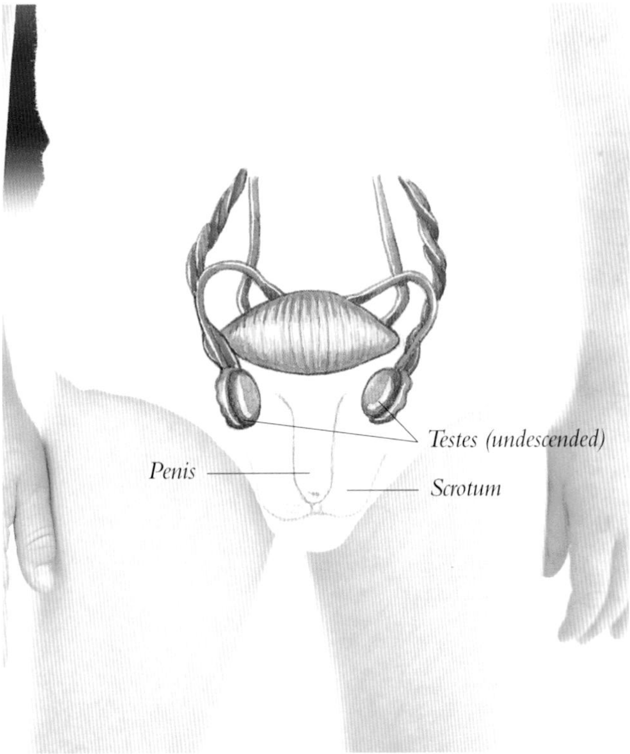

Prior to birth, the testes generally migrate from the abdomen into the scrotum via the passageway called the inguineal canal. If they are undescended (a condition known as cryptorchidism) by the time the baby is six to eight weeks of age, the baby may require a small operation (orchidopexy) to manoeuvre them into position.

Complementary Treatment

Chinese herbalism can stimulate liver energy to mature and descend the testes. The liver channel circulates around the genitals and has an influence on all genital problems. It may avoid the possibility of surgery. **Homeopathy** offers specific remedies: Clematis 30c (*Clematis erecta*, virgin's bower) when the left testicle has not descended but the right one has; and Aurum 30c (*Aurum metallicum*, gold) when neither testicle has descended. Remedies are to be given twice a day for two months. If the testicles do not descend after this, you should see a homeopath.

Circumcision

What is it ?

Male circumcision is a surgical operation to remove the foreskin of the penis, which at birth is joined to the head, or glans, of the penis. Left alone, by 12 months the foreskin of around half of all baby boys has separated from the glans naturally, and for the majority this has occurred by the age of three years. In relatively few cases the foreskin cannot be pulled back until the boy becomes a teenager.

Once your son reaches the age of seven or so, it is sensible to teach him to pull back his foreskin gently (as long as there is no resistance) while he is in the bath, clean the area around the glans and then replace the foreskin. This stops white, cheesy secretions gathering under the foreskin and may possibly protect him against cancer of the penis as an adult. However never forcibly pull back the foreskin; this may tear the delicate membranes underneath, leaving scar tissue.

Reasons for circumcision

The most frequent reasons for circumcision are religious or social. Jewish boys are circumcised on the eighth day of life while Muslims are treated between the ages of one and fifteen years. The only medical reasons for performing a circumcision are that the foreskin cannot be drawn back, or the foreskin is too tight (phimosis), which can lead to repeated inflammation (balanitis, see page 299). Circumcision may prevent this. It may also be associated with a reduced incidence of urinary tract infection in the first year.

The surgical procedure

A plastic device, the Plastibell, is often used in operations on newborn infants. After freeing the foreskin the device is inserted over the glans and a ligature applied. The foreskin falls off after a few days. In older children circumcision is usually carried out as a daycare operation requiring a general anaesthetic. During surgery the inner and outer layers of the foreskin are carefully cut away and the edges stitched together. The surgeon may leave the penis exposed or apply a dressing. The dressing may be removed while the child is in hospital, as removal later at home when the wound has dried can be very painful. Alternatively the genital area may be protected with a biodegradable dressing, which will make removal unnecessary.

Aftercare

The penis may be so tender following circumcision that your child may not want to wear pants for a few days, in which case a long tee-shirt will protect his modesty. If your child is still in a nappy, smear petroleum jelly on to the nappy to stop it sticking to the penis. The surgeon may prescribe an anaesthetic jelly and/or painkillers; some surgeons will also prescribe an antibiotic ointment to prevent sores developing on the newly exposed and very sensitive glans. Your child can have a bath on the day after surgery as long as it isn't too uncomfortable. Taking two or three baths a day helps the healing process.

The cut usually heals in seven to ten days, but in quite a proportion of boys it becomes infected. Signs of infection include reddening, swelling, a discharge, bleeding and difficulty passing urine. If these signs develop contact your doctor for antibiotic treatment.

Alternative treatment

A simpler operation, causing less discomfort afterwards, is preputial plasty, which means a widening of the foreskin. This is an alternative for boys with mild or moderate phimosis. Alternatively, a foreskin that is stuck down can be loosened under a general anaesthetic.

Complementary Treatment

Complementary treatments will be confined to emotional problems associated with surgery. The **Bach flower remedies** may help to alleviate fear and anxiety and the emotional aspects of recovery. **Homeopathic remedies** that can be given prior to surgery include Aconite 30c (*Aconitum napellus*, blue aconite) for the child who is panicking and has a great fear of surgery, and Gelsemium 6c (*Gelsemium sempervirens*, yellow jasmine) if the child is very apprehensive, weak and trembling. Phosphorus 6c (phosphorus) can be given to relieve vomiting following surgery; and Arnica 30c (*Arnica montana*, leopard's bane) to relieve pain and prevent infection. Arnica should be followed by the remedy Staphisagria 6c (*Delphinium staphisagria*, stavesacre). These remedies should be given every half hour for up to ten doses.

URINARY TRACT INFECTIONS

What are they ?

Infections of the urinary tract are common in children and are caused most often when bacteria that normally live in the bowel enter the urinary tract. Once the bacteria, most commonly *E-coli*, reach the bladder they multiply and can develop into an infection in the urinary tract. In a proportion of children the problem is made worse by anatomical faults in the tubes and valves that make up the urinary system.

On the whole urinary tract infection is more likely to occur in girls because the openings to the rectum and urethra are so close together. However in babies, boys are more commonly affected by urinary tract infections than girls, but by school age infections are much more common among girls. At any age a urinary tract infection should be taken seriously.

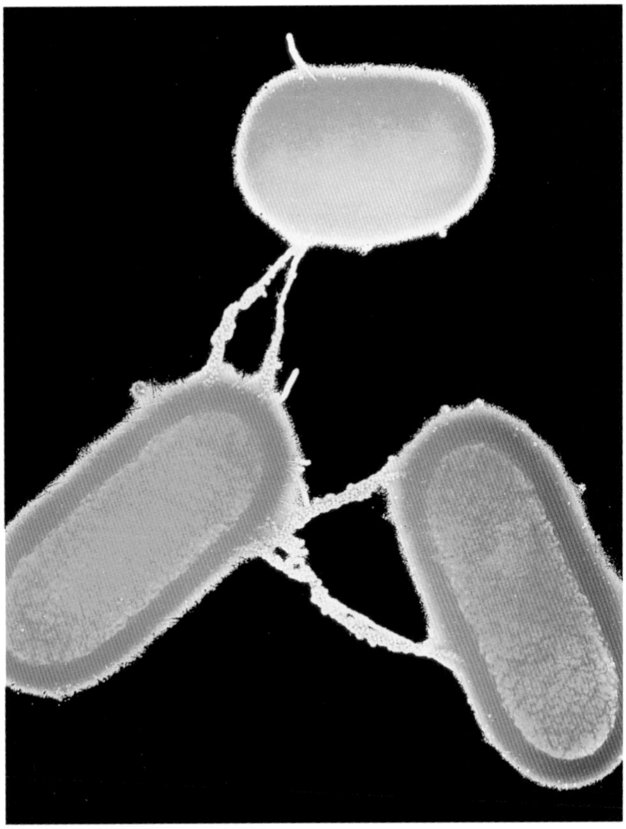

A male E-coli *bacterium (lower left) conjugates with two female* E-coli *bacteria. These organisms normally live in the gut, but under certain circumstances they can migrate to or be transferred into the bladder, where they multiply by sexual reproduction.* E-coli *is one of the common causes of urinary tract infection, which is more common in girls than boys, as the urethra and the rectum are close together.*

You may notice

In young babies

- *New babies may remain jaundiced for longer than expected (neonatal jaundice usually fades by the age of two weeks)*
- *They may lose more weight after birth than expected. They may fail to thrive*

In children

- *The younger the child, the vaguer the symptoms. Some children feel well while others run an unexplained fever. They may seem off-colour and irritable*
- *Other children have a sudden fever. They look pale, lose interest in food and may develop vomiting and diarrhoea, or constipation*
- *Some children start to wet again during the day or at night*
- *Wriggling with discomfort during urination or holding on to avoid pain*
- *Instead of flowing out in a strong stream urine may dribble out. It may look hazy or cloudy. Sometimes infected urine has a foul, fishy smell*

Diagnosis

Take a child with any sign of a urinary tract infection to the doctor. Wash the genital area first and give a drink of water or dilute juice a couple of hours before the appointment so it is easier to produce a urine sample on demand. The doctor will give you a sterile container.

To give an accurate picture of the urine in the child's bladder a mid-stream urine specimen is needed. However this is often difficult to collect.

The first few millilitres of urine passed are not collected as they may contain micro-organisms from the perineal area (the area enclosed by the thighs and lower buttocks, including the external genitalia). The idea is to get your child to urinate a little, then stop.

The next flow of urine is then collected in the sterile container. This is easier for boys, but a girl may achieve it by holding the container to catch the urine as she urinates. Obviously hands need to be washed thoroughly after this task; alternatively the doctor or practice nurse may provide protective gloves.

To collect a specimen of urine from a baby, your doctor can give either you either a bag or a urine collection pad and a syringe with which to draw up the urine, as well as a sterile container in which to put it.

A diagnostic strip dipped into the urine can detect the presence of infection, giving a positive result if there are white cells, nitrites, protein or blood in the urine.

Many children who have had a diagnosed urinary tract infection will be referred to hospital for tests. This may include an X-ray of the abdomen and an ultrasound examination to show the structure of the urinary tract, the kidneys and the bladder. A DMSA scan will show how the kidneys are functioning. This test involves injecting a minutely radioactive substance of DMSA (dimercaptosuccinic acid) into a small vein. The substance passes through the blood stream and into the kidneys. When the kidneys are X-rayed the shape, size and function show up clearly.

Some young children may also have a micturating cystourethrogram - a special X-ray taken while the child is passing urine. A fine tube is inserted into the urethra and a contrast dye passed along it. The X-rays are taken during urination; they show whether any urine is flowing back into the kidneys as the bladder contracts. Once a child is toilet-trained a DTPA scan can be used. This is similar to a DMSA scan but the radioactive substance (diethylene triamine pentacetic acid) is filtered out of the kidneys and a series of pictures is taken to record its passage through the urinary tract.

Abnormalities

The most common abnormality found is vesico-ureteric reflux. Instead of draining straight out of the bladder down the urethra, some urine flows back towards the kidneys. Children usually grow out of reflux but in the meantime they need long-term antibiotics in a low dose to protect them against infection. It is important to take the antibiotics because if left untreated reflux can permanently scar the kidneys. Children also need regular check-ups with the doctor as well as annual scans to ensure the kidneys are developing normally and healthily. Any children under the age of seven who do not grow out of reflux can have a simple operation to correct it, after which the danger of damage has generally past. Reflux can be inherited, so any brothers or sisters may benefit from referral to a paediatrician for assessment.

Treatment

Once a urine sample has been taken the doctor will probably start the child on an antibiotic drug immediately, usually even if other tests need to be carried out. A few days after the course of antibiotics is finished the doctor should check the urine again to see if it is clear of infection.

What else?

Children with a urinary tract infection should drink extra clear fluids in order to keep their urinary system well flushed out. Tap water is a perfectly suitable drink as many boiled waters contain inappropriate quantities of salts. However some mineral waters are considered suitable for babies (ask your doctor to recommend a brand) and so can be given, as can very well diluted fruit juices or squash.

Avoid irritants such as bubble baths and nylon underwear. Buy underwear with a cotton gusset and avoid tights and snug leggings.

Soft toilet paper wipes more efficiently than hard paper. Teach girls to wipe their bottom from front to back. This avoids harmful micro-organisms from the anus being wiped over the vulva.

Encourage your child to take showers rather than baths as they cleanse more efficiently. If baths are taken, wash hair separately under the shower. If your child catches worms, treat the infestation immediately as worms can result in a urinary tract infection (see Threadworms, page 268).

Children who hang on when they need to urinate may make it more likely that urine will flow back from the bladder. Encourage a toddler to go to the toilet every two or three hours at most, and always before going out. Keep them amused while they are there so that they don't rush off before they have properly emptied their bladder.

Complementary Treatment

Western herbalism will prescribe herbs to be applied topically, used in douches and taken internally. **Chinese herbalism** can be very helpful in acute conditions and will support orthodox treatment when the condition is chronic. **Acupuncture** and **homeopathy** can also be effective. **Aromatherapy** oils applied to the abdominal wall in compresses or during massage may relieve pain and stimulate diuresis. This is best carried out by a nurse or physiotherapist who has been trained in the practice of aromatherapy.

Warning: Essential oils should not be used on or by patients who also have renal disease or must maintain a strict fluid balance.

SEE ALSO KIDNEY DISEASE (PAGE 294)

KIDNEY DISEASE

What is it ?

The kidneys perform many vital functions, such as filtering waste products out of the blood into the urine and regulating fluid levels and salts in the body. They maintain the balance between acid and alkaline substances and help to keep the blood pressure constant. The kidneys also produce the hormone erythropoietin, which stimulates the bone marrow to make red blood cells and another hormone, renin, which is important in controlling blood pressure. Therefore any inflammation or damage to the kidneys will have wide-ranging effects throughout the body.

Reflux

The kidneys may be affected if an organism that has caused an infection further down the urinary tract travels up the ureter. This is much more likely to happen if the valves at the junction between the bladder and the ureter are faulty. In the condition called vesico-ureteric reflux, when the bladder contracts in order to excrete urine, some urine travels backwards up the ureter and into the kidneys. After passing urine, the bladder relaxes, allowing the refluxed urine to return. However a constant reservoir of urine remains in the bladder, acting as a focus for infection. Any obstruction in the urinary tract tends to make the problem worse.

Effects and treatment

Refluxing urine can damage the kidneys before birth and certainly in early childhood. Any scarring is permanent and in certain children can lead to serious kidney damage and failure – which is why a young child with a urinary tract infection and any child with repeated urinary infections should always be investigated by a paediatrician or paediatric nephrologist. As the bladder wall matures and thickens with age, reflux improves, but as the scarring is permanent, all affected children should receive protective antibiotic drugs. If infections continue, an operation may be performed to re-site the ureters in the bladder.

Haemolytic Uraemic Syndrome

This disorder, which is now the most common cause of acute kidney failure in children, and appears to be increasing in frequency, affects young children much more often than adults. It may follow an attack of gastroenteritis caused by the bacterium *E-coli*, frequently found in undercooked meat, particularly that used in hamburgers. In a child who is severely affected, small blood vessels in the kidney clot and cause temporary kidney failure.

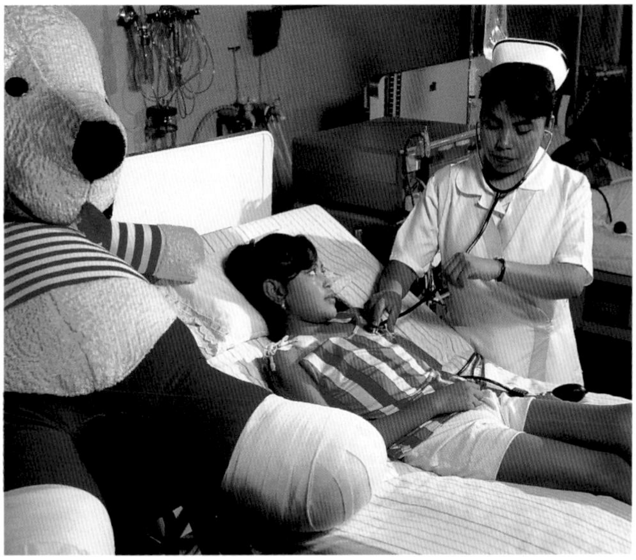

Children whose kidneys are no longer operating as efficient filtration units may need short- or long-term dialysis to remove accumulating waste products from the blood. Children who need short-term dialysis for acute kidney failure can normally expect to use a kidney machine in the hospital. Otherwise dialysis is carried out in an outpatient centre or even in the child's home.

You may notice

- *Acute diarrhoea, often blood stained*
- *Vomiting*
- *Abdominal pain*
- *Pale skin*
- *Very little urine is passed*

What to do

Contact your doctor immediately. The child will be taken into hospital where intravenous fluids and, if necessary, a blood transfusion can be given. Dialysis can take over the functions of the kidneys if they fail temporarily. In many cases dialysis is only needed for a few days, after which the kidneys often recover completely.

Kidney Failure

In kidney failure the kidneys cannot perform their normal functions. In children this is rare, and if one kidney is damaged the other usually takes over its work. Very occasionally both kidneys fail – most often because of congenital kidney abnormalities; following severe kidney scarring as a result of reflux; or less often haemolytic uraemic syndrome.

You may notice

- *After at first being very thirsty (most obvious during the night) and passing much more urine than normal, the child passes much less urine*
- *The child may lose both energy and appetite*
- *The pace of their growth will slow down*
- *Their skin will become dry and dull*

What to do

Consult your doctor, who will refer your child to a hospital specialist for detailed investigations. The child's treatment will depend on the cause, but a good diet is important – one that is low in protein and has supplements of vitamin D. However this may be difficult to achieve as children with kidney disease are often fussy eaters. Most children recover, but in a minority of cases long-term dialysis or a kidney transplant will be necessary.

Kidney dialysis

Dialysis is a method of by-passing the kidneys by using a machine to remove toxic waste products from the blood. Two different systems are available. In the first, haemodialysis, the child's blood is passed down a tube from a blood vessel in the arm to a kidney machine. Once in the machine the blood is cleaned and then returned to a vein to circulate around the body. Dialysis sessions take around four hours to complete, which allows time for the accumulated poisonous waste substances in the body to filter into the blood and be cleaned out in the kidney machine. Haemodialysis is difficult to carry out for a child at home. This makes the process particularly time-consuming and restrictive.

In the second type, peritoneal dialysis (CAPD), a dialysis cleansing fluid is put into the peritoneum, the membrane lining the abdominal cavity. The fluid is left in the peritoneum for approximately four hours during the day or overnight, and is then drained off, taking with it poisonous waste products that have accumulated in the blood.

CAPD can be used at home and is as successful with very tiny babies as well as with older children. However any form of dialysis is exhausting and demanding not only for the patient but for the whole family, and improvements in organ transplants mean that for most children a transplant will eventually be the best solution.

Glomerulonephritis

In this condition the glomeruli in the kidneys become inflamed. The glomeruli are the filtering units where waste products are removed from the blood and pass into the tubules in the kidneys. The cause may not be known or the inflammation may be caused by a streptococcal infection or by a virus. When glomerulonephritis follows an infection, typically tonsillitis or scarlet fever, the symptoms usually first appear seven to ten days later. Children with glomerulonepthritis need hospital treatment and the infection normally clears in about a week.

You may notice

- *Your child passes noticeably less urine than usual*
- *The urine is smoky, pink or red. The colour change is caused by blood in the urine*
- *Possibly a headache, fever and being generally unwell*
- *Possibly slight swelling around the face and perhaps the ankles (oedema)*

What to do

If you notice that your child's urine is an odd colour and has reduced in quantity, consult your doctor immediately. The doctor may test the urine and check the child's blood pressure. If glomerulonephritis is diagnosed, your child will be admitted to hospital. As well as urine tests and blood pressure checks, the child's fluid levels will be monitored.

Treatment

Treatment is likely to consist of relieving the strain on the kidneys by giving your child a low-fluid. low-protein and low-sodium diet. Your child will also be weighed regularly to check that any fluid retention is clearing. Antibiotics will be prescribed if the cause is bacterial. If your child develops high blood pressure, this will be treated with medication.

Who can help?

The psychological effects of kidney disease in children are far-reaching, and both parents and children will benefit from outside support. For organizations who can offer help and support see the Directory.

Complementary Treatment

Chinese herbalism offers supportive treatment to stimulate the kidneys; tonics, often in pill form, are given as long as the child will tolerate them and at intervals during the growing years. **Homeopathy** and **osteopathy** may also be beneficial. **Nutritional therapy** may trace the cause to nutritional deficiencies or a long-term toxic overload.

INGUINAL HERNIA

What is it ?

A hernia, or rupture, is a protrusion of an organ from its normal compartment in the body into another part. It occurs where there is a weakness, for example in a muscle, that allows the organ to push through. In an umbilical hernia, which affects newborn babies, the intestine protrudes through the abdominal muscle at the naval. In an inguinal hernia, the most common type of hernia, a loop of the bowel pushes through into the inguinal canal, along which the testes travelled down from the abdomen to the scrotum. Inguinal hernias are particularly common in boys and can occur when the baby is only a few weeks old.

You may notice

- *A painless swelling in the leg crease at the bottom of the child's abdomen, or in the scrotum. The swelling may appear on one side or both. It is more common on the right side, but sometimes appears on the left. It can be small or very large*
- *The swelling becomes larger when the baby cries, coughs or strains. It may disappear completely when the child is relaxed and lying down. It does not usually cause discomfort or pain*
- *The child may suddenly develop a large swelling that cannot be pressed back. It may feel tender, making him very irritable. He may also vomit. This occurs if a small part of the bowel becomes trapped. It is called a strangulated, or incarcerated, hernia. Strangulated hernias must be treated as a medical emergency*

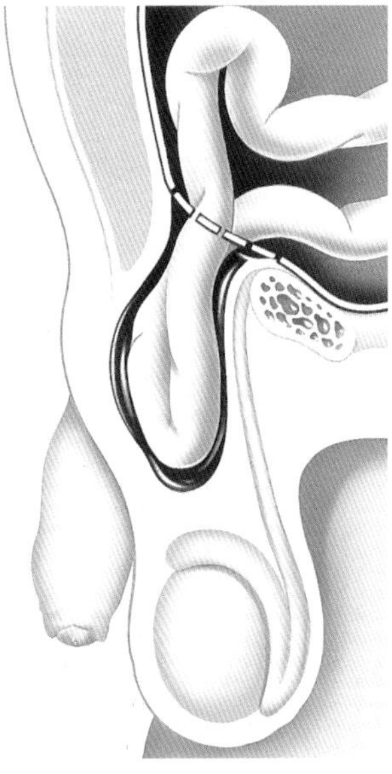

A loop of intestine is seen protruding through the muscle wall of the abdomen, causing swelling at the top of the scrotum above the testis. The potential danger in this situation is obvious – that the neck of the intestine loop becomes obstructed, cutting off a length of bowel. To avoid this serious complication any child with a suspected inguinal hernia should be seen by a doctor within a day or so.

What to do

Contact your doctor, who should refer the child to a paediatric surgeon for an operation to repair the hernia. The doctor should also tell you about the signs to look for if the hernia becomes incarcerated while your child is awaiting surgery.

Treatment for hernias in babies and older boys involves a herniotomy, in which the defect in the wall of the abdomen is repaired. This is a straightforward operation and is usually performed as day surgery. After an operation such as this there is always some post-operative pain and the your child will have a dressing over the wound. After two or three days the child can take a bath, which will help to soak the dressing and make it easier to remove.

What else?

There is no need to restrict your child's activity after the operation, but try to avoid anything that could squeeze or knock the operation site. An older child will normally be well enough to return to school within a week.

The policy of referring all children with a hernia for surgery is carried out in order to prevent the complication of an incarcerated hernia. However, if one does develop, an urgent operation is needed to release the part of the bowel that has become trapped and surgically repair the hernia.

Complementary Treatment

Complementary treatment will be supportive of the orthodox treatment and will usually concentrate on the emotional issues that are associated with surgery. **Homeopathic remedies** the homeopath may recommend include Nux 6c (*Strychnos nux vomica*, poison nut tree), and Aesculus 6c (*Aesculus hippocastanum*, horse chestnut). Remedies are to be given four times a day for up to two weeks while awaiting surgery. **Kinesiology** may also be helpful.

SEE ALSO UMBILICAL HERNIA (PAGE 269)

HYDROCELE

What is it ?

A hydrocele is a collection of fluid around the testis on one or both sides of a boy's scrotum. It is a harmless condition and is often noticed at birth or soon afterwards. In children it is more common in premature babies than in full-term babies or older boys. In adults it is more common among older men.

Causes

Although a large hydrocele can look quite alarming, it is not a serious condition and rarely causes the baby any discomfort. Childhood hydroceles are usually caused before birth when the testes descend from the abdomen into the scrotum. As they descend, they are accompanied by a pouch, or pocket, of peritoneum (the membrane that lines the abdominal cavity), which normally closes off around the time of birth and disappears completely during the first year or two of life. Sometimes, however, this pouch remains open, allowing fluid in through its narrow entrance. The fluid collects in the pouch. In some (communicating) hydroceles the fluid can flow back and forth, while in others (non-communicating) the fluid remains within the hydrocele.

When the paediatrician examines the newborn immediately following birth, they may shine a light through the scrotum. Because hydroceles are filled with fluid they are translucent, which allows the paediatrician to examine what is inside the scrotum and identify any problems.

You may notice

- *The scrotum looks swollen. This is different from the normally swollen scrotum of a new baby and is easier to see if the swelling is on one side only*
- *In a large hydrocele the scrotum may be so stretched that you can see the tiny blood vessels just under the skin*
- *The hydrocele may become larger when your baby cries and then shrink when he is relaxed*
- *The hydrocele may enlarge during the day, so that it is markedly bigger by the evening, indicating a communicating hydrocele*

Treatment

A hydrocele that occurs in a newborn baby and remains the same size will disappear on its own, frequently within a few months or, in most children, by the age of two years. If the problem is a communicating hydrocele, in which fluid can still flow into the scrotum, a surgeon will perform a simple operation to tie off the entrance to the pouch and drain away the fluid. This is usually done as a day case so the child does not need to stay in hospital overnight. A child who develops a swelling in the scrotum, or any infant whose hydrocele does not recover spontaneously by the age of six months, should be seen by a doctor.

The hydrocele may be linked with an inguinal hernia and will require surgery. The cause of a scrotal swelling in an older boy may be injury and although the swelling will reduce without treatment the testes will be checked for damage.

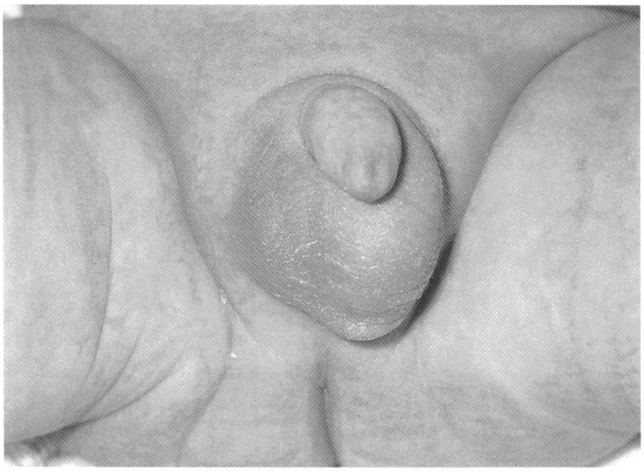

This one-sided swelling in the scrotum is caused by the failure of the inguinal canal connecting the scrotum with the abdomen to close normally soon after birth. As a result, fluid collects inside the scrotum, causing a swelling that is quite painless. A hydrocele is harmless and disappears naturally, but a swollen scrotum should always be checked by a doctor just in case there is a more serious cause.

Complementary Treatment

Homeopathy offers specific remedies including Arnica 30c (*Arnica montana*, leopard's bane) where an injury has caused swelling; Bryonia 30c (*Bryonia alba*, white bryony) if the Arnica is ineffective; and Rhododendron 6c (*Rhododendron chrysanthum*, Siberian rhododendron) if the testicle aches when there is thundery weather. The remedies are to be given three times a day for up to three weeks. **Acupuncture** might also prove to be helpful.

Hypospadias

What is it ?

A few boys are born with the opening that is normally at the end of the penis, on the underside, a condition known as hypospadias. The hole may be anywhere from the underside of the tip to the end of the penis where the scrotum begins. In some boys the hole is the normal size, and passing urine is no problem. In others the opening is very tight, so when the child tries to pass urine the foreskin balloons out, a condition that is known as phimosis.

In some babies with hypospadias the penis curls downwards. This condition, called chordee, is caused by the urethra being shorter than the penis. Sometimes there is a blind hole at the penis tip that looks at first sight like the opening of the urethra.

Diagnosis

Hypospadias will be noticed by the paediatrician who checks your new baby at birth. As long as the hole is on the glans (the tip of the penis) and the penis is straight, treatment is not usually needed. If it is further down, surgery will be necessary. If the hole is so tiny that urine cannot flow properly a surgeon will perform an operation, called a meatotomy, to enlarge the opening of the urethra.

Occasionally a boy with severe hypospadias and the opening of the penis situated far down towards the body also has a small scrotum and undescended testes. As there is a question mark over the true sex of a baby with these abnormalities, he will be investigated very soon after birth.

Treatment

Surgeons vary in their thinking about the most suitable age at which to correct hypospadias. Some paediatric surgeons like to do a one-stage operation before the baby becomes mobile. Others complete surgery when the boy is around three to four years. All operations should be finished before the child starts school. Boys with hypospadias should not be circumcised, because the foreskin is used in the corrective surgery. As soon as the child can pass urine normally and direct its flow, he will be able to go home.

Following surgery the penis is sore and swollen for quite a few days. A fine tube will be fixed in place to allow the child to pass urine and site of the wound will be dressed. Keeping the dressings in position and hygienic can be difficult. Ask your practice nurse or health visitor for help, including anaesthetic gels and antiseptic sprays if they are not offered. After a week to ten days the dressings will be removed in hospital. This can be uncomfortable so ask in advance what pain relief your baby can have. The stitches that are usually used will not need removing as they will dissolve naturally.

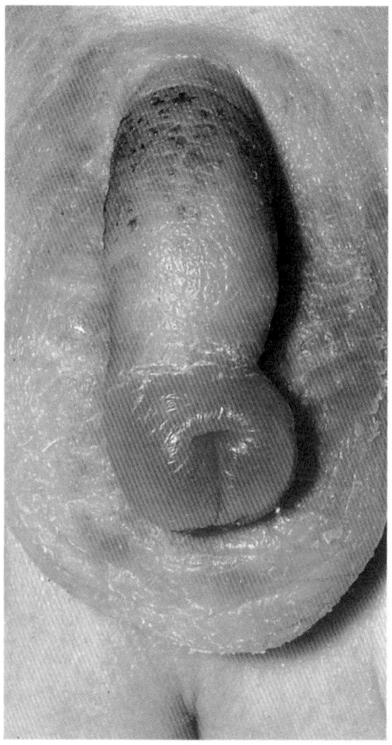

In a mild case of hypospadias, the opening is still found on the glans at the end of the penis, and if any correction is needed, the surgery, using skin from the foreskin, is straightforward. Where the opening is found closer to the scrotum an operation becomes essential, sometimes straightening out the curved shaft of the penis at the same time.

Who can help?

For organizations who are able to offer help and support see the Directory.

Complementary Treatment

Complementary treatments will be confined to emotional problems associated with surgery. The **Bach flower remedies** may help to alleviate fear and anxiety and the emotional aspects of recovery. **Homeopathic remedies** that can be given prior to surgery include Aconite 30c (*Aconitum napellus*, blue aconite) for the child who is panicking and has a great fear of surgery, and Gelsemium 6c (*Gelsemium sempervirens*, yellow jasmine) if the child is very apprehensive, weak and trembling. Phosphorus 6c (phosphorus) can be given to relieve vomiting following surgery; and Arnica 30c (*Arnica montana*, leopard's bane) to relieve pain and prevent infection. Arnica should be followed by the remedy Staphisagria 6c (*Delphinium staphisagria*, stavesacre). These remedies should be given every half hour for up to ten doses.

SEE ALSO PHIMOSIS (PAGE 298)

PHIMOSIS

What is it ?

Phimosis is a narrowing of the opening of the foreskin, so that it cannot be drawn back over the end of the penis. In the newborn male infant the foreskin is joined to the tip, or glans, of the penis. For about half of all baby boys it separates from the glans by the age of about 12 months, and for most boys by the age of 3 years. However in a small minority the foreskin cannot be pulled back until the boy reaches puberty. This too is perfectly normal. In all cases it is important not to pull the foreskin back forcibly or the delicate membranes underneath can be torn, leaving scar tissue, which can cause phimosis.

Phimosis may also develop as a result of balanitis (see Sore penis, page 289) or other inflammation of the foreskin. Occasionally boys are born with a natural phimosis, where the foreskin is so tight that it cannot be drawn back at all.

A tight foreskin causes problems when the opening to the penis is so narrow that the boy cannot pass urine in a steady stream. Instead, the urine balloons inside the foreskin and trickles or sprays out. Because it is difficult to wash the genital area efficiently, infections of the foreskin and glans are more likely to recur.

A secondary problem, paraphimosis, can arise if a tight foreskin has been pushed back under pressure. It may then form a tight band around the end of the penis and prove impossible to push forward again.

You may notice

- *Urine does not come out as a steady stream but dribbles out. At the same time you can see ballooning at the end of the foreskin. Urine then sometimes sprays out in all directions, and sometimes leaks out later. Leaking urine is more common in boys in middle childhood, that is, around the ages of five to ten*
- *Repeated infections of the glans. It is difficult to keep the glans clean, even with daily baths, so secretions build up inside the foreskin and become infected*
- *After retracting the foreskin during washing you find it will not go back. The end of the penis is trapped and becomes sore, red and swollen*

What to do

If the foreskin has trapped the end of the penis, wring out a face cloth in cold water and lay it over the penis to reduce the swelling. After a few minutes it may become possible to gently pull the foreskin forward again. If not, contact a doctor who may be able to squeeze the penis, thereby allowing the foreskin to move.

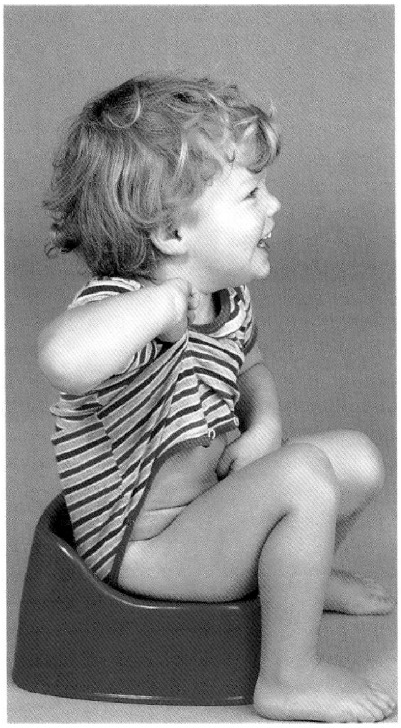

The inevitable spraying of urine that results from a foreskin with an unusually small outlet can be a source of delight to a toddler – although not to his parents! If the outlet does not enlarge with age a small operation to widen it may be all that is necessary. Some doctors will recommend circumcision.

See your doctor if you are at all concerned about your son's phimosis. The doctor may be able to reassure you that the foreskin will eventually enlarge. Meanwhile infections of the glans are usually treated with an antibiotic cream and regular bathing. However the standard treatment for boys with phimosis is circumcision.

Complementary Treatment

Complementary treatments will be confined to emotional problems associated with surgery. The **Bach flower remedies** may help to alleviate fear and anxiety and the emotional aspects of recovery. **Homeopathic remedies** that can be given prior to surgery include Aconite 30c (*Aconitum napellus*, blue aconite) for the child who is panicking and has a great fear of surgery, and Gelsemium 6c (*Gelsemium sempervirens*, yellow jasmine) if the child is very apprehensive, weak and trembling. Phosphorus 6c (phosphorus) can be given to relieve vomiting following surgery; and Arnica 30c (*Arnica montana*, leopard's bane) to relieve pain and prevent infection. Arnica should be followed by the remedy Staphisagria 6c (*Delphinium staphisagria*, stavesacre). These remedies should be given every half hour for up to ten doses.

SEE ALSO CIRCUMCISION PAGE 291

Vaginal Discharge

What is it ?

Newborn females may have a heavy, white discharge, which gradually lessens and disappears within a week. Some newborn infant girls also lose a small amount of vaginal blood a few days after birth, but this ceases spontaneously. Young girls often have a slight discharge from the vagina that may be colourless or pale. As girls approach puberty the natural discharge again becomes heavy enough to stain underwear. However an unusually heavy discharge can be a sign of threadworms (which occasionally carry infection from the anus) especially if the child scratches her bottom. Some girls are also highly sensitive to chemicals in washing powders or in bath products, particularly before the sex hormones that are produced at puberty thicken the vaginal skin, and the lips of the labia become larger, protecting the vagina. A thick white discharge together with redness, itching and soreness is most likely to be thrush, which is caused by the fungus *Candida albicans*, particularly if the girl has been taking a course of antibiotics or has diabetes.

Diabetes itself can cause itching around the vulva, but this would not be the only symptom as thirst and frequent urination would be more readily apparent.

You may notice

- *Stained underpants or signs of a white discharge in a newborn infant*
- *An unpleasant-smelling discharge, which may be also thick and yellow*
- *The child complains of the vagina feeling itchy and sore*
- *Passing urine may be painful*
- *There may be bleeding from the vagina as well*

What to do

Try to find the cause of the discharge. To check for worms, use a torch to inspect your child's bottom while they are asleep. Alternatively lay a small strip of butterfly tape over the anus or press some blu-tak over it. In the morning this may reveal threadworms – thin, white thread-like creatures approximately 12.5 mm/½ in long that come out at night to lay their eggs.

Check that your daughter is taking a daily bath or shower and giving herself enough time to wash and carefully dry her vagina. Simple hygiene may be all that is needed to clear the discharge. Some girls are very sensitive to bubble baths and the enzymes in biological washing powders. Encourage your daughter to bath in plain water, use non-biological powders and cotton-gusseted underwear.

Ask your daughter if she has pushed anything into her vagina – such as a tampon that she has not been able to retrieve. Ask sensitively to spare embarrassment.

Treatment

If your daughter has pushed something she cannot retrieve into her vagina, she should see the doctor, who will need to give an internal examination using a speculum (a smaller version of the instrument used when taking a cervical smear). Your doctor may be able to retrieve the object and avoid the need for a visit to hospital. Otherwise your child may need to have the object removed under general anaesthetic.

The doctor may take a swab of the discharge and a urine sample for laboratory analysis. The result will show the bacterium responsible and will help the doctor to choose the most appropriate antibiotic cream or oral antibiotic. If thrush is diagnosed – much more common in teenagers than in younger children – your child will be prescribed an antifungal preparation, probably as cream and pessary.

What else?

Make sure your daughter always wipes her bottom from front to back, using soft paper, to prevent harmful micro-organisms entering the vagina.

Complementary Treatment

Chinese herbalism can be beneficial, as can **acupuncture**. Western herbalists will prescribe herbs for douches and for internal application. **Homeopathy** offers recommendations for self help and specific remedies to be taken six times a day for up to five days. These include Carbo an 6c (*Carbo animalis*, animal charcoal) for a burning yellow discharge; Calcarea 6c (*Calcarea carbonica*, calcium carbonate) for a milky discharge causing the vulva to itch; and Pulsatilla 6c (*Pulsatilla nigricans*, pasque flower) for watery and cloudy discharge causing smarting and soreness.

SEE ALSO THREADWORMS (PAGE 268) AND DIABETES (PAGE 147)

TOXIC SHOCK SYNDROME

What is it ?

Toxic shock syndrome (TSS) is an extremely rare but serious type of blood poisoning. It is caused by a poison produced by the bacterium *Staphylococcus aureus*. These bacteria live naturally and usually quite harmlessly on the skin and in the nose, armpit, groin or vagina of many people. However under certain circumstances the bacteria have the ability to manufacture a poison called TSST-1, which can enter the blood stream and multiply rapidly. Precisely why only a few of the many people – one in three – who carry the bacteria should develop an infection is not yet fully understood. It is considered possible that the people who succumb to toxic shock syndrome lack protective antibodies against the toxin. Most cases of toxic shock syndrome make a sufferer very ill very quickly, and are emergencies. If treatment is started rapidly a full recovery should be made. However in the rare serious cases where no treatment is given, toxic shock syndrome can be life threatening.

Causes

Approximately half of all cases of toxic shock syndrome are associated with tampons, and all tampon boxes now carry warnings that tampons should be changed every four to eight hours. Some cases have been associated with the use of contraceptive sponges, caps or diaphragms. However toxic shock can affect individuals of any age. It can start with an abscess, an insect bite, a burn or a surgical incision, or when a graze develops into a staphylococcal infection.

You may notice

- *Symptoms develop quickly, in a matter of hours.*
- *Sudden high fever (39°C /102.2°F or more)*
- *Vomiting and diarrhoea*
- *A red, sunburn-like rash*
- *Dizziness and fainting as the blood pressure drops*
- *Aching muscles*

Treatment

If a child develops any illness that becomes worse very quickly, always contact a doctor or hospital. Should your daughter be wearing a tampon when she develops a combination of these symptoms, take the precaution of asking her to remove it. This is not to act in an unduly alarmist manner, but rather to remove any possibility that she has toxic shock syndrome. If toxic shock syndrome is suspected, the child will be admitted to hospital and staff will start treatment immediately. Large doses of antibiotics may be given intravenously, together with fluids to correct dehydration and shock. Should any of the major organs of the body be involved, the child will be admitted to an intensive care unit. In some units children are given the antibody immunoglobulin in an attempt to boost their resistance to the toxin.

When given the above treatment, the child will usually recover fully from the infection within a few weeks. As the fever is reduced and the rash fades, the skin on the hands and feet will begin to peel.

What else?

Toxic shock syndrome is extremely rare. As long as women and girls take the recommended precautions when using tampons or contraception, it is very unlikely to develop.

Always use the lowest absorbency tampon appropriate. Change tampons every four to eight hours and alternate with sanitary towels, in compliance with the manufacturer's instructions. However strong the flow of blood, warn your daughter not to put in more than one tampon at a time. If she needs extra protection, then a tampon can be used in conjunction with a sanitary towel. Remind her also to remove the last tampon at the end of the period.

If a tampon is used overnight a fresh one must be inserted just before going to bed and removed immediately on waking. Wash hands thoroughly before and after inserting tampons.

If your daughter has had toxic shock syndrome she should never use tampons again, or any contraceptive device such as a cap, sponge or diaphragm.

Who can help?

For organizations offering help and advice, see the Directory.

Complementary Treatment

Kinesiology may be useful during diagnosis and the **Bach flower remedy** Rescue Remedy can be very helpful. Both **Chinese herbalism** and **acupuncture** could be effective, possibly when they are used together. Consultation with a **homeopath** would be preferable to relying on specific remedies without taking a homeopath's advise.

WETTING

What is it ?
Bedwetting, or enuresis, is extremely common, with most three-year-olds still wet at night. At five, wetting the bed is still common, especially among boys, and half a million six to sixteen-year-olds are still not reliably dry. The majority of these children are late developers. More rarely there is a medical condition that causes the wetting. However recent research has confirmed a strong family tendency to bedwetting in childhood.

Children usually become dry during the day between the ages of two and three, and at night a few months later. However, some children wet in the daytime or at night for a much longer period. Some of these children have been previously dry for a time, while others have never achieved dryness. (Wetting in the daytime is perceived by children as the third most stressful thing that can happen to them, rated only after the death of a parent and going blind.)

Before a child can stay dry at night they need to know what a full bladder feels like and learn how to control it. The dry-at-night child holds on until morning or long enough to get to the toilet. The bedwetting child responds instantly to the urge to urinate.

Below the age of seven, bedwetting for which there is no medical causes should be regarded as no more than a normal variant of development and treated with encouragements and rewards for success. However once a child has reached her seventh birthday, she may well benefit from more active treatment, such as using a burner or an alarm to wake her at night as she begins to wet the bed.

How to help
In a child of three or four
- Leave the child in nappies. Once they want to stop wearing a night nappy, put their pants on at night instead, leave their potty on a non-slip surface by their bed and leave a light on nearby. Give lots of encouraging cuddles and praise. If the child is wet every night for a fortnight, put them back in nappies without comment and try again in three to four months

In a child of five or six
- Check that the child is not in pain when they're urinating, that they aren't unusually thirsty and that their urine doesn't have a fishy smell. Any of these signs mean there might be a physical reason for the bedwetting, so consult your doctor. Otherwise, make being dry as easy as possible. If the child gets dry nights, praise them and do your best to ignore wet sheets. Give them rewards even for small achievements, such as going to the toilet before bed or helping to change the bedding

In a child of seven or older
- Ask if the child wants to be dry and talk about the things they can do when they are, such as staying over with friends. Practise daytime holding on exercises: counting to ten or singing a song before urinating. Set an alarm clock for an hour or two before normal waking time if you know that the child wets early in the morning

If child has started wetting again after being dry
- See what has disturbed the child. A new baby, starting school, rows, separation or divorce, and bullying can start a child wetting again

What to do
You should consult your doctor if: the child is as wet in the day as they are at night; the child is very thirsty or finds urinating painful; the urine has a fishy smell. The doctor will examine the child and check the urine for sugar, suggesting diabetes, or protein, suggesting kidney problems or a urinary tract infection.

Children over seven may be helped by a bedside or body alarm that wakes them up as they start to dampen the sheets.

Some doctors prescribe a nasal spray or tablets containing the anti-diuretic hormone desmopressin; this will help a child who wants to go away or stay with a friend to stay dry overnight. Antidepressants are used less commonly because of side effects and the risk of accidental poisoning. For children who deny that they are wetting, a pants alarm can be worn, but only at home.

Daytime wetting

Occasional tell-tale damp patches on the trousers of three and four-year-old boys are common and best ignored. Damp knickers are less visible but even more frequent as day wetting is more common in girls.

What to do

Contact your doctor who may well want a specimen of urine to check for infection. If the day wetting persists, he may refer your child to a paediatrician for investigation of any urinary tract abnormalities. Some children with an unstable bladder benefit from a drug that calms the bladder's muscle activity.

If there is no physical problem, try to train by encouragement. Make sure your child drinks six or seven cups of fluid day as drinking too little makes the bladder adjust to holding less. Dress your child in clothes that are easy to get off, such as trouser with elastic waists. Encourage your child to go to the toilet regularly, ideally every 1½ hours, and always before they go out.

Cognitive bladder training

One approach to daytime wetting where the child has no underlying abnormality (such as continuous wetting, bowel problems or repeated urinary tract infections) is a psychological approach known as cognitive bladder training. The aim is to teach children to respond to early signals from the bladder and to urinate regularly, approximately seven times a day. Training is given by a specialist nurse and the programme usually has to be followed for several weeks before the first signs of success are evident.

Children are usually seven years of age or over when they start cognitive bladder training and are motivated by the desire to be dry. In some schemes children are paired to compete with each other. First they learn how the bladder works, using a 'My body' type of book or a soft anatomical doll. They then learn to listen for the signals from the doll's bladder, as if they were listening to a telephone ringing. Next they are taught how to sit in a relaxed manner on the toilet with the feet flat on the floor or steps. They try to pass all the urine in one steady stream, instead of stopping and starting. A child who is in the habit of dashing off before finishing can be taught double micturition, which simply means having another attempt to urinate. After going to the toilet once, they go to their room, count to 30 and then come back for a second attempt. Children learning to urinate regularly need to drink plenty of fluids every day, taking extra drinks to school if this is necessary.

To remind them to urinate, children need a series of daily prompts, such as mental messages or numbered stickers to put on a chart. Charts full of stickers can be used as a basis of a reward system. Some children defy the evidence by denying that they are wetting. A pants alarm acts as a reminder that they cannot ignore, but it should only be worn at home.

Complementary Treatment

Chinese herbalists give astringent herbs such as schisandra (*Schisandra chinensis*) to give support to the liver and kidney energy, which will prevent urine from overflowing in the night. **Bach flower remedies** will focus on emotional causes and are chosen according to individual needs and the issues prevailing. **Western herbalism** will prescribe to restore the normal nervous function, and calm excess anxiety. **Homeopathy** may offer constitutional treatment (treatment according to the personality, temperament and mood of the child concerned) where infection is the main cause. Specific remedies to be taken at bedtime include Equisetum 6c (*Equisetum hyemale*, horsetail) when the child wets the bed during dreams; and Causticum 6c (*Causticum Hahnemanni*, potassium hydrate) when the child wets the bed during first sleep, which becomes worse when the child has a cough and/or when the weather is dry and clear. The remedies are to be taken for up to two weeks. **Play and music therapy** could be beneficial where wetting does not have a medical cause, particularly if it is caused wholly or in part by anxiety, or if other signs of anxiety are present. The problem would not be addressed directly, and improvement would possibly be slower than with the popular behavioural methods.

SEE ALSO SOILING AND ENCOPRESIS (PAGE 256)

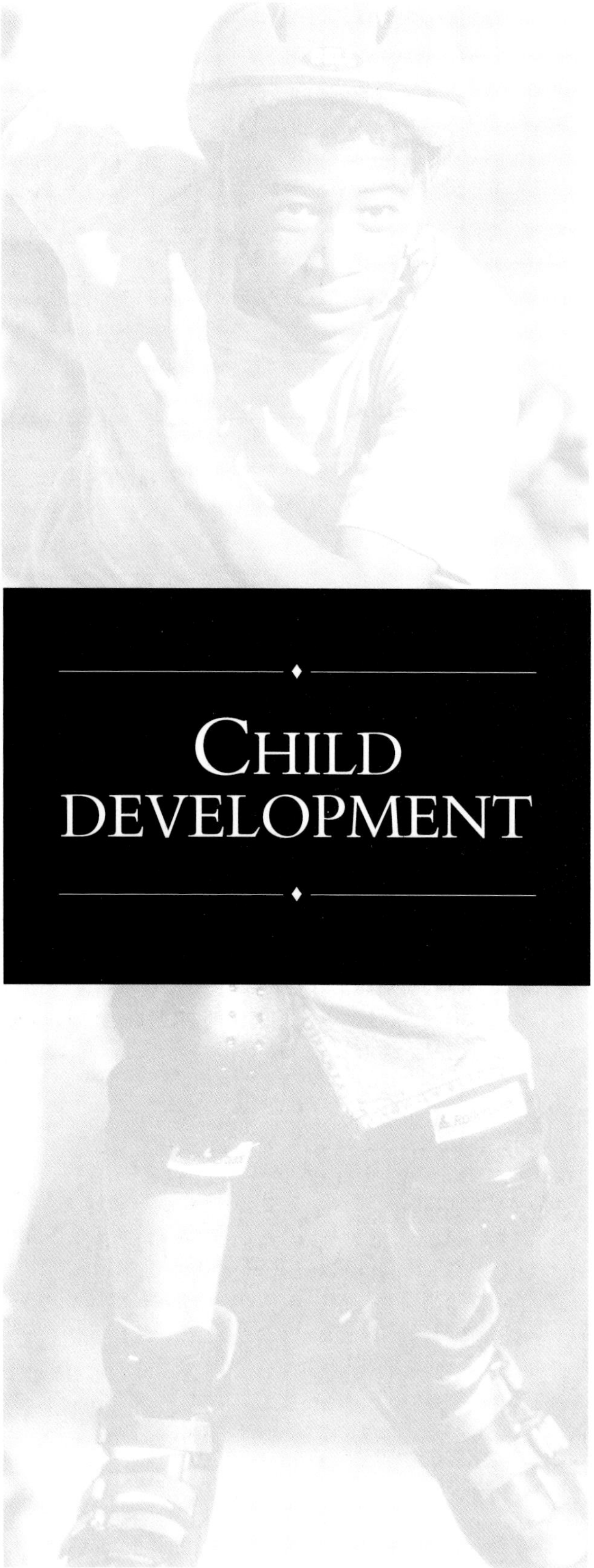

CHILD DEVELOPMENT

Babies and children are naturally programmed to develop in a reasonably orderly sequence. They put on weight, grow, smile and laugh, recover from colic and their first cold, develop teeth, learn to sleep through the night and then become risky little people as they start to crawl and walk around the furniture. In the early years children's achievements and milestones come thicker and faster than ever again. Parents may feel tempted to take the credit for these achievements – and so they should. In the nature-nurture debate, no one denies the impact that a stimulating, loving and opportunity-rich home life can have on children.

Children's experiences mould them from birth, and in all probability prior to birth. Babies who are at the receiving end of much chatting and talking from adults frequently grow into children who talk early and fluently. Children who live in homes with a flight of stairs learn to negotiate them earlier than children who live in flats. Children who are taken outdoors on foot as toddlers learn to walk further and more robustly than those who are always ferried by car or push chair. The best two-year-old walkers I ever came across were twin boys, just two years older than their twin sisters. With four children under two-and-a-half, their mother could simply never carry them. They walked everywhere.

However experience is not everything. Personality makes all the difference between the child who grasps an opportunity, learns from the experience and moves on to the next stage, and the child who needs endless coaxing and repetition before they can feel confident.

The pace of development

Children develop and learn at different speeds – some faster, some slower. The pace at which a child can take on a new learning experience depends partly on their personality, genetic make-up and environment, and partly on any particular difficulties they may have. For example a baby who has a visual problem will smile later than a baby who can see their mother's face from birth. A child whose hearing is impeded by bouts of glue ear may well speak late. One of the main reasons for the development reviews regularly offered for your child is that the doctor can identify any particular problems your child may face and help to overcome them.

Parents instinctively know their own child best and health professionals are aware of this. In many places parents are given a child health record to keep throughout their baby's childhood. You should be encouraged to record your observations in it and share these with your health visitor or doctor. In this way everyone keeps track of your child's medical progress and physical development. Whenever you take your child to the clinic, either at the doctor's surgery or at the hospital, take the child health record with you.

Assessing child development

When assessing a child's development, health professionals now tend to ignore rigid tests and charts. Instead, by talking to you and carefully watching your child play, they can form an idea of the child's level of development. It is undoubtedly true that parents are the first people to spot any problems, but health professionals have a better idea of what is normal for a child at any particular age.

Before a health review, let the doctor or your health visitor know if your child has been under the weather recently, as this will affect how the child behaves. If the child was born prematurely, remind your doctor or health visitor of this. The rule that children develop at very different rates holds particularly true of children who were premature babies, and allowances are usually made until they are two years old. If you are still concerned about your child's progress at the end of the review, ask if a second review is necessary or if a referral to a specialist can be arranged.

Now that parents are advised to lay their infants on their backs to protect against sudden infant death, it is important to allow infants to play on their stomachs. The front-down position allows infants to develop strength in the neck, shoulders and trunk, ready for crawling.

The neonatal examination

The doctor or midwife who performs the neonatal examination will ask about the family history and any problems during pregnancy or birth. They will also ask you if you have any particular worries, so this is an opportunity to express any concerns you may have.

The infant is examined for any obvious physical abnormalities. The heart is checked, as well as the infant's general colour and breathing rate. A male infant's genitalia are examined to see whether the testes have descended. The infant is weighed and, if possible, measured, and the head circumference noted. The fontanelles – those areas where the skull has not yet fused – are felt.

The doctor or midwife will test the hips to see if they are dislocated or can be easily dislocated. The eyes are checked for major structural problems, such as a cataract, and the inside of the mouth is checked to be sure there is no cleft in the palate. In some health areas the baby's hearing is checked.

The health review at six to eight weeks

The infant has a second examination at six to eight weeks. The doctor or health visitor weighs and measures the infant and their head circumference. This gives helpful information about how the infant is feeding and growing, as most infants lose some weight in the first few days following birth.

The infant has a thorough physical check, which will include assessing whether the hips can be dislocated and possibly checking the legs and arms for muscle tone. Even in such a small space of time, the baby's muscles will have started to strengthen. The doctor may well show this graphically by gently pulling the infant from a lying to a sitting position and watching how the head no longer flops back, but follows the movement of the back.

The eyes will be examined and checked for any signs of a squint or other abnormality, which might have been missed at birth. The doctor will test to see if the infant can follow a moving toy to right and left and back again; to see if the infant is interested in looking at brightly coloured objects, that the eyes move smoothly; and the infant has started to smile.

The doctor will want to know about the infant's hearing, and will ask if your baby responds to your singing or talking voice, is quiet when talked to, and whether the baby reacts to sudden loud noises or soothing sounds. The infant's heart and, in male boys, genital area are checked again, and if the baby's testes have not yet descended, the doctor will arrange a referral to a paediatric surgeon. Babies who are exclusively breastfed may be given an extra dose of oral vitamin K.

The health review at six to nine months

By the time infants have their health review at six to nine months, they are very different individuals. Your baby will be starting to eat real food, sitting up and taking notice of the world and may be babbling. At this review the infant can be weighed if you are concerned that your baby is putting on weight too fast or not fast enough, and measured if you are not certain your baby is growing at a normal rate.

The baby's hips and legs are checked again for any signs of dislocation, as hip dislocation occasionally develops after the neonatal period. The baby's eyes are assessed for any squint (which, if present at the last check, should have disappeared by now) and to see that the infant focuses well when a toy is held some 3 m/10 ft away, and that the infant can follow with their eyes a toy moving at a distance of around 3 m /10 ft.

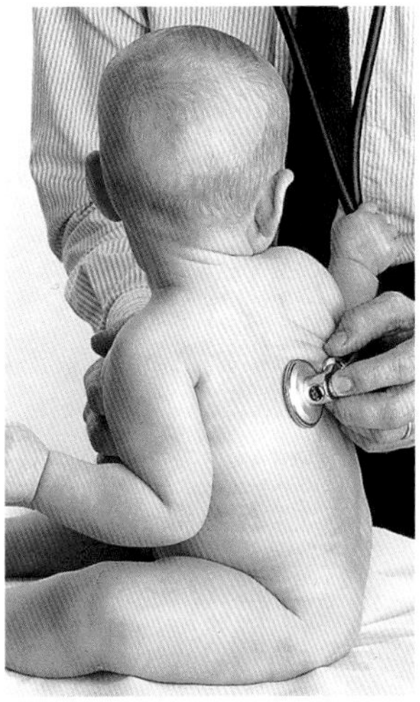

Between six and nine months of age most infants acquire enough muscle control and balance to sit up straight while turning their head. Suddenly the world is a more interesting place in which to live.

The doctor will usually perform a distraction test to assess the baby's hearing. A sound is made from a position beyond the baby's field of vision to see if the baby turns towards it. An infant who has a cold or is tired – or can't hear – will have a second assessment, and if they can't hear on that occasion they will be referred to a specialist in children's audiology.

The infant's sounds are noted (at this stage the infant may well be making *a-ga, dada* sounds). The doctor or health visitor will also notice how interested the infant is in listening to parents speak, and how the infant manages to attract their parent's attention.

Balance will be checked to see if it is good enough for the infant to sit alone. There will also be a check to find out what attempts the infant is making to become mobile, and to see if they can bear weight on the feet when you hold their hands.

You may also be asked questions about how your baby is getting on. Concerns that can loom large in the second half of the first year often include feeding, manipulating finger foods, holding a cup and sleeping, as well as the baby's general health, including any episodes of wheezing.

The health review at 18 to 24 months

By the time of this health review the erstwhile infant has probably turned into a mobile toddler who is into everything. The health visitor or doctor will check that the child is walking properly and ask about general development and speech. They will explain that at this age understanding and being interested in making social contact is more important than talking. By now a toddler's vision is mature, so they can see fine detail. Health professionals will be able to judge from the child's behaviour and from asking questions about books, pictures and television whether there are any serious difficulties.

If the child had any earlier problems with slow growth the child may be weighed and, if necessary, measured.

The health visitor may well ask about play and activities such as walking up and down stairs, running and jumping. Your toddler may not have mastered these skills yet, but by now they will have good control over muscles and will be making steady progress with hand-eye coordination. The idea is to spot any problems early.

The doctor or health visitor will also talk about toilet training, eating and the child's behaviour – if major problems are to arise this is usually when they will happen.

The pre-school health review

This review is carried out to check that the child is well and able to benefit fully from education at school. It may be done at the same time as the child is given pre-school booster immunizations: diphtheria, tetanus, polio, measles, mumps and rubella.

The health visitor or possibly doctor will discuss any worries you may have about the child's eyesight and might ask your child to perform a simple task, such as threading bricks, in order to check hand-eye coordination. In some health regions the child may be asked to do a simple test, during which each eye is covered separately to check for any signs of a latent squint.

The health visitor will ask whether the child can now speak clearly enough for anyone outside the home to understand them. The child will only need a hearing assessment if they have problems with speech or if parents are concerned.

The doctor or health visitor will measure the child and plot their height on a chart, but they will only weigh your child if you want them to, or if there has been any concern in the past about growth. If your child shows signs of clumsiness or falls frequently, this is an opportunity to mention it.

By this age most children are dry by day although some, especially boys, are still wet at night. This is a good opportunity for parents to air any concerns they may have.

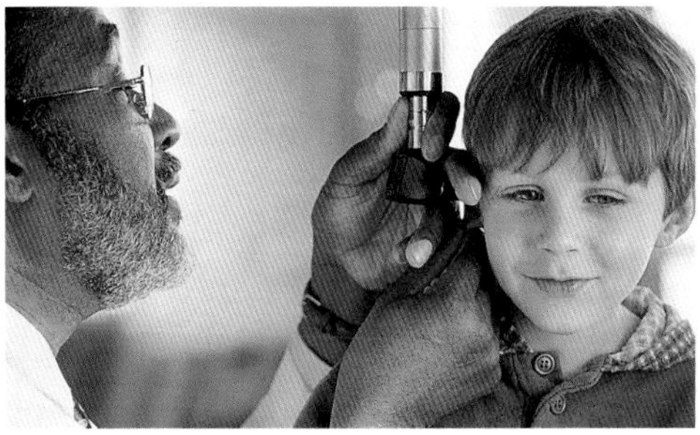

Most children will be given a hearing test when they start school, but they will only need a thorough examination of the ears and further tests if the doctor finds that there is a problem.

STAGES OF DEVELOPMENT

It is fascinating to see how babies develop. The guidelines given below, which indicate the various stages of achievement, can serve as a basis for developmental activities that parents can enjoy with their children. However parents should remember that each baby is unique and, within a broad span of 'normal', will develop at their own pace.

The one-month-old infant

Moving If you pull your baby into a sitting position, the back will curve and the head will need support to stop it from flopping forwards or backwards. When lying on the stomach, your baby will turn the head to one side or the other. However you should only lay them on their stomach to play when you are with them. If you hold them under the arms over a hard surface such as a table, your baby will press down with their feet and make apparent walking movements. This is not real walking, however; it is one of the reflex actions with which babies are born. Another one is stepping; if you hold your infant with the top of their foot held against a table edge, for example, they will step up on to the table.

Hearing and speech The month-old infant responds to loud noises by appearing startled, blinking or stiffening. When they are at peace they may make tiny throaty or cooing noises, especially if they are 'talking' to you.

Seeing At this age infants blink in response to light and turn their head towards a source of light. They are interested in the difference between darkness and light and can stare at lights for a long time. However your baby will be most interested in your face, which they will watch intently as they feed. From around four to six weeks they start to smile.

The three-month-old infant

Moving Lying on their back, infants wave their arms symmetrically and kick with both legs together, or 'cycle'. If you pull them up into a sitting position, they will hold their head still for a few seconds before it wobbles forwards. Do lay them down to play on their stomach; by now your baby can lift the head and chest up to look around them.

Hearing and speech As long as the baby is not crying, they will quieten and appear to listen when they hear your voice or an interesting sound such as a bell or a rattle. They make noises when you speak to them and when they are alone. If the baby is trying to discover where the sound is coming from, they may move their eyes or even roll their head from side to side.

Handling objects At first your baby could not hold an object without letting it go, but by now, if you place a toy or rattle in their hand, they can hold it for a few moments and may move it towards their face, often hitting themself. Your baby is starting to reach out for objects and starting to put their fingers into their mouth. Everything else also goes into the mouth for investigation. Dribbling becomes obvious.

Seeing Babies are very interested in human faces at this age and follow them constantly. They can perceive colours as well as shades and variations in shade. If a ball or brightly coloured toy is held and moved about 20 cm/8 in away from the face, the baby can follow its movement. Soon they start to watch their own hands and to recognize the activities that precede a feed.

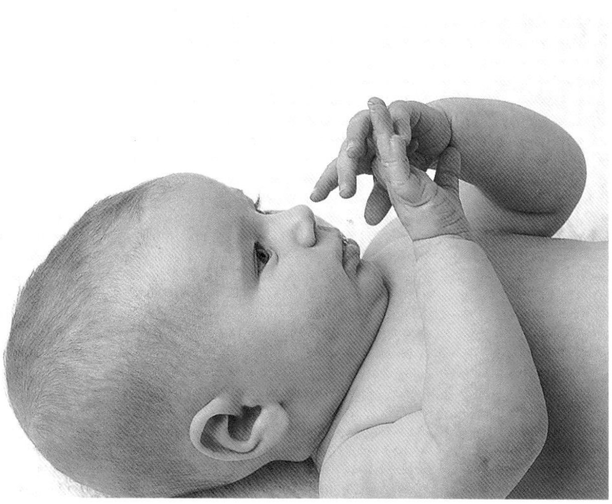

By three months of age your baby will be able to focus on close objects, such as her hands, and, fascinated, will begin to play with them. At this stage of development she will be able to hold a small object in her hands for a short time and also have control over her head movements.

The six-month-old infant

Moving Lying on the back, your baby can lift their head to look at their feet. As long as the baby is supported in their cot or chair, they can sit up and turn their head from side to side to see the world around them. Their back is straight and they can support their head well. Your baby has probably learned to roll over by now – from front to back or back to front. Hold them under the arms and you will find that their feet press down on the surface you hold them above, and they may start to bounce up and down.

Hearing and speech Your baby turns when they hear your voice. Soon they will be able to turn to a quiet noise made on either side of them, as long as there is not something more interesting to attract their attention. They will sing to themself and laugh and chuckle while playing. A child who is annoyed or frustrated can scream.

Handling objects Your baby can grasp a toy and pass it from hand to hand.
Seeing Your baby can see across a room and follow activities with interest. They are aware of depth and distance and can see in 3-D; this is important because your child is about to become more mobile. Once they can sit up they can be offered finger foods.

The nine-month-old infant
Moving At nine months infants can sit on their own on the floor for quite a few minutes and lean forward to pick up a toy without toppling forward. They may be on the move, either crawling or commando crawling across the floor, and may be strong enough to pull themself to a standing position, but then fall backwards with a bump.
Hearing and speech At this age infants babble in long strings of tuneful sounds, such as '*dadada*' or '*mumumum*'. They can also imitate other sounds such as coughing or smacking their lips in a pretend kiss. They know the meaning of words such as 'no' and 'bye bye'.
Handling objects Babies can stretch out to grasp a toy or other object if offered, then let go to give it to you, but can't put it down yet. They can also pick up small objects between their finger and thumb. They can poke at something close to them, and are starting to point at objects a little further away from them.
Seeing If something falls off the high chair, the baby will be able to watch the direction in which it falls.

The one-year-old infant
Moving The one-year-old infant can sit on the floor for as long as they want, crawl, bottom-shuffle or bear-walk on their legs and arms. When they pull themself into a standing position they can let themself down gently or side-step around the furniture, still holding on for support. However if you hold their hands they may be able to step out across the floor. Some babies can walk by now, others can just stand alone, while others are ready to learn to crawl upstairs.
Hearing and speech The one-year-old knows their own name and chats, although you may not understand a word. They can understand a simple instruction or words that are familiar to them in their context. They may even be able to give you a named object such as a shoe or cup.
Handling objects They can pick up small objects and feed themself competently with finger foods, throw objects and can point to things that interest them. They will soon start to feed themself with a spoon – which is extremely messy at first – and take off clothes such as socks.
Seeing At this age infants can look in the right direction for things that roll out of sight or disappear from their view. They are beginning to enjoy looking at pictures, so you can spend some time looking at picture books with them.

The two-year-old toddler
Moving The two-year-old can run without falling over and have a go at kicking a large ball. They can walk up and down stairs using two feet to each step, as long as they steady themself on the wall or banisters. They can squat on the floor and climb on to furniture, sit on a tricycle and push themself forwards with their feet on the floor, but they are not able to use the pedals yet.
Hearing and speech The two-year-old's vocabulary has grown to around 50 words and they can link two words into a meaningful phrase. They ask what things and people are called and can join in with songs, jingles and nursery rhymes. The toddler can now point to parts of the body on request and, depending on their mood, can obey commands such as 'Go and pick the letters up'.
Handling objects At this age toddlers can grip objects and may hold a pencil correctly between the thumb and first two fingers. Their drawings are becoming more interesting – they can imitate a vertical line and their scribbling becomes more circular. When they are looking at a book, they can turn the pages one by one. If something interesting such as a wrapped sweet is placed in front of them, they will unwrap it without too much difficulty. Hand preference is usually clear.
Seeing They can appreciate the fine detail in the pictures in their favourite stories. They may be able to recognize themselves in photographs.

Children usually start to draw people with a circle to which eyes, mouth and later a nose is added. Legs come next, followed by arms sticking straight out of the head or halfway down the body. Eventually the child reaches the separate gender sophistication of this drawing.

The three-year-old child

Moving Three-year-olds can walk upstairs one foot to a step and down again two feet to a step. When they reach the bottom they can jump off the bottom step. They love climbing frames and slides and are usually perfectly confident using them. They can use the pedals on a tricycle and, given enough space, can steer it around corners. They can kick a ball, stand on tiptoe and stand just for a second or two on one foot. They can also throw a ball and catch a large one with both arms.

Hearing and speech People outside the family can understand what a three-year-old says, although some of their sounds are still not quite adult and they make regular and endearing grammatical errors. At this age children adore stories and have their own repertoire of nursery rhymes and rote learning, such as numbers up to ten.

Handling objects Children are fairly manually dexterous by now. They can eat with a fork and spoon and wash their hands, although they may still need help with drying them. They can pull their own pants up and down, but may need help with buttons. They can thread wooden beads on a lace and play competently with different construction toys. They can use (round-ended) scissors and can hold a pencil correctly and use it to draw a circle, a V-shape, imitate a cross and simple letters such as H. They can draw a man with a head and usually some other body parts as well, and can paint with a large brush.

The four-year-old child

Moving Four-year-old children can walk up and down stairs, climb ladders and trees, ride a tricycle with ease, hop, stand and run on tiptoe and sit with their legs crossed, and are quite expert with a ball and even a bat.

Hearing and speech By now children speak clearly although they still make mistakes with certain sounds. They ask many questions, make up long stories and enjoy jokes.

Handling objects Four-year-olds can draw quite expertly, often people and houses. They can use a knife and fork.

The five-year-old child

Moving The five-year-old child can walk steadily down a line, skip on alternate feet, hop on each foot and play all sorts of ball games.

Hearing and speech The only sounds which children may still have problems with are usually *s*, *f* or *th*. They can tell you their full name, age and address as well as their birthday. They love stories and often act them out.

Handling objects At five years of age children are able to thread needles and to sew. They can write and draw with pencils and brushes, and the people they draw have a large number of features.

SPEECH AND LANGUAGE

Children who have a good mastery of speech and language have experienced many interesting conversations with adults at home. However it is true that there are factors outside a parent's control that can interfere with a child's fluent acquisition of speech and language – for example a physical problem such as glue ear or an unusual speech disorder. It is also true that genetic influences play an important role in deciding how fast a child will acquire and use language, and that in speech as in all other areas of development, some children mature more quickly than others. Yet the greatest contribution parents can make to their child's speech and language development is to speak to their child.

It is neither necessary nor desirable to make conversation a special event. Talking as often as possible to children about what interests them at that moment is more helpful. Speak clearly, using short sentences and simple but not babyish language. Making two-way conversation encourages babies and young children to participate, especially if the noises they make are interpreted as real speech. Busy parents who do not have time to sit down and talk face-to-face can give a running commentary on what they are doing.

You should limit the background noise from the video, television and radio so that the child can hear speech clearly. Draw their attention to other noises around them – a bird in the garden, traffic or even silence. Listening, like speaking, is an acquired skill.

In an important recent study researchers found that a large proportion of nine-month-old babies showed signs of delayed speech. The researchers suspected that babies in homes where the television or video was on all the time were likely to be at greatest risk of speech delay, and their evidence proved them right. When parents were advised to reduce the time the television was on, and to set aside half an hour a day to play and talk to the child, the results at the age of three showed a great improvement. Children whose parents had followed the advice were at least a year further ahead in their language development than the children of parents who did not.

This does not mean that the television has to be turned off permanently. It depends on your circumstances at home, although the study found the greatest progress in the children who not only benefited from extra adult attention but also had the television off during the day. The problem with continuous television is thought to be two-fold: it makes it difficult for children to distinguish background noise from speech, and it reduces the number of times children interact in a social way and have conversations with adults. However sitting down to watch a programme with a child and talking about it can increase the child's vocabulary, while watching a video (usually the same video) again and again can help young children to appreciate the way in which events follow on from each other.

Specific types of language, such as nursery rhymes, help the child to develop an awareness of sounds. This acuity can then be helpful in learning to read.

The bilingual family

Increasing numbers of children in many parts of the world are brought up in bilingual families, and some parents worry that coping with two languages will slow down the acquisition of speech, as well as lead to problems. However there is no evidence that this is the case. Until the child is three or four years of age the parents should use their mother tongue or the language with which they feel most comfortable to express emotions. It is easier for children if the parent uses only one language with them or if certain situations are linked with certain languages.

Childhood speech problems

The most common speech problems that occur in childhood are the following.

The child's speech cannot be understood Either the child cannot hear the differences between sounds or cannot say them. The most common reasons for being unable to discriminate between sounds are a hidden hearing loss, frequently caused by glue ear, and a lack of clear one-to-one conversation at home. If adults outside the family have difficulty understanding a three-year-old child, an assessment by a speech therapist may prove helpful.

The child cannot hear properly In children under the age of five the most common cause of deafness is glue ear. Children vary enormously in their ability to compensate for the fluctuating hearing loss that glue ear brings. If speech is clearly immature or unclear there is often an additional factor or the glue ear is severe. Children with glue ear should be spoken to face to face, using language they can understand and without background interference from television or radio. They should also have a hearing test and possibly treatment with grommets (see page 202).

The child lisps By the time children reach their first birthday they have learned to discriminate between all the sounds of their mother tongue. However every language has its stumbling blocks and in English these are the sounds *s*, *f*, *th*, *w* and *y*. Many children do not sort these out until the first or second year of primary school, but the lisp is endearing rather than worrying. When a child pronounces a sound in the wrong way, just say it correctly, in an approving tone of voice.

The child has started to stammer As children gather speed with their speech – frequently around the age of three or four – it is amazingly common for them to pause, repeat themselves or get stuck midway. Speech therapists call this nonfluency, but it is stammering to everyone else. Listen to what the child is trying to say, give them your full, patient attention and resist any temptation to finish the sentence for them. The stammer often dies away in a month or two. If other people in the family stammer, or if the stammer lasts more than six weeks or is very severe, ask for a speech therapy assessment.

Speech therapy should be fun for the child. This five-year-old boy has had a cleft palate repaired and is practising blowing to increase his control of air pressure inside his mouth. Speech therapy sessions are held individually or in small groups.

Complementary treatment

Music therapy has proved to be particularly beneficial in cases of specific speech delay, and speech and language therapists will sometimes recommend it. It can explore psychological causes, build confidence and establish rewarding patterns of nonverbal communication, as well as encourage verbal communication at a developmentally appropriate level. Music therapy may also offer help and support in cases of stammering that arise from anxiety. Emotional causes of stammering may be helped by the **Bach flower remedies**: Mimulus for shyness; Larch for lack of confidence; Centuary for inassertiveness; Vervain for over-excitement; and Impatiens for impatience. Both **play** and **drama therapy** can be beneficial in cases of speech and language delay, and play therapy for stammering.

How speech develops

- Soon after birth infants may make quiet breathy sounds such as *heh*
- By four to eight weeks infants may respond by starting to coo if you leave a gap in your speech
- At three to five months infants often enjoy making a variety of different noises when spoken to and may start a 'conversation' themselves
- By six months infants can squeal, chuckle and scream. Tuneful babbling starts soon, at first with single sounds such as *goo* and moving on to double sounds such as *ama* or *uduh*
- By 12 months infants often make sounds that could be words and even conversations. Listen carefully and you will hear most of the consonants and vowels
- By 18 months toddlers can say between five and twenty words or more, and understand many more. They try to sing and join in nursery rhymes and can point out parts of the body
- By two years of age children use 50 or more words and understand far more. They string them together in at least two-word sentences, ask constant 'What's that?' questions and understand instructions such as 'See why the baby is crying'
- By three to three-and-a-half years of age children can build complex sentences and stories linked by 'and', and ask endless questions. However many sounds are still childish, as are speech forms such as 'I bringed it.'
- By four to four-and-a-half years of age children are sophisticated communicators with an active vocabulary of over 1000 words and a wider passive vocabulary. They still muddle sounds (*r* and *w*, *l* and *y* or *p* and *th*, *s* and *f*, or *t* and *k*). They can talk about the past and the future
- By five years children are fluent, using nearly all the correct sounds except for *s*, *f* and *th*. They understand abstract words and jokes and can tell stories using subordinate clauses
- Beyond the age of five years children learn to connect their speech fluently using linking words such as however, for instance, perhaps and really. They learn different registers of language for school, home and the playground. By late primary school, children have a vocabulary of 10,000 to 20,000 words – still a mere fraction of the million and more words in the English language

Learning difficulties

A child with a learning difficulty is a child who has significantly greater difficulty in learning than most children of the same age, and/or has a disability that prevents or hinders them from making use of the educational facilities available to children of the same age.

Some children with a learning difficulty find learning most things difficult. They may have been slow to sit up and walk and they are very likely to have been late talkers They may be quite unresponsive to noises and speech, so there are early concerns that they may be deaf. Parents are usually the first to notice their child's difficulties when they compare them with other children of the same age. Sometimes a health visitor or a doctor who sees the child for a development review notices the learning delay before the parents.

Many children with learning difficulties have physical difficulties as well. Children with Down's syndrome (see page 316) or fragile X syndrome (see page 313) all experience some degree of learning problem. Some, although not all, children with cerebral palsy also have difficulty in learning. A minority of babies born prematurely, in particular babies born with a very low birth weight, have a general or specific learning difficulty that may be accompanied by cerebral palsy. Damage to the brain before, during or after birth can leave a legacy of learning problems, although the brain has a remarkable ability to compensate when even large areas are damaged. However no cause is ever found for 50 per cent of children who have difficulty in learning.

What to do

Discovering that a child has a learning difficulty is upsetting for all parents, particularly if the discovery follows months or years of uncertainty. In the initial stages parents require a good deal of information, which is sometimes not easy to obtain. Many parents report that parents of children with similar difficulties are the best source of information. Voluntary organisations (see the Directory, page 366) can also provide advice, information and support.

Children with a learning difficulty are entitled to assessment and help. As a second problem, for example, with hearing or vision can compound their problems, they should receive regular checks. Therapy depends on the cause but parents are always kept closely involved.

Once it comes to schooling, some children can attend a mainstream school with additional one-to-one support, while others thrive better in a special school. In the school population of the United Kingdom, one child in five needs some level of extra help to cope with the curriculum. These children are held to have a special educational need (SEN), which in many cases can be met in school by the teacher, with support where necessary from outside bodies. Some children catch up quickly when given specialist help and are able to keep up with their classmates. Others continue to need help and support.

Predicting the outlook for children with learning difficulties is not easy. Children generally improve, although some have a problem in a particular area for the rest of their lives.

Dyslexia

One of the most common specific learning difficulties, dyslexia represents a disorder in processing symbolic information. People with dyslexia have difficulty making sense of words and symbols, getting them in the right order and recalling them. This leads to difficulties with reading, spelling and writing. Number and organization skills and coordination may also be involved. However it is important to remember that dyslexia is not related to intelligence, culture, class or socio-economic background.

Dyslexia is thought to be four times more common in boys than girls and can often be inherited; genetic markers for it have been found on two chromosomes, numbers one and fifteen. The condition may have its roots in slight differences in brain structure and organization. Neurobiology has shown that in some dyslexics the right and left hemispheres of the brain are unusually symmetrical.

A dyslexic's fundamental difficulty is usually with the sounds of spoken words (the phonology), so that the child has difficulty breaking words into syllables and in knowing whether they rhyme or not. Typically, a child with dyslexia has difficulty with verbal short term memory; finding the right word; and distinguishing similar sounds such as *t* and *d*.

A number of children with dyslexia have additional visual problems that contribute to difficulties with reading and writing, and make schoolwork extremely frustrating. Detailed eye tests are vital and the use of coloured overlays on reading text can result in unexpected progress.

Children with dyslexia should always have an eye examination, because subtle defects of vision may contribute to the condition, although they are not the primary cause. For example, visual problems with focusing over a wide range of distances, and with eye coordination, are more common in dyslexics than in other children. Some experience eyestrain and visual distortions when reading, a condition known as scotopic sensitivity syndrome (also known as Mearles-Irlen syndrome), which can be helped by using coloured filters.

Dyslexia usually becomes obvious when a child is struggling with reading and writing at school. However there are early signs. When present on their own they are not evidence that a child is dyslexic, and many children who are not dyslexic show some of the signs. However a pre-school child with many obvious and persistent signs deserves observation. This is especially true if someone else in the family has dyslexia.

You may notice

Pre-school

- *The child is markedly better at some things than others. They may be good with construction toys and craft activities, but have no interest in pre-reading and pre-writing activities and skills*
- *The child is late in talking clearly. They confuse the names of objects and directions (in/out; up/down) and have difficulty in remembering nursery rhymes*
- *The child cannot clap in time and may be clumsy*
- *The child cannot remember easily more than one instruction at a time*

At school

- *A child eight years of age or less may show particular difficulty learning to read or write, may persistently reverse letters and numbers and/or find it hard to remember information sequences, such as multiplication tables, the alphabet or days of the week. Concentration may be difficult and frustration may lead to behavioural problems*
- *A child aged nine to twelve years may still make mistakes reading and spelling, take longer than expected over written work and have difficulty copying from the blackboard or taking down oral instructions. There may be increasing frustration and a growing lack of self confidence*
- *A pupil over the age of 12 years may read inaccurately, spell inconsistently and have difficulty planning and writing essays. They may have difficulty with verbal instructions and foreign languages. Self-esteem may be low*

What to do

If your child shows most of the signs above, ask the teacher whether the child needs extra support at school and whether there are any helpful activities that can be done at home. If the school agrees that your child has a special educational need, an individual education plan may be drawn up describing their difficulties, the action to be taken and the support the child can expect, as well as targets to be reached in a given time. This may be enough for the child to keep up with classmates. If it is not, the child may need a full assessment, followed by help from special educationalists. There are many approaches to dyslexia, but children learn best from a structured programme to literacy that uses a variety of senses, ideally taught by a teacher with a special qualification.

You should also make arrangements through your doctor for your child to have a detailed vision and hearing assessment, and make arrangements through the school for an educational psychologist to assess the child.

At home, stress what your child is good at and praise them for it. Avoid drawing attention to failures, as children with dyslexia experience enough of that at school.

Never accept diagnosed dyslexia as an excuse for not trying. Success just takes longer and is harder to achieve. Be patient and remember that trying hard is stressful.

Who can help?

For organizations that offer an information and referral services to local associations see the Directory.

Complementary Treatment

Musical activities devised by teachers may support specialized teaching methods. The **Bach flower remedies** may be helpful in dealing with emotional problems associated with the condition.

Fragile X syndrome

Fragile X syndrome is a common inherited cause of learning disability. As accurate tests have only recently become available, the incidence is not yet agreed, but it is thought to affect approximately one boy in four thousand. It has remained a hidden cause of learning disability because people with fragile X are often not immediately identifiable, although they do have typical physical characteristics. In the same way, the amount of learning disability and behaviour problems fragile X causes vary widely from child to child.

The fragile X condition is transmitted on the X chromosome, one of the chains of genetic material that control inherited characteristics. Examined under a microscope, the tip of the X chromosome appears to be breaking off. This occurs at the site of a particular gene, FMR 1, where a genetic change has resulted in a small segment of the gene being repeated many times. Some people have a large change (a full mutation) in the gene and consequently have fragile X. Others have a small change (a pre-mutation) which does not usually cause symptoms, but is likely to increase, possibly into a full mutation, when the gene is passed on by a woman to the next generation. Pre-mutations in men do not increase in size when passed on.

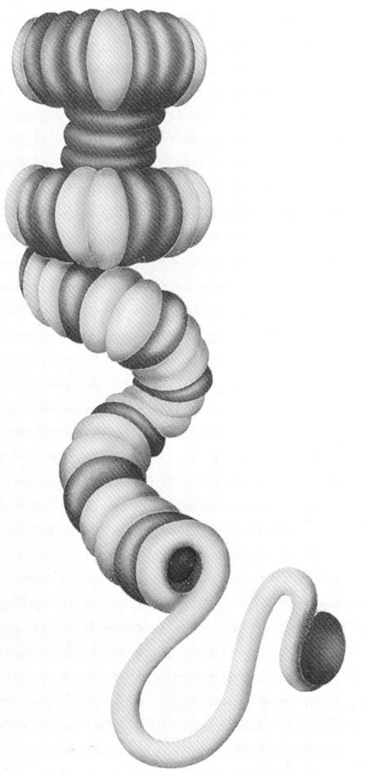

If you examine under a microscope the X chromosome of a boy with fragile X syndrome, you will see that the end of the chromosome seems to be breaking off, as reflected in this illustration.

Males have one X and one Y chromosome: females have two X chromosomes. A woman with a fragile X chromosome is likely to have a second, normal X chromosome, and it seems that the normal chromosome protects her from some of the effects of the fragile one. Therefore the woman will have no fragile X symptoms. However such women have a 50 per cent chance of passing the condition on to their children.

Fragile X can be diagnosed accurately from a blood sample, which can identify both affected children and carriers. The condition can usually be detected prenatally at 11-12 weeks of pregnancy by chorionic villus sampling. However a full discussion with a genetic counsellor is recommended before becoming pregnant.

Children with fragile X may show only some of the following symptoms, and to an extremely varied degree.

You may notice

- *Learning difficulties, such as specific difficulties with number work, thinking in 3-D and processing sequential information*
- *Speech may be rapid, with poor rhythm control and may be difficult to understand*
- *Difficulties concentrating, and the child is easily distracted*

- *Impulsive behaviour*
- *High activity levels, restlessness*
- *Babies may be noticeably floppy*
- *Some people with fragile X develop epilepsy*

Strengths Some children with fragile X understand words surprisingly well and have excellent memories. In terms of behaviour, children may combine being happy, friendly and likable with certain autistic-like features such as avoiding eye contact, hand-flapping and speech and language delay.

What to do

Early diagnosis does help children with fragile X, because appropriate support and therapy – particularly speech therapy and, later on, special educational support – can be given. As many children take in what they see better than what they hear, a demonstration is often more helpful than instruction, and a practical, concrete teaching approach helps.

Behaviour modification – rewarding desired behaviour and ignoring undesirable behaviour – helps. Preparing children gently for change is important, and supporting them with social skills is beneficial.

The family should receive genetic counselling so that the risks of future children being affected can be explained and the implications discussed.

Complementary Treatment

The Bach flower remedies may be helpful in dealing with the emotional problems that may be associated with the condition.

Attention deficit disorder

All children are sometimes overactive, restless and difficult to handle. However children with attention deficit disorder (ADD) are so inappropriately impulsive, overactive and/or inattentive for their age that their behaviour impedes their social activities, development or educational progress. ADD is not a fixed syndrome but an evolving concept, therefore ideas about it are constantly changing as more is discovered about the causes and most effective treatments.

Current thinking holds that ADD can have many causes. Genes play an important part and brain scans of affected children have shown underactivity in areas of the brains, particularly in the frontal lobes, the command centres for self control. Usually a variety of factors adds up to a final picture of hyperactivity, commonly including a restless and impulsive temperament and a delay in developing the ability to concentrate. For a small number of children allergies to certain foods or ingredients play a role. Three to four times as many boys as girls are affected. In the United Kingdom one child in two hundred is thought to have the disorder, while in the United States as many as one child in twelve has been diagnosed with attention deficit disorder.

Children usually improve as they mature and learn ways of coping. However they may grow out of the overactivity and impulsiveness while the inability to concentrate may be more difficult to overcome.

Behaviour that is appropriate in a young child can signal an attention deficit disorder in an older child. Unceasing and sometimes purposeless activity is an early indication that the child's behaviour may need to be looked at by a professional.

Although ADD is diagnosed most frequently around the age of seven when educational demands on young children increase, some symptoms may be clear from earliest childhood. The following are some of the most common features.

You may notice

- *Frequent disorganized and aimless activity. Pointless, forbidden and even painful actions are repeated*
- *Constantly changing activities*
- *Constantly waking in the night*
- *Difficulty acquiring self-control. Possibly aggressive play*
- *Difficulty following instructions, learning to cope with a new situation or fitting in with a group*
- *The child is clearly different from their unaffected brothers and sisters*
- *Possibly extreme temper tantrums*
- *Some children show signs that commonly accompany the hyperkinetic syndrome – a severe type of hyperactivity. These may include being slow to talk and clumsiness*

Diagnosis
Many of the typical features of ADD are common and normal in young children. A paediatrician, psychologist or psychiatrist diagnosing ADD or the hyperkinetic syndrome will look for clear signs. These include six of the following symptoms denoting lack of concentration, all six lasting for more than six months and being inappropriate for the child's age. The symptoms are: often being careless and failing to pay attention to detail; losing concentration quickly at play or work; not appearing to listen to what is said; not following instructions or completing tasks; not being very good at self organization or organizing activities; an avoidance or dislike of tasks that need a sustained mental effort; losing things that are needed for work or games; being easily distracted; and being frequently forgetful.

The doctor will also look for signs of overactivity or impulsiveness, including frequent fidgeting or squirming when sitting; getting up and leaving the seat when expected to stay still; frequent running or climbing about; being inappropriately noisy; being unable to hear the whole question before blurting out the answer; and having difficulty waiting in turn.

What to do
Children who cope best are often the children of coping parents. Try to encourage self control, establish and adhere to clear house rules and plan structured days.

Be positive, encourage and reward good behaviour, including small achievements such as sitting still at the table. Use the child's best time of day to teach new skills.

Ask for help when the child's activity levels become too much for you to bear.

Treatment
No single treatment works for all children and doctors often combine different approaches. A small number of children respond to changes in diet. Some children with attention deficit disorder are thought to suffer from food allergies, while others cannot metabolize certain substances in food or drugs, especially artificial colours, some preservatives and salicylates. Cows' milk, chocolate, fizzy drinks and food additives are believed to be common culprits. A few children improve when they avoid a wide variety of manufactured, processed and frozen foods. Others respond to a diet that does not contain caffeine.

Drugs used for severely affected children include stimulants, such as methylphenidate hydrochloride (Ritalin), which appear to increase concentration. However this is not a cure and is not suitable for children under the age of six. The drug is thought to help nerve cells in the brain carry messages to other cells, allowing children to filter out unwanted information. Medication does not help all children and can have adverse effects, including headaches, appetite and weight loss and poor sleep. However when it is effective the child is able to concentrate, learn and behave sociably and respond to the behaviour or cognitive therapies that should always accompany drug therapy.

Other approaches to hyperactivity include psychological treatments. Behavioural and cognitive therapy are the most common; treatment plans are drawn up individually for the child. Behavioural therapy includes reward schemes and positive encouragement. Cognitive therapy can help children manage their own reward schemes, control their impulses and solve problems in an ordered way.

Who can help?
For organizations offering help and advice, see the Directory.

Complementary Treatment
Children with mild to moderate symptoms may benefit from **music therapy**, developing concentration and commitment through musical activities when they are unable to tolerate educational ones. Severe cases may benefit from receptive music therapy to encourage relaxation. The **Bach flower remedy** Vervain is often useful for over-excited, over-enthusiastic children who cannot switch off, wind down or relax. Cherry Plum is helpful if there is a tendency to lose emotional control and Impatiens for those who become impatient, irritable and do everything in a hurry. **Play** and **drama therapy** can also be beneficial.

Autism
Autism is a developmental disorder that interferes with a child's social and communication skills. Four times as many boys as girls are affected and most, although not all, have learning difficulties. The cause is not yet understood, although events before, during or shortly following birth may be involved. Genetic traits appear to be an important factor in many children; however the sites of any relevant genes have yet to be identified.

Children with autism live in a world of jumbled fragments of information, which means they cannot assess other people's feelings or reactions. This makes their behaviour and responses appear bizarre, unsociable and at times unpredictable. In an affected child patterns of behaviour are already odd enough for a diagnosis by the age of three years. Sometimes the typical lack of response is visible from infancy. All children with autism show the following three features. First, they ignore other people or approach them but pay no attention to their response (some children want to be sociable but don't know how). Second, they have difficulty communicating using either words or gestures and expressions, and they do not listen to others. Third, they have difficulty developing pretend or imaginative play.

You may notice

- *Your baby turns from your gaze, dislikes being picked up and prefers to be left alone*
- *They appear deaf and you are left with an uneasy feeling that something is wrong*
- *They are probably slow to reach their milestones and are not only late to develop speech but respond inappropriately to sounds. However, as they develop they may be good at certain tasks such as jigsaws and sorting shapes*
- *As a child they insist on a precise routine and find it extremely difficult to accommodate change*
- *Other signs shown by some, but not all, children with autism include: looking past people rather than straight at them; a tiptoe walk; flapping hands; indifference to pain; laughing in the wrong situation; erratic sleeping; and seemingly uncontrollable behaviour problems.*

What to do

A health visitor or doctor may refer your child to a psychiatrist or psychologist for assessment. Autism cannot be cured, but careful education, care and support can improve behaviour and develop life skills. A range of approaches is used when working with people with autism, but as the disorder is both complex and quite individual in its effects, there is no single definitive treatment. Children should be assessed and regularly reviewed at a child development centre. By school age a child will need appropriate education and support. Some people with autism lead successful working lives, often in areas requiring a particular attention to factual detail.

Asperger syndrome

Asperger syndrome is a type of autism in which children often have average or above average intelligence, but in other ways share many of the characteristics of children with classic autism. Language skills tend to be better developed and children may have a tendency to talk at people whether they are interested or not, as well as to be over precise and very literal in their understanding of language.

Children with this syndrome often have a narrow range of obsessive interests and dislike even small changes in their lives. Some children with Asperger syndrome are clumsy and find it difficult to learn skills requiring coordination, such as riding a bicycle.

Because of their intelligence and language skills, some children with Asperger syndrome may go undiagnosed for many years. Others are educated in special schools. With appropriate support and education, children can go on to lead full and fulfiling adult lives, and may be especially valued for their reliability and their dedication in a sympathetic and informed workplace.

Who can help?

For organizations who can offer advice, support and help, see the Directory.

Complementary Treatment

The **Bach flower remedies** would be helpful in a supportive role when chosen to suit the personality, mood and temperament of the child. **Drama** and **play therapies** can be helpful. **Music therapy** can be particularly beneficial, as music is a dynamic language rich in emotional nuance, and requires no understanding of verbal language. The child may become more accessible, manageable and contented.

Down's Syndrome

Down's syndrome is a genetic condition involving an extra chromosome. In each cell in the body the majority of people have 46 chromosomes, which carry all the information about characteristics they have inherited from their parents. People with Down's syndrome have 47 chromosomes, with the extra chromosome inherited either from the mother or the father. Children with Down's syndrome are unique, but share certain typical features. They generally develop more slowly than other children and reach their milestones later. All have some degree of learning disability, but it is not possible to look at a baby and predict the ultimate level of achievement. Some babies with Down's syndrome have more of the characteristic physical features of the condition, but this is no guide to eventual attainment.

Diagnosis in pregnancy

The first sign that a foetus may have a major chromosome abnormality may be detected on an ultrasound scan in the 11th to 13th weeks of pregnancy. Among other features, this early scan may show extra fluid at the back of the foetal neck. This is not a diagnosis, but may indicate the need for further tests, as it is more common in foetuses with Down's syndrome. In a few centres, the scan may be combined with blood tests to give a more accurate prediction. At around 16 weeks of pregnancy a blood test for chemical markers in the mother's blood (the Double, Triple or Quadruple test) can be used to calculate the chances of the infant having Down's syndrome. Results are rated screen-positive or screen-negative: screen-positive women are offered further tests. The

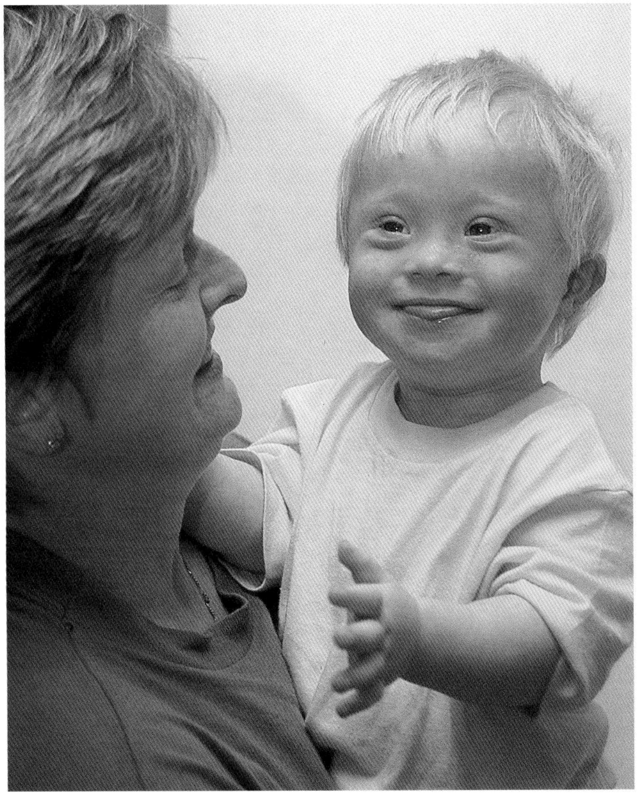

It is a truism that children with Down's syndrome are happy little people. Because of this they are capable of bringing happiness into many people's lives, not only their own family's. Yet the discovery that a child has Down's syndrome or any other major disorder is always accompanied by shock and grieving for the wished-for child. Love for the child as she is follows later.

diagnosis can be confirmed by testing the foetus's own cells, either at 10-12 weeks of pregnancy by chorionic villus sampling, or at 15-18 weeks by amniocentesis.

Diagnosis at birth

Signs of Down's syndrome are usually clear at birth, although babies are quite individual and look and behave like other babies. Typical features include being small for dates, and subsequently growing more slowly. Other signs are: the back of the head is unusually flat; the outside corners of the eyes slope up and the inside corners are often invisible beneath a fold of skin; there may be a third soft spot on the top of the head; and the palms of the infant's hands are crossed by a single crease.

Potential associated problems

Feeding a baby with Down's syndrome may be difficult, and the baby's tongue may get in the way of the nipple or teat; in addition, co-ordinating the feeding action may be hard for a baby with Down's syndrome. One child in three has a heart defect – in some cases quite minor but in others it will require surgery – and some have a narrowing of the intestine. Down's syndrome children may develop long-term glue ear as a result of repeated ear infections, to which, like chest infections, they are prone. Appropriate health checks and, where necessary, surgery, keep these problems to a minimum, and many babies make slow but steady developmental progress during their early years.

What you can expect

Children with Down's syndrome have a wide range of ability. Some do best in a special school, but others thrive with special needs support in a mainstream school where they can mix with their peers. In the United Kingdom children with Down's syndrome are entitled to extra help with learning. Despite their learning difficulties, Down's syndrome children respond warmly to the play and stimulation you would give to any child you love, and grow into adults who can lead rewarding and semi-independent lives.

Who can help?

For organizations offering help, support and advice, see the Directory.

Complementary Treatment

Music therapy is an ideal intervention for addressing specific secondary emotional and communication problems frequently associated with the condition. However educational and recreational music when carefully adapted to the child's abilities, is often sufficient to foster the development of which the child is capable. **Bach flower remedies** would be helpful in a supporting role, chosen according to the child's personality, mood and temperament. **Drama therapy** may also be beneficial.

THE PRE-SCHOOL CHILD

During the pre-school years children develop from infants who are dependent on others for their very survival into children who have practised at home all the skills they need to launch themselves into the world beyond the family. How do they manage it?

For their physical and psychological survival infants have one overwhelming need: the committed, loving care of an adult. They need care to survive physically, and love and commitment to survive psychologically. A child who is deprived of this relationship in the earliest years, before the age of three, is very likely to grow into an adult who cannot make relationships with other people.

An overview

Initially infants see themselves as a single unit with the mother. Only in the second half of the first year does the awareness of their separateness dawn, and for the first two or three years children's security is tied in with the constancy of their care. Learning to separate is a key experience of the pre-school years and one that many children find hard to handle. However as children approach school age, they do get better at it. They still need a replacement for the mother, and the social grouping they find easiest to cope with remains an enlarged substitute family. Many pre-school children – and quite a few school children – need a prop when they are without their habitual emotional support. The cuddly or transitional object stands for the absent caretaker, whether it takes the form of a well-sucked thumb or a silky blanket.

During the pre-school years this simple, fundamental need for a securely anchored emotional life is increasingly counterbalanced by the child's desire for independence. This powers the drive to acquire the simple but basic skills that turn a baby into a child – self-feeding, attending to daily tasks, toilet training. It takes time to learn these skills and this, together with an unbridled impulsiveness, can lead to the frustrations, moods and tantrums that can characterize two- and three-year-old children.

Emotions in very young children are extremely strong. Prey to jealousy, anger, love, fear and excitement, they have neither the words to express how they feel nor the understanding that others feel as they do. This can leave them open to quite marked fears and anxieties at an age when the demarcation between reality and fantasy is not yet clear.

Perhaps the single most important skill pre-school children acquire is language. Once their language blossoms they can use words to think. Words and stories help children give their emotions shapes and names and teach them that others have felt as they do. By the age of four, some children are using language to grapple with the larger issues of death, love and eternity in a way that is unthinkable in the pre-verbal child.

Threading through the pre-school child's career is the unfolding of their personality. Discernible from the earliest days, it is clear by the age of two whether a child is outgoing and confident or adopts a more tentative and thoughtful approach to life. While early childhood experiences can moderate differences – by boosting the child's self-esteem, for example – watching the child's unique individuality develop is one of the most exciting rewards of parenthood.

Attachment and separation

The earliest bonds infants form with people around them will serve them for life. Their early attachments – to their mother, their father and a range of other important people in their world – provide the secure basis for their emotional development. Their first experience is dependence, and from this they learn whether or not their needs will be attended to.

In the early years children may venture towards independence, but only with a backwards glance to be sure that their mother (or other attachment figure) is still there. A well-known piece of research showed how a one-year-old in a new environment would venture 7 m/23 ft from their mother and a two-year-old 15 m/50 ft. With each succeeding year the distance would grow.

Separation can be difficult for parents as well as children, but a confident and loving farewell is more helpful than wavering uncertainly. And it is usually the case that, once the mother has left, the child very soon forgets his unhappiness at separating and becomes immersed in an absorbing activity.

By the second year forces are already tugging the child in contrary directions, as the need to depend intertwines closely with the wish for independence. As demands on toddlers increase – for appropriate behaviour or even skillful performance – toddlers start to assert themselves. Excessive demands can lead to defiance, and even reasonable requirements often meet negativity and refusal. This is the age of food fads and manipulation, followed swiftly by the demand 'I want mummy'.

Inevitable separations have to be handled sensitively. Young children need to be told of them in advance, and they need to know that the parent is returning. At first their separations need to be very short – just minutes. Ideally, during separation from the parents, they should stay with a person who is one of their attachment figures, so that their experiences are reassuring.

Even so, not all children respond positively to separation. Children who are clingy may be too young to separate. After the age of three, children start to cope better with separation and there is plenty of evidence that spending time away from home in a group nursery environment helps the child's development. By the age of four most children no longer need physical proximity, although throughout childhood they continue to fear losing one of their prominent attachment figures.

At each stage of transition it will be easier for the child if they are accompanied by someone or something familiar. If they start school with a friend, they will cope better. Other factors that make separation easier are: a secure mother-child bond; an harmonious atmosphere at home; the child's growing awareness of past and future; their use of language to explain and express their emotions; and good experiences.

Complementary Treatment

Music therapy is highly recommended where separation presents particular problems, as the relationship with the therapist can re-enact the damaged or delayed process of separation from the primary carer without substituting a new dependency. **Play therapy** can also be very helpful. Recommended **Bach flower remedies** are: Chicory for the clinging child; Walnut for adjustment; and Mimulus or Rock Rose where there is fear.

Temper tantrums

Temper tantrums are usually a feature of pre-school behaviour, often triggered by frustration, tiredness or by over-excitement. Although they are extremely common, not all children develop them; personality and home circumstances are important underlying factors. The peak years are 18 months to 3 years of age.

A child having a temper tantrum can become very frightened, especially if the adult also loses control. Remaining calm and holding the child firmly helps him to feel secure and confident. Be sure to cuddle him as soon as his body relaxes.

The following strategies appear to be the most effective methods of coping with tantrums.

Prevention Prevent a temper tantrum in a supermarket by providing an apple for the child to eat, rather than have a fight beside the sweet display. Give your child as much loving attention as you can spare when they are behaving well.

Distraction When a temper tantrum is brewing, try to draw the child's attention to something interesting.

Ignoring the tantrum Try not to explode yourself; when your child has a temper tantrum in public, ignore any comments or disapproving looks from other people.

Time out Either leave the child somewhere safe but boring for a short while so they can calm down, or remove yourself. Between three and five minutes is usually enough. This approach is known as 'time out from positive reinforcement'. As an alternative to time out, hold the child firmly but calmly until they have calmed down.

The response to guard against is changing your reaction because of the temper tantrum. This merely teaches the child that they have only to throw a tantrum whenever they want their own way.

Note that tantrums may be more severe in a child with a hidden difficulty – such as glue ear or speech delay – that affects their ability to communicate.

Complementary Treatment

Rescue Remedy, a **Bach flower remedy**, can be useful in relieving some of the frustration and tension, but other remedies, chosen on an individual basis, may be more effective. They include Vine for very strong-willed children; Holly for tantrums that develop as a result of jealousy; Willow for the self-pitying, resentful element; and Chicory if the tantrum is used to manipulate or gain attention. **Music therapy** will have a dual function where tantrums are a response to a genuinely frustrating situation, either internal or external. It provides an alternative and creative method of expressing frustration and offers fulfiling and less frustrating activities to build confidence. Both **drama** and **play therapy** can also provide support.

Fears and phobias

Fears in children are common. All children are afraid of being abandoned by a parent or of a parent simply walking out. Young children typically fear darkness and shadows; animals and insects; monsters, witches and ghosts. Older children's fears are more obviously rooted in the challenging experiences they face at school. They may be fearful of teachers, tests and coping with their schoolwork. They also learn to fear social rejection – for example, being the last child to be picked for the team. During the teenage years fears become more similar to adult fears – of closed or open spaces and of social situations such as losing their role in their peer group or being the subject of ridicule.

Some children are born more fearful, while others learn fearful ways of behaving from their parents. Pre-school children are particularly prone to insecurities because of their lack of knowledge and experience of the world; they also have powerful imaginations, which can transform everyday events into terrifying ordeals; and they have very little control over events. The things of which they are frightened – insects, animals, darkness, abandonment – are all quite logical if one remembers that it is not long since humans lived in a far more hostile environment than they do today.

With an unclear dividing line between reality and fantasy, pre-school children are particularly prone to imaginary fears – of ogres, monsters and witches. Some psychologists believe that such creatures embody children's powerful emotions at an age when rage, jealousy or hatred is intense. The embodiment helps young children to give shape to their feelings and to imagine them as separate from themselves. In this way, they learn to cope with what would otherwise be overwhelming emotions.

What to do

Some parents belittle fears, try to distract their children's attention or make allowances. If the child is afraid of the dark, they turn on the light rather than exploring with the child gently and gradually how safe darkness is. It is important to respect a child's fear and consider how best to approach it, agreeing a planned approach in which the child stays in control. Reflective listening is helpful, opening the subject with a statement such as 'I know it seems hard to get into the water . . .'. Once children have realized that nothing awful happens when they confront their fear, it will fade.

Another technique is to give children something they like to do – such as eating crisps or sweets – at the same time as they confront their fear, so that the child is being rewarded for confronting it and learning to associate something pleasant with a previously frightening situation. Role playing the frightening situation (with people, toys, drawing or writing) helps to desensitize the child in advance or to rework the situation afterwards. Many children do this instinctively themselves through play, repeating an experience again and again until they get used to it. For older children who can acknowledge and talk about the fear but still cannot control it, simple breathing exercises and relaxation techniques are helpful.

A phobia is a fear that is so intense that it prevents the child from doing normal things. A child who is afraid of the dark, for example, won't get out of bed in case something grabs them. A child with a phobia about darkness sleeps in full light and starts to fear even small shadows. As it is possible to prevent their fears from developing into phobias by judicious intervention, it is important that parents are sensitive to a child's developing fears.

The phobias that unfortunately do develop in children and teenagers follow certain patterns. In older children phobias about their appearance are relatively frequent and can become extreme (see Eating disorders page 248), as can social phobias, school phobia (see page 327) and the phobias common in adults, such as agoraphobia and claustrophobia. If you are aware that your child's fears are becoming more intense, your doctor can refer the child to a child or adolescent psychiatrist or a clinical psychologist.

Complementary Treatment

Music therapy can be an effective alternative or possible adjunct to verbal forms of psychotherapy where phobias result from traumatic stress disorder or other forms of anxiety. A child may be supported in the exploration and resolution of the anxiety in musical terms, with or without words. **Drama** and **play therapy** may also help in this way. The **Bach flower remedies** offer Aspen for fear of the unknown, Rock Rose for terror and terrifying dreams, and Rescue Remedy for combined elements of panic, fear and shock.

Comfort habits

Children's comfort habits often leave parents feeling guilty. Are they a sign of insecurity or of unmet emotional need? Should parents wait until the child grows out of the habit – even if that seems to take forever – or should they help the child to move on by intervening in their dependence on the comfort object or habit? And will one bad habit just be replaced by another?

While it is not clear why some children develop comfort habits when others do not, it is reassuring to know that, within reason, comfort habits seem helpful to children, acting as an emotional crutch at times of transition. There are thought to be only three times when they are not advantageous psychologically: when a normal, moderate dependency becomes acute; when the child persistently turns to the comforter while rejecting the mother; and when an older child suddenly takes up a comfort habit.

Comfort blankets

These are the pieces of cloth that usually originate in the cot, and on which young children become passionately fixated. They are a middle-class phenomenon, and the association for the child is with a comforting permanence while the mother is not there. Over the years they become unrecognizable scraps or rags, or the attachment is transferred to another object, so that silk ties, large underwear labels, powder puffs and cuddly toys become the child's constant companion. Although children are most dependent on their cuddlies between the ages of two and three, especially at times of stress or change (such as bedtime or starting nursery school) the passion can last until the teenage years. Boys of 11 have been found with terry nappies under their pillows, and toy shops do a steady trade in soft toys to university students. Eventually the scorn of their peers usually puts a stop to the dependence, but meanwhile research shows that children who have had a transitional cuddly in their pre-school years are better adjusted and more sociable later.

There is a surprising consistency in the comforters that children take to bed with them. Blankets and soft toys are the universal favourites of many, including this girl. Dummies, rags, sheets, clothing and fluff that has been fiddled from clothes are all popular. Parents should be reassured that the comforter is a useful emotional tool; they therefore should not discourage their child from making use of them.

Sucking habits: thumbs, fingers, bottles, dummies

Even in the uterus, foetuses show a difference in their wish to suck. Later, some suck hard and strong while others are happy to be spoon-fed. Such differences may be innate.

Individual differences apart, virtually all babies need to suck for sustenance in the first six months and many need extra comfort in the early weeks. Sucking objects, like cuddlies, stand in for an absent mother, and it is easy to encourage the habit in babies. Some children give the habit up without difficulty; others need persuasion. Research suggests that a persistent sucking habit may not be quite as supportive as a persistent cuddly. Four-year-olds who were still regularly sucking thumbs or fingers were found in one study to be more awkward and moody as teenagers. However, reassuringly and perhaps surprisingly, they were not any more likely to have started smoking.

Holding something like a dummy in the mouth for years rather than months is thought by some psychoanalysts to hold children in the infantile oral phase of development and to discourage the development of speech. For example, as a dummy fills the front of the mouth, it is impossible for children to make the sounds *t* or *d* properly. Beyond this, some dentists believe that dummy-sucking children are more prone to tooth decay because at night the saliva, which normally acts as a mouthwash, dries out if the child's mouth is open, allowing plaque to build up more quickly. As persistent and strong sucking really does pull teeth out of alignment there is every good reason to encourage a child of seven or eight to stop thumb or finger sucking.

For thumb and finger sucking, the most successful strategies involve motivating the child (telling them they will look more grown up); choosing a good time, such as school holidays; and providing a big reward and a 30-day star chart with smaller rewards at the end of each week's unbroken non-sucking. To encourage a child to give up a dummy, keep it for sleeping only and pay special attention when the child is talking, because they will not be able to talk properly with a dummy in their mouth.

Nail-biting

There is reassurance for parents of nail-biters: there is no evidence that children who bite their nails are more poorly

Nail biting may very well be a sign of stress, but it does not indicate any deep-seated emotional or psychological problem. There is a genetic component to the habit, with identical twins more likely to bite their nails than non-identical twins.

adjusted than others, although it is true that children do bite their nails under stress. It is an extremely common childhood habit affecting one school-age child in three. The tendency is probably inherited and children often stop and later relapse.

Masturbation

Very many pre-school children discover the pleasure that touching their genitals bestows. In one study, researchers found that over half the pre-school boys and one in six girls masturbated. However at this age there is no sexual connotation. For many the activity is no more than a reassuring habit at a time of stress. Others discover the pleasures of rhythmic stimulation – even babies have been known to rub against cot bars so frantically that they appear to be having a fit. Tell a child who is old enough to understand that this is an activity to keep private. Otherwise turn a blind eye.

Head banging

Rhythmic head banging frightens parents, who fear either that their child is disturbed or that it will lead to brain damage. In a normal child with no other diagnosed difficulties neither is the case – the child is usually having a massive tantrum or is bored. If the head banging is part of a tantrum the child may hurt themself and never try again, or they may continue to get whatever they want as a result of a tantrum (see Temper tantrums, page 319). Ignore it.

Children who headbang towards the end of the day may be acting to release a build-up of tension. Spending time quietly with the child before they are over-tired may successfully avert a storm or frenzied behaviour.

Sleep

Infants and children need anything from ten to sixteen hours sleep. The amount of sleep they need drops as they grow older, until by puberty they reach adult levels. At first infants sleep in snatches varying from a few minutes to five hours, regardless of day or night. By the age of three months they have often developed a pattern of a longer sleep at night as well as having three or four periods of sleep during the day. By six months of age babies no longer need to have a night feed, and with luck and encouragement they may even sleep through an abbreviated night. At this stage parents choose between late nights and early mornings – but some unlucky ones get both.

How well young children sleep is culture-dependent. Recent research from Pennsylvania State University established that Kenyan babies who are expected to wake several times a night do, while babies in Los Angeles do what their parents expect and sleep through the night from the time they are a few months old.

Average sleep requirements

Note that there are enormous individual variations.

Age	Number of night hours spent sleeping	Total number of hours in 24 spent sleeping
6 months	10-12	14½
1 year	11	14
2 years	11	13
3 years	11	12
4 years	11½	11½
5 years	11	11

Night waking

Parents do not need to be told that problems in settling the child down to sleep and night waking are the commonest sleep difficulties. Night waking is strongly conditioned by what parents do in response. There are three basic strategies: checking that the baby is all right but disturbing them as little as possible, and repeating this as often as it takes until the baby settles; lifting the baby out of the cot and doing what the baby appears to want – feeding, nappy change, cuddle – before putting them back down; and taking the baby into the parental bed (see The family bed, page 20).

A good night's sleep

The following tips can help to get your child to sleep through the night.

- From the earliest days, feed the baby, then lay them in the cot to sleep while they are still awake. Try not to allow your baby to fall asleep while feeding
- Create a suitable sleep environment and set up a daily bedtime routine, such as tea or a feed followed by some quiet play, a bath, story, drink and, finally, bed
- For a period of two weeks write down when the child sleeps, what wakes them and what their response is. This will make you more aware of what is really going on
- Use behavioural methods to train a child who is mature enough to sleep through the night to do so. When the child wakes one of the parents goes in, checks the child is all right and then leaves. If the child continues to cry or comes out of their room, they are taken back and the parent checks that they are all right every five minutes. The intervals may extend to 10 or 15 minutes until the child finally goes off to sleep
- A doctor may prescribe a sedative such as promethazine (Phenergan) or trimeprazine (Vallergan) that is suitable for children and encourages them to sleep for a few nights to give parents a rest

All babies wake at least occasionally at night, but their persistence in staying awake varies. For some families the only workable solution is the family bed.

Night terrors

Night terrors occur during deep sleep and most often affect young primary school children. The child behaves as if they are really terrified, screaming, shouting, sweating and even running away from danger. They remain asleep throughout the experience, which usually lasts about 10 to 30 minutes. During the terror the child cannot be woken, and in the morning remembers nothing. Night terrors are quite unconnected with emotional problems. If they recur at a predictable time, as they often do (usually in the first three hours after falling asleep) try waking the child 15 minutes beforehand. Alternatively, wake the child when they appear restless. If the terrors arrive at unpredictable times, stay with the child as the night terror occurs. Switch on a light or turn on a favourite tape. It is best if the child remains in bed, but if they get out do not stop them. Night terrors usually fade quite quickly.

Sleepwalking

Sleepwalking often happens during the first hours of deep sleep. A sleepwalking child has their eyes open but is clearly asleep and can walk around the house, up and down stairs, opening and closing doors. Many sleepwalking children take themselves back to bed. If they do not, lead a sleepwalking child gently back to bed and stay quietly with them until they fall asleep again. They probably won't acknowledge you or wake. For the future, secure the bedroom windows and the stairs. Sleepwalking is most common between the ages of five and ten years, and children eventually grow out of it. It does not indicate emotional disturbance, although your child may start to sleepwalk during a particularly anxious time.

Nightmares

Nightmares are very common, particularly in pre-school children. They usually occur during light dream sleep. When the child wakes up, or if you decide to wake them, remain with them and let them talk if they wish.

Nightmares can be triggered by experiences that are frightening to a child, if not to an adult. One three-year-old had nightmares when his baby sister developed an eye condition in which her eyes moved uncontrollably.

A child who has enjoyed a full and active day, followed by a quiet, familiar bedtime routine, may well reward her parents with an unbroken night's sleep – for herself and them. Making the bedroom as comfortable and welcoming as possible may well persuade the child to remain there, rather than get up to enjoy the company of her parents.

Other children may react to frightening videos and films, so it is wise not to allow young children to watch videos or television programmes that stimulate the imagination an hour or two before bedtime. Soothe the child in their own room so that they learn to associate their bedroom with stillness and calmness. The nightmares will reduce in intensity as the child's anxiety levels fall, but in some vulnerable children they will linger well into adulthood.

Complementary Treatment

Music therapy can be an effective alternative or possibly an adjunct to verbal forms of psychotherapy where nightmares and night terrors result from traumatic stress disorder or other forms of anxiety. A child may be supported in the exploration and resolution of the anxiety in musical terms, with or without the use of words. **Drama** and **play therapy** may also help in this way. The **Bach flower remedies** offer Aspen for fear of the unknown, Rock Rose for terror and terrifying dreams, and Rescue Remedy for combined elements of panic, fear and shock.

Jealousy and sibling rivalry

For many young children the three most stressful life events are separating from their mother, starting full-time education and the birth of a brother or sister. Given that a young child views their relationship with their mother as similar to that of a married couple, the arrival of a baby might be seen as tantamount to an extra-marital affair, in which the girl or boy friend is brought into a ménage à trois. From this inauspicious beginning a loving sibling relationship is expected to develop. Parents should not be surprised when it does not, but instead leads to intense jealousy and rivalry for parental affection that can thread through childhood into adult life.

Certain children are especially vulnerable to jealousy. They include: children with low self-esteem and lack of confidence; children with intense emotions; the eldest child; and children who feel under threat from more than one direction – for example, if the arrival of the new baby coincides with a time when they are having particular difficulties with their own friendships.

What to do

It is sensible to anticipate these events and let a young child, particularly an only child, down gently. Children need to know about the birth in advance, although telling a child under five around the sixth or seventh month is enough for their needs. Involving your child in preparations may help to stop them feeling excluded. Throughout the preparations you need to take the child's level of understanding into account. A very young child who is told that they are going to have a brother or sister to play with can only be bitterly disappointed at the outcome of childbirth. Using their own baby book, or photographs spanning their own babyhood to the present, will help the child to realize that the baby will eventually become a playmate.

It is also important to protect children from other major sources of stress. This is not the time to move the child from a cot to a bed, to enrol the child in a playgroup, to start potty-training, to have the child admitted to hospital for any procedure that could be delayed, to spend nights away from home, nor to start school.

Once the baby is born you should continue your daily routines as normally as possible, respecting the child's individual needs rather than projecting on to them a new role as the older brother or sister of the new baby. It is one thing to be a big boy or girl; quite another to be a big brother or sister. Big boys and girls do, however, require compensatory privileges, such as a later bedtime or special outings. It is also sensible, if for no more than self-preservation, to avoid blatantly provocative actions, such as breastfeeding the baby in front of your older child in the first few weeks.

Preparation will not sanitize a young child's feelings; it will just soften the blow, as will developing the child's relationship with the father. Your child's feelings of jealousy will almost inevitably come out: early reactions may include aggressive or clingy behaviour, desperately seeking attention or regressing to infantile behaviour. Behind all these is a fear of exclusion, so being angry only increases the child's insecurities. Research shows that jealousy tends to persist where parents punish children for behaving meanly or aggressively.

What else?

Encouraging the child to talk about their feelings helps – even children as young as three can be helped to find words to express what they feel. Tell them how jealous you used to feel as a child. Read children's books that reflect their experiences. Set aside a special time every day for each child in the family. Fifteen minutes when the child knows that no one will interrupt may be all that is needed. Protecting the child's possessions and space matter as well.

A natural emotion

Despite all parents' endeavours, a certain level of jealousy and rivalry will persist. It is natural, and part of growing up. Troubled teenagers can feel as threatened as toddlers and may be barely more articulate. In one study, one-third of five- and six-year-olds said they would prefer not to have a brother or sister. Two-thirds fought or came to blows regularly. Jealousy may produce superficial discord, but psychologists tend to view it as helpful, as quarrels that are played out in the safety of the family home are rehearsals for coping with rivalries in the outside world. Jealousy only becomes harmful if it reflects a situation where one child is always more successful, competent or preferred to another.

Complementary Treatment

Interactive **music therapy** offers the enriching experience of being noticed, valued and competent, as well as addressing any anxiety, and can help to compensate for any actual emotional impoverishment in the child's past or present experience. The **Bach flower remedies** Holly is useful for jealousy and hatred, and Chicory for the desire for attention. **Drama** and **play therapies** may also be particularly beneficial.

Dealing with a jealous child

- Parents need to be even-handed with their children, but this does not mean giving them all the same thing, the same privileges or responsibilities. Some children need more cuddles, others need more challenges. Children understand if privileges and responsibilities are consistently applied and can be justified
- Particularly avoid comparing the jealous child with other (less jealous) children. Nothing is better calculated to increase the jealous child's sense of insecurity than believing that their parents think they are inferior
- Above all, avoid direct comparisons between children. It is tempting to try to get one child to behave better or do better at school by pointing out how well the other child does, but these comparisons usually misfire. In any case, children know perfectly well how good their brothers and sisters are, and this may be the cause of their disaffection. It is better to use the one child's superior abilities to bring on the other child, so, for example, the child who dances beautifully can teach the less able child the steps
- Notice and praise the times when the children cooperate. It is terribly easy not to notice when they are getting on well, but praise in the end works better than being told off when children area at odds with each other

THE SCHOOL YEARS

The early years in school mark a gradual transition from the secure protection of the family to the more challenging world outside. At the same time, those basic infant skills that were built on in the pre-school years are fine-tuned and differentiated. Latent aptitudes, parental encouragement and dogged perseverance contribute to the widening skills and differences in ability that develop between children in their early primary school years.

The early school years: four to seven

From a social point of view, classes in the early years of education are organized so that children can identify the teacher as a parent-substitute, which helps those children who are still experiencing difficulties separating from their mother. (How many young schoolchildren have inadvertently called the teacher 'Mummy'?) At the same time children now have to cope for the first time with being one of a very large group of children.

Parent participation in the school can be very helpful in breaking down large groups into more manageable units, and in easing the child's transition from home to school. It can also help children with another new task that faces them: integrating what may be two quite different worlds – school and home – with possibly different languages, accents, expectations, attitudes and beliefs. In this atmosphere of change, children like to know what is expected of them. They like clear rules, which make them feel safe.

Coping with new situations

As children settle at school, academic demands increase, and at this age subtle or specific learning difficulties begin to become evident. Success and failure loom large in the child's life, and it is important for parents to maintain a balance. If a child is experiencing unavoidable difficulties at school as they try to grapple with new and difficult concepts, parents need to provide compensation. Can the child swim? Are they good with animals? Can they join a junior football course?

A few children react to increasing pressures, or stress at home, by exhibiting a reluctance to attend school. At this age reluctance is not entrenched, and if you can spend time listening to whatever is worrying your child, it can usually be managed. You may need to liaise with the school to make sure your child still attends (see School phobia, page 327).

The friends of pre-school children are still in part chosen by their parents, but once at school children start to forge their own friendships. Most children have at least one best friend at this age, but friendships can be fickle and sometimes change almost daily. It is unusual for a child between four and seven years of age to be unsociable, so the child who appears to spend all their school playtimes alone may need sensitive observation by school staff. Solitary pursuits with pets, on the computer or watching television can compensate, but do not help the child to practise their social skills.

As they mature children learn to stand up for their own point of view. This can lead to quarrels with friends and siblings and parents have to decide whether to intervene. It is usually better to allow equally matched children to sort their quarrels out themselves, but watch for rough fighting or any actions that could hurt a younger or weaker child.

Four- to seven-year-old children are still avidly curious, asking endless questions and unable at first to cope with the notion that the parent or teacher does not know all the answers. As their widening vocabulary enables them to think in an abstract way, their still unfettered curiosity prompts deep abstract questions about death and eternity. This is the age when you should encourage your children to search for knowledge themselves and give them the means to find it.

By the age of seven children can be amazingly competent. They can usually cook simple meals, play an instrument and look after the needs of a younger brother or sister for hours on end. However their competence depends on opportunity. Parents in a position to offer their seven-year-olds a chance to pursue their interests do them a service. Many activities will be dropped later, but the skills remain, as does the self esteem that comes with their acquisition.

The middle school years: eight to ten

The years of increasing independence are now beginning. For many children this is symbolized by having pocket money, sometimes earned, which they have the freedom to spend according to their own judgement. The judgement of children at this age is quite refined; they know the rules of the activities that fill their lives and they can believe fervently in right and wrong. At this age it is not unusual for a passion for good causes to emerge. Children of this age like rules and following them may underpin favourite activities, such as playing board games and joining in team games.

By the age of eight years many children have the perseverance to learn and practise a musical instrument, and while they will not, on the whole, become professional or even talented musicians, they acquire self confidence by having a skill that they realize other children do not necessarily possess.

The more stable friendships often become extremely important at this age, and clubs assume a new role. Many children organize their own, partly to formalize their own alliances but also partly to exclude other children – even if it is only a tiresome three-year-old sister. Children of this age also like to join organized activities and to wear uniforms and badges as marks of achievement.

By the middle school years most children have the confidence to stay away from home overnight, in a group such as Brownies or Woodcraft, or with a special friend. Children's friendships develop quite independently of family intervention, but home is still vitally important for support and continuity. The more home remains the same as ever, the better.

At this age some children appear to be quite independent and secure, although in fact they are not. They need back-up when things go wrong – when they forget their pencil case for school or on those days that they come home feeling completely friendless.

Once children reach the age of ten they have acquired an impressive range of abilities that can help to support their independence. Many can cycle safely on a road, others can be allowed to undertake short, familiar journeys – to school and back – alone. With supervision they can try out dangerous activities, such as abseiling and canoeing, on adventure holidays organized in the school holidays or during term-time. Their physical skills are now advanced and complex; if you watch any team game organized within a primary school you can see children's acute awareness of justice and fairness.

By now children are aware that home and school may have very different rules. As children become increasingly conscious of differences between themselves and other children, they may use them to create stereotyped images. At best, and with a little prompting from adults, children will learn to celebrate differences. At worst, they use them as a means to single out victims for bullying (see page 328).

Puberty

By the age of 11 many girls have entered puberty, while the majority of boys have not. Girls may be growing taller, leaving boys of the same age behind. As breasts begin to develop, periods start and, eventually, hips widen, girls are more likely to be upset by body changes than are boys. Research suggests that on the whole boys experience fewer problems at the onset of puberty.

By the time these changes begin children are quite independent within the family. They are able to look after themselves and to choose and regulate their own friendships. They can play a part in the running of the home, and in many families are expected to shoulder quite considerable responsibilities. Yet they are not old enough to be completely independent. Eleven-year-olds can still be immature; they are only just old enough to coordinate the many skills required to reliably cross a road safely. They have not had enough experience of life to know the right thing to do at all times. Therefore they still need a firm, consistent and supportive home.

Children frequently fight – physically or verbally – to sort out arguments and problems. Before intervening, adults should observe and decide whether the children are in fact play-fighting and have no intention of hurting each other, or are engaged in a real fight.

Such a home is particularly important, as at the age of 11 most children begin secondary school, with its less family-centred and more challenging environment. School children of this age need to be able to organize themselves and to cope with the stress and extra work that are imposed by matters such as exams and homework.

Friendships may now take the form of gangs. Many friends of this age have known each for years, and the groupings no longer change as much as they did in the past. At this age children sometimes make friends for life.

Members of certain groups can be extremely unkind to outsiders, to newcomers, people they wish to exclude and members of other groups. Boys in particular can be competitive and argumentative and resort to physical fighting to sort out their differences.

School fear or phobia

At some point during their school years many children decide that they do not want to go to school. They may claim to be ill or may appear unhappy and afraid. They may simply refuse to go or, if dragged to school, try to run away or hide. This is school refusal and, when it is taken to extremes, it can become school phobia.

There are two chief triggers for school refusal, circumstances at home and circumstances at school. Children sometimes fear leaving home for school if they feel unsure what to expect when they return; if past separations have been stressful or upsetting; if they are very dependent on protective parents; or if a parent is depressed.

Children who are afraid of going to school may be being teased or bullied; they may have specific difficulties with

Studies show that a disinclination to go to school is more common in boys, especially if they feel that they are failing there. With patience and persistence the reason behind the child's reluctance usually becomes clear.

work, playtimes, other children, friends, physical activities, school dinners or even the toilets.

What to do

It is worth trying to get the child to continue attending school so that any fears are not magnified. You may have to talk to someone at the school so that you can work out a combined strategy. Forcing a child to attend instead of examining the underlying issues will simply make matters worse.

Helpful strategies include keeping the atmosphere at home secure and calm; maintaining a regular morning routine; arranging for someone at the school to welcome the child and, if necessary, take the child into the building. Make an arrangement with the school to have someone contact you if the child turns out to be genuinely unwell (always a possibility). Going to school with another child can also be helpful, as it avoids the need for the fearful child to arrive alone. Alternatively, you could ask another parent, neighbour or educational social worker to accompany the child. The child who does go to school should receive a positive reward.

Solving the underlying difficulty usually means spending time discovering why the child is frightened. The class teacher or the assistants who supervise lunchtime play may have some ideas. Listening to the child and believing what they say is important.

If your child refuses to go to school you will need to liaise with the education social work service. A gradual approach involving activities for you and your child, such as meeting children from school at home, helps to expose the child to the experience of school without increasing their anxieties. Other school children can be told that the child who is refusing to go to school has been ill, in order to spare the child embarrassment when they return. You will almost certainly need some support from an outside agency such as a child and family consultation unit.

Complementary Treatment

In **drama** and **play therapy**, specific phobias might be successfully dramatized or played out and then gradually resolved. Useful **Bach flower remedies** include Mimulus for known fears, and Aspen where the child is frightened of something, but does not know what. Red Chestnut is useful where the child is anxious for the safety or health of others, such as their parents, siblings or pets.

Bullying

Bullying is aggressive behaviour consistently and deliberately directed towards another child. It can start in the early years at primary school but is more likely to start in the final years, in children aged between nine and eleven. Common types of bullying include: name calling and teasing; threats to injure the child; threats to exclude the child from a group of friends; hitting, hair-pulling and scratching, kicking and throwing things; stealing; demanding money or (with younger children) toys; and racial or sexual harassment.

The bullied child tends to be physically weaker than others their own age and is different from other children in an obvious way. For example, they may be overweight, have the wrong accent or a different skin colour. They tend to be sensitive, intelligent children who have little experience of conflict at home and are unprepared to deal with it at school, and they experience bullying as confirmation of their inadequacies.

Signs of bullying may include any of the factors listed below.

You may notice

- *An unwillingness to go to the playground or take a certain route home for fear of meeting the bully*
- *Your child makes excuses to avoid attending school*
- *Their possessions, clothes or books are damaged. Victims may be scratched or bruised themselves*
- *The child loses confidence and becomes withdrawn, or they become aggressive, anxious or distressed*
- *The child cries easily and has nightmares*
- *The child begins to bully other children*

What to do

Bullying is never acceptable. Addressing it requires an atmosphere of openness and trust between adults and children, which enables children to feel free to tell adults about it and to know that their worries will be dealt with discreetly but effectively. Victims usually feel ashamed and unwilling to admit to being bullied, so the enquiring adult needs to be clear and direct, making a statement such as 'I think you are being bullied and I am worried about it. Let's talk about it.'

First, believe what the child says, and if the bullying is taking place at school talk to a teacher or head teacher. All schools should have a written policy on bullying that parents can read and of which children are aware. Some schools operate a system of counsellors – adults or older children to whom younger children may turn with their worries.

Second, work out ways you can protect your child. You can meet them discreetly on the way home from school; if the bullies have been identified at school, they can be kept in until other children have arrived home. Parents can help by making the home more secure, warm and friendly during a spell of bullying.

Victims can sometimes be helped by being encouraged to act self-confidently so they do not invite trouble. KIDSCAPE (the UK children's charity dealing with bullying) suggests that they can practise assertiveness techniques – saying 'No' or 'Leave me alone'. They can be encouraged to stay in a group, to avoid places where bullying often occurs and to ignore the bullying or defuse it with humour.

Bullies can sometimes be helped if they are encouraged to excel at something. The younger the child is when the problem is addressed, the more likely they are to improve.

What makes a bully?

KIDSCAPE has found that bullies often share the following characteristics.

- They often feel inadequate
- They are bullied at home within the family
- They come from families that accept or even praise bullying types of behaviour
- They are victims of some types of abuse
- They are unable or not allowed to show their feelings and have low-self esteem
- Some bullies are self-confident and spoilt children who are prepared to bully to get their own way

Who can help?

For organizations and agencies offering help, advise and support, see the Directory.

Complementary Treatment

Drama and **play therapies** may help the child face up to their antagonist. The **Bach flower remedy** Mimulus is useful for victims who are shy and nervous, Centaury for a child unable to stand up for themself; and Larch for the child who lacks confidence. Holly is useful for a child who bullies because they are envious, and Vine for a child who bullies because they are full of hate. Children who bully may also benefit from **music therapy**.

Handedness

Handedness is a clear preference for using one hand rather than the other for skills needing fine coordination, such as writing or using scissors. It is related to the division of the brain into two hemispheres, each of which controls sensation and movement on the opposite side of the body. A preference for one hand or the other may be obvious when an infant is 15 months old, and is usually clear by the age of two. However children up to the age of 12 who suffer damage to the dominant side of the brain can change their preference for which hand they use.

Almost nine children out of ten are right-handed, while the rest are left-handed or ambidextrous. Left-handedness is more common among boys, twins, and babies born before 32 weeks of pregnancy. Of children with a clear hand preference, some are very strongly left- or right-handed, while others are

Handedness only becomes obvious when a child is faced with a manually demanding task. For simple actions such as pointing, either hand may be used, while more difficult tasks such as writing demand that the child uses his more skillful hand.

more confident about using either hand. The preferred hand is often linked with the preferred foot – the one that kicks the ball or presses the pedal first – but not necessarily with the preferred eye. Around one-third of left-handed children have a left dominant eye, and this is usually associated with a preference for the left ear for listening.

The left side of the brain usually relates to language ability and logic and the right side to emotions and spatial awareness. However attempts to infer from this that right-handed children are more logical or have better language abilities, while left-handed children are better at appreciating and understanding art and architecture, are disproved by reality. In 70 per cent of left-handed people, the speech centre is on the right side of the brain.

What to do

Handedness has the following main effects. Children who are very strongly right- or left-handed have difficulty acquiring skills that need two hands, such as playing the piano, or catching, but not throwing, a ball. Left-handed children need to cut with left-handed scissors or to be taught by someone who is also left-handed how to use right-handed scissors. They also need to be taught the most efficient way to cut food with a knife and how to position their hand and paper when learning to write.

Complementary Treatment

In rare cases where there has been damage to the dominant hand, **music therapy** might provide motivation for free and specific exercises to develop skills in the unaffected hand. Musical activities might also be useful in the early identification of handedness.

Depression

In children depression occurs as a reaction to severe emotional stress, and frequently takes the form of pure misery, rather than the complex set of symptoms exhibited by adults. It is particularly common in adolescents, in whom it combines with feelings of self depreciation, creating inner turmoil. Sadness is of course part of everyday life and learning to cope with it is part of growing up. However sadness that cannot be overcome or which interferes with normal activities could be a warning sign of depression.

The following are among the common reasons for children and adolescents to feel depressed: the loss of a special person, a parent or a pet; bullying; changing school or moving house; living with a parent who is depressed; family tensions, such as rows, a new baby, divorce or joining a step family; academic or social problems at school; and physical, sexual or emotional abuse.

You may notice

In very young children

- *Being unresponsive and finding it hard to settle*
- *Tearful, clinging behaviour, nightmares and waking at night, appetite loss*
- *Very demanding behaviour or temper tantrums*

All these signs are common in perfectly well adjusted children. The difference to watch for is a change in the child's behaviour. The length of time the symptoms last is also important.

In school-age children

- *Difficulty concentrating, possibly school refusal, irritability or hard-to-handle behaviour*
- *Lack of confidence*
- *Negative or destructive behaviour, for example stealing or playing truant*

In teenagers

In teenagers who are often moody, the difference between feeling depressed and teenage moodiness is important. Distress and feeling depressed are common in teenagers, and these are possible signs:

- *Extreme moodiness and irritability*
- *Social withdrawal. Losing interest in school and in outside activities; losing touch with friends*
- *Not looking after themselves; a change in eating pattern*
- *Low self esteem*
- *Sleeping too much or not sleeping soundly*

Teenagers may act out their feelings by living dangerously, taking drugs or drinking too much. They may contemplate suicide and, if they are very depressed, they may attempt it or try to harm themselves.

What to do

If the feelings of depression do not lift in a couple of weeks, speak to your doctor, or encourage your child to do so. The doctor can discuss treatment options and possible referral to a child and adolescent mental health service. Counselling for child and family can be helpful. Many psychiatrists prefer to reserve antidepressants for severely depressed children.

Who can help?

Children who are depressed need to talk to someone about their unhappiness. If they cannot talk to a person they know they may be able to use a confidential telephone helpline. See the Directory for details.

Complementary Treatment

Music therapy may alleviate some of the distress of acute depression.

Stealing

Stealing is extremely common in young children, partly because they do not have the rigid rules about property that adults do. Very young pre-school children do not have fully developed ideas of possession, particularly when it comes to shared property such as nursery crayons and toys. When they are found in a child's pockets at home they should just be returned openly to the nursery with an explanation that it was a mistake. This will also be a good opportunity to explain to the child very clearly, but not in a punitive manner, the rules about not taking other people's property home.

Later in childhood more serious types of stealing may develop. Comfort stealing affects children who do not feel sufficiently loved. They may steal from their parents or from outside the home, taking comfort in possessions or in the particular objects of which they feel they have been deprived. This may be the motive behind stealing at home, rather than outside. This type of stealing is sometimes also seen in children whose parent has died, and who are trying to adjust to a new step family.

Older children may steal in groups, partly as a dare and partly to gain status among their peers and guarantee themselves a place in the gang. Such children are frequently boys and tend to come from families without a consistently enforced code of moral conduct.

A child who steals when she self-evidently knows it is wrong may be acting as part of the gang, or may have been put up to it by an older child or a teenager. Alternatively, she may steal as a form of compensation for love she feels she is not getting – a type of behaviour known as comfort stealing.

What to do

If you find your child has taken something by mistake or stolen it, say quite simply but clearly that it must go back.

Give your child pocket money so that they learn to value and manage resources. Point out how bad they would feel if someone stole from them.

Set a good example. Adults rarely steal, but they often keep things they find or they keep the wrong change at the supermarket. Give it back and explain your reasons for doing so to your child.

Complementary Treatment

If psychological investigation suggests an emotional cause (in addition to any faulty socialization) **music therapy** might be one element in a programme of correction. **Bach flower remedies** may be helpful in dealing with any underlying emotional issues. Both **play** and **drama therapy** may also be beneficial.

Lying

To suggest that a child who is too young to distinguish fantasy from reality is capable of lying is not reasonable. To lie, a child needs to intend to deceive, and this is not something that children under the age of three or four can do. The two perfectly normal and largely universal types of lie that come later are boastful lies and lies to get out of trouble.

Boastful lies are lies to the outside world that make a child's life, home or background seem more interesting than it really is. Later on in childhood, children of demanding parents develop a variant of the boastful lie in recounting their school exploits. As virtually all children tell these lies, it is inappropriate to suggest that they stem from low self-esteem. However they are best countered by stressing what the child is good at and has to be proud of.

Lies to get out of trouble and avoid punishment are by no means the exclusive province of children. Virtually all adults are also capable of abandoning their moral principles if the punishment seems too threatening. Parents who punish severely tend to reinforce lying, particularly if they punish a child who is found out. This will usually lead to the child becoming a more skillful liar. Parents should always stress the importance of trust and respond warmly when a child confesses to having lied.

Complementary Treatment

If psychological investigation suggests an emotional cause (in addition to any faulty socialization) **music therapy** might be one element in a programme of correction. **Bach flower remedies** may be helpful in dealing with any underlying emotional issues. **Play therapy** may also be beneficial.

Stress

Stress is a fact of modern life, and although it can be harmful it is not always bad. A certain amount of stress helps to prime both children and adults for challenges. It only becomes a problem when it is excessive, clouding a child's entire life or making them focus on a single activity, such as taking exams.

Children respond to the same stressful pressures as adults, and in much the same ways. Family rows, starting school, the death of a loved relation or friend, not doing well at school, and rejection are all stressful. So are events that might seem on the surface to be pleasant, such as joining a club or going on holiday. Personality, age and experience all play a role in determining what is experienced as a stressful situation, so that a situation that can seem crushing to one child may be insignificant to another.

Studies show that children subjected to a string of stressful events are more likely to catch minor infections and may also be more accident-prone. However other studies have shown that children who cope with minor stressful experiences are strengthened by the experience and better able to manage major stressful experiences.

What can parents do to get the stress level just right and help a child feel that they can cope?

What to do

Avoid stressful situations when the child is young, such as leaving your child alone in an unfamiliar environment, and try to avoid more than one stressful experience occurring at the same time. Parents who arrange for a separation or divorce just before a major exam are certain to create unnecessary problems for their children.

Anticipating events and discussing the feelings they may cause will help, as will devising problem-solving approaches. For example, if the child feels homesick while they are staying with their best friend, discuss what they can do to alleviate the stress. The options will most likely be to telephone home, tell the friend's parents or come home. Knowing the options and finding ways to manage the new experience will help your child take control of the situation.

Listening to your child and reflecting on what they tell you will help the child cope with a stressful situation after it has taken place. Comments such as 'You must have felt awful when . . .' are a useful technique. So is acting out stressful situations at home in order to investigate different approaches to the problem.

Encouraging the child with gentle praise when they have coped well offers the child an extra reward in addition to the flush of pride they will feel knowing that they have managed. And it is just as important to ignore situations in which your child fails to cope.

Family rows, particularly those between parents that occur in front of the children, can be extremely stressful for the child. Stress that is experienced over a long period can have adverse effects not only on the child's emotional health, but also on their physical well being, causing minor infections and even making the child accident prone.

Complementary Treatment

Relaxation techniques can be very helpful in dealing with stress, as can massage allied with **aromatherapy**. **Drama** and **play therapies** can also help to relieve the condition.

Common causes of stress in children

- Starting school full-time
- Changing schools – especially from primary to secondary school – and having to make new friends, especially if the child has to integrate into an existing friendship group
- Preparing for school tests and exams
- Family rows
- Divorce or separation
- Parents arguing about money, employment and, for young children, politics
- Parents needing reassurance from the child, rather than the other way round
- Death

If you are aware from your child's difficult behaviour that they are under stress but can't pinpoint the cause, keep a two-week diary, noting your child's behaviour as well as potentially stressful events. A pattern may emerge.

CARING FOR A SICK CHILD AT HOME

Parents know instinctively when their child is unwell. The early signs are subtle but unmistakable, and always mark a difference in what you know you can expect from your child. Early pointers to illness are often a mixture of physical and behavioural symptoms. A baby or child who has a particularly restless night or takes less interest in the world around them may alert you to watch them attentively. Some children look paler or more flushed than normal (for how to assess and treat fever, see page 83). Others have an odd look around the eyes or are whiny, irritable or clingy.

Children who are unwell usually have a very short attention span and will want to play with relatively babyish toys. Try to provide sufficient variety to deep them amused and relax your standards about television viewing. This stage of the illness usually only lasts for a day or two.

You will almost certainly find that when your child is ill they will want you to care for them. Children who are unwell tend to be demanding, but take your lead from your child. Some sick babies want to be picked up and cuddled all the time, while others just want to be left alone. Not many children want to be banished to their bedroom and most prefer to lie in a bed or on a settee downstairs. This gives you the advantage of being able to observe your child regularly for any change in their condition.

Boredom is a problem for ill children. Keep a treasure box of spare toys and activities – stocked from party bags, sales and unwanted or duplicate presents, as well as any outgrown toys. Children who are sick choose toys that are slightly young for them and need endless variety, as they don't concentrate on anything for long – except possibly videos.

What to do

If a young child wants to lie on the settee, put a waterproof cover underneath them in case of accidents; if the child is sleepy cover them with a duvet. Keep the room comfortably warm. If the child has any respiratory symptoms, make sure that the air does not dry out. You can moisten the atmosphere simply and cheaply by laying a towel, previously dampened and wrung out, over a radiator. Alternatively, place a bowl of cold water beneath the radiator.

If you want to stay close to your child at night, put your child's cot or a temporary bed near yours or take up residence in the child's room. If you stay in your own bedrooms, use a baby monitor to alert you to restlessness or coughing at night. Letting a sick child sleep in bed with you is tempting but can allow a feverish child to overheat. If you do allow your sick child to share your bed, and many parents do, be firm about returning them to their bed once they are well.

What else?

In the first day or two of a minor infection children often lose their appetites. Fluids are more important than solid food because children can be at risk of dehydration if they are feverish or have diarrhoea, especially if they are also vomiting. Tempt a sick child to drink with their favourite clear drinks, giving rehydration fluids first if they are needed. For variety, freeze drinks into cubes or fun-shaped ice lollies.

Offer the breast frequently to a breastfed baby and express and store surplus milk until the baby's appetite returns. Make your own juices – rhubarb freezes to an attractive pink. Once your child starts to take solid food again, try soft, bland foods such as ice cream and yoghurt, which contain a lot of liquid.

Should you call a doctor?

Faced with a child who is obviously sick, it's clear to even an inexperienced parent what to do. Frequently, however, it is difficult to interpret the signs of illness. Is it just a snuffle, or the start of a serious infection? Will the pain go away or will it get worse? Younger children usually suffer more seriously from the effects of infections. In babies in particular, signs of illness can be quite non-specific.

Being worried about your child is a good enough reason in itself to call your doctor. Nobody knows your child better than you do. Some parents are concerned about bothering the doctor unnecessarily, but if they are able to set your mind at rest that is a perfectly good reason. Yet there are certain occasions when it is imperative that your child is seen by a medical professional. See Emergency situations on page 335.

The family medicine chest

Keep all medicines in a 'child proof' medicine chest well out of reach of even a child standing on a chair. The following are essentials for any family:

- Children's sugar-free paracetamol or soluble tablets for older children. The brand does not really matter, so choose whatever brand your child prefers
- Oral rehydration sachets. These are useful for making up balanced drinks should your child develop diarrhoea
- Calamine lotion to soothe itchy rashes such as those that occur with chickenpox
- Aqueous cream to moisturize dry skin
- Vaseline or petroleum jelly to protect noses, lips and chins during a cold
- Any prescribed drugs that do not need to be kept in the fridge
- A fever strip and a mercury or digital thermometer (see page 83)

A parent's calm and reassuring presence is just what a child needs when she is unwell. Illness can be frightening to young children when they feel extremely feverish, or if their breathing is affected.

Giving your child medicine

When collecting a prescription, always ask the chemist for a sugar-free preparation. If one is not available, chase the medicine down with a drink of water or juice and clean the child's teeth thoroughly afterwards. Make sure that you know what you need to about the medicine. Ask the chemist or doctor the following questions.

- Exactly how much should be given and when. Whether it has to be given with meals or feeds
- Whether the medicine is likely to have any side effects. For example, some cough medicines and some antihistamines make children sleepy
- Whether it is safe to give paracetamol at the same time. Paracetamol produces different effects to antibiotics and should be given to lower fever and control pain until the antibiotics start to work
- Whether it is necessary to finish the course or whether it only needs to be given while symptoms last

When giving medicine, be matter-of-fact but positive. If your child resists forcibly, ask your doctor if it can be given in another formulation

Medicines by mouth

To measure liquid medicines accurately use an oral syringe, a medicine tube or a spoon, ensuring that a spoon is the type that stands flat. To draw medicine into the syringe, fit the adaptor supplied on to the bottle and tip the bottle up, withdrawing the plunger until the dose is correct. Sit a young child on your lap with their head in your elbow or put a baby in their carry seat. Press the syringe plunger slowly or tip the spoon, aiming towards the back of the cheek. Don't squirt the medicine in too quickly or the child will choke. Chase the medicine down with a drink. If you find it easier, put the measured dose of medicine into a small cup for your child to drink. However, never mix it in with the drink as the child may not take it all.

Medicines by inhaler

Correct inhaler technique can only be shown in person by your child's nurse or doctor.

Children under three Use a face mask as well as a spacer with their spray inhaler. Get everything ready before you put on the mask. Make sure it is in place on your child's face and check that the spacer is upright. Shake the inhaler, then for each separate puff, spray once and count slowly out loud to ten. This gives the child time to take five or six breaths. If the mask slips or your child tugs it off repeat the dose.

Children aged three to five need a spacer but no face mask. Get everything ready, shake the inhaler and give one puff. Count out loud as your child takes five big breaths in and out. If you sit opposite your child they can copy you as you take five big long breaths. Repeat puffs as prescribed.

Older children should be offered different devices until they find one that is easy for them to use.

Ear drops

Ear drops can feel cold, so ask the chemist if they can be warmed to body temperature (never above) by standing the bottle in a bowl of warm water for a few minutes. Lay your child down on one side, holding their head still, then squeeze the bulb close to the ear so the drops fall into the ear canal. Keep the child still for a minute or two before turning them over to do the other ear. Some children find it easier if they can watch this process in a mirror.

Eye drops

Lay your child down with a cloth or towel under their head. Rest your hand holding the dropper on their forehead. When the child sees the dropper coming the child will instinctively close their eyes, so ask them to keep one eye shut, the other open, or to look for patterns on the ceiling. Put the drops into

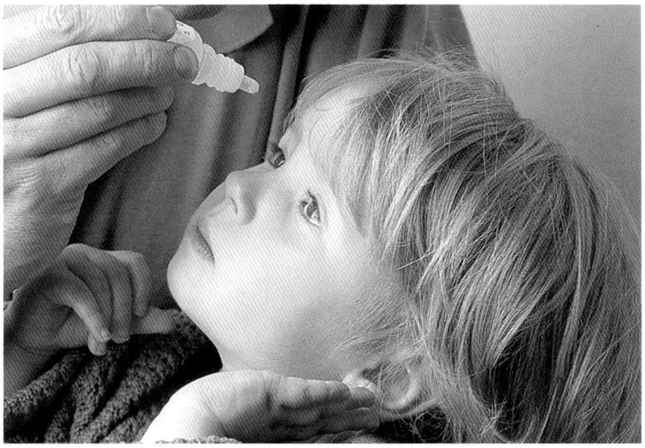

Giving a child eye drops calls for a steady hand and a trusting relationship. It is a difficult task until you are confident, so if you are unsure, ask your doctor or practice nurse to show you how to give them. If you feel nervous, try not to show it, as your child may be reluctant to allow you to put in the drops.

the inner corner of the eye, so that as the child blinks the drops are swept across the eye. Hold the dropper steady so it doesn't touch the eye. Ask an older child to blink ten times afterwards. Warn your child that things will look hazy for a minute or two.

Use exactly the same approach for eye ointment, pulling down the lower lid slightly and squeezing a little ointment on to the lower lid.

Nose drops

Lay a baby across your lap, keeping the head supported with your hand. Get an older child to blow their nose first and then lie down flat with the head tilted slightly over the edge of the bed. Support their head with one hand, and with the dropper near the nostril, squeeze in the drops. Count as you squeeze, repeat in the other nostril, then wait a minute or two before encouraging the child to sit up. An older child or adult should also lie on their back on the bed, but after putting in the drops, should turn over with their head over the edge and bend their head as if looking for slippers under the bed.

Emergency Situations

Call the doctor immediately if:

- You cannot rouse your child or baby. Being difficult to rouse is not the same as being sleepy: on this occasion, when you handle your child or talk to them, they do not respond
- Your baby or child turns very pale or blue. If you notice a bluish-grey tinge around the mouth or tongue, this is an emergency
- Your baby becomes quiet and lethargic or droopy and hot
- Your child's temperature rises to over 39.5°C/103.1°F and paracetamol does not keep it under control
- Your child has any difficulties in breathing or has noisy, grunting or fast breathing or cannot speak or drink
- Your child has a pain severe enough to stop them in what they were doing. The child cannot be comforted
- Your child has a pain on breathing in
- Your baby or child cannot keep drinks down
- A baby or a young child has diarrhoea and is vomiting
- A baby or young child develops watery diarrhoea Your child has been vomiting and is now ill
- Your child is vomiting and the stomach looks swollen
- There is any blood in the vomit
- Your baby or child has a convulsion
- Your child vomits for more than an hour
- Your child develops a rash of violet spots that do not fade when you apply pressure
- Your baby cries in an very odd, weak or high-pitched way
- You are worried, even if you cannot explain exactly why you are worried

THE CHILD IN HOSPITAL

Every year an estimated three million children in England and Wales go to Accident and Emergency, and over one-third of all children under the age of five have day surgery or stay in hospital for at least one night. Staff make every effort to welcome children and their families, and all wards provide facilities for parents to stay overnight. Yet going into hospital is still daunting for a child; studies have shown that children are afraid of going in and feel lonely and frightened when they get there. Procedures such as blood tests that seem quite routine to hospital staff, and even some parents, can be very traumatic, especially for young children. In an unfamiliar environment children cannot predict what will happen to them and this increases their anxiety.

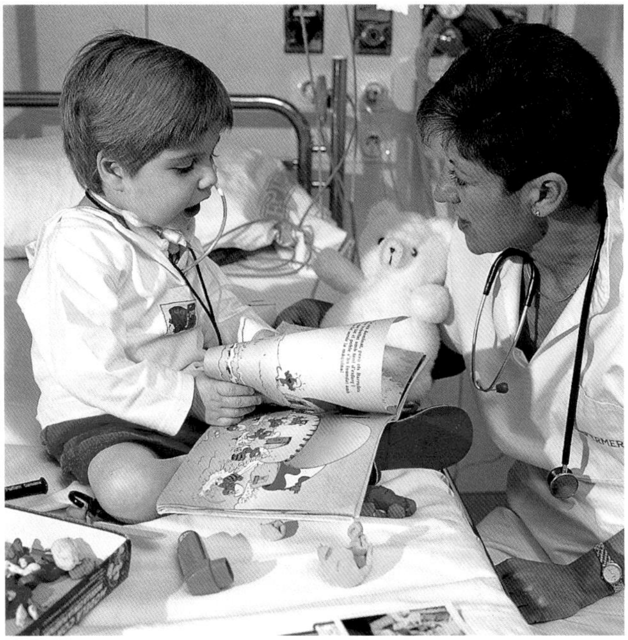

Young children can find their dependence on support systems extremely tiresome. Babies tend to loosen or pull out catheters unless they are restrained, and even older children need constant distraction. This child is suffering from a rare respiratory disease in which the normal breathing reflex does not work overnight.

Preparing for admission

Find out everything you can about your local hospital before your child is admitted.

If you are visiting someone who is in hospital, take your child with you.

Ask whether the hospital has open days. A few children's wards hold open sessions in their playroom for children who are booked in for surgery the following week. Your child may be able to join in.

When explaining to the child about going into hospital, tell a young child only a day or two in advance and always include information about getting better and coming home. Children worry that they won't recover. Don't, however, promise a precise day for returning home if you don't know one.

Going to Accident and Emergency

Many hospitals have a separate area in Accident and Emergency that is set aside especially for children, with a separate waiting room and staff who have been trained to look after children. Within a few minutes of arrival children are assessed by a triage nurse, but they may then face a long wait or series of waits to have further investigations or treatment.

If you have time, before you set off for hospital pack a bag containing cash and overnight essentials in case you need to stay until the following day. However reassure the child that this is 'just in case'. Most children who go to Accident and Emergency come home the same day.

A common reasons for children's admission to Accident and Emergency is broken bones. Diagnosis involves at least two periods of waiting – first for X-rays, and then for the X-ray films to be sent to the attending staff. The child will be given pain relief before a plaster cast is applied to the fracture. If the bones need re-aligning before the plaster is applied, an anaesthetist will give your child a general anaesthetic. The plaster cast will be removed later with an electric saw. Many children find this frightening; ask if a fine hand saw or cutters can be used for the layers nearest the skin.

Toys and puppets help in therapeutic role-play in hospital, with puppets entrusted with important messages, while treatments can be role-played on toys, allowing child to come to terms with feelings of anxiety or anger.

Hospital essentials bag

- The child's health record, including information about any illnesses, such as asthma. Any drugs the child takes
- Your child's favourite comforter, teddy or bottle. It doesn't matter if it is scruffy – most are
- Light day and night clothes, socks, trainers, slippers or shoes
- Money, including coins or cards for public phones. (You can't use mobile telephones in all hospitals)
- Telephone numbers of family and friends
- Small rewards for bravery
- Washing bag with toothbrush and toothpaste, soap, face cloth, hairbrush, towel
- Your child's favourite drink
- Toys and books and a walkman for an older child. However limit valuable possessions as hospitals are public places

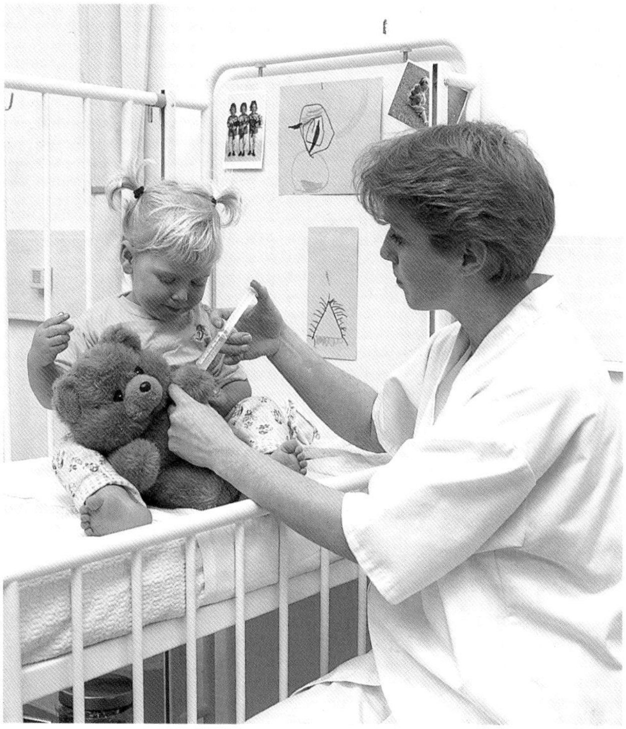

Play specialists are central to children's preparation for many hospital experiences. They can explain and act out procedures, and use diversionary tactics even when the anaesthetic is administered. Integrating play with therapy relaxes children and makes their hospital admission a more positive experience.

Going to a clinic

In many hospitals outpatient clinics are designed with children in mind and may be connected to the children's department. There should be a play area but toys may be limited, and as waiting periods between different investigations are almost inevitable, it is worth bringing a supply of activities, toys or games that do not require too much concentration. You should be seen within 30 minutes of arrival, and if you are not you should be told why. It is very helpful if you bring your child's health record with you as well as any drugs your child is taking. Most children in outpatients are likely to be examined, so dress your child in clothes that are easy to remove. If you think your child may be upset by tests or treatment take a small reward with you to give for bravery.

Planned admissions

Some hospitals have a member of staff who is in charge of establishing links with children's families and who will contact you before admission. If not, ask if you can visit the hospital before your child is admitted.

It is important, if at all possible, to stay in hospital with your child. Sick children are known to get better much faster when they have the confidence and security of having their parents near them. Hospitals make overnight accommodation provision for parents, which may be free of charge. In a regional centre or in special circumstances there may be accommodation for the rest of the family.

On arrival at the hospital the ward clerk will take down basic details, and the nurse who will be looking after your child will draw up a care plan. After basic checks – temperature, pulse, weight – have been carried out the nurse will give your child a hospital wristband. The doctor who admits the child will carry out an examination, reviewing the reason for which admission is necessary and, if the child is to have surgery, examine the child's chest. The anaesthetist may visit the child as well.

Boredom and restlessness are major problems both for children and parents. There may be a play specialist who can help prepare the child for medical procedures such as blood tests or an anaesthetic and provide alternative activities during the day. A store of undemanding games and activities from home is helpful, and if the child is in hospital for longer than a day or two, it may be necessary for the child to keep up with school work. Primary schools are particularly good at building a class member's stay into the learning process. If the teacher has not suggested it, take the initiative.

Access to a telephone as well as a walkman makes all the difference to an older child confined to bed. Older children also like to keep up with their friends by watching their favourite television programmes.

Parent partnerships
While you are with your child you can look after them as you would at home – washing and feeding, playing and settling the child for sleep. If your child is to be hospitalized for more than a very short while, nursing staff may show you how to help with some of the caring procedures, such as taking and recording temperatures. The longer the stay, the more you will do. Staff should also observe and learn from you.

Stay with the child when they most need you – when they are having investigations or treatments, or when they are in the anaesthetic room or the recovery room following surgery. Observe your child's responses sensitively. Children often don't feel brave enough to speak up for themselves in hospital, in which case the parents need to speak up for them.

One disadvantage of staying in hospital with a child is that you can feel trapped. Living in hospital is tiring and often boring. Bring plenty of activities that are not too demanding for yourself, and take a break at least once a day, if possible while your child has a visitor.

Surgery
Surgery may be elective or an emergency. Sometimes you have time to prepare your child briefly – for example, if surgery is needed to re-set a fractured bone. An elective operation is one that is planned, so there is ample time to prepare the child. Children and parents are told what is likely to happen, either during a session with the play therapist or during discussions with the surgeon.

Preparation for day surgery may take place at a weekend session before admission; otherwise it usually takes place on the day of the operation. Individual hospital practices vary, but you can usually expect the following sequence of events. Children may have to fast overnight, or at the least have no milk or solid food for four hours prior to surgery and no clear drinks such as apple juice or water for two hours before. They will have a bath and dress in suitable clothing. If your child's nightwear or T-shirt is cotton or mainly cotton, they may be able to wear their own clothes if that is how they feel most comfortable. However hospital gowns are easier to remove and may be preferable if clothes are likely to get stained during surgery. Jewellery or nail varnish will have to be removed.

Just before surgery staff will put an anaesthetic cream on the back of the child's hand and may give a sedative drink, although this is often not needed for a day surgery procedure. Children are usually allowed to take a favourite object to the anaesthetic room and choose how they go – in their parent's arms, on foot, on a trolley or on a hospital bed The anaesthetic may be given as gas from a mask or as an injection. For young children gas is often preferred. If the anaesthetic is given into a vein, simply asking the child to cough can be sufficiently distracting so that they do not notice the needle entering the vein. Parents are asked to leave the anaesthetic room once the child is unconscious.

In deciding whether or not to remain in hospital with your child, you should consider whether he is used to group play and whether he is old enough to go on holiday without you. If the answer to either of these is no, you should stay with him if you can. Hospitals can be frightening places even for adults, more so for a child.

Following surgery you will be able to sit with your child in the recovery room. If the child is asleep it is better not to wake them. When the child does wake, offer a drink. After day surgery, once the child is able to walk again, go to the toilet, drink, eat and is comfortable, you can help them get ready to leave. This is usually two to four hours following surgery. Before you leave you should be given an information leaflet, a follow-up appointment and instructions explaining how to give any prescribed drugs. You should also be given the name and telephone number of a staff member whom you can contact if you are worried. Try not to use public transport and do not let your child play outside for the rest of the day, as it can take 24 hours for the full effect of an anaesthetic to wear off.

Pain and pain relief
Procedures that are painful for most children include anything involving needles – blood tests, immunizations or injec-

tions; recovery from surgery; fractures; and having dressings changed. Such pain can usually be prevented, but fear and anxiety make pain worse, so no child should ever have to wait for pain relief. Parents can help by asking about analgesics when they see their child is in pain. Signs include a change in behaviour – the child may be noisier or quieter than usual or look flushed or pale.

Pain relief without drugs

Pain relief without administering drugs may be appropriate while waiting for the next scheduled drug dose, or in circumstances when drugs are not available or are contraindicated.

Warmth eases pain, and a child who is generally in pain may be helped by sitting in a warm bath if this is practical. A well-wrapped hot water bottle can temporarily ease toothache or earache. If a procedure is going to be painful, children should be told and given an explanation. For a mild, brief pain such as an injection, numbing the skin with ice cubes for a second or two may be all that is needed.

You can prepare a child for a painful procedure by keeping them calm and relaxed. Deep breathing, stroking and massage help some children. Blowing bubbles helps to control breathing; alternatively count four slow breaths in and four slow breaths out. Distraction with a story tape, video or hand-held computer game is helpful, particularly if the child is in charge of the controls. A simple appeal to the child's imagination (imaging) can have powerful results (see Relaxation, page 60.

Control is an important part of pain. If children know that they can stop the pain with a pre-arranged signal, then they will feel better about allowing a certain amount of it.

Pain relief with drugs

For mild pain, paracetamol works quickly, building up to maximum effect within 30-45 minutes. Alternatives for moderate pain include the anti-inflammatory drugs diclofenac and ibuprofen (but these should be given only when directed by hospital staff). For a local procedure such as a blood test, an anaesthetic gel or cream numbs the skin. For a short but painful procedure such as having a dressing changed, the pain can be lessened if the child takes a warm bath. A child who is old enough to cooperate may be able to breathe in nitrous oxide (Entonox). For severe pain, such as that experienced from a fracture, morphine works quickly and, taken as part of treatment, is not addictive. It can be given as an injection, intravenously (when it works in 10 minutes) or by use of a device that allows the child to control their own pain relief. This is known as patient controlled analgesia (PCA). It can be used by some children over five years of age who are in severe pain. When the child experiences the onset of pain they press a button, which activates the device to release a dose of the pain-killing drug.

Children should not wake up in pain following surgery. Immediately after surgery they may be given an injection of local anaesthetic into the wound or into a nerve to a specific area. A caudal block is one type of nerve block, in which anaesthetic is injected around the nerves at the base of the spinal cord, numbing the genital and buttock areas. The effect lasts for four to six hours.

Hospital tests

Some tests carried out in hospital are completely painless, while others are uncomfortable. For any which are painful a child will be offered pain relief. The parent's presence is, however, often the best form of pain relief and the best form of reassurance child can have.

Blood tests

Blood tests can provide important information about the state of a child's health. Children who are hospitalized may need to give blood samples to help doctors diagnose illness such as anaemia or evaluate the efficacy of treatment. If only a small amount of blood is needed it can be taken from a capillary just under the skin. In babies it is usually taken from the side of the heel, while in older children it can be taken from a finger or thumb. Taking blood like this does cause a pricking sensation, and if a child needs repeated blood tests their fingers can become tender. Keeping the child warm taking blood helps children to relax, and it also helps to keep their blood vessels dilated.

A larger blood sample is usually taken from a vein, often on the inside of the elbow. A few ice cubes held against the area prior to inserting the needle provide instant numbness. Otherwise a child can have a local anaesthetic cream or gel applied to the site half an hour to an hour in advance. This is almost always done before an injection into a vein, or when a cannula (a very fine tube) is to be inserted into a vein, in which case the wriggling of the tube can feel uncomfortable. A cuff similar to a blood pressure cuff may be put around the child's arm to help the veins stand out. Children deserve a reward afterwards – even if it is just a cuddle.

X-rays

X-rays do not hurt, but children can feel frightened by the size of the machine, particularly if it has to come very close to them. They also have to lie or stand quite still and may have to adopt an uncomfortable position so that the technician can obtain a clear picture. Parents can normally stay with their child during the procedure, but they must wear a lead apron to protect their reproductive organs. Any mothers who might be pregnant will not be allowed into the X-ray room with the child but can watch through a glass screen. To reassure them, you can tell them that the X-ray machine is large and will come close to them, but never comes very close, and that it never hurts.

Radio isotope tests

These tests are used specifically to find out whether the kidneys are functioning normally. The child lies on a table which has a large isotope camera underneath it. Anaesthetic cream is rubbed on to the back of their hand and a fine tube is inserted into a vein. The child is then given an injection of liquid containing a tiny amount of radioactive substance; this is tracked by the X-ray camera under the bed. While the X-ray pictures are being taken staff will usually ask the child to take up different positions. To help them lie quite still the nurse or technician may tie light straps around the child's body.

MCUG

The MCUG (a micturating cysto-urethrogram) shows how well the bladder and its outlet are functioning. It specifically checks whether any urine is flowing back from the bladder towards the kidneys instead of draining out normally. The test does not hurt, but it is uncomfortable and takes about 30 minutes. The child lies on a table in the X-ray room. After cleaning the genital area, the doctor inserts a catheter into the child's urethra and bladder. Fluid is then passed into the bladder until the bladder distends. X-rays are taken when the child urinates. Urinating after the catheter has been removed may cause a stinging sensation, but drinking quantities of fluid will help to relieve this.

Barium swallow or meal

These tests are carried out to investigate structures in the digestive tract. The child swallows a white, chalky liquid containing barium; X-rays are taken as the barium travels through the digestive tract. For a barium swallow, the baby or child is X-rayed in an upright position, but when taking a barium meal they lie down. The test can cause constipation, which you can help to prevent by giving the child plenty to drink for the next 24 hours. When the child does pass stools, you may notice tiny white pieces or streaks, which are the remains of the barium. They will soon disappear.

EEG (electroencephalogram)

An EEG measures the patterns produced by tiny electrical impulses in the brain. It is useful for diagnosing epilepsy. The child usually wears between 16 and 20 small electrodes attached to their head. The electrodes pick up the impulses, which are enlarged in the computer and then either viewed on a monitor or printed on to paper. There is no pain involved – the electricity goes from the brain to the machine, not vice versa. It takes 30-90 minutes, depending on how still the child can lie.

During the recording staff may ask the child to open and close their eyes and breathe deeply in and out; a light may be flashed in their eyes. As the electrodes are sometimes fixed in place with a special glue, the child will need to have their hair washed after the test. Some children have the test at night to examine their brain waves while they are asleep. Many hospitals can offer children a portable EEG, which allows recordings to continue at home.

CT scan (computed tomography)

A CT or CAT scanner records images of the brain or other soft parts of the body. The child lies on a table that slides into a tubular disc – scanner – that rotates around the patient, building up a scan of the brain by means of X-rays. A computer then integrates the images to build up slices or cross-sections of the part of the body X-rayed. The test is painless but as the X-rays are taken the machine sometimes produces sounds, which the child may find disturbing. As the child has to lie very still for the test they may be given a sedative, or possibly a brief general anaesthetic.

MRI (magnetic resonance imaging)

As far as the child is concerned, this is very like a CT scan, because the child has to lie quite still on a table in a tubular structure rather like a tunnel while images are recorded. However the images show far more detail than X-rays and more than a CT scan.

The scan takes about 30 minutes. The MR scanner looks frightening and is noisy, and as the child has to lie alone and perfectly still inside, they are usually given a sedative or general anaesthetic. An older child or teenager who is not sedated can communicate through an intercom with the staff operating the machine.

ECG (electrocardiograph)

The child undresses to the waist and lies down while patches are stuck to their arms, legs and chest. These are attached to a machine that picks up the heart's electrical impulses and records them as a printout or on a monitor, showing the rhythm and rate of the heartbeat. The test is completely painless and normally takes about five minutes.

Echocardiogram

This is like the ultrasound used in pregnancy. A picture of the heart, its structure and blood flow is produced on a screen. The procedure takes between 15 and 60 minutes.

The care of premature babies

About one baby in ten in the United Kingdom needs extra medical care immediately after birth. Of the 70,000 babies a year who spend time in special care units in British hospitals, some 52,500 are premature. Most have a low birth weight; more than one per cent of babies born in England and Wales in 1995 weighed less than 1500 g/3 lb 5 oz. Yet in recent years the prognosis for very premature babies has steadily improved. A few babies survive at 23 weeks and from 24 weeks survival rates start to climb steeply.

The cause of some premature births is still not understood, but it is possible that some otherwise inexplicable premature births are triggered by a common vaginal infection, bacterial vaginosis. In some pregnant women the membranes break before term, or the foetus begins to grow too slowly or stops growing altogether, and the doctor decides that they would thrive better outside the uterus.

Predicting prematurity is the subject of much current research. A range of tests is now being investigated, including swabbing the vagina to detect infection, screening for fibronectin (a foetal protein that usually disappears by the fifth month) and scanning the cervix for early signs of changes that herald labour. If delivery can be delayed long enough to give the mother a steroid drug to protect the baby's lungs, the chances of any breathing problems developing later on can be halved.

Special care baby units

All babies are different, but a baby born after 36 weeks can usually be treated like a normal term baby and will not need special care. A baby born between 33 and 36 weeks should have few difficulties, but may find coordinating sucking and swallowing too difficult for normal breast- or bottle feeding. Babies born between 28 and 32 weeks have immature lungs, and those born before 27 weeks need support for many of their body systems.

Until the baby is 32 to 34 weeks old the lungs are physically very small. They do not produce surfactant, the substance that allows expansion when the lungs fill with air. In some babies the breathing control in the brain is still immature. Ventilators therefore take over the breathing by gently inflating the lungs.

Some premature babies receive negative pressure ventilation, which reduces the air pressure around the baby and makes breathing easier. Others receive oxygen-enriched air through nasal prongs (rubber tubes, which are inserted into the baby's nostrils, while others lie with their head in a transparent headbox containing oxygen-enriched air. Babies are often given artificial or animal-derived surfactant at birth. Research is under way into liquid ventilation, in which the lungs are not filled with air or oxygen but with a fluid in which oxygen is dissolved.

Paediatricians balance the amount of ventilation the baby needs with the knowledge that ventilation over a long period, especially at a high pressure, can damage the internal surfaces of the lungs, giving rise to a condition called chronic lung disease (also called bronchopulmonary dysplasia or BPD). Babies who do develop this condition have a tendency to catch respiratory infections and to wheeze in their first few years; however they outgrow their difficulties by late childhood.

Premature babies lose heat very quickly, so they need to be kept extremely warm, either in an incubator or, if they need constant medical attention, under an open radiant heater.

Until coordinated sucking and swallowing develop around 34 weeks, babies can be fed essential nutrients by intravenous drip directly into the bloodstream, or given milk through a tube that passes through the nose and down the oesophagus into the stomach.

The major impact on parents who have a baby in special care is emotional. At first parents often feel shocked (at not having produced a healthy, full-term baby), anxious (about the baby's immediate health and long-term development) and perhaps either alienated or fiercely protective of a baby who depends on high-technology medicine to survive. Staff in neonatal units are acutely aware of parents' difficulties. When it is appropriate, parents are encouraged to become involved in the baby's care and to talk to, possibly touch or even hold them. Some units foster kangaroo care, in which the baby is placed on the parent's chest in an upright position, warm inside their clothing, for up to an hour a day.

Outcome

The development of babies born prematurely depends on many factors but most grow up with no long-term difficulties. Because development may initially be delayed or follow an unusual pattern, in the first two years of life allowances are usually made for the child's prematurity. Beyond the age of two years the effects of having been premature are less noticeable, although a minority of children are left needing long-term support. It is impossible to predict the outcome for any individual baby, but generally speaking, the closer the baby was to term the more unlikely they are to have long-term disability. Babies born after 32 weeks have a 98 per cent chance of developing in a perfectly normal way.

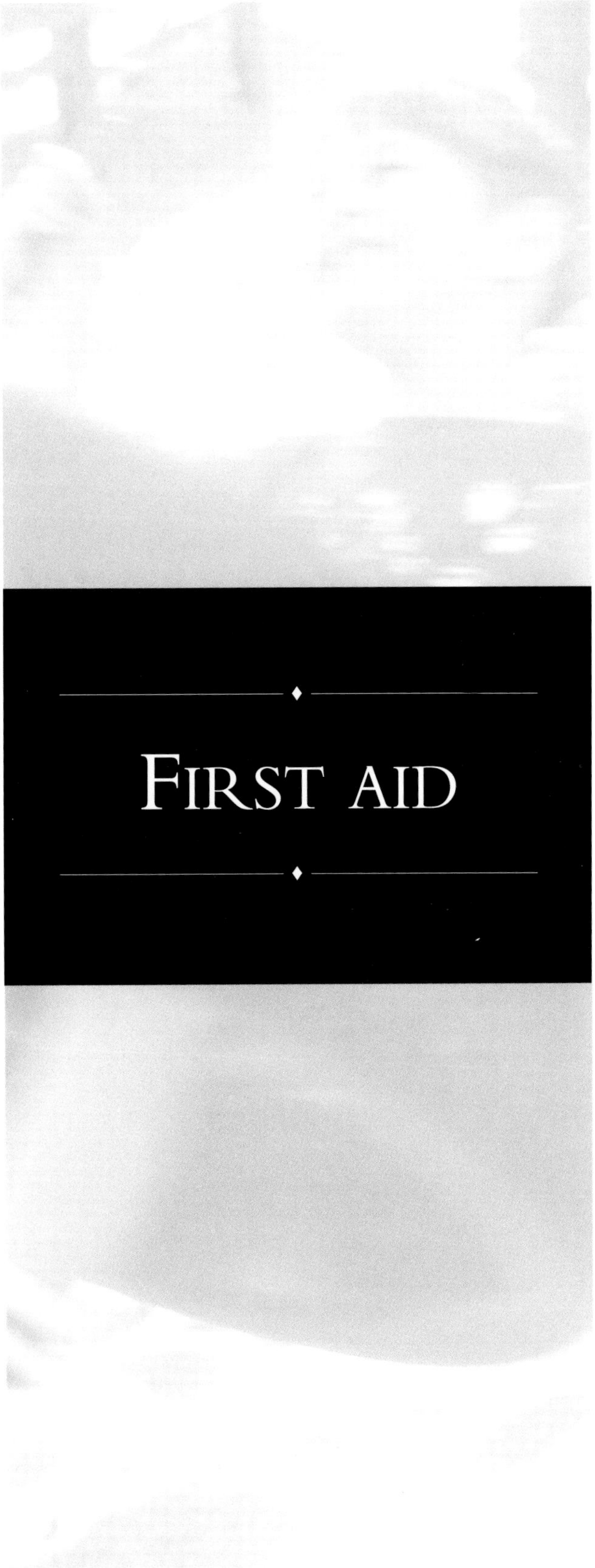

FIRST AID

FIRST AID

First aid cannot be taught from a book. The best way to learn is to attend a recognized training course and to update your training regularly. However as the information here is to hand take the opportunity to read through these pages in case an accident or emergency occurs.

The advice given in this section is fully up to date at the time of publication, and the topics that have been selected are those that are especially relevant to infants and children.

If after an accident there is no danger to life, and professional help will be quickly available, the best course of action may be to wait for help to arrive. Note that in the following instructions, baby = 0–12 months and child = 1–7 years.

RESUSCITATION

ABC of resuscitation
A = Airway. Blockage of the air passage by foreign bodies, vomit or the tongue when a child is unconscious but breathing. The airway must be clear.
B = Breathing.
C = Circulation (the pulse caused by the beating of the heart).

Assess:

1. Is the baby/child conscious? Shake the child gently, and call his/her name. Pinch the skin. If there is no response lay the baby/child flat on a firm surface.
2. Is the **airway** clear? Kneel beside the child's head. Check for and remove anything obvious that may be causing a blockage, but **DO NOT put your fingers down the back of the throat. Open the airway** (fig.1). Place one hand on the forehead and one (**for a baby**) or two (**for a child**) fingers of the other hand on the bony part under the chin. Gently tilt the head back. Be careful not to overextend a baby's neck.
3. Is the baby/child **breathing?** Put your cheek close to the nose and mouth while looking along the chest. Look, listen and feel for breathing sounds or movements for up to ten seconds.

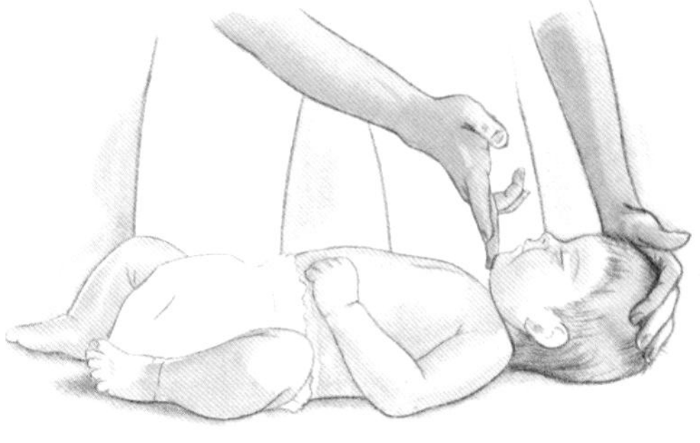

fig. 1 Open the airways

If the child is breathing place him/her in the **recovery position** (page 345).

If there is no breathing:

1. **For a baby:** seal your lips around the mouth and nose (fig. 2).
2. **For a child:** seal your lips around the mouth and pinch the nostrils. Breathe into the mouth until you see the chest rise.

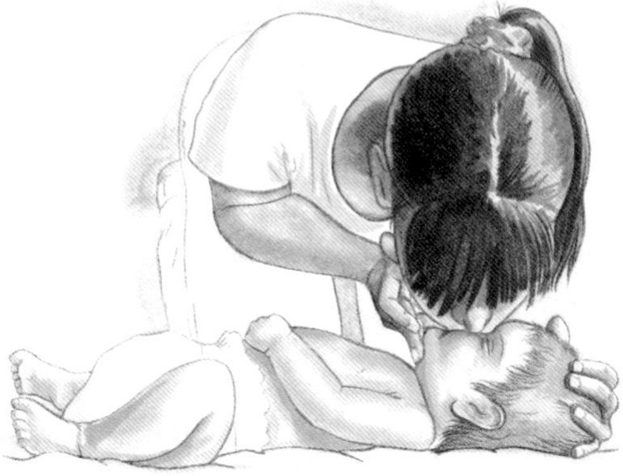

fig. 2 Seal the mouth and nose

3. Do this five times. This is mouth-to-mouth ventilation. Check for the **circulation.** Is there a **pulse**?

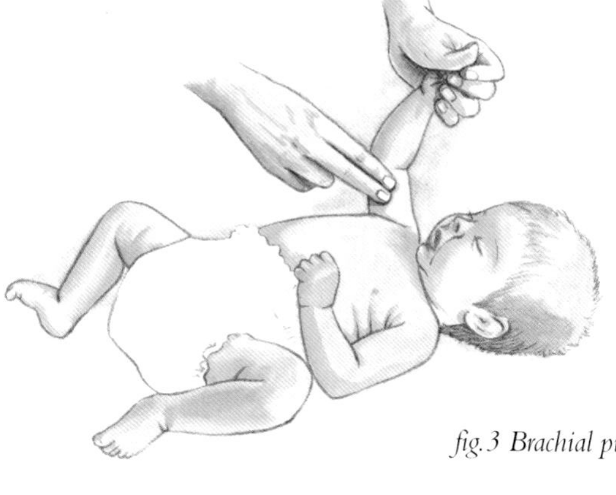

fig. 3 Brachial pulse

For a baby: press with two fingers on the inside of the baby's arm halfway between the elbow and shoulder for the brachial pulse (fig. 3). Check for up to ten seconds.

For a child: feel the windpipe and slide fingers into the groove beside it for the carotid pulse (fig. 4).

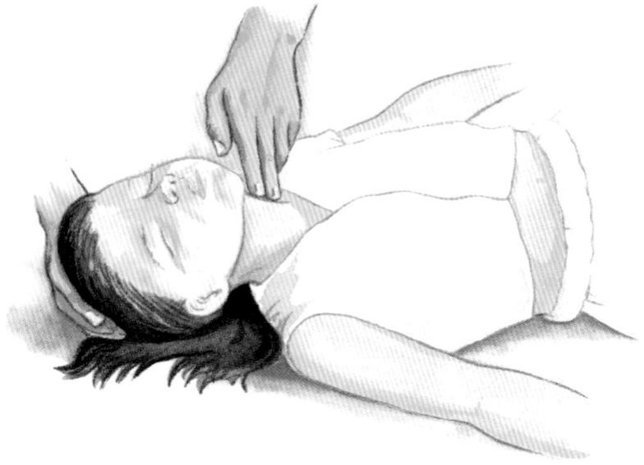

fig. 4 Carotid pulse

If there is no pulse, or the pulse is less than 60 beats per minute in a baby: You must restart the circulation by commencing cardiopulmonary resuscitation (CPR).

1. **For a baby:** place two fingertips below the nipple line on the lower half of the breastbone (fig. 5).

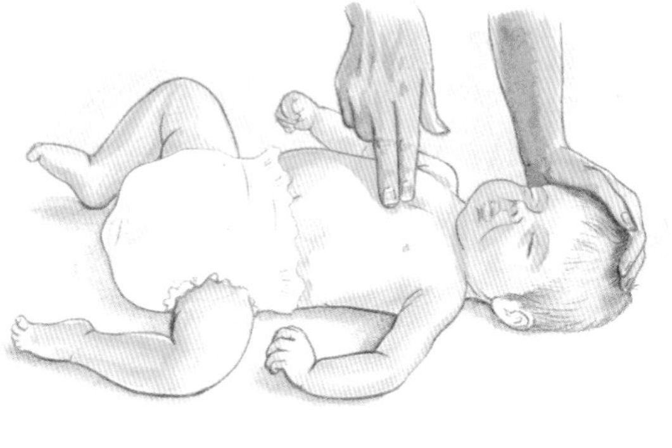

fig. 5 Place two fingertips below the nipple line

2. **For a child:** put your middle finger where the ribs meet the breastbone, put the index finger of the same hand beside it on the breastbone and slide the heel of your other hand down beside the fingers. Remove fingers. Do the compressions with the heel of one hand (fig. 6).
3. Press down sharply to one-third of the depth of the chest five times, at a rate of almost two compressions a second.
4. Give one breath of mouth-to-mouth ventilation.
5. Repeat sequence of five chest compressions and one breath for one minute.
6. **Call an ambulance**, or get someone to call one for you. If you have to do this yourself, take the baby/child to the phone with you if necessary.
7. Continue CPR until the ambulance arrives.

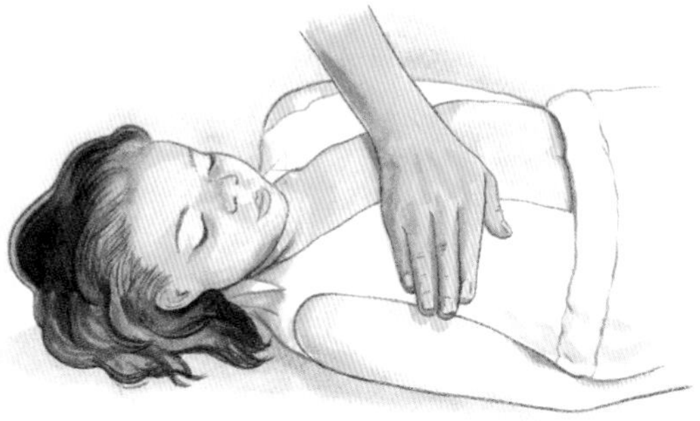

fig. 6 Do compressions with the heel of the hand

For older children (8+) and adults:

1. Do the airway and breathing checks.
2. If the child is not breathing **call an ambulance**.
3. If breathing failure is caused by injury or drowning check the circulation and, if necessary, resuscitate for one minute before going for help. In either case use the same resuscitation technique as that for children, except: use two hands for compressions and a ratio of two breaths to fifteen compressions.

UNCONSCIOUSNESS

In a child:

Assess the situation to ensure your own safety. If a child is unconscious, the most important action is to keep the airway open and check that the child is breathing.

1. Shake the child gently, call his/her name and pinch the skin to rouse him/her.
2. Shout for help.
3. Check the mouth and remove any obvious obstruction.
4. With two fingers under the chin raise the jaw. Place the other hand on the forehead and tilt the head back gently. Lean close to the child's mouth and nose and feel for breath on your cheek (fig. 7). Watch the chest for breathing movements.
5. If necessary, carry out resuscitation (see page 343).
6. Check for bleeding or major injury. Treat if necessary.
7. Turn the child into the recovery position (see opposite).
8. **Call an ambulance.** Remain with the child and monitor them until medical help arrives.

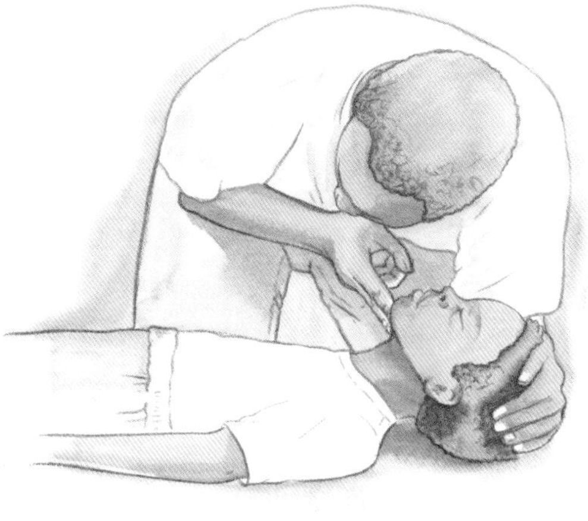

fig. 7 Feel for breath on your cheek

In a baby:

1. Try to rouse the baby gently.
2. Shout for help.
3. Check for any obvious obstruction in the mouth. **Do not push your finger down the throat.**
4. With one finger under the chin tilt the head back slightly. Be careful not to overextend the baby's neck, as this will block the airway.
5. Listen and feel for breathing sounds and movement.
6. If necessary check the upper arm pulse. If the baby is unconscious but breathing, keep the airway open.
7. **Call an ambulance**, taking the baby to the phone if you can.

RECOVERY POSITION

A child who is unconscious but who is breathing should be placed in the recovery position (fig. 8) so she cannot choke on vomit or on her tongue.

For a child:

1. Kneel down beside the child and open the airway. Check breathing (see ABC of resuscitation, page 343).
2. Keeping the child's arm nearest to you straight, put it under her thigh with the palm facing upwards.

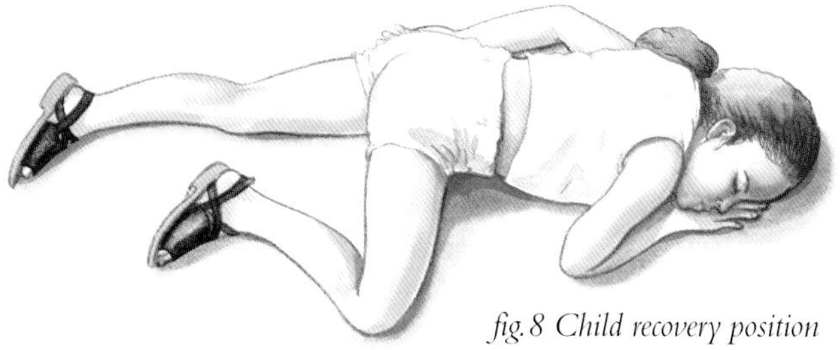

fig. 8 Child recovery position

3. Remove anything from the pockets that might hurt the child when you roll her.
4. Place the back of the other hand against the child's nearest cheek and hold that hand (palm to palm) to protect the head as you roll her over.
5. Bend up the knee of the leg furthest from you until the foot is flat on the ground.
6. Pull the thigh of the bent leg towards you. The child will roll over on to her side.
7. Support her against your knees to stop her going right over on to her front.
8. Tilt the head back to keep the airway open.
9. Bend the upper leg at right angles to the hip and knee to support the child.
10. Ensure the child is not lying on her lower arm and that her palm is facing upwards.
11. **Call an ambulance.**
12. Carefully assess the child's breathing and circulation until the ambulance arrives.

For a baby:

If a baby is unconscious but breathing hold him across your chest (fig. 9). Then tilt his head downward so that his airway is kept open.

fig. 9 Hold the baby across your chest, then tilt the head downwards

BLEEDING

Bleeding can be external, as in a cut, or internal, when it can cause shock (see page 355). Bleeding from small blood vessels (capillaries) is usually easily controlled, but if the wound is serious, direct pressure must be applied and, if possible, the wound must be raised above the level of the heart.

1. Check that there is nothing embedded in the wound. Press on top of the wound for ten minutes using a clean, non-fluffy cloth or pad. If blood soaks through the pad, add another layer.
2. If the wound is on a limb, raise the wounded part above the level of the child's heart (fig. 10).
3. Lay the child down, keeping constant pressure on the wound to reduce shock.
4. Once the bleeding eases, cover the pad with a dressing and bandage the dressing firmly but not tightly into place. Keep the wounded part raised, using a sling if necessary. **Take the child to hospital.**

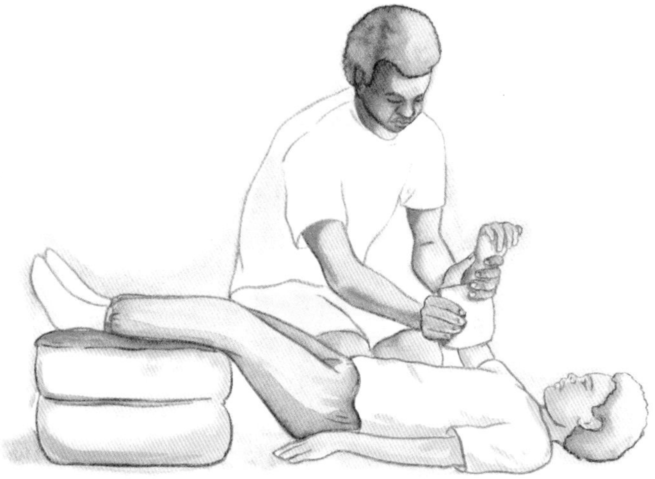

fig. 10 For a wound on a limb, raise the limb above the level of the child's heart. If the child feels faint, lay him down and raise the legs. Use this position too for severe bleeding while awaiting an ambulance

5. If the bleeding continues put another dressing on top of the first, maintain pressure over the wound and support the child's legs above the level of the heart.
6. **Call an ambulance.**
7. Watch for signs of shock (see page 355).

FAINTING

Fainting is caused by a brief restriction in blood flow to the brain, which usually corrects itself quickly. Children may faint out of hunger, fear or pain, or if they have to stand without moving for a long time.

1. **Watch for:**
   - *Signs of dizziness, sickness or weakness*
   - *Very pale face*
   - *Briefly losing consciousness*
   - *Slow pulse*
2. Lie the child down, raise his/her legs and support them.
3. Loosen tight clothing at the waist, chest and neck.
4. Ensure there is fresh air: open a window and/or fan the face.
5. As the child comes round, sit him/her up gradually and reassure him/her. Do not give the child anything to drink until s/he is fully conscious.
6. If the child does not come round quickly, assess his/her airway and breathing (see resuscitation, page 343).

If your child feels faint, but has not lost consciousness, get her to sit on the floor or on a chair and put her head between her legs for several minutes. This will allow oxygenated blood to flow more quickly into her head. A child who has fainted should be placed in the position that is shown in figure 10 (left).

7. **Call an ambulance.**
8. If the child is breathing, place him/her in the recovery position (page 345) and monitor until help arrives.

BURNS AND SCALDS

Burns are caused by heat, cold, the sun, chemicals or hot liquids. Burns are always serious as tissues under the skin are frequently damaged. In a baby or child any burn larger than 25 mm/1 inch in diameter should be seen by a doctor or taken to Accident and Emergency.

1. Remove the child from the cause of burning (see Electrical burns, right) without endangering yourself.
2. Hold the burn under cold water for at least 10 minutes.
3. If the burn is minor, remove clothing from the affected area.
4. If the burn is more serious, remove clothing only if it is not stuck to the burn and you can do so easily and without doing more harm. Do this after cooling with water.
5. Loosen tight clothing and remove any jewellery, because the burnt area may swell.
6. Cover the burn with clingfilm or a clean, non-fluffy cloth (a handkerchief, pillow case or linen/cotton tea towel). Or put a clean plastic bag over a foot, hand, arm or leg.
7. Do not apply any lotions, creams or fats.
8. Do not burst blisters or use adhesive dressings.
9. **Take the child to the nearest Accident and Emergency.**
10. Watch for signs of shock (page 355).

Chemical burns

Household cleaners (such as bleach, oven cleaners, ammonia and paint stripper) and glues are the most frequent causes of chemical burns in young children. The child's eyes are especially vulnerable.

1. **Watch for:**
   - *Complaints of stinging or burning*
   - *Redness and soreness*
   - *A blistering or peeling and swelling of the skin as the burn develops*
2. Put on rubber gloves. Wash off the chemical with copious running cold water for at least 20 minutes.
3. Remove the child's clothes, making sure you do not touch any other part of the body with chemical-impregnated clothing.
4. Cover the burned area with clean, non-fluffy material, such as a handkerchief, pillow case or linen/cotton tea towel.
5. **Take the child to the nearest Accident and Emergency straightaway.** Keep a note of the name of the chemical.
6. **If the eye is affected** wash the affected eye under gently running cold water for at least ten minutes. If this proves difficult, pour water from a jug. Pull the eye open to ensure that water goes inside. Make sure the water drains away from the other eye. Cover the eye with a clean pad, bandage into place and **take the child to hospital.**

ELECTRICAL BURNS

Children are at risk of electrical burns if they play with flexes, plugs or electric sockets. Electrical burns can be more serious than they first appear, because the tissues underlying the skin can be burned.

1. If the child is in contact with an electrical appliance, switch off the power at the mains. If this is not possible, stand on a newspaper, a rubber mat or a large book and remove the source of electricity with a wooden broom handle (fig. 11), or move the child away from the source. Alternatively, without touching the child directly, twist a large dry cloth around his ankles and pull him away. **Avoid becoming a victim yourself.**
2. Check for consciousness and, if necessary, follow the steps for resuscitation (see page 343).
3. Electrical burns occur where the current enters and leaves the body. Cool the burns under cold water for at least 10 minutes.
4. Cover the burns with clingfilm, a clean plastic bag or non-fluffy material.
5. **Take the child to Accident and Emergency.**
6. Watch for signs of shock (see page 355).

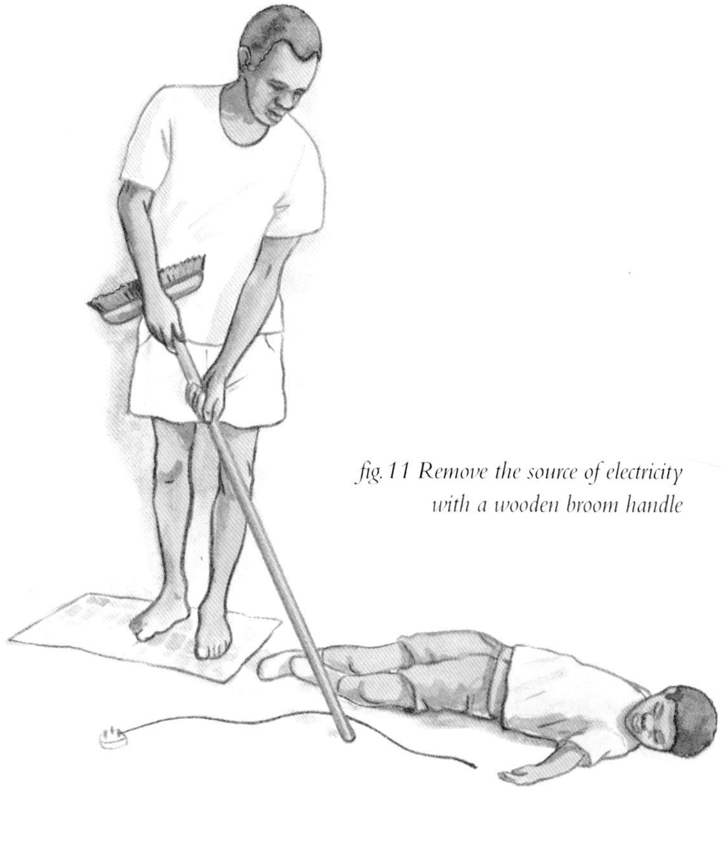

fig. 11 Remove the source of electricity with a wooden broom handle

CHOKING

Children can choke if they put objects in their mouths or if they don't chew properly and food enters the airway.

1. **Watch for:**
 - *Inability to breathe, cry or speak*
 - *Face turning blue*
 - *Child clutching at his/her throat*
2. Encourage the child to cough.
3. **Lay a baby** face down along your arm (fig. 12), supporting his head and shoulders.

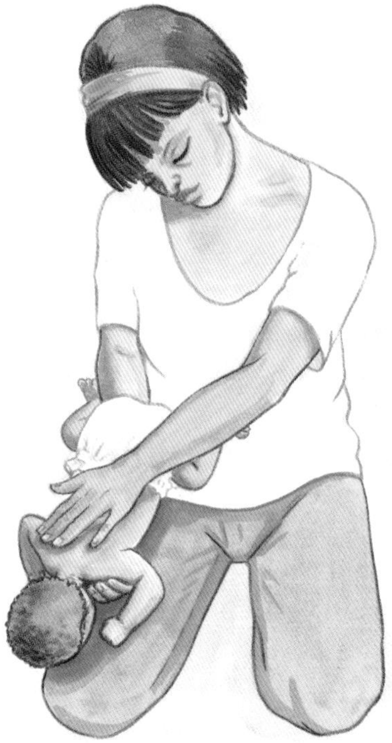

fig. 12 Lay a baby face down along your arm

4. **Lay a small child** across your lap with the head well down. **Bend an older child** forward so that his/her head is lower than the chest.
5. Give five sharp slaps between the shoulder blades.
6. Check the mouth for obvious obstruction. **Never stick a finger down the throat.**

If a baby is still choking:

1. Turn the baby face upwards along your arm, still supporting the head. Place two fingers in the middle of the chest, just below the nipples. Thrust sharply downward five times. Check the mouth. **Do not** do abdominal thrusts on a baby.
2. **Call an ambulance.**
3. Continue with the above until help arrives or the obstruction is cleared.

If a child is still choking:

1. Stand or kneel behind the child.
2. Make a fist and, with the other hand over the top of it, press sharply inwards on the lower half of the breastbone. Do this up to five times every three seconds.
3. Check the mouth again.
4. Try five more back slaps.
5. Make a fist and place your other hand over your fist at the top of the child's abdomen. Press inwards and upwards sharply five times.
6. **Call an ambulance**.
7. Repeat the above steps until the obstruction is cleared or until help arrives.

If a child becomes unconscious:

Check the airway, breathing and circulation (see ABC of resuscitation, page 343) and give resuscitation if necessary .

If the airway is still blocked:

1. Check the child's mouth again.
2. Roll the child on to his/her side and give five back slaps.
3. Roll the child on to his/her back and give five thrusts on the lower half of the breastbone to one third the depth of chest once every three seconds.
4. Give five more back slaps then five more abdominal thrusts with one hand.
5. Repeat until the obstruction clears or help arrives.
6. If the child or baby begins to breathe put him/her in the recovery position (see page 345).

CONCUSSION

Concussion occurs if the brain is shaken hard inside the skull. It may be caused by a violent blow to the head or active shaking of a baby or child.

1. **After a blow to the head watch the child for:**
 - *Abnormal behaviour*
 - *Loss of consciousness*
 - *Nausea and dizziness as the child comes round*
 - *Forgetting events just before the accident*
 - *Mild headache*
2. **Call the doctor** even if s/he passes out for only a few seconds.
3. Encourage the child to rest and watch him/her. If child is not fully back to normal in 30 minutes **call an ambulance.**

4. If unconsciousness, check the airway, breathing and pulse (see ABC of resuscitation, page 343) and lay the child in the recovery position (see page 345). **Call an ambulance**.
5. The child may have a delayed reaction. Bleeding inside the skull after a head injury can compress the brain.
   Watch for:
   - *Confusion*
   - *Severe headache*
   - *Increasing sleepiness*
   - *Uneven pupils*
6. If you notice any of the above signs **call an ambulance**. Watch the child closely and be ready to resuscitate him/her.

CONVULSIONS

In a pre-school child convulsions (fits, seizures) can be brought on by a rapid rise in temperature. In a child who is not feverish, the convulsion is more likely to be linked with epilepsy.

1. **Watch for:**
   - *Fever*
   - *Trembling or twitching of the arms or legs*
   - *The eyes rolling upwards, squinting or being fixed*
   - *The body stiffening or turning rigid*
   - *Unresponsiveness. The child may pass out, turn blue or pale or limp*
2. Clear a space around the child while s/he is fitting to prevent him/her from injuring him/herself.
3. Stay with the child. If the s/he is still conscious and feverish, remove the clothes.
4. If the child is unconscious, remain with him/her until the body relaxes, then turn him/her gently into the recovery position.
5. **Do not** put anything in the child's mouth or give anything to eat or drink.
6. **Call a doctor or ambulance.**
7. Reassure the child.

MOUTH AND TOOTH INJURY

A blow to the mouth can cause cuts or bleeding from the tooth socket. Bleeding may be profuse, as the blood supply to the mouth is rich. A blow or fall may knock out a tooth.

1. Sit the child with his/her head forward over a bowl to catch any blood.
2. Press a pad in place over the wound for ten minutes or until bleeding stops.
3. Do not let the child rinse out his/her mouth with water as this may disturb forming clots.
4. If a milk tooth is knocked out and the socket is bleeding, place a thick pad over the socket and apply pressure for ten minutes to stop the bleeding.
5. Look for the tooth to be sure the child has not inhaled or swallowed it.
6. Have the gum checked by a dentist.
7. If a permanent tooth is knocked out, pick it up by the crown and if you can, press it quickly back into the socket. Make sure it is the right way round. Put a pad between the bottom and top teeth and get the child to bite against it to stop the bleeding and keep the tooth in place.
8. Get the child to a dentist as quickly as possible.
9. Alternatively, get the child to bite on a thick pad to staunch the flow of blood, and put the tooth in a container of milk or water to keep it moist while you **get the child to a dentist or Accident and Emergency.**

EYE INJURY

Injury to an eye needs prompt attention. A blow near the eye can burst blood vessels, causing a black eye. If a sharp object enters the eyeball or makes a cut in the region of the eye, then the child will need emergency treatment.

1. Following a blow to the eye lay a clean face cloth that has been wrung out in cold water over the eye to limit bruising.
2. For chemicals in the eye, (see Chemical burns, page 347).
3. For a foreign object in the eye, see page 350.
4. If the eye has been injured by a sharp implement, bandage a pad over it for protection and then bandage the other eye to limit movement (fig. 13).

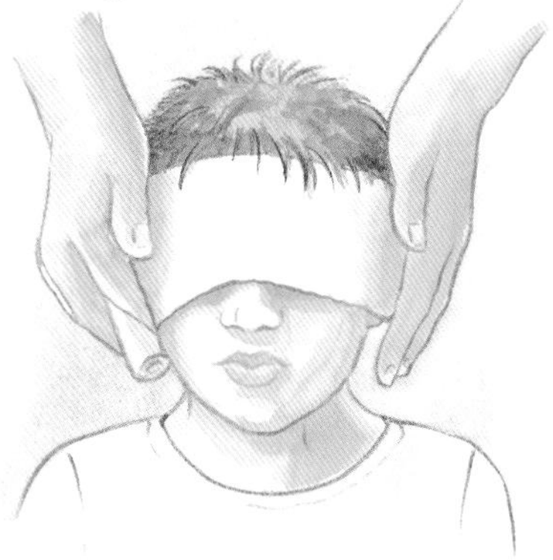

fig. 13 Place a bandage over both eyes

5. Reassure the child.
6. **Take the child to the nearest Accident and Emergency.**

FOREIGN OBJECT IN THE EAR

Young children may push objects, such as tiny parts of toys, into their ears. Insects may fly into the ear.

1. Sit the child down and examine the ear in a good light.
2. If there is an insect in the ear, lay a towel over the child's shoulder and pour tepid water from a jug into the ear to float it out (fig. 14).
3. Never try to remove anything else from the ear canal. It is only too easy to push the object further down into the ear canal and cause further damage.
4. Reassure the child and **take him/her to the Accident and Emergency.**

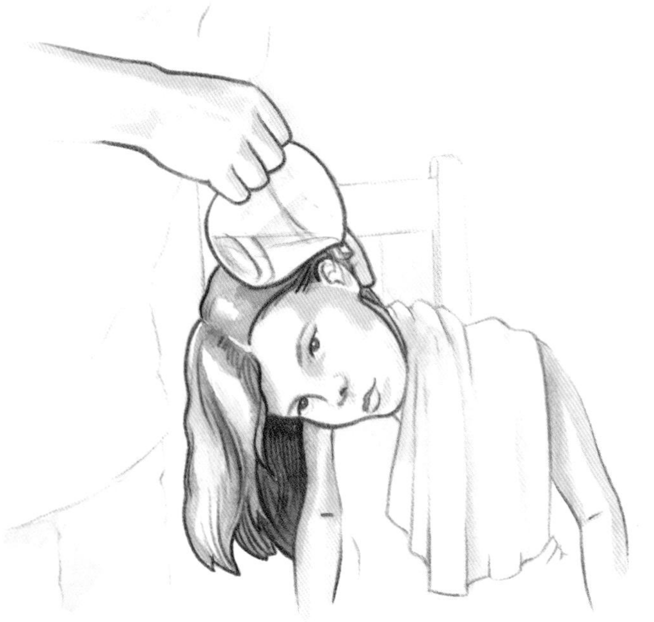

fig. 14 Pour a little tepid water into the ear

FOREIGN OBJECT IN THE EYE

Particles of dust or grit often get into the eye and it is usually quite simple to remove them. However, anything embedded in the eye or sticking to the coloured part of the eye (the iris or pupil) must not be touched.

1. If the particle is on the coloured part of the eye and does not move when the child blinks, cover the eye with a pad and bandage it into place. Treat as for an eye injury (page 349).
2. If the particle is on the white of the eye or under a lid, gently pull down the lower lid and ask the child to move the eye up, down and across until you see the particle.
3. Tilt the child's head so the affected eye is on the lower side. Then pour a small amount of water from a jug into the eye to wash out the particle (fig. 15).

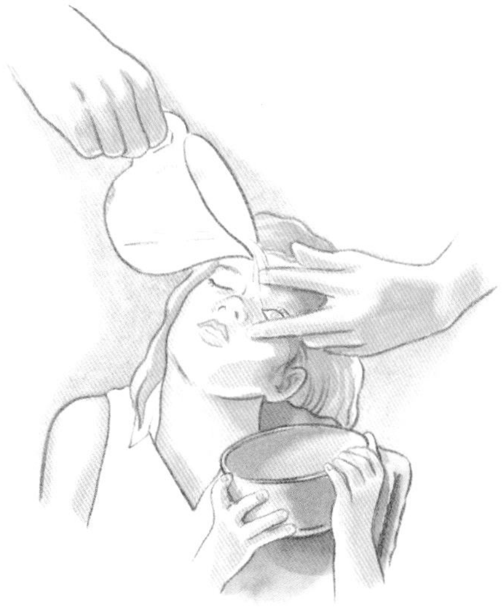

fig. 15 Pour a little tepid water into the eye

4. If the particle is not washed out, lift it out using a moistened folded corner of a tissue or a clean handkerchief.
5. If the particle is under the upper lid, pull the upper lid down over the lower lid and ask the child to blink. This may remove it. An older child can do this herself (fig. 16).
6. If the particle remains in the eye, cover with a pad, bandage it into place and **take the child to a doctor.**

fig. 16 Pull the upper lid over the lower one

SCALP WOUND

The blood in the scalp is rich, so wounds bleed profusely.

1. Cover the wound with a cloth or dressing and press gently to control bleeding (fig. 17).
2. Sit or lay the child down and reassure him. If he is lying down, raise the head and shoulders.

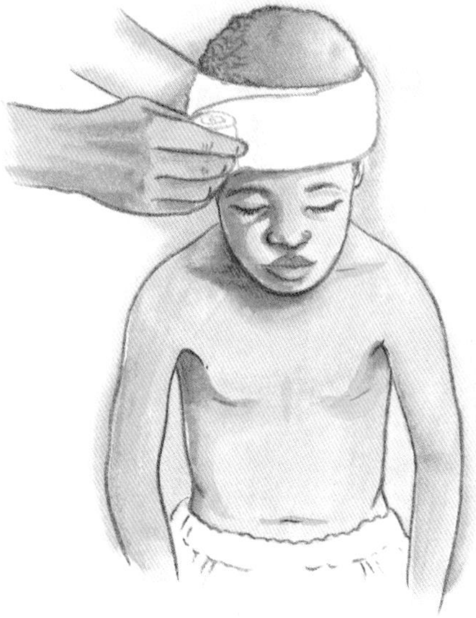

fig. 17 Cover the wound with a dressing and press gently

3. Add dressings if needed, pressing gently but firmly. Fix the dressing in place with a bandage or scarf.
4. If the child has had a blow to the head, **call a doctor.**
5. Watch the child carefully. If he becomes drowsy, if his behaviour is abnormal or if he loses consciousness, follow the steps for the ABC of resuscitation (see page 343) and **call an ambulance**.

HEAD INJURY

The majority of children who bump their heads do only superficial damage and recover quickly. Because the blood supply is rich, scalp wounds usually bleed copiously (see above) and bumps sometimes produce dramatic swellings.

Nevertheless, for any suspected head injury, you should always assess the child immediately in case the head injury is serious and requires medical attention. The child may be concussed or have another type of head injury.

Concussion

1. **Watch for:**
   - *Abnormal behaviour*
   - *Any loss of consciousness, even brief*
   - *Inability to remember events immediately beforehand*
2. Sit the child down. Lay a cold compress gently over the bump. If the child loses consciousness, even for a few seconds, **call a doctor.** If the child comes to, but is not back to normal in 15–30 minutes, **call an ambulance.**

Head injury

1. **Watch for:**
   - *Unusual behaviour or deterioration in responsiveness*
   - *A soft area on the scalp*
   - *Clear fluid coming from the ear or nose*
   - *Blood showing in the eye*
   - *Severe headache*
   - *Unequal size of pupils*
2. **Call an ambulance.**
3. Assess the child's airway, breathing and circulation (see ABC of resuscitation, page 343).
4. Keep the child still and comfortable. Stay with him/her. If s/he loses consciousness, move him/her gently into the recovery position (see page 345).
5. Monitor breathing and circulation.
6. The child may have a delayed reaction. This can show several hours (or even days) later.
   Watch for:
   - *Increasing sleepiness, difficult to rouse, confusion*
   - *Repeated vomiting*
   - *Severe headache, visual disturbance*
   - *Irritability, continuous crying, can't be settled*
   - *Unequal size of pupils*
   - *Any attack that could be a fit*
7. **Call an ambulance or take the child to the nearest Accident and Emergency immediately.**

BACK AND NECK INJURIES

Injuries to the back and neck are associated with traffic accidents, falling from a height and sports such as rugby, riding, diving or gymnastics.

1. If the child or baby is conscious s/he must be encouraged or made to keep still. Reassure him/her.
2. If the child is unconscious but breathing put him/her in the modified recovery position, keeping the head and trunk in line and supporting the head and neck at all times (fig. 18). If there are several people to help, use a log roll (fig. 19).

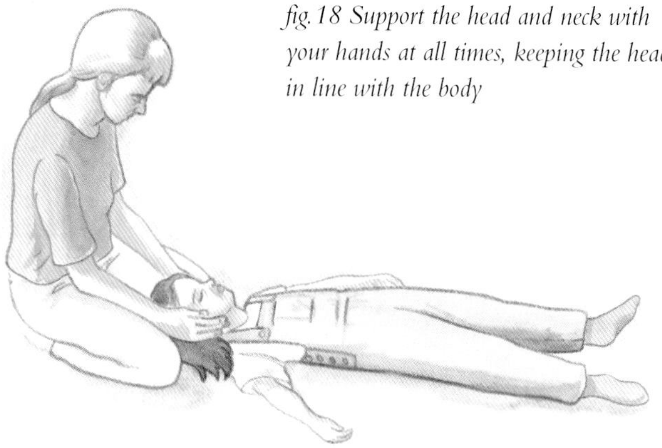

fig. 18 Support the head and neck with your hands at all times, keeping the head in line with the body

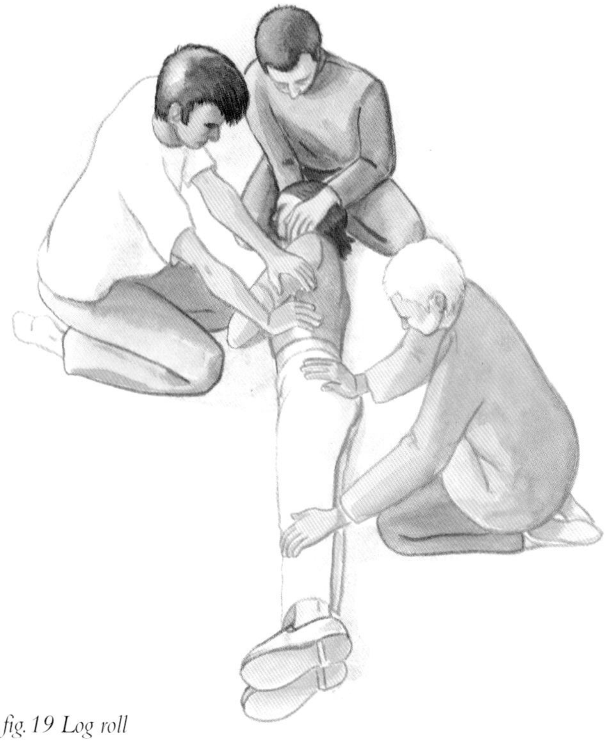

fig. 19 Log roll

3. **Get someone to call an ambulance.**
4. If the child's breathing becomes difficult, place two fingers under the bony part of the chin and very gently lift the lower jaw forward and up while keeping the head still. Support the head with the other hand. This helps to keep the airway open. If the breathing becomes difficult, tilt the head back very slightly.
5. If breathing stops, follow the steps for the ABC of resuscitation (page 343), and resuscitate if necessary, turning child on to his/her back, keeping head and trunk in line as you do so.

CRUSH INJURY

Crush injuries happen when objects heavy enough to immobilize a child fall on top of them. They also occur in road traffic accidents.

1. **Call an ambulance.**
2. If the child has been crushed for over ten minutes, leave the heavy object where it is. Removing it could do more harm.
3. If the accident has just happened, remove the object. Control any bleeding by pressing directly on the wound.
4. If a fracture is suspected, make the child comfortable, but do not move him/her until help arrives.
5. Observe the child carefully for signs of shock (page 355).

AMPUTATION

Severed fingers, toes and limbs can now be successfully reattached in some circumstances. The operation is more successful the quicker the child and the severed parts get to hospital.

1. Staunch the bleeding by placing a clean pad or sterile dressing on the injury and pressing firmly. Raise the injured part if at all possible.
2. Treat for shock (page 355).
3. **Call an ambulance. Tell the operator there has been an amputation.**
4. Do not be tempted to remove the dressing. Bandage or tape it into place and support the limb, if appropriate, in a sling.
5. Cover the severed part with clingfilm or place it in a clean plastic bag. Wrap this in soft material and place it in a plastic bag containing ice. Seal this in another plastic bag, labelled with the child's name and the time of the accident.

TRAPPED FINGERS

Small children often trap their fingers in doors and in swinging doors.

1. Release the fingers from the door quickly, causing as little extra pain as possible.
2. Hold the child's hand under running cold water to reduce swelling and to clean any wounds.
3. Apply a cold compress if pain or swelling persist.
4. Raise the injured hand (put it in a sling) to reduce the pain and the swelling.
5. Apply a plaster to any cuts or breaks in the skin.

6. If the fingers are still swollen or the child finds it difficult to move them after half an hour, **take the child to hospital** to check for fractures.

CUTS AND GRAZES

Cuts and grazes with broken skin, tissue damage and bleeding are very common in children. Minor cuts and grazes can easily be treated at home.

1. Wash your hands with soap and water and wear gloves as appropriate.
2. Sit or lie the child down while you examine the wound.
3. Wash the wound carefully under running water until it is clean. Gently pat the skin dry.
4. Press gently with a clean pad or cloth to stop any bleeding.
5. Cover with a non-stick dressing and adhesive tape or a plaster larger than the wound.
6. If the edges of a cut gape open or it is on the head, **take the child to hospital.**

INFECTED WOUND

Any wound can become infected with germs from the cause of the original injury, from the air or from the hands of people who have treated the wound. Therefore, hand washing before first aid procedures is extremely important.

1. **Watch for:**
   - *Absence of any sign of healing within 48 hours*
   - *Increasing tenderness*
   - *Redness and swelling*
   - *Possibly pus*
2. Cover the wound with a sterile dressing.
3. If the wound is on a limb, raise it in a sling if possible to help reduce swelling.
4. **Take the child to a doctor or to hospital.**

BROKEN ARM

A broken arm may be obvious, with swelling, distortion and extreme tenderness. Children who have a partial break in the bone (a greenstick fracture) may have less clear signs. Any child who has an accident and then has tenderness over part of the bone should be investigated. Fractures involving the elbow are especially common in children.

1. Sit the child down and support the injured arm.
2. Place a pad of folded cloth between the arm and the chest.
3. Gently move the arm across the chest to the most comfortable position and immobilize it using a triangular bandage or a headscarf (fig. 20).

fig.20 Immobilize the arm using a triangular bandage or a headscarf

4. For extra support, tie a second bandage around the chest and the sling.
5. **Take the child to hospital.**

BROKEN LEG

A broken leg may cause swelling, distortion and extreme tenderness. Children who have a partial break (greenstick fracture) may show less clear signs. Any child who has an accident and then has tenderness and swelling over part of the bone should be investigated.

1. Support the leg while helping the child to lie down.
2. Immobilize the leg with your hands (fig. 21) or rolled blanket.

fig.21 Immobilizing a broken bone prevents movement, which can cause pain, bleeding and shock

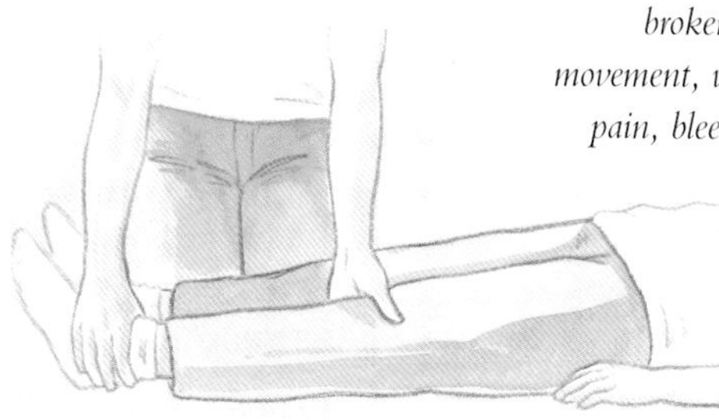

3. **Call an ambulance.**
4. Bandage for support only if the ambulance is going to be delayed – it is better to let trained personnel do this.
5. Keep the child still. Do not give him/her anything to eat or to drink.
6. If you need to move the child, first support and splint the broken leg moving the good leg to the injured one (fig. 22).
7. Treat for shock if necessary (see page 355).

fig.22 Support and splint the broken leg to the good leg

SPRAINED ANKLE

A sprain is a tear in the ligaments and tissues around a joint, which causes pain and swelling. The injury may be minor or it can be so extensive that it is difficult to distinguish it from a fracture. If there is any doubt, a sprain should always be treated as a fracture.

1. Help the child to sit or lie down. Support the ankle in a comfortable resting position.

fig.23 Bandage the ankle and keep it raised

2. Gently remove footwear and socks.
3. Lay a cloth that has been wrung out in cold water over the ankle and put an ice pack (or bag of frozen vegetables) on top to reduce pain and swelling.
4. Wrap a thick layer of cotton wool round the ankle. Bandage this into place to provide support and cushioning.
5. Keep the ankle raised (fig. 23).
6. If you are unsure whether the injury could be a fracture, **take the child to hospital.**

HYPOTHERMIA

Young infants can easily develop hypothermia because their thermal regulation system is immature. Older children can become very chilled outdoors if they are not properly clothed or if they fall into cold or icy water.

The child may shiver at first. As hypothermia deepens, the skin turns pale and cold. The child will behave oddly and be unusually quiet and drowsy, and possibly confused. A baby may look pink and well, but his/her skin feels cold and s/he is hard to rouse and will not feed.

For a child:

1. Remove wet clothes and if the child is well enough, warm him/her up in a warm (not hot) bath.
2. Dress in warm clothes and put him/her into a warm bed.
3. Give warm drinks.
4. Contact the doctor if you are at all worried about the child's condition.

For a baby:

1. Warm the baby gradually by wrapping him/her in blankets, putting his/her hat on and cuddling him/her close to you.
2. **Call a doctor.**
3. Do not use hot water bottles. It is important to warm the baby up gradually.

INSECT STING

Most insect stings cause sharp pain, but are not serious. If a child is stung inside the mouth the resultant swelling may cause breathing difficulties. This requires emergency treatment. On very rare occasions a child may develop an allergic reaction, anaphylaxis, to an insect sting. This also requires emergency treatment (see Anaphylactic shock, page 356)

Wasps never leave a sting behind; bees sometimes do. If there is a sting visible, remove it as quickly as you can using tweezers, holding them as near to the skin as possible.

1. Rinse the area under cool running water or put a cold compress on it for a few minutes to reduce pain and swelling.
2. If the sting is inside the mouth give an ice-cold drink to sip or ice cubes to suck.
3. If the swelling gets worse or the child's breathing is affected **call an ambulance** and monitor the child's airway, breathing and circulation (see ABC of resuscitation, page 343) until the ambulance arrives.

POISONING

Poisoning is most often the result of a child swallowing medicines, berries or plants, or alcohol.

1. **Watch for:**
   - *Burns or redness around the mouth*
   - *Empty or part-empty containers or plants or berries near the child*
   - *Abnormal behaviour*
   - *Drowsiness*
   - *Unconsciousness*
2. Remove any visible berries, plant pieces or pills from the child's mouth. If the child is old enough to spit out, give him/her water to rinse out his/her mouth.
3. Give sips of cold water or milk to alleviate burning to the lips, mouth or throat.
4. Do not make the child sick as this may do more harm.
5. Find out what the child has taken and, if possible, how much they have taken.
6. **Call a doctor.**
7. If the child becomes unconscious, assess his/her airway, breathing and circulation (see ABC of resuscitation, page 343) and respond accordingly.
8. **Call an ambulance.**

DROWNING

Drowning causes asphyxia by water getting into the lungs. To help a drowning child, you must be safe. Drowning can also cause hypothermia, so a rescued child needs warming.

1. Carry the child out of the water with the head lower than the chest.
2. Get another adult to **call an ambulance.**
3. Don't bother trying to get water out of the lungs. The child will cough it out as she starts to breathe.

If the child is conscious:

1. Wrap her in dry clothes, coats or towels and get her to shelter. Then change her into dry clothes.
2. **Take her to hospital**. She might have inhaled some water, which may damage her lungs.

If the child is unconscious:

1. **Call an ambulance.**
2. Assess her airway, breathing and circulation (see ABC of resuscitation, page 343).

fig.24 Carry the child with the head lower than the chest

3. If she is breathing, lay her in the recovery position (see page 345). Remove her clothes and cover with a dry towel, coat or clothing. Be ready to start mouth-to-mouth ventilation.
4. If she is not breathing, start resuscitation (see page 343).
5. Monitor the child carefully until help arrives.

SHOCK

Shock can occur in a child as a result of severe bleeding (page 346), a serious burn (page 347) or scald (page 347). The injuries should be treated without delay.

1. **Watch for:**
   - *Pale, cold, sweaty skin*
   - *Rapid pulse, getting weaker*
   - *Shallow, fast breathing*

   As the child deteriorates:
   - *Restlessness, thirst*
   - *Nausea*
   - *Yawning*
   - *Unconsciousness*
   - *The heart stopping*

2. Reassure the child. Do not give him/her anything to eat or drink. Moisten the child's lips with water if she is thirsty, but do not allow her to drink.
3. Lay the child flat and support his/her legs above the level of the heart. Turn the child's head to one side (fig. 25).

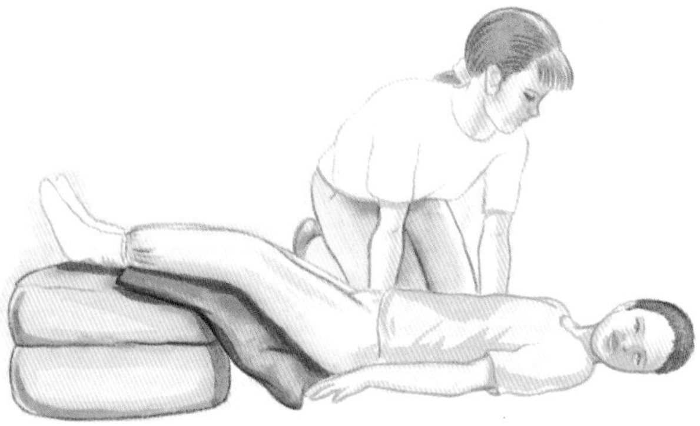

fig.25 Position for a child suffering from shock

4. Treat any obvious cause, such as bleeding.
5. Loosen clothing at the neck, chest and waist.
6. If possible get someone else to **call an ambulance.**
7. If the child is cold, cover her with a blanket/coat.
8. Do not use direct heat.
9. Stay with the child and reassure her constantly.
10. If the child loses consciousness, assess his/her airway, breathing and circulation (see ABC of resuscitation, page 343).
11. Resuscitate if necessary (see page 343).
12. If the child is breathing, place him/her in the recovery position (page 345).

ANAPHYLACTIC SHOCK

Anaphylaxis is an acute, severe allergic reaction requiring immediate medical attention. It can develop within minutes of the child coming into contact with the allergen.

1. **Watch for:**
   - *Anxiety*
   - *Swelling of the throat or tongue*
   - *Swelling around the face, eyes, neck*
   - *Blotchy, flushed skin*
   - *Difficulty swallowing or breathing*
2. **Call an ambulance immediately.**
3. If the child loses consciousness, check whether s/he is breathing. If s/he is, place him/her in the recovery position and monitor his/her pulse and breathing.
4. If the child is not breathing, resuscitate him/her (see ABC of resuscitation, page 343).
5. A child who has had one anaphylactic shock reaction is often prescribed a syringe ready-loaded with adrenaline. This should be given.

SMOKE INHALATION

Smoke inhalation most commonly occurs during house fires, when people are often overcome by fumes. Foam furniture and synthetic coverings give off toxic fumes, and these can quickly overcome a child.

1. Without putting yourself in danger, remove the child to fresh air as quickly as possible.
2. **Call an ambulance.**
3. Lay the child down. Open the airway by placing one hand on the forehead and two fingers of the other hand under the chin. Tilt the head back and lift the jaw. Watch the chest for breathing movements. Place your cheek near the nose and mouth to feel for breathing.
4. Place a child who is breathing in the recovery position (see page 345). If the child is not breathing, follow the steps for the ABC of resuscitation (page 343).

SPLINTERS

Splinters of wood or metal commonly get embedded in the skin, especially if the child walks barefoot on wooden floors.

1. Wash gently round the wound with soap and water.
2. If the end of the splinter is visible remove it with tweezers. Sterilize them by holding them in a match flame (fig. 26).

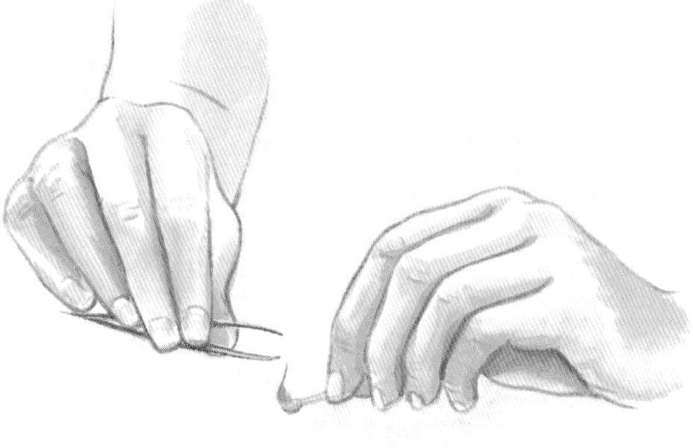

fig.26 Sterilize tweezers in a naked flame

Let the ends cool, but don't wipe off the black part. Holding the tweezers close to the skin, pull the splinter out.
3. Encourage the wound to bleed a little by squeezing it. This will wash out any remaining dirt.
4. Clean the wound again, dab dry and cover with a plaster.
5. If the splinter will not come out or if it breaks off, **take the child to the doctor.**

BLISTERS

Blisters form when the skin surface is rubbed or burned but not broken. Serum from the tissues gathers under the bubble of skin. New skin gradually reforms under the blister and the serum is reabsorbed into the tissues. The skin from the blister eventually peels off.
1. As a blister is a sterile environment, **do not burst it**. Pricking it introduces infection.
2. Clean the area around the blister with water and pat it dry.
3. If the blister is likely to be rubbed or broken, cover it with a non-adhesive dressing larger than the blister.
4. For a blister caused by a burn, see Burns (page 347).

STRANGULATION

Strangulation occurs when external pressure squeezes the airway shut.
1. Support the child's body if it is hanging.
2. Remove the restriction from the neck, cutting the child free if necessary (fig. 27).

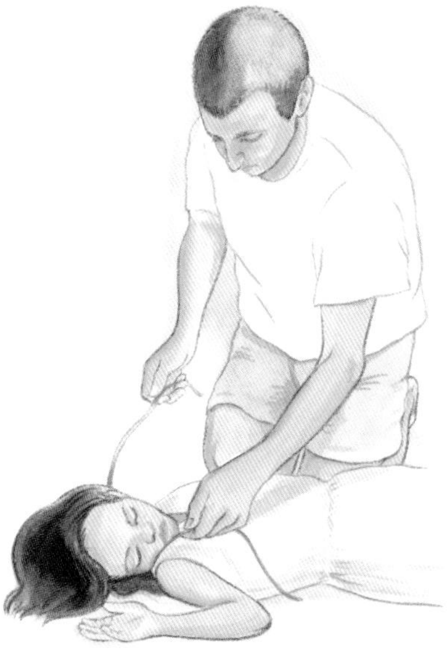

fig.27 Remove the restriction from the neck

3. Lay the child on her back. Put one hand on her forehead and two fingers of the other hand beneath her chin bone. Tilt her head back and lift the jaw.
4. Listen for breathing. Place your cheek near the child's nose and mouth to feel for breathing. Look down her chest for any breathing movements.
5. If the child is breathing, lay her in the recovery position (see page 345) and **call an ambulance.**
6. If the child is not breathing check her airway, breathing and circulation. Resuscitate (see page 343).
7. **For suffocation**: remove the object suffocating child. Follow from step 3, above.

SUNBURN

Despite the knowledge that sunburn in children increases the risk of skin cancer developing in adulthood, children and teenagers still get sunburned.
1. The skin becomes red and extremely sore. It may blister.
2. Cover the child immediately; move him/her into the shade.
3. Give him/her a drink of cool water.
4. Gently cool the reddened skin with cold water for ten minutes. Apply calamine lotion or an after-sun cream.
5. Dress in loose, soft clothing.
6. If the skin has blistered, **take advice from your doctor.**

HEAT EXHAUSTION AND HEAT STROKE

A child who has been in strong sunshine for too long or who has overexerted him/herself can lose so much water from the body that his/her temperature rises; s/he feels dizzy, and develops a headache and nausea; and his/her skin becomes clammy and pale. The pulse will become weak and very fast.
1. Move the child somewhere cool and shady.
2. Lay him/her down with his/her feet slightly raised and make sure s/he is cool.
3. Give him/her a drink of water, juice or oral rehydrating drink.
4. If the child is not better within an hour, **contact a doctor.**
5. If the child's condition gets worse **call an ambulance.**
6. If the child's skin feels hot and dry, s/he could be suffering from heatstroke. Remove his/her clothing and sponge him/her with tepid water to cool him/her down.
7. **Call an ambulance.**

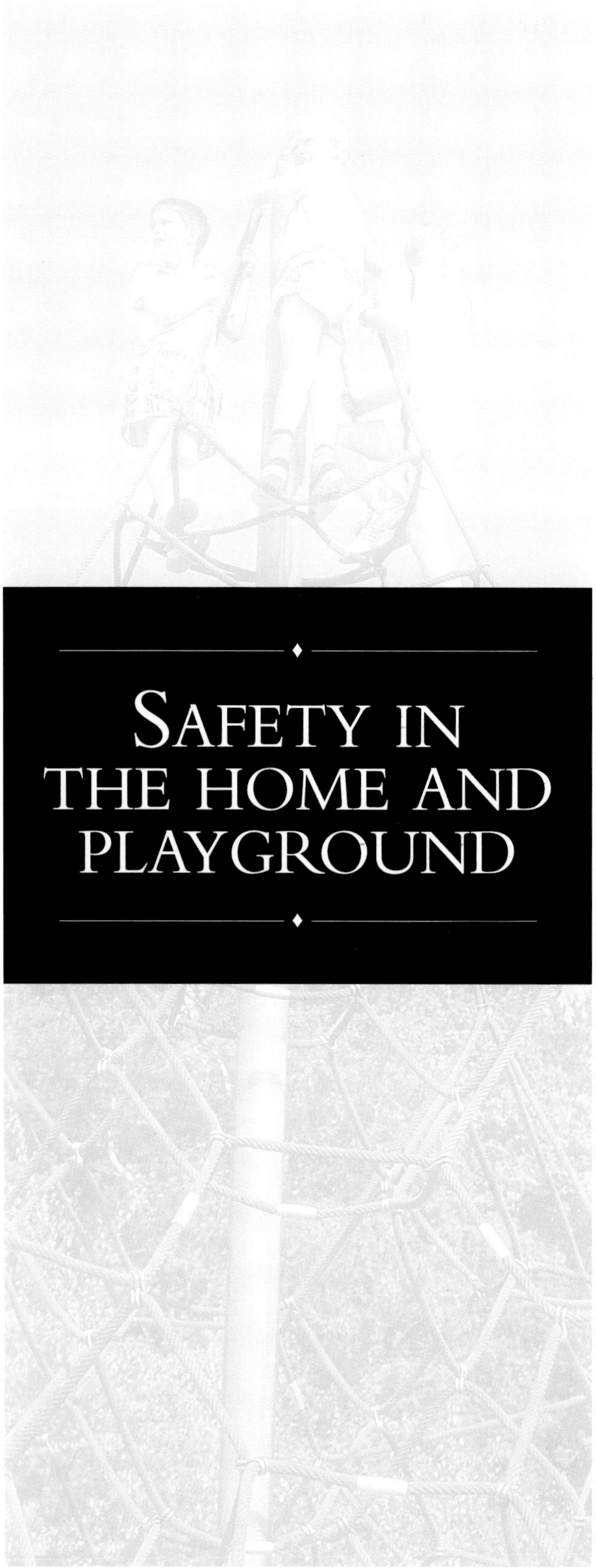

SAFETY IN THE HOME AND PLAYGROUND

It is unwise, not to say potentially dangerous, to bring a child into a home where no thought has been given to the child's safety. Parents, and others who frequently have children in their homes as guests, should be constantly aware of the dangers to which children can fall victim. The safety notes given here and on the following pages can and should be used as a guide to check and improve the safety of your home.

Safety in all rooms

- Fix socket covers on all electric sockets
- Don't use cords on blinds or curtains
- Fix trailing flexes to the wall with cable retainers
- Make sure carpets are not frayed and don't have holes. Fix non-slip webbing under loose rugs
- Fix smoke detectors
- Keep toys tidied away in boxes
- Keep all medicines in child resistant containers

Accidents to children

Accidents among children are frequently minor – but serious incidents do occur. A key target of the United Kingdom's Health of the Nation strategy is to cut by one-third fatalities from accidents to children by the year 2000. In young children accidents usually happen at home. The type of accident is often related to the child's age, with young children frequently one step ahead of their expected abilities. While many aspects of home safety depend on parents being reasonably vigilant, others require equipment that can be expensive and difficult to install. In some areas parents have access to free distribution of safety devices, so always ask your health visitor or family doctor first. In addition, over one million children are injured annually away from home in parks, playgrounds and while using sporting facilities.

Safety considerations are as important in the choice of children's toys as they are in children's environments. Among other things, babies should never be given anything to play with that is small enough to go into their mouth.

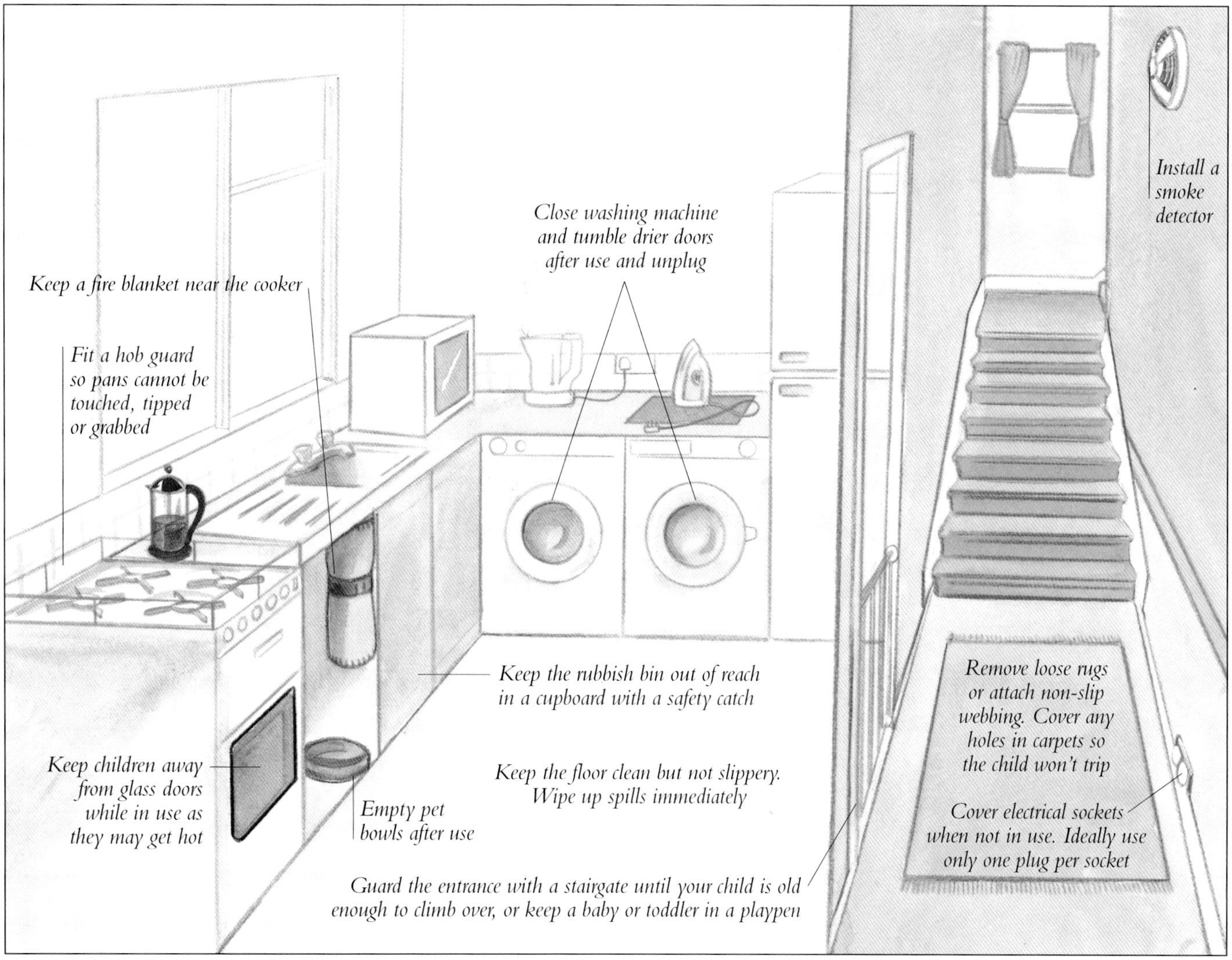
Install a smoke detector
Close washing machine and tumble drier doors after use and unplug
Keep a fire blanket near the cooker
Fit a hob guard so pans cannot be touched, tipped or grabbed
Keep the rubbish bin out of reach in a cupboard with a safety catch
Remove loose rugs or attach non-slip webbing. Cover any holes in carpets so the child won't trip
Keep children away from glass doors while in use as they may get hot
Keep the floor clean but not slippery. Wipe up spills immediately
Empty pet bowls after use
Cover electrical sockets when not in use. Ideally use only one plug per socket
Guard the entrance with a stairgate until your child is old enough to climb over, or keep a baby or toddler in a playpen

SAFETY IN THE KITCHEN

For a young child the kitchen is the most dangerous room in the house. It is full of exciting but hazardous possibilities, and parents may be too busy preparing meals or doing other chores to keep a close eye on what is happening. It is safest to keep a toddler outside the kitchen altogether, but if you allow a child in, don't let them sit on the floor between you and the work surfaces, and don't allow them to spread toys over the floor where you may trip over them.

Use the back rings of a cooker if possible and keep pan handles turned inwards so they cannot be grabbed. Keep children away from oven doors, which can get hot enough to burn.

Don't allow children under the age of eight to use a microwave on their own. However use your judgement about your own child's maturity; it is too easy to put in a metal container by mistake. Other containers can be surprisingly hot and so can microwaved food that is eaten without standing or stirring it first.

Use a cordless kettle or one with a short or curly flex. Empty spare hot water after boiling. Turn off and unplug the iron after use. Leave to cool well out of reach. Store at the back of the work surfaces, and never leave a trailing flex.

Keep hot liquids out of reach at the back of work surfaces. A hot drink will remain at a scalding temperature for 30 minutes after it has been poured. Never have a drink with a child on your lap. Use mugs, not cups.

Keep all heavy or breakable objects at the back of the work surfaces. Fix child resistant safety catches to prevent children gaining access to sharp knives, mixer blades, matches, cleaning materials, fridge and freezer. Don't store medicines in the fridge, and keep a lock on a chest freezer.

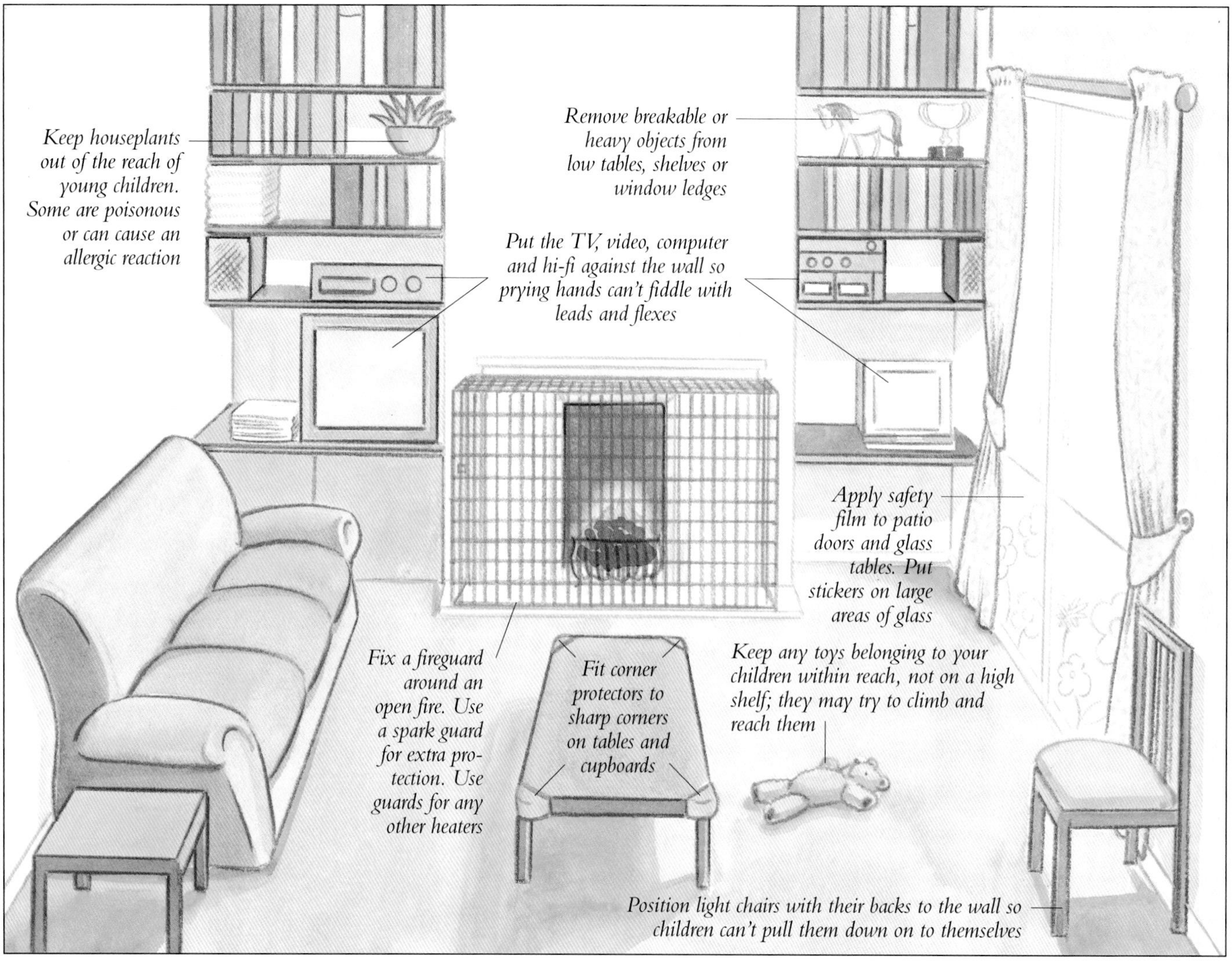

Keep houseplants out of the reach of young children. Some are poisonous or can cause an allergic reaction
Remove breakable or heavy objects from low tables, shelves or window ledges
Put the TV, video, computer and hi-fi against the wall so prying hands can't fiddle with leads and flexes
Apply safety film to patio doors and glass tables. Put stickers on large areas of glass
Fix a fireguard around an open fire. Use a spark guard for extra protection. Use guards for any other heaters
Fit corner protectors to sharp corners on tables and cupboards
Keep any toys belonging to your children within reach, not on a high shelf; they may try to climb and reach them
Position light chairs with their backs to the wall so children can't pull them down on to themselves

SAFETY IN THE SITTING ROOM

Before a baby becomes mobile, put away valuables and breakables. This is a room where you want to relax, not be constantly worrying whether the baby is destroying family heirlooms and irreplaceable software.

Run flexes behind furniture and fix along skirting boards. Where there are several flexes together, run them in a plastic tunnel. Use a video guard to prevent a young child sticking their hand into the cassette cavity. Tuck away curtain cords and blind pulls that could entangle or even strangle a child. Make sure that curtains and upholstery are made from flame retardant material.

Remove any tablecloths and use mats instead. Children can pull the tablecloth and the entire contents of the table on top of themselves. Lock all bottles of alcohol away. Never leave hot drinks, glasses or alcohol within reach on a coffee table, low shelf or television.

Never leave a young child alone in a room with a fire.

Don't assume that your child can't climb; the chances are that if they are inquisitive enough they will view shelves or tables and chairs as a challenge to their ingenuity. If the child is still most mobile close to the ground, make certain that your floor is clear of small objects that they will otherwise 'hoover up' and try out for taste.

The greatest single danger in the sitting room is heating devices. Even radiators can burn, so use room thermostats to control the temperature. Shield children from solid fuel, wood burning stoves, electric and even decorative gas fires with a fireguard. Turn off the electricity supply of an electric fire and remove the plug when not in use. Fires kill more children in the home than any other single hazard.

Fix a safety catch to the window, but make sure it can be opened in case of fire
Keep lights away from curtains or bedding in case they catch fire
Fit a pluglight, nursery light or dimmer switch so you can check on the children without waking them
Keep a thermometer in a baby's room to make sure the temperature stays around 18°C /65°F
Keep the space below the window free of furniture so the child cannot climb to the window. If you have sash windows, fix the bottom one in the closed position
Install a listening device.
Don't let children play on top bunks or use the structure as a climbing frame. Make sure the child on the top bunk is not too close to wall or ceiling lights
Changing a baby on the floor is safest as the baby can roll off a changing table or bed if you turn away for a second

SAFETY IN THE BEDROOM

The bedroom is probably the only room where babies spend time alone. It is also where they spend much of their time when they are young, so as soon as they become mobile, safety becomes all-important. In other people's bedrooms, make sure cosmetics, pills (including vitamin pills and contraceptives), perfume, deodorant or hairsprays are kept in a drawer (ideally, locked) well out of reach.

A baby's cot must be deep enough to stop a baby climbing out. There should be a space of at least 50 cm/20 in from the top of the mattress to the top of the cot; the gap between the cot and the mattress edge should be no more than 3 cm/1⅛ in. The spaces between the bars should be no more than 6 cm/2¼ in wide so the baby's head cannot get stuck. Make sure the clasps on the dropside are strong enough to resist inquisitive hands. If you use a cot bumper, keep the ties short, so the baby can't twist them around their fingers.

Once the baby can sit up, remove the bumper and any large toys they could use to try to climb out. Any mattress or bedding cover must be made of breathable fabric in case the baby's head gets trapped inside. Never use a pillow for a baby under the age of 12 months because of the possibility of suffocation. Instead of a duvet, which babies could kick over their face, or become overheated underneath, use a sheet and cellular blankets. Once a child has tried to climb out, move them to a bed with a side guard or take off a removable cot side to create a three-sided bed.

Children under six years of age should sleep in a bed or on a bottom bunk. Top bunks must have safety rails on both sides. The gap between the bottom of the rail and the mattress must be no more than 6-7.5 cm /2¼-3 in.

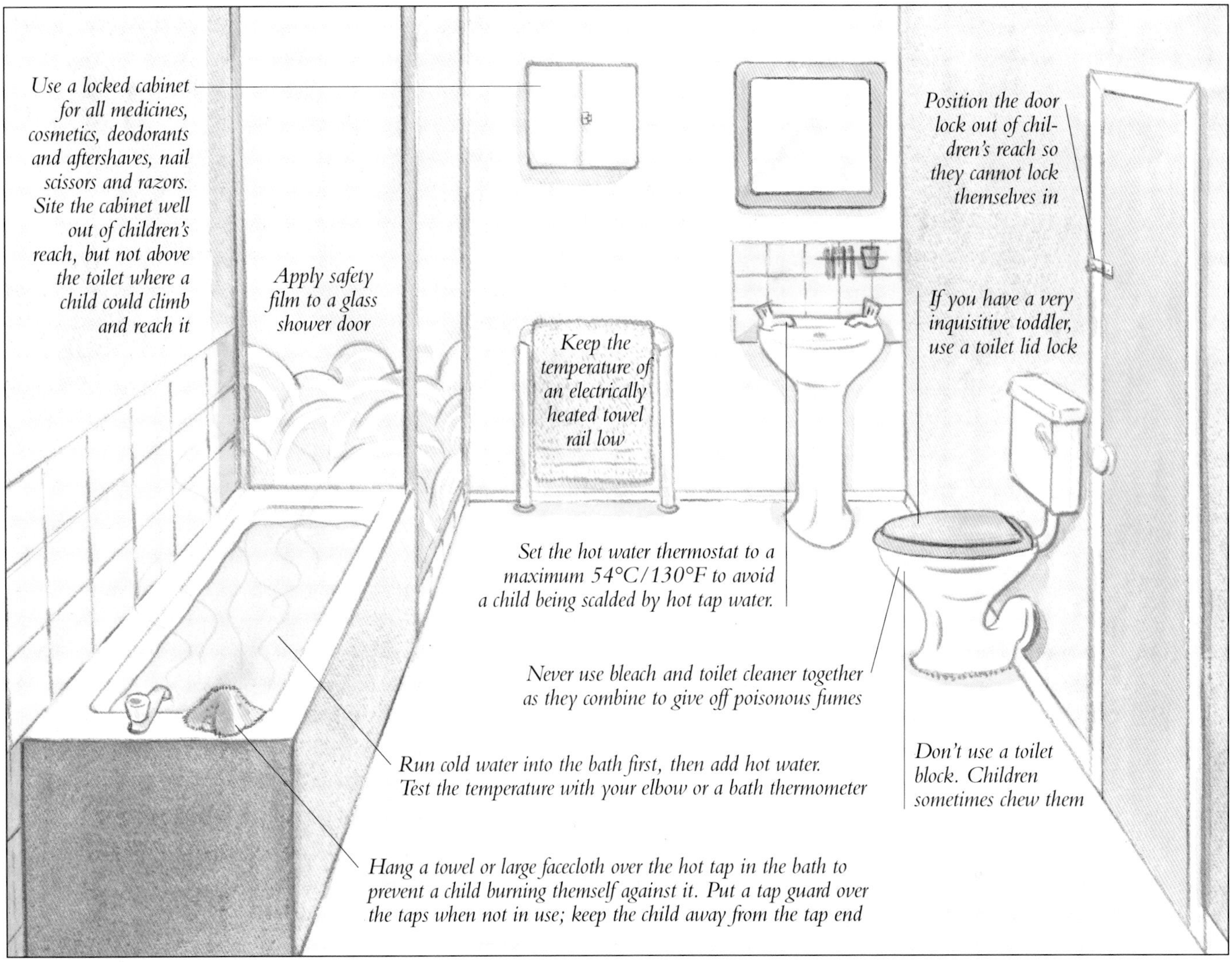
Use a locked cabinet for all medicines, cosmetics, deodorants and aftershaves, nail scissors and razors. Site the cabinet well out of children's reach, but not above the toilet where a child could climb and reach it
Apply safety film to a glass shower door
Keep the temperature of an electrically heated towel rail low
Position the door lock out of children's reach so they cannot lock themselves in
If you have a very inquisitive toddler, use a toilet lid lock
Set the hot water thermostat to a maximum 54°C/130°F to avoid a child being scalded by hot tap water.
Never use bleach and toilet cleaner together as they combine to give off poisonous fumes
Run cold water into the bath first, then add hot water. Test the temperature with your elbow or a bath thermometer
Don't use a toilet block. Children sometimes chew them
Hang a towel or large facecloth over the hot tap in the bath to prevent a child burning themself against it. Put a tap guard over the taps when not in use; keep the child away from the tap end

SAFETY IN THE BATHROOM

To a child, the bathroom is an exciting and dangerous place – doubly so if they are not allowed to play in there alone. Water is fun, but all wet surfaces are slippery and hot water scalds. Young children can drown in minutes in only a couple of centimetres of water.

Playing with cosmetics is also appealing to a child, but aftershaves and perfumes are poisonous, as are bathroom cleaning materials.

Children who know they are playing forbidden games are more than capable of locking themselves in, so keep the bathroom door shut as a discouragement.

Don't allow children to walk around with a toothbrush in the mouth; they may slip, and it may cause a very painful cut.

The bathroom is one of the most hazardous rooms in the home for small children. Babies and toddlers should never be left unattended in a bathroom, and even when an adult is present safety precautions should always be uppermost in the mind.

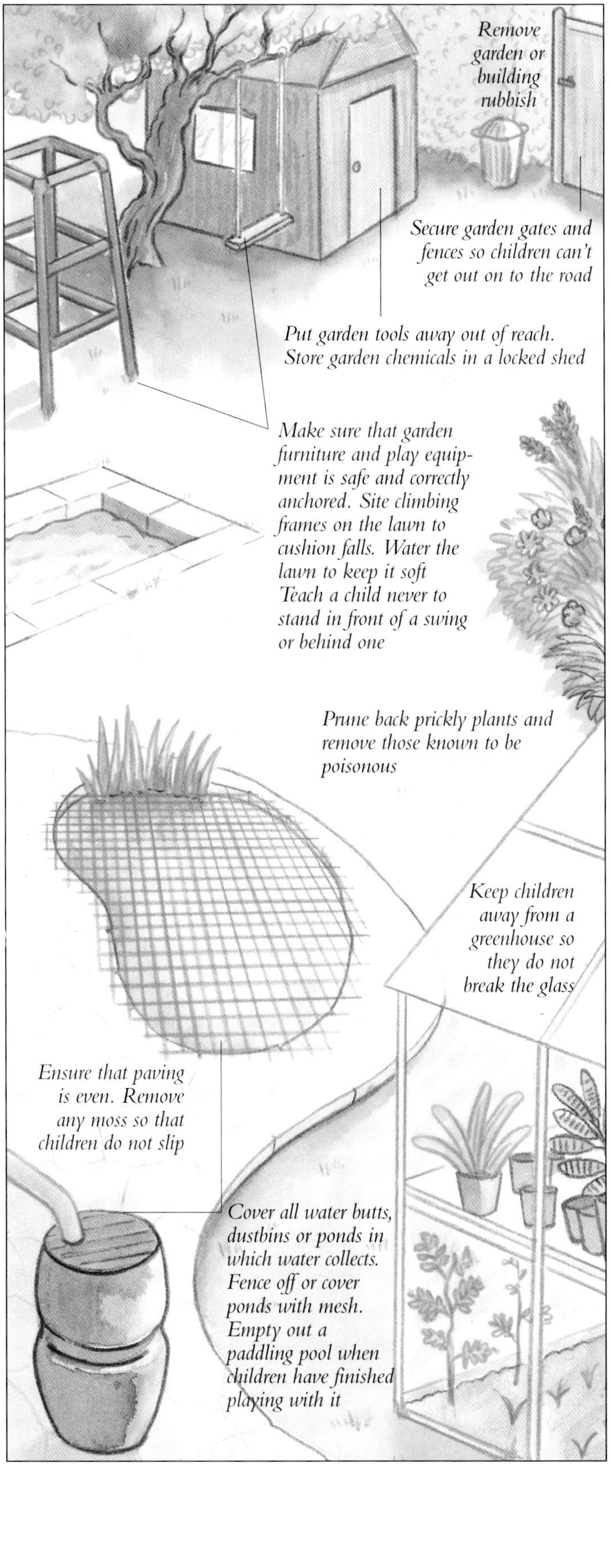

Remove garden or building rubbish
Secure garden gates and fences so children can't get out on to the road
Put garden tools away out of reach. Store garden chemicals in a locked shed
Make sure that garden furniture and play equipment is safe and correctly anchored. Site climbing frames on the lawn to cushion falls. Water the lawn to keep it soft Teach a child never to stand in front of a swing or behind one
Prune back prickly plants and remove those known to be poisonous
Keep children away from a greenhouse so they do not break the glass
Ensure that paving is even. Remove any moss so that children do not slip
Cover all water butts, dustbins or ponds in which water collects. Fence off or cover ponds with mesh. Empty out a paddling pool when children have finished playing with it

GARDEN AND PLAYGROUND SAFETY

Gardens and playgrounds are exciting places for children to play. Of course they are also hazardous, particularly for children of school age, who have more mishaps and accidents outside and in the garage than in any one room in the house. It is unrealistic and unreasonable to try to think of every possible hazard that could befall children outside and to protect them from injury. However taking sensible precautions and teaching basic outdoor safety rules from the start allows children to gain confidence and allows parents to build up trust.

In the playground, do not allow older children to play in a toddler area.

Make sure a child who is roller-skating, roller-blading or skate-boarding wears protective elbow and knee pads and, if appropriate, a helmet.

Do not allow a young child to climb out of reach on a climbing frame.

Never encourage a child to undertake something that scares them, such as coming down a very high slide. Never allow children to stand upright on slides.

Public playgrounds

Before letting your child use a public playground, check that it is free of dog mess, glass and litter. Ensure that it is fenced off from the roads and car parks, and that the gate is wide enough to get a pushchair through. The surface should be even, with equipment sited on impact-absorbent materials and well-spaced so that children don't collide and hurt themselves. Teach your child never to throw sand or bark chip; both materials can damage the eyes.

Many playgrounds designed for children are made unsuitable by poor maintenance and vandalism. contact other disgruntled parents and complain to your local authority.

An adventure playground provides children with many opportunities for exploration and imaginative play. However play should always be supervized by an adult – either a trained attendent or the child's parent.

DIRECTORY

The directory contains useful addresses and, where possible, telephone numbers for organizations and agencies offering help, advice and support in the various fields of child health. Also included is information on how to find qualified and experienced complementary practitioners, together with the addresses of their official regulating bodies or centres of study. Organizations and agencies in Australia and New Zealand are listed on pages 370-371. Although every effort has been made to check the addresses before publication, the publishers cannot accept responsibility for associations who have changed their address or phone number in recent months.

INFANT HEALTH

BONDING

BLISS
17–21 Emerald Street
London WC1N 3QL
Tel 0171 831 9393
Helpline 0500 618140

SUDDEN INFANT DEATH SYNDROME

Foundation for the Study of Infant Deaths
14 Halkin Street
London SW1X 7DP
Tel 0171 235 0965
Helpline 0171 235 1721

CHILDREN OF MULTIPLE BIRTHS

Multiple Births Foundation
Queen Charlotte's and Chelsea Hospital
Goldhawk Road
London W6 0XG
Tel 0181 383 3519

Twins and Multiple Births Foundation
PO Box 30
Little Sutton
South Wirral L66 1TH
Tel 0151 348 0020
Helpline 01732 868000

CHILD HEALTH

ROAD SAFETY

Royal Society for the Prevention of Accidents
Edgbaston Road
353 Bristol Road
Birmingham B5 7ST
Tel 0121 248 2000

VEGETARIAN CHILDREN

The Vegetarian Society
Parkdale
Dunham Road
Altrincham
Cheshire WA14 4QG

HEALTHY EATING

The publication *Eight Guidelines for a Healthy Diet* is published by, and can be obtained from, the Department of Health, Health Education Authority, The University of Agriculture, Food Sense, London.

TEENAGE HEALTH

EXERCISE AND SPORT

English Sports Council
16 Upper Woburn Place
London WC1H 0QP
Tel 0171 273 1500

DRUG AND SUBSTANCE ABUSE

For families and friends of drug users:
ADFAM
Waterbridge House
32–36 Loman Street
London SE1 0EE
Helpline 0171 928 8900

For parents of drug users:
Families Anonymous
Tel 0171 498 4680

National Drugs Helpline
Tel 0800 776600

TEENAGE SEXUALITY

British Pregnancy Advisory Service
Austy Manor
Wootton Wawen
Solihull West Midlands B95 6BX
Tel 01564 793225
Helpline 0345 304030

Brook Advisory Centre
165 Grays Inn Road
London WC1X 8UD
Tel 0171–833 8488
Helpline (office hours) 0171 713 9000; (24-hour computerized information) 0171 617 8000

Family Planning Association
2–12 Pentonville Road
London N1 9FP
Tel 0171 837 5432
Helpline 0171 837 4044

SMOKING

QUIT
Victory House
170 Tottenham Court Road
London W1P 0HA
Tel 0171 388 5775
Quitline 0800 002200

ALCOHOL

Drinkline Youth
Tel 0345 320202

COMPLEMENTARY MEDICINE

How to find a qualified practitioner:
The British Register of Complementary Practitioners, administered by The Institute of Complementary Medicine (ICM), holds lists of qualified practitioners.

British Register of Complementary Practitioners
PO Box 194
London SE16 1QZ

Further information about complementary medicine can be obtained from the ICM at the address above. Alternatively, contact any of the organizations and associations listed below.

HOMEOPATHY

For medical doctors who are also qualified homeopaths:

British Homeopathy Association
27A Devonshire Street
London WC1N 1RJ
Tel 0171 935 2163

For a list of qualified homeopaths who are not doctors send a large sae to:
Society of Homeopaths
2 Artizan Road
Northampton NN1 4HU
Tel 01604 21400

BACH FLOWER REMEDIES

The Dr Edward Bach Centre
Mount Vernon
Bakers Lane
Sotwell
Wallingford
Oxfordshire O10 0PZ
Tel 01491 834867

To contact other practitioners who use the Bach flower remedies, contact the British Register of Complementary Practitioners.

AROMATHERAPY

Aromatherapy Organisations Council
3 Latymer Close
Braybrooke
Market Harborough
Leicester LE16 8LN
Tel 0185 434243

International Federation of Aromatherapists
Stamford House
2-4 Chiswick High Road
London W4 1TH
Tel 0181 742 2605

NUTRITIONAL THERAPY

The Society for the Promotion of Nutritional Therapy
PO Box 47
Heathfield
East Sussex TN21 8ZN
Tel 01435 8670007

Institute for Optimum Nutrition
Blades Court
Deodar Road
London SW15 2NU
Tel 0181 877 9993

OSTEOPATHY

Osteopathic Information Service
PO Box 2074
Reading
Berkshire RG1 4YR
Tel 01491 875255

Osteopathic Centre for Children
4 Harcourt House
19a Cavendish Square
London W1M 9AD
Tel 0171 495 1231

CHIROPRACTIC

British Chiropractic Association
Equity House
29 Whitley Street
Reading
Tel 01734 757557

REFLEXOLOGY

Association of Reflexologists
Flat 6
Sillwood Mansion
Sillwood Place
Brighton BN1 2LH
Tel 01273 771061

WESTERN HERBALISM

National Institute of Medical Herbalists
56 Longbrooke Street
Exeter EX4 8HA
Tel 01393 426022

MASSAGE

British Massage Therapy Council
Greenbank House
65a Adelphi Street
Preston PR1 7BH
Tel 01772 881063

APPLIED KINESIOLOGY

Association of Systematic Kinesiology
The Secretary
A S K
39 Browns Road
Surbiton
Surrey KT 8ST
Tel 0181 399 3215

RELAXATION

British Register of Complementary Practitioners
PO Box 194
London SE16 1QZ

ARTS THERAPIES

Association for Dance Movement Therapy
c/o Arts Therapies Department
Springfield Hospital
61 Glenburnie Road
London SW17 7DJ
Tel 0181 672 9911

British Association of Art Therapists
11a Richmond Road
Brighton BN2 3RL

British Association of Dramatherapists
The Secretary
The Old Mill
Tolpuddle
Dorchester
Dorset DT2 7EX

Association of Professional Music Therapists
The Administrator
Chestnut Cottage
38 Pierce Lane
Fulbourn
Cambridge CB1 5DL
Tel 01223 880377

PLAY THERAPY

Qualified play therapists have undergone a two-year course and are registered with the British Association of Play Therapists, who offer training and have a published code of ethics on conduct.

British Association of Play Therapists
PO Box 98
Amersham
Buckinghamshire HP6 5BL

ACUPUNCTURE

For qualified acupuncturists specializing in the treatment of children, contact the British Register of Complementary Practitioners or any of the following:

British Acupuncture Association and Registrar
34 Alderney Street
London SW1V 4EU
Tel 0171 834 1012

British Medical Acupuncture Society
Newton House
Newton Lance
Lower Whitley
Warrington
Cheshire WA4 4JA
Tel 01925 730727

Council for Acupuncture
10 Panther House
38 Mount Pleasant
London WC1X 0AN

CHINESE HERBALISM

Register of Chinese Herbal Medicine
PO Box 400
Wembley
Middlesex HA9 9NE
Tel 0181 904 1357

TAI CHI/CHI KUNG

Tai Chi Union for Great Britain
102 Felsham Road
London SW15 1DO
Tel 0181 352 7716

GROWTH

Child Growth Foundation
2 Mayfield Avenue
London W4 1PW
Tel 0181 994 7625

Cranio-facial Support Group
Trem Hafren
Earlswood
Chepstow
Gwent NP6 6AN
0129-1641547

Failure to Thrive Consultancy
3/4 New Road
Chippenham
Wiltshire SN15 1EJ
Tel 01249 446436

Marfan Association
Diane Rust
6 Queen's Road
Farnborough
Hampshire GU14 6DH
Tel 01252 810472/617320

Microcephaly Support Group
43 Randall Road
Kingsley
Northampton NN2 7DJ
Tel 01604 722407

Restricted Growth Association
PO Box 8
Countesthorpe
Leicester LE8 5ZS
Tel 0116 247 8913

The Turner Society
Child Growth Foundation
2 Mayfield Avenue
London W4 1PW
Tel 0181 994 7625/995 0257

COMMON AILMENTS

INFECTIONS

Children with AIDS
2nd Floor
111 High Holborn
London WC1V 6JS
Tel 0171 242 3883
24-hour AIDS helpline 0800 567123

Malaria Information Line
Tel 0891 600350

SENSE
11–13 Clifton Terrace
London N4 3SR
Tel 0171 272 7774

Toxocara Information:
Community Hygiene Concern
160 Inderwick Road
London N8 9JT
Helpline 0181 341 7167

BRAIN, NERVES AND MUSCLES

Action for ME
PO Box 1302
Wells BA5 2WE
Tel (office hours) 01749 670799;
(24-hour information line) 0891 122976

Association for Spina Bifida and Hydrocephalus
42 Park Road
Peterborough PE1 2UQ
Tel 01733 555988

British Epilepsy Association
Anstey House
40 Hanover Square
Leeds LS3 1BE
Tel 01132 439393
Helpline 0800 309030

British Migraine Association
178a High Road
West Byfleet
Surrey KT14 7ED
Tel 01932 352468

Dyspraxia Foundation
8 West Alley
Hitchin
Hertfordshire SG5 1ED
Tel 01462 454986

Encephalitis Support Group
Pasture House
Normanby
Sinnington, York YO6 6RH
Tel 01751 433318

ME Association
Stanhope House
High Street
Stanford-le-Hope
Essex SS 17 0HA
Tel 01375 642466
Information line 01375 361013

Meningitis Research
Old Gloucester Road
Alveston
Bristol BS12 2LQ
Tel (office hours) 01454 282822; (24-hour helpline) 01454 413344

Migraine Trust
45 Great Ormond Street
London WC1N 3HZ
Tel 0171 831 4818

Muscular Dystrophy Group
7–11 Prescott Place
London SW4 6BS
Tel 0171 720 8055

National Meningitis Trust
Fern House
Bath Road
Stroud
Gloucester GL5 3TJ
Tel (office hours) 01453 751738; (24-hour supportline) 0345-538118

National Society for Epilepsy
Chalfont Centre
Chalfont St Peter
Gerrards Cross
Bucks SL9 0RJ

Scope (formerly Spastics Society)
12 Park Crescent
London W1N 4EQ
Tel 0171 636 5020
Helpline 0800 626216

BONES AND JOINTS

Children's Chronic Arthritis Association
47 Battenhall Avenue
Worcester WR5 2HH
Tel 01905 163556

Lady Hoare Trust for Physically Disabled Children
Mitre House
44–46 Fleet Street
London EC4Y 1BN
Tel 0171 377 7567

Perthes' Association
42 Woodlands Road
Guildford
Surrey GU1 1RW
Tel 01483 306637

REACH
12 Wilson Way
Earls Barton
Northamptonshire NN6 0NZ
Tel 01604 811041

Scoliosis Association UK
2 Ivebury Court
325 Latimer Road
London W10 6RA
Tel 0181 964 5343

STEPS
Lymm Court
11 Eagle Brow
Lymm
Cheshire WA13 0LP
Tel 01925 757525

Young Arthritis Care
18 Stephenson Way
London NW1 2HD
Tel 0171 916 1500

HORMONES AND GLANDS

British Diabetic Association
10 Queen Anne Street
London W1M 0BD
Tel 0171 323 1531

Hypothyroidism Support Group
47 Crawford Avenue
Tyldesley
Manchester M29 8ET
Tel 01942 874740

SKIN, HAIR AND NAILS

Acne Support Group
PO Box 230
Hayes
Middlesex UB4 0UT

Action against Allergy
PO Box 278
Twickenham TW1 4QQ
Tel 0181 561 6868

For camouflage:
British Red Cross Society
9 Grosvenor Crescent
London SW1X 7EJ
Tel 0171 235 5454

For Bug Buster Kit for the treatment of headlice:
Headlice
Community Hygiene Concern
160 Inderwick Road
London N8 9JT
Tel 0181 341 7167

Naevus Support Group
58 Necton Road
Wheathampstead
Hertfordshire AL4 8AU
Tel 01582 832853

National Eczema Society
163 Eversholt Street
London NW1 1BU
Helpline 0171 388 4800

Psoriasis Association
7 Milton Street
Northampton NN2 7JG
Tel 01604 711129

EYES

Royal National Institute for the Blind
224 Great Portland Street
London W1N 6AA
Tel 0171 388 1266

EARS, NOSE, THROAT AND RESPIRATION

Cystic Fibrosis Research Trust
Alexandra House
5 Blyth Road
Bromley
Kent BR1 3RS
Tel 0181 464 7211

Defeating Deafness (Hearing Research Trust)
330–332 Gray's Inn Road
London WC1X 8EE
Tel 0171 833 1733

DELTA (Deaf Education through Listening and Talking)
PO Box 20
Haverhill
Suffolk CB9 7BD
Tel 01440 783689

National Asthma Campaign
Providence House
Providence Place
London N1 0NT
Helpline 0345 010203 (Mon–Fri 9am–9pm)

National Deaf Children's Society
15 Dufferin Street
London EC1Y 8PD
Tel 0171 250 0123
Helpline 0800 252389 (2pm–5pm)

MOUTH AND TEETH

CLAPA
(The Cleft Lip and Palate Association)
134 Buckingham Palace Road
London SW1W 9SA
0171 824 8110

FEEDING AND DIGESTION

British Allergy Foundation
Deepdene House
30 Bellegrove Road
Welling
Kent DA16 3PY
Tel 0181 303 8525
Helpline 0181 303 8583

British Digestive Foundation
3 St Andrew's Place
London NW1 4LB
Tel 0171 486 0341

Children's Liver Disease Foundation
138 Digbeth
Birmingham B5 6DR
Tel 0121 643 7282

Coeliac Society
PO Box 220
High Wycombe
Buckinghamshire HP11 2HY
Tel 01494 437278

Crohn's in Childhood Research Association
Parkgate House
356 West Barnes Lane
Motspur Park
Surrey KT3 6NB
0181 949 6209

Eating Disorders Association
103 Prince of Wales Road
Norwich
Norfolk NR1 1DW
Tel 01603 621414
Youth helpline 01603 765050 (Mon–Fri 4pm–6pm)

Galactosaemia Support Group
31 Cotysmore Road
Sutton Coldfield
West Midlands B75 6BJ
Tel 0121 378 5143

National Association for Colitis & Crohn's Disease
4 Beaumont House Sutton Road
St Albans
Hertfordshire AL1 5HH
01727 844296

National Society for Phenylketonuria
7 Southfield Close
Willen
Milton Keynes MK15 9LL
Tel 01908 691653

Research Trust for Metabolic Diseases in Children
Golden Gates Lodge
Weston Road
Crewe
Cheshire CW2 5XN
Tel 01270 588815
Helpline 01270 250221

For colic:
Serene
London WC1N 3XX
Cry-sis helpline 0171 404-5011

HEART, BLOOD AND CIRCULATION

Association for Children with Heart Disorders
26 Elizabeth Drive
Helmsmore
Rossendale
Lancs BB4 4JB
Tel 01706 213632

Association of Children with Heart Disorders
Killieard House
Killiecrankie
Perthshire PH16 5LN
Tel 01796 473204

British Heart Foundation
14 Fitzhardinge Street
London W1H 4DH
Tel 0171 935 0185

Cancer and Leukaemia in Childhood
12/13 King Square
Bristol BS2 8JH
Tel 0117 924844

Children's Heart Federation
115 Gloucester Place
London W1H 3PJ
Tel 0171 935 4737

Haemophilia Society
123 Westminster Bridge Road
London SE1 7HR
Tel 0171 928 2020

Heartline Association
Rossmore House
26 Park Street
Camberley
Surrey GU15 3PL
Tel 01276 675655

Leukaemia Care Society
14 Kingfisher Court
Venny Bridge
Pinhoe
Exeter EX4 8JN
Tel 01392 464848

Leukaemia Research Fund
43 Great Ormond Street
London WC1N 3JJ
Tel 0171 405 0101

Sickle Cell Society
54 Station Road
London NW10 4UA
Tel 0181 961 7795

UK Thalassaemia Society
19 The Broadway
London N14 6PH
Tel 0181 882 0011

GENITAL, URINARY AND KIDNEYS

British Kidney Patient Association
Bordon
Hants
Tel 01420 472021/2

ERIC
34 Old School House
Britannia Road
Kingswood
Bristol BS15 2DB
Tel 01179 603060

Hic-Ups (Hypospadias Information Centre)
PO Box 2132
Wells
Somerset BA5 2WE
Tel 01179 432563

HUSH (Haemolytic Uraemic Syndrome)
c/o Howe & Co
Tel 0181 840 4688

National Kidney Research Fund and the Kidney Foundation
3 Archers Court
Stukeley Road
Huntingdon
Cambs PE18 6XG
Tel 01480 454828

Toxic Shock Syndrome Information Service
24–28 Bloomsbury Way
London WC1A 2PX
Advice line 0171 617 8040

STAGES OF DEVELOPMENT

Exploring Parenthood
4 Ivory Place
20A Treadgold Street
London W11 4BP
Tel 0171 221 4471
Advice line 0171 221 6681 (10am–2pm)

SPEECH AND LANGUAGE

British Stammering Association
16 Old Ford Road
London E2 9PJ
Tel 0181 983 1003

LEARNING DIFFICULTIES

ADD/ADHD Family Support Group
1a High Street
Dilton
Westbury
Wiltshire BA13 4DL
Tel 01373 826045

AFASIC
347 Central Markets
London EC1A 9NH
Tel 9171 236 3632

British Dyslexia Association
98 London Road
Reading
Berks RG1 5AU
Tel 01189 662677
Helpline 0990 134248

CHILD DEVELOPMENT

Down's Syndrome Association
155 Mitcham Road
London SW17 9PG
Tel 0181 682 4001

Fragile X Society
53 Winchelsea Lane
Hastings
East Sussex TN35 4LG
Tel 01424 813147

Genetic Interest Group
Farringdon Point
29–35 Farringdon Road
London EC1M 3JB
Tel 9171 430 0090

Hyperactive Children's Support Group
71 Whyke Lane
Chichester
Sussex PO19 2LD
Tel 01903 725182

KIDSCAPE
152 Buckingham Palace Road
London SW1W 9TR
Tel 0171 730 3300

LADDER
PO Box 700
Wolverhampton WV3 7YY
Tel 01902 336272

National Autistic Society
393 City Road
London EC1V 1NE
Tel 0171 833 2299

Parent Network
44–46 Caversham Road
London NW5 2DS
Tel 0171 735 1214

Young Minds
102–108 Clerkenwell Road
London EC1M 5SA
Tel 0171 336 8445
Parents information service 0345 626376

THE SCHOOL YEARS

ChildLine
Tel 0800 1111

The Samaritans
Tel 0345 909090

THE CHILD IN HOSPITAL

Action for Sick Children
Argyle House
29–31 Euston Road
London NW1 2SD
Tel 0171 833 2041

Association for Children with Life Threatening or Terminal Conditions and their Families
65 St Michael's Hill
Bristol BS2 8DZ
Tel 01179 221556

Contact A Family
170 Tottenham Court Road
London W1P 0HA
Tel 0171 383 3555

In Touch Trust
10 Norman Road
Sale Cheshire M33 3DF
Tel 0161 962 4441
(This organization acts as an umbrella group for associations for rare diseases)

FIRST AID AND SAFETY

FIRST AID

Anaphylaxis Campaign
PO Box 149
Fleet
Hampshire GU13 9XU

SAFETY IN THE HOME AND GARDEN

Child Accident Prevention Trust
Clerks Court
18 Farringdon Lane
London EC1R 3AU
Tel 0171 608 3828

USEFUL ADDRESSES AUSTRALIA

GENERAL

Association of Drug Referral Centres
91 Pittwater Road
Manly NSW 2095
Tel 02 9977 0711

Australian Dental Association
75 Lithgow Street
St Leonards NSW 2065
Tel 02 99064412

Australian Medical Association
42 Macquarie Street
Barton ACT 2600
Tel 02 9231 2092

Australian Psychological Society
1 Gratton Street
Carlton Vic 3053
Tel 03 9663 6166

Children's Medical Research Institute
214 Hawkesbury Road
Westmead NSW 2145
Tel 02 9687 2800

Health Information Management Association of Australia
51 Wicks Road
North Ryde NSW 2113
Tel 02 9887 5001

Royal Children's Hospital Research Foundation
Flemington road
Parkville Vic 3000

COMPLEMENTARY MEDICINE

Australian Acupuncture Association
Suite 2
77 Vulture Street
West End Qld 4101
Tel 07 3846 5866

Australian Institute of Homeopathy
7/29 Bertran Street
Chatswood NSW 2067
Tel 02 9415 3928

Australian Natural Therapists Association
1/126 Bulcock Street
Caloundra Qld 4551
Tel 07 5491 9850

Australian Nutrition Foundation
1-3 Derwent Street
Glebe NSW 2037
Tel 02 9552 3081

Chiropractors' Association of Australia
459 Great Western Highway
Faulconbridge NSW 2776
Tel 047 51 5644

COMMON AILMENTS

Allergy Information Network
Suite 14/370 Victoria Avenue
Chatswood NSW 2067
Tel 02 419 7731

Asthma Australia
69 Flemington Road
North Melbourne Vic 3051
Tel 03 9326 7088

Australian Federation of Aids Organizations
Level 8
33 Bligh Street
Sydney NSW 2000
Tel 02 9231 2111

Dental Health Education and Research Foundation
1-3 Derwent Street
Glebe NSW 2037
Tel 02 9351 3219

National Heart Foundation
cnr Denison Street & Geils Ct
Deakin ACT 2600
Tel 02 6282 2144

USEFUL ADDRESSES NEW ZEALAND

GENERAL

Community Alcohol Drug Service
Grafton Road
Auckland
Tel 09 377 0370

New Zealand Psychological Society
Level 2, Fogel Building
22 Garret Street
Wellington
Tel 04 801 5414

National Child Health Research Council
297 Rosebank Road
Avondale
Tel 09 828 5155

COMMON AILMENTS

Allergy Awareness Associaton
P.O. Box 12701
Penrose
Tel 09 303 22024

Auckland Asthma Society
581 Mt Eden Road
Auckland
Tel 09 630 2293

Auckland Dental Association
3 St Mark Street
Remuera
Auckland
Tel 09 524 2778

COMPLEMENTARY MEDICINE

Karori Acupuncturist
92a Karori Road
Wellington
Wellington
Tel 04 426 2765

New Zealand Institute of Classic Homeopathy
P.O. Box 7232
Wellesley Street
Auckland

South Pacific Association of Natural Therapy
28 Willow Ave
Birkenhead
Auckland 10

New Zealand Nutrition Foundation
12-14 Northcroft Street
Takapuna
Auckland
Tel 09 486 2036

GLOSSARY

A

Adrenaline
'Fight or flight' hormone secreted by adrenal glands; also given by injection for anaphylactic shock.

Allergen
Substance that is normally harmless but provokes an inappropriate response by the immune system in individuals who are susceptible.

Alveoli
Collections of air sacs at the end of the bronchioles. Carbon dioxide and oxygen are exchanged through the walls of the alveoli.

Amblyopia
Faulty visual acuity not caused by a structural abnormality or disease of the eye. In young children, amblyopia is commonly caused by a squint.

Amino acids
Chemicals that are responsible for the break down of proteins in the body. Twenty amino acids are present in protein, eight of which are essential for health.

Anabolic
Promoting growth of body tissues.

Antigen
A substance recognized as foreign by the immune system. An antibody is then produced. If an innocuous substance is recognized as harmful, the body mounts an allergic reaction.

Asphyxia
Suffocation, caused by obstruction of the airway, breathing in too little oxygen or too much of a poisonous gas such as carbon monoxide.

Ataxia
Lack of coordination and clumsiness, causing an unsteady walk and uneven, jerky movements.

Atherosclerosis
Disease in which fatty deposits form on the inside walls of the arteries.

Atopy
The tendency to mount allergic reactions to normally harmless substances.

Autonomic nervous system
That part of the nervous system that controls involuntary functions of the body – such as the heart beat, digestion and sweating.

B

Binocular vision
The ability to focus both eyes together so that the brain receives a single image.

C

Cartilage
Tissue that is softer than bone but forms an important part of the body's structure. There are three types: soft, elastic cartilage (e.g. in the ears); smooth, hard hyaline cartilage that lines joints; and strong fibrocartilage (e.g. in the discs between the vertebrae).

Central nervous system
The brain and spinal cord, which together with the peripheral nervous system receives messages from receptors and organs all around the body, decodes the information and signals a response.

Cerebrospinal fluid
The fluid that circulates around the brain and spinal cord, acting as a shock absorber.

Chorionic villus sampling
A test in early pregnancy in which a small sample of the developing placenta is removed to check for abnormalities in the foetus.

Cilia
Hair-like projections on the cells lining the airways that beat continuously to sweep out mucus and any unwanted particles.

Cryotherapy
Freezing.

Curettage
Scraping off, for example, a verruca.

D

Decongestant
Medication used to reduce congestion in the nose. Decongestants narrow superficial blood vessels; this reduces swelling and mucus.

Desmopressin
A drug that acts to regulate water output in the urine.

Dilatation
Widening or stretching a hollow or open part of the body.

Dyspraxia
Developmental disorder, leading to poor co-ordination and clumsiness.

E

Electrocautery
Electrical heat treatment occasionally used to destroy warts.

Emphysema
Abnormal collection of air in the tissues of the body. In pulmonary emphysema, the alveoli are damaged, causing breathlessness.

Endocarditis
Inflammation of the lining of the heart, often caused by a bacterial infection.

Endocrinologist
Doctor specialising in disorders of the hormone-secreting endocrine glands.

Enzyme
A type of protein that acts as a catalyst, speeding up and regulating the rate of biochemical reactions in the body.

Erythrocyte
Red blood cell.

F

Ferritin
A protein that combines with iron to store it in the body.

Follicle
A small sac or cavity, such as the follicle from which a hair grows or the cavities in the ovary where eggs develop.

G

Glans
Acorn-shaped end of the penis, normally covered by the foreskin.

Glucagon
Hormone produced in the pancreas that causes blood sugar levels to rise.

Glycogen
The principal form in which carbohydrate is stored in the body, in the liver and muscles. It can be easily broken down to glucose to maintain the blood sugar level.

Gonadotrophins
Hormones secreted by the pituitary gland that stimulate the gonads (the ovaries and testes) to produce sex hormones. In pregnancy the placenta produces human chorionic gonadotrophin.

Griseofulvin
Antifungal drug often used to treat tinea infections. such as ringworm.

H

Histamine
Chemical released from the cells in an allergic reaction, giving rise to inflammation, itching and a narrowing of the airways.

Hypotonia
Excessive muscle slackness, causing floppiness in infants.

I

Ileum
The last section of the small intestine before it joins the large intestine.

Immunoglobulin (Ig)
A type of protein that acts as an antibody. Immunoglobulins are produced by white blood cells (B-lymphocytes) and attach to substances recognized as foreign bodies or antigens. There are five classes of immunoglobulin: IgA, IgD, IgE, IgG and IgM. Immunoglobulin can be obtained from the blood of convalescing patients for passive immunization against certain diseases.

Immunosuppressive
Drugs that suppress the production of infection-fighting lymphocytes and so reduce the body's natural immunity.

Incisors
The four front teeth.

Incubation period
The interval between exposure to an infection and the appearance of the first symptoms.

Inflammation
Response to infection or injury with redness, swelling, heat and pain.

Innocent
Harmless, benign.

Insulin
Hormone produced in the pancreas in response to the blood sugar level.

Intolerance
A reaction, usually to a type of food, in which the immune system is not involved.

Intraocular lens
Replacement artificial lens fitted into the eye.

K

Keratin
Tough, fibrous protein found in nails, skin and hair.

Kernicterus
A condition in which very high bilirubin levels in a newborn baby with jaundice can cause brain damage.

L

Labyrinthitis
Inner ear inflammation; causes vertigo,

Larva
The immature developmental stage of some worms and insects,

Leucocyte
White blood cell, mainly involved in protecting the body against infection.

Ligament
Band of tough fibrous tissue holding bone ends together, limiting their movement and strengthening the joint.

Lumbar puncture
A test, often for meningitis or leukaemia, in which a small amount of cerebrospinal fluid is drawn out of the spinal canal through a hollow needle.

Lymph nodes
Small organs (also known as lymph glands) found along the lymphatic system. They consist of lymphoid tissue and act as filters for the lymph, destroying bacteria and preventing them from entering the bloodstream.

Lymphocyte
A type of white blood cell vital to the immune system. B-lymphocytes produce antibodies; T-lymphocytes act to destroy abnormal body cells.

M

Metabolic disorder
A disorder in which the body's chemistry is upset. The inborn errors of metabolism are a large group of inherited disorders, each individually rare. A single genetic defect causes malfunction of an enzyme essential to normal metabolism.

Metabolism
Activity in cells that either releases energy from nutrients in food or else uses energy to create other substances, Chemical processes in the body.

Mucus
Fluid consisting of water and proteins secreted by cells in the mucous membrane. Mucus lubricates and moistens internal surfaces, dilutes noxious substances and in the airways helps to trap and clear particles.

Mucous membrane
Moist membrane that lines many parts of the body, including the mouth and the respiratory tract, the digestive system, the eyelids, parts of the nose, and the genital and urinary tracts. Cells in the membrane secrete mucus.

N

Nebuliser
Machine that delivers medication as a fine mist of droplets to be breathed in, often using a face mask.

Neural tube
The structure in the embryo from which the spinal cord and brain develop.

Nystagmus
Involuntary and often jerky movement of the eyes.

O

Orchidopexy
Operation to bring undescended testes down into the scrotum.

Orthodontist
Dentist specialising in correcting irregularities in the positioning of teeth.

Orthopaedics
Surgical speciality concerned with correcting damage or disease affecting bones and joints.

P

Papule
Small, raised spot or abnormality less than 5 mm/¼ in across.

Parasite
An organism that lives in or on another organism without beneficial effects. Parasites spend all or part of their life depending on their host organism.

Pessary
Device designed to introduce medication into the vagina.

Peripheral nervous system
The nerves and nerve cells that connect the central nervous system to all other parts of the body.

Phagocytes
Cells found in the blood, lymph nodes, spleen and alveoli that are able to surround and destroy bacteria, viruses, dust, foreign particles and cell debris.

Phenylalanine
Amino acid that is normally converted to tyrosine. In phenylketonuria this conversion does not take place because of an inherited enzyme defect.

Pigment
Colour-giving substance, found in the skin, the iris, the blood and bile.

Plasma
The fluid in which blood cells are suspended.

Podiatrist
Chiropodist.

Polycystic ovaries
A condition caused by an imbalance of hormones from the pituitary gland, leading to excessive testosterone output from the ovaries, hirsutism, a lack of ovulation and scanty or absent periods.

Portoenterostomy
Hepatic portoenterostomy is an operation to repair or reconstruct the ducts that drain bile away from the liver; also known as the Kasai operation.

Prepuce
Foreskin.

Puberty
Development of the physical changes that accompany sexual maturity.

R

Rebound congestion
Congestion occurring in the nose after treatment with decongestants has stopped.

Rectum
The last section of the large intestine, where faeces are stored before defecation.

Refractive error
Defect in the eye, which means that light rays do not come to focus precisely in the retina.

Remission
Improvement or temporary disappearance of symptoms of a disease.

Rheumatic fever
An inflammatory disease initiated by a streptococcal infection that can cause permanent damage to the heart.

S

Salivary glands
One of three pairs of glands which secrete saliva into the mouth.

Scrotum
The sac containing the testes.

Sebum
Oily and mildly antibacterial secretion from sebaceous glands, which lead into the hair follicles.

Secondary sexual characteristics
Physical characteristics of developing sexual maturity. In girls, they include breast development, female body shape and pubic and underarm hair; in boys, the deepening of the voice, enlargement of the penis and testes and growth of body, pubic and facial hair.

Septicaemia
Blood poisoning caused by a rapid increase in the numbers of bacteria in the blood. The bacteria spread through the body and cause extensive damage.

Serotonin
A substance widely distributed through the body in the bloodstream, the digestive tract and in the brain where it is involved in transmitting nerve impulses and in mood regulation.

Speculum
Instrument to hold open a part of the body while it is examined.

Sputum
Phlegm, or mucus produced by cells in the respiratory tract.

Staphylococcus
Type of bacterium that is harmlessly present on most people's skin, in the nose and throat, but can cause infection under certain circumstances.

Stenosis
Narrowing of a passage or opening.

Strabismus
Squint.

Streptococcus
Bacterium that often lives harmlessly in the nose and throat but can also cause a range of common infections.

T

Traction
Applying a pulling force to position two adjoining body structures to align correctly so that healing can take place.

Tendon
Tough fibrous cord that usually attaches a muscle to a bone.

Tibial tuberosity
A protuberance at the top of the tibia, to which tendons are attached.

UVW

Ulceration
Formation of sore, inflamed patches of skin or mucous membrane.

Ureter
Tube linking the kidneys and bladder.

Urethra
The outlet tube leading from the bladder to the outside of the body.

Ventricle
One of the two pumping chambers of the heart, or one of four fluid-filled cavities in the brain.

Weal
Red, raised and often itchy patch of skin.

INDEX

Italic page numbers refer to diagrams and **bold** *numbers to main entries.*

ACKNOWLEDGEMENTS

MEDICAL CONSULTANTS

Publishers and author would like to thank the following for their invaluable help and advice during the preparation of this book.

Dr Alex Habel, MB, ChB, FRCP
Dr Alex Habel qualified in 1967 and lectured in Child Life and Health at Edinburgh University. In 1978 he became Consultant Paediatrician at West Middlesex University Hospital, and more recently at Great Ormond Street Hospital for Children, where he is holistic paediatrician to the cleft palate team. His textbooks, *Synopsis of Paediatrics* (1993), *Aids to Paediatrics for Postgraduates* (1993) and *Aids to Paediatrics for Undergraduates* (1995) are used worldwide. He is married with four children.

Professor Charles G D Brook, MA, MD, FRCP, DCH Director, London Centre for Paediatric Endocrinology and Metabolism

Dr John Buchan, MBChB, MRCGP, DRCOG, DPD, DFFP General Practitioner and Founder Member of the Primary Care Dermatology Society

Dr Joanne Clough, DM, FRCA, MRCP Senior Lecturer in Paediatric Respiratory Medicine, Southampton University

Dr Anne Cobbe, MB, MRGP, DRCOG, DCH General Practitioner, London

Dr Brian Colvin, MA, MB, FRCP, FRCPath Consultanat Haematologist, The Royal Free Hospital, London

Lynda Davies, RGN, RM, HV Health Visitor, London

Dr Keith Dodd, BSc, MB, BS, FRCPCH, FRCP, DCH Consultant Paediatrician, Derbyshire Children's Hospital

Miss D Eastwood, MB, FRCS Consultant Orthopaedic Surgeon, Royal National Orthopaedic Hospital and the Royal Free Hospital, London

Michele Elliott, Director, Kidscape

Dr Bruce Evans, BSc (Hons), PhD, FCOptom, DCLP, FAAO Senior Lecturer, Institute of Optometry, London

Tam Fry, Hon. Chairman Child Growth Foundation, London

Dr Jane Goodman, BDS, FDS, RCS Consultant in Paediatric Dentistry, Eastman Dental Hospital, London

Ann Mills, RSCN

Dr Jacqueline Morrell, MBBS, MRCPsych Consultant Child Psychiatrist, Park Royal Centre for Mental Health, London

Dr David Murfin, MPhil, FRCGP, DRCOG, General Practitioner, Former Vice-Chairman of The Royal College of General Practitioners, Member of the Standing Committee on Medicines for Children

Susan Pinkney, Child Accident Prevention Trust

Adelaide Tunstill, RN, RSCN, BA(Hons) Clinical Nurse Specialist, Cardiac Unit, The Great Ormond Street Hospital for Children, London

Sue Vernon, BA(Hons), RGN, RSCN Research Associate, Regional Children's Urinary Tract Infection Audit, Sir James Spence Institute of Child Health, Royal Victoria Infirmary, Newcastle-Upon-Tyne

Dr Lee Wadey, MBBS, MRCP, MRCPCH Specialist Registrar in Paediatrics, St Thomas' Hospital, London

Professor John Walker-Smith, MD, FRCP, FRACP Chair of Paediatric Gastroenterology, The Royal Free Hospital, London

Andrea Woolley, RGN, BSC(Hons) Health & Safety Consultant

THE COMPLEMENTARY PRACTITIONERS

The following practitioners have made a valuable contribution by supplying information on the field of complementary medicine in which they work and how it may help to relieve specific ailments and conditions.

kinesiology (Diagnostic Therapist)

Brian H Butler, BA
Brian Butler is President of the Association & Academy of Systematic Kinesiology. In 1975 he became the first English person to train in Applied Kinesiology in the USA. He has pioneered AK training in Britain and Europe and has run the Kinesiology for Health and Wellbeing Clinic in Surbiton since 1975, formulating a lay programme for anyone wishing to take responsibility for their health. He has also written books on kinesiology including An Introduction to Kinesiology and Kinesiology for Health and Wellbeing, published by Task Books.

western herbalism

Mark Evans, B Phil
Mark Evans is the Director of the Bath Natural Health Clinic, a multi-disciplinary centre for complementary medicine, and Principle of the Bath School of Massage. He runs practices in Bath and Bristol offering herbal medicine, massage, aromatherapy and reflexology. He is a Fellow of the national Institute of Medical Herbalists and a former President and council member. He holds a B Phil in Complementary Health Studies from Exeter University, and has had research papers published in the *European Journal of Herbal Medicine* and the *British Journal of Phytotherapy*.

chinese herbalism

Helen Fielding MRCHM

Helen Fielding graduated from The College of Traditional Acupuncture in 1984 and since then has received diplomas in Traditional Chinese Medicine, Traditional Chinese Herbal Medicine and paediatric acupuncture. She is a practitioner and teacher of Tai Chi Chuan and Chi Kung and lectures in post graduate studies in acupuncture and herbal medicine for the treatment of children, in the UK, USA and Europe. Helen now runs an Acupuncture and Herbal Medicine practice in central London and Croydon, Surrey.

relaxation and aromatherapy

Carol Horrigan

Carol Horrigan began training in complementary therapies in 1963 and added nursing qualifications from 1977. She has studied and now uses in her practice: relaxation and visualization therapies, massage, reflex therapy, therapeutic touch, chakra balancing, reiki, Bach flower remedies, aromatherapy, clinical hypnosis, Fleming method and yoga. From 1988 she developed the posts of Lecturer in Complementary Therapies at Bloomsbury college of Nursing and at the Institute of Advanced Nurse Education at the Royal College of Nursing. She has also contributed to several books and is currently writing a new advanced textbook for nurses and therapists.

bach flower remedies

Judy Howard

Judy Howard qualified as a nurse in King's Lynn in 1980 and as a midwife in London in 1982. She then qualified and worked as a Health Visitor in Nottingham before returning to Oxfordshire where she grew up. She has been a consultant at the Bach Centre since 1985 and is also one of its directors and trustees. She co-runs the teaching programme of the Dr Edward Bach Foundation, which is responsible for the training and international registration of practitioners, and prepares the remedy mother tinctures along with her family and colleagues. Judy has written several books on the Bach Flower Remedies, has been involved with various forms of media interest in the Bach Centres, and is the mother of twins.

osteopathy

Stuart Korth DO FICO MRO

Stuart Korth is Director of Osteopathy at the Osteopathic Centre for Children and is in private practice. He graduated from the British School of Osteopathy in 1964, taught there and at the European School of Osteopathy. His present teaching is at post-graduate level both in the UK and abroad, except for occasional visits to the European School of Osteopathy as Consultant to their Children's Clinic. He is a member of both the General Council and Register of Osteopaths, and the Osteopathic Association of Great Britain, and a Fellow of the Institute of Classical Osteopathy.

tai chi chi kung

Master Lam Kam Chuen

At present Master Lam Kam Chuen teaches Tai Chi and practises Chinese herbalism at the Lam clinic in London's Chinatown. He is trained in martial arts, and he also studied Chi Kung. Using his medical knowledge of Chi Kung, Master Lam developed a new form of Tai Chi known as Lam Style Tai Chi. He came to the West in 1976 and became the first Tai Chi instructor to teach for the Inner London Education Authority. He has written *The Way of Energy*, which is published by Gaia Books.

nutritional therapy

Linda Lazarides

Linda Lazarides is widely recognized as one of Britain's top nutritional therapists, and is one of the few in her profession who has worked for the National Health Service. She is director of the Society for the Promotion of Nutritional Therapy, founder of the British Association of Nutritional Therapists, and author of Principles of Nutritional Therapy and The Nutritional Health Bible, published by Thorsons. She is also an adviser to the Institute for Complementary Medicine, bacup, and Here's Health magazine.

acupuncture and acupressure

Stuart Lightbody

Stuart Lightbody has been the Director of the Halifax Clinic of Natural Medicine in West Yorkshire since 1979. He qualified as a Master of Acupuncture in 1985 and is a member of the Traditional Acupuncture Society and the British Acupuncture Council. He studied at the College of Traditional Chinese Medicine in Chengdu, China, in 1984 and also in San Francisco in 1986. He has also made some appearances on television.

With thanks also to Steven Guthrie, MBAcC of Brighton Children's Clinic, for his help with this subject.

homeopathy

Dr. Andrew Lockie

Dr Andrew H Lockie, MB, ChB, MF Hom, Dip Obst RCOG, MRCGP

Dr Andrew Lockie is a founder member of the Homeopathic Physicians Teaching Group and is a member of the Faculty of Homeopathy. He qualified in medicine at Aberdeen University in 1972 before studying at the Royal London Homeopathic Hospital in 1973–74. He then took house officer posts in obstetrics, gynaecology and paediatrics in various hospitals before training as a general practitioner in Southampton. He is the author of several books including *The Family Guide to Homeopathy*, published by Hamish Hamilton, and is a Consultant Editor of the *Journal of Alternative and Complementary Medicine*.

massage

Clare Maxwell-Hudson

Clare Maxwell-Hudson is the director of the Institute of Health Sciences in London and principal of The Clare Maxwell-Hudson School of Massage. A registered massage therapist, she teaches doctors at the British Post Graduate Medical Association and runs courses for nurses at two major London teaching hospitals. She contributes to radio and television, and has written for newspapers and journals. Her books include *The Complete Books of Massage*, *The Aromatherapy Massage Book* and *Massage for Stress Relief*, all published by Dorling Kindersley.

play therapy

Nancy Secchi, MA, RDTH

Nancy Secchi is a registered and practising play therapist and a qualified but non-practising drama therapist. She teaches on the post-qualifying diploma course in play therapy at the University of York and is an external examiner on the post-graduate diploma course in Art and Therapeutic Play for Children at Roehampton Institute. She is also a qualified social worker.

music therapy

John Strange BA, DipEd, ARCO, ARCM, DipMTh, RMTh

John Strange taught in an inner city comprehensive before retraining as a music therapist. He has practised for twelve years in schools for students with moderate to profound learning difficulties. He has chaired the Association of Professional Music Therapists and he represents the UK on the European Music therapy Confederation.

chiropractic

Susan L Steward, Dip Chp, NLP

Susan Steward is a chiropractor in private practice, a former President of the British Chiropractic Association (1987–1990), a member of the British Chiropractic Association and of the new General Chiropractic Council. She received the Diploma Doctor of Chiropractic from the Anglo-European College of Chiropractic in 1976 and also holds the Diploma and Advanced Diploma in Eriksonian Clinical Hypnosis, Cognitive Psychotherapy and Neuro-linguistic Programming. She regularly writes on chiropractic and lectures widely.

reflexology

Mo Usher, MAR, MGCP

The former Chairperson and President of the Association of Reflexologists, Mo Usher is now an Honorary Life Member. She is on the advisory board of the *Journal of Alternative and Complementary Medicine*, and is a member of the Royal Society of Medicine. She has been president of the International Council of Reflexologists and on the executive committee of Reflexology in Europe. She has broadcast on reflexology on radio and television.

The publishers would also like to thank Michael Endacott, Research Director, The Institute for Complementary Medicine, London for his help and advice.

PHOTOGRAPHIC ACKNOWLEDGEMENTS:

Bubbles/Claire Camm 101/William Crees 242/Pauline Cutler 145/Jacqui Farrow 254/Nikki Gibbs 299/Perry Joseph 31 Bottom/Amanda Knapp 249/Lynne McEwan 246/Rex Moreton 248/Claire Paxton 271/David Robinson 46, 264/Dr Hercules Robinson 45/Frans Rombout 13, 21, 23, 94, 245, 289, 337, 338/Loisjoy Thurston 12 Right, 50, 74, 137, 151, 152, 214, 233, 305, 307, 334, 335/Ian West 90, 173, 178, 187, 188, 193, 209, 250, 267, 331/Jennie Woodcock 22 Bottom, 25, 33, 86, 105, 142, 154, 165, 172, 202, 203, 232, 257, 302

Child Growth Foundation 70

E.T. Archive 48, 54

Reed Consumer Books Ltd./Gary Holder 57, 69, 81, 107, 125, 139, 141, 149, 181, 189, 195, 198, 206, 222, 223, 224, 227, 239, 260, 265, 268, 273, 287 Bottom Right, 287 Bottom Left, 287 Top, 290

Angela Hampton/Family Life 15 Bottom, 15 Top, 18, 19, 22 Top, 26, 28, 31 Top, 35 Right, 40, 52 Bottom, 56 Right, 56 left, 61, 63, 78, 79, 92, 100, 102, 110, 113, 114, 127, 130, 144, 146, 157, 158, 159, 167, 170, 179, 185, 186, 190, 215, 231, 234, 235, 251, 252, 256, 263, 270, 280, 314, 317, 321, 322 Bottom, 322 Top, 323, 327, 336 Right, 358 Right, 358 left

Image Bank/Barros & Barros 17/Andre Gallant 153/L. D. Gordon 332/Infocus Int'l 328, 333/Going Jacobs 95/Blue Lemon 324/David de Lossy 44, 262/G + M. David de Lossy 119/Michael Melford 96/Anne Rippy 120/Schmid/Langsfeld 319/Turner & Devries 306 Top/Ross Whitaker 281, 362/Yellow Dog Productions 363

Kobal Collection/New Line 36

Children's Liver Disease Foundation 266

Niall McInerney 39

Science Photo Library 85, 163, 175, 298/John Bavosi 296/Tim Beddow 112/BSIP, Pourdieu 244/Dr L. Card 292/Kairos, Latin Stock 313/CC Studio 128/CC Studio 201/CC Studio 275/Mark Clarke 143, 213, 217/CNRI 164, 211/Custom Medical Stock Photo 16/Mike Devlin 133, 136/A. B. Dowsett 197/Dr H.C. Robinson 169/Simon Fraser/Royal Victoria Infirmary 283/Simon Fraser/RVI, Newcastle-Upon-Tyne 199/John Heseltine 237/Phil Jude 176/Mehau Kulyk 91/Damien Lovegrove 123/Dr P Marazzi 88, 89, 93, 98, 103, 155, 160, 174, 192, 212, 297/Dr Gopal Murti 104/David Parker 177/Alfred Pasieka 99/Princess Margaret Rose Orthopaedic Hospital 77, 131, 132/Dr H. C. Robinson 166, 168, 229/Saturn Stills 118/Blair Sweitz 200/Jame Shemilt 191/Simon Fraser 72/Sheila Terry 156/Geoff Tomkinson 294, 336 left/Garry Watson 220/Hattie Young 49, 310

Tony Stone Images/Jon Bradley 308/Michael Busselle 243/Dennis O'Clair 12 left/Tessa Codrington 117/Peter Correz 11/Robert F Daemmrich 71/James Darell 208/Mary Kate Denny 37/Ken Fisher 38 left/Tim Flach 97/Sara Gray 115/Bruce Hands 62 Top/Graeme Harris 38 Right/Paul Harrison 8/Mitch Kezar 312/Mark Lewis 329/Ian O'Leary 53, 258/Rosanne Olson 121/Lori Adamski Peek 134, 304 /Steven Peters 84, 306 Bottom, 318/Peter Poulides 60/RNHRD NHS Trust 76/Martin Rogers 7, 342 /Andy Sacks 24 left, 35 left/Don Smetzer 122/David C. Tomlinson 87/Penny Tweedie 43/Terry Vine 135/Charlie Waite 52 Top/David Young Wolff 42/Keith Wood 24 Right

John Walmsley 62 Bottom, 218